The People's Voice:

A Populist Cultural History of Modern America

The People's Voice:

A Populist Cultural History of Modern America

David A. Horowitz

Portland State University

2008
Sloan Publishing
Cornwall-on-Hudson, NY 12520

Library of Congress Control Number: 2007926260

Horowitz, David A.
  The People's Voice: A Populist Cultural History of Modern America
    p.   cm.
  Includes bibliographic references and index.
  ISBN 1–59738–013–X

Cover designer: Amy Rosen
Cover photo: "MR. SMITH GOES TO WASHINGTON" © 1939, renewed 1967
Columbia Pictures Industries, Inc. All rights reserved. Courtesy of Columbia
Pictures.

Printed in Canada
10 9 8 7 6 5 4 3 2 1

ISBN 1–59738–013–X

To the hundreds of scholars, biographers, journalists, and other writers whose works comprise the basis for this compilation.

Contents

About the Author

Born in the West Bronx, New York, David A. Horowitz is a graduate of Antioch College and the recipient of a History Ph.D. from the University of Minnesota. He is a professor of History at Portland State University, where he has taught since 1968. His publications include *Beyond Left and Right: Insurgency and the Establishment* (1997); *Inside the Klavern: The Secret History of a 1920s Ku Klux Klan* (1999); and *America's Political Class Under Fire: The Twentieth Century's Great Culture War* (2003). He currently resides with his wife, Gloria E. Myers, in Portland and Arch Cape, Oregon.

Preface

Expressive Culture and Populist History

The People's Voice: A Populist Cultural History of Modern America is a textbook devoted to imaginative expressions of U.S. culture since the 1890s that have addressed the everyday experiences and aspirations of ordinary people. Starting with the legacy of Walt Whitman, Mark Twain, and Stephen Foster, the book offers a chronological sampling of fiction, poetry, journalism, memoir, painting, photography, animation, comedy, drama, dance, film, radio, television, and music framing the nation's public life since the late nineteenth century.

Populism normally refers to a democratic political faith in the wisdom and integrity of the common people and hostility to perceived elites. *The People's Voice* employs the term "populist" in reference to expressive forms designed for the consumption of ordinary Americans, favorably commenting upon their lives, or rendered in their name. For purposes of this text, "ordinary people" designates members of the working or middle classes who see themselves outside the nation's more privileged or powerful economic, political, or cultural circles.

Although populist cultural expression frequently appears within the realm of "popular culture," it may not necessarily pursue the latter's drive for commercial success. Beyond celebrations of the commonplace, the cultural products described in these pages have sought to engage as broad an audience as possible by incorporating "vernacular" or informal language, unadorned and representational modes of presentation, and widely shared social and spiritual values. The examples of expressive culture embraced by this text often strive for identification with ordinary people through explicit references to geographical place, family ties, or cultural roots.

As an introductory text, *The People's Voice* draws from hundreds of scholarly monographs, reference books, biographies, journalistic studies, and other publications. Ample lists of sources and suggested readings at the end of each of the twelve chapters provide the opportunity for further study. Designed as an accessible survey and reference work for both college students and general readers, the book shies away from excessively theoretical formulations. Yet as an exploration of cultural history, *The People's Voice* addresses several challenging issues. First, it raises questions concerning the interaction between expressive culture and the consumer economy. Second, the book describes the role of race, ethnicity, social class, and gender in shaping cultural expression and its reception. Third, the text explores the manner in which expressive styles frequently assume modified forms before winning broad acceptance. Finally, it touches upon the complex relationship between those speaking for "the People" and those they profess to represent.

The originality of *The People's Voice* rests upon its ability to inventory in a single volume those aspects of modern American expressive culture immersed in the joys, sorrows, and varied experiences of everyday life. By tracing the vitality of such articles of the democratic faith, the book seeks to provide readers with a deeper sense of the nation's rich cultural legacy. The author hopes that these pages may serve as a starting point for the social healing that might contribute to a reconciliation of the bitter political divisions of recent decades.

ACKNOWLEDGEMENTS

Preparation of *The People's Voice* occurred during a 2005–2006 sabbatical leave, a grant of free time facilitated by Portland State University and the Department of History, as well as Oregon taxpayers. The author wishes to thank Michael G. Horowitz and Lawrence E. Hussman, Jr., for assistance in locating relevant Internet sources, Jeff Brown for vital technical support, and reviewers Robbie Lieberman (Southern Illinois University, Carbondale) and William H. Mulligan, Jr. (Murray State University) for their valuable comments and suggestions during the writing process. Production of the book owes a great deal to the vision of publisher Bill Webber and the enormous contributions of copy editor Serena Hoffman. Most of all, the author extends heartfelt appreciation to Gloria E. Myers, whose mission of "feeding, watering, and exercising" her spouse during the year at the Oregon Coast went far beyond the call of love and duty.

1

On the Brink of the
People's Century

As Chicago's business elite inaugurated the World's Columbian Exposition of 1893 to commemorate four centuries of European settlement in the New World, the United States appeared to be on the cusp of the modern age. In the years following the Civil War, powerful national corporations and banks had created an impressive industrial and technological infrastructure centered in the most populated cities. The Chicago Fair celebrated the new era's scientific innovations and cultural progress with sixty-five thousand exhibits distributed over nearly seven hundred acres of Lake Michigan frontage. Within five months, over fourteen million visitors would flock to its gates to sample the bright attractions of the future paradise.

ALONG THE MIDWAY

The heart of the Exposition consisted of an electrically illuminated Court of Honor known as the White City. Surrounding a pristine pond and grounds laid out by landscape architect Frederick Law Olmsted, the designer of New York City's Central Park, a series of classically inspired "temples of civilization" represented twelve departments of applied knowledge and scientific innovation. Several exhibits featured electrical appliances and other future consumer commodities. Imbued with a purified and harmonized view of the social order, the White City contained no references to industrial workers, agricultural laborers, or ethnic minorities. Participation by distinguished

1

African American diplomat and author Frederic Douglass, in fact, was confined to the Haitian exhibit. In keeping with the new science of anthropology, which contrasted tribal primitivism and modern progress, dozens of oriental, tropical, and ancient village replicas were arrayed on the adjoining "Midway Plaisance." Visitors to the mile-long boulevard could observe the quaint artifacts and costumes of "exotic" and "backward" peoples such as Africans, Asians, and American Indians.

The racist and elitist messages of World Fair planners, however, frequently lost their resonance within the diversity of cultural expression thriving on the Midway. In order to maximize Exposition attendance and please commercial vendors, officials sponsored the addition of a Ferris Wheel to the strip's collection of exotic villages and permitted the spread of a variety of ethnic cafes, food stalls, and open-air bazaars. A number of side-shows, curiosity exhibits, coin arcades, variety theaters, and music halls soon appeared alongside these attractions. The Midway hosted appearances by strongman Eugene Sandow and "Buffalo Bill" Cody's *Wild West Show.* Its most popular draw was "Little Egypt," a performer who staged an exotic belly-dance or "cooch" at the "Streets of Cairo" that quickly spread to the burlesque theaters of Chicago and New York, where it became known as the "hootchy kootchy."

Fair administrators liked to distinguish between the refined arts of the White City and the base amusements of its unofficial counterpart. Yet the Exposition's free cultural exhibits and classical music recitals were not nearly as well-attended as the commercial attractions of the Midway. The democratic diversions of the strip helped to popularize the existence of an informal or vernacular popular culture rooted in everyday language and experience. "After the Ball" (1892), the first significant hit to come out of the mass-production sheet music industry, owed much of its fame to the exposure it received in Chicago. Early forms of ragtime music came to public light when played by itinerant African American musicians at boulevard cafes. The spread of turn-of-the-century diversions such as the amusement park, the vaudeville theater, and the musical cabaret all could be traced to the explosion of cultural expression to be found on the notorious Midway.

The Columbian Exposition's outpouring of popular culture pointed to the importance of vernacular representations of ordinary life in American society. In the preceding half-century three creative giants—a poet, a storyteller, and a songwriter—had led the way in bringing the distinct voices of the populace to national awareness. Although their efforts were constrained by their own prejudices as well as prevailing social mores, each would leave a lasting impact on cultural expression in the United States. In their attempt to erase the boundaries between the formal arts and commercial entertainment, these pioneers brought middle-class Americans far closer to the experiences of everyday people than social convention normally allowed. Their efforts helped to set in motion a revitalization of culture and social values that would profoundly alter the nature of modern American society and institutions.

THE PEOPLE'S POET

Walt Whitman died only one year before the inauguration of the White City. Born in 1819 to an egalitarian Long Island carpenter and an ethically principled Quaker mother, Whitman grew up in Brooklyn before leaving school at thirteen to become a printer's helper. After holding several teaching positions, he arrived in New York City at the age of twenty-two to become a writer. Finding work with several newspapers and magazines, he published *Franklin Evans* (1842), a short populist temperance novel addressed to working-class readers. Four years later Whitman became editor of the *Brooklyn Eagle* but lost the position for denouncing the Democratic Party's failure to oppose slavery expansion to the western territories. After further stints as a journalist, bookstore clerk, printer's assistant, and carpenter, the brash adventurer used his own funds in 1855 to secure publication of the first edition of his initial collection of poetry, *Leaves of Grass.*

Whitman had been inspired by essayist Ralph Waldo Emerson's insistence that poetry embrace the whole range of human emotions and lift the mundane to the level of beauty. Emerson argued that American literature needed to reflect the language of conversation—the "vascular and alive" speech of common men at work. Great verse, he declared in an 1854 lecture, reflected "the beauty of the common sights and sounds." The older writer's declarations confirmed the feel for everyday life that Whitman often

Walt Whitman

experienced in afternoon strolls along the "populous pavements" of Broadway. These excursions convinced the would-be poet of his talent for conversing with ordinary people. He was particularly taken with Lower Manhattan's rowdies, petty criminals, and the Bowery B'hoys—an assortment of streetwise butchers and workers sporting soap-greased clipped hair, carelessly placed stovepipe hats, loosely fastened ties, flared trousers, and cigars or tobacco chaw.

The colorful idioms and slang expressions of the city's African Americans and white poor fascinated Whitman. Terms like "pal," "chum," blowout," and "so long," never before used in polite literature, easily worked their way into his vocabulary. This informal spirit of the sidewalks infused the appearance of *Leaves of Grass*, whose title page boldly displayed the name of the book in large block letters with "Brooklyn, 1855" listed below. An engraved portrait of the author with open-necked white shirt and tilted hat graced the opposite page. Printed in small type, an untitled preface followed. Here Whitman laid out the democratic premise that poets were "no better" than the populace. America's greatness rested with ordinary people, he wrote, specifically their manners, speech, dress, and friendships—"the freshness and candor of their physiognomy—the picturesque looseness of their carriage … their deathless attachment to freedom." As his poetry "absorbed" the nation, the young bard hoped it could be a cohesive force in overcoming the wrenching debate over slavery and the prospects of disunion.

Leaves of Grass consisted of twelve untitled poems set in newsprint topography. Written in an irregular prose style free of rhyme or meter and replacing normal punctuation with ellipses, the work captured authentic rhythms of feeling and voice. "In all people I see myself," declared Whitman, "none more and not one a barley-corn less." This also meant that no one was the writer's superior. By addressing the reader as "you," the poet sought to break down formal boundaries between the audience and himself. Using descriptive language to convey sounds like "the blab of the pave, tires of carts, sluff of boot-soles, talk of the promenades," Whitman introduced the texture of working life to formal literature. In the belatedly entitled "I Hear America Singing," he celebrated "the varied carols" of mechanics, carpenters, masons, ploughboys, mothers, and wives. Of the Yankee woman sewing machine operator, the factory or mill hand, the road-builder, the sign-painter, the canal boy, and the shoemaker, he boasted in the collection's opening piece, "I weave a song of myself."

An 1856 edition of *Leaves of Grass* contained a congratulatory note from Ralph Waldo Emerson. Celebrating Whitman as "an American, one of the roughs, a kosmos," Emerson enthused that the book's "free and brave thought" ranked as "the most extraordinary piece of wit and wisdom that America has yet contributed." Its "fortifying and encouraging" spirit, he contended, stood in stark contrast to "the sterile and stingy nature" of much of the country's poetry. Whitman inspired such praise by tying his boisterous personal identity to the unlimited potential of the American populace. "I celebrate myself," he wrote, "my own master total and absolute," adding that "every atom belonging to me as good belongs to you." By questioning authority, mocking privilege, and pointing to the worth of every person, Whitman expressed a profound faith in democratic values. Despite the fact that he was no abolitionist, such egalitarianism extended to African Americans. The narrator of "Song of Myself," for example, turns into a fugitive bondsman, while portions of "I Sing the Body Electric" refer to the private thoughts of a slave on the auction block.

Whitman associated the promise of democratic progress with industrial technology, which he viewed as a liberated expression of the energy and vitality of the human spirit. Much of the concrete imagery of "I Hear America Singing" came from reciting the terms for the machinery that Whitman found in iron foundries and mines, steam printing presses, electric telegraph facilities, locomotives, factories, tool shops, and steamships. "Chants Democratic," a poem added to *Leaves of Grass* in 1860, turned the reader's attention to the West. On the Great Plains, "where the broad fat prairies spread," and in the Rocky Mountains, and on the Pacific Slope, Whitman imagined "a free original life" where a simple diet and "clean and sweet blood" had produced a people of "clear eyes and perfect physique." The youthful pioneers of the western territories were inaugurating a new order based on the simplicity of nature.

The pristine West produced Whitman's common-man hero and national redeemer: Abraham Lincoln. During the Civil War, the poet served as a volunteer nurse for the Union Army in Washington, D.C. Hospital visits not only offered the chance to establish emotional intimacy with male soldiers, but validated Whitman's vision of ordinary citizens as heroic cleansers of the republic. Lincoln perfectly represented this spirit of sacrifice. A homely and humbly born self-made lawyer, the former rail splitter and boatman embodied the virtues of hard work, humility, tolerance, and integrity idealized in *Leaves of Grass*. Lincoln's strength and moral leadership were complemented by his folksy tenderness, low-brow humor, and taste for popular entertainments like minstrels. The president's assassination brought forth Whitman's classic elegy, "When Lilacs Last in the Dooryard Bloom'd." Casting aside the brash tone of earlier work, the poet portrayed the salvation of the Union by a plain man who had become the nation's unifying symbol. Its imagery lingered on "the silent sea of faces and the unbared heads" saluting the crepe-draped Lincoln funeral train.

Whitman rarely touched on all-encompassing themes after the Civil War. In a collection entitled *Drum-Taps* (1865), he employed conventional rhythms to mount a patriotic defense of the Union cause. "Passage to India," published six years later, saw potential in the souls of "common people," but its celebration of "captains, voyagers, explorers, engineers, architects and machinists" seemed more in tune with the unifying force of technology than with the inherent talents of ordinary citizens. A similar emphasis dominated "Song of the Exposition," a work inspired by New York's national industrial fair of 1871. Whitman now applied his eye for concrete detail to contemporary wonders like the Atlantic Cable, the transcontinental railroad, oceanic steamships, petroleum and natural gas refineries, and the construction of the Brooklyn Bridge. In "The Prairie States" (1879), the poet combined a love of primal nature with the conviction that the railroads were the engines of western progress.

Sustaining a romantic view of the common people proved difficult for Whitman in later years. A series of essays in *Democratic Vistas* (1871) restated the poet's distrust of cultural elites with the complaint that refinement threatened "to eat us up, like a cancer." The writer was particularly offended by the "parcel of dandies ... dapper little gentlemen from abroad, who flood us with their thin sentiment of parlors, parasols, piano-songs, tinkling rhymes." Calling for the creation of a classless democratic culture that did not exclude the populace, Whitman castigated American writers for failing to speak to the nation's "interminable swarms of alert, turbulent, good-natured, independent citizens, mechanics, clerks, young persons." Yet he held the masses as responsible as business figures for the corruption and sterility of the years following the Civil War. It was impossible to sustain a government of equal rights for all, he argued, given "the crude, defective streaks in all the strata of the common people ... the ignorant, the credulous, the unfit and uncouth, the incapable, and the very low and poor."

By the 1880s, the people's bard was something of an enigma. His formal patriotic odes and celebrations of industrial might had endeared him to the social elite, with whom he was increasingly comfortable in his old age. The industrialist Andrew Carnegie even helped to subsidize the aging poet's income. Meanwhile, a tobacco company adopted Whitman's face as a logo to market a cigar named "Blades o' Grass." Surprisingly, such adulation did not significantly diminish when Boston municipal officials banned several sexually explicit poems from the 1882 edition of *Leaves of Grass*. Nevertheless, Whitman was saddened by the failure of his poetry to win widespread readership and regretted that his work was not published in portable pocket books accessible to the populace he idealized. "The people—the crowd," he lamented in his declining years, "I have had no way of reaching them. I needed to reach the people ... but it's too late now."

TALES OF THE HEARTLAND

Like Walt Whitman, Samuel Clemens served as a bridge between ordinary Americans and the literary establishment. Yet the relationship was not always a smooth one. Asked in 1877 to deliver a speech at a Boston dinner honoring the poet John Greenleaf Whittier, Clemens told of paying a call to a miner's cabin in the Nevada hill country and identifying himself as Mark Twain. Unimpressed, the prospector recalled that he had been visited the previous night by "a rough lot" who introduced themselves as Ralph Waldo Emerson, Henry Wadsworth Longfellow, and Oliver Wendell Holmes. Before reciting their poetry, he recalled, they had eaten his food, drank his whiskey, and stolen his boots. "I ain't suited to a literary atmosphere," the man had protested.

Samuel Clemens (Mark Twain)

Born in 1835, Samuel Langhorne Clemens was raised in Hannibal, Missouri, where he left school at the age of twelve to become a printing apprentice. Traversing the Midwest and East, Clemens found several jobs as a journeyman printer before training to be a Mississippi riverboat pilot. In 1861 he joined up with a Confederate volunteer company, only to desert a week later to follow his brother to Nevada to prospect for silver. When nothing came of these effort,s he accepted a position as a reporter for a Virginia City newspaper. It was at this point that the self-assured twenty-six-year-old newcomer assumed the persona of an irreverent, skeptical, irresponsible, humorous, and unpretentious western adventurer. To secure the new identity Clemens took the river pilot's term for safe water at two fathoms and renamed himself Mark Twain. He was interested in "simple-hearted" and straightforward ordinary people, he informed newspaper readers, and was willing "to use the language of the vulgar, the low-flung and the sinful" even if it shocked "the ears of the highly civilized."

Twain found humorous possibilities in topics normally forbidden by polite society. When he relocated to San Francisco in 1864, he expanded upon this formula by reporting on horse races, theatrical performances, political meetings, and sensational crimes. He supplemented these accounts with magazine sketches of clerical accountants, romantic lovers, and excessively sentimental nature admirers. Twain had stumbled upon a lucrative vein. Assuming the guise of an old western storyteller with a long career as a miner, sea captain, or riverboat man, his narratives captured what he later described as "the vigorous new vernacular of the occidental plains and mountains." Twain won instant attention when newspapers across the country ran his tall tale, "The Celebrated Jumping Frog of Calaveras County," leading to publication of a collection of similar stories in 1867. Two years later, in his first novel, *Innocents Abroad*, the author took his western hero overseas to contrast the literary pretensions and conventions of the Old World and its genteel tourists with the democratic ways of the American homeland.

As Mark Twain turned his travels into the subjects of a popular lecture series, he published *Roughing It* (1872), an account of his early Nevada adventures. Like the short stories of Bret Harte, the novel contrasted the pretentious civilization of the East with the relative freedoms afforded white men on the unruly frontier. Twain's drinking, smoking, card-playing, and foul-mouthed old tricksters and sinners pointed to the folly of reforming ordinary people, a constant theme of the writer's work. The following year brought *The Gilded Age* (1873), a satiric novel in which Twain and co-author Charles Dudley Warner parodied the rampant financial corruption and materialism of the post-Civil War elite. Nostalgia for the days of the pristine republic became more explicit in Twain's next two books. Set in an environment reminiscent of Hannibal in the early 1840s, *Tom Sawyer* (1876) contrasted the repressive moral conformity of conventional adulthood with the innocence of childhood. *Life on the Mississippi* (1883), in contrast, presented an idealized recollection of the author's organic relationship to the river as a prewar steamboat pilot.

Long heralded as "the people's author," Twain produced one of the masterpieces of American literature in 1884 with *The Adventures of Huckleberry Finn*. The novel's originality rested on its narration by a semi-literate, ignorant, poor Missouri white boy who spoke in southern dialect. Although some contemporary critics characterized the book's prose as rough, coarse, and inelegant, Twain had become the nation's first writer to fully utilize the potentialities of the American language. Through Huck's vernacular expression and humor, the author conveyed unprecedented degrees of irreverence, skepticism, and personal honesty. Although disguised as a simple exploration of childhood innocence, *Huck Finn* broke new ground by presenting realistic accounts of an adult world shadowed by insanity, murder, thievery, betrayal, feuding, lynching, and racism.

Without having read *Tom Sawyer*, Huck begins, "You don't know about me but that ain't no matter." From then on, the deadpan narrator tells the reader everything that has happened before him and exactly what he has experienced. In doing so, he unintentionally exposes the callous and cruel behavior of his elders, forever destroying the notion of innocence in the hearts of men. Yet the reader's faith is rehabilitated through Huck's magnificent ability to see through the foibles of others and transcend his surroundings.

Abandoned by his drunken, thieving, and murdering father, the young boy is civilized into middle-class mores by the Widow Douglas. Despite this, he comes to see that mechanical prayer does not substitute for compassion in a small town enslaved by arbitrary rules and rigid morality. Neither is piety its own reward. When Huck contemplates the death of a young woman known for bleak Victorian sketches and poems, we learn that he "reckoned, that with her disposition, she was having a better time in the graveyard."

Slavery is the supreme hypocrisy of the local culture, a symbol of the impulse that allows humans to justify brutality in the alleged name of moral conscience. Escaping middle-class propriety, Huck finds himself on a river raft with "Nigger Jim," a runaway slave. Instead of doing his duty and turning the illegal fugitive over to justice, however, he gradually develops an appreciation of Jim as a fellow human being. In what remains one of the single most elevating moments of American literature, Huck comes to the realization that a sound heart is more important than a poorly trained conscience schooled by religious orthodoxy. "All right, then, I'll *go* to hell," he agonizes when deciding to disregard the slavery laws. "And so there ain't nothing more to write about," the young narrator ultimately concludes, "and I am rotten glad of it, because if I'd 'a' knowed what a trouble it was to make a book, I wouldn't 'a' tackled it, and ain't a-going to no more." Then Huck informs the reader that he has "to light out" for the western territories "because Aunt Sally she's going to adopt me and sivilize me, and I can't stand it. I been there before."

Huck Finn captured Mark Twain's profound ambivalence about American society. A leading critic of Gilded Age materialism, Twain nevertheless associated himself with a tenuous entrepreneurial scheme to develop a typesetting machine. In part, he undertook his next novel, *A Connecticut Yankee in King Arthur's Court* (1889), to raise capital for the project. At the same time, the author sought to use his comic skills to attack British snobbery and elitism. *Connecticut Yankee* presented a populist satire of an enslaving sixth-century English church and arrogant aristocracy. The story's protagonist, a good-natured, time-traveling American enterpriser named Hank Morgan, introduces medieval civilization to modern progress by building schools and factories. Yet when the superstitious and ignorant people turn against him, his only response is to harness the ruthless efficiency of industrial technology toward their total annihilation. As an anti-utopian parody, the book not only hinted at the limits of benevolent uplift, but implied that the scientific doctrine of progress was an empty illusion incapable of eradicating human evil.

Despite misgivings about ordinary people, Twain saw himself as an ally of the underdog. In a tribute in 1886 to the Knights of Labor union movement, the popular novelist called for greater respect for the American wage earner. He expressed impatience with cultural elites two years later by denouncing genteel sentimentalism in contemporary fiction, in contrast to his own work aimed at "the deriding of shams, the exposure of pretentious falsities." Following the Spanish-American War of 1898, Twain became a leading opponent of U.S. imperialism and complained of the moral arrogance of American missionaries in China. Populist sensibilities continued to infuse his writing in *Pudd'nhead Wilson* (1894), a novel mocking southern hysteria over miscegenation (interracial sexual intimacy). A short piece entitled "Corn-Pone Opinions" (1901) reproduced the oral folk wisdom of a former slave. Yet Twain's most memorable works of the early twentieth century suggested a loss of the faith in the democratic promise of the people coloring his earlier work.

Beginning as another comical tall tale in the western tradition, the short story entitled "The Man That Corrupted Hadleyburg" (1900) pointed instead to inherent greed in the American small town. The novel *What Is Man?* (1906) drew another portrait of people as essentially selfish. In the posthumously published *The Mysterious Stranger* (1916), set in sixteenth-century Europe, the author implied that life was nothing more than a dream.

More than any writer of his time, Mark Twain incorporated the language and experiences of ordinary people, particularly those of the Border States, Deep South, and Frontier West. Nevertheless, when the greatest of American storytellers died in 1910, he had experienced personal financial disappointment, feared that he had not fully achieved literary respectability, and never had accepted the disappearance of the pre-Civil War life of his youth once immortalized by his prose.

SONGS OF THE STREET

Fashioning himself as a man of the people, Mark Twain once ridiculed the piano as an instrument "for love-sick girls who lace themselves to skeletons." In contrast, Twain associated the African-derived banjo with "*genuine* music," whimsically comparing its rough sound to "a bad quarter, … strychnine whiskey, … the measles, … the pinfeather pimples on a pickled goose." Walt Whitman was equally enthusiastic about musical expression from the lower ranks. Insisting that the taste for melody among the masses indicated a "native elegance of soul," Whitman promoted himself as a singing bard whose verse captured vernacular musical phrasing and imagery. His favorite melodic inspirations were Italian opera, traditional family singing ensembles, and the raucous songs and dances of the minstrels.

The distinctively American genre of minstrelsy became the nation's first form of popular commercial entertainment in the second half of the nineteenth century. Growing out of the frontier humor of the tall tale, minstrels first surfaced as rustic comic songs that strung together improbable and loosely associated images in a rambling, improvisational manner. A central feature of the performance was the use of burnt-cork makeup to simulate a "blackface" appearance. By using slapstick comedy to portray African Americans as rambunctious, lazy, and sensual, white imitators established a bond of imagined racial superiority with working-class audiences. Yet the guise of minstrelsy also involved nostalgia for the simpler life of the pre-industrial order, allowed the expression of uncensored antisocial attitudes and behavior, and offered a protest against the effete affectations of upper-class morality.

Blackface musical comedy was first staged in the 1820s by George Washington Dixon, a white Virginian who sported an oversized coat and presented ditties like "Long Tail Blue" and "Zip Coon." In 1832 Thomas Dartmouth "Daddy" Rice, an Irish American, borrowed a nonsensical song and shuffle dance entitled "Jump Jim Crow" from an elderly black performer and introduced it to great acclaim at New York's Bowery Theater. Eleven years later Dan Emmett's Virginia Minstrels mounted the nation's first blackface show in Boston with a series of rousing dances, jokes, skits, and pithy songs in which the banjo and fiddle shared the melody, and rattling bones and large tambourines provided rhythm. It was Emmett who subsequently popularized and took copyright credit for the minstrel standard "I Wish I Was in Dixie's Land" ("Dixie's Land"), a nostalgic tribute to the Old South written by Ben and Lew Snowden, two African American musicians. Meanwhile, Christy's Minstrels, a troupe originating in a Buffalo tavern for Erie Canal boatmen, toured the South and the West before initiating a ten-year run on the Bowery in 1846.

Traversing the country in three theatrical circuits, minstrel productions assumed uniform characteristics by mid-century. The first part of the show would be hosted by a white master of ceremonies who introduced a number of light-hearted blackface songs and dances accompanied by an ensemble chorus. The second segment normally featured several novelty acts, including speeches by burnt-cork actors that parodied white intellectual pretension and piety or "uppity" black oratory. The finale usually consisted of a one-act slapstick comedy skit or plantation frolic. Minstrelsy was partly a manifestation of the Democratic Party's pre-Civil War alliance between southern planters and Irish American workers in northern cities. Accordingly, the minstrels mixed sentimentalized treatments of southern slavery and comic racial caricatures with elements of earthy populism and folk humor designed for non-elite audiences.

Although blackface extravaganzas did not assert overt political stances threatening to the social order, their sardonic style of comedy often targeted the custodians of formal culture. Through the use of the black mask and boastful figures like Jim Crow, burnt-cork performers could stage irreverent treatments of white authority figures, from staunch preachers, female moral reformers, charity officials, politicians, and the newly arrived rich to anyone who looked down on working people. Other routines mocked the pretentiousness of touring European opera and classical music artists.

Minstrelsy's outrageous mimicry and daring improvisations received fullest play in the theatrical setting of the plantation, a carnival-like arena whose conviviality suggested a world free of social rank, privilege, and prevailing norms. The character foibles, common-sense virtues, survival tools, and nostalgia for the rural past demonstrated by blackface characters resonated among marginalized whites with origins in the Irish, German, or American countryside. In short, minstrel spectacles conveyed both fear and envy of those it subjected to racial caricatures.

Creating the foundation for a national popular culture, late-nineteenth-century minstrelsy became the favorite stage entertainment of the American people. Although performers began to tone down lyrics and moderate the use of dialect as early as the 1850s, blackface productions persisted in making light of African American culture while absorbing its vernacular musical styles. Borrowed techniques included the punctuated phrasing of lyrics, simple delivery, syncopated dance rhythms, and widespread use of folk melodies. The minstrels also popularized a narrative structure in which the verse recounted a story commented upon by the chorus. Stephen Foster proved to be the most successful student of these traditions. The nation's leading mid-century lyricist and composer and the first American to earn a living from songwriting, Foster fused the harmonies and rhythms of minstrel music into widely acclaimed ballads that won the hearts of middle-class patrons. In doing so, he laid the groundwork for American popular music as a multi-ethnic hybrid crossing class boundaries.

THE PARLOR MINSTREL

Stephen Foster was born into an Irish American family outside Pittsburgh on July 4, 1826—the fiftieth anniversary of the signing of the Declaration of Independence and the same day presidents John Adams and Thomas Jefferson died. When Foster's father, a state legislator and land developer, suffered severe financial reverses, the family lost its rural home and was forced to live in rentals, boarding houses, and relatives' quarters. At thirteen the impressionable Foster was devastated by the news that his musical mentor, a beloved older sister who loved to play the piano and sing melancholy melodies, had died of malaria. Rather aimless as a young man, he would drop out of college after only a few days of classes. At the age of twenty, Foster moved to Cincinnati to become a bookkeeper, a vocation he never relished. Having performed Negro songs at home and subsequently sung in blackface ensembles, he began publishing dialect compositions like "Loui'siana Belle," a sentimental tribute to a slaveowner's mistress. Yet it was not until "Oh! Susannah" that Foster discovered the enormous commercial potential of minstrelsy.

Initially performed in a Pittsburgh ice cream parlor in 1847, the upbeat polka described a slave's riverboat journey in the nonsensical language of the minstrel tradition: "I come from Alabama with my banjo on my knee," the song began in burnt-cork style, "I'se gwine to Louisiana, my true lub for to see." "It rained all night de day I left, de

Stephen Foster   *(Foster Hall Collection, Center for American Music, University of Pittsburgh Library System.)*

wedder it was dry," the lyric continued with a touch of the tall tale, "the sun so hot I froze to def, Susannah don't you cry." A less well-known second verse expressed anxiety over modern technology with demeaning blackface imagery. As the narrator jumped aboard the steamboat "and tumbled down de ribber," he sang, "de lectrick fluid magnified, and killed five hundred Nigga." As "Susannah" won major exposure on the New York stage, "49-er" gold prospectors added their own lyrics to the tune and made it the unofficial anthem of the California mining camps.

Foster's rapid success allowed him to leave his bookkeeping job and become a songwriter for the Christy Minstrels. Just over the age of twenty-two, the young composer began to tailor his blackface pieces to middle-class taste and abandoned the crudest racial caricatures. "Uncle Ned" (1848) described the death of an elderly slave in respectful and compassionate terms. "Nelly Was a Lady" (1849) portrayed a black man's dignified love for a Negro woman. "Camptown Races" (1850) offered a minstrel tribute to the legendary horse races of a ramshackle settlement outside Pittsburgh. Punctuated by rhythmic shouts of "doo-dah! doo-dah!" the upbeat number captured the excitement of the free-spirited event without the slightest hint of self-consciousness.

During the 1850s Foster produced some of America's most beloved ballads. In "Old Folks at Home" (1851), a blackface narrator expressed mournful regret for the parents and surroundings he had left behind "way down upon" the "Swanee River." Through the guise of minstrelsy, Foster was able to speak to the common experience of abandoning one's birthplace and loved ones in an ever-mobile society. "Massa's in de Cold Ground" (1852), another sad lament of the South, portrayed the death of a patriarchal planter from a slave's decidedly ambivalent perspective. In 1853 Foster scored one of his greatest hits with "My Old Kentucky Home." At the age of twenty-seven, the composer had never ventured South except for a riverboat excursion to New Orleans. When Foster decided to write a song based on Harriet Beecher Stowe's *Uncle Tom's Cabin* (1852), however, he dropped blackface dialect from the final version and eliminated references to the book's lead character. What emerged was a work of timeless nostalgia over lost families, homes, and childhood captured by the haunting choral refrain, "Weep no more, my lady,/Oh! Weep no more today!"

Despite his successes, Foster remained ambivalent about his minstrel repertoire, which accounted for about 10 percent of the two-hundred pieces he wrote throughout his lifetime. On one hand, he believed that he had "done a great deal to build up a taste for the Ethiopian songs among refined people by making their words suitable to their taste, instead of the trashy and really offensive words which belong to some songs of that order." Yet he also anguished whether he should abandon the "negro idiom" and produce a "higher kind of music" for "white" men. To preserve his reputation as a composer of respectable parlor ballads, Foster had requested that his name be left off his works published in *Christy's Plantation Melodies*. Seeking to broaden his career opportunities, he moved to New York City in 1853, where he attempted to market his compositions as "American" songs.

One of the first results of the move from southern themes and blackface was "Old Dog Tray" (1853), a best-selling number whose melody originated with a minstrel Foster had written sometime earlier. He followed this hit with "Jeanie with the Light Brown Hair" (1854), a tribute to his estranged wife that sold poorly as a sharp depression took effect, but ultimately became an American classic. In the same year, Foster completed "Hard Times Come Again No More," possibly inspired by Charles Dickens' *Hard Times,* a Victorian novel then appearing in serial form. Neither a plantation ditty or parlor ballad, the dirge-like composition portrayed a genteel and virtuous white "maiden" reduced to an impoverished life of toil. Although the lyric embodied an excessive degree of sentimentality, its stark call for compassion for the unfortunate demonstrated the author's potential for spiritual and emotion maturity. "Let us pause in life's pleasures and count its many tears," it began, "while we all sup sorrow with the poor." "While we seek mirth and beauty and music light and gay," it continued, "there are frail forms fainting at the door."

"Hard Times" was presented by the popular Charles White's Minstrels as a "Negro Extravaganza." Yet by the time the ballad was published, Foster had completely abandoned the blackface format. Most of his remaining compositions would attach mawkish lines about remote beauty, child-like innocence, or premature death to recycled melodies. Two exceptions defied this pattern. "Old Black Joe" (1860), a melancholy meditation about the prospects of meeting one's loved ones in another life, approached the dignity and understated solemnity of an African American spiritual without recourse to dialect. "Beautiful Dreamer" (1862), Foster's siren song, offered an exquisitely honest metaphor of personal dissolution and escapist fantasy with a haunting melody that would be his greatest legacy.

As the Civil War broke out, Foster tried to exploit prevailing martial fervor, but his maudlin approach to the conflict elicited little interest. The composer then produced nearly thirty Sunday-school hymns, a difficult task when he no longer retained religious faith. A group of light-hearted theatrical songs, while anticipating later vaudeville forms, may have been too far ahead of their time. Increasingly in debt, Foster signed away royalties to borrow money from publishers, leading to further impoverishment. The last years of his life were spent in a dingy room on the Bowery near the German grocery and bar where he took his meager meals, wrote his last creations, consumed increasing amounts of liquor, and occasionally entertained fellow drinkers with heartfelt renditions of "Hard Times." Early in 1864 Foster gashed his neck in a bad fall. In a weakened state from a series of alcoholic binges, he failed to recover from the extensive bleeding and died at the age of thirty-seven. At Bellevue Hospital the emptied pockets of his tattered suit held three cents and a handwritten sheet of paper with the words, "dear friends and gentle hearts."

Following the close of the Civil War, Foster's songs returned to public favor as parlor, campfire, and concert entertainment. Negro choral groups like the Fisk Jubilee Singers performed several renditions of the composer's works. *Uncle Tom's Cabin,* the late nineteenth century's most popular theatrical production, invariably included Foster selections as musical instrumentation. No less an authority than African American scholar W.E.B. Du Bois would praise the composer for incorporating slavery-era melodies into songs like "Old Folks at Home" and "Old Black Joe." Early-twentieth-century classical composer Charles Ives would work Foster's musical themes into his Second Symphony (1901–02) and produce an "Elegy for Stephen Foster" (1915) that built upon motifs from "Old Black Joe."

Single-handedly, Foster had transformed crude white minstrel characterizations into lyrical parlor ballads that humanized African Americans and acknowledged their emotional depth. "They are heart songs and the finest feelings of human nature are expressed in them," abolitionist Frederick Douglass had said of the composer's creations as early as 1855. Like the street cries of Walt Whitman and the comic tales of Mark Twain, the popular lyrics and melodies of Stephen Foster helped to set the foundations of American vernacular culture and give expression to the voices of ordinary people as the nation approached the twentieth century.

SOURCES AND SUGGESTED READINGS

The Chicago World Fair's relationship to the emergence of consumer capitalism comprises the focus of James Gilbert, *Perfect Cities: Chicago's Utopias of 1893* (1991). See also the chapter on the "White City" in Alan Trachtenberg, *The Incorporation of America: Culture and Society in the Gilded Age* (1982). The cultural significance of the Exposition is the subject of Erik Larson, *The Devil in the White City: Murder, Magic, and Madness at the Fair That Changed America* (2003).

David S. Reynolds provides invaluable context for the contributions of the nineteenth century's greatest poet in *Walt Whitman's America: A Cultural Biography* (1995). See also Roger Asselineau, *The Evolution of Walt Whitman: The Creation of a Book* (1962). A useful study of the populist orientation of the work of Samuel Clemens appears in Everett Emerson, *The Authentic Mark Twain: A Literary Biography* (1984).

Cultural analyses of the multilayered issues of nineteenth-century minstrelsy abound. Helpful sources include Eric Lott, *Love and Theft: Blackface Minstrelsy and the American Working Class* (1993); W.T. Lhaman, *Raising Cain: Blackface Performance from Jim Crow to Hip Hop* (1998); Dale Cockrell, *Demons of Disorder: Early Blackface Minstrels and Their World* (1997); and William J. Mahar, *Behind the Burnt Cork Mask: Early Blackface Minstrelsy and Antebellum American Popular Culture* (1999). Michael Rogin's *Blackface, White Noise* (1996) places the minstrel tradition in a broad historical setting. Nicholas E. Tana, *High-Minded and Low-Down: Music in the Lives of Americans, 1800–1861* (2000) presents an overview of pre-Civil War song. For a nuanced view of the nation's first popular music giant, see Ken Emerson, *Doo-dah! Stephen Foster and the Rise of American Popular Culture* (1997).

Lawrence W. Levine, *Unpredictable Past: Explorations in American Cultural History* (1993) and Michael Kammen, *American Culture American Tastes: Social Change and the 20th Century* (2000) offer insights into American expressive culture since the nineteenth century. For literature, see James D. Hart, *The Oxford Companion to American Literature*, 6th ed. (1995) and Cathy N. Davidson et al. eds., *The Oxford Companion to Women's Writing in the United States* (1995). Portraits of minority writers appear in Henry Louis Gates and Nellie Y. McKay, eds., *The Norton Anthology of African American Literature* (1997) and Kathy J. Whitson, *Native American Literatures: An Encyclopedia of Works, Characters, Authors, and Themes* (1999). See also Nicolás Kanellos, *Hispanic Literature of the United States: A Comprehensive Reference* (2003) and Lawrence J. Trudeau, ed., *Asian American Literature: Reviews and Criticism of Works by American Writers of Asian Descent* (1999). A useful synthesis of socially oriented painting appears in Francis Pohl, *Framing America: A Social History of American Art* (2002).

LeRoy Ashby, *With Amusement For All: A History of American Popular Culture Since 1830* (2006) offers the most comprehensive account of the development of mass entertainment. See also Jim Cullen, *The Art of Democracy: A Concise History of Popu-

lar Culture in the United States (1996). For the history of commercial music, see Larry Starr and Christopher Waterman, *American Popular Music: From Minstrelsy to MTV* (2003); Ian Whitcomb, *After the Ball: Popular Music from Rag to Rock* (1982); and Charles Hamm, *Yesterdays: Popular Song in America* (1979) and *Putting Popular Music in Its Place* (1995).

2

The Strenuous Life of Ragtime America

The classical façades of the Chicago World's Fair could not hide the persistence of cultural ferment in late-nineteenth-century American life. Even before the onslaught of the economic depression of 1893–97, upper-class leaders had sought to universalize habits of self-control and discipline through the creation of city parks, libraries, and other uplifting public institutions. Yet innovations like the urban department store and the advent of the affectionate family contributed to the erosion of traditional moral values within the middle class. With the growing importance of self-fulfillment, emotional satisfaction, and leisure pursuits, affluent Americans increasingly turned to immigrant and African American sources for inspiration, entertainment, and styles of cultural expression. From the popular press to big-city sports, from amusement parks and Tin Pan Alley to ragtime, blues, and jazz, from burlesque, vaudeville, and the Broadway revue to motion pictures, the early twentieth century was significantly shaped by the quest for "authentic" and vital cultural forms from below.

THE ZEST FOR AMUSEMENT

As American cities tripled their population between 1890 and 1920, the urban metropolis emerged as the prime site of economic activity. The concentration of wealth in locations like New York City, where there were 1,368 millionaires in 1892, contributed to a contest for influence between recently enriched entrepreneurs and established families. Seeking to civilize the new rich while instituting proper decorum in the working class, patrician leaders turned to formal culture as an instrument of societal cohesion. Through the creation of public museums, libraries, concert halls, opera houses, schools, and parks, civic elites hoped to diffuse knowledge, taste, and refinement among the lesser orders, while reinforcing habits of personal decorum, religious duty, and social deference.

Steel magnate Andrew Carnegie, the nation's leading philanthropist, sought to reconcile the contradictions between high and low culture. The son of a radical Scots hand-loom weaver, Carnegie arrived in the United States with his struggling family at the age of thirteen. Abandoning a detested textile factory job, the ambitious young man found work as a telegraph messenger and operator by the time he was sixteen. During the Civil War he became director of telegraph communications and superintendent of military transportation for the Pennsylvania Railroad. Becoming a venture capitalist, he invested in steel production during the Depression of 1873. By adopting the efficiencies of the Bessemer process, Carnegie Steel dramatically improved quality and cut prices, allowing the firm to become a vertically organized monopoly dominating every phase of the industry. In 1892, however, company managers violently suppressed a strike at the firm's home plant in Homestead, Pennsylvania. Demoralized by events, Carnegie sold the corporation to financier J.P. Morgan in 1901.

Freed from business affairs, Andrew Carnegie fulfilled a life-long dream of using his riches to better the lives of others. A persistent critic of the "debasing" nature of money worship, Carnegie was known for a fierce hostility to monarchy and a passion for republican ideals. An admirer of the Scots dialect verse of Robert Burns and a close friend of both Mark Twain and religious free thinker Robert Ingersoll, he considered Walt Whitman to be America's greatest poet. Carnegie even compared his own tributes to capitalist technology in *Triumphant Democracy* (1886) to the spirit of Whitman's poetry. Three years later the industrialist published the "Gospel of Wealth," a tract encouraging the rich to become trustees of God's abundance through charities designed "to produce the most beneficial results for the community." Acting accordingly, Carnegie donated nearly 90 percent of a $400 million fortune after 1901 to 2,500 public libraries and an assortment of religious, educational, and peace causes.

While a minority of wealthy patrons bestowed the gift of culture on those beneath them, a larger number of urbanites began to taste the fruits of the emerging consumer revolution on their own. By the early twentieth century, salaried white-collar employment had become far more prevalent among middle-class men than independent enterprise, leading to a lessening of business responsibilities and more relaxed attitudes toward leisure and pleasure. The emphasis on self-realization and individual fulfillment was reinforced by a trend toward smaller families knit together by emotional ties of intimacy and affection. As a result, the new middle-class family tended to function more as an agent of economic consumption than a unit of production. Rather than serving as a test of moral character and competitive will, the market increasingly afforded affluent men the opportunity to earn money to be spent in pursuit of life's enjoyments.

The reorientation of the middle-class family coincided with enhanced spending on amusements, leisure pursuits, clothing, cosmetics, canned goods, home decorations, furniture, and telephones. A significant portion of these expenditures occurred through the department store, a retail institution that combined lower prices, wider choices, and autonomy for female shoppers with sophisticated merchandising of new products like phonographs, typewriters, and packaged soaps. Presenting commodities in a magical and glamorous setting, merchandisers helped to make shopping itself a leisure-time activity. As Henry Ford's mass-produced and relatively affordable Model-T automobiles entered the national marketplace in the 1910s, retail installment purchase plans expanded consumer ranks even further.

The consumer revolution also impacted the working class. Ready-made clothing, produced in New York City's garment trade, contributed to the democratization of American fashion by eliminating the high cost of custom tailoring. Gradual wage increases and working-hour reductions, particularly for women abandoning domestic service for factory or mill employment, also opened up consumption opportunities. Expanding upon these possibilities, economist Simon Patten suggested in *The New Basis of Civilization* (1909) that American society was moving from an age of scarcity to one of abundance. Patten predicted that industrial laborers would submit to work-place discipline in order to earn sufficient income to gratify the "zest for amusement." The "craving to be amused," he insisted, could serve as the basis of an efficient and cohesive social order. In advancing a rationale for consumer democracy, the economist had asserted the important principle that social harmony need not be imposed from above, but could flow from the choices of ordinary people.

IRISH AND GERMAN ACCENTS

Urban politics provided one of the first arenas for contesting elite hegemony. Following the Civil War, a series of immigrant electoral machines displaced the Anglo-Protestant political leaders of many of the nation's largest cities. In New York, Boston, Chicago, and San Francisco, rule by Irish American political professionals became legendary. As the initial wave of a massive trans-Atlantic migration, nearly 5.5 million Irish nationals fled impoverished conditions and British colonialism to come to the United States in the one-hundred years after 1815. Originally consigned to menial labor positions or domestic service, Irish immigrants saw many of their American-educated children work their way into white-collar employment. With the advantages of English language facility and support systems in the Roman Catholic Church and urban social institutions, the Irish made an easy transition into municipal governance through political clubs like New York's Tammany Hall.

By exchanging social services, jobs, and city contracts for political loyalty and using public payrolls to distribute wealth among constituents, Irish American Democratic bosses built up powerful political machines from the bottom up. The most publicized of these power brokers was George Washington Plunkitt, a Tammany Hall district leader from Manhattan's Middle West Side. Born to immigrant parents in 1842, Plunkitt quit school at eleven and spent time as a construction contractor until he discovered that politics was a more lucrative pastime. At the age of thirty-eight, he held simultaneous positions as assemblyman, alderman, and county supervisor and was known for conducting public consultations from a bootblack stand at the county court house. In 1905 William L. Riordon, a New York Irish American journalist, pieced together a variety of newspaper stories about the urban boss and reworked them into a book entitled *Plunkitt of Tammany Hall.*

Plunkitt recently had lost a bid to retain his state senate seat to a Republican reformer who claimed that the leader had mortgaged the district to railroad and corporate interests. Riordon set out to defend Tammany against such charges by expanding upon literary stereotypes of the genial urban boss. The forty-four-year-old political reporter already had published fifteen newspaper interviews with Plunkitt, which he reorganized and supplemented with fresh quotes. Riordon also used existing literature on ethnic electoral machines for information on the social services normally offered by local operatives. Finally, he constructed a fictitious Plunkitt diary, published in a last segment of the book, that borrowed a phrase from President Theodore Roosevelt to describe the "Strenuous Life of the Tammany District Leader."

In an effort to profile Plunkitt as a colorful character, Riordon had the district leader describe the difference between "honest" and "dishonest" graft, a distinction that separated the intelligent foresight of a Wall Street investor from a thief stealing funds from the municipal treasury. Plunkitt was pictured as someone whose personal fortune resulted from convenient access to useful information, prompting the boss to suggest that his epitaph should read "He Seen His Opportunities and He Took 'Em." Riordon's book was careful to emphasize the unpretentious qualities of a successful Tammany operative. Officeholders were advised to live like their neighbors, since "puttin' on style don't pay in politics." One needed to "talk the language the people talk" and reach "the heart" of voters, Plunkitt was quoted as saying. The only way to hold a district, readers learned, was "to go among the people, see them and be seen … to go right down among the poor families and help them in the different ways they need help."

One year after Riordon's populist characterization of George Washington Plunkitt, Irish American journalist Finley Peter Dunne published his sixth collection of the wit of an irreverent Chicago bartender known as "Mr. Dooley." The son of lower-middle-class Irish immigrants, Dunne was born in Chicago in 1867 and worked as a newspaper office boy by the time he was sixteen. Turning sportswriter the next year, he won a following for his colorful prose and the invention of baseball slang terms like "southpaw" for left-handed pitchers. After a stint as a political reporter and editor, Dunne began to write a series of "Martin Dooley" pieces in 1893. Modeled on James McGarry, an Irish saloonkeeper whose establishment was frequented by reporters and politicians, the fictional character spoke with a heavy brogue, conveniently disguising his creator's satires of pretense and hypocrisy as good clean fun. Once Dunne's features achieved popularity and were syndicated in the late 1890s, he changed the name of his protagonist to "Mr. Dooley" and placed him on "Archey Road."

As Dooley relayed stories of local firemen and police to his chief listener—a steel mill worker named Hennessy—readers learned to relish his crusty powers of description. This was particularly so when discussion turned to the world of politics, usually introduced by Mr. Dooley's ritualistic "I see by the 'papers." At that point, anything and anyone was fair game. It was Mr. Dooley who fashioned the immortal caveat that "the Supreme Court follows the election returns." More often, his targets were prominent figures who took themselves too seriously. "I wonder if two hundred years from now people will cease to talk of William Jennings Bryan," he speculated about the populist Democrat and free-silver advocate. "He won't, but will they?" Commenting on corporate corruption in politics, Dooley marveled that "a man expects to be elected President of the United States ... for the fine qualities that the rest of us use only to keep out of the penitentiary." "We may be a tough gang over at the City Hall," he later observed, "but, thank the Lord, no man ever accused us of being life-insurance presidents."

Wealth was a favorite topic for Mr. Dooley, who referred to the legendary baron of the Rockefeller oil realm as "Jawn D." "Getting money and behaving yourself don't always go together," he explained, noting that riches required a person to "cash in" their friends, relatives, health, and happiness. The poor, in contrast, were simply "people that've been out at work when opportunity knocked." Dunne's cynicism was particularly sharp when it came to reform. "The more ye see it the better ye like it," Dooley said of vice. No one really wanted to reform themselves, he declared. "He'll reform other people gladly.... But a healthy man'll never reform while he has the strength." At another point Dunne's host relayed an observation from the fictional Father Kelly that Thanksgiving was founded by the Puritans to give thanks for being preserved from the Indians, and that "we keep it to give thanks we are preserved from the Puritans."

Like the Irish, nineteenth-century immigrants from Germany sustained Old World traditions while adjusting to the political opportunities and popular culture of the United States. In adopted cities such as Cincinnati, Milwaukee, and St. Louis, German Americans created intricate networks of benevolent societies, sports clubs, beer gardens and taverns, cultural institutions, and political reform associations. German newspapers played a central role in sustaining immigrant nostalgia for serious theater, high-minded literature, symphonic music, and grand opera. Meanwhile, New York's *Morgen Journal,* a German language daily owned by newspaper publisher William

Randolph Hearst, helped to acclimate German Americans to mass culture innovations such as the amusement park, spectator sports, the vaudeville stage, and the movies.

NEW IMMIGRANTS

By the 1880s, a second wave of immigration had begun to populate the United States with unprecedented numbers of laborers and peasants from the rural villages of eastern, central, and southern Europe. Attracted to unskilled and semi-skilled positions in the industrial sector, newcomers arrived at an average rate of a million a year by the early twentieth century, although some returned home. By the end of World War I, foreign-born Americans and their children constituted nearly 60 percent of the residents of cities with over a hundred thousand people. Like their predecessors, the new immigrants settled in urban neighborhoods where they could establish ethnic stores, banks, newspapers, cooperatives, mutual-aid societies, and in the case of the Italians and Poles, receive the social services and spiritual support of the Catholic Church. The "poor man's club" of ethnic saloons offered blue-collar workers a refuge from industrial discipline in a relaxing atmosphere that enhanced male camaraderie and collective self-esteem.

The most numerous of the new arrivals were eastern and central European Jews, some two million of whom came to the United States between 1880 and 1917. Like the Irish, the Jews were fleeing oppressive political and economic conditions in a homeland to which it was virtually impossible to return. This meant that entire families and communities participated in the exodus, accounting for the fact that women constituted half the number of migrants, and that significant numbers of religious, cultural, and mercantile leaders joined the migration. Since two-thirds or more of Jewish immigrants identified themselves as skilled workers with the ability to read and write, many were prepared for jobs in the industrial economy. When one million Jewish newcomers settled in New York City, half on Manhattan's Lower East Side, they provided both the entrepreneurs and the labor force for the burgeoning ready-to-wear garment trades.

Forced into overcrowded tenements, the new immigrants conducted much of their social life in the streets. By the turn of the twentieth century, the Lower East Side was not only known for its colorful pushcarts, open-air markets, and ethnic shops, but for its rich array of cafes, newspapers, concert halls, and theaters. The common language of the quarter was Yiddish, a German-based dialect whose written form used the Hebrew alphabet. An extremely expressive hybrid, Yiddish lent itself to socialist, trade union, and Zionist rhetoric. It also was incorporated in the secular poetry, song, humor, and drama that thrived in the new environment. Catering especially to recently arrived immigrants, New York's inexpensive Yiddish theater attracted between five and seven thousand patrons every night. By depicting continuities between traditional social values and the American way of life, stage plays and Yiddish newspapers often functioned as agents of acculturation for predominately working-class audiences.

To outsiders like Hutchins Hapgood, author of *The Spirit of the Ghetto* (1902), the culturally endowed poets and artists of the Lower East Side were vital subjects of human interest. Jewish writers tended to be more circumspect. In *Yekl: A Tale of the New York Ghetto* (1896), Yiddish newspaper editor Abraham Cahan mounted a brief for traditionalism by suggesting that manliness meant taking care of one's family and religious duties. Yet in *The Rise of David Levinsky* (1917), Cahan told the story of a garment worker who deserts his comrades to become a dress manufacturer. The American city, he wrote, was a land "of fantastic experiences, of marvelous transformations." Similar fervor permeated Mary Antin's memoir, *The Promised Land* (1912). In Israel Zangwill's *The Melting Pot* (1909), a play published in book form in 1914, the United States was depicted as "God's Crucible," a place where "all the races of Europe" were "melting and re-forming." In contrast, essayist Horace Kallen held that America's umbrella of "cultural pluralism" allowed ethnic peoples to maintain their distinct traditions.

THE PENNY PRESS AND THE COMICS

The mix between immigrant and native-born cultures appeared most clearly in big-city journalism. By the 1880s twelve-thousand newspapers appeared each day in the United States. Through innovations in mechanical production and graphic imaging, mass-production techniques gradually took over late-nineteenth-century journalism. However, it was not until St. Louis publisher Joseph Pulitzer purchased the *New York World* in 1883 and geared advertising rates to the number of readers that the age of mass-circulation dailies officially began. To maximize newsstand sales, Pulitzer used bold headlines and half-tone photographs to highlight human interest stories on the idle rich, powerful trusts, corrupt political bosses, sensational crimes, and urban poverty. The *World* also cultivated New York's huge working class by devoting increased space to sports, affordable women's fashions, and comic strips.

Pulitzer's leading competitor was William Randolph Hearst. The son of a California railroad and mining millionaire, Hearst had convinced his father in 1887 to let him run the near-bankrupt *San Francisco Examiner.* The twenty-four-year-old publisher wasted no time in hiring quality staffers such as humorist Ambrose Bierce and editorial cartoonist Homer Davenport. He also convinced Ernest Lawrence Thayer, with whom he had served on the *Harvard Lampoon,* to produce contributions for the Sunday supplement, one of which turned out to be the classic ballad "Casey at the Bat" (1888). Adopting Pulitzer's mass- marketing techniques, Hearst proceeded to align the *Examiner* with a variety of populist causes. Consequently, by pushing for regulation of the trusts, public ownership of utilities, lower transit fees, and progressive tax policies, he raised the newspaper's circulation from a mere thirty thousand to eight hundred thousand. Fresh from this triumph, the young entrepreneur bought the *New York Journal* in 1895, initiated a price war with Pulitzer's *World,* and reduced newsstand prices to a penny.

In an effort to dominate the New York newspaper market, Hearst recruited Richard Felton Outcault, Pulitzer's leading comic strip artist. A university graduate who had studied art in Paris, Outcault was the creator of a Sunday feature called *Down in Hogan's Alley*, a title taken from the first line of a popular Irish American song. The strip presented a colorful portrait of the residents of a New York Irish tenement, among them a primitively drawn, unnamed, single-toothed, bald-headed young street urchin. When Hearst ran *Hogan's Alley* in a multicolored Sunday comics supplement in 1896, Outcault's character appeared with a yellow nightshirt, prompting readers to christen him "The Yellow Kid" and inaugurating the term "yellow journalism" to describe the crowd-pleasing tactics of the mass-circulation papers.

By introducing a permanent cast of characters whose activities appeared in adjoining pictorial frames, Outcault pioneered the modern comic strip. Capable of being read in two minutes, the feature attracted a loyal following by carrying on a sequential narrative from one installment to the next. In 1897 Hearst inaugurated *Katzenjammer Kids,* a frolicking portrait of working-class immigrant life drawn by Rudolph Dirks, a nineteen-year-old German American artist. Dirks developed the thought balloon, thereby providing a clue to his characters' inner thinking. Two years later the *Journal* introduced Frederick B. Opper's *Happy Hooligan.* The son of Austrian immigrants, Opper perfected the use of the speech balloon to convey the dialogue of a mundane but witty and lovable clown who wore a tomato soup can on his head, patiently endured misfortunes and cruelties, and usually wound up the butt of his own best intentions.

As publishers syndicated comics in the early twentieth century, the focus on ordinary characters and immigrant life proved highly popular. In 1908 Harry Conway Fisher's *Mutt and Jeff* began a run as the first successful daily strip. Mutt was a compulsive gambler and poolroom shark who had rescued his buddy Jeff from an insane asylum. Through these zany but believable characters. Fisher introduced common phrases such as "fall guy," "inside stuff," "got his goat," and "this is going to be a scream." George McManus' *Bringing Up Father,* debuting in 1913, followed the exploits of Jiggs, a working-class Irish American who seeks refuge from his snobbish wife at the local saloon and billiards hall and invents the expression "let George do it." In contrast, *The Newlyweds,* the first family-oriented strip, shifted the focus to more affluent protagonists. Other middle-class sagas included *Hazel the Heartbreaker,* the story of a young woman trying to marry up the social ladder, and *Abie the Agent,* a humorously sympathetic account of a Jewish family head and business figure.

AMUSING THE MILLIONS

Coverage of athletic contests remained an essential ingredient of the mass-circulation press with particular emphasis on prizefighting, the preferred contest of working-class men. Boxing flourished in immigrant communities as a test of physical prowess, courage, intelligence, and manly honor. The overwhelming majority of late-nineteenth-century fighters were Irish Americans, many of whom had learned to defend themselves in urban street brawls. In the post-Civil War era, commercial bouts were most often fought in taverns, gyms, or athletic clubs. Since the sport was financially dependent on gambling revenues, it quickly fostered ties to bookmakers and political machine operatives. Denounced by social reformers for excessive violence and a culture of corruption, boxing was outlawed in most states until the 1890s. Nevertheless prizefighting thrived as a simultaneous agent of Americanization, ethnic identity, and working-class social mobility.

The greatest boxer and athletic hero of the nineteenth century was John L. Sullivan. Known as the Boston Strongboy, the hefty Irish American was famous for a free-swinging style and powerful punches. After winning the heavyweight crown in 1882, the "Great John L." slugged it out in a legendary match in Mississippi five years later that earned him a reputation as the "people's champion." Embodying the survival of the fittest creed on the most basic terms, Sullivan toured the nation's vaudeville circuits in the 1880s, offering fifty dollars to any challenger who could last four rounds with him.

By popularizing the use of gloves and modernizing the sport, Sullivan attracted admirers outside the working class. Yet prizefighting would not draw large numbers of upscale fans until the 1920s. In contrast, professional baseball elicited a broader range of support. Baseball had functioned on amateur lines up through the 1850s. Following the Civil War, however, teams began charging admission and paying salaries, creating the first commercial sport whose merits rested primarily with the game itself, rather than with gambling. By the 1880s a variety of ethnic benevolent societies, labor unions, political parties, and civic-minded breweries had sponsored professional squads. The sport reached a turning point in 1876 with the advent of the National League. By gradually instituting uniform contracts requiring proper behavior on and off the field, the League assumed the right to blacklist players for insubordination or moral offenses like drinking or gambling. When the National and American Leagues merged in 1903, the game solidified its image as a legitimate American sport.

Like all competitive athletics, baseball could be praised for advancing egalitarian virtues such as fair play, individual discipline, self-sacrifice, and teamwork. As the sports press promoted the game as a cohesive force of American social democracy rooted in pastoral tradition, baseball became the subject of hundreds of works of romantic juvenile fiction by authors such as Frank Merriwell. The reality, however, was more complicated. Analyses of early-twentieth-century team rosters reveal that one-third of major leaguers came out of the skilled manual laboring class, 44 percent from white-collar families, and another fifth from farming backgrounds. Yet with the exception of several American Indians and a few German Jews competing under assumed names, the overwhelming majority of players were of Irish, German, or native-born white Protestant backgrounds. Virtually no offspring of "new immigrants" partic- ipated in organized baseball in its early stages, and no African Americans were permit- ted in the game for nearly a half-century after 1898.

Baseball fans tended to come from the same backgrounds as players, particularly as enterprising owners responded to the sport's popularity by investing in expensive, fire-resistant stadiums in the 1910s. To maximize revenues, franchises established three admission price categories, confining a small number of the cheapest seats to the open-air "bleachers." Attendance at a baseball game and the ritualistic consumption of hot dogs, pretzels, and beer offered a welcome release from the enforced discipline of industrial labor. But even after Chicago White Sox owner Charles Comiskey initiated Sunday competition in 1900, most teams were required to conform to state or local "blue laws" prohibiting professional sports contests on the Sabbath, thereby depriving most workers of the chance to attend games on their day off. Baseball's quasi-populist appeal, nevertheless, was captured in "Take Me Out to the Ballgame" (1908), a popular waltz in which a young woman begs to join the crowds rooting for the home team.

From the 1890s on, mixed-sex diversions came to play an increasing role in American popular culture. One of the first to do so was the amusement park. Seeking to fill seats on weekends, trolley car companies began to assemble end-of-the-line attractions on city outskirts. Establishments such as Brooklyn's Coney Island emulated the Chicago World's Fair Midway with mechanized rides like carousels and roller coasters, food con-

The beach at Coney Island *(photo by Irving Underhill, courtesy of the Brooklyn Public Library —Brooklyn Collection)*

cessions, arcade installations, bathing facilities, vaudeville theaters, band pavilions, beer saloons, and dance halls. As the parks spread to nearly every major population center, their uninhibited atmosphere proved extremely popular among young people seeking freedom from parental supervision, particularly single working women. In a holiday atmosphere of relative anonymity, familiarity between strange men and women could take place in a harmless context. By suspending conventional proprieties and lessening personal restraints, urban recreational facilities like the amusement park provided welcome entertainment and emotional release for ordinary Americans.

RAGGING RHYTHMS

Amusement park music halls normally featured performances of popular numbers from the variety stage and musical theater. With the advent of mass-produced pianos and broad dissemination of sheet music, the same selections often found their way into middle-class homes. By the 1890s a sizable music publishing industry had coalesced on Manhattan's West 28th Street. Once songs were promoted by in-house song "pluggers," sheet music sales could be enhanced with the endorsement of well-known entertainers. The cacophony of tingling pianos accompanying these auditions led journalists to refer to the district as Tin Pan Alley, a name that continued to identify the popular music business for decades.

Most turn-of-the-century music publishers were first- or second-generation Jewish immigrants who tailored most of their output to middle-class tastes. Sheet music production often leaned toward sentimental waltzes and parlor ballads such as "When You Were Sweet Sixteen" (1898) and "Sweet Adeline" (1903). Yet the vitality of urban and ethnic influences rapidly made their way into popular song. In 1892 Charles K. Harris, a self-taught Jewish musician who played "by ear," translated an encounter observed at a Chicago dance hall into a wistful ballad entitled "After the Ball," a piece that sold ten million sheet music copies over the next twenty years. Instead of a declaration of pure love, the lilting waltz warned of the consequences of moralistic rigidity with the story of a young man who witnesses his sweetheart kissing a stranger, only to learn years after he has cut off all contact that the interloper was her brother.

Irish Americans provided a particularly lucrative marketing niche for Tin Pan Alley tunesmiths. One of the pioneers of the genre was Edward ("Ned") Harrigan, a New York song-and-dance man whose ballads described life in the working-class Five Points district of Lower Manhattan. By the 1890s, however, many of Harrigan's imitators sought to broaden the appeal of their work by abandoning ethnic dialect and stereotypes while maintaining a distinctive Irish flavor. This was evident in some of the decade's biggest hits, including "Sweet Rosie O'Grady" (1896) and "My Wild Irish Rose" (1899). Other perennial favorites like "The Sidewalks of New York" (1894) made reference to obvious Irish characters like "me and Mamie O'Rorke," while "The

Band Played On" (1895), the signature song of the period, described an Irishman named "Casey" who waltzed the night away with a strawberry blonde.

Despite the persistence of subsequent favorites like "Let Me Call You Sweetheart" (1910) and "Down By the Old Mill Stream" (1910), popular music reflected a less-idealized approach to romance in the first two decades of the new century. The vernacular phrasing and emotional intimacy of songs like "Melancholy Baby" (1912), "You Made Me Love You" (1913), and "For Me and My Gal" (1917) mirrored the informal tone of ragtime, the musical craze that swept the nation after 1900. Ragtime traced its origins to the African American minstrel troupes that played northern cities in the late 1850s. In the years after the Civil War, professional black singers, dancers, comedians, and musicians achieved widespread acclaim by presenting themselves to white audiences as untrained and guileless minstrels. African American composers such as James Bland even adopted minstrel racial imagery in popular dialect tunes such as "Carry Me Back to Old Virginny" (1878).

The grand finale of minstrel shows revolved around the high-stepping cakewalk, an up-tempo dance routine rooted in slave imitations of white pretensions. African American minstrelsy also produced the comic "coon song," a syncopated send-up of black urban dandies. Another form of parody surfaced in the 1870s and '80s when black piano players in boisterous Mississippi River towns such as Memphis and St. Louis began to mock European and American music by rhythmically improvising or "ragging" melodies. Keyboard musicians now replaced the clapping accents of the cakewalk with a steady bass beat, while using the right hand to syncopate the normal phrasings of the banjo, violin, or vocal lead. Ragtime verses, often rendered in dialect, sketched a narrative followed by choral commentary. Yet the music was mainly intended for dancing. A fusion of European composition and African American rhythmic techniques, ragtime brought the traditional shouts, spirituals, and work songs of the black South into line with the more frenetic tempos of urban-industrial America.

Although African American composer Jesse Pickett's "Dream Rag" initially debuted at the World's Fair Midway, ragtime more often surfaced in the saloons, gambling houses, and brothels of the adjoining vice district, where musicians such as W.C. Handy and Scott Joplin briefly performed. Born in northeast Texas in 1868, Joplin was the son of a former slave who worked on the railroad and a free-born black woman employed as a domestic servant. His childhood was spent in Texarkana, where he took piano lessons from a German immigrant before taking to the road in his twenties as an itinerant musician. In 1896 Joplin arrived at the railroad nexus of Sedalia, Missouri, where he studied music at a local college and supported himself by playing piano at black night spots. As the ragtime vogue gathered momentum, publishers began to print sheet music versions of hits such as Ben R. Harney's "Mister Johnson, Turn Me Loose" (1896) and Kerry Mills' "At a Georgia Camp Meeting" (1899). Yet it was Joplin's "Maple Leaf Rag" (1899) that revolutionized American popular music.

Scott Joplin

Dedicated to the black railroad workers' saloon where the musician normally entertained, the instrumental was released by a German publisher in Sedalia and sold a half-million sheet music copies over the next ten years. On the basis of this initial sensation, Joplin toured the Middle West as the "King of Ragtime." Classifying his music as "classic ragtime," the composer continued to infuse subsequent pieces such as "The Easy Winners" (1901), "The Entertainer" (1902), and "The Strenuous Life" (1902) with the elegant styling that marked his first creation. Joplin published more than forty ragtime pieces and some seventy piano and vocal numbers, as well as an opera entitled *Treemonisha* (1911) fusing classical phrasing with African American folk motifs.

By the turn of the twentieth century, musicians in New Orleans had begun to supplement ragtime piano harmonies and cakewalks with elaborate horn orchestrations. Known for a Creole mixture of Latino and African cultures, the multi-ethnic Crescent City provided a free-wheeling environment that encouraged a variety of musical styles. As a manufacturing center of wind instruments, New Orleans featured a tradition of brass and reed musicianship evident in the performances of Mexican American ensembles, military bands, and circus processions. Local musicians readily incorporated such instrumentation into funeral entourages, street parades, weddings, lodge events, and religious carnivals. The result was an improvised instrumental music with strong rhythmic accents, deviating pitch, varying intonations, and strong emotion that ultimately came to be known as jazz.

New Orleans jazz derived its economic base from the cabarets, brothels, dance halls, saloons, and gambling joints of the city's Storyville vice district. As racial segregation codes tightened in the 1890s, Creole musicians were barred from performing with white counterparts and forced to ply their trade in the African American community. The consequent explosion of musical expression would lay the groundwork for the twentieth century's most unique art form. A key participant in these efforts was the Creole cornet player Buddy Bolden, creator of the classic New Orleans jazz ensemble. Beginning in the mid–1890s, Bolden led a band that featured intense collaboration between two cornets, a clarinet, a trombone, a stand-up bass, a guitar, and drums, interspersed with improvised solos. Other Creole jazz pioneers included clarinetist Sidney Bechet, cornetist Joseph "King" Oliver, and composer and pianist Jelly Roll Morton. Native son Louis Armstrong would emerge from the impoverished African American quarter of New Orleans to become the central figure of jazz history.

RAGTIME IN BLACK AND WHITE

"Got ragtime habits and I talk that way," the lyrics of a popular contemporary ditty proclaimed, "I sleep in ragtime and rag all day." Ragtime music and dance highlighted white society's fascination with African American cultural forms. As early as 1893, Czech classical composer Antonin Dvorak, the creator of the folk-infused *New World Symphony,* had predicted that the future of American music would be "founded upon what are called the Negro melodies." Twenty-one years later playwright Israel Zangwill noted that ragtime and its accompanying dances had created a "spiritual miscegenation" between whites and blacks that would permit the culture of "ex-Africans" to continue defining the United States. Vaudeville promoters even heralded ragged rhythms as "the folk-music of the American city." Given hardening white racial attitudes in the 1890s and after, however, cross-fertilization between the two cultures involved a complex process that went beyond the ease of such generalizations.

Like contemporary chronicles of western outlaws, black popular music offered a taste of the forbidden to white consumers. As much as society stereotyped African Americans as hapless inferiors, whites perceived black performers as transmitters of an authentic folk tradition their own culture lacked. As a result, a few black songwriters experienced a degree of commercial success. In 1896 lyricist and composer Ernest Hogan synthesized ragtime and "coon song" styles into a ditty entitled "All Coons Look Alike to Me," a comic piece describing a proper young woman's rejection of unsavory urban dandies as appropriate suitors. Not surprisingly, Hogan's number came to serve as the basis of racial taunts when its chorus was whistled on city streets by hostile whites.

As dialect selections came to dominate turn-of-the-century Tin Pan Alley, scores of white imitators worked the "coon song" formula into demeaning odes to southern "darkies" and plantation life. Yet African American composers built upon Hogan's combination of ragtime syncopation and vernacular lyrics in numbers like "Hello! Ma Baby" (1899), a spirited piece by Joseph E. Howard and Ida Emerson, and Hughie Cannon's classic "Bill Bailey, Won't You Please Come Home?" (1902). "Under the Bamboo Tree" (1902), a piece composed by black vaudeville entertainer Bob Cole with lyrics by James Weldon Johnson, sought to elevate African American popular music to higher levels of artistry by cleaning up racial caricatures and toning down offensive dialect. The song was a major hit, selling nearly a half-million sheet music copies.

Despite the sporadic success of black composers, it fell to a European immigrant to ensure overall white acceptance of African American popular music. Born in Russia in 1888 as Israel Baline, the songwriter later known as Irving Berlin migrated with his family at the age of four to New York's Lower East Side. When his father, a former cantor who worked in a kosher meat factory, died four years later, young Izzy quit school to hawk newspapers on the Bowery. For amusement he began to perform songs for customers learned through the open doors of neighborhood restaurants and saloons. When Berlin's mother disapproved of the street urchin's plans to become a singing waiter, he ran away from home. Finding work as a publisher's song "plugger," he made a living introducing musical numbers to vaudeville theatergoers. At the age of sixteen, Berlin achieved his goal of becoming a singing waiter. When asked to write a publicity number for his employers at Nigger Mike's Chinatown restaurant, he initiated a fifty-year career as America's most prolific and famous tunesmith.

Berlin published his first lyric at nineteen and followed it with a minor Italian dialect hit. It was not until 1911 that he made his mark as a songwriter. It was then that Berlin turned his ear for vernacular idiom and African American syncopation into the infectious "Alexander's Ragtime Band." Although the number was not strictly in ragtime meter, its short, punctuated bugle-call phrasing, jagged breaks, internal rhymes, and slang contractions captured the genre's democratic irreverence. "Oh, ma honey, Oh, ma honey," the verse began in mild dialect, "ain't you goin', ain't you goin',/to the leader man, ragged meter man?" The booming chorus beckoned the listener to "come on and hear, come on and hear,/it's the best band in the land, … just the bestest band what am, honey lamb." A second refrain referenced the minstrels by promising a ragged version of "The Swanee River." By introducing African American slang and ragtime music to white audiences, Berlin served as a key transition figure. Initially performed in blackface by Al Jolson, "Alexander" quickly sold a million sheet music copies.

Many white Americans first heard ragtime rhythms in commercial dance establishments. An outgrowth of neighborhood social clubs, the dance hall offered young people freedom from family and community ties. In New York City, where five hundred such facilities proliferated by 1910, dance halls attracted single female garment workers, domestic servants, and retail clerks, many under the age of twenty. Beyond the physical pleasures of movement and the excitement of dressing up, the establishments provided opportunities for romantic flirtations or even sexual encounters, particularly when ballrooms were adjacent to saloons. Instead of the patterned movement of feet featured in European dancing, patrons preferred the "tough dances" associated with black night life or the vice districts. These included numbers with suggestive names like the Slow Rag, Two-Step, Turkey Trot, Grizzly Bear, Texas Tommy, and Bunny Hug. Moral reformers agonized about the erosion of propriety when frenzied partners clung to each other in crouched positions and provocatively learned to "shimmy" their hips.

Ragtime soon found its way to larger dance palaces and cabarets. A hybrid of the opulent hotel saloon and disreputable male vice den, the refurbished cabaret featured risqué entertainment, drinking, and dancing to live music. By moving performers from the stage to the dance floor and encouraging them to mingle with patrons, the cabaret presented itself as a sociable and democratic gathering place for fun-loving couples. Both nightclubs and ballrooms outpaced the dance hall in social status because they catered to both second-generation Americans and the native-born middle class. Here, overtly sexual aspects of African American dances like the Charleston and the Black Bottom were subject to modifications to preserve perceived standards of decorum. Dance instructors Irene and Vernon Castle introduced and legitimized the new dances in the most prestigious venues with demonstrations known for restraint, refinement, and grace. Irving Berlin's composition of a drag called "Play a Simple Melody" for *Watch Your Step* (1914), a Broadway revue featuring the Castles, soon established a national dance craze.

VAUDEVILLE AND THE BLUES

Ragtime easily took to the American stage. Mid-nineteenth century theatrical productions had appealed to a broad public spectrum by mixing melodramatic readings from Shakespeare with a variety of magicians, dancers, singers, acrobats, minstrels, and comics. Original plays often exploited common nostalgia for the rural past by pitting innocent virtue against the corruptions of urban life and privilege. Adaptations of Harriet Beecher Stowe's best-selling antislavery novel, *Uncle Tom's Cabin: Life Among the Lowly* (1852), were among the most popular productions. By 1900 five hundred companies were performing action-oriented versions of the piece before American audiences. Yet as urbane elites rallied behind a consolidated "highbrow" culture of classical music and high drama, public performances segmented along class lines. Instead of seeking mere entertainment, refined theatergoers sought to demonstrate higher social status by approaching art as a genteel route to aesthetic discipline and spiritual elevation.

Rejecting the high-minded cultural pretensions of the prosperous classes, many Americans preferred less elevated forms of amusement. By 1902, ninety-eight traveling circuses were bringing a touch of slightly disreputable adventure and excitement to big cities and small towns alike. Burlesque offered another alternative to refined gentility. First appearing in the United States in the late 1860s with a tour by English performer Lydia Thompson and her "British Blondes," burlesque theater originally offered parodies of conventional gender roles in which women sang and danced in revealing tights or short men's tunics. A series of risqué female musical revues and women's minstrel shows followed in the next decade. By the late 1880s the hefty May Howard ranked as America's undisputed "queen" of the genre. As entrepreneurs discovered that working men experienced a vicarious sense of mastery through the erotic display of women's bodies, they consolidated the industry into two national circuits that played to the cheap theaters and saloons of white male vice districts.

By the start of the twentieth century, vaudeville had replaced minstrels and burlesque as the nation's most popular entertainment. Like its predecessors, its roots lay in big-city concert saloons and music halls. During the Civil War, impresario Tony Pastor had staged Bowery and Broadway variety shows in which topical lyrics about war, labor issues, and women's fashions were pegged to familiar melodies. In 1879, Irish American performers Edward Harrigan and Tony Hart produced *The Mulligan Guards.* Centered in a Bowery saloon, the play combined catchy songs and dances, slapstick ethnic comedy, and real-life portraits of local toughs, newsboys, flower girls, and saloon patrons. A similar mix filled the bill at Tony Pastor's vaudeville house, known in the 1890s for personalities such as ex-sheetmetal worker John W. Kelly ("The Rolling Mill Man") and Maggie Cline ("The Irish Queen"). The daughter of a shoe factory foreman, Cline performed feisty ditties such as "When Hogan Pays the Rent" and the boxing saga "Throw Him Down, McCloskey."

Seeking to expand the vaudeville audience beyond blue-collar male workers, entrepreneurs began to eliminate on-site liquor sales and to purge routines of overt sexuality and rough humor. These changes became the norm in the 1890s, when Benjamin Franklin Keith and Edward Albee organized a nationwide syndicate of thousands of vaudeville "palaces." With continuous shows from 9:30 a.m. to 10:30 at night, each of the chain's venues offered a highly structured menu of dramatic readings, opera and popular song solos, animal acts, ballets, comedy skits, sexual impersonations, magic presentations, toned-down burlesque routines, and musical extravaganzas. The rapid-fire pace of the shows was maintained by limiting most acts to ten minutes, reserving twenty-to-thirty-minute segments for featured "headliners." Such tactics appeared to be successful. A New York City survey of 1911 reported that while manual laborers continued to comprise 60 percent of vaudeville house audiences, women accounted for about a third of ticket holders and clerical workers 36 percent.

Vaudeville's commercial secret lay in its universal appeal. Audiences were fascinated by the drama of self-liberation staged by Harry Houdini, a Hungarian Jewish im-

Sophie Tucker

migrant, who carried out incomprehensible escapes from locked boxes, safes, strait-jackets, and handcuffs. Eva Tanguay, the buxom "Queen of Perpetual Motion," offered a taste of burlesque by singing uninhibited and humorous ditties with a lusty sexuality. Tanguay invariably topped off her act with a manic version of the cooch dance, followed by her signature song, "I Don't Care." Russian-born Sophie Tucker, a working-class Jew who grew up in Hartford and began her career as a blackface "coon shouter," presented herself as an earthy, humorous, and world-wise Red Hot Momma. A heavy-set woman with a raucous voice who did not pretend to be sexually desirable, Tucker parodied marriage, but conveyed an honest desire for the joys of physical love. Her fame rested upon her rendition of "Some of These Days" (1910), a betrayed lover's fantasy of revenge written by black lyricist and musician Sheldon Brooks.

One of vaudeville's most important functions involved the acculturation of immigrants and their children. Through humor and self-parody, ethnic comedians softened the difficulties of abandoning Old World religious, family, and folk traditions for the harsh realities of modern life. Adolph Phillip's "Dutch Act," which made fun of newcomers fracturing the English language, was an enormous hit among German Americans. In a similar fashion, comedy performers like Eddie Cantor, George Burns, George Jessel, and (Joe) Weber and (Lew) Fields commented on the ironies and contradictions of the Jewish American experience with impeccable timing, wordplay, and delivery. Irish immigrants were able to laugh at their own foibles while taking pride in their ethnic and American identities through versatile entertainers like George M. Cohan or comedians (Ed) Gallagher and (Al) Shean. Even Chinese Americans found a place on the variety stage with acts like the Chung Hwa Comedy Four and the song-and-dance team of Harry Gee Haw and Dong Fong Gue.

Although vaudeville performers most often came from families of working people or European immigrants, audiences embraced a mix of social classes. Respectable venues like Oscar Hammerstein's Victoria Theater or B.F. Keith's Palace helped to introduce more affluent patrons to the boisterous world of amusement and leisure beyond the home and family. Ethnic humor and stereotyping also taught native-born Americans about the cultural traits of immigrants, while making them appear fully human and vulnerable. In accomplishing these tasks, the variety theater functioned as a public ritual for a generation coming to terms with urbanization and the growing ethno-cultural complexity of early twentieth century life.

For all its ethnic diversity, vaudeville operated on racially segregated lines. Accordingly, most African American entertainers performed in all-black minstrel tent shows, traveling carnivals and circuses, honky-tonks, or vaudeville theaters. Sometime after 1900, a new vernacular musical form began to emerge from these venues. Borrowing the call-and-response pattern of plantation work chants, field hollers, peddlers' cries, and religious shouts, solo vocalists employed a structure in which a four-beat line was sung twice and resolved with a rhyming third line. Improvising from familiar phrases already in the language of ordinary people, singers incorporated African falsetto, guttural, and rasping tones, distorted the fifth and seventh notes of each scale, and deployed a complex polyrhythm. Lyrics usually described sexual relationships as the source of grief and the simultaneous requirement for happiness and self-esteem. Infused with uncompromising honesty, the music later known as the blues offered an epic mixture of stoicism, irony, fatalism, self-ridicule, and personal empowerment.

The first known interpreter of the blues was Gertrude ("Ma") Rainey, a Georgia vaudeville performer who toured the South in a song-and-dance team. In 1902 at the age of sixteen, claimed Rainey, she first heard the blues performed by an itinerant black female street singer in Missouri. Within a few years, the African American vaudeville circuits of the South, West, and large northern cities featured a number of black women vocalists whose repertoires drew upon a mixed bag of ragtime, popular music, and blues. As the form became commonly recognized in the 1910s, several piano-guitar duos took to the road, and white vocalists like Marion Harris, known for the first version of "I Ain't Got Nobody" (1915), began performing the music as well. By that time W.C. Handy, an Alabama-born black minstrel musician and band leader, had introduced the genre into popular music. Borrowing phrases learned in the Mississippi Delta, the self-styled father of the blues responded to a request for a political campaign song with "The Memphis Blues" (1912), followed by the sensational "St. Louis Blues" (1914).

ETHNIC BROADWAY

Spurred by the energetic impact of ragtime, black music quickly made its way to the Broadway stage. In 1898, the African American team of composer Will Marion Cook and poet Paul Laurence Dunbar mounted a forerunner of the American musical comedy with *Clorindy, the Origin of the Cakewalk.* Combining ragtime songs, dances, and everyday subject matter with elements of a consistent plot and characterization, the show traced the cakewalk to Louisiana of the 1880s. *Clorindy* featured African American composer and vaudeville star Ernest Hogan and won an enthusiastic reception during its run on the roof garden of Broadway's Casino Theater. Several subsequent black musical productions starred the vaudeville team of George Walker and Bert Williams. In *Senegambian Carnival* (1898) Walker played the urbane Jim Dandy, while Williams took the role of the country bumpkin. The duo's next hit was *In Dahomey* (1902), a free-wheeling production about an African colonization scheme. With a score by Will Cook, the show was the first full-length Broadway musical written and performed by blacks.

Despite such contributions, New York's musical theater still had a predominantly Irish face at the turn of the twentieth century. Edward Harrigan and Tony Hart's *Mulligan Guards* continued to prosper until ending its thirty-year run in 1909. By then, George M. Cohan had become the most significant fixture on Broadway. Raised in vaudeville by his song-and-dance-team parents, Cohan began his adult career as a coon singer. Intuitively in touch with the sensibilities of working-class and immigrant audiences, he discovered that syncopated music and a vernacular idiom could help to undermine Viennese and British domination of the musical stage. Cohan stormed Broadway in 1904 with *Little Johnny Jones*. Fashioning short, punctuated colloquial phrases into snappy hits like "Give My Regards to Broadway" and "Yankee Doodle Boy," he cleverly merged Irish American verve and humor with patriotism. In a single stroke Cohan had manufactured an identity as a jaunty ethnic cosmopolite and made New York City the symbol of the nation's democratic ideals.

Two years after his initial success, Cohan scored another triumph with *Forty-Five Minutes from Broadway.* Set among the suburban rich, the comedy portrayed an ex-horse player and a maid as the only characters with moral integrity. The show's homage to traditional virtues was elegantly conveyed in the sentimental "Mary's a Grand Old Name." *George Washington, Jr.,* a second Cohan production that season, expressed the scorn of street-tough but lovable urban types toward effete European culture. Cohan's instinctive feel for working-class nationalism was responsible for the musical's hit number, "You're a Grand Old Flag." When the United States entered World War I in 1917, Cohan recycled the patriotic formula and produced "Over There," the song that became the unofficial anthem of U.S. troops in France.

One year after Cohan scored simultaneous hits on Broadway, Florenz Ziegfeld presented the first of his Follies. The son of a prosperous Chicago classical music concert impresario, Ziegfeld ran away with Bill Cody's *Wild West Show* at the age of sixteen before his father brought him back home. Working in the family business, the young man developed a flair for showbusiness promotion. When the elder Ziegfeld's classical recitals failed to draw crowds at the Chicago World's Fair, the son recruited strong man Eugene Sandow to compete with the attractions of Little Egypt. Three years later, Ziegfeld brought Parisian siren Anna Held to the United States amid enormous publicity and created a sensation by having her take a milk bath on stage.

The *Follies of 1907* were modeled on fast-paced Parisian revues known for comedy, extravagant production numbers, and beautiful women. Sensing that upscale audiences were tired of melodramatic plots and the shallow story lines of musicals, Ziegfeld sought to provide brief and tantalizing examples of glamour in an elegant setting. There was no better example of the graceful sensuality of the Follies than Irving Berlin's "A Pretty Girl Is Like a Melody" (1919), which became the theme song of all subsequent productions. Ziegfeld succeeded in presenting a vision of the city as a land of pleasure in which gorgeously adorned chorus girls served as playful representations of freedom and unlimited possibility. With tickets selling for as much as five dollars, the Follies catered to an elite audience. Yet throughout the revue's extravagant twenty-year run, Ziegfeld introduced an incredible array of talent with roots that ranged from the nation's dusty heartlands to its cities and immigrant streets.

African American standup comic Bert Williams was one of Ziegfeld's most brilliant performers. Williams was born in the Bahamas in 1874. His family roots were Danish, Spanish, and African. Growing up in Riverside, California, he launched a show-business career in 1893 by joining a theatrical band that brought blackface entertainment to northern California logging camps. Recruited for a San Francisco minstrel show, Williams met actor George Walker, who became a troupe regular at one of the city's roughest music halls, the Midway Plaisance. The duo then went on to produce the series of all-black musicals that made them top vaudeville stars in a trio that included Walker's wife, Aida Overton. Williams added to his reputation by composing the music for African American lyricist Alex Rogers' "Nobody" (1905), a plaintive song that expressed the human need for admiration, love, and acceptance. Joining the Follies as a solo act in 1910, Williams became the first black regular featured in a Broadway revue.

A master of timing, which he taught to white colleagues like Eddie Cantor, Williams was known for droll wit and a solemn on-stage demeanor. Although still wearing blackface, he broke new ground by discarding minstrel-style plantation roles and portraying modern-day African American characters like gardeners, porters, golf caddies, or taxi drivers. Williams' earthy brand of humor permeated all these characterizations, resulting in one of his most popular songs, "White Folks Call It Chantecler, But It's Just Plain Chicken to Me." When the writer and actor played the Palace Vaudeville Theater in 1913, he expanded his repertoire to include a brilliant pantomime of a solo poker game, as well as parodies of Mexican revolutionary

Pancho Villa, Shakespearean drama, and classical ballet. Williams always empha-sized character development. "The man with the real sense of humor," he explained, must "put himself in the spectator's place and laugh at his own misfortunes," leading the audience to identify with him.

Fanny Brice also joined the Follies in 1910. Born Fannie Borach in 1891, the daughter of a Brooklyn saloon-keeper initiated her career at thirteen at an amateur night. Although barely able to understand Yiddish, she soon began singing ethnic parodies and "coon" songs in a burlesque house, where Ziegfeld discovered her. Brice's self-deprecatory humor and humble pathos touched anyone who heard her. She claimed that audiences spoke "so much louder than my mind" in terms of what they wanted and seemed to lose herself in their responses. Unlike many comics, Brice laughed with people, not at them. This became evident in her dialect version of "Lovey Joe," a "coon" song written by African American composer Will Marion Cook and rag-time pianist Joe Jordan. When Fanny entered a darkened stage in a simple black dress in 1921, hushed audiences broke into sobs and cheers when they heard her sing "My Man," a fiery torch song that seemed to describe her own troubled marriage to racketeer Nick Arnstein.

ZIEGFELD'S TRICKSTERS

Rope-twirler and cracker-barrel philosopher Will Rogers began appearing in the Ziegfeld Follies in 1915. Born in the Oklahoma Territory in 1879, Rogers proudly ac-knowledged that he was one-quarter Cherokee. Will learned roping tricks at an early age from a Negro employee of his father's cattle ranch who was a former cowboy. When the young boy was eleven years old, however, his mother died. Plagued with a lack of self-discipline and a restless frame of mind, Rogers fared poorly at a number of private boarding schools and military academies. After seeing Buffalo Bill's *Wild West Show* at the World's Fair and observing the roping techniques of Mexican cowboys (vaqueros), he began attending class in western attire until he warranted expulsion from one institution for lassoing the headmaster's colt. The irreverent and slow-talking youngster left military school at the age of nineteen to work on a Texas ranch owned by one of his father's friends.

Rogers loved living on horseback with his own saddle and bedroll, breaking and training horses, rounding up and branding calves, and trading stories with crusty cow-hands. Participating in extended cattle drives to Kansas and California, he perfected a dry wit and relaxed conversational style that would serve as the stepping-stone of a long career in show business. Rogers first appeared as a rodeo roping entertainer in St. Louis in 1899. He then traveled to Argentina and South Africa, where he signed on as a *Wild West Show* roper, blackface comic, and Indian entertainer. After touring New Zea-land, Australia, China, and Japan and performing at the St. Louis World's Fair of 1904,

Rogers began appearing in midwestern burlesque houses. Combining comic patter and rope tricks, the diffident Oklahoman delivered rambling observations on anything that crossed his mind. He had discovered the humor of common sense. When the lariat-twirling cowboy accompanied a *Wild West* troupe to New York's Madison Square Garden in 1905, he remained behind to find his way into vaudeville.

Initially billed as a roper, Rogers began talking to explain his mistakes. As the act caught on, he toured vaudeville circuits across the United States and Europe. In 1912 Rogers ascended to the legitimate stage as "a poet with a lariat" during a scenery change of *The Wall Street Girl*. Three years later Ziegfeld inserted him into the *Midnight Frolic,* a Follies supplement staged on the roof of the New Amsterdam Theater. At first Rogers confined his comments to the showgirls and performers, but soon extended his sway to current events and the self-righteous behavior of the powerful. "Well, folks," he liked to begin, "all I know is what I read in the papers." Promoted to the Follies in 1916, Rogers perfected a satire of smugness and self-satisfaction. "I generally hit a fellow that's on top," he once observed, "because it isn't fair to hit a fellow that's down."

Critics have compared Rogers' shrewd pessimism to the writings of Mark Twain. By purposely disregarding the rules of grammar, punctuation, and spelling, and confining himself to colloquial expressions, the Oklahoma roper seemed to speak for ordinary Americans. This reputation took dramatic hold during World War I, when audiences were desperate for laughter. "Our soldiers can win wars faster than our diplomats can talk us into them," Rodgers noted. After good-natured bantering about Woodrow Wilson's diplomatic notes to Germany and military preparedness, the star won national acclaim when the president and his new wife came backstage to meet him. Yet Rogers remained stubbornly bipartisan. "The Democrats are investigating the Republican slush funds," he commented in 1920, "and if they find where it's coming from they want theirs."

Comedian W.C. Fields joined the Follies the same year as Will Rogers. Born in Philadelphia as William Clark Dukenfield in 1880, Fields was of English and German background. His father, a former bartender, made a respectable living as a vegetable produce distributor. Fields left high school for an assortment of menial jobs in a cigar store, a clothing shop, an oyster restaurant, and a pool hall, as well as working as a newsboy and an iceman's assistant. He debuted in show business in 1898 at Miner's Bowery Theater with a comic juggling act in conjunction with an ensemble known as the Monte Carlo Girls. As Fields moved up from burlesque to the vaudeville stage in the next two years, he took on a tramp's costume and perfected a series of cigar box tricks and other visual routines. On the American vaudeville circuit in the following years, he also toured Europe, South Africa, and Australia.

By the time Fields joined the Follies, he was an accomplished performer. His physical humor rested on the illusion of moving through a hostile world that could never be trusted. The joke was that even his own body would not obey his will. The Follies sketches that Fields wrote and enacted all centered on slapstick expressions of the human predicament. Consequently, the one-time juggler mastered the art of the sight gag, whether in the pool room, the tennis court, the golf course, the dentist's office, or in a crowded elevator. The cumbersome Fields usually augmented these comic scenes with rambling monologues that tailed off into absurdity. When teamed with Fanny Brice, the effect could be exhilarating.

Two years after Fields debuted at the Follies, Eddie Cantor joined the fold. Born Israel Iskowitz on the Lower East Side in 1892, Cantor spent his childhood in a basement apartment where his grandmother raised him after his immigrant mother died of a lung disease when he was a year old and his father deserted him. Taking to the streets, the young urchin learned to pacify street gangs by acting as the local clown. Two years after he dropped out of school at thirteen, Cantor took up with a nineteen-year-old married Polish woman. His entertainment debut came as a female impersonator at amateur night at the Bowery Theater, where he quickly learned to deal with hecklers. Cantor then moved on to a job in a burlesque house and a singing waiter's position at a Coney Island saloon where Jimmy Durante played piano. His vaudeville career began as a blackface performer in small-time theaters in 1911. The next year Cantor became part of an act called "Kid Kabaret," touring the circuit with comedians George Jessel and Will Rogers.

Cantor first made the big time at the age of twenty-four in the *Midnight Frolics*. Introducing himself as Ziegfeld's plumber who had accidentally wandered on stage, he caused a sensation by using famous audience members like William Randolph Hearst and racketeer Diamond Jim Brady as "stooges." Promoted to the Follies in 1917, Cantor teamed up for a skit with Bert Williams in which he took the part of railroad porter Williams' effeminate son returning from college to Grand Central Station, much to the embarrassment of the porter, who has boasted to his friends of his football-playing offspring. Cantor embodied an assertive Jewish persona that balanced impudence with earnest determination. By striking an air of familiarity with audiences regardless of their money, fame, or social status, he assumed the role of the lovable underdog who succeeds by pure will and determination.

BIRTHING HOLLYWOOD

As Eddie Cantor and his mentor, Bert Williams, made plans to share a private late-night turkey dinner after a New Year's Eve show in 1917, Williams could not help commenting on the fact that hotel policy required him to use the back elevator. "It wouldn't be so bad, Eddie, if I didn't still hear the applause ringing in my ears," Cantor remembered his colleague as saying. In a period in which Jews and blacks were helping to shape popular music, comedy, and live theater, Jewish entertainers tended to feel a special relationship with African Americans. These ties derived in part from the perception that both Jews and blacks conveyed the oppression and pain of their historical experience through emotionally tinged music and song. As marginalized people who nevertheless had white skins, Jewish performers often saw themselves as expert translators of vernacular cultural expressions into generic American forms. Popular music's emphasis on romantic love offered this rootless group of outsiders a particularly lucrative avenue to assimilation and integration.

Vaudeville star Al Jolson offered a prime example of the relationship between Jewish and African American entertainment. Born into a poor family of religious Russian Jews in Washington, D.C. in 1886, young Asa Jolson sang Stephen Foster songs on the streets for spare change. At the age of fourteen he ran away with the circus and soon was performing a blackface act in burlesque and vaudeville. As Jolson played to makeshift theaters following the San Francisco earthquake of 1906, he fashioned his famous line, "You ain't heard nothin' yet." Joining a minstrel troupe, he helped to popularize "Alexander's Ragtime Band." In 1911, he depicted a "colored aristocrat" in a Broadway revue staged at the Schubert Brothers' Winter Garden Theater. As a seasoned veteran, Jolson realized that material had to have "snap and swing," and that audiences laughed at simple and short jokes about things they had experienced and knew about. Seeking to foster intimate rapport, he used the Winter Garden runway to maximize personal interaction with adoring crowds.

Jolson showcased the explosive qualities of his singing style when he recorded "You Made Me Love You" in 1913. Returning to the Winter Garden as the star of *Sinbad* (1918–21), he consolidated his reputation as the nation's leading blackface artist with three musical show-stoppers. Both "Rockabye Your Baby With a Dixie Melody," a powerful tune with a bluesy feel, and Irving Caesar and George Gershwin's "Swanee" paid homage to the legacy of Stephen Foster with explicit references to "Old Black Joe" and "Old Folks at Home." But it was the melodramatic "My Mammy," introduced in 1920, that ensured Jolson's place in entertainment lore when the blackface performer sank to his knees and delivered a quivering dialect tribute to motherhood.

By the time *Sinbad* appeared, live theater and vaudeville were facing a major competitor in the silent film industry. The American movie industry had its origins in 1893 with Thomas Edison's development of a motion picture camera and projector. Since Edison's kinetoscope only permitted individual viewing, the first movies appeared as curiosities in vice district penny arcades and tended to be one-reel excerpts of newsreels, boxing matches, vaudeville skits, or peep shows. Edison's production of the vitascope in 1896 enabled motion pictures like *The Great Train Robbery* (1903) distribution to larger audiences. By 1905 nickelodeons began to permeate the tenement storefronts of big-city immigrant neighborhoods. Charging five cents for entry to "democracy's theater," operators exhibited a variety of ten-to-fifteen-minute features, half of which were imports from France, Germany, or Italy. European films frequently titillated working-class audiences with frank portraits of pre-marital sex and adultery as examples of inevitable human weakness.

By 1910 tens of millions of Americans were attending the continuous showings of the nation's ten thousand nickelodeons at least once a week. In New York City, where there were six hundred of the five-cent movie theaters, surveys found that three-quarters of audiences were working class, 40 percent of whom were women. Movies offered workers an escape from the drudgeries of long labor, while providing married and older women a safe environment free of the male saloon culture. Many featured films were simply replicas of vaudeville routines and popular melodramas. Yet a large number of comedies dealt with social relations between the sexes and stressed the links between personal freedom and an invigorating hetero-sociality.

The explicit sexual themes of nickelodeon fare deeply disturbed Edison, who organized a consortium of producers in 1908 to cooperate with censorship groups, control film production, raise admission prices, and eliminate cheap theaters. Yet several Jewish entrepreneurs with Eastern European backgrounds refused to defer to the Edison Trust. Entering the realm of motion picture production and distribution after 1910, the "independents" contested the motion picture monopoly by producing multi-reel films appealing to popular taste. Renegade moviemakers often entered business partnerships with exhibitors, who built new theaters in the style of classical public buildings to legitimize the new industry and expand their clientele. Relocating to southern California in the next several years, these business visionaries created the Hollywood studio system.

Independent filmmakers were able to trump Edison's efforts because of extensive experience in dealing with changing consumer whims. Louis Mayer, the creative force behind MGM, was a one-time burlesque impresario. Movie pioneer Sam Goldwyn offered another case in point. The son of a poor peddler, Goldwyn was born Schmuel Gelbfisz in the Warsaw Jewish ghetto in 1879. When his father died, the young man of sixteen walked to Hamburg, made his way to Great Britain, and arrived in the United States three years later. After changing his name, Goldwyn found work as a three-dollar-a-day glove cutter in upstate New York, studied English at a business nightschool, and became a top glove salesman. By 1913 Goldwyn had pooled his modest earnings with his brother-in-law to form Jesse L. Lasky Feature Plays, which established its headquarters in an abandoned barn in Hollywood.

Jack Warner had a similar background. The son of a Polish Jewish cobbler and peddler who settled in Youngstown, Ohio, Warner opened a bicycle shop with his three brothers at the start of the century. Beginning in 1904, the Warner family put on traveling motion picture shows, ran a small movie theater in Newcastle, Pennsylvania, and entered the film distribution business. Finally, Jack and Sam Warner began to produce motion pictures in 1912, thereby laying the foundation for the creation of the Warner Bros. studio in the 1920s. Adolph Zukor offered another variation of the same theme. The grandson of a rabbi, Zukor was born in Hungary in 1873 but was orphaned as a child. Migrating to the United States at the age of sixteen, he started as a furrier's apprentice and became a successful merchant. In 1903 Zukor opened a New York City penny arcade with Marcus Loew and a movie theater the next year. Desiring to produce and distribute the works of filmmaker Edwin S. Porter, he created Famous Players in Famous Plays in 1912, the forerunner of Paramount Pictures.

Hollywood's trail-blazing moguls succeeded in consolidating the casting, filming, distribution, and exhibition of motion pictures. As Eastern European Jews, the movie independents enjoyed relative immunity from Victorian moral values, leading them to see marriage and procreation as healthy practices, sexual fulfillment for women as a positive good, emotional vitality as a natural expression of communal settings, and gambling and liquor as an essential part of social ritual. Most of all, liberation from Old World traditions opened these entrepreneurs to the expression of romantic fantasies. Through their guidance, the possibility of the good life would be conveyed to Americans of all social backgrounds in an industry that packaged itself as the national dream factory.

SILENT SCREEN HEROES AND HEROINES

Movies of the twentieth century's initial decade targeted the working-class audiences of the nickelodeons. Westerns were among the most popular features. Interest in western films originated with the popularity of late-nineteenth-century dime novels, stage plays, and Wild West shows. The first westerns had been railroad features designed to attract tourists to scenic Colorado. After 1900, however, filmmakers began to situate crime stories in western landscapes. *The Great Train Robbery* contributed to the maturation of the genre by employing rapid cuts, dissolves, and multiple cameras. Nickelodeon audiences relished the crude violence of movies, with vicious Indians or Mexicans and brutal chase scenes and gunfights. As women came to comprise a substantial part of the movie audience by 1910, however, western heroes began to appear as manly cowboys who espoused Victorian virtues of God, country, home, and family.

Edwin Porter's *Great Train Robbery* depicted lawmen as brutal as the criminals. Porter sustained such elements of social criticism in *The Kleptomaniac* (1906), a film in which a poor woman steals food from a storefront to feed her starving child, while a wealthy socialite takes valuable merchandise from a store on impulse. After a prostitute cheerfully accepts her courtroom prison verdict, the poor woman is given a stiff sentence, while her affluent cohort is reprimanded but let go. A scale of justice appears on the screen with one side weighted down by a bagful of dollars. Porter's *From the Submerged* (1912) presented the story of homeless people who steal bread and sleep on park benches to survive. Although Progressive reform era movies often sentimentalized the poor as people of middle-class virtues who simply lacked money, directors like Porter undoubtedly deployed such contrivances to augment sympathy for the disadvantaged.

D.W. Griffith, the filmmaker whose explicit racial caricatures in *The Birth of a Nation* would stir major controversy in 1915, had a long record of pursuing populist themes. In 1909 Griffith had released *A Corner in Wheat,* the screen version of a short story by naturalist novelist Frank Norris. The twelve-minute feature opened with a view of impoverished farm laborers trudging across a field with grain sacks hung from their bent and knotted shoulders. When relief lines are suspended in the city, hungry people rush the bread shop, only to be met by police violence. In the end, the grower accidentally falls into a grain shaft and is buried, a symbol of the ruin of the rich land by monopolists and trusts. Griffith's *The Song of the Shirt* (1910) and *The Lily of the Tenements* (1911) shifted the focus to the modern city by portraying the troubles of lowly paid seamstresses victimized by the sexual advances of rapacious employers. In *A Child of the Ghetto* (1910), the director depicted residents of the Lower East Side as being capable of survival and mutual assistance without the aid of police or charity.

The quest for realistic depictions of the working class led Griffith to produce America's first gangster movie. *Musketeers of Pig Alley* (1912) cast Lillian Gish and Elmer Booth as a young couple caught in a web of crime. The nervous energy and quick gestures of the two protagonists perfectly mirrored the life of city streets. Like Griffith's classic, Thomas Ince's *The Gangsters and the Girl* (1914) explored the slum area pool halls and surroundings that nurtured crime, allowing an occasionally positive cast of criminal types. Empathy for the downtrodden was even more explicit in Ince's *The Italian* (1914), a film about an immigrant bootblack who slaves away in the poverty and grime of Manhattan's Little Italy. Saving enough to send for his fiancé, he is devastated when their baby falls ill from oppressive heat and malnutrition. Robbed of the little money he has when he goes out to buy milk, the protagonist searches for the assailants, only to be beaten and arrested by the police. While he is in prison the baby dies. The brutality of the streets had seldom been so graphically depicted.

As the nation's number of female workers doubled between 1890 and 1910, socially conscious films often dramatized the plight of impoverished women. *Shoes* (1916), directed by former actress Lois Weber, dealt with a young woman compelled to prostitute her body to support her family, as did *The Wages of Sin* (1914). Yet few films about the struggles of ordinary women reached the popularity of those featuring Mary Pickford. Of English and Irish background, Pickford was born in Toronto in 1892 as Gladys Louise Smith. Touring the United States as a child actress with her mother and sister, she learned to stress "heart" in performances and to identify completely with audiences. After breaking into movies with D.W. Griffith's Biograph studio in 1909, Pickford leaped to stardom in *Tess of the Storm Country* (1914), a production of Adolph Zukor's Famous Players.

Tess presented the story of a poor young woman in love with a divinity student. Discovering that her beau's sister has been impregnated out of wedlock by his best friend, Tess takes the woman into her shack and pretends to be the child's mother to save the

Mary Pickford   (*New York Public Library*)

aspiring clergyman from family shame. When the baby dies and a minister refuses to baptize a "creature of sin," she storms into the church and performs the rite herself. Pickford's characters often relied on toughness and resiliency to overcome poverty, adversity, or social humiliation. Other roles included that of a mother of an illegitimate child in *Hearts Adrift* (1914), a homeless orphan sleeping in the park with stray dogs in *The Foundling* (1916), a sweatshop worker in *The Eternal Grind* (1916), an orphan in *Daddy Long-Legs* (1919), and a Cockney laundry worker in *Suds* (1920). These portraits often contrasted the honor of working-class life with the arrogance and hypocrisy of the rich. Even *Poor Little Rich Girl* (1917) contrasted the spiritual purity of a young daughter with the materialism and social climbing of her wealthy parents.

Two of Pickford's greatest performances came in two films made in 1918, *Amarilly of Clothes-Line Alley* and *Stella Morris*. In the first, the actress played the daughter of a Lower East Side laundress who gets a job as a cigarette girl in a dance hall. Pursued by an upper-class patron, she is forced to confront the young man's family at a snooty social gathering when her suitor's aunt conspires to break up the relationship. Losing both her admirer and her job at the dance hall, Pickford nevertheless demonstrates defiance and resolves to go on. In *Stella Morris* the actress played both a homely servant girl and the invalid woman with whom her employer is in love. When her master's alcoholic wife savagely beats her, Stella regains the use of her legs. Discouraged, however, by the cruelty and poverty surrounding her and seeking happiness for the employer whom she loves, she shoots her abusive mistress and then ends her own life.

The male equivalent of Pickford's plucky protagonist was the cowboy. Tom Mix provided some of the first western movie heroes. Born in Pennsylvania in 1880, Mix served with U.S. military forces in the Spanish-American War, the Philippines, and China before wrangling cattle in South Africa, Texas, Oklahoma, and Kansas. After some rodeo appearances and a stint in law enforcement, Mix bought an Oklahoma ranch that was used as the setting for a documentary film. From there the itinerant cowboy drifted into a career in Hollywood, starring in over seventy one- or two-reel features between 1911 and 1917, many of them comedies utilizing his horse-riding stunts. Signing with Fox in 1917, Mix won top billing in an additional sixty movies. "I ride into a place owning my own horse, saddle, and bridle," he once explained. "It isn't my quarrel, but I get into trouble doing the right thing for somebody else." "When it's all ironed out," the hero never gets any monetary reward, although sometimes the script allows him to become ranch foreman or "get the girl."

Mix's only competitor was William S. Hart. Born in 1870 in Newburgh, New York, Hart was the son of a miller who settled in the Dakotas, where the young boy made friends with Sioux Indian children from a nearby reservation. After a stint as a trail-head cowboy in Kansas, Hart returned east with his family at age fifteen and launched a career as a theatrical actor in New York. He began appearing in two-reel westerns in 1914 and soon started directing them. Several of these scenarios concerned westerners coming east and using common sense and physical brawn to overcome duplicitous city slickers. Invariably, Hart features concluded with a subtitle in which the hero announces, "I'm goin' back to the country, where I belong." Yet in *Hell's Hinges* (1916), Hart demonstrated gritty realism in a portrait of a hero who protects a church in an anarchic, dusty, deglamorized western town when the minister falls prey to the temptations of decadence. In *The Aryan* (1916) and *The Toll Gate* (1920), moreover, the actor took the role of amoral outsiders reformed by good women.

FILM COMEDY: DEMOCRACY'S ART

The silent screen's most popular genre proved to be comedy: one-third of all features produced before 1912 fell within this category. Some of the earliest comic films took an ethnic angle. Two versions of *Yiddisha Cowboy* in 1908 and 1911 described a character named Ikie who sets up pawnshops out west where he must use wit and cleverness to overcome endemic anti-Semitism. *Becky Gets a Husband* (1912) presented a light-hearted account of the obstacles faced by a Jewish-Irish couple. In the years after 1912, however, the most widely attended silent comedies assumed a more generic approach to the human predicament. Hollywood's success with comic movies owed much to Mack Sennett. A veteran film actor of working-class and Irish-Catholic background, Sennett formed his own renegade Keystone studio to challenge the power of the Edison trust. Between 1912 and 1917 his company would be responsible for dozens of the fast-paced comedy features that would attract millions to motion picture theaters.

Borrowing crusty performers from the circus, boxing, and vaudeville, Keystone utilized abrupt cutting to accent the slapstick humor it drew from French films and burlesque. Sennett's movies delighted audiences by tromping on social proprieties, a tendency outrageously illustrated by the Keystone Kops series inaugurated in 1913. Using a group of hapless policemen to illustrate the foolishness, corruption, and mindless violence of authority figures, Sennett brazenly employed bad taste, sexual innuendo, and vulgarity in amoral treatments of subjects like drunkenness, suicide, adultery, and prostitution. His movies were famous for their frolicking "bathing beauties," by which the director promoted an unprecedented exposure of women's skin. In its anarchic view of American society, Keystone took on purity reform, schooling, marriage, middle-class manners, and all institutions standing for social order.

Mack Sennett's greatest discovery was Charles Chaplin, a British actor who appeared in thirty-five Keystone features in 1914. A product of London slums who schooled himself in the pantomime techniques of the English music hall, Chaplin first came to the United States at the age of twenty-one as part of a London dance troupe. His initial Keystone appearance came in a ten-minute one-reel film entitled *Making a Living* (1914). He followed this with *Kid Auto Races at Venice,* the film in which he first assumed the comically sad persona of "the Tramp." Sent to the wardrobe department, the young actor had emerged with an oversized coat, baggy pants, a tight-fitting derby, overly large shoes, and a springy bamboo cane. The lowly character that Chaplin invented could mischievously pick up a cigarette butt, steal candy from a baby, or deliver a kick in the pants to a lady. But as he told Sennett, the Tramp was also "a gentleman, a poet, a dreamer, a lonely fellow, always hopeful of romance and adventure."

Although critics paid little attention to Chaplin's talents as an actor at Keystone, audiences came to appreciate the Tramp's ability to magically transform himself, thereby reaffirming the possibility that ordinary people could make of themselves what they willed. By 1915 Chaplin had switched studios and was writing and directing his own movies. He now refined the character drawn from the comedy and pathos of working people's lives and dreams and produced *The Tramp,* the movie that created a national Charlie Chaplin craze. Described by the press as humble and modest, Chaplin insisted that "I am no one—just a plain fellow." The film pitted Chaplin's character in competition with a man of higher social status for the hand of a woman. Forced to renounce his love, his tender self-sacrifice is unrewarded. Nevertheless, the Tramp's sprightly step in the final frames speaks to his resolve to go on despite disappointment.

Differences of social class also permeated Chaplin features such as *Work* (1915), *The Bank* (1915), and *Police* (1915). Signing with the Mutual studio, the actor-director produced some of his greatest work between 1916 and 1917. In *The Vagabond,* Chaplin played an itinerant street musician who saves a woman he has fallen in love with from a

Charlie Chaplin and Jackie Coogan in *The Kid* (1920)

brutal gypsy, but she becomes interested in an artist who paints her portrait. In the end, Chaplin's tender and vulnerable protagonist resigns himself to her loss, but she returns and they reunite in romantic bliss. *Easy Street* (1916) presented Chaplin as a vagrant who falls in love with a social worker at an urban mission. To win her approval, he becomes a police officer to clean up the neighborhood of bullies, drug fiends, and criminals.

Joining the First National studio in 1917, Chaplin starred in *The Immigrant,* a poignant portrayal of penniless newcomers arriving in an uncaring city. He followed this by playing a harmless hobo whose life paralleled that of a stray animal in *A Dog's Life* (1918). In *Shoulder Arms* (1918), Hollywood's leading celebrity offered a hilarious portrait of a boot camp recruit who has difficulty learning to march and handle a rifle. Yet Chaplin's genius countered physical humor with well-honed pathos. Crestfallen that he has received no mail, the film's protagonist looks over the shoulder of a comrade reading a letter from family or a loved one.

Chaplin appeared to attain the apex of his artistry in *The Kid* (1920). The story centered a deserted woman who is turned out of a charity hospital and leaves her infant in a luxurious sedan outside a mansion. When the car is stolen, the child is abandoned a second time, only to be discovered by the Tramp, who cares for it and raises it as his own. As "the Kid" reaches the age of five, he breaks windows so his father can get work repairing them. County officials respond by threatening to take the boy away from his impoverished "father." Meanwhile, the mother of the youngster has become a successful actress and advertises for the return of her child with an ample reward. Seizing this opportunity, an unscrupulous flop-house operator steals the boy for the prize. In the end, Chaplin's protagonist reunites with "the Kid" at his mother's mansion, but the doors close on the camera and the resolution of the story remains unclear.

SOURCES AND SUGGESTED READINGS

One of the first explorations of early-twentieth-century consumer values appeared in several of the essays contained in Warren I. Susman, *Culture as History: The Transformation of American Society in the Twentieth Century* (1984). See also the relevant portions of Alan Trachtenberg, *The Incorporation of America: Culture and Society in the Gilded Age* (1982). For middle-class fascination with consumer lifestyles, see William R. Leach, *Land of Desire: Merchants, Power, and the Rise of a New American Culture* (1993), as well as the initial chapters of Lary May, *Screening Out the Past: The Birth of Mass Culture and the Motion Picture Industry* (1980).

Two Irish-American urban icons receive profiles in William L. Riordon, *Plunkitt of Tammany Hall,* ed. by Terrence J. MacDonald (1994) and Grace Eckley, *Finley Peter Dunne* (1981). For a view of the Italian and Polish Catholic immigrant community, see the early chapters of John Bodnar, et al. *Lives of Their Own: Blacks, Italians, and Poles in Pittsburgh, 1900–1960* (1982). Gerald Sorin, *A Time for Building: The Third Migration, 1880–1920* (1992) and Susan A. Glenn, *Daughters of the Shtetl: Life and Labor in the Immigrant Generation* (1996) describe Jewish city life in the century's initial period.

For the acculturating role of newspapers geared to a Euro-American readership, see Peter Conolly-Smith, *Translating America: An Immigrant Press Visualizes American Popular Culture, 1895–1908* (2004). Ben Procter's *William Randolph Hearst: The Early Years, 1863–1910* (1998) contextualizes the growth of mass circulation journalism. The advent of the newspaper "funny pages" comprises the focus of Ian Gordon, *Comic Strips and Consumer Culture, 1890–1945* (1998). Jerry Robinson, *The Comics: An Illustrated History of Comic Strip Art* (1974) remains a useful source.

Steve A. Riess describes a key element of early twentieth century spectator amusements in *Sport in Industrial America: 1850–1920* (1995) and *Touching Base: Professional Baseball and American Culture in the Progressive Era* (1999). See also the early chapters of Jeffrey T. Sammons, *Beyond the Ring: The Role of Boxing in American Society* (1988) and John P. Rossi, *The National Game: Baseball and American Culture* (2000). For the development of amusement parks, see John F. Kasson, *Amusing the Million: Coney Island at the Turn of the Century* (1978) and the more recent Michael Immerso, *Coney Island: The People's Playground* (2002). Joy S. Kasson, *Buffalo Bill's Wild West: Celebrity, Memory, and Popular History* (2000) and Bluford Adams, *E Pluribus Barnum: The Great Showman of U.S. Popular Culture* (1997) analyze two of the period's most popular spectator amusements. For theatrical productions of *Uncle*

Tom's Cabin, see the first chapter of Linda Williams, *Playing the Race Card: Melo-dramas of Black and White from Uncle Tom to O.J. Simpson* (2001).

The roots of American popular music receive extended treatment in Jon W. Finson, *The Voices That Are Gone: Themes in Nineteenth-Century Popular Song* (1994). For the development of Tin Pan Alley, see the relevant portions of Ian Whitcomb, *After the Ball: Popular Music from Rag to Rock* (1982) and Charles Hamm, *Yesterdays: Popular Song in America* (1979). Useful introductions to the early twentieth century's prime musical revolution appear in Edward A. Berlin, *Ragtime: A Musical and Cultural History* (1980) and *King of Ragtime: Scott Joplin and His Era* (1994). See also Susan Curtis, *Dancing to a Black Man's Tune: A Life of Scott Joplin* (1994). For the social background of Joplin's music, see the relevant chapter of David Thelen, *Paths of Resistance: Tradition and Democracy in Industrializing Missouri*, 2d ed. (1991). The first segments of Philip Furia, *Irving Berlin: A Life in Song* (1998) deal with the resourceful lyricist and composer's use of ragtime themes in pre-World War I popular music.

Descriptions of the origins of the blues appear in the relevant portions of William Barlow, *Looking Up at Dawn: The Emergence of Blues Culture* (1989); W.T. Lhaman, *Raising Cain: Blackface Performance from Jim Crow to Hip Hop* (1998); and Lawrence W. Levine, *Black Culture and Black Consciousness: Afro-American Folk Thought from Slavery to Freedom* (1977). Elijah Wald, *Escaping the Delta: Robert Johnson and the Invention of the Blues* (2004) describes the interracial dimension to early blues performance. For the advent of America's most significant art form, see Burton W. Peretti, *The Creation of Jazz: Music, Race, and Culture in Urban America* (1992).

Profiles of the denizens of ragtime cabarets appear in David Nasaw, *Going Out: The Rise and Fall of Public Amusements* (1993) and Randy D. McBee, *Dance Hall Days: Intimacy and Leisure among Working-Class Immigrants in the United States* (2000). Kathy Peiss, *Cheap Amusements: Working Women and Leisure in Turn-of-the-Century New York* (1986) and Louis Erenberg, *Steppin' Out: New York Nightlife and the Transformation of Culture* (1981) delineate the gender mix in the dance establishments of the nation's largest city.

An extensive literature on vaudeville includes Robert W. Snyder, *The Voice of the City: Vaudeville and Popular Culture in New York* (1979) and Henry Jenkins, *What Made Pistachio Nuts? Early Sound Comedy and the Vaudeville Aesthetic* (1992). Two of Broadway's greatest performers receive treatment in Simon Louvish, *Man on the Flying Trapeze: The Life and Times of W.C. Fields* (1997) and Eric L. Smith, *Bert Williams: A Biography of the Pioneer Black Comedian* (1992). For burlesque, see Robert C. Allen, *Horrible Prettiness: Burlesque and American Culture* (1991). Jewish and Chinese performers, respectively, comprise the focus of Ted Merwin, *In Their Own Image: New York Jews in Jazz Age Popular Culture* (2006) and Krystyn R. Moon, *Yellowface: Creating the Chinese in American Popular Music and Performance, 1850s–1920s* (2005). The Follies receive a full description in Richard and Paulette

Ziegfeld, *The Ziegfeld Touch: The Life and Times of Florenz Ziegfeld* (1993) and Linda Mizejewski, *Ziegfeld Girl: Image and Icon in Culture and Cinema* (1999).

For the origins of the movies, see the relevant segments of Lary May, *Screening Out the Past: The Birth of Mass Culture and the Motion Picture Industry* (1980); Robert Sklar, *Movie-Made America: A Cultural History of American Movies*, rev. ed. (1994); and Neal Gabler, *An Empire of Their Own: How the Jews Invented Hollywood* (1988). A useful work on the first three decades of the movies is William Everson, *American Silent Film* (1978). Andrew Smith, *Shooting Cowboys and Indians: Silent Western Films, American Culture, and the Birth of Hollywood* (2003) and the opening chapters of George N. Fenin and William K. Everson, *The Western: From Silents to Cinerama* (1962) describe the development of one of the industry's central genres.

For film comedy, see Walter Kerr, *The Silent Clowns* (1975) and Charles J. Maland, *Chaplin and American Culture: The Evolution of a Star Image* (1989). See also Scott Eyman, *Mary Pickford: America's Sweetheart* (1990). Early Hollywood's sociological focus receives consideration in Kevin Brownlow, *Beyond the Mask of Innocence* (1990) and Steven J. Ross, *Working-Class Hollywood: Silent Film and the Shaping of Class in America* (1998). For America's first great director, see Scott Simmon, *Films of D.W. Griffith* (1993) and the chapter on *Birth of a Nation* in Linda Williams, *Playing the Race Card: Melodramas of Black and White from Uncle Tom to O.J. Simpson* (2001).

3

Chronicles of the American Multitude, 1893–1920

The dynamic popular culture of early-twentieth-century America drew much of its substance and vitality from European immigrants, African Americans, and working people. Yet commercial entertainment did not fully embrace the nation's cultural diversity and social agendas. It is not surprising that representations of ordinary life marked the output of several groups seeking public sanction amid widespread social and political change. Advocates for social justice advanced their concerns by telling the stories of people society appeared to ignore. Their efforts coincided with the social vision of a number of realist novelists, regional fiction writers, big-city poets, and urban painters. In the West writers with American Indian, Asian, and Hispanic roots sought to create appropriate forms to describe the historical experiences of their people. Black authors and intellectuals struggled to carve out a dual role as African Americans and citizens. Finally, a host of bohemians, feminists, and political radicals sought to link their visions of a new society to proletarian interests and sentiments.

PROTEST AND EXPOSÉ

"Make right the immemorial infamies/Perfidious wrongs, immedicable woes," announced "The Man with the Hoe," a widely reprinted poem by Edwin Markham published in a San Francisco newspaper in 1899. Based on French painter Jean Francois Millet's *The Gleaners*, the piece compared the plundered and disinherited American farm laborer to the European peasant. Markham's verse spoke to the prevalence of agrarian unrest and anti-monopoly fervor in late-nineteenth-century America. Henry George's *Progress and Poverty* (1879), which sold two million copies, proposed to equalize economic opportunity by limiting taxation to the "unearned increment" resulting from land speculation. Edward Bellamy's million-seller *Looking Backward: 2000–1887* (1888) envisioned the replacement of a ruthlessly competitive social order with one based on shared abundance and ethical cooperation. Similar notions emanated from the Farmers Alliances of the 1880s and the People's (Populist) Party, formed in Omaha in 1892. Opposed to high transportation, distribution, and finance costs, Populist lecturers, cooperatives, newspapers, and political figures built an adversarial movement culture.

Anxieties over elite rule were brilliantly addressed by journalist and Minnesota Alliance leader Ignatius Donnelly, whose apocalyptic novel *Caesar's Column* (1891) depicted a future plutocracy that brutally exploited the masses through physical terror. Degraded by their treatment, workers responded with bloody revenge, even turning on their own leaders. Civilization could only be preserved, warned Donnelly, through a redeeming transformation of collective life based on solidarity and equality. Subsequent works of Populist fiction included William Harvey's *Coin's Financial School* (1894), an account of a debate in which a young boy shatters the arguments of monetary gold-standard proponents, and Elliott Flowers' *The Spoilsman* (1903), a morality tale of financial corruption. The most eloquent treatment of these themes, however, came in the novels of Hamlin Garland.

Born in Wisconsin and raised in Iowa, Garland arrived in Boston in 1884 at the age of twenty-four. Sleeping in a cockroach-infested eight-by-ten-foot room, he spent most of his time at the Boston Public Library devouring the works of William Shakespeare, Henry George, and Walt Whitman. *Leaves of Grass*, he said, taught him the "the spiritual significance" of American democracy. A sincere but gawky westerner, Garland was hired as a literature instructor at the Boston School of Oratory and soon took on guest lecture and magazine writing assignments. In the late 1880s he visited the Dakota Territory, where he had briefly lived with his family. Observing the "lack of color, of charm in the lives of the people" and "the tragic futility of their existence," he wondered why such "stern facts" had never worked their way into American literature.

Although eastern publishers preferred charming love stories, Garland decided that realism was a higher goal than beauty. The time had come, he believed, to "tell the truth about the barn yard's daily grind"—"the mud and the sweat and the dust" as well as "the hard wear of wind and toil." *Main-Traveled Roads* (1891), the writer's first book, brought together an assortment of stories depicting the struggle against nature and greedy speculators on the Northern Great Plains. The narrative flow of Garland's sketches featured authentic detail and an ear for regional dialect. No author had ever delved so completely into the slop and mud of farming, the weariness of plowing, the emptiness and drudgery of agrarian labor, or the impact of the region's grasshopper infestations and hailstorms. Yet Garland also extolled the simple beauties of the land and occasional instances of human decency and fellowship. In 1892, the author published a second group of stories in *Other Main-Traveled Roads*, as well as a political novel entitled *A Spoils of Office.* As he moved toward heroic western romances in the late 1890s, however, Garland never recaptured the artistic depth or descriptive accuracy of his initial work.

Reformer Henry D. Lloyd also supported the Populist Party's attack on corporate and financial concentration. Graduating from Columbia University in 1869, Lloyd was admitted to the New York State Bar before becoming financial editor of the *Chicago Tribune.* In 1881 he explored the abusive practices of John D. Rockefeller's Standard Oil Company in an *Atlantic Monthly* article on the erosion of free competition. Lloyd further detailed the operations of the firm and called for public ownership of all monopolies in a widely read polemic entitled *Wealth vs. Commonwealth* (1894). Coming to the defense of independent farmers and industrial workers, he was one of the first American writers to promote the press as a lever for social justice and to push religious leaders toward embracing proposals for humane social welfare.

Building on Lloyd's work, investigative journalist Ida Tarbell published the first of a series of exhaustive articles on Standard Oil in 1902. Tarbell's widely heralded exposé appeared in *McClure's* magazine, the creation of Samuel Sidney McClure. Brought to the United States by his widowed Irish mother when he was nine, McClure grew up in poverty in Indiana and worked his way through college. After serving as a bicycling magazine and book editor in Boston and New York, he organized the nation's first literary syndicate, distributing articles and stories by Mark Twain, William Dean Howells, Joel Chandler Harris, and others. Seeking to bring literature to the masses, the ambitious entrepreneur co-founded *McClure's* in 1893 and hired a stable of well-educated young reporters. By using halftone photo-engraving to reproduce images, taking advantage of cheaper paper sources, and increasing ad sales, McClure initiated a price war that broadened the basis of American magazine readership. When Ida Tarbell's human interest portrait of the early life of Abraham Lincoln appeared in the magazine in 1895, circulation leaped above 250,000.

As writers like Hamlin Garland and Henry Lloyd piqued middle-class interest in social issues, McClure responded. Since "the public is the people," he once reflected, there was no one left to enforce the law "but all of us." Sensing widespread anxiety over the dominance of corporate trusts, McClure assigned Tarbell to write the full story of Standard Oil in order to explore the inner workings of big business. The daughter of a western Pennsylvania independent oil producer, the journalist understood the point of view of Rockefeller adversaries. Yet she saw herself as an objective analyst. Pouring over documentary evidence from government reports, civil suits, newspaper accounts, and personal interviews collected during five years of research, Tarbell described Standard Oil as a model of efficiency and organization whose business practices neverthe-less were bound up with bribery, fraud, coercion, and violence. The "mother of all trusts" was a threat to small business and ordinary workers, she reported. "Nothing, however trivial," she concluded, "must live outside of its control." Tarbell's nineteen articles, published as a book in 1904, helped to shape public taste for the advent of "muckraking" journalism.

SOCIAL UPLIFT

"Jesus Christ knew a great deal ... about organizing society," declared Columbus, Ohio Congregational minister Solomon Washington Gladden, the author of *Applied Christianity* (1887). Gladden helped to popularize the Social Gospel, a doctrine calling for the use of religious principles in solving the problems of the industrial order. An unrelenting critic of sweatshops and child labor, the minister established a settlement house to provide social services for the poor, reorganized local charities, supported labor's right to organize, and inspected local housing to alleviate slum conditions. Interest in the Social Gospel undoubtedly figured in the popularity of *In His Steps* (1896), a parable written by Topeka, Kansas, Congregational minister Charles M. Sheldon. The novel told the story of a Chicago church whose members vow to follow the example of Jesus in all things when a dying vagrant tells the congregation his life story. Never assigned a copyright and appearing under the imprint of sixteen American publishers, Sheldon's book ranked only second in sales to the Bible in its time.

No single author enhanced middle-class interest in the poor as much as photo-journalist Jacob Riis. Born to a struggling Jewish family in Denmark, Riis migrated to the United States at the age of twenty-one and became a police reporter for New York newspapers. In 1887 he began to deliver lectures dramatizing the conditions of urban poverty on the Lower East Side, with a focus on the need for tenement housing reform and city parks. Part ideology and part entertainment for church congregations and other middle-class audiences, Riis' widely attended presentations were illustrated with a collection of lantern photography slides he published in *How the Other Half Lives: Studies Among the Tenements of New York* (1890, 1901).

Although Riis saw himself as an objective reporter, his images were chosen to highlight the crime, misery, and sinister depravity of the slums and underworld. Some, like the portrait of shady, back-alley characters in *Bandits' Roost, 39½ Mulberry Street*, were staged presentations of scenes that other photographers had previously shot; others, like *"Knee Pants" at Forty-five cents a Dozen—a Ludlow Street Sweater's Shop* and *Police Station Lodging Room: two women* were designed to place their subjects in as dependent and demeaning a position as possible. Riis' ghetto residents tended to be representative "types" who were either victims or gangsters. In an imitation of comic strip narratives, images were placed in a consciously designed order so that Fifth Ave-

Jacob A. Riis, *Bandits' Roost, 39 ½ Mulberry Street.*, 1887   (*Museum of the City of New York, The Jacob A. Riis Collection*)

nue mansions could be contrasted to filthy Lower East Side dives, and "saved" children could be distinguished from ragged street ruffians.

The Riis lectures invariably contained the warning that failure to alter the slum environment would result in the spread of disease, disorder, and massive social upheaval. "The sea of a mighty population," he admonished, "heaves uneasily in the tenements." The journalist was particularly concerned about immigrant entrepreneurs who invested meager sums in buildings and were only interested in maximizing profits. Yet as a reformer, Riis believed the problem could be solved by appealing to the conscience of landlords and through appropriate state legislation. As a tour guide who shocked comfortable audiences with the barbarism of the slums, Riis assumed dual roles as humanitarian crusader and stern protector of society's interests.

As the Riis presentations demonstrated, the impact of poverty on children was particularly distressing to middle-class Americans. Two works by socialists, Robert Hunter's *Poverty* (1905) and John Spargo's *The Bitter Cry of the Children* (1906), addressed these concerns. Yet few treatments of the subject achieved the exposure of Lewis Hine's photographic profiles of child labor. Raised above his family's restaurant in Oshkosh, Wisconsin, Hine hauled furniture thirteen hours a day, six days a week, when his father's death forced him into a factory at age eighteen. When the plant closed during the Panic of 1893, he took on a variety of jobs before starting to work his way through Illinois Teachers College at twenty-five. Placed as a geography and nature instructor at a progressive private school in New York, he earned an M.A. in Education at night. Hine then took up photography as a hobby. At the suggestion of a mentor, he began taking portraits of Ellis Island immigrants for classroom use. Assignments followed from social welfare organizations interested in documenting slum living and working conditions.

Approached by the National Child Labor Committee in 1908, Hine quit teaching and became a full-time photographer. By that time some two million children under the age of sixteen were part of the American work force, most putting in six-day weeks of twelve or more hours each. Employed as field hands or in dusty, sooty, damp, and poorly ventilated cotton plants, textile mills, glass and shoe factories, coal yards, mines, canneries, and laundries, children worked for lower wages than adults and seldom complained. For ten years after 1908, Hine used his box camera to document the existence of child labor. Traveling fifty thousand miles a year by auto and train, he recorded the name, age, hours of work, earnings, and schooling of every child he encountered. Yet it was the pictures of sooty-faced boys in coal mines and small girls working giant machines that became the focus of the pamphlets, booklets, photo exhibits, and lecture slide collections that Hine assembled and brought to public attention.

Between 1909 and 1914 Lewis Hine's *Pittsburgh Survey* compiled an ambitious documentation of industrial work and life. In a period in which employees were threatened by scientific management, technological innovation, and a loss of worker autonomy, labor union affiliation steadily increased. By 1914 the American Federation of Labor, organized along skilled craft lines, claimed more than two million members. The "labor question" became a focal point of *McClure's* in 1902, when the magazine ran an eight-part series by Ray Stannard Baker. The Michigan-born journalist had forged a reputation with a sympathetic portrait of "Coxey's Army," the march of unemployed men that had petitioned the federal government to fund public works in 1894. Covering the anthracite strike of 1902, Baker went into workers' homes and union meetings, only to express sympathy for those not manning the picket lines. At the same time, he concluded that although union racketeering had assumed a national scope, labor corruption was merely a response to deteriorating ethics in the corporate community.

Upton Sinclair sought to bring the public entirely into labor's camp. Born into a family of declining southern gentry, the young Sinclair was shuttled between cheap boarding houses and wealthy relatives. His childhood was not made any easier by the fact that his father, a salesman, had a drinking problem, and that his mother was a snobbish Puritan. Working his way through the City College of New York and Columbia University by writing for comic newspapers and adventure magazines, Sinclair aspired to becoming a poet. One year after coming out with his first novel in 1901, however, he joined the Socialist Party, hopeful that a liberated social order would be more conducive to artistry. When Chicago stockyard workers went on strike in 1904, Sinclair published a pamphlet in *The Appeal to Reason,* a Kansas-based socialist magazine with a circulation over 300,000. Once the strike was lost, the magazine offered him $500 to live among the workers and write about their lives. Sinclair spent seven weeks in Chicago before returning to his New Jersey home to compose *The Jungle* (1906).

Although social realist Robert Herrick had recently published *Web of Life* (1900), a sympathetic portrait of Chicago's South Side working class, Sinclair was staking out new territory by placing his story around the work place. Realizing that the meatpackers were immigrants following the American Dream, he decided to open the novel with the joyous dancing of a Lithuanian wedding in a "back of the yards" saloon. He then contrasted the celebration with an environment in which men toiled from early morning to late at night in ice-cold cellars with a quarter inch of water on the floor. All this, he reported, earned each employee $300 a year. Writing of smells and sights he had observed first hand, Sinclair described how the packers were compelled to process diseased and boil-covered cattle and hogs, and how sausage products often were infested with rats and refuse. He relayed accounts of slashed and dismembered fingers and even cases in which men had fallen into the open boiling vats used to make lard. Finally, Sinclair showed how the agents of the beef trust dominated the local police, politicians, and underworld.

As the author struggled to find a suitable ending to the story, he joined with writer Jack London in organizing a socialist organization for college students. Sinclair's political commitments may have colored the resolution of *The Jungle,* which took on a decidedly polemical tone. When the book finally went into print, however, readers focused on the dozen pages depicting the grisly details of meat production. Contrary to his intentions, the socialist labor activist had become a muckraking reformer whose work proved instrumental in passage of the Pure Food and Drugs and Meat Inspection Acts of 1906. "I aimed at the public's heart," Sinclair concluded with an unusual degree of irony, "and by accident I hit it in the stomach."

TALES OF THE UNDERWORLD

Middle-class readers were also fascinated by exposés of urban vice, crime, and political corruption. Some of the earliest of these appeared in 1900 in *McClure's* "True Stories from the Underworld," a series of pieces by reformer Alfred Hodder and writer Josiah Flynt. The following year Flynt authored another feature called "The World of Graft." The son of a liberal newspaper editor and nephew of temperance leader and feminist Frances Willard had run away from home in his early teens to tramp around the country and learn the ways of hobo culture. After a stint in reform school and study at the University of Berlin, he traveled across Europe, meeting leaders of the English literary and artistic decadence movement like Oscar Wilde and Aubrey Beardsley. A man of the world drawn to both extraordinary people and the seamy side of life, Flynt pursued a dual existence between respectability and raw poverty. Once he returned to the United States, he went by the nickname of "Cigarette" and spent time in grimy dives drinking and talking with professional thieves, vagrants, and social outcasts.

Having abandoned the Willard family name, Flynt published sketches of the vagabond life in respectable magazines, leading in 1899 to the release of his first book, *Tramping with Tramps*. Written in clear and economical prose, the collection portrayed homeless people in their natural surroundings instead of jail, and showed them to be no different in psychological make-up than anyone else. Flynt then assembled the *McClure's* series on corruption into a second volume, *In the World of Graft* (1901). Discarding sentiment and morality, the thirty-two-year-old author relied on the language of the streets. The term "graft," he explained, came from the argot of criminals. Grafters made their living through theft and illegal practices, whether within the letter of the law or not. Emphasizing how collaboration between police and criminals sustained urban lawlessness, Flynt described crooked businessmen and politicians as "unmugged" grafters. "Crime is like water," he concluded in *My Life* (1908), a memoir published a year after he died at the age of thirty-eight—"it seeps from the top."

Like Josiah Flynt, Lincoln Steffens was an educated member of the affluent classes with acute listening habits. Raised in Sacramento, Steffens matriculated near the bottom of his class from the University of California at Berkeley in 1889. After graduate studies in experimental psychology and ethics in Germany and France, he returned to the United States, only to be cut off from financial support by his father. Hired as a police reporter for a New York daily in 1892, Steffens found "life as it is lived" to be more intriguing than a college education. His on-the-job tutors included civic activist and city police commissioner Theodore Roosevelt, anti-vice crusader Reverend Charles H. Parkhurst, and tenement-housing reformer Jacob Riis. It was Riis who emphasized the importance of tracing the causes of crime and other problems to social conditions.

Steffens reported on labor strikes, interviewed political bosses, and mingled with the common people, seeing an essential humanity in everyone. Covering the Lower East Side, he came to see crime as an inevitable part of the chaos and poverty of immigrant life. Yet his writing never sank into ethnic stereotypes or caricatures. Beyond the "dark, dismal, and ill ventilated" tenements that Riis had described, Steffens observed the vitality and spirit of the district's residents. His articles conveyed details of Jewish religious rituals, as well as samples of the Italian culture of the cafés, park benches, and street festivals. Writing with wit and irony about petty law-breakers, thieves, and pickpockets, Steffens demonstrated that many criminals were artists with a sense of honor who took pride in their craft. He also distinguished between corrupt police higher-ups and the rank-and-file who shared a working-class background with criminals. The top brass, he explained, protected vice, gambling, and prostitution in return for a percentage of the profits. In contrast, beat officers were shrewd and street-wise participants in graft but not responsible for the results of a corrupt "system."

When New York reformers were voted out of power in 1896, Steffens discovered that police wages were too paltry to prevent corruption. Furthermore, the business community opposed closing the vice industries and welcomed the efficiency of corrupt political bosses. This led the journalist to conclude that so-called "good men" in the Anglo-Protestant middle class wanted bad government, while dishonest individuals in Tammany Hall were at least truthful about their interests. Steffens built on these insights once he became managing editor of *McClure's* in 1901. After publishing several pieces about police and politicians, he was sent into the field to learn how staff writers did their work. The first result was "Tweed Days in St. Louis," which appeared in 1902. Through interviews with St. Louis prosecutor Joseph W. Folk and his own research, Steffens came to realize that collusion between "good business men" and grafting politicians was not confined to New York. His path-breaking article passed on Folk's insight that government no longer represented "the people" when commercial interests paid for city franchises, licenses, exemptions, and privileges.

Steffens' six *McClure's* articles became the basis for *The Shame of the Cities* (1904). Each installment of the series read like a detective story in which the "shameful facts" and descriptions of secret deals were manipulated for dramatic effect. These well-documented pieces helped to lay the foundations of the Progressive reform movement. As an advocate for social justice, Steffens criticized the "moral weakness" of the average citizen. But he had little love for upper-class uplift or elitist charity efforts and held upstanding Anglo-Protestants as responsible for corruption as immigrants. Steffens also humanized the bosses by describing them as intelligent, generous, congenial, and willing to acknowledge their faults. In later years, the author reminisced about being called to the bed of a dying Philadelphia machine politician. Asked why he thought the man's behavior was "so rotten wrong," Steffens replied that he was a "born leader of the common man" but had betrayed his trust to "rich business men and other enemies of the people." In *Upbuilders* (1909), the great muckraker concluded that the poorer classes were "the first, last, and best appeal in all great human cases."

LITERARY REALISTS

Much of muckraking journalism and protest literature involved a concerted effort to reject Victorian sentimentalism. The trend toward social realism in American letters had been propelled by novelist William D. Howells. Born to a middle-class family of Ohio communitarians, Howells left school at the age of eleven to become a typesetter in his father's printing office. After several years as a political journalist, he produced an 1860 presidential campaign biography of Abraham Lincoln, for which the Republican Party awarded him a consulate appointment in Venice. Upon returning to the United

States, Howells worked at the *Nation* before moving to the *Atlantic Monthly,* which he edited between 1871 and 1881. After writing a number of romantic novels and chastising authors for ignoring "the smiling aspects" of American life, Howells began to call for the infusion of realism in literature. Democracy could be extended into fiction, he insisted, if authors offered a "truthful treatment of commonplace material" and portrayed daily life "in the most exact terms possible with an absolute and clear sense of proportion."

Resigning from the *Atlantic Monthly* in 1881 and moving from Boston to New York, Howells took on the subject of divorce and journalistic ethics in *A Modern Instance* (1882). Three years later he published *The Rise of Silas Lapham,* a morality tale about a self-made paint manufacturer who rises above greed and selfishness, thereby demonstrating the innate honesty and dignity of the American character. After experiencing a mental breakdown in 1885 and discovering the work of Leo Tolstoy, however, Howells dedicated himself to writing about the destructive impact of industrial capitalism and class warfare. His semi-autobiographical novel, *A Hazard of New Fortunes* (1890), presented the "frantic panorama" of New York City life through a series of rough-edged, slang-speaking characters and the lead protagonist, a newly hired magazine publisher. Pulling no punches, Howells introduced readers to the "shabby diversity" of Lower East Side slums, to rampant vice, to labor strikes, and to the dire consequences of economic depression. "The real suffering of the world," remarks one character, was "the daily portion of the poor."

Hazard climaxes with a violent streetcar workers strike that takes the life of the publisher's idealistic son. In the end, Howells' protagonist wonders about "the absence of intelligent, comprehensive purpose in the huge disorder and the violent struggle to subordinate the result to the greater good." After contemplating the meager possibilities for equality in a society obsessed with material success, the character concludes that people must do their best to live by values of love, reason, and charity, although disharmony and evil are not easily eliminated in a complex world. As Howells found himself moving toward an ethic of social cooperation and Christian socialism amid a depressed economy, he published *A Traveler from Altruria* (1894), a utopian novel outlining the benefits of a rationally organized social order for ordinary Americans.

Henry Blake Fuller's *The Cliff-Dwellers* (1893) was the second American novel to describe modern city life. Fuller was an unlikely prospect for such an undertaking. His banker father, an original Chicago white settler, traced the family lineage back to the Mayflower. After receiving part of his education at a classical academy and working as a store clerk and bank employee, Fuller made three trips to Europe between 1879 and 1892. These excursions resulted in publication of a collection of romantic Italian vignettes and travel sketches, as well as a novel describing the Americanization of the European aristocracy. Imbued with Old World aestheticism, Fuller returned to Chicago to write about the neoclassical structures of the World's Fair, which had been criticized by progressive architect Louis Sullivan as "snobbish and alien to the land." Taken by the city's bustle, he wound up producing an epic novel. The story centered on a fictional eighteen-story skyscraper employing four thousand people. By following a newcomer's attempt to succeed in finance and high society, readers were exposed to the blind ruthlessness of business competition and the social pretensions that surrounded it.

What gave Fuller's work enhanced scope, however, was the attention he paid to a broad range of characters, from the building scrubwomen to top executives. One of the book's central protagonists was Cornelia McNabb, a working-class migrant from Wisconsin who finds a job as a boarding house waitress, takes courses in shorthand and typewriting, follows the newspaper society columns, and wins a position as stenographer to a rising bank vice-president whom she marries. McNabb's energy and determination to succeed provide an exact replica of the drive of her business-oriented male counterparts. In the end, Fuller decries the shallowness of capitalist materialism, observing that men will build skyscrapers to bask in the admiration of ambitious women, even though "a hundred others are martyred in it."

In the same year that *The Cliff-Dwellers* appeared, twenty-two-year-old New York journalist Stephen Crane self-published *Maggie, A Girl of the Streets* (1893) under an assumed name. Writing in simply constructed sentences, Crane broke new ground by focusing on the pre-rational motives and emotions of characters instead of mere thought. Going beyond Howells' emphasis on the social setting, the novel presented the story of an innocent child of the Bowery slums surrounded by the evils of poverty and despair. *Maggie* heralded the rise of literary naturalism, an attempt at social realism that placed primitive forces such as heredity and environment at the heart of human affairs. In the stark world of the naturalists, individual will was often an illusion, yet only the strongest survived.

Frank Norris' fiction embodied the most recognizable features of the naturalist school. Born in Chicago in 1870 to a successful wholesale jeweler and a former teacher and stage actress, Norris accompanied his family to San Francisco at age fifteen. As a boy he loved the open-air markets, saloons, and bustle of neighboring Polk Street. Sent to study art in London and Paris, he returned to enroll in college at Berkeley, where he discovered the work of French novelist Emile Zola. After attending English classes at Harvard, Norris served as a war correspondent, magazine writer, and publishing house employee. His second novel, *McTeague* (1899), merged fascination with the lower-middle-class life of the Bay Area with the conviction that internal drives and external forces shaped human behavior. The story centered on a dim-witted, brutish dentist who gives in to sexual passion, only to lose desire for the woman who becomes his wife. When she wins the lottery and hoards her fortune in gold coin, he tracks her down to the school where she scrubs floors, kills her with his bare hands, and steals the treasure. McTeague then suffers a violent death in the California desert defending his ill-begotten gains.

Norris' next book, *The Octopus* (1901), continued to trace the consequences of self-indulgence, greed, pride, and lust for power. Although the novel's sympathy for the victims of corporate arrogance seemed to place it within the framework of protest literature, its message was far murkier. The lead character of the story was a romantic poet whose heart was with "the people," but who is repelled by the "uncouth brutes" of California's ranching communities. Faced with the financial machinations of the powerful railroad, valley wheat farmers organize a protective league. Yet the growers turn out to be as greedy as their capitalist foes when they attempt to bribe a railroad commissioner to side with their interests. When the official sells out to the company, a shoot-out ensues, a ranching leader loses his life, and the farmers are defeated and thrown back into poverty. Norris has the railroad magnate attribute the tragedy to "forces" and "conditions," while the poet surveys the wheat and marvels at nature's eternal qualities. Neither of these perspectives seems to sum up the author's view that selflessness and humanitarianism were the only routes to self-fulfillment in a world devoid of meaning.

In an essay entitled "The Novel with a Purpose" (1902), written shortly before Norris died of a ruptured appendix at the age of thirty-two, the author castigated affluent consumers of literature who refused to read stories about human suffering. Published posthumously the following year, his last work addressed such themes. *The Pit* (1903) described the Chicago grain market as a symbol of national energy and vitality. Yet it also pointed to the contrast between the cosmopolitan elite and homeless souls "shivering in rags and tattered comforters." Two years earlier, Norris had encouraged the twenty-nine-year-old Theodore Dreiser to publish *Sister Carrie* (1900), another Chicago epic. This story of a young woman from a small western town who comes to work in a city sweatshop and shoe factory became the most controversial American novel of the early twentieth century. Breaking the conventional formulations of polite fiction, it conveyed a profound compassion for ordinary people and treated them as complex characters striving to satisfy their contradictory longings.

Raised in Indiana, Dreiser was the son of an impoverished German Catholic mill worker. Like Jacob Riis and Lincoln Steffens, his intellectual training came as a police reporter, but he was also influenced by the Social Gospel, evolutionary social theory, and the writings of French novelist Honoré de Balzac. Fascinated with the frenzied pursuit of happiness in the American city, he created a resilient female protagonist in *Sister Carrie* who embodied a mix of self-interest and compassion. After having an affair with a salesman, Carrie slips into a relationship with a married restaurant manager. As her lover experiences gradual degeneration, she rises to fame and fortune as a New York actress but finds no fulfillment of her dreams. For Dreiser, primal drives for sex, fame, or money could not satisfy the fundamental needs of human beings. Nevertheless, the book's hazy distinctions between crime and honesty and its frank treatment of sex led the publisher to limit printing to a thousand copies. Dreiser's reputation did not rebound until publication of *Jennie Gerhardt* (1911), the story of an allegedly amoral woman's unselfish service, at which point *Sister Carrie* reappeared in a new edition.

CITY PAVEMENTS

As novelists like Frank Norris and Theodore Dreiser realized, working-class Chicago offered an apt setting for examining the lives of ordinary people. Journalist George Ade proved to be a master of this genre. The son of a middle-class banker, Ade grew up in post-Civil War Indiana and graduated from Purdue University. Hired by a Chicago newspaper in the 1890s, he worked his way up to a column called "Stories of the Streets and of the Town." *Artie* (1896), Ade's first book of sketches, described a brash office boy given to fast talk and ambitious schemes for instant wealth. "No matter what you've got in your hand," the character advised, "play it as if you had a royal flush for a bosom holdout." When readers liked the hero's captivating qualities, Ade produced *Pink Marsh* (1897), a series of pieces about a shy, likable African American bootblack given to dialect philosophic musings on topics ranging from boxing, to love, to cakewalks. Ade followed up with a more structured collection of episodes in *Doc' Horne* (1899), an assortment of tall tales, detailed observations, and characterizations delivered by a talkative roomer in a cheap boarding house inhabited by shabby but genteel residents.

Increasingly drawn to the use of vernacular language, Ade published *Fables in Slang* in 1900. He described the subjects of these stories as "nobodies"—ordinary people with human foibles who were gullible, trapped by circumstances beyond their control, or simply cynical. Employing lean and simple sentences and commonplace images, the breezy prose of the collection assumed a slightly satirical stance toward hypocrisy and material values. One story concerned a thirty-four-year-old woman who aspired to high culture and marriage to a literary figure, who nevertheless settles for a janitor by the name of Earnest. Another told of a homely girl who studiously completed her daily piano exercises while the neighborhood boys crowded around the house of the girl across the street. Other tales described the experience of awkward farmers in the big city. *In Babel: Stories of Chicago* (1903) offered additional sketches of everyday people from a canny working-class perspective.

"What infinite use Dante would have made of the Bowery," Theodore Roosevelt once observed. Owen Kildare sought to satisfy public interest in the mysteries of the city with *My Mamie Rose: The Story of My Regeneration* (1903), a memoir of a self-educated Skid Row tough, complete with a map of the district. The best New York tales could be found in the sketches of O. Henry. The son of a self-educated North Carolina physician and a mother from the southern gentry, America's greatest short story writer was born William Sydney Porter in 1862. After clerking in a local drug store, Porter made his way to Texas, where he hired on as a sheep ranch hand. He then became an architectural draftsman in the state land office before accepting a position as an Austin bank teller. During the 1890s Porter began to publish reports on Texas life and other sketches in newspapers and magazines in Detroit and New York. He even edited an iconoclastic weekly called *The Rolling Stone* for a couple of years. A free spirit, the aspiring writer liked to "go bumming" with friends after work. Disdaining the "higher classes," he preferred to mingle in the streets, shops, and cafes in search of interesting story ideas.

Porter's life at the bank ended in 1898, when he was convicted of embezzling less than $900 for unknowingly participating in a corrupt transaction initiated by superiors. Sentenced to five years at the federal penitentiary at Columbus, Ohio, he was released in 1901. While his experience taught him cynical lessons about the rich and powerful, he developed compassion for the downtrodden poor and sympathy for ordinary men who had gone wrong. Porter published three stories while in prison, including "Whistling Dick," a morality tale set in a hobo camp whose residents serve beef-stew meals out of a five-gallon kerosene tin. With an ear for vernacular expressions like "swiped," the piece captured the atmosphere of the camps and illustrated a superb talent for storytelling.

Released from prison, Porter relocated to Pittsburgh, where he worked for a newspaper, lived in a rooming house, and consumed a nightly ten-cent sandwich, soup, and beer at a local saloon. Producing at least a story a week, he sold several pastiches and character studies to national magazines. In 1902 Porter moved to New York, the city he dubbed Baghdad on the Hudson. Within a year he had published seventeen pieces under the name of O. Henry. Using a steamer trunk as his desk, he lived in residential hotel rooms in Manhattan's Tenderloin, Hell's Kitchen, and the Bowery. O. Henry claimed to write only to obtain money for beer, food, clothes, and rent, and insisted that he was too close to those on the bottom to pose as a reformer. Never looking in obvious places for material, he studied salesgirls when they were out in public squares and parks. Some of his best tales, like "The Furnished Room," described the city life of young working women. In "An Unfinished Story," O. Henry portrayed a shop clerk named Dulcie, who must choose between living off a box of crackers and pot of strawberry jam in her room or accepting a dinner invitation with a predatory character her friends have named Piggy.

Between 1903 and 1906 O. Henry published weekly stories in the *New York World* and issued two collections—*Cabbages and Kings* (1904) and *The Four Million* (1906). In "A Little Local Color," a tour guide and a visiting author come across a slang-filled sidewalk political discussion that turns out to be a debate between a university professor and a distinguished social economist. Seeking the "real thing," they repair to the Bowery where they meet an old-time resident who addresses them in perfect diction. Their source informs them that the district's famed argot was an invention of "literary 'discoverers'" and that the locals "had adopted the patois forced upon them in order to deal with the tourist trade." Asked to have a drink, the man responds that he's too busy observing Bowery life for his second book. O. Henry's intimate characterizations of Irish Americans and other city folk were enriched by frequent visits to cabarets, vaudeville shows, burlesque houses, social clubs, boxing matches, Greenwich Village haunts, and Coney Island. "I never met a man but what I could learn something from him," he told an interviewer in 1909, one year before he died at the age of forty-eight.

URBAN REALISTS ON CANVAS

The increasing popularity of representational literature carried over into the visual arts. Spurred by the development of photography in the 1840s and '50s, a democratic ethos began to shape American painting. While artists of the Hudson River School rendered unadorned versions of the natural world, so-called "genre" portraitists preferred to profile rural Americans such as farmers, trappers, hunters, and riverboat men. The West offered ample opportunity for such experimentation. During the mid-nineteenth century George Catlin completed colorful canvases of Great Plains Indian buffalo hunters and costumed warriors. His work was succeeded by the illustrations and paintings of Frederic Remington, a New York born graduate of the Yale School of Fine Arts who spent two winters as a Kansas sheep rancher, and Charles Russell, an action painter from St. Louis with a passion for depicting cowboys, Indians, and wild horses. Meanwhile, realists like Winslow Homer and Thomas Eakins were straying beyond the moral pretensions of academic art, sentimental landscapes, and classical imitations with profiles of contemporary life focused on active working figures and athletes.

Representational art leaned toward social realism. One of the early practitioners of the genre was Robert Koehler, the German-born son of a Milwaukee machinist trained in the United States and Europe. In 1886, the same year Koehler became director of the Minneapolis School of Fine Arts, he completed *The Strike,* the first American painting to depict labor-management conflict. Suggested by the violent railroad walkouts of 1877, the huge oil showed working men and women ominously gathering before a capitalist figure.

Not all realism was as politically edged as Koehler's work. Mary Cassatt, who grew up in upper-middle-class Philadelphia before moving to Paris, influenced the use of Impressionist approaches to color and light in American painting. Assigned to do two murals for the Woman's Building at the Chicago World's Fair, Cassatt completed a panel of female fruit pickers and another of "Modern Woman" engaged in the pursuit of art, music, and dance. Known for posing servants, friends, and relatives, she developed a reputation for intimate portraits of nurturing mothers and canvases featuring independent and assertive young city women in cafes and cabarets.

Elizabeth Sparhook Davis' painting of female sales clerks in *Shoe Shop* (1911) replicated Cassatt's view of the city as an arena for women of all social classes. The urge to go out in the streets and reproduce life as found was advanced by a group of urban realists led by the painter Robert Henri. Raised in Nebraska, Henri studied art in Philadelphia and Paris. His intellectual influences ranged from Zola, Balzac, and Tolstoy to Thomas Paine, Ralph Waldo Emerson, and Walt Whitman. *Leaves of Grass* had led him to the beauty of ordinary existence, he recalled. Insisting that art and life were interconnected, Henri advocated that painting be drawn from one's experience. When he began teaching at the New York School of Art in 1900, he instructed students to study "life in the raw" by making sketches of scenes in restaurants, boxing rings, parks, theaters, saloons, and neighborhood shopping districts. There was "character and meaning and even beauty in a crowd of east side children tagging after a street piano or hanging over garbage cans," he once observed. The city was a spectacle—visible in scenes of Lower East Side immigrants or in the bustling commerce of the streets.

Henri's most celebrated paintings included *Cumulus Clouds, East River* (1901–02), a depiction of the working waterfront; *Portrait of Willie Gee* (1904), a presentation of a young African American bootblack or newsboy in a quiet pose; and *Salome* (1909), a sexually infused portrait of a young woman that threatened accepted distinctions between art and vulgarity as well as culture and commerce. By taking on subjects from popular culture and everyday life normally treated in mass-circulation newspapers and magazines, Henri and his followers addressed their work to a broad audience beyond the art world. Consequently, the realists were heralded in the press as purveyors of democratic art and linked to the literary naturalists. Painting no longer was to be confined to the pursuit of beauty. Instead, the rebel painters directed their energies to expressing the special circumstances of their time and portraying the complexity of the human condition.

Although the realists would not be known as the "Ashcan School" until the 1930s, they came to public attention in 1908 when Henri helped to organize a gallery exhibit advertised as "The Eight." Besides featuring the work of the movement's leader, the show included paintings by students and associates John Sloan, George Luks, William Glackens, and Edward Shinn. Born to a struggling family of cab makers in Lock Haven, Pennsylvania, Sloan quit high school to become a cashier in a bookselling firm. After study at the Pennsylvania Academy of Art, he began a career as a Philadelphia newspaper illustrator. By the late 1890s, however, photographs were replacing drawings as the main source of graphic imagery in metropolitan dailies. Moving to Manhattan's Chelsea district in 1904, Sloan compiled a diary of notes on the second-generation Irish Americans of his neighborhood, as well as working people frequenting the parks, movie theaters, and other entertainments of the Tenderloin, Madison Square, and Coney Island. Like the other artists in Henri's circle, he preferred to see these subjects as real people, instead of preconceived types or objects of apprehension.

Between 1905 and 1908 Sloan completed a series of urban etchings that consciously rejected condescending charm. He pursued this approach in *Sixth Avenue and Thirtieth Street* (1907), an oil painting of a prostitute in a red-light district adjusting her glove. *Election Night* (1907) portrayed the elevated subway and crowded streets. *South Beach Bathers* (1907–08) caught the uninhibited feel of working-class revelers as they prepared steamed clams and hot dogs at a Staten Island outing. *Three A.M.* (1909) conveyed a warm and intimate approach to the lives of ordinary people by showing two

George Luks, *Hester Street* (1905)   (*Brooklyn Museum. 40.339. Dick S. Ramsay Fund*)

women roommates, either bohemians or prostitutes, smoking and sipping from a tea-cup in a relaxed moment of late-night fellowship. *Pigeons* (1910), observed from the rooftop of Sloan's studio, depicted a man and boy ingeniously establishing recreational space in the most unlikely of places, while *Scrubwomen, Astor Library* (1910–11) offered a seldom-seen perspective on the underside of a great city. Sloan did not sell his first painting until 1913, when he was forty-two years of age, one year before initiating a twenty-four-year career as an instructor at the Art Students League.

Although he was the son of a cultured physician, George Luks was raised in a working-class mining district of Pennsylvania. After receiving formal art training, Luks arrived in New York and became a sketch reporter for the *New York World*. Taking over the cartoon responsibilities of *Hogan's Alley* (the "Yellow Kid") in the mid–1890s, he developed the character of the wisecracking Mickey Dugan. Luks' paintings depicted vigorous physical energy through bold brushwork. He was particularly interested in urban immigrants and the slum environment. Yet the painter was more concerned with his subjects' individual character and attempts at self-improvement than their poverty. "Down there people are what they are," he once remarked. Some of Luks' striking works included *Hester Street* (1905), a colorful view of a crowded Lower East Side market; *Bleeker and Carmine Streets, New York* (1905), a night-time scene of a Greenwich Village corner filled with socializing working-class Italian immigrants; and *Allen Street* (1905), a sympathetic portrait of an evicted tenant.

William Glackens, another Philadelphian, settled in New York in 1906 to become a magazine illustrator for *Harper's Weekly*. Some of his best work appeared in *Far from the Fresh Air Farm* (1911), a pencil and watercolor treatment of a tenement street crowded with pushcart vendors, market produce, and garment workers transporting goods. The fifth Philadelphia exile of Henri's group was Edward Shinn, another news illustrator whose contrasts between wealthy glamour and the plight of the poor often combined line drawings with splashes of color. Shinn's pastels and watercolors took on such subjects as Lower East Side tenements, building fires, river docks, traffic accidents, elevated subway structures, and late-night newsboys. In *Cross Streets of New York* (1899) the artist skillfully contrasted an array of orange-brick tenements with their snowy surroundings. *Tenements of Hester Street* (1900) depicted poor tenants sleeping on the roof and fire escapes to avoid the sizzling heat of summertime. In Shinn's illustration *The Laundress* (1903), a woman hangs clothes among the outhouses and storage sheds of a tenement backyard.

George Bellows, the only non-Philadelphian of the six leading urban realists, was born in Columbus, Ohio, and came to New York to study with Henri at the age of twenty-two. Bellows was drawn to painting muscular laborers, competitive athletes, and the life of the tenements. Fixated on concrete imagery, his descriptive emphasis defied the idealizations of academic art while steering clear of abstract symbolism. In *Forty-Two Kids* (1907), Bellows pictured slum youngsters diving off a broken East River pier for a summer swim. The more somber *Excavation at Night* (1908) offered a view of the construction site for the new Pennsylvania Station in which workers appear in the deep pit as mere specks. Boxing paintings like *Stag at Sharkey's* (1907) and *Both Members of the Club* (1909) convey a sense of struggle and conflict inside the ring in the presence of almost grotesque crowds. *Men of the Docks* (1912), in turn, offered a portrait of dockworkers quietly waiting for the day's assignment alongside a giant freighter.

FICTIONAL REGIONALISTS

The emphasis on local color in realist painting reflected a broad interest in regional imagery and culture. As the nation moved toward an integrated industrial economy, curiosity about sectional folkways appeared to deepen. White southerners delighted in Joel Chandler Harris' *Uncle Remus: His Songs and Sayings* (1880), published in several sequels. A Georgia journalist, Harris had collected plantation tales, legends, and proverbs from African American sources that he reproduced in original dialect. George Washington Cable's short stories about traditional Creole life also charmed middle-class whites. Ellen Glasgow's *The Battle-Ground* (1902) and *Virginia* (1913) offered far more realistic views of the troubled South. Yet the region's most influential fiction came from the pen of Thomas Dixon, a white populist whose North Carolina family of small planters had been uprooted by the Civil War and Reconstruction. In *The*

Leopard's Spots (1902) and *The Clansman* (1905), Dixon pictured the South's white yeomen farmers as defenders of civilization against brutish former slaves and greedy Yankees. The inflamed racial imagery of Dixon's work would form the basis of D.W. Griffith's *The Birth of a Nation.*

Sarah Orne Jewett wrote regional fiction about New England. In *The Country of the Pointed Firs* (1896), a group of stories set in Maine's declining seaports, Jewett demonstrated how the genre could lend itself to profound psychological insight. Edith Wharton provided another example. Born in 1862 into an established New York family, Wharton spent six years of her childhood in Europe and was educated by private tutors. Marrying a wealthy Boston banker in 1885, she moved to Paris for the rest of her life. After publishing several fictional portraits of New York's upper crust, Wharton completed *Ethan Frome* (1911), a novella serialized in *Scribner's* magazine. Set in a bleak Berkshire Mountains village, the tightly written tale described the plight of a poor New England farmer married to an ailing woman and in love with his spouse's niece. When his wife announces that the woman will be sent away, the lovers vow to kill themselves by crashing a sled into a tree. The plan goes awry, however, when the protagonist is merely lamed and the niece is crippled for life. Now recovered, Frome's wife presides over the tragic household of three.

The emotional depth achieved by Wharton could also be found in the early Great Plains fiction of Willa Cather. Born in 1873 and raised in Nebraska, Cather graduated from the state university and served as a Pittsburgh newspaper editor and arts critic for several years. Moving to New York to become managing editor of *McClure's* between 1906 and 1911, she published forty-three short stories before becoming a novelist. Cather's second book, *O Pioneers!* (1913), combined social realism and romance in depicting the epic struggles of a Nebraska Swedish woman immigrant. *My Antonia* (1918) used the author's childhood memories of another immigrant, a woman she cherished as a Bohemian earth mother, to recount the taming of the prairie.

The most popular regionalist of the early twentieth century may have been Booth Tarkington. Born in 1869, Tarkington was the son of a prosperous Indianapolis attorney; his mother hailed from an old New England Presbyterian family. Reading and writing ceaselessly as a child, the young boy nevertheless was a frequent public school truant. After transferring to Phillips Exeter Academy, Tarkington spent a year at Purdue University, where he befriended George Ade. Trying his luck at Princeton, where he was ineligible for a degree, he jumped into campus social activities and became editor of three student publications. At the age of thirty, Tarkington produced his first novel, *The Gentleman from Indiana* (1899). Serialized in *McClure's* at the urging of Hamlin Garland, the commonplace tale described an eastern writer who comes west to save a run-down newspaper and turn it into a crusader against local corruption. Infused with entertaining humor, sentimental optimism, and local Hoosier dialect and color, the book became a national best-seller.

Tarkington next turned his down-to-earth characterizations to juvenile fiction. *Penrod* (1914), a second best-seller, wove the author's boyhood memories and imagination into the creation of a new American folk hero. Assembling a series of self-contained incidents, the novel revealed how everyday characters could do ordinary things in extraordinary ways. Tarkington's protagonists compensate for a lack of power over their lives by day-dreaming. Resenting parental authority and seeking peer approval, they strive to release spirits hemmed in by school and society and manage to survive crisis after crisis. After publishing a group of stories about thwarted juvenile romance in *Seventeen* (1915), Tarkington returned to adult themes with the Pulitzer Prize-winning novel, *The Magnificent Ambersons* (1918), the story of a Victorian family's adjustment to the modern age, and *Alice Adams* (1921), a second Pulitzer winner that presented a realistic account of a young woman's failed effort to climb the social ladder of a small town. Rejected by an affluent young bachelor at the end of the novel, Alice resolutely takes her place among the multitude by entering business school.

THE WESTERN

No region of the country captured the public's imagination more than the West. As the meeting place between civilization and nature, as well as law and anarchy, the western territories were the subject of thousands of dime novels produced by New York publishers from the 1860s on. Fictional western heroes like the semi-comic Seth Jones represented the world of rugged individualism, violent masculinity, and democratic male bonding. Deadwood Dick and Calamity Jane, two additional icons of the genre, translated their humble origins, dearth of formal education, and lack of inherited wealth into feats of will and courage to overcome the corrupt and hypocritical scions of the established order. As the range industry spread north from Texas over the Great Plains after the Civil War, the cowboy became the celebrated hero of western lore. Dime novels attributed traits of generosity, bravery, honesty, and honor to weather-beaten cattle drivers. The most colorful of these fictional figures was "Buffalo Bill," a character based on William Frederick Cody, a former messenger, wagon driver, trapper, Pony Express rider, meat supplier, and U.S. Army scout.

As early as the 1860s, journalist and author Ned Buntline helped to place Cody's versions of his illustrious deeds in magazine serials and dime novels. In 1872 Buntline arranged for his friend to star in *The Scouts of the Prairie*, an autobiographical stage play that pictured its protagonist as a pioneer of civilization and agent of progress. Ten years later the celebrated hero was chosen as Grand Marshall of a July 4th celebration in North Platte, Nebraska, cattle country. Cody soon incorporated the event's outdoor exhibitions of hunting and fighting skills into his own *Wild West Show.* Touring the United States and Europe, the extravaganza featured circus acts, ethnic group displays, biographical theatrical dramas, and staged battles between the Cavalry and Indian warriors. Cody later shared the spotlight with sharpshooter Annie Oakley and Sioux Indian leader Sitting Bull. A celebration of the pioneering white man, Buffalo Bill's Wild West also introduced the general public to elements of Latin American cowboy culture and Native American arts.

Alfred Henry Lewis preferred to write about Arizona cattlemen. Raised in Cleveland, Lewis practiced law until his health broke down and he found his way to the Southwest to spend five years working on cattle ranches. He eventually resumed his law career in Kansas City, but began sending western sketches to the newspapers, which he transformed into two books, *Wolfville* (1898) and *Wolfville Days* (1902). Having an individualistic and rough temperament himself, Lewis understood taciturn western prospectors and cowboys who played cards and drank, held life cheap, disparaged Indians, Mexicans, and blacks, and shared a placid irony. The "Old Cattleman" was "rude, storm-beat and of shaggy roughness," he explained in the Preface to one of his volumes. Regretting the "personal ungrace and want of elegance" of his storyteller's dialect tales, the author reminded readers that "one may not be other or different than one is." Anticipating adverse reviews, Lewis dismissed critics as "book invalids" who were not as trustworthy as the public, "whose tastes run true."

The action in mythical Wolfville centered on the Red Light Saloon where the Old Cattleman offered hearty rounds of commentary. "Cow-punchers is queer people," he mused. "They need a heap of watchin' an' herdin'." A gambler had to "play his system through, an' with no more conscience than cows, no matter who's run down in the stampede." Attorneys were "law coyotes." The morality of "church sharps" was "a matter of health" since "sick folks usual is a heap more moral" than healthy ones. Beyond the narrator's maxims lay a host of stories about colorful characters like Doc Peets, Texas Thompson, Cherokee Hall, Curly Ben, Toothpick Johnson, Grief Mudlow, Rainbow Sam, Tucson Jenny, and Whiskey Billy. In later years Lewis rehashed these tales in the back room of a Times Square saloon in the company of a prizefighting referee, former Dodge City sheriff Bat Masterson, a boxer named Kid McCoy, the actor Eddie Foy, a famous criminal, a police detective, and the western landscape painter Charles Russell.

In the same year that *Wolfeville Days* appeared, Harvard graduate Owen Wister published the archetypical western novel. Wister was an unusual candidate for such a task. His mother, a leading Philadelphia cultural activist and writer, had tutored her son in Victorian manners and refined tastes, while his father tried to steer him toward a business career. Forced into a banking slot, Wister was stricken with a nerve disease and went west to heal at a Wyoming ranch. Returning during summers in the early 1890s, he began to place short stories in leading magazines, publishing several collections in book form. *The Virginian* (1902), Wister's first novel, adamantly rejected the culture of eastern propriety, formal education, and class distinction. Reflecting a harsh western environment that highlighted physical sensation, violence, and the need for domination, its cattle-roping, sharp-shooting, range-riding protagonists found the meaning of life in a job well done. The West required manly qualities like self-discipline, will-power, skill, ingenuity, and judgment. Accordingly, Wister's gruff characters were given to understatement and the belief that actions spoke louder than words.

The climax to *The Virginian* occurs when the hero defies his eastern fiancé to engage in a Main Street gunfight in which he kills the outlaw and wins back his bride. Wister understood the attractions of male comradeship in the confrontation with death and the need to act courageously. In contrast to the elevated religious sentimentality of popular women's fiction, his stories offered no refuge of domesticity. The saloon, not the home or church, provides the only indoor locale of the classic western. Wister even provided a satire of female reformers in a chapter on Em'ly, the blue-legged and "manly-lookin'" hen who reminds the narrator of "an old maid at home" who was a church worker and member of a group opposed to cruelty to animals. Nature and manhood are the only divinities in Owen Wister's world. Combining notions of Anglo Saxon social dominance with a populist celebration of the rough-and-tumble open spaces, *The Virginian* sold 1.5 million copies in its extended lifetime and established the modern western as one of the leading genres of American fiction and male fantasy.

If Owen Wister invented the western novel, Pearl Zane Grey perfected its form. Raised in Zanesville, Ohio, a town founded by his family, Grey devoured dime novels and boy adventure stories as a youth. After winning a baseball scholarship to the University of Pennsylvania, he practiced dentistry in New York. Yet his true love was writing. Living off his wife's inheritance, Grey authored several rejected novels between 1903 and 1908. Then he accompanied an old Plains hunter on a trip west and met Jim Emmett, the character upon whom most of his stories would be based. *Riders of the Purple Sage* (1912) was originally rejected for publication, but went on to become the most famous western novel of all time. Dropping his first name, Zane Grey used a sparse narrative style stripped of intensive expressions and superlatives to depict the region's rugged deserts and arid mountains. Fascinated with the wildness of Nature and Man, he sketched out adventure heroes whose craggy character replicated the unforgiving western landscape and whose ability to withstand pain mirrored its durability.

INDIAN STORYTELLERS

American Indians often were victims of the western conquest celebrated in popular fiction and film. Eager to demonstrate Native American willingness to embrace white civilization, officials of the Chicago World's Fair had invited Simon Pokagon, a southwest Michigan Potawatomi Indian, to deliver a welcoming address at the White City. The son of a chief and a graduate of Oberlin College, Pokagon had previously negotiated a federal financial settlement for lands the Potawatomi once held along Lake Michigan near the site of Chicago. Yet tribal members had accused him of self-serving dealings and disowned his efforts. Whether or not the controversy had sensitized Pokagon to the need for mediation between white and Native American cultures, his address took such a direction. Proclaiming that "we are as human as they are," the diplomat and writer pleaded that Indians had suffered long enough at the hand of others, and that it was time to stake their own claims to progress and prosperity. This could only be accomplished, he emphasized, if native people rejected the tribal way of life, assimilated into white society, and swore complete allegiance to the United States.

Although praised by white authorities for such sentiment, Pokagon was far from a rank apologist for dominant interests. His posthumously published novel, *Queen of the Woods* (1899), a sentimental temperance romance with autobiographical elements, candidly addressed the difficulties of reconciling tribal traditions with an expansive American culture. At Chicago, Pokagon sold copies of his pamphlet "Red Man's Greeting," published several months earlier as "Red Man's Rebuke." In eloquent but blunt language, the author assumed the guise of an Indian "word sender" who characterizes reality with unblinking honesty. America's original inhabitants had no cause for celebrating the opening of the continent to the "pale-faced race" that had usurped their land and homes, declared Pokagon. Instead, the arrival of Christopher Columbus had marked "our funeral," he confessed, one in which "our inheritance was cut off, and we were driven and scattered as sheep before the wolves." It had been left to "weeping parents" to convey the sad history of native peoples to succeeding generations.

Simon Pokagon's divided loyalties were rooted in the plight of Indian peoples. Through military conquest, railroad expansion, and the elimination of the buffalo, Native American political sovereignty and cultural autonomy were nearly obliterated in the West by 1890. Numbering less than 300,000, the American Indian population had fallen by half in the previous one hundred years. To aggravate matters, the Dawes Act of 1887 had extended citizenship to male Indians who accepted individual property allotments, but repudiated tribal structures by opening communally owned lands to commercial agriculture. The U.S. Supreme Court legitimized Congress' right to abrogate tribal treaties in *Lone Wolf v. Hitchcock* (1903). Meanwhile, the federal government's mandatory Indian boarding schools required young Native American men to leave their reservations for extended periods of time, abandon Indian names and languages, and adhere to rigorous and petty codes of military discipline.

Seeking broad citizenship rights, legal empowerment, and improved opportunities for schooling, a group of educated activists formed the Society of American Indians in 1911. Leaders like Seneca anthropologist Arthur C. Parker spoke out against the moral hypocrisy of white civilization proponents in the federal bureaucracy and boarding schools. Reginald Oshkosh, a Menominee graduate of the Carlisle, Pennsylvania, Indian academy, bitterly denounced the fact that native peoples remained wards of the federal government. At the same time, acculturated Native American elites were torn between the desire to pass on English language proficiency and vocational training and the fear that a narrowly focused education might discourage the emergence of independent-minded community leaders. Several Indian writers responded to this dilemma by plotting out a middle alternative that sought to bridge the traditional heritage of the past and modern American civilization.

One of these transitional figures was Francis La Flesche, an educated writer and anthropology researcher from a prominent family of French and Omaha Indian background. La Flesche's anecdotal memoir, *The Middle Five: Indian Schoolboys of the Omaha Tribe* (1900), contrasted the humanity of his Native American childhood peers with the oppressive environment of a Presbyterian boarding school. When asked to entertain visitors on one occasion with an Indian song, the author recalled, students broke into an Omaha victory chant, only to have the performance dismissed as "savage." Laura (Minnie) Cornelius Kellogg, a formally educated Oneida Indian born on a Wisconsin reservation, turned her writing and speaking talents into a spirited campaign against the boarding institutions. There was "something behind the superb dignity and composure of the old bringing up, something in the discipline of the Red Man," she protested, that a mastery of Latin and algebra could not replace.

Reverence for Indian cultural heritage prompted Gertrude Bonnin, the daughter of a Yankton mother and a white Dakota trader, to take the Lakota name for Red Bird when she began to publish short stories about traditional Sioux life. A graduate of Quaker schools and Earlham College, Bonnin often contrasted paganism and the voice of the Great Spirit with what she saw as the bigoted and empty pieties of the Christian faith. In 1901 she published *Old Indian Legends,* a collection of stories she described as "relics of our country's virgin soil." These narratives, she insisted, provided evidence of the kinship of Native Americans with the rest of humanity. Celebrating "the loving mystery round about us," Bonnin released a second anthology entitled *American Indian Stories* in 1921.

The most celebrated Indian author of the early twentieth century was Charles Eastman. A Santee Sioux from South Dakota, Eastman went from a Presbyterian training school to Dartmouth College to Boston University Medical School. After serving as an agency physician at the Pine Ridge reservation, a YMCA organizer, an Indian Office official, and a lecturer on Native American affairs, Eastman began writing sketches for children's magazines. His efforts resulted in *Indian Boyhood* (1902), a memoir in which the author assumed the role of a traditional storyteller. He followed this with a series of reflections on Native American culture in *The Soul of an Indian* (1911). Eastman's full-length autobiography, *From the Deep Woods to Civilization* (1916), sought to capture the vitality of the Indian way. "Our simple lives were so imbued with the spirit of worship," he recalled, "while much church-going membership among white and nominally Christian Indians led often to such very small results." If everything was a gift from God, Eastman was asked by a tribal elder, why didn't white followers of Jesus acknowledge that food and land were "free as sunshine and rain" and could not be owned?

Charles Eastman

HISPANIC AND ASIAN SAGAS

One of the most significant results of the commercialization of the West was the disruption of the ranching culture of the region's indigenous Spanish speakers. When California substituted land values for income as the basis of tax assessments in the 1890s, Mexican American property owners often were dispossessed during periods of drought or crop losses. In New Mexico, where sixty thousand people traced their land titles back to sixteenth and seventeenth century Spanish grants, territorial governments conspired to transfer huge amounts of property to Anglo-controlled mining and ranching interests. Meanwhile, some 270,000 immigrants fled Mexican poverty and political repression between 1900 and 1910 to become agricultural wage laborers, miners, and construction workers in Texas, New Mexico, Arizona, Colorado, and California.

Confronted with an aggressive Anglo culture, southwestern Hispanics struggled to maintain an ethnic identity. Preserving the Spanish language often presented the best way of resisting the dominant culture. In the New Mexico territory alone, sixty-one Spanish-language newspapers thrived between 1880 and the early twentieth century. Yet a sizable proportion of the creative writing published by these periodicals consisted of romantic verse by anonymous poets aspiring to a bicultural identity. Between 1900 and 1910, Maria Cristina Mena became the first author to write for a wider audience when her English-language stories about Mexican American life appeared in *The Cen-*

tury and *American* magazines. Until the 1940s, Hispanic literature would be dominated by the quest for cultural and political accommodation among writers of similarly privileged backgrounds.

Mexican American folklore offered the most important outlet for working-class themes. Spanish-language newspapers often documented the exploits of "social bandits" such as New Mexico's *La Mano Negro* or *Las Corras Blancas*, known for guerrilla attacks on Anglo landowners and colluding government officials. The oral traditions of Hispanic folk music, however, provided the most accessible stories of resistance. *Tejano* (Texan) laborers favored the dance music of *conjunto* accordion ensembles, whose repertoire ranged from country love ballads, to religious and philosophic meditations, to social commentaries. The most popular selections of Mexican troubadours often turned out to be the *corridos*. These epic narratives helped to consolidate a sense of cultural solidarity by celebrating the feats of legendary anti-Anglo heroes such as Gregorio Cortez of Texas and California's Joaquin Murrieta.

Like Hispanics, Asian Americans found themselves in hostile circumstances. Recruited to Hawaii and the mainland as a cheap labor force, immigrants from China, Japan, and the Philippines hired out as plantation laborers, railroad crewmen, miners, factory operatives, and cannery workers. More than 600,000 Asian migrants came to the United States between 1868 and 1917, where they faced rampant discrimination and sporadic violence. In 1882 Congress singled out the Chinese with the first immigration exclusion law. Such a climate encouraged Chinese shopkeepers, merchants, and small business operators to develop separate commercial enclaves and self-help networks. Chinatowns in San Francisco, Los Angeles, and New York featured ethnic groceries, herb shops, clothing stores, newspapers, theaters, barbershops, restaurants, temples, after-hours religious schools, and family association centers. The difficulties of acculturation to mainstream society were described by Edith Maud Eaton, the daughter of a Chinese mother and English father, who wrote for American magazines as Sui Sin Far before publishing a collection of short stories entitled *Mrs. Spring Fragance* (1912).

Writing under the Japanese name Onoto Watanna, Eaton's sister Winnifred authored fifteen novels before going to Hollywood in the 1920s. Since immigration from Japan had only taken on substantial proportions in the 1890s and was limited by the Gentlemen's Agreements of 1907–08, the small Japanese American community struggled to define itself. Racial discrimination often resulted in a greater commitment to ethnic solidarity and independent economic enterprises like shop-keeping and farming. Yet cultural loyalties took on divergent paths. While traditional Japanese ethics stressed family duty, mutual obligations, and the virtues of endurance, many parents saw education in American ways as the key to overcoming discrimination. Accordingly, Japanese-language schools encouraged both knowledge of the homeland and assimilation of U.S. customs and manners. Japanese civic organizations even pressed women to walk alongside their husbands instead of behind, and urged workers to wear American clothes and eat American food on the job. Americanized in the public schools and among peers, young Japanese Americans nevertheless maintained traditional cultural ties at home.

THE SOULS OF BLACK FOLKS

Every African American, black intellectual W.E.B. Du Bois wrote in 1903, was both "an American, a Negro, two souls, two thoughts." The son of a domestic servant from western Massachusetts, Du Bois was the first student of color to earn a Harvard Ph.D. in History. After completing a pioneering sociological study of the African American community of Philadelphia, the young scholar became a professor of economics and history at Atlanta University, a predominantly Negro institution. As rigid racial segregation codes took hold in the South, and black men were subjected to political disenfranchisement and an epidemic of public lynching, Du Bois broke from the accommodating strategies of educator Booker T. Washington, the most important Negro conduit to the white political and business establishment. Highlighting the necessity of protest amid deteriorating race relations, the Atlanta professor called for a "talented tenth" of black leaders to form the vanguard of a civil rights struggle. "The problem of the twentieth century is the problem of the color line," he asserted in 1900.

One year later, Washington published his autobiography. *Up from Slavery* (1901) held out hard work, economic improvement, and self-help as the salvation of the black working class. Du Bois responded with a series of essays in *The Souls of Black Folks* (1903). The Negro, he said, was "a sort of seventh son, born with a veil and gifted with second sight in this American world." Yet the double-consciousness and dual identity of African Americans could be made whole, he insisted. Du Bois sought to encourage this process by drawing attention to the distinctive artistic traditions, expressive culture, and social values—the "soul"—that black people shared. This involved an appreciation of African American spiritual aspirations through folklore, music, religious faith, and the quest for social justice. Once enunciating the meaning and passion of black religion in the preface, Du Bois headed each chapter of the volume with an excerpt from a Negro spiritual, the "sorrow songs" he described as "the most original and beautiful expression of human life and longing yet born on American soil." These hymns, he wrote, were "the singular spiritual heritage of the nation and the greatest gift of the Negro people."

The Souls of Black Folks presented an unprecedented analysis of the importance of African American folklore and oral tradition. White readers were already familiar with Joel Chandler Harris' collection of plantation lore in *Uncle Remus*. The stories Harris assembled relied on characters like Br'er Rabbit to show how duplicity, guile, and cunning were essential to an underdog's survival, but were in jeopardy of undermining by excessive pride. The first African American novelist to explore these themes was

Charles W. Chesnutt. Born in Cleveland to free black parents in 1858, Chesnutt grew up in North Carolina during Reconstruction. After serving as a teacher and assistant principal at a Negro normal school, he moved back north, passed the Ohio Bar, and established a successful court reporting firm. With no literary training, Chesnutt published a dialect story in the *Atlantic Monthly* in 1887 that featured a conjuror from black folk tradition and a shrewd narrator who outsmarts her white employer.

Twelve years after this initial success, Houghton Mifflin published a collection of Chesnutt's short stories entitled *The Conjure Woman* (1899). Writing with realism and sympathy for his slave characters, the author offered profiles of canny survival among people who never lost their human dignity or fortitude. At the same time, Chesnutt stripped away stereotypes to reveal complex individuals with flaws as well as strengths. One year later *The House Behind the Cedars* (1900) told the tale of two African Americans who pass for white in the post-Civil War South. A second novel, *The Marrow of Tradition* (1901), used the setting of the 1898 Wilmington, North Carolina, race riot to offer a plea for racial justice. *The Colonel's Dream* (1905), the author's final work, dealt with a failed attempt to revive an economically depressed Carolina town. Addressing powerful racial themes within the broad canvas of black life, Chesnutt found little commercial success among the affluent white reading public. Nevertheless, the writer, who returned to court reporting rather than compromise his principles, was among the first Negro novelists to come to terms with the African American experience.

Black poet and fiction writer Paul Laurence Dunbar fared much better with the white public. The son of former Kentucky plantation slaves, Dunbar was born in Dayton, Ohio in 1872. The only black student at his public high school, he was elected graduating class president. Yet when refused jobs in newspaper and legal offices, Dunbar was forced to work as an elevator operator. Influenced by the white midwestern regionalist poet James Whitcomb Riley, the young writer felt the call to "interpret my own people through song and story." In 1893 he subsidized the publication of his first book of verse, *Oak and Ivy.* Seeking to enlighten readers without alienating them, Dunbar published *Majors and Minors* in 1895, a collection of poems that received high praise from novelist and literary critic William Dean Howells, who served as its patron. The book included a brutally honest portrait of role-playing in black life with the title of "We Wear the Mask." The writer followed this triumph with *Lyrics of Lowly Life* (1896), his best-selling book, and with sixteen editions of poetry and fiction in the next ten years.

Dunbar broke fresh ground by freeing black poetry from the religious clichés of the African American experience. Yet publishers were eager to capitalize on white interest in black southern folklore, and therefore insisted that he write in dialect and conform to the "plantation school" of characterization. Dunbar and composer Will Marion Cook tested the boundaries of racial convention in 1898 with the popular black Broadway musical *Clorindy, The Origin of the Cakewalk.* The following year the poet revealed his more somber side in a poem entitled "Sympathy." "I know why the caged bird sings!"

Dunbar declared in a line that would be considered his greatest contribution. He then turned to realist fiction with *The Sport of the Gods* (1902), a novel describing both the advantages and disadvantages of the migration north and the first African American work to describe the life of the emerging northern black ghetto.

The most celebrated African American folk hero of the early twentieth century was not a writer but the professional boxer Jack Johnson. The son of a former Maryland slave who supported his family as a janitor, Johnson was born in a modest house in Galveston, Texas, in 1878. When the young boy was victimized by schoolyard bullies, his mother insisted that he learn to fight back. Following five or six years of elementary school, Johnson took on an assortment of jobs as a wagon painter, horse trainer, longshoreman, baker's assistant, porter, and barber's helper. He also participated in degrading Battle Royal free-for-alls, in which naked young African Americans fought each other for the amusement of white spectators who threw coins at the last man standing. Johnson roamed the country as a sparring partner and common laborer through the mid–1890s before moving to Los Angeles and becoming a professional prizefighter.

Taking on a series of white opponents, most of whom were Irish American, Johnson earned a reputation as a defensive and deceptive boxer. Understanding that the ring was white man's territory, he allowed aggressive rivals to overextend themselves and become vulnerable to efficient counterattacks, which he often punctuated with derisive laughter. "Papa Jack," as he soon became known to fans and "lady friends," shaved his head for a more intimidating look and began to sport the expensive clothes, cane, and golf cap of a successful ragtime musician. By 1908 the boxer was in line to contest the heavyweight championship against Tommy Burns, a German Canadian who shared the racist assumption that black fighters lacked courage, skill, and tactical ability. Nevertheless, the match was propelled by sports writers who believed that athletics was an isolated arena of equal opportunity, and by white supremacists convinced that a Johnson defeat would teach African Americans to maintain their subordinate place.

Held in Australia, the fight was stopped by police in the eighth round after Johnson's quick footwork allowed him to punish Burns with a variety of precisely directed jabs accompanied by a barrage of sexually tainted verbal insults. When the champ defended his title five times in the following year, boxing promoters searched for the "great white hope" to defeat him. Finally, former champion James L. Jeffries agreed to come out of retirement for a match in Reno, Nevada, on July 4, 1910. Entering the ring in a silk robe, blue trunks, and American flag belt, Johnson prolonged the fight to humiliate his aging opponent, taunting him with cries of "How do you like it?" Finally, after two nine-count knock-downs, the champion finished off his rival with a fifteenth-round knockout. In response, white race riots broke out across the country, and fifteen states and the District of Columbia banned all boxing films to preserve public order. Newspaper editorialists now warned that African Americans were incapable of distinguishing between a sports contest and social reality.

Perceived by whites as a threat to social decorum and stable race relations, Johnson became a folk hero to working-class blacks and a forerunner of the "New Negro." Not since Nat Turner's slave insurrection had an African American public figure so recklessly defied the deferential racial codes of white society. Ostentatiously traveling with white women and consorting with prostitutes, the glib-talking champion paraded his wealth with fancy clothes, fast cars, and a love of literature and music. Boasting that he was the greatest lover, talker, and boxer in the world, "Papa Jack" took on the guise of celebrated black heroes like Railroad Bill, a turpentine worker who shot a white Alabama policeman in 1893, and the legendary Stagolee, the blues and ballad protagonist who kills a man for winning his hat in a card game. Exploiting such notoriety, the fighter participated in a vaudeville tour of the East and northern Middle West in 1910 in which he entertained audiences with his favorite stories.

Johnson's relationships with white women resulted in an arrest by federal officials for violations of the White Slave Traffic Act of 1910. Convicted in 1913 of aiding prostitution and debauchery and engaging in unlawful sexual intercourse, the boxer escaped on bond and traveled to Canada and Europe. Two years later the champ was defeated by Jess Willard in a twenty-sixth-round knock-out in Havana. Johnson finally agreed to return to the United States in 1920 and did nearly a year's time in a federal penitentiary. He never fought major bouts again, but remained a prominent figure in the Harlem nightlife of the 1920s and a legendary African American folk hero.

BOHEMIAN DEMOCRACY

The plight of black people captured the imagination of several significant white figures. In 1908 muckraking journalist Ray Stannard Baker published *Following the Color Line,* a path-breaking exposé of racist practices seen through the eyes of a white man disguising himself as a Negro. One segment of Gertrude Stein's experimental novel *Three Lives* (1909) was devoted to a stream-of-consciousness monologue that employed vernacular language to describe the life of an illiterate African American servant girl. Midwestern poet Vachel Lindsay's widely recited "The Congo: A Study of the Negro Race" (1914) purported to synthesize the emotional totality of black life through rhythmic intonations depicting African origins, a cakewalk celebration, and Negro spirituality. In the realm of social activism, W.E.B. Du Bois prompted a group of prominent white socialists, social workers, and reformers to join him in 1909 in forming the rights-oriented National Association for the Advancement of Colored People (NAACP).

Despite such interest, race relations were not the central concern of most white cultural activists between the 1890s and World War I. During this period a number of young American writers, artists, and intellectuals strove to build a democratized social order built on avowed principles of socialism, sexual equality, and cultural progress. Repudiating nineteenth-century concepts of hierarchy and propriety, the rebels fashioned themselves as ideological and cultural revolutionaries mounting a wholesale challenge to genteel customs, morality, and art. In large cities such as Chicago, San Francisco, and New York, like-minded dissidents established creative communities in imitation of the nonconformist bohemians of Paris. Searching for fresh ideas, invigorated art forms, and an emotionally infused intelligence, America's self-styled bohemians relished unbounded conversation, personal honesty, and vital contact with selected representatives of the white working classes.

Along California's Barbary Coast, an area stretching from San Francisco Bay to Carmel, writers like Jack London sought to give voice to new protagonists as they mingled in brothels, cafes, and saloons with sailors and rough adventurers. New York's Lower East Side also served as a favorite inspiration for realist painters, photographers like Alfred Stieglitz, and authors. Hutchins Hapgood's *The Spirit of the Ghetto* (1902) offered a definitive guide to the city's vibrant Yiddish culture, while Jewish characters figured as central figures in the writings of David Graham Phillips, Lincoln Steffens, Bruno Lessing, and others. Yet by the 1910s, Chicago had become the most important meeting ground of creative literature and vernacular culture. Through modest outlets such as Harriet Monroe's *Poetry, a Magazine of Verse* and Margaret Anderson's *Little Review* regional writers sought to translate the rugged power of the lakefront city into print. Serving as self-conscious heirs to the legacy of Walt Whitman, the small journals reached out to a broad audience with poetry and fiction that reflected the rhythms of jazz, the conversational tone of common speech, and the experiences of ordinary people.

Carl Sandburg offered a prime example of the shift in literary style. The son of a semi-literate Swedish immigrant who supported his family as a blacksmith in a small northwestern Illinois town, Sandburg left school after eighth grade. After becoming a shoeshine boy and holding a variety of odd jobs, he bummed around the Midwest at the age of nineteen. Sandburg then enlisted in the Spanish-American War infantry. Returning to briefly attend college in his hometown, he learned about Walt Whitman and took to the road again for five years, riding the rails and finding work as a casual laborer. At the age of twenty-nine, the young drifter finally settled down in Milwaukee as a socialist organizer. In 1913 he moved to Chicago to write for a movement newspaper that folded. Sandburg then took on a variety of journalism jobs, including one as an entertainment columnist. Describing his poetry as "verse of massive gait," Harriet Monroe published the first samples of his work the following year. A collection of Sandburg's free verse followed in book form in *Chicago Poems* (1916).

Known as a "people's poet" who let his hair grow shaggy, wore string ties, and dressed informally, Sandburg identified himself as a successor to Walt Whitman. He even shared the bard's fascination with Illinois folk hero Abraham Lincoln. Combining vernacular phrasing with fellowship for the common person and sympathy for the poor,

Carl Sandburg

the poet characterized beaten-down laborers in "Masses" as "patient as the darkness of night." Another poem, "They Will Say," paid tribute to those who "work, broken and smothered" for "a little handful of pay on a few Saturday nights." In "Child of the Romans," Sandburg contrasted an Italian railroad laborer eating dry bread and bologna by the side of the tracks with the wealthy passengers in the dining car of a passing train.

Despite such instances of class consciousness, Sandburg seemed to prefer celebrating the laughter and joy of working life and the beauty of the industrial landscape. In "Happiness," he depicted "a crowd of Hungarians under the trees with their women and children and a keg of beer and an accordion." The collection's odes to the writer's adopted town established Sandburg's reputation. One poem memorably represented the Chicago fog coming in "on little cat feet ... on silent haunches." In the most widely quoted selection of the book, Sandburg memorialized the city as "Hog Butcher for the World,/Tool Maker, Stacker of Wheat, ... /Stormy, husky, brawling,/City of the Big Shoulders." He turned such optimism to his prairie homeland in *Cornhuskers* (1918). "I was born on the prairie," the poet wrote, "and the milk of its wheat, the red of its clover, the eyes of its women, gave me a song and a slogan ... I speak of new cities and new people." Two years later Sandburg published *Smoke and Steel* (1920), which mixed images of spring fields and autumn leaves with smoke rising from steelmill roofs. "Pittsburgh, Youngstown, Gary," he exclaimed, "—they make their steel with men."

The *Little Review's* most important prose stylist was Sherwood Anderson. Born in Camden, Ohio, in 1876, Anderson worked as a laborer in a Chicago warehouse at age twenty, served in the Spanish-American War, and returned to his adopted city to write advertising for five years. After running businesses in Ohio and attempting to publish four novels, Anderson suffered an emotional breakdown and moved back to Chicago in 1912 to devote his life to writing. The first result was *Mid-American Chants* (1918), a collection of Whitman-inspired verse whose intention, he said, was "to bring God home to the sweaty men on the corn rows." The following year Sherwood published his first successful novel, *Winesburg, Ohio* (1919). Influenced by Whitman's poetry, Impressionist painting, and Gertrude Stein's use of vernacular phrasing, the book penetrated beneath the surface of a small town to expose the grotesque realities of its inhabitants' inner lives. Sherwood penetrated into the minds of his characters with a profusion of descriptive detail and dialogue that captured midwestern color and cadence.

RADICAL ACTIVISTS AND THE PROLETARIAT

Many American bohemians also identified themselves as feminists. Although a coalition of female church activists, social workers, and labor union advocates supported woman's suffrage, the vote was not the central goal for those women more concerned with economic independence, education rights, cultural autonomy, and sexual freedom. Inspired by images of liberated female figures in popular theater, the mass-circulation press, and literature, cultural and political radicals like Crystal Eastman and Louise Bryant aspired to genuine comradeship and universal fellowship with men. Advocating self-realization and free speech about previously censored topics like birth control, activists such as Margaret Sanger pictured themselves in the image of the New Woman.

Talk of sexual equality, especially among men, may frequently have been rhetorical, but the subject had resonance beyond the cosmopolitan classes. In "The Woman Who Toils," an article appearing in *Everybody's Magazine* in 1902, writer Marie Van Vorst and her sister-in-law had depicted the degrading experiences of labor in a Pittsburgh pickle works, a New York State clothing mill, a southern cotton plant, and a Lynn, Massachusetts, shoe factory. A more ambitious attempt to describe women's working conditions came from Rheta Childe Dorr, who had deserted a secure marriage to come to New York to be a journalist. Taking work as a laundress, seamstress, and factory hand, Dorr sent reports to her editor at *Everybody's* but had to sue to get her name on the byline, and discovered that her story of female bondage had been altered to demonstrate the triumphant march of women into industry. Moving on to *Hampton's Magazine,* Dorr published a new series that resulted in *What Eight Million Women Want* (1910), a book that focused on the suffrage campaign, the influence of women's clubs, and the fight against the sexual double standard. It sold a half-million copies.

Anarchist Emma Goldman's combination of populism and feminism made her one of the most electrifying public speakers of the pre–World War I period. A Russian Jewish immigrant attracted to radical circles in New York and Chicago in the 1880s, Goldman founded *Mother Earth* magazine in 1906. Combining Yiddish ethnicity, radical bohemianism, labor militancy, and sardonic invective, she established a bond with listeners by asserting that "spiritual hunger and unrest" drove people to rebel. Goldman sought to unite working-class interests with those of the more affluent by pointing to the vulnerabilities of capitalism and by aligning herself with women's rights, free speech, and sexual freedom. Her popular lectures not only attracted respectable audiences but rallied politically active artists such as John Sloan, Robert Henri, and George Bellows.

Several realist painters contributed drawings to the radical magazine *The Masses*. Edited by Columbia University philosophy professor Max Eastman with help from John Reed, Waldo Frank, and Floyd Dell, *The Masses* advocated a revolutionary mix of free love, racial and women's equality, birth control, socialism, and labor justice. Its stripped-down topography and uniform font represented a departure from the ornamental styles used in traditional printing, as did Art Young's sparse political cartoons. Contributors saw socialism as a humane alternative to the dehumanizing qualities of the capitalist order. Intellectual interest in a socialized economy dated back to politically conscious writers such as William Dean Howells, Henry D. Lloyd, and Jack London. Growing up fatherless in Oakland, California's waterfront district, London had worked as a newsboy, oyster pirate, and bowling alley pin setter before setting sail as a merchant seaman at seventeen. After joining the Alaska Gold Rush in 1897, he began publishing short stories about his adventures, leading to publication of *The Call of the Wild* (1903), the story of a dog's cunning survival in the Arctic bush.

London's subsequent novels pitted primitive and instinctual ordinary supermen against effete intellectuals and cultural custodians. Having been exposed to socialist ideas during a brief stint at the University of California at Berkeley, the writer believed that class struggle would lead workers to ultimate emancipation. London published his radical lectures and essays in *The War of the Classes* (1904), and described the future evolution of capitalism into an oppressive oligarchy in his most political novel, *The Iron Heel* (1907). In contrast, Winston Churchill, the author of eight best-selling works of fiction, offered a milder version of the cooperative commonwealth for more genteel audiences. *The Inside of the Cup* (1913) described the conversion of an Episcopalian minister to the Social Gospel and the belief that each individual was potentially divine and capable of personal responsibility. In *A Far Country* (1915), Churchill presented a socialist hero who preached the gospel of love and the free spirit of man.

While novelists like London and Churchill experimented with radical doctrines, a grass-roots socialist culture thrived among radical Germans and Scandinavians of the Upper Midwest and among tenant farmers in the Old Southwest. Socialist encampments in early-twentieth-century Oklahoma frequently attracted ten thousand people for speeches by leaders including Eugene V. Debs and Mother Jones, hymns and songs like "The Farmer Is the Man," and access to magazines and newspapers like *The Appeal to Reason*. Both socialists and anarchists were attracted to the Industrial Workers of the World (IWW). Organized in 1905 to place production under worker control by any means necessary, the radical labor union declared that "the working class and the employing class have nothing in common." Most effective in recruiting western miners, loggers, and migrant workers, the IWW created a loosely affiliated hobo culture that celebrated folk heroes like its own Big Bill Haywood. Parodies of religious hymns by organizers like Utah's legendary Joe Hill, executed for murder in 1914, and by Ralph Chaplin, the creator of "Solidarity Forever" (1915), furthered the "Wobbly" mystique.

IWW and bohemian energies intersected in New York in 1913 when Bill Haywood and writer John Reed collaborated on a Madison Square Garden Pageant to support a silk workers' strike in Paterson, New Jersey. Raised by a prominent Portland, Oregon, family, Reed settled in Greenwich Village in 1910 after graduation from Harvard, where he published several magazine stories about city life and working women. Arrested as a bystander in Paterson, Reed completed a series on the strike for *The Masses*. Committing himself to the workers' struggle, he enlisted former classmate Robert Edmond Jones, a student of Berlin's avant-garde theater, to direct the Madison Square Garden event and asked John Sloan to design the sets. Thousands of workers joined the cast, in which they listened to long speeches delivered through bullhorns. The pageant proved to be a financial bust, and the strike ultimately was lost. Yet Reed went on to become the foremost journalist of his generation, with first-hand reporting on Poncho Villa's military exploits during the Mexican Revolution, the Eastern Front of the Great War, and the Bolshevik uprising that created the Soviet communist state in 1917.

World War I and its aftermath would sever the tentative ties between revolutionary political consciousness and cultural experimentation and lead to a widened gap between segments of the intelligentsia and the public at large. For that reason, the period between 1893 and 1920 stands out as one in which writers, poets, and artists strove to identify their efforts with "the people," even if they sometimes assumed a patronizing tone. In an era sensitive to the requirements of reform and readjustment, the cosmopolitan classes seemed anxious to establish legitimacy by proving their connections to the ordinary American, however defined. The dynamic period following the European war would provide unanticipated but lucrative means for furthering such an agenda.

SOURCES AND SUGGESTED READINGS

The definitive treatment of late-nineteenth-century protest literature appears in John L. Thomas, *Alternative America: Henry George, Edward Bellamy, Henry Demarest Lloyd and the Adversary Tradition* (1983). Reform-minded journalists of the Progressive era receive chapter profiles in Louis Filler, *The Muckrakers*, rev. ed. (1976).

Leading examples of the genre appear with critical commentary in Ellen F. Fitzpatrick, ed., *Muckraking: Three Landmark Articles* (1994). See also Leon Harris, *Upton Sinclair: American Rebel* (1975) and Patrick F. Palermo, *Lincoln Steffens* (1978). The subjective nature but enormous impact of documentary photography marks the focus of the early chapters of Maren Stange, *Symbols of Ideal Life: Social Documentary Photography in America, 1890–1950* (1989) and Russell Freedman's *Kids at Work: Lewis Hine and the Crusade Against Child Labor* (1994).

Social realism in Progressive era fiction is the focus of John Pilkington, Jr., *Henry Blake Fuller* (1970) and the relevant chapters of David W. Noble, *The Eternal Adam and the New World Garden: The Central Myth in the American Novel Since 1830* (1968). See also Kenneth S. Lynn, *William Dean Howells: An American Life* (1971) and the treatment of Hamlin Garland in Henry Nash Smith, *Virgin Land: The American West as Symbol and Myth*, rev. ed. (1970). For the Naturalists, see Lawrence E. Hussman, Jr., *Harbingers of a Century: The Novels of Frank Norris* (1999) and *Dreiser and His Fiction: A Twentieth Century Quest* (1983). Two of the most popular urban writers of the period receive insightful profiles in Lee Coyle, *George Ade* (1964) and David Stuart, *O. Henry: A Biography of William Sydney Porter* (1990).

Progressive era realist painters are the subject of Rebecca Zurier, et al. *Metropolitan Lives: The Ashcan Artists and Their New York* (1995) and John Loughery, *John Sloan: Painter and Rebel* (1995). See also the relevant segments of Francis Pohl, *Framing America: A Social History of American Art* (2002). Works on regional fiction writers and poets include Rex Burbank, *Sherwood Anderson* (1994); R.W.B. Lewis, *Edith Wharton: A Biography* (1985); Keith J. Fennimore, *Booth Tarkington* (1974); and the early chapters of North Callahan, *Carl Sandburg: His Life and Works* (1987). For the evolution of the western genre, see the first segments of Jane Tompkins, *West of Everything: The Inner Life of Westerns* (1992) and treatments of vernacular fiction in Henry Nash Smith, *Virgin Land: The American West as Symbol and Myth*, rev. ed. (1970) and Michael Deming, *Mechanic Accents: Dime Novels and Working-Class Culture in America* (1987).

An excellent collection of early-twentieth-century Native American writing appears in Frederick E. Hoxie, ed., *Talking Back to Civilization: Indian Voices from the Progressive Era* (2001). For Asian-American literary efforts and historical background, see the relevant entries in Lawrence J. Trudeau, ed., *Asian American Literature: Reviews and Criticism of Works by American Writers of Asian Descent* (1999) and segments of Ronald Takaki, *Strangers from a Different Shore: A History of Asian Americans* (1989). Latino expressive culture receives coverage in Nicolás Kanellos, *Hispanic Literature of the United States: A Comprehensive Reference* (2003) and in the opening segment of Manuel Peña, *The Texas-Mexican Conjunto: History of a Working Class Music* (1985).

David Levering Lewis, *W.E.B. DuBois: Biography of a Race, 1868–1919* (1993) profiles the Progressive era's leading AfricanAmerican author and intellectual. Portraits of the period's two most significant black creative writers appear in Sylvia Lyons Render, *Charles W. Chesnutt* (1980) and Peter Revell, *Paul Laurence Dunbar* (1980). For the controversial career of black heavyweight boxing champion Jack Johnson, see Randy Roberts, *Papa Jack: Jack Johnson and the Era of White Hopes* (1983); Geoffrey Ward, *Unforgivable Blackness: The Rise and Fall of Jack Johnson* (2004); and the relevant sections of Jeffrey T. Sammons, *Beyond the Ring: The Role of Boxing in American Society* (1988).

Progressive cultural revolutionaries receive comprehensive treatment in Christine Stansell, *American Moderns: Bohemian New York and the Creation of a New Century* (2000). For the radical shift in gender roles among affluent women, see Susan Glenn, *Female Spectacle: The Theatrical Roots of Modern Feminism* (2000) and June Sochen, *The New Woman: Feminism in Greenwich Village, 1910–1920* (1972). Experimental art and radical politics come together in Martin Green, *New York 1913: The Armory Show and the Paterson Strike Pageant* (1988). See also Robert A. Rosenstone, *Romantic Revolutionary: A Biography of John Reed* (1990).

4

The Romance and Nostalgia of America's Jazz Age

Buoyed by a vibrant consumer economy, American popular culture took on new importance in the period following World War I. With more than half the population living in urban areas, the frenzied era known as the Jazz Age inspired the spread of cosmopolitan values and practices. Novelists, short story writers, and poets helped to popularize some of the irreverent social attitudes of the times. Yet the 1920s also brought Prohibition, immigration restriction, and a resurgence of traditional values. Contradictory portraits of ordinary Americans in literature, journalism, blues, jazz, the Broadway stage, Hollywood, and rural music helped to shape the Jazz Age as a period of widespread ambivalence toward social innovation and one of divided cultural allegiances.

STORIES OF THE BIG TOWN

As the corporate economy experienced a period of relative prosperity between 1922 and 1929, a consolidated domestic market stimulated a consumer ethic that equated democratic choice with the pleasurable ownership and use of commodities. Through mass-circulation newspapers and magazines, radio, the movies, nationwide advertising, the phonograph, and other innovations, Americans immersed themselves in a thriving popular culture that glamorized abundance, leisure, and self-indulgence. The attractions of consumerism extended beyond the affluent. By 1929 some 30 percent of the population was comprised of first- or second-generation immigrants, while 36 percent was Roman Catholic. An influx of Mexican laborers and the migration of southern whites and African Americans to the cities contributed to the mix of ethnicities and social classes that gave a decidedly egalitarian and democratic feel to public culture.

As syndication of newspaper features became common practice, comic strips took on added significance as embodiments of everyday life. In contrast to the slum-dwelling characters from the early twentieth century, a second wave of cartoons focused on lower-middle-class underdogs who retained a stubborn faith in democratic opportunity and happy endings. Using folk themes, humorous exaggeration, sight gags, and tightly expressed wit and farce, "the Funnies" presented fables of modern life to tens of millions of readers. Several popular Twenties comics dated to the preceding decade. *Polly and Her Pals,* begun in 1912, chronicled the life of a white-collar heroine. *Judge Rummy and Indoor Sports,* first appearing in 1916, popularized slang terms like "hot dog," "bum's rush," "the cat's pajamas," and "baloney." *The Gumps,* inaugurated the next year, recounted the antics of Andy, a struggling family head endowed with eternal optimism and self-pride. *Gasoline Alley* and *Barney Google* both debuted in 1919. The first pictured the zany life of an average American family; the second told the story of a "fall guy" who found himself perennially pushed around by more powerful adversaries.

In the early 1920s the tabloid *New York Daily News* introduced another set of comics. *Winnie Winkle,* which first ran in 1920, focused on the romances of a working woman. *Smitty,* appearing in 1922, chronicled the experiences of a humble office boy and his kid-brother Herbie. *Moon Mullins,* which the *News* began to publish in 1923, reflected the hardened experience of cartoonist Frank Willard, a high school truant who had been busted in military rank on three occasions before running hamburger stands at county fairs. Capturing the low-brow humor of gritty pool hall regulars and fast-buck hustlers, *Mullins* presented a slapstick portrait of a congenial anti-hero with no luck when it came to cards, dice, or women. The most popular strip of the Twenties may have been *Little Orphan Annie,* which debuted on the comic page of the *Chicago Tribune* in 1924. Tracing the plight of a plucky little girl continually separated and reunited with her foster father, the mercenary but lovable Daddy Warbucks, the feature offered a backhand tribute to the rugged individualism, hard work, and courage of the American Dream.

For male readers, the sports page was as popular a feature as the comic strips. In the increasingly bureaucratized and corporate postwar years competitive athletics took on enhanced allure as an arena for individual accomplishment and heroism. Although college football stars like University of Illinois halfback Harold ("Red") Grange helped to romanticize campus culture, the greatest sports heroes came from the European ethnics and rural whites who competed in professional baseball and boxing. No single athlete of the era achieved the fame of New York Yankees slugger Babe Ruth. Born into an impoverished German American family in a third-floor apartment over a saloon on the Baltimore waterfront, Ruth was sent to a Catholic industrial school at the age of seven. Working in the facility's shirt factory in pursuit of a tailor's trade, he learned that his talent for baseball could provide a potential route out of poverty. The barely literate ballplayer signed his first contract at nineteen and by 1920 was a Yankee star. His powerful homeruns helped to restore baseball's luster after gambling interests had brought scandal to the game by fixing the 1919 World Series.

The affable Ruth elicited adoration from working-class fans familiar with their hero's exploits at the ballpark, on the radio, or in the press. His homely round face, hefty physique, bandy legs, and tastes for gambling, sex, drinking, and fine clothes furthered the mystique. Ruth helped to perpetuate such loyalty by signing his name to newspaper articles, delivering product endorsements, visiting children's hospitals, and even spending one off-season touring small towns with a vaudeville troupe. The only athlete who approached the Yankee hitter's popularity was the Irish American boxer Jack Dempsey. Raised in Manassa, Colorado, Dempsey spent years as a hobo and barroom brawler before entering the ring. Promoted as "Jack the Giant Killer" and the "Manassa Mauler," he beat reigning heavyweight champion Jess Willard in an upset victory on July 4th, 1919. Dempsey permanently reinforced the underdog image when he lost the title to clean-living college man Gene Tunney in 1926, and suffered a second defeat in the "long count" match the next year when he failed to retreat to a neutral corner after flooring his opponent.

The heroics of athletic personalities were conveyed to the public through an expanded sports media. Writers like Heywood Broun, Grantland Rice, Ring Lardner, and Damon Runyon brought a rare degree of literary eloquence to the hard-bitten genre. Coming out of an affluent background in Niles, Michigan, Lardner initiated his writing career as a baseball reporter in South Bend, Indiana. Assigned a column in the *Chicago Tribune* in 1913, he began to build stories around the colorful, humorous, and dramatic incidents involving baseball personalities. In "Busher's Letters," a series published in the *Saturday Evening Post* the following year, Lardner fused midwestern dialogue and baseball lingo in the guise of a left-handed pitcher describing games to a pal back home. The feature expanded into *You Know Me, All* (1916), an assortment of observations in which a down-to-earth ballplayer assumed the attributes of an average American.

Sports writing taught Lardner that ordinary characters with familiar faults could be rendered with considerable sympathy. When the writer moved to New York in 1919, he began a column containing the common-sense ruminations of a pedestrian middle-class family man. Casting his protagonist with a cynical but congenial sense of humor, unpretentious innocence, and natural shrewdness, Lardner was able to produce satiric barbs that otherwise may have appeared ill-tempered. On occasion he managed to strike a note of simple poignancy. "The Golden Honeymoon," for example, lovingly detailed an elderly couple's fiftieth anniversary trip to Florida. Lardner's newspaper stories and sketches were collected in two successful volumes, *The Big Town* (1921) and *How to Write Short Stories* (1924).

Damon Runyon came out of a far less protected background than Ring Lardner. Born in Manhattan, Kansas, as Alfred Damon Runyan in 1880, he was the son of a hard-drinking itinerant printer and newspaper publisher. When the boy's mother died shortly after the family moved to Pueblo, Colorado, father and son holed up in a hilltop shed and the youngster freely roamed the downtown streets and bars. In his teens Alfred took on a variety of local newspaper jobs. His first story assignment came at fourteen, when he was asked to cover a lynching. Made a full-time reporter, he learned to chain-smoke Turkish cigarettes, devour large quantities of Red Eye whiskey, and tout a six-shooter for show. When the budding journalist received his first byline at age seventeen, the printer misspelled his name as Runyon, a designation that remained for his entire writing career.

After returning from volunteer military service in the Philippines, Runyon hopped freights around the country, learned hobo language and lore, and spent the next ten years with newspapers in Colorado and across the West. In 1910 he took a job as a "breather," accompanying a corpse by train to New York, where he sold verses and hobo sketches to magazines and traded story lines to a newsman acquaintance for room and board. Hired the next year as a sportswriter for William Randolph Hearst's *American,* Runyon took over the New York Giants baseball beat. With cohorts Grantland Rice and Heywood Broun, he shaped modern sports journalism by infusing features with humor, personalized observations, and human interest. Runyon's descriptions of Casey Stengel legging out a homerun in the 1923 World's Series and spitball pitcher "Bugs" Raymond's elaborate ploys to retrieve beer into the clubhouse took on legendary status for contemporaries.

Runyon's stories were spiced with a variety of vernacular expressions, a skill he learned from boxing reporter Tad Dorgan. Drawn to the gambling crowd that circled around sports figures, he spent increasing amounts of time at Broadway saloons, nightclubs, and racetracks, and published his sketches in national magazines and a book he called *Guys and Dolls* (1931). The gamblers or "home boys" who inhabited these accounts included humorous street characters like Harry the Horse, Educated Edmund, Dave the Dude, Solid John, Dopey Goldberg, Philly the Weeper, Joe the Joker, Lost Card Louie, Feets Samuel, horse trainer Hymie Banjo Eyes, ex-fighter Milk Ear Willie, floating craps game operator Nathan Detroit, tap dancer Billy Perry, and striptease performer Miss Dawn Astra. True to their working-class origins, Runyon's tales cautioned that there were no sure things in life, and that no one stayed ahead of the game for keeps.

LITERARY AMERICANA

Although most creative writers of the post-World War I era were products of affluent families and sensibilities, a broad rebellion against moral sentimentality encouraged widespread use of everyday language and characterizations. F. Scott Fitzgerald depicted the cultural rebellion of middle-class youth in *This Side of Paradise* (1920) with news of "a new generation ... grown up to find all Gods dead, all wars fought, all faith in man shaken." John Dos Passos relied upon a collage prose style and verbal jazz rhythms to mirror the urban landscape in *Manhattan Transfer* (1925). Theodore Dreiser used a realist's view of slum life as the foundation for *An American Tragedy* (1925). In *The Sun Also Rises* (1926) and *A Farewell to Arms* (1929), Ernest Hemingway wrote of wartime anti-heroes who spoke in common speech. He strove for the exact word instead of the decorative adjective. Discarding moral abstractions, Hemingway's characters insisted that only concrete terms like names had any meaning. The use of bare syntax suggested the belief that life's pleasures derived from simple appetites, skills, or ritualized actions, and that a novelist should simply record the sequence of events that led to specific emotions.

The direct treatment of subjects, concise phrasing, and rhythmic prose of authors like Hemingway borrowed a good deal from imagist poetry, a genre that traced its roots to the 1910s. Imagists insisted that poets should not intrude into their work, should refrain from using objects as symbols, should present particular images without explaining them, and should speak plainly in rhythmic cadence without "poetic" diction. Such devotion led writers like Amy Lowell, Hart Crane, Edna St. Vincent Millay, and Ezra Pound to experiment with vernacular speech and unrhymed verse while expressing irreverence toward conventional morality. Leadership of the movement in the United States fell to Lowell, a heavy-set, cigar-smoking descendant of one of New England's aristocratic families. At the age of fifty-one, the former civic activist and public lecturer published *What's O'Clock* (1925), a collection that received the Pulitzer Prize in poetry.

Influenced by the imagists, physician and poet William Carlos Williams chronicled the life of Rutherford, New Jersey, the place of his birth and life-long residence. After studies in the United States and Europe, Williams began practicing family medicine in 1910. Influenced by modern French painting, realist art, and photography, he sought to place avant-garde forms within an American context. In 1914 Williams painted a self-portrait in which he appeared with a wide-open collar and tousled hair reminiscent of Walt Whitman. By then the full-time physician had come under the influence of Carl Sandburg and other urban poets. Opposed to the Genteel Tradition of idealized pastorals, he sought to write truthful verse that would strip away external trappings and emphasize the particular locale in which the author lived. Williams' early work offered bare descriptions of Negroes, children, working men, drunks, wildflowers, weeds, crooked trees, and his grandmother. "The Wanderer" (1914) referenced Whitman once again with an ode to a young poet on a Hudson River ferry. Two other pieces about nearby Paterson described a crowded main street and striking silk workers in a bread line.

In *Spring and All* (1923), Williams sought to counter fears that America was sinking into drabness by celebrating the universal elements of his immediate surroundings.

Poems like "Rapid Transit," a work comprised of short lines, included advertising slogans and other trivia. Poetry was "a rarest moment in the language around us," Williams later reminisced, "in the actual words as we hear them spoken under all circumstances." Yet he cautioned that it was "likely to appear under the most unlikely disguises." This philosophy was elucidated in "This Is Just To Say," a late-night apology for eating plums intended for breakfast. "I take what I find," the poet explained to his wife. "No one believes that poetry can exist in his own life. But everything in our lives, if it is sufficiently authentic … and touches us deeply enough with a certain amount of feeling, is capable of being organized into a form which can be a poem."

Robert Frost's verse also captured the rhythms of colloquial discourse and the beauty of the mundane. Born in San Francisco in 1874, Frost was the son of a hard-drinking newsman and a mother who was a religious seeker. After the boy's father died when he was ten, the family moved to his grandfather's in Lawrence, Massachusetts. An excellent high school student, Frost enrolled for a brief spell at Dartmouth College, but dropped out to teach, work in a textile mill, travel through the South, and write. Following two years at Harvard in the late 1890s, he settled on a New Hampshire farm and taught English at secondary schools to make ends meet. The aspiring poet relocated to England in 1912, where at the age of thirty-nine he published his first book. Partly autobiographical, *A Boy's Will* (1913) rendered the cycle of the seasons with the archaic phrasing of traditional verse. Frost's next work, *North of Boston* (1914), which

Robert Frost

he privately described as a "Book of People," made better use of everyday language. "What help he is there's no depending on," he mused about an old derelict in "The Death of the Hired Man." "After Apple-Picking" described the joys of completing a simple task.

Returning to the United States in 1915, Frost took on teaching positions at several New England schools and colleges and lived on nearby farms. While his poetry strove toward universal truths, it was increasingly imbued with the taciturn expressions and dry humor of its rugged rural Yankee characters. Frost's imagery also drew its texture from the rocky fields, stone fences, old houses, and lush woods of the landscape. Intimately phrased meditations like "The Need of Being Versed in Country Things," which appeared in the Pulitzer Prize-winning *New Hampshire* (1923), provided clear evidence of Frost's love of his environment. The collection also featured "Stopping by Woods on a Snowy Evening," a working farmer's tribute to the wonders of nature and ultimate promise of death that would take its place as a literary classic.

While Frost's New England pastorals conveyed a comforting tone, novels like Evelyn Scott's *The Narrow House* (1921), Edith Summers Kelley's *Weeds* (1923), and Ellen Glasgow's *Barren Ground* (1925) described protagonists who were stunted or crushed by rural life. The confrontation between naturalistic forces and ordinary people was most graphically depicted in O.E. Rölvaag's *Giants in the Earth: A Saga of the Prairie* (1927). Born into a family of fishers near Norway's Arctic Circle, Rölvaag immigrated to the South Dakota frontier at age twenty. After completing his education in Minnesota and the University of Oslo, he returned to the United States to teach college. Identifying with the Upper Middle West's Norwegian community, Rölvaag dedicated himself to the preservation of his cultural heritage. Beginning in 1904, he published several novels in Norwegian that contrasted Old World ways and New World demands. Not until 1927 was *Giants in the Earth* translated into English.

Telling the story of the Norwegian migration to the Dakotas in the 1870s, Rölvaag's masterpiece described the human costs of western empire-building through Per Hansa, a male character who looked forward, and his wife Beret, who gazed backward. Replete with Biblical references to the desert wanderings of the ancient Hebrews, *Giants* invoked the endless prairie to construct a metaphor of human struggle and the fate of man in an uncaring universe. Per Hansa cleverly draws on Norwegian folklore, innate shrewdness, and a curious mind to cope with the extreme climate and hostile environment. In contrast, Beret is driven insane from the drudgery and cultural isolation of the barren Plains. Rölvaag's epic incorporated both humor and a sense of tragedy into as insightful an account of working life ever encountered on the printed page.

Novelist Sinclair Lewis also dealt with the Middle Border. Raised in Sauk Center, Minnesota, Lewis graduated from Yale in 1908 and became a popular magazine writer. His literary recognition came with the publication of *Main Street* (1920), a satire of midwest hypocrisy, smugness, conformity, and materialism that won broad commercial success. Lewis compared the dullness of his small-town protagonists to "the contentment of the quiet dead who are scornful of the living for their restless walking." In *Babbitt* (1922), the author memorably profiled the superficial aspirations of a village "booster," thereby contributing a new term to the national vocabulary. Beneath both stories, however, lay an appreciation of the candor and common sense that Lewis saw as inherent to Plains culture. His penchant for describing the physical detail of his characters' lives and for capturing the nuances of everyday speech attested to the writer's love of Americana and the potential for freedom if people would only retain faith in themselves.

Postwar America's most complex explorations of ordinary life appeared in the novels of Mississippi author William Faulkner. After attending the state university at Oxford for two years and serving as its postmaster for two more, Faulkner published a volume of poetry in 1924, followed by two novels on postwar disillusionment. In 1929 he began to chronicle the story of a declining southern family with some resemblance to his kin. Two of these works, *The Sound and the Fury* (1929) and *As I Lay Dying* (1930), were completed while the young writer worked as a janitor and a fishing boat deck hand. Although Faulkner buttressed his tales with layers of allegory and symbolism, he drew key characters from the impoverished whites and rural blacks he had known all his life. *The Sound and the Fury* illustrated a family history through the perspective of a simple-minded idiot. *As I Lay Dying* infused folk humor and tall tales into a profile of poor white opportunists whose selfishness and spiritual arrogance led to the rejection of essential human ties and moral responsibilities.

TENEMENT DREAMS

Faulkner's rich tapestries pointed to the variety of perspectives to be found among the multiplicity of America's people. The need to acknowledge cultural diversity had been most notably advanced by bohemian writer Randolph Bourne, a disciple of educator and philosopher John Dewey. Writing before World War I, Bourne had envisioned a "Trans-National America" of open borders and mutual toleration. As sentiment for immigration restriction legislation mounted after the war, the pluralist banner was taken up by social critic Horace M. Kallen in *Culture and Democracy in the United States* (1924). Yet the case that European immigrants had much to offer was best illustrated by Jewish writer Anzia Yezierska. Arriving on the Lower East Side in the early 1890s with her Russian-Polish family, Yezierska graduated from Columbia University Teacher's College with a degree in domestic science. Nevertheless, she could only find work in a sweatshop, a laundry, and a restaurant, and did not publish a story until 1915. The young author's first book, *Hungry Hearts* (1920), introduced readers to a collection of personal narratives based on experiences inside the crowded tenements and beyond.

Yezierska's sketches dealt with characters caught between their Jewish heritage and admiration for American culture. "Soap and Water" described a harried student who is rejected for teaching certificate candidacy because of her unkempt appearance resulting from her eight-hour daily labor at a laundry. "The Free Vacation House" contrasted a Jewish woman's pride in her way of life with the burden of caring for six nagging children and boarders in a cramped apartment full of unwashed dishes. In "Hunger" an immigrant factory girl yearns for fulfillment beyond material satisfactions, a common theme in Yezierska's writing. The notion that art could be found in ordinary gestures is captured in "The Lost Beautifulness" when a laundry worker expresses the splendor of life in the single act of ironing clothes. In "My Own People" the author contrasted the cold cruelty and arbitrary rules of charity workers with the vitality of immigrant clients. The prize-winning "Fat of the Land" described a mother's despair when her new uptown neighbors don't care about each other, and her children are ashamed of her Old World ways. Yet she realizes she can no longer tolerate the ghetto's cold, mice, and foul odors.

Yezierska was consumed by her need to explain the immigrant woman's plight to the American public. In "How I Found America" she pictured the Lower East Side's "narrow streets of squeezed-in stores and houses, ragged clothes, dirty bedding oozing out of the windows, ash-cans and garbage cans cluttering the sidewalks." Yet when the story's factory girl is fired for protesting a wage cut, she finds inspiration to strive for "the soul – the spirit of America" from a friendly mentor. Seeking to express such optimism to a greater audience, Yezierska sold *Hungry Hearts* to the movies, but was disillusioned by the isolation of her brief stay in Hollywood. Her next book, *Salome of the Tenements* (1923), told the story of a scheming immigrant heroine who induces a well-meaning Gentile aristocrat to wed her, only to experience a loveless marriage. After her divorce she falls to the bottom of the social ladder, but reconstitutes her life as a successful dress designer, marries a man she loves, and opens a non-profit Lower East Side clothing shop so that poor women can have access to beautiful things.

In *Children of Loneliness* (1923), Yezierska pursued her obsession with the conflict between cultural tradition and Americanization. The protagonist of one story finds that she "can't live with the old world" but feels she is "too green for the new." To complicate matters, her social worker admirer romanticizes ghetto folk and deals with them as "social types." These themes were taken a step further in *Breadgivers* (1925), a novel pitting the virtues of religious tradition, material comfort, family, and home against self-fulfillment, artistic expression, and intellectual achievement. As a young woman struggles to free herself from the protective but tyrannical bonds of Jewish patriarchy, she comes to accept her father's human qualities and see him as a frightened old man whose faith and learning cannot adapt to American realities. At the same time, she realizes that family ties can support as well as imprison, and that if Jewish tradition restricts its followers, it also gives them the faith to go on. Finally, as

Yezierska's protagonist returns to the ghetto, she acknowledges the genuine hold of tradition and family, but in a final twist also becomes aware of the guilt impelling her to re-establish her ties.

By 1925 many of Yezierska's readers had begun to tire of her moralistic treatments of both ghetto life and Americanized Jews and found more excitement in the fiction of the more commercially inclined Fannie Hurst. Born in St. Louis to middle-class German American Jews in 1885, Hurst got her initial taste of the world as a volunteer for a local settlement house. Her first published story about two shop girls appeared in a St. Louis literary magazine. One year after graduating from Washington University in 1909, she convinced her parents to let her go to New York, where she worked at assorted jobs, absorbed the weight of humanity on endless walks, wrote incessantly, and received a modest allowance from home. Identifying with the "new women" of Greenwich Village bohemia and convinced that feminism and socialism would liberate the working classes, Hurst became fascinated with "little unknown people" and their "drab little tragedies." Her interest in ordinary life attracted her to the Lower East Side, where she remembered that despite pervasive crime, poverty, and drudgery, "the life and hope of these sodden streets tingled through the soles of my shoes."

Hurst published sixty short stories between 1912 and 1923, by which time three Broadway plays and eight movies derived their plots from her work. Her sketch ideas were rooted in real-life observations of Jewish immigrants, boarders, and shop girls, and speculation as to how particular characters might react to imaginary conditions. Praised by William Dean Howells for "penetrating to the heart of life," Hurst was heralded as a master of vernacular literature in the tradition of Mark Twain and O. Henry. In 1919 *Cosmopolitan* published "Humoresque," a short story about a Russian Jewish couple's struggles through poverty and the support of eight children to raise a violin prodigy. The piece became the lead story of a volume of sketches published later in the year. Hurst's first novel, *Star-Dust: The Story of an American Girl* (1920), traced the New York experiences of a pregnant German Jew from St. Louis forced to survive on her own wits.

Lummox (1923), Hurst's next book, offered a portrait of a domestic servant's life along the lines of Gertrude Stein's *Three Lives*. Raped by her employer's son, the protagonist is falsely accused of theft and deprived of references for further work. Another women's tale followed with *Back Street* (1931), the saga of an illicit affair between an intriguing married woman and an investment banker. Four of Hurst's books were translated to the screen in diluted form in the 1920s. As a commercial success, however, she often received criticism for excessive sentimentality. A striking woman with jet-black hair, she wore heavy amounts of lipstick, favored exotic jewelry, and sported outlandish clothing. Her much-publicized trial marriage to a choreographer and her friendship with and financial patronage of African American folklorist Zora Neale Hurston helped to make Hurst a controversial but celebrated Jazz Age public figure.

HARLEM RENAISSANCE

When Alain Locke introduced an anthology of black art, literature, and criticism in 1925 by proclaiming that Negro life was "finding a new soul" with "an unusual outburst of creative expression," he sought to include African Americans in an expanded framework of cultural diversity. A Harvard Ph.D. and the first black recipient of a distinguished Rhodes fellowship, Locke had been invited to edit a special "New Negro" edition of the social work journal *Survey Graphic*. The enhanced stature of African Americans was partly a result of the Great Migration of 1915–1928, an exodus of 1.2 million blacks from the South to the industrial centers of the North and Midwest. Locke believed that the postwar focus on artistic expression and cultural self-determination reflected a new Negro psychology that would lead to the eradication of remaining barriers to achievement. Like poet and political activist James Weldon Johnson, he insisted that people with great art and literature could never be considered inferior. The New Negro would rediscover the beauty of the black experience hidden by prejudice and caricature.

Locke's celebration of African American vitality coincided with the rise of a race-conscious artistic phenomenon subsequently known as the Harlem Renaissance. The movement's fiction and poetry embraced the full scope of black life, from the rural folk cultures of the South to the cosmopolitan cabarets, supper clubs, and jazz haunts of the North. Novelists such as Nella Larsen and Jessie Redmon Fauset focused on the plight of northern middle-class Negro women. Other writers, like the poet Countee Cullen, explored African American life while retaining conventional literary forms in highly acclaimed works such as *Color* (1925), *Copper Sun* (1927), and *The Ballad of the Browngirl: An Old Ballad Retold* (1927). Some of the most well-known Renaissance authors, however, sought to reproduce black vernacular expression in as direct a manner as possible and welcomed the resulting controversy generated by their work.

James Weldon Johnson served as elder statesman of the movement. Johnson had written dialect poetry in the 1890s before teaming up with his brother Rosamond as a successful vaudeville composer-performer and co-writer of "Lift Every Voice and Sing" (1900), the hymn later recognized as the Negro national anthem. Johnson also was the anonymous author of *The Autobiography of an Ex-Colored Man* (1912), the story of a light-skinned black who lives as a Negro and then passes for white, only to experience the psychological costs accompanying a loss of racial identity. After serving as U.S. consul to Venezuela and Nicaragua, Johnson became the lead editorial writer for New York's oldest black newspaper and then joined the NAACP as the organization's first African American executive secretary. In 1917 he returned to poetry with *Fifty Years*, a collection whose title piece described "a race ten million strong" standing erect without fear.

Seeking to draw attention to the African American cultural heritage, Johnson edited *The Book of American Negro Poetry* in 1922. The genius of black folk, from Uncle

Remus tales to the spirituals and slave songs to ragtime and the cakewalk, he asserted, had produced the only genuinely American art. Johnson called upon Negro poets and writers to "express the racial spirit by symbols from within rather than by symbols from without" their realm. As an aspiring poet at the turn of the century, he had begun to emulate Walt Whitman's free verse. Johnson also had come to believe that dialect phrasing suffered from too many emotional restrictions to be other than sad or funny. In "The Creation" (1920), he attempted to free vernacular verse from racial caricature. "And God stepped out on space," the poem read, "And he looked around and said:/I'm lonely—/I'll make me a world." *God's Trombones—Seven Negro Folk Sermons* (1927), illustrated by Harlem's Aaron Douglas, borrowed from the loose rhythms of black oral tradition to present a series of verses infused with the cadence and imagery of a rural preacher. "Your arm's too short to box with God," proclaimed Johnson's minister.

By the time Johnson published an informal inventory of African American contributions to the arts in *Black Manhattan* (1930), the Harlem Renaissance was in full swing. One of its most critically acclaimed writers was Jean Toomer. Born in Washington, D.C. in 1894, Toomer had been reared in a white neighborhood by his strict grandfather, a former Louisiana black Reconstruction governor. After attending several colleges and holding an assortment of jobs, he was hired as substitute principal of an all-Negro manual trade school in Georgia. Hearing black folk songs in the rural community, Toomer was inspired to describe the people and landscape of the South and capture the "souls of slavery." Modeled on *Winesburg, Ohio,* his masterpiece *Cane* (1923) merged poetry with colorful and sensual prose sketches and vignettes. Sensitive to African American spirituality and the region's physical beauty, Toomer nevertheless confronted white southern violence and black victimization. The poem "Portrait in Georgia" eerily described a white woman's hair as "braided chestnut/coiled like a lyncher's rope." Another line offered "her slim body, white as the ash,/of black flesh after flame."

The second half of *Cane* suggested that refuge in the North offered its own problems. A prose poem entitled "Seventh Street" mourned the loss of folk culture among migrants who tried to offset a sterile and destructive modern existence by adopting morally dissolute lifestyles. Despite praise for its passion and sympathy for the full dimensions of African American life, *Cane* sold poorly, and Toomer relocated to France to study mysticism and transcend racial identity.

Another Renaissance writer living abroad was Claude McKay. The son of prosperous West Indian peasants, McKay wrote dialect poetry before leaving Jamaica in 1912 to attend college in the United States. He soon found editorial positions with the radical *Liberator* and *The Masses* magazines, but supported himself as a boarding house dishwasher and railroad dining car waiter. McKay's first publication was *Harlem Shadows* (1922), a volume of poetry chronicling the intimate joys and sorrows of urban life. One of its selections, "The Harlem Dancer," offered an apt guide to the poet's reliance on vernacular imagery by comparing the "perfect, half-clothed body" of a young prostitute to a "proudly swaying palm."

McKay left New York for Paris in 1922, where he received financial support from bohemian writer Louise Bryant to complete *Home to Harlem* (1927). This landmark novel sought to reveal the beauty of those elements of working-class and peasant culture that appeared untouched by the modern world. It told the story of a black soldier who deserts from World War I and returns to New York, where he learns to live by his wits and instincts. McKay's hero is entranced by "the sugared laughter" and "honey-talk" of the Harlem streets and the powerful sounds of ragtime and blues emanating from its cabarets and dives. Celebrating the primitivism of the black working class, the novel placed nearly all its action within an all-night world of jazz dancing, drinking, fighting, and flirtation.

No other Renaissance writer captured the feel of blues and jazz as much as Langston Hughes. Hughes was born in Joplin, Missouri, in 1902 and raised by a stern grandmother. After graduating from high school in Cleveland, he published his first poem, "The Negro Speaks of Rivers" (1920). Hughes attended Columbia University for a year and shipped out as a freighter steward in 1923. Shortly thereafter, he won an *Opportunity* magazine prize for "Weary Blues," a poem published in a collected volume three years later. Merging the vernacular phrasing of Walt Whitman and Carl Sandburg with African American oral and musical traditions, Hughes projected a commonplace quality into his verse. "Negro Dancers," for example, described "Soft lights on the tables./Music gay,/ Brown-skin steppers/In a cabaret." "Jobs are just chances," he began in "Elevator Boy" (1926), "Like everything else,/Maybe a little luck now,/Maybe not." "We cry among the skyscrapers," he exclaimed in *Fine Clothes to the Jew* (1927), "As our ancestors cried among the palms in Africa/Because we are alone./It is night/And we're afraid." "I'm black like that old mule," he confessed in another verse, "Black and don't give a damn."

One of Hughes' closest associates was Zora Neale Hurston. Born in 1891, Hurston was the fifth child of Alabama tenant farmers who moved to the black community of Eatonville, Florida, where her father served as a carpenter, minister, and mayor. Inspired by her mother to follow her dreams, she came north to study anthropology and black folklore at Howard University, Barnard College, and Columbia. After three years in New York, however, Hurston returned to Florida between 1928 and 1930 to collect field data for the folklore collection that would comprise *Mules and Men* (1935). "The unlettered Negro" had made the best black contributions to American culture, she insisted. By incorporating the feel of the blues and the rhythms of southern African American speech into her writing, Hurston sought to convey the respect that black people had for their own songs, stories, sayings, and dances. At the same time, her nostalgic engagement with folk traditions typified a tendency among some Jazz Age cosmopolitans to romanticize southern Negroes as pre-industrial primitives.

Langston Hughes

BLACK ARTISTRY, BLUES QUEENS, HOT JAZZ

Langston Hughes shared Hurston's belief that the common people were the prime inspirations for great art. Yet critics such as W.E.B. Du Bois and Black Nationalist Marcus Garvey complained that too much Harlem Renaissance writing presented degrading portraits of Negro life that perpetuated slanderous white racial stereotypes. In an exchange appearing in the *Nation* magazine in 1926, Hughes responded that the black working class did not care whether they were like white folks. "Let the blare of Negro jazz bands and the bellowing voice of Bessie Smith singing blues penetrate the closed ears of the colored near-intellectuals," he declared, until they listened and caught "a glimpse of their own beauty. We younger artists … intend to express our individual dark-skinned selves without fear or shame." Seeking independence from white publishers and black censure, the poet joined with Hurston and novelist Wallace Thurman in 1926 in forming the literary journal *Fire!!* The new magazine, promised the editors, would be "flaming, burning, searing, and penetrating far beneath the superficial items of the flesh to boil the sluggish blood."

Beneath its title in oversize font, the red cover of the inaugural edition of *Fire!!* featured a primitive African print by Harlem's Aaron Douglas. Visual artists like Douglas saw themselves in the tradition of Henry Ossawa Turner, the first African American painter of major repute. The son of a prominent Philadelphia minister, Turner had trained under Thomas Eakins in the early 1880s before studying in Paris. His oil painting *The Banjo Lesson* (1893) countered racial stereotypes of comic black figures with a solemn portrait of a father passing on cultural knowledge to his son. The work of black painter Archibald J. Motley, Jr. also shaped Harlem Renaissance art. Motley's feel for everyday life was evident in *Mending Socks* (1924), a portrait of an elderly servant woman in a shawl who is seated in a wooden rocking chair quietly concentrating on the task before her. *Jockey Club* (1929) presented a black doorman greeting white patrons on a crowded sidewalk outside a Paris night club.

Douglas was particularly influenced by the sparse West African aesthetic popularized by contemporary black sculptors Richmond Barthé and Malvina Hoffman. Arriving in Harlem in 1924 after graduation from the University of Nebraska and a stint as a high school art teacher in Kansas City, the painter learned to fuse European modernism with African forms under the guidance of German immigrant Winold Reiis, a fervent supporter of the black arts movement. Both mentor and student completed illustrations for *The New Negro*. Douglas' silhouette drawing *Ma Bad Luck Card* (1926) also accompanied publication of Langston Hughes' "Hard Luck" in *Opportunity*. The young artist would go on to become one of Harlem's most prominent public muralists.

Few African American image creators had the impact of pioneer filmmaker Oscar Micheaux. Shunned by most Harlem Renaissance writers and intellectuals, Micheaux nevertheless shared the premise that black people would only gain acceptance when they were perceived as having their own culture. Starting out as a Pullman porter at age seventeen, the young disciple of Booker T. Washington purchased 160 acres of land in South Dakota. Within eight years, he had more than tripled his holdings, prompting him to self-publish an autobiographical novel, *The Conquest: The Story of a Negro Pioneer* (1913). When no one showed any interest in converting the book into a movie, Micheaux formed his own motion picture production company. Relying upon black amateur actors from all walks of life and people's homes for sets, the neophyte producer released *The Homesteader* in 1919.

Micheaux believed that the mass medium of film could be a major force of racial pride, empowerment, and uplift. Responding to an outbreak of anti-black rioting after World War I, he produced *Within Our Gates* (1920), a movie depicting the lynching of a black family by ordinary white town folk. *The Symbol of the Unconquered* (1920) then exposed the resurgent Ku Klux Klan. In *The Gunsaulus Mystery* (1921), Micheaux pictured the plight of an African American man wrongfully accused of murdering a white woman. Race relations and the specter of miscegenation also dominated screen versions of Charles Chesnutt's *The House Behind the Cedars* (1925) and *The Conjure Woman* (1926). Micheaux's most controversial feature was *Body and Soul* (1924), a film starring Paul Robeson about a black criminal who escapes jail, poses as a minister, and uses religion to viciously exploit the community. In this drama of intraracial strife and corruption, skin color was not a reliable indicator of character or morality.

Micheaux's films attracted a large black following, but his moral emphasis often proved intrusive. In contrast, the popular black blues artists of the 1920s struck a closer relationship with audiences. The first blues recording, "Crazy Blues" (1920), had been cut by vaudeville performer Mamie Smith for the Okeh label. Two years later Alberta Hunter recorded "Down Hearted Blues," an original song covered the next year by vaudevillian Bessie Smith. Born in Chattanooga, Tennessee, in 1900, Smith performed through most of her teens in tent shows, carnivals, and honky-tonks. Initially targeted for a black southern audience, her first record became a national best-seller, leading to the sale of more than two million of her discs within a year. Known as "the Empress of the Blues," Smith fulfilled audience expectations by dressing in gaudy costumes, flaunting her dark black skin, and delivering truthful, wise, and comic observations about daily life. She bonded with people by expressing the sexual bravado and vulnerability of female newcomers to the Black Metropolis. "I'm a young woman and ain't done runnin' round," Smith sang in "Young Woman's Blues," "I ain't high yeller, I'm a deep killa brown."

Benefiting from the consolidation of the black vaudeville circuit by the Theater Owners Booking Association (TOBA), Bessie Smith earned an unprecedented $1500 a week in stage appearances by the mid–1920s. Smith and other blues stars also appeared in the *Midnight Frolics* arranged by TOBA for all-white audiences in black theaters across the South. By mid-decade, specially designated "race" labels were selling five to six million blues records a year, including some to white customers. Nostalgia for the South among urban African American migrants and the nationalizing influences of vaudeville and the record industry helped to inspire a musical mix of rural folk traditions and urban innovations. Just as entertainers like the Smiths, Ma Rainey, and Ethel Waters adopted the styles and techniques of rural black musicians, the latter learned songs or verses off the records of the nation's top African American vaudeville stars.

Blind Lemon Jefferson was one of the most significant of the southern male performers to emerge in the Twenties. An itinerant Dallas street-corner singer with a rough-hewn style and an ability to improvise original guitar licks, Jefferson was invited to Chicago to record at mid-decade. Like the blues queens, he inspired a sense of collective solidarity by singing about commonly experienced personal problems like dislocation and loneliness. Other blues performers included John Lee "Sonny Boy" Williamson and Lonnie Johnson. A New Orleans guitar virtuoso, bar musician, and riverboat jazzman, Johnson employed a suave delivery appealing to women listeners. The blues man's popularity, in turn, prompted the studios to search for urbane soloists who could produce upbeat party music. The conversational style of blues crooner Leroy Carr, an Indianapolis pianist, fit the desired style perfectly, as did the Chicago duo of Tampa Red and "Georgia Tom" Dorsey, known for the suggestive "It's Tight Like That" (1928).

By the end of the 1920s, blues music often seemed indistinguishable from jazz. With the close of the Storyville vice district during World War I, black musicians had moved north to Kansas City, Chicago, and New York. In the process, ragtime evolved into the music later called Dixieland. The transformation involved the substitution of the stand-up string bass for the tuba, the use of the guitar instead of the banjo, the inclusion of the saxophone, and reliance on muted horns. As the four even beats of early New Orleans music gave way to the off-beat accents of the blues, jazz seemed to embody both the emotional qualities of African American experience and the dissonance and abrasiveness of modern society.

Jazz came north with bands led by New Orleans legends King Oliver, Kid Ory, and Jelly Roll Morton. South Side Chicago boogie-woogie musicians Pine Top Smith and Meade Lux Lewis and Harlem stride pianists Eubie Blake, James P. Johnson, and Willie "The Lion" Smith added to the mix. Yet no single jazz figure approached the originality of Louis Armstrong. Born out of wedlock to a New Orleans turpentine factory worker and a Louisiana woman, Armstrong grew up in the city's poorest district. Receiving his first musical training at reform school at age twelve, he began playing cornet for local marching bands, dances, and river cruises. When he was twenty-one, Armstrong joined King Oliver's Creole Jazz Band in Chicago, settled in the South Side's Bronzeville section, played in Prohibition speakeasies, and accompanied night-

Louis Armstrong

club floor shows, dances, and silent movies. After marrying Oliver's pianist Liz Hardin, he relocated to New York to join the Fletcher Henderson Band, and then returned to Chicago to organize Armstrong's Hot Five. The band's recording of "West End Blues" (1928) established the lyrical musician as the leading improvisational jazzman of his time.

WHITE JAZZ HEAVEN

The informal spirit and syncopated rhythms of jazz complemented Prohibition's thriving cabaret culture. Cities like New Orleans, Memphis, Detroit, and Kansas City continued to sustain live music scenes throughout the era. In Los Angeles, African American professionals and the domestic servants of the Hollywood elite often caught the latest bands at Culver City's trendy Cotton Club. Chicago's State Street boasted a number of jazz hot spots, while the South Side's basement hideouts were perfect for after-hours jams. Yet Harlem's profusion of gangster-operated speakeasies and nightclubs made it the center of the jazz world. Cabarets such as Small's Paradise and larger venues like the Roseland Ballroom, the home of the Fletcher Henderson Band, provided the laboratory giving birth to swing music. By mid-decade the Harlem rent party had become an additional force for the spread of jazz. For twenty-five cents admission to a private apartment, patrons could purchase bootleg whiskey, order southern-styled fried fish and chitlins, and dance or listen to the music of a stride piano player or small combo.

Jazz attracted a small circle of white musicians, including Chicago hipster Mezz Mezzrow, the legendary Davenport, Iowa, cornet player Bix Beiderbecke, and Indiana pianist and songwriter Hoagy Carmichael. Hearing a "hot Negro band" at a high school dance in Bloomington, Carmichael took his place among the "jazz maniacs" and began writing dreamy and sentimental portraits of southern black life. His first tune, "Riverboat Shuffle" (1925), was written for Beiderbecke's band, the Wolverines. Despite such enthusiasm, jazz remained a controversial fixture of American popular culture. In 1924 the *New York Times* editorialized that the music had no structure or form, was produced by incompetents, and merely expressed the mechanical sterility of modern urban life. Cultural critic H.L. Mencken compared jazz to the "sound of riveting." As social moralists charged that New Orleans music nurtured vulgarity and uncontrolled sensuality, sixty American cities banned its performance in public dance halls.

Most whites who expressed a fondness for jazz leaned toward a diluted and sweetened style they perceived as less "barbarous" than the original. The first jazz record had been made in 1917 by five white New Orleans café musicians who called themselves the Original Dixieland Jass Band. Three years later Paul Whiteman introduced the genre to a mass constituency with his instrumental version of "Whispering" (1920), a path-breaking record that sold 1.8 million copies. Born in Denver in 1890, Whiteman was a classical musician who first heard the New Orleans sound at the San Francisco World's Fair of 1915. Leading several large dance bands after World War I, he strove for a listenable and danceable sound by arranging separate charts for brass, reeds, and rhythm sections. Whiteman marketed himself as the "King of Jazz." His business skills soon opened opportunities at smart big-city dance clubs, live performances on radio, and the burgeoning record industry. Intent on heralding jazz's compositional advances and "melodious" forms for a respectable audience, Whiteman presided over the 1924 New York concert in which pianist George Gershwin debuted *Rhapsody in Blue.*

Jazz also found its way to Broadway. In 1921 black stride pianist Eubie Blake joined the Noble Sissle Orchestra in providing the accompaniment for *Shuffle Along,* the African American vaudeville revue that introduced white audiences to the hip and pelvic thrusts of the Charleston and Black Bottom. Broadway patrons also flocked to see *Hot Chocolates* (1929), a revue that featured Louis Armstrong singing Andy Razaf and Fats Waller's rollicking "Ain't Misbehavin'." The most celebrated showcase of black talent, however, was Harlem's Cotton Club. Built to house a vaudeville theater and dance hall in 1918, the facility had been purchased by boxer Jack Johnson, who converted the second story into a supper club. When Johnson entered into a partnership with gangster Owney Madden's syndicate in 1923, the new operators renamed the establishment, expanded seating capacity to seven hundred, and instituted a jungle décor and plantation setting to attract an exclusive whites-only clientele.

The Cotton Club was designed to appeal to white fantasies about African American expressiveness and eroticism. Serving a cuisine that included fried chicken and barbecued spare ribs, the upscale facility boasted light-skinned chorus girls who were at least five-foot six-inches tall, able to carry a tune and dance, and below the age of twenty-one. Its semi-annual floorshows were Ziegfeld-styled, quickly paced revues staged around a two-tiered horseshoe formation of tables. Productions featured the snappy lyrics and up-tempo melodies of Cotton Club songwriters Dorothy Fields and Jimmy McHugh, a white duo responsible for extravagant novelty numbers such as "Diga Diga Doo" (1928). Between 1927 and 1932, Duke Ellington and the Washingtonians served as the cabaret house band, forever associating the Mecca of uptown night life with the sophisticated blend of harmonies and rhythm that evolved into black swing.

"Harlem was in vogue," Langston Hughes commented of Jazz Age fascination with perceived qualities of African American primitivism. Predominantly white theatergoers were treated to such themes in the 1924 Broadway production of *The Emperor Jones*, a Eugene O'Neill drama starring black actor Paul Robeson. The play offered a psychological portrait of a Pullman porter who gains control of a Caribbean island through brutality and terror. After being plagued by voodoo spells and hallucinations, the central character faces an uprising and is assassinated for his crimes by a witch doctor. Robeson also appeared in *All God's Chillun's Got Wings* (1924), an O'Neill drama depicting the internal tensions of a racially mixed marriage.

The most controversial white interpreter of the African American psyche was Carl Van Vechten. Born in Cedar Rapids, Iowa, in 1880 to well-educated parents who were sympathetic to women's and Negro rights, Van Vechten graduated from the University of Chicago in 1906 and moved to New York. Serving as a newspaper music and drama critic, he frequented the fashionable bohemian salons of Greenwich Village. Beginning in 1922 Van Vechten published six socially oriented novels with urbane protagonists. The fifth and most serious of the lot was *Nigger Heaven* (1926). A supporter of Negro theater and a Bessie Smith admirer, Van Vechten had often co-hosted mixed-race parties with his wife, befriended James Weldon Johnson, and spent considerable time in Harlem bars and cabarets. Seeking to explore what it meant to be a Negro in America, he produced a book that dealt with a cross-section of New York African American life from the richest individuals to members of the mundane middle class.

Although Van Vechten sought to picture the terrible impact of racial prejudice, he utilized unsavory characters like a wealthy numbers racketeer to point to the internal weaknesses and divisions within the African American community. One of the main figures of *Nigger Heaven* was an aspiring young writer whose moral downfall provided the central tragedy of the novel. Losing the love of a young middle-class woman, the protagonist is seduced into a life of sex and drugs that the book outlines with explicit detail. Beneath her educated veneer, in turn, the young woman yearns for a connection to African roots. Split between the music of Schumann and the spirituals, she symbolizes the human conflict between the primitive and the civilized. Van Vechten's affluent black folk only differ from other Americans of their class through their inclinations toward sensuality. Although Western civilization pretended to discard such feelings, the author implied, it secretly hoped to recapture them.

Harlem intellectuals delivered a split verdict on *Nigger Heaven.* Critics like W.E.B. Du Bois condemned the book for demeaning Negro life with undue focus on vice-ridden and crime-infested cabarets. In contrast, James Weldon Johnson praised Van Vechten for dealing with African Americans as fully developed characters, and Langston Hughes celebrated the writer's colorful use of jazz settings and vernacular speech. The controversy escalated as *Nigger Heaven* sold a hundred thousand copies within months, and white "slumming parties" flocked to the ghetto to taste the pleasures the book had described. Although Van Vechten and his allies defended the novel as a work of sociological fiction, its exploration of the underside of African American life established formulized expectations for black literature that would be difficult to overcome.

BROADWAY CLAMOR

Prohibition era fascination with organized crime invaded the legitimate theater when playwright Maxwell Anderson's *Outside Looking In* opened on Broadway in 1925, with James Cagney in his first dramatic role. The son of a Lower East Side bartender,

Cagney had attended Columbia University for a year under the auspices of the army training corps before making it to Broadway and the vaudeville stage as a song-and-dance man. Anderson's play was based on Jim Tully's *Beggars of Life* (1924), a memoir of life among railroad hoboes. As gangster Little Ned, Cagney incorporated the quick gait, rapid-fire slang, and abrupt movements that came to be associated with the urban tough guy. The following year a production entitled *Broadway* (1926) used a nightclub setting to feature a diversity of big-city characters who spoke in underworld jargon.

The Broadway stage offered a mild version of Jazz Age pluralism. Since the early years of the century, American Jews had used popular music and theater to strive for acceptance as legitimate citizens. Dramatic plots emphasizing the triumph of love over social convention often conveyed the virtues of assimilation, toleration of differences, and acceptance of outsiders. Romance also underscored the democratic relevance of free choice and independence from outmoded social hierarchies. These themes received reinforcement in Samson Raphaelson's *The Day of Atonement* (1925), a play later brought to the screen as *The Jazz Singer* (1927), the film that would inaugurate the movie career of Al Jolson and introduce synchronized sound. The original story concerned a blackface performer who was the son of a Jewish cantor. On the brink of the singer's big break in vaudeville, which happened to fall on the eve of the Yom Kippur holy day, his ailing father asks him to take over duties at the synagogue. In an act of loyalty to his family and religion, the entertainer honors the request, thereby receiving praise for the performance from his producer, who hopes that he will soon return to the stage.

The Day of Atonement resolved the tensions of assimilation by suggesting that one could maintain an ethnic and religious identity and still be an American, and that family obligations did not prevent success as a popular culture icon. Ziegfeld trouper Eddie Cantor represented the drama of Americanization in a far lighter vein in *Kid Boots* (1923), a frenzied musical comedy about a caddy who sells bootleg liquor. Playing a streetwise character whose drive for success resonated with Broadway audiences, Cantor mixed naughtiness with youthful innocence in musical numbers such as "If You Knew Susie" and "Dinah." The Lower East Side hero triumphed again in 1928 with a starring role in *Whoopee!* Based on a play *The Nervous Wreck*, the Ziegfeld musical farce featured a Jewish hypochondriac sent to heal in California, where he helps a rancher's daughter escape an unwanted marriage. As Cantor is pursued by the woman's tormenters, he disguises himself as a cook, a blackface minstrel, and an Indian. The plot finally resolves on a reservation when the heroine weds her true love, who turns out not to be an Indian as once thought, and the revitalized New York neurotic marries his nurse.

As exotic Ziegfeld girls paraded as Indian maidens, *Whoopee!* offered the haphazard plots and thin characterizations usually seen in Broadway musical fare. Yet the sophisticated score by lyricist Gus Kahn and composer Walter Donaldson added an element of emotional realism to the show. "I in-tend to be ind-e-pen-dent-ly blue," belted out sultry performer Ruth Etting in "Love Me or Leave Me," one of the production's monumental musical hits; "I'd rather be lonely than happy with somebody else." Involved in a troubled marriage to a man with ties to the Chicago underworld, Etting brought undeniable authenticity to the role of a scrappy but defiant victim. The show's second crowd-pleaser was "Makin' Whoopee!" a hilariously cynical commentary on sex, marriage, adultery, and divorce that sold two million copies when Cantor recorded it. Taken from a line by newspaper columnist Walter Winchell, the title of the number became a Jazz Age catch-phrase for carnal intimacy.

As Broadway songwriters aspired to be democratic interpreters of American culture, musical revues and comedies broke the genteel traditions of European light opera by merging everyday speech and imagery with the casual approach of blues and jazz. In a period in which the radio and phonograph catered mainly to solo listeners, intimate songs like "It Had to Be You" (1924) and "Am I Blue?" (1929) set the style for Broadway productions. Irving Berlin brought these attributes to the Twenties musical stage in his work for the Ziegfeld Follies and several variety revues. Skillfully setting the slang expressions of ordinary life to lilting melodies, Berlin composed gems of simplicity like the colloquial "What'll I Do?" (1924).

Lorenz Hart was another master of the conversational lyric. The product of a respectable middle-class Jewish family from Manhattan's Upper West Side, Hart was initially fascinated by the idiomatic language, crisp rhymes, and ironic detachment of society verse. At the age of eighteen, the young poet met fellow Columbia University student Richard Rodgers when they both worked as counselors at a summer camp. Two years later, the duo teamed up to write the songs for Columbia's varsity show of 1920. Recycling their collegiate enthusiasm, Rodgers and Hart developed the numbers for several amateur musical revues in the following years. In 1925, however, the two secured a place on Broadway with the score for the *Garrick Gaieties*.

Produced by a troupe of unemployed college graduates as a theater company fund-raiser, the show presented a series of satirical sketches on recent Broadway musicals. The hit number turned out to be "Manhattan," a parody of love songs set in exotic locales. Lifted by Rodgers' gushing melody, the Hart lyric depicted a young couple without the means to escape the New York summer. Carried away by romantic euphoria, they trumpet the delights of the subway's "balmy breezes" and euphemize the Lower East Side "in July" with "sweet pushcarts gently gliding by." The tribute to the attractions of bustling Delancey Street, the Bronx Zoo, Central Park, Coney Island, and other commonplace sites tops off with the exclamation that "the city's clamor can never spoil, the dreams of a boy and goil." Rodgers and Hart solidified their reputation for witty numbers about self-pitying but ironic lovers with Broadway show classics like "My Heart Stood Still" (1927) and "You Took Advantage of Me" (1928).

The duo's main rival in vernacular lyrical and musical phrasing was the team of George and Ira Gershwin. Born Jacob and Israel Gershowitz, the brothers grew up on

George and Ira Gershwin   (*Photofest*)

the Lower East Side. As a boy George discovered jazz standing outside the doors of Harlem cabarets. Leaving high school at the age of fifteen, he worked at a series of Tin Pan Alley piano-playing jobs. When Al Jolson introduced the young musician's "Swanee" at the Winter Garden in 1919, Gershwin moved a step closer toward his goal of bringing quality popular music to the theater. Ira began writing society verse as a young man but was convinced by an English playwright to incorporate American slang into his work. He soon became adept at fitting common jargon into the rhythmic turns of music. After providing the words for George's melody in "The Real American Folk Song (Is a Rag)" (1918), Ira did not collaborate with his brother until 1924, when the two worked on the score for *Oh, Lady, Be Good!* for the brother-and-sister song-and-dance team of Fred and Adele Astaire.

"I'm alone in this big city," the lead male sang in the title number of *Lady Be Good!* Over the next six years George and Ira Gershwin excelled in capturing both the exhilaration of romantic freedom and the terrors of rejection and abandonment. The secret to their success lay in the ability to infuse Tin Pan Alley lyrics and melodies with blues and jazz intonations. The upbeat "Fascinating Rhythm" (1924) and *Girl Crazy's* "I Got Rhythm" (1930) each combined syncopated verbal collage fragments with nervous musical accents. "'S Wonderful" (1927), another up-tempo tune, demonstrated Ira's playful use of colloquial contractions. "The Man I Love" (1924), inexplicably cut from the Astaire show, described a wistful woman's search for emotional security. Both "Somebody Loves Me" (1924) and "Someone to Watch Over Me" (1926) offered plaintive hopes of romantic fulfillment. "But Not for Me" (1930) provided a disarming expression of vulnerability and melancholy. In "Embraceable You" (1930), one of the team's most intimate love songs, the repetition of the conversational "come to papa, come to papa, do" merged perfectly with George's restrained but insistent melody.

AMERICA'S OPERA

When Florenz Ziegfeld hired Oscar Hammerstein II and Jerome Kern to write the songs for a Broadway adaptation of Edna Ferber's *Show Boat* in 1927, the American musical stage took a giant step toward freeing itself from the revue format. Counting Negro principals among its characters, Ferber's novel dealt with intensely controversial issues such as miscegenation and racial prejudice. Hammerstein was a German American Jew from a New York family involved for two generations in producing opera, operetta, and vaudeville. After studying law at Columbia, he had written the libretto for European-style light operas by Rudolf Frimi and Sigmund Romberg. Kern was a middle-class New York Jew who had studied at conservatories in the United States and abroad. Schooled in English and European art songs, he had returned home in 1904 to learn the music business by working as a song plugger, salesman, and rehearsal pianist. Between 1912 and 1918 he composed several musical comedies whose melodious songs were tightly knit into the plots. After scoring a hit with the title number from Ziegfeld's *Sally* in 1921, Kern collaborated on several more commercially successful revues.

Hammerstein set out to create simply rhymed lyrics for *Show Boat* that allowed characters to sing the way they talked, draw images from daily life, and express the musicality of the song. For his part, Kern already was convinced that musical selections should carry the action of the play and contribute to character development. He also knew that however complex the score, audiences wanted songs rendered in an effortless and casual manner. Set in the 1880s and '90s, *Show Boat* opens with black Mississippi River dockworkers musically lamenting the back-breaking task of loading cotton. The scene then shifts to Julie, the lead female entertainer of the *Cotton Blossom*, who is ordered off the boat with her white husband because she is discovered to have a Negro ancestor and therefore has broken the miscegenation laws. Once she and her spouse ritualistically prick their fingers to mix their blood, Julie sings the bluesy but stoic "Can't Help Lovin' Dat Man." "Fish gotta swim, birds gotta fly," she warbles, "I gotta love one man til I die." As the captain's daughter joins the refrain, black and white characters sing together for the first time in American musical stage history.

Hammerstein's folksy lyrics and Kern's dignified and soulful melodies resulted in an intimate union between speech and song. Nowhere was this better illustrated than in the musical meditation delivered by Joe, the black stevedore who serves as a choral commentator on the play's action. In a stark ode to human frailty and resignation with the solemnity of a religious hymn, "Ol' Man River" brought audiences face to face with a mature African American man with psychological depth and a painful awareness of injustice. The song is framed on the contrast between human suffering and the strength and endurance of the Mississippi. "What does he care if de world's got troubles?" the narrator asks of the river in the song's opening verse, "What does he care if de land ain't free?" "Colored folks work on de Mississippi," he sings, "Colored folks work while de white folks play."

The cryptic references to the river are repeated in the tightly constructed chorus. "Don't plant 'taters, don't plant cotton," Joe croons in a low register, "and them that plant 'em are soon forgotten." From there the intensity rises to a musical bridge that is nearly shouted: "You an' me we sweat an' strain/Body all achin' an' racked with pain./Tote dat barge! Lift dat bale!/Get a little drunk an' you land in jail." The choral reprise once again assumes a tone of resignation, but as with the blues, the act of singing is itself a gesture of affirmation. "I git weary/An' sick of tryin'/I'm tired of livin'/an' skeered of dyin/," the vocalist cries, "But ol' man river, he just keeps rollin' along."

Show Boat's successful run on Broadway gave it an emotional power rivaling that of *Uncle Tom's Cabin.* Although Joe's stevedore was not fully integrated into the story, the production demonstrated that an American musical could combine native themes, characters, and songs in intelligent and moving art. By focusing on the interaction of blacks and whites on the Mississippi River—the original home of the blackface minstrel—American show business was returning to the theme of its first vernacular form. Nevertheless, Kern and Hammerstein had created a new genre—the popular opera—that democratized and naturalized the classical traditions of Europe with no sacrifice of lyrical or musical quality.

HOLLYWOOD DEMOCRACY

Show Boat's release as a sound motion picture in 1929 also marked a new departure in cinema. The same year witnessed the debut of King Vidor's *Hallelujah,* a film starring African American musical stage personality Nina Mae McKinney in an all-black cast, supplemented by two thousand extras from Memphis-area plantations. Promising to bring "real Negro folk culture" to the screen, Vidor set the shoot in the swamps of Tennessee and Arkansas. Relying substantially on conventional archetypes, the movie told the story of a religious man corrupted by a rowdy cabaret dancer. Its narrative pitted the jazz bands, predatory gamblers, abundant liquor, and exotic women of the urban vice dens against the spiritual purity and idealism of rural people. After abandoning his family and church, the protagonist experiences total degradation, only to return a repentant man as the reassuring voices of the Dixie Jubilee Choir welcome him home. Despite *Hallelujah's* well-worn plot, however, an enthusiastic cast brought life and urgency to the production.

Although theaters in the South and elsewhere segregated African Americans in the balcony, and motion pictures seldom took black characters seriously, the industry portrayed itself as offering a universal form of entertainment accessible to the average person. Seizing upon the fact that all seats were priced the same and said to be equally comfortable, exhibitors boasted that movie houses were "shrines to democracy." By 1920, in fact, more Americans went to see a film on Sunday than attended church. By the close of the decade, weekly motion picture attendance surpassed seventy million. Meanwhile, eight studio giants doubled the total worth of their assets to $2 billion to create the fifth largest enterprise in the nation. The key to such success lay in sustaining the silver screen's attraction to working-class constituencies and continuing to expand its appeal among more affluent viewers.

Western drama offered Hollywood a proven route to mass patronage. The first western epic, James Cruze's *The Covered Wagon* (1923), used documentary styling to portray a pioneer wagon trek to California. Although the movie was plagued by poor character development and plot construction, it inspired the young John Ford, the director of thirty-nine previous western shorts, to make *The Iron Horse* (1924), a sweeping account of the building of the transcontinental railroad. Born John Martin Feeney in 1895 near Portland, Maine, Ford was the fourteenth child of an Irish Catholic saloon keeper who often assisted immigrants in finding jobs. Coming to Hollywood as a prop man, Ford began to direct movies in 1917. A devout Catholic, he used western motifs to focus on the family, law, traditional moral values, and the American Dream. Films like *Three Bad Men* (1926) and *Four Sons* (1928) portrayed tightly knit male communities often torn between individualism and cooperation. Known for a quiet camera, the director relied on body language and spare dialogue to reveal inner character. Ford's ensemble approach to directing sought to capture what he called "the excitement of the commonplace."

The Goldwyn studio approached westerns in a far lighter vein when it signed Will Rogers to a contract at the end of World War I. *Laughing Bill Hyde* (1918) used the humorist's natural style to tell the story of an ordinary thief whose acts of loyalty and kindness lead to his redemption. A second feature, *Jubilo* (1919), revolved around the plight of a carefree tramp framed for a train robbery. Proclaiming that he was "the ugliest fella" in movies, Rogers developed a reputation as Hollywood's leading populist. "More people should work for their dinner instead of dressing for it," he once cracked. Audiences enjoyed the former roper's good-natured and awkward cowpokes to such an extent that the studio continued featuring him in western-style comedies throughout the Twenties. Not satisfied, Rogers spread his talents elsewhere. His accomplishments included three return engagements to the Ziegfeld Follies, authorship of *The Illiterate Digest* (1924) and *Will Rogers' Political Follies* (1929), a syndicated newspaper column that ultimately reached forty million readers, extensive lecture tours, and the inauguration of one of radio's most illustrious careers.

Beyond westerns, Hollywood offered a variety of urban dramas. Erich von Stroheim's *Greed* (1924), an adoption of Frank Norris' *McTeague,* used realistic settings from the San Francisco Bay area to portray the seamy life of its lower-middle-class protagonists. Movies such as *The Exciters* (1923), *While the City Sleeps* (1928), *Come Across* (1929), and *Alibi* (1929) depicted big-city gangsters who defied the moral restraints of Prohibition and flaunted their sexuality, often crossing social class barriers to seduce society women. *The City Lights of New York* (1928), the first all-talking feature film, used the Brooklyn accents of its characters to portray ethnicity as the dark side of modern urban culture. Josef Von Sternberg presented the story of a gang leader in *Underworld* (1927), while his *Docks of New York* (1928) conveyed the bleak environment of the crime-ridden waterfront and its fishnet-strewn outdoor stairways, dark alleys, and dreary saloons. Meanwhile, William Wellman's *Beggars of Life* (1928) profiled a hobo who takes to the streets with a young woman who has killed a farmer who attempted to rape her. By 1929 Hollywood was producing more gangster movies than cowboy films.

Cross-class fantasies permeated the 1920s screen with varying results. In Cecil B. De Mille's *Saturday Night* (1922) a marriage between an Irish laundress and a playboy meets disaster, just as one between a neighboring Irish chauffeur and a young debutante suffers a similar fate. In the end, the laundress and the chauffeur find each other. "I like Tom," the young woman explains in the subtitles, "because he likes Gum, and Hot-Dogs, and Jazz!" instead of "High-Brow Opera and Olives—and such." In King Vidor's silent classic *The Crowd* (1928) a young couple struggles to survive in the city, only to find that Coney Island offers the only escape from the dehumanizing routine of the workaday world. Several stories featured Joan Crawford, Gloria Swanson, or Clara Bow as independent-minded and self-assured department store clerks, secretaries, or stenographers looking to break out of the dull life of the working girl. A world-wise product of the Brooklyn tenements, Bow graduated from bit parts to her defining role in *It* (1928), where she played a lingerie store clerk who wins the boss' love.

The fate of the ordinary person was most graphically conveyed in Hollywood's silent film comedies. Performers like Buster Keaton, Harry Langdon, Harold Lloyd, and Charles Chaplin perfectly embodied the poor but proud underdog who is nurtured in adversity but clings to self-respect. Facing repeated threats and dangers, these weak and vulnerable characters manage to prevail through cleverness, agility, courage, and even accident. Never defeated by life, they embody a surrealist humor based on exaggeration and the contrast between their grave personas and the chaotic circumstances in which they find themselves.

Born in Kansas, Buster Keaton joined his parents' vaudeville act at the age of three and continued to tour with the family for almost twenty years. After playing minor roles in Hollywood comedies, Keaton was extended the freedom to write, develop, and direct his own films. He used this opportunity to cultivate a character whose deadpan expression and quiet stoicism perfectly complemented the actor's superb timing, acrobatic skills, and execution of sight gags. Keaton's famed parodies of heroism included *Cops* (1922), *The Navigator* (1924), and *The General* (1927). Yet his masterpiece proved to be *Sherlock, Jr.* (1924), the story of a movie projectionist who dreams himself onto the screen. Sweeping up the theater, the hero finds a dollar, which a young woman soon claims. When a tearful older lady inquires about a lost bill, the projectionist gives her a dollar out of his own pocket. Spotting a threatening-looking man sifting through the trash, he resigns himself to handing over his last bill in anticipation of the request.

Harry Langdon perfected the role of the optimistic "little man" whose naïve faith in humanity was constantly flattened by fate. Langdon's baby face and trusting demeanor brought enormous box-office success for Frank Capra's *The Strong Man* (1926) and *Long Pants* (1927). Another mild-mannered optimist was portrayed by Nebraska's Harold Lloyd, who built hundreds of films around the character of a bespectacled and bumbling protagonist. Lloyd reached the pinnacle of his brilliance in *Safety Last* (1923, the tale of a small-town bumpkin who comes to the city to earn wealth and status so that he can marry the girl back home. Finding a job as a department store sales clerk, he pretends to have been promoted to management. When his loved one comes to visit, the hero seeks to impress her by having a daredevil climb the walls of the store, but when the performer is chased away by a policeman, Lloyd's character must accomplish the feat himself. The satire on upward mobility leads to one of the most heralded comic stunts in film history.

As a co-founder of independent United Artists, Charles Chaplin wrote and directed several of his own Twenties comedies. *The Pilgrim* (1923) told the story of a prison escapee who steals a preacher's clothing and assumes the role of a Texas minister in a small town, where he discovers the community's hypocrisies and cruelties. When a fellow ex-convict shows up, however, the hero's cover is blown and he is arrested, although the sheriff takes him to the Mexican border to escape. Just as Chaplin's character prepares to leave the country, he is caught in the middle of an outlaw's shoot-out. The movie ends as the hero waddles along the border with one foot on each side of the boundary. *The Gold Rush* (1925), another Chaplin classic, is set in the Klondike of the 1890s, where the actor's bumbling character winds up eating a Thanksgiving dinner of boiled shoe and spaghetti shoe strings. When the dance-hall girl that he loves fails to arrive for the New Year's Eve dinner he has prepared, he fantasizes an intimate rendezvous. All ends happily, however, when the prospector strikes it rich and reunites with his love on the ship home.

COUNTRY ROADS

Hollywood's reluctance to dramatize the experience of non-European ethnics reflected prevailing social attitudes. For Native Americans, normally the objects of caricature in western movies, the 1920s were a particularly difficult period. As tribal lands continued to be exploited by outside interests, and the federal government campaigned to abolish "pagan" religious rituals like the Plains Sun Dance, several Indian leaders sought to reassert Indian cultural identity. Founded in 1918, the Native American Church combined the use of peyote, a hallucinogen extracted from the stem of the cactus plant, with precepts of monogamy, sobriety, and hard work. The Church's program had substantial appeal for Indian boarding school graduates seeking to fit into reservation life. Another attempt to strengthen traditional practices centered on the efforts of Anglo reformer John Collier. Forming the American Indian Defense Association in 1923, Collier pressed the federal government to permit young men to leave the boarding schools to participate in tribal religious ceremonies. Meanwhile, Native American writers and artists extolled the virtues of an indigenous culture in jeopardy of extinction.

In *My People the Sioux* (1928), *My Indian Boyhood* (1931), *Land of the Spotted Eagle* (1933), and *Stories of the Sioux* (1934), Lakota author Luther Standing Bear used memories of childhood to instruct a general audience that Indians were not a "savage" race, but fellow human beings whose time-honored cultural practices were as worthy of respect as those of modern civilization. Standing Bear's celebrations of traditional family practices, religious rituals, and tribal ties were replicated in the paintings of Carl Sweezy, an Arapaho artist who brought the reservation life of the Great Plains onto canvas. Likewise, Ernest L. Spybuck, a self-taught Oklahoma Shawnee painter, built a nationwide reputation for colorful and vibrant portraits of Indian ceremonies and social scenes. Widespread interest in Native American art led to participation by six New Mexico Pueblo painters in the Prague Congress of Folk Arts in 1928 and the New York Exposition of Indian Tribal Arts three years later.

As southwestern agriculture expanded its reliance upon Mexican American field labor after World War I, an informal Hispanic culture rapidly spread from the region to other communities. By 1930, 1.6 million people of Mexican descent lived in the United States, half speaking no English. Although cities like Detroit, Chicago, San Antonio, and Los Angeles attracted large numbers of migrants, Mexican American cultural identity was primarily sustained through the popularization of rural musical forms, a process accelerated by Spanish-language recording studios, widespread phonograph use, and a variety of Spanish-idiom radio stations. The most commonly heard musical genre was the *canción-corrido*. Performed by traditional accordion ensembles, these emotional ballads combined the narrative structure of the *corrido* with intense lyrical imagery. Instead of celebrating legendary heroes, however, *canción* performers addressed the pathos of everyday life, particularly the hardships of physical labor and an uprooted existence. Foremost among such practitioners was Los Hermanos Bañuelos, a Los Angeles band that sang about dishwashers, railroad trackmen, contract laborers, and field workers.

The recording industry and radio also helped to popularize white rural music. With roots in the southern Appalachians, country music mixed traditional Anglo-Celtic folk songs, ballads, religious hymns, dances, and instrumentals with selections from medicine acts, tent shows, minstrels, circuses, vaudeville, and ragtime. The indigenous musical heritage of the hill country had initially been described by Tennessee's Emma Bell Miles, author of *Spirit of the Mountains* (1905). Miles pointed out that revered old ballads like "The Wagoner's Lad" often had been kept alive by women singing at work or by mothers teaching songs to their children. Between the early and late nineteenth century, the dulcimer, fiddle, banjo, and guitar each took their place as instrumental accompaniments to mountain vocalists. Like the folk tunes from which it was derived, rural music was a democratic form of expression whose narratives of death, sadness, and self-pity were not far removed from the personal experience of its creators.

As record companies sent talent scouts across the South, the first commercial country recording was made in 1923 by Fiddlin' John Carson, a Georgia cotton mill worker who often performed with his daughter, Moonshine Kate, a brassy mountain comic and country blues vocalist. By mid-decade, studio executive Ralph Peer was marketing the ballads and songs of rural white southeasterners as "hillbilly" music. The genre's first unlikely star was Vernon Dalhart, the son of a prominent Texas rancher who had a background in light opera and popular music. In 1924 Dalhart recorded a standard folk tune, "The Wreck of the Southern 97." Yet it was the flip side that established the singer's reputation and ultimately allowed the record to sell twenty-five million copies. "If I had the wings of an angel," implored the poignant lyrics of the "Prisoner's Song," "over these prison walls I would fly." In the brief period that Dalhart teamed up with Kansas guitarist Carson J. Robison, the composer of the classic "My Blue Ridge Mountain Home" (1927), he was the hillbilly genre's most popular entertainer.

Live radio performances provided the showcase for country music. In 1924 a Chicago radio station inaugurated the National Barn Dance, a weekly Saturday night fixture that subsequently brought performers like Kentucky folk balladeer Bradley Kincaid to a wide audience. Yet the spiritual home of mountain music gradually shifted to Nashville's Ryman Auditorium, the site of the radio show christened as the Grand Ole Opry in 1927. Sponsored by a life insurance company, the Opry specifically directed its down-home offerings to southern working people and their families. Early installments of the program featured a healthy assortment of vaudeville and ragtime numbers, as well as Uncle Jimmy Thompson's traditional fiddle tunes, Uncle Dave Macon's minstrel style banjo picking and comedy, vocalist Alcyone Bate Beasley's sentimental ballads, and Eva Thompson Jones' versions of Stephen Foster parlor songs.

Audiences were particularly moved by the traditional harmonies of singing string bands like the Stoneman Family. A Blue Ridge Mountain group from western Virginia who performed in straw hats and overalls, the Stonemans scored mid-Twenties hits like "The Titanic," "Dying Girl's Farewell," "In the Shadow of the Pines," and "Katy

Kline." The Carter Family, another Virginia hill country band, recorded their first songs in 1927. Group leader Alvin (A.P.) Carter brilliantly synthesized fragments of lyrics and images from traditional mountain music into modern standards whose harmonies seemed conducive to a backwoods church or a front-porch get-together. A.P.'s wife Sara played autoharp and guitar and sang in a resonant alto that conveyed depths of repressed emotion, haunting regret, and loneliness. Maybelle, Sara's cousin and A.P.'s sister-in-law, popularized the use of the guitar as a lead instrument by having her thumb pick out the melody on the bass strings while the other fingers stroked the rhythm. Within two years the Carters produced such classics as "The Wildwood Flower" (1928), "Wabash Cannonball" (1929), and "I'm Thinking Tonight of My Blue Eyes" (1929).

At the age of thirty, country music performer Jimmie Rodgers also cut his first record for Ralph Peer's label. Rodgers had been born north of Meridian, Mississippi. When the boy's mother died before he was six, he was taken on the road with his father, a railroad gang foreman. A year after joining a medicine show at thirteen, Rodgers began a fourteen-year stint as a railroad crewman. Picking up the vocabulary and music of fellow laborers, including blacks, he often entertained crews on break with a guitar or banjo and occasionally played with African American musicians in town. Rodgers finally left the railroad at age twenty-eight to become a blackface entertainer with a traveling medicine show touring the mountain and hill country of the Upper South and Ohio River Valley. The Bristol sessions marked the start of a brief but fruitful career in which he recorded one hundred eleven songs and sold twelve million records.

Rodgers sang in a nasal tenor with a Delta drawl, but his unique synthesis of blues and yodeling made him the father of modern country music. Wearing a cowboy hat at a jaunty angle and presenting himself as a rambler, "the singing brakeman" toured the South as a top-billed vaudeville star and frequent guest on local radio stations. Rodgers' unaffected demeanor and relaxed informality appealed to an audience of railroad workers, truck drivers, laborers, farmers, and small-town folk. He often appeared alone on stage, hunched atop a stool with a guitar cradled in his arms. Lengthening or shortening words for emotional effect in the style of a blues singer, the Mississippi troubadour conveyed the impression that he had lived the music he created. "It's gotta have pathos," Rodgers once instructed musicians at a recording session. While the entertainer's blue yodels eloquently captured the pain of unrequited love, a song like "In the Jailhouse Now" (1928) demonstrated unabashed familiarity with the roguish characters on the disreputable side of town. "I told him once or twice/to quit playin' cards and shootin' dice," its lyric stated with mock solemnity. In "Waiting for a Train" (1929), the singer pictured himself as a hobo, "a thousand miles away from home, sleeping in the rain."

Ever ready to perform for flood victims or unemployed workers, Rodgers endeared himself to fans with extravagant personal spending habits and a love of whiskey. His undisciplined lifestyle, however, weakened resistance to the tuberculosis overtaking his lungs. Two days before the disease finally killed him in 1933, months short of his thirty-sixth birthday, the performer held his last recording session in New York. When the train carrying Rodgers back to Meridian finally approached the station late at night, the engineer blew his whistle in a long moaning wail that intensified to a shrill pitch as it reached the depot, and the singer forever assumed his place as a country music legend.

SOURCES AND SUGGESTED READINGS

Lynn Dumenil, *The Modern Temper: American Culture and Society in the 1920s* (1995) provides an excellent introduction to the Jazz Age. Two of the period's most popular chroniclers of the urban scene appear in Tom Clark, *The World of Damon Runyon* (1978) and Donald Elder, *Ring Lardner* (1956). Twenties boxing is the subject of Bruce J. Evensen, *When Dempsey Fought Tunney: Heroes, Hokum, and Storytelling in the Jazz Age* (1996). See also Brian Booth, ed., *Wildmen, Wobblies & Whistle Punks: Stewart Holbrook's Lowbrow Northwest* (1992). For two significant Jewish women literary figures, see Carol B. Schoen, *Anzia Yezierska* (1982) and Brooke Kroeger, *Fannie: The Talent for Success of Writer Fannie Hurst* (1999). The popularity of newspaper cartoon strips in the Twenties receives treatment in the relevant segments of Reinhold Reitberger and Wolfgang Fuchs, *Comics: Anatomy of a Mass Medium* (1972) and Ian Gordon, *Comic Strips and Consumer Culture, 1890–1945* (1998).

Among the distinguished poets of the 1920s, Robert Frost and William Carlos Williams excelled in portraits of everyday life. See Jeffrey Meyers, *Robert Frost: A Biography* (1996) and James Guimond, *The Art of William Carlos Williams: A Discovery and Possession of America* (1968). For the culture and creative expression of ethnic Americans, see the relevant portions of Ronald Takaki, *Strangers from a Different Shore: A History of Asian Americans* (1989); Frederick E. Hoxie, ed., *Talking Back to Civilization: Indian Voices from the Progressive Era* (2001); and Manuel Peña, *The Texas-Mexican Conjunto: History of a Working-Class Music* (1985). See also the reference works listed at the end of Chapter 1.

Black poets, fiction writers, and painters sought to describe ordinary people under the rubric of the Harlem Renaissance. See Janet Witalec, ed., *Harlem Renaissance: A Gale Critical Companion*, 3 vols. (2003) and the relevant entries in Henry Louis Gates and Nellie Y. McKay, eds., *The Norton Anthology of African American Literature* (1997). General works on the flowering of black creativity in the Twenties include Cary D. Wintz, *Black Culture and the Harlem Renassiance* (1988) and David Levering Lewis, *When Harlem Was in Vogue* (1981). For female writers, see Cheryl A. Wall, *Women of the Harlem Renaissance* (1995). The relationship between black artists and white patrons receives treatments in segments of Ann Douglas, *Terrible Honesty: Mongrel Manhattan in the 1920s* (1995) and Kobena Mercer, *Welcome to the Jungle: New Positions in Black Cultural Studies* (1994).

African American visual arts of the 1920s are covered in Haywood Gallery, et al. comps., *Rhapsodies in Black: Art of the Harlem Renaissance* (1997); Amy Helene Kirscke, *Aaron Douglas: Art, Race, and the Harlem Renaissance* (1995); and the relevant portions of Francis Pohl, *Framing America: A Social History of American Art* (2002). For the leading African American film director of the period, see Pearl Bowser and Louise Spence, *Writing Himself into History: Oscar Micheaux, His Silent Films, and His Audiences* (2000).

The most important post-World War I African American popular culture form comprises the focus of Kathy J. Ogren, *The Jazz Revolution: Twenties America and the Meaning of Jazz* (1989). See also several of the contributions in Marc H. Miller, ed. *Louis Armstrong: A Cultural Legacy* (1994). Jazz music's place in Twenties nightlife receives treatment in the relevant segments of Ronald L. Morris, *Wait Until Dark: Jazz and the Underworld, 1880–1940* (1980) and in Jim Haskins, *The Cotton Club* (1977). For the era's male and female blues artists, see portions of Elijah Wald, *Escaping the Delta: Robert Johnson and the Invention of the Blues* (2004) and Peter Guralnick, *Feeling Like Going Home: Portraits in Blues and Rock 'n' Roll* (1999).

Jazz Age musical revues and comedies comprise the focus of the relevant sections of Gerald Mast, *Can't Help Singin': The American Musical on Stage and Screen* (1987) and Andrea Most, *Making Americans: Jews and the Broadway Musical* (2004). See also Ted Merwin, *In Their Own Image: New York Jews in Jazz Age Popular Culture* (2006). For two of Broadway's most popular performers, see Ray Robinson, *American Original: A Life of Will Rogers* (1996) and Herbert G. Goldman, *Banjo Eyes: Eddie Cantor and the Birth of Modern Stardom* (1997). The cultural influence of the Follies concerns Linda Mizejewski, *Ziegfeld Girl: Image and Icon in Culture and Cinema* (1999). See also Billie Melman, *Women and the Popular Imagination in the Twenties: Flappers and Nymphs* (1988).

Works on the lyricists and composers of the musical stage include Frederick Nolan, *Lorenz Hart* (1994); John Peyser, *The Memory of All That: The Life of George Gershwin* (1993); Philip Furia, *Irving Berlin: A Life in Song* (1998) and *Ira Gershwin: The Art of the Lyricist* (1996). For background on *Show Boat*, see the initial chapters of Hugh Fordin, *Getting to Know Him: A Biography of Oscar Hammerstein II* (1986). Twenties Tin Pan Alley garners coverage in the relevant sections of Charles Hamm, *Yesterdays: Popular Song in America* (1979) and *Putting Popular Music in Its Place* (1995); Philip Furia, *The Poets of Tin Pan Alley: A History of America's Great Lyricists* (1990); and Jeffrey Melnick, *A Right to Sing the Blues: African Americans, Jews, and American Popular Song* (1999).

General works on 1920s Hollywood include William K. Everson, *American Silent Film* (1978) and the relevant portions of Robert Sklar, *Movie-Made America: A Cultural History of American Movies*, rev. ed. (1994). For Twenties cowboy icons, see segments of George N. Fenin and William K. Everson, *The Westerns: From Silents to*

Cinerama (1962). Working-class and crime dramas are the focus of Kevin Brownlow, *Beyond the Mask of Innocence* (1990) and Steven J. Ross, *Working-Class Hollywood: Silent Film and the Shaping of Class in America* (1997). For comedy, see Walter Kerr, *The Silent Clowns* (1975) and Henry Jenkins, *What Made Pistachio Nuts? Early Sound Comedy and the Vaudeville Aesthetic* (1992). Two masters of film comedy warrant profiles in Robert Knopf, *The Theater and Cinema of Buster Keaton* (1999) and Charles J. Maland, *Chaplin and American Culture: The Evolution of a Star Image* (1989).

Bill C. Malone, *Country Music U.S.A.*, 2nd rev. ed. (2002) offers the most definitive account of the growing popularity of rural music in a chapter on the 1920s. For the social environment from which the genre sprang, see the appropriate sections of Peter W. Williams, *America's Religions: Traditions and Cultures* (1990) and Anthony Harkins, *Hillbilly: A Cultural History of an American Icon* (2004). The music's commercialization comprises the focus of Richard A. Peterson, *Creating Country Music: Fabricating Authenticity* (1997) and Charles K. Wolfe, *A Good-Natured Riot: The Birth of the Grand Ole Opry* (1999).

5

Documenting People's Stories:
The 1930s

"There are heroes then—among the plain people," poet Carl Sandburg exclaimed in *The People, Yes* (1936). Following the Stock Market Crash of 1929, a growing number of American writers and artists responded to the traumas of the Great Depression by making common cause with working people. "There is no longer I—there is WE," declared the humorist Dorothy Parker. Literary critic Alfred Kazin observed that writers were determined to recognize the possibilities of art in daily experience. Whether in journalism, fiction, poetry, theater, ballet, folk music, painting, photography, or non-commercial film, no period of the nation's history displayed a greater emphasis on documentary portraits of ordinary life. The eagerness of many creative figures and government officials to identify with "the people" often had political ramifications. Whatever the roots of such affinity, socially conscious cultural expression elevated the common man and woman to new heights in the austere 1930s.

NATIONAL INVENTORY

"The struggle for the emancipation of society from the blight of capitalism is not only an economic question," proclaimed a group of artists and writers supporting the Communist Party in 1932, "it is a cultural question as well." Social critics such as Edmund Wilson and Lewis Mumford insisted that even a prosperous market provided no coherent purpose or mission to life beyond mere materialism. It was the duty of middle-class

124

intellectuals, they believed, to support the proletarian struggle to replace the collapsing capitalist order with a worker's state in which production would be responsive to social needs instead of profit. Many members of the intelligentsia preferred to function as mere "fellow travelers" of the communist movement, and others remained independent socialists, liberals, or even conservatives. Yet the Depression enhanced the Party's viability as the only legitimate critic of an economic system in which 90 percent of investment had evaporated and the gross national product had fallen by half.

Documentary journalism provided socially conscious writers with the opportunity to break out of the isolation of 1920s bohemianism. As reporters they could chronicle the facts of everyday existence, record ordinary dialogue, and detail the specifics of local situations. Taking to the road for the liberal *New Republic* early in the Depression, Edmund Wilson composed a series of articles about the despair of impoverished families in northern industrial communities that he collected in *American Jitters: A Year of the Slump* (1932). Two of the country's most prominent novelists, Theodore Dreiser and John Dos Passos, covered the bitterly contested Kentucky coal mining strikes supported by the Communist Party. Publishing their findings in *Harlan Miners Speak* (1931), the authors pictured the protesters as traditional mountain folk ready to fight for their rights as their ancestors had done during the Revolutionary War.

Dos Passos and writer Malcolm Cowley also reported on the Bonus Army of 1932—a march of jobless World War I veterans to the Capitol to demand early payment of their service annuities. The radical *New Masses* published Minneapolis fiction writer and single mother Meridel Le Sueur's "Women on the Breadline" that same year. Le Sueur described waiting on an empty stomach in the employment bureau for work as a domestic that never materialized. As joblessness rose to 25 percent in 1933 and Franklin D. Roosevelt's New Deal drew attention to the "forgotten man," first-person accounts of misery multiplied. Writing under the name of Lauren Gilfillan, Smith College graduate Harriet Woodbridge visited western Pennsylvania mines and homes to compile the material for *I Went to Pit College* (1934). Edward Anderson's *Hungry Men* (1935) retold the adventures of a reporter who "rode the blinds" of gondolas and cattle cars and "slept in welfare flops, ten-cent hotels, parks, and darkened churches." Clara Weatherwax, the descendant of an old New England family, offered a first-person account of work in low-paying white-collar and factory jobs in *Marching! Marching!* (1935).

One of the most ambitious print documentaries of the early Thirties came from the pen of *Winesburg, Ohio* author Sherwood Anderson. When Anderson had made the suggestion that President Roosevelt use the radio to talk to the American people at least once a week, a White House aide had responded that citizens needed to communicate with leaders as well. Urged to "go out through the states as Walt Whitman used to and talk to people and write what they say and what you think of what they say," he published *Puzzled America* (1935). Anderson described his book as offering first-hand accounts by "mill workers, tenant farmers, the unemployed, the plain, simple people."

Fashioning himself as a mere recorder whose simple descriptions would put the facts to work, the author said his aim was "to see all I can of how people live their lives." Praised for a realistic eye and lack of doctrine, Anderson nevertheless conveyed a faith in American democracy that, like many Depression works, tended to sentimentalize "the people."

Erskine Caldwell's *Some American People* (1935) chronicled a similar journey. A Georgia native, Caldwell was the author of *Tobacco Road* (1932) and *God's Little Acre* (1933), two highly celebrated novels detailing how the southern tenant farming system ravaged the soil and tore apart poor white families. Starting in central Oregon and driving east to Maine, the writer recorded a year's worth of observations and conversations. Caldwell said that he sought to gain "a sympathetic understanding" of other human beings and hear "the stories of the people." "The people and their activity" were the things to see in America, he explained. Although several of the book's segments dealt with unemployed Detroit autoworkers, its main emphasis lay with the southern cotton tenants that the author knew so well. As Caldwell presented brief notations about impoverished rural whites from Arkansas to Georgia, readers were confronted with images of ragged children in cold, barren shacks near the point of starvation.

At the end of the decade, a second wave of literature advanced the drive toward social realism. Louis Adamic, a Slovenian immigrant who had come to the United States in his teens and gone on to publish a history of labor violence, culminated one-hundred thousand miles of travel with *My America* (1938). Adamic noted how many of the Depression's unemployed male breadwinners lost self-esteem, but how other families came together in the crisis. In contrast, Leonard Q. Ross (Leo C. Rosten) offered light-hearted reports on daily life in locations ranging from New York's Chinatown to Chicago's strip-tease clubs to a big-city maternity ward in *The Strangest Places* (1939). Ross seemed particularly attuned to the casual political conversations of jobless men idly passing the time on park benches. Another compendium of working people's tales appeared in *The People Talk* (1940), a work by Benjamin Appel, a Polish American novelist who infused gangster stories like *Brain Guy* (1934) with the slum jargon of his Hells' Kitchen youth. Working-class life was tied to the bleak northeastern industrial landscape in the sparse *U.S. 1* (1938), a collection of poetry by Muriel Rukeyser.

ROMANCING THE PROLETARIAT

Calling for stories from working people, *New Masses* editor Michael Gold advised would-be contributors to "write for us as you would write a letter to your best friend." Gold envisioned a magazine of "workers' correspondence" that would embrace confessions, diaries, and concrete accounts from hoboes, peddlers, chambermaids, night club waiters, stenographers, steel workers, miners, sailors, convicts, and strikers. The *New Masses*, he predicted, would ultimately produce a "Jack London or a Walt Whitman ... the son of working-class parents, who himself works in the lumber camps, coal mines, and steel mills, harvest fields and mountain camps of America." Gold was instrumental in the formation of the Communist-sponsored John Reed Clubs in 1929. Adopting the slogan "Art is a Class Weapon," the organization sought to foster a collective identity for radical intellectuals by developing a proletarian culture of novels, plays, and poems by, for, and about workers. Proletarian literature also included those forms of expression that espoused class-conscious radicalism or were forged out of "working-class" politics.

The John Reed Clubs mainly attracted second-generation European ethnics and urban African Americans who wanted to improve writing skills and break into journalism. Members often favored the tenement pastoral—a proletarian narrative employing vernacular language to describe the process of growing up in big-city slums. Nevertheless, these works normally were the work of writers who had long since left the ranks of manual labor. One of the genre's earliest examples was Gold's own *Jews without Money* (1930), an anecdotal memoir of a Lower East Side childhood marked by the injury of the author's father in a house painter's fall that led to the family's descent into poverty. Other examples included Henry Roth's *Call It Sleep* (1934) and Daniel Fuchs' *Summer in Williamsburg* (1934) and *Homage to Blenhort* (1936), each of which described growing up in a Jewish Brooklyn household. H.T. Tsiang's *And China Has Hands* (1937) told the story of a young Chinatown hand-laundry man, while the narratives of John Fante's *Wait Until Spring, Bandini* (1938) and Pietro di Donato's *Christ in Concrete* (1939) featured the sons of Italian bricklayers as lead protagonists.

The first proletarian novelist to depict working-class struggle from a woman's perspective was Josephine Herbst. Born in Sioux City, Iowa, in 1897, Herbst worked her way through the state university and the University of California. Arriving in Greenwich Village in 1920 to pursue a career as a writer, she supported herself as a magazine editor before relocating to Europe, where she published two novels. As the Depression deepened, Herbst returned to the United States and compiled reports for the *New Masses* and other radical outlets on labor unrest and the Iowa dairy farmers' strike of 1932. Her trilogy, *Pity Is Not Enough* (1933), *The Executioner Waits* (1934), and *Rope of Gold* (1939), described three generations of midwestern women family members as representations of working-class survival and the strengths of ordinary people. Building a narrative around her own family's letters and clippings, Herbst portrayed women who learn to ground their social analysis on personal experience in the household. The third installment of the trilogy concluded with the emergence of the autobiographical protagonist as a radical woman writer.

A second genre of proletarian fiction set itself entirely in the Depression social environment. Edward Newhouse's *You Can't Sleep Here* (1934) offered the autobiographical tale of a revolutionary college dropout and newspaper reporter who had lost his job, ridden freights for twenty thousands miles, spent weeks in a "Hooverville" homeless camp in Queens, New York, and "picked up change by contributing to highbrow magazines and other sordid methods." Tom Kramer's *Waiting for Nothing* (1935) adopted a similar posture. The son of factory workers, Kramer had worked his way through three years of college in West Virginia, labored in the Kansas wheat fields, and had taken to hopping freights during the Depression. Dedicating his book to "Jolene who turned off the gas," the author described a young drifter's life on the road that supposedly had been recorded on scraps of paper.

Kramer insisted that his novel was versed exclusively in hobo jargon. "Our home is a garbage heap," he wrote of the camp. "When I am looking at those stiffs by the fire, I am looking at a graveyard." Nevertheless, *Waiting for Nothing* often wavered between Hemingway's "tough-guy" prose and the Biblical spouting of benevolent prostitutes and lost migrants. In contrast, Nelson Algren's *Somebody in Boots* (1935) presented a raw and unedited portrait of boxcar existence. "The people were moving about" though "no one knew why," its narrator explained. "It's the big trouble everywhere," a young girl observes. At one point the drifter hero describes a town with "the hungriest jailhouse and the cruelest bulls in all southern Texas." Another slice of realism appeared in Horace McCoy's *They Shoot Horses, Don't They?* (1935), a novel picturing the grim ritual of an Ocean Pier dance marathon contest as a death camp for the Depression's lost souls.

The most political form of proletarian fiction was the strike novel. Mary Heaton Vorse's *Strike!* (1930) and Grace Lumpkin's *To Make My Bread* (1932) were based on sympathetic views of the Communist-supported 1929 textile workers' protest in Gastonia, North Carolina. Jack Conroy's *The Disinherited* (1933) offered a story based on the mining experiences of the author's father, his mother's life of drudgery, and his own work in a Missouri mill. Conroy's protagonist distrusted abstract communist ideology until the final pages of the book, when he accepted the Party as the only vehicle able to deal with the state's ability to prop up the capitalist system through force. Robert Cantwell's *The Land of Plenty* (1934) told a similar story through the author's autobiographical tale of a strike in a Pacific Northwest sash-and-door mill.

Unlike the positive portraits of working-class resistance offered in most proletarian fiction, James T. Farrell's *Studs Lonigan* trilogy (1932–35) struck a far more pessimistic tone. Born in Chicago in 1904, Farrell was the son of a teamster but was raised by his middle-class grandparents. After attending the University of Chicago, the young writer renounced his Catholic upbringing and embraced urban realism and literary naturalism. Set in the Irish-Catholic neighborhoods of Chicago's South Side, *Studs* portrayed people as victims of social circumstances who then embodied cruelty, violence, ignorance, and moral dissipation. Farrell's main character was a listless product of the slums who victimized racial and ethnic minorities, rejected any hint of social conscience or labor solidarity, and identified with the heroes of drugstore novels and gangster movies. A remorseless accounting of the sordidness and desperation of working-class life, the trilogy was devoid of any sentimentality about the revolutionary potential of the proletariat. Its most appropriate image may have been the sight of its realistically drawn protagonist half-heartedly searching for an elusive job on a dreary rainy day.

John Dos Passos' *U.S.A.* trilogy (1930–36) hardly offered more hope. Having written several antiwar novels in the early Twenties, Dos Passos had come to believe that only the working class was free of pervasive greed and corruption. Seeking a distinctively American radicalism by forging an alliance between Greenwich Village and the working class, he collaborated with Michael Gold in founding the *New Masses* in 1926. When Italian American anarchists Nicola Sacco and Bartolomeo Vanzetti were executed the following year for an armed robbery in which a paymaster and a guard were killed, Dos Passos set out to write the story of the "little people" and small producers swallowed up by the "big money." His trilogy followed the lives of twelve fictional characters, half of whom were women stenographers or retail clerks. Dos Passos filled in the details of the social landscape with "Newsreel" excerpts from newspapers, films, ads, popular songs, speeches, and picket signs, and a series of poetic biographical sketches of the century's leading figures. Several stream-of-consciousness "Camera Eye" pieces conveyed the author's personal experiences for the period encompassed by the narrative.

U.S.A. conveyed a romantic longing for America's traditional individualism. "Bring back (I too Walt Whitman) our story book democracy," pleaded Dos Passos. The trilogy's historical heroes included John Reed, antiwar senator "Fighting Bob" La Follette, socialist Eugene Debs, and Wobblies "Big Bill" Haywood and Joe Hill. Its narrative structure set up an innate conflict between craftsmanship and profit, between honest work and exploitation. The American spirit was diseased, the author suggested, a decline evident in the deterioration of character and in the senseless chatter of "hired hacks and publicity men." "America our nation has been beaten by strangers," Dos Passos proclaimed as Sacco and Vanzetti were executed, "who have turned our language inside out who have taken the clean words our fathers spoke and made them slimy and foul … all right we are two nations." The only redeeming note of the trilogy appeared in a prologue added in 1938, when Dos Passos had completely rejected a fellow-traveler relationship with the Communist Party. "But mostly *U.S.A.* is the speech of the people," it read, "the turn of a joke, the singsong fade of a story, the gruff fall of a sentence."

THE CULTURAL FRONT

U.S.A.'s nostalgia for democratic heroes resonated with progressive cultural politics. Responding in 1935 to the need for a united stance against global fascism, the Communist International called for radicals to form Popular Front alliances with liberals and democratic forces. The communist-led American Writers' Congress soon moved in this direction. Seeking to broaden the left's appeal, literary critic Kenneth Burke urged the movement to invoke common national values and classless symbols. Since populism was basic to American folkways, the Popular Front was to replace "the worker" with "the people" as the focal point of its imagery and organizing. A unified national culture could then mobilize working men and women of all races and nationalities behind a progressive political agenda of labor solidarity, racial justice, antifascism, and New Deal reform.

Radical theater provided an appropriate venue for the Popular Front's renewed interest in culture. The precedent for people's drama had been set by Elmer Rice's Pulitzer Prize-winning *Street Scene* (1929). Born Elmer Leopold Reizenstein in 1892, Rice grew up in a New York City slum and dropped out of high school after two years. While working his way through night law school, he published his first story in a pulp magazine and soon abandoned his studies. Rice's first dramatic production was *On Trial* (1914), a courtroom drama whose flashback scenes addressed the moral callousness induced by wealth. Converted to utopian socialism by World War I, the writer suffered a lean period of creativity until the Theater Guild produced *The Adding Machine* (1923), an expressionist drama about marriage and dehumanization versed in everyday language.

Rice continued to rely on vernacular dialogue in *Street Scene*, a play set entirely in a New York tenement structure. Reproducing the rambling speech of ordinary people about commonplace experiences, the drama sought to explore the inner emotional life of the building's lower-middle-class tenants. Such an intention was immediately apparent in the opening scene, when several characters lean out their windows to comment on the summer evening's heat and gossip amidst the noise of the street and the sounds of children playing. The dialogue soon reveals two strands of the plot: a romance between a young Irish American woman and the son of a dogmatic Jewish radical and a tragic tale of adultery and murder. Through the telling of these stories, the audience is forced to confront the costs of emotional possessiveness and intolerance, as well as the psychological toll wrought by blind materialism. The drama resolves, however, with a reassertion of human dignity, and the life of the tenement resumes with new characters.

When Rice sought to impart more political meaning in his work in the 1930s, he experienced little success. In contrast, Clifford Odets came to be the American playwright most commonly associated with radical drama. Born to eastern European Jews in Philadelphia in 1905, Odets grew up in the Bronx, where he dropped out of high school. Seeing himself as a revolutionary disciple of Thomas Jefferson, Walt Whitman, and Abraham Lincoln, he joined New York's radical Group Theater, an ensemble whose socially relevant presentations were produced at popular prices. Odets' first triumph was *Waiting for Lefty* (1935), a one-act "agit-prop" (agitation-propaganda) play based on a recent New York City taxi strike. The turning point of the story comes when the union representative is killed and the drivers have to decide how to proceed. "It's war. Working class, unite and fight!" someone yells. The production then climaxes when a labor organizer played by actor Elia Kazan leaps to the stage and brings the audience to its feet with "spontaneous" chants of "STRIKE! STRIKE! STRIKE!"

As the Depression and the competition of sound motion pictures cut into Broadway revenues, productions such as *Waiting for Lefty* demonstrated the increased attractions of emotional realism and politicized drama for a more narrowly defined audience. Odets' second work, *Awake and Sing!* (1935), dealt with a working-class Jewish family in the Bronx. When the lead character's Marxist grandfather commits suicide to enable his loved ones to receive his life insurance, the hero decides to use the money for the betterment of the community. Infused with streetwise humor, moments of wistful hopefulness, and touches of poetry, the production explored how ordinary families could be trapped by financial and social circumstances or the superficial attractions of money and status. These themes found their way into the playwright's subsequent hits, *Golden Boy* (1937) and *Rocket to the Moon* (1938).

Musical theater offered another intriguing venue for Popular Front dramatists. Up through the early 1930s, the Communist Party equated revolutionary music with the doctrinaire lyrics and formal orchestrations of Eastern European workers' choruses. With the formation of Party-affiliated composer collectives, radical artists strove to create "progressive" (avant-garde) concert pieces and May Day anthems free of "bourgeois" melodic harmonies or commercial influences. It was not until 1937 that Marc Blitzstein attempted to reach a broader audience by fusing modernist compositional techniques with colloquial popular music in a revolutionary political operetta that would be based on working-class themes.

Born in 1905 into an affluent Philadelphia Jewish banking family, Blitzstein had studied in Berlin with composer Arnold Schoenberg. Joining the communist movement's Composers Collective after 1929, he became fascinated with the political musical theater of the German cabarets. *The Cradle Will Rock* (1937) presented an idealized view of labor's use of sit-ins to organize the steel industry. Set in "Steeltown, U.S.A.," the production featured characters such as Joe Worker, Larry Foreman, and capitalist Mr. Mister, as well as a host of singing cab drivers and tough guys. It combined the story of a prostitute, a portrait of middle-class life, and a tribute to industrial unionism by mixing classical recitations, avant-garde arias, and atonal choruses with fragments of torch numbers, blues, and popular tunes. Yet although the songs were addressed to working people, they were not sung by them. "How many toiling, ailing, dying, piled up bodies,/Brother, does it take to make you wise?" the chorus asked.

Originally conceived under the auspices of the Federal Theater Project, *The Cradle Will Rock* was banned from its opening performance for excessive partisanship. Producer John Houseman and director Orson Welles responded by loading a rented piano onto a truck and leading a procession of patrons to a new site, where Blitzstein provided on-stage keyboard accompaniment as the actors recited their lines from the audience. Converted to an oratorio, the production moved to Welles' Mercury Theater and enjoyed considerable support from Popular Front supporters. Its seven-record album set became the first full-length Broadway cast recording of a musical. Building on such success, Blitzstein returned to the stage with *"Not for an Answer"* (1941), a play centered on a group of service workers attempting to unionize a resort town. The main protagonist of the production was the working-class chorus, whose short, clipped musical phrasing of vernacular expressions commented on the plight of a hobo, an immigrant laborer, and a working girl. Yet the show never gained the broad following of its predecessor.

In contrast to Blitzstein's attempt to create art out of proletariat experience, Harold Rome's *Pins and Needles* (1937) attracted far larger working-class audiences. The son of a Jewish coal company operator, Rome was born in Hartford, Connecticut in 1908. He began writing popular tunes while a summer-camp counselor in his teens. Graduating from the Yale School of Architecture in 1934, Rome fruitlessly tried to sell topical songs to Tin Pan Alley publishers while working as an unpaid drafting office assistant. His big break came when the socialist International Ladies Garment Workers Union (ILGWU) needed someone to create the score for an amateur production. Rome's New Deal political consciousness and music talents provided the perfect fit for the job.

The cast of *Pins and Needles* was drawn entirely from the predominantly female labor force of the clothing industry. Replete with witty agit-prop sketches, burlesque comedy routines, and vaudeville musical numbers, the show satirized Tin Pan Alley clichés, commercial advertising, snooty department store patrons, patriarchal fascists, and the drudgery of women's toil. One number, "What Good Is Love?" featured a struggling garment employee bemoaning the uselessness of romance without "all that makes life worth living." The revue's Popular Front stance was best expressed in "Sing Me a Song of Social Significance," a musical manifesto in which a female union loyalist compels her beau to "Sing me of wars and sing me of breadlines,/Sing me of strikes and last minute headlines … or I won't love you." Meanwhile, the idyllic "Sunday in the Park" offered a softened view of labor with a celebration of the single day of rest from the weekly grind.

AMERICAN BALLADEERS

As Popular Front cultural politics broadened its scope, folk music gradually found an accepted place within the movement. The Communist Party initially had rejected IWW parodies, "hillbilly" tunes, and folk songs as insufficiently class conscious, progressive, or proletarian. Yet by the mid-Thirties the Party was publishing "workers' song books" rooted in a variety of sources, and classically trained Seattle composer and activist Earl H. Robinson had formed the American People's Chorus to perform traditional folk tunes in fine-art style. Meanwhile, cultural historian Alan Lomax, the assistant director of the Folk Music Archives of the Library of Congress, had begun to record southern black prison songs for his father, folklorist John Lomax. Through these sessions, Lomax discovered guitar player, singer, and songwriter Huddie Ledbetter ("Leadbelly"), the Louisiana-born creator of American classics such as "The Midnight Special" and "Goodnight Irene." Lomax also transcribed black folksinger Josh White's rendition of "John Henry," a traditional African American ballad about a mythic steel driver who competes against a steam-powered drill and dies of exhaustion.

Between 1935 and 1939 Lomax recorded 150 songs from labor activist Aunt Molly Jackson. The daughter of a Kentucky preacher, miner, and union organizer, Jackson had been married at fourteen. In the following years, mining accidents claimed the lives of her husband, son, and one brother, while blinding her father and another brother. Evicted from the coal fields in 1931, she sought to publicize the miners' crusade by composing Appalachian-style protest ballads. "The bosses ride fine horses while we walk in the mud," she sang in "I Am a Union Woman," "their banner is a dollar sign while ours is stripped with blood." Another miner's wife, Florence Reece, was responsible for the most famous labor anthem of the 1930s. Supporting the Communist-led National Miners Union strike in the Kentucky coal fields in 1932, Reece inscribed the words to "Which Side Are You On?" on a wall calendar. "They say in Harlan County,/There are no neutrals there:" the song began, "You'll either be a union man/Or a thug for J.H. Blair."

The Popular Front sympathies of folklorists such as the Lomaxes, Charles Seeger, and Benjamin A. Botkin led them to view folksongs as authentic "people's music." Accordingly, they sought to preserve the simple and direct expressions of ordinary Americans who were creating their own culture outside the parameters of high art or the corrupting pressures of commercialism. The egalitarian orientation of folk music provided a way for the communist movement to communicate to outsiders. Performers such as Josh White, who found ideological music artistically stultifying, had become convinced that audiences tired of political sloganeering. It was more effective, believed folklorists like Alan Lomax, to describe an unjust situation, celebrate an act of resistance, or show how beauty, love, and decency occasionally triumphed over poverty and oppression. Representing and articulating the ideas of working people, therefore, offered a far more fruitful approach to political music than telling workers what to think.

One of the most effective practitioners of such an approach was Earl Robinson. A University of Washington graduate, Robinson had traveled to New York and joined the Workers Laboratory Theater and the Composers Collective. As the musical director of a radical summer camp in 1936, he was asked to compose the accompaniment to a poem written in the Twenties about IWW martyr Joe Hill. "I dreamed I saw Joe Hill last night,/Alive as you or me," the lyric stated, "Says I 'But Joe, You're ten years dead,' 'I never died,' says he, 'I never died,' says he." Robinson's haunting melody turned "Joe Hill" into a movement anthem. Yet the composer won even broader acclaim with another Popular Front classic in 1938 when he converted lyricist John LaTouche's "Ballad for Americans" into a "Whitman cantata" for a Federal Theater Project revue.

Although the work was never performed as originally planned, it was broadcast over network radio the following year and recorded by African American baritone and activist Paul Robeson. A perfect embodiment of progressive values, "Ballad" merged traditional folk melodies, concert music, and patriotic imagery into a celebration of American freedom and egalitarian democracy. The subject of the piece was "America"—a mix of all races, religions, nationalities, and occupations, whose members' names were recited in an exhaustive choral litany. In response to persistent queries as to his identity, the anonymous narrator answers that he is "nobody who was anybody … anybody who was everybody." Prodded further, he finally declares, "You know who I am: the people!"

The virile populism of "Ballad for Americans" also characterized *Billy the Kid* (1938), a ballet choreographed by twenty-seven-year-old Wisconsin native Eugene Loring. Based on a best-selling novel, the production told the story of New Mexico's legendary desperado of the 1870s. Placed within a background of corrupt politics and moneyed interests, however, Billy was portrayed as an innocent—a friend of the people turned into an outlaw by the violent forces of the American frontier. *Billy the Kid* marked Aaron Copland's first significant composition. Born Aaron Kaplan in Brooklyn to Russian Jewish immigrants in 1900, he was taken to burlesque houses at any early age and received piano lessons from his sister when he was eleven. Copland devoured Whitman's poetry in high school but decided to study music. After pursuing training in Paris in the 1920s, he returned to New York, where he joined the literary and artistic avant-garde rallying behind Alfred Stieglitz's "Affirm America" banner. Praising the simplicity and naturalness of Stephen Foster melodies, Copland sought to convey "a largeness of utterance wholly representative of the country that Whitman had envisaged."

Although the composer's piano and orchestral pieces of the late 1920s frequently borrowed jazz themes, his work was highly abstract. Even when Copland joined a communist-affiliated collective in 1932 and won the competition for a May Day anthem score, his music followed modernist lines. By 1934, however, he had begun to experiment with the use of folk themes, popular melodies, and Mexican harmonies, and come to the realization that people responded to music on a personal and instinctive level. "I don't compose, I assemble materials," he later acknowledged. Fusing philharmonic traditions and vernacular motifs, Copland integrated six American cowboy songs and Mexican dance rhythms into *Billy the Kid* to evoke the spirit of the West. The halting

and simple chords of "The Open Prairie," the ballet's opening and closing proces-
sional, hinted at the vast spaces of the production's setting. After a successful run in
Chicago, the performance debuted in New York to crowds stretching four blocks long.

HARD TRAVELIN'

Socially conscious artists and musicians sought to combine folk motifs and high art in
behalf of a populist and democratically oriented Popular Front sensibility. Yet cantatas,
operettas, ballets, and musical revues appeared to be somewhat removed from the contemporary experiences of everyday Americans. The movement's increasing desire for
legitimate working-class forms of cultural expression helps explain the tremendous enthusiasm that Woody Guthrie began to generate in the late 1930s progressive community. Named after President Woodrow Wilson, Guthrie was the son of an Oklahoma
land speculator and courthouse politician. As the elder Guthrie's business interests deteriorated, the family moved to a shotgun shack on the east side of town, and Woody became a notorious "alley cat" scavenger and the class clown. When his mother was
institutionalized for a nervous disorder, the boy found himself on his own at age fifteen.
Two years later he hitch-hiked south, staying in hobo camps with migratory wheat farm
workers and joining his father to run a disreputable boarding house in Pampa, Texas.

Claiming to have received his first harmonica from a "colored shoeshine boy" in a
barber shop, Guthrie had learned a variety of cowboy songs from Oklahoma oil workers. In Texas he joined a country music trio that entertained at dances and house parties. After marrying a local woman at the age of twenty-two, he scraped by as a soda
jerk, commercial sign painter, and barroom caricature artist. As the Texas panhandle
suffered its fourth consecutive year of drought in 1935 and dust storms ravaged the
region, Guthrie wrote "Dusty Old Dust" ("So Long, It's Been Good to Know Yuh").
"This dusty old dust is getting my home," the lyric went, "And I've got to be drifting
along." Leaving Texas with his guitar in tow, the young troubadour rode the rails as a
hobo, learning songs as he traveled. Hitting the Denver Skid Row bars, Guthrie performed original "Okie" anthems like "Lonesome Road Blues" for spare change.
When he sang "I'm goin' down the road feelin' bad," his audience knew what he was
talking about.

One of a half-million California refugees from the Dust Bowl, Guthrie arrived in the
Bakersfield hobo camps in 1936, where he met old Wobblies and found a copy of the
IWW songbook. He soon began to parody old country tunes to protest police treatment of
migrants and wrote a series of "talking blues" about life on the road. In "Talking Dust
Bowl" he sang of "tater" stew that was almost thin enough for a politician to see through.
On a second trip to California, Guthrie attempted to be a singing cowboy but had diffi-
culty riding a horse. Nevertheless, he got a job on the radio mixing homespun patter with

Woody Guthrie   *(Courtesy of the Woody Guthrie Foundation and Archives)*

renditions of mountain standards and hillbilly tunes. The singer's popularity among displaced midwesterners prompted him to write new lyrics, such as "Philadelphia Lawyer," "Do Re Mi" (slang for cash), and "Oklahoma Hills." When Guthrie toured migrant labor camps to promote a newspaper belonging to the populist owner of his Los Angeles radio station in 1938, however, songs like "Dust Bowl Refugees" began to take an even sharper political tone. Supporting the San Joaquin cotton pickers' strike, the balladeer wrote "I Ain't Got No Home" to describe the plight of itinerant workers.

Guthrie's involvement in labor causes impressed a correspondent for the Communist Party *People's World,* who had never met a "progressive hillbilly." Creating a sensation in performances for Popular Front fund-raisers, he received solo billing as a radio host and wrote a crop of new songs about outlaws as populist heroes. "The Ballad of Pretty Boy Floyd" (1939) described a legendary Depression bank robber who killed a sheriff in a fair fight for insulting his wife. "Every crime in Oklahoma was added to his name," the lyric instructed. The song then pictured Floyd as a hero to poor farmers who provided the renegade with food and shelter and sometimes found their mortgages paid or a thousand dollar bill left on the kitchen table. "Some will rob you with a six-gun/And some with a fountain pen," warbled Woody, but "as through this life you roam/You will never see an outlaw/Drive a family from its home."

As Guthrie's constituency shifted to the Popular Front, he found he was most successful when coming across as an uneducated rube. Billed as "the voice of his people" and the new Joe Hill, the singer toured labor camps with radical movie actor Will Geer in behalf of the Communist Party. He also adopted a proletarian persona in articles for the *People's World* that reflected Party views on national and world affairs. Loyal to people who worshipped him as a representative of the proletariat, Guthrie defended the 1939 peace pact between the Soviet Union and Nazi Germany. When his radio station fired him for pro-Communist leanings, the singer decided to leave Los Angeles for New York, where a vibrant left-wing movement presented more opportunities for a folk singer.

THE PEOPLE, YES

As John Steinbeck's novel *The Grapes of Wrath* (1939) demonstrated [see Chapter 6], the image of "the people" resonated profoundly in Depression America. By no means was such populism defined exclusively in political terms. A fellow traveler like poet William Carlos Williams, for example, remained skeptical of the possibilities of social revolution. Nevertheless, Williams was sufficiently moved by the impact of the economic crisis to focus much of his work on the urban poor and the essential worth of everyday people. In "Proletarian Portrait" (1935), the bard adopted Whitman's use of free verse in a series of succinct casual lines about a bedraggled woman holding her shoe to find the nail embedded in its sole. Another poem, "View of a Lake" (1936), pictured three children standing on a slope of cinders along a railroad track beside "the weed-grown chassis of a wrecked car." Excluding nothing from his realm, the New Jersey physician had come to believe that a poet's emotions and judgments were best expressed through concrete detail, no matter how commonplace, tawdry, or sordid. Yet he insisted on portraying the downtrodden without excessive sentimentality, idealization, or political ideology.

In *Adam and Eve and the City* (1936), Williams looked to the proletarian surroundings of his New Jersey hometown. Beyond sympathy for victims of the Depression, he saw the poor as symptomatic of humanity's struggles. Williams detected enormous reservoirs of spiritual courage among the unfortunate. But he believed that poor people often were ignored because of the same prejudices and stereotypes that excluded literary treatment of the "un-poetic." Nevertheless, the poet's socially oriented verse was rejected by leftist magazines because it failed to adhere to formula depictions of oppressed workers and class struggle. Experimenting with short stories in the late 1930s, he began to put together a collection of poems that used nearby Paterson as a setting for an exploration of the universal qualities of the human condition.

Like Williams, Carl Sandburg used the democratic tradition to work common experience into poetry. Sandburg had forged populist credentials with collections such as *Shades of the Sunburnt West* (1922) and *Good Morning America* (1928). His biography, *Abraham Lincoln: The Prairie Years* (1926), and *The American Songbag* (1927), a folk song anthology, further underscored the poet's feel for the vernacular. *The People, Yes* (1936), Sandburg's great Depression work, sought to catalogue the nation's folk wisdom. "The people is Everyman, everybody," it proclaimed, "Everybody is you and me and all others." Acknowledging the "flaws and failings" of fellow Americans, Sandburg nevertheless celebrated common virtues like patience, sacrifice, and devotion. The people was "a cauldron and a reservoir/," he proclaimed, of "the human reserves that shape history." Hope, he wrote, was "The evening star inviolable over the coal mines,/The shimmer of northern lights across a bitter winter night/The blue hills beyond the smoke of the steel works." "Who shall speak for the people?" the poet asked. They would accept no idea, he answered, unless it had "a promise of roots/Twisted deep in the heart of man."

Sandburg's brand of democratic romanticism re-appeared in the work of fellow Illinois poet Archibald MacLeish. A graduate of Yale University and Harvard Law School, MacLeish had published several works of verse while in France as a Twenties expatriate. His epic *America Was Promises* (1939) offered an unabashed celebration of the westward migration and commonplace virtues such as love, reason, justice, liberty, self-respect, and decency. "America was always promises," the poet declared, its dynamic people consumed with "Building liberty a farmyard wide." "For whom the promises?" asked MacLeish. The answer was that the potentialities of American life belonged to the people until they were taken from them.

The details of ordinary life framed some of the most important fiction of the 1930s. William Faulkner continued to extract local color from the South to explore moral issues with universal significance. *Sanctuary* (1931) presented a metaphor of southern society as a brothel. *Light in August* (1932), an allegory of human imperfection, traced the tale of a "fallen" woman's plight in a Puritan society alongside the descent of a mulatto male character into self-hatred and self-destruction. In *Absalom! Absalom!* (1936) Faulkner turned his attention to a poor white man's obsession with obtaining possession of land.

Another southern novelist, Thomas C. Wolfe, offered detailed descriptions of the everyday life and secrets of his Asheville, North Carolina, birthplace in *Look Homeward, Angel* (1929), a semi-autobiographical account of his youth. Wolfe's fourth book, *You Can't Go Home Again* (1940), however, adopted a broader social scope. The novel centered on a protagonist cast as "Everyman" who returns to the scene of his upbringing and is dismayed to discover how speculative business practices have led to economic devastation. "America went off the track somewhere," he muses, "corroded at the heart of its power with easy wealth and graft and special privilege." Back in Depression New York, Wolfe's hero vows to share "the common life of man" and watches homeless people hovering for warmth in public latrines and idle loiterers on street corners. Through all this, the book's narrator sees life's beauty, hope, and bounty along with its harshness, terror, and ugliness. "I believe that we are lost in America," he confides, "but I believe we shall be found ... I know that America and the people in it are deathless, undiscovered, and immortal, and must live."

THE HEART OF MAN

Some of the most poignant explorations of Depression America appeared in the stories of William Saroyan. The son of Armenian immigrants, Saroyan was born in Fresno, California, in 1908. When he was three years old his father died, leading to the boy's five-year stay in an orphanage. After holding jobs as a newsboy and telegraph messenger and being forced out of high school for disciplinary problems, the young Saroyan worked in a relative's vineyard. A year later he moved to San Francisco to take a position as a railroad clerk and telegraph office manager. Haunting public libraries and devouring the work of Whitman, Emerson, and Sherwood Anderson, he began to publish sketches, short stories, and poetry about the immigrant working people and farmers of the California valleys. Saroyan described the focus of his first collection, *The Daring Young Man on the Flying Trapeze* (1934), as "everyday material." Written in an accessible style, the book's poetic fragments and ironic humor conveyed an acceptance of human variety and personal foibles and a relentless faith in humanity that would become his trademark.

"Seventy Thousand Assyrians," one of the book's most acclaimed selections, was set in San Francisco's Skid Row, a district "of men and boys, out of work, hanging around smoking Bull Durham, talking about the government, waiting for something to turn up, simply waiting." Although the story centered on a disaffiliated and socially marginalized Armenian barber, the narrator insists on intruding upon the reader's attention. "I am deeply interested in what people remember," he states. "A young writer goes out to places and talks to people." Saroyan's storyteller insists that he wants to write "a letter to the common people, telling them in simple language things they already know." "I do not believe in races," he states. "I do not believe in governments. I see life as one life at a time ..." Using italics for emphasis, the narrator protests that *"It is the heart of man I am trying to imply in this work."*

Inhale and Exhale (1936) consisted of stories from Saroyan's childhood and tales of drunks, wrestlers, communists, vineyard workers, sailors, actors, reformers, and others. "The laughter of the homeless and half starved is the center of our greatness," the reader learns in "The Great American Novel." In "International Harvester" the narrator marvels that with ten million unemployed, there are "no riots, no trouble, no multi-millionaire cooked and served with cranberry sauce." Building on the use of irony to portray the intrinsic goodness of all people, Saroyan published *My Name is Aram* (1940), another look at his Fresno raising. Writing about a willful, independent, and adventurous young boy with a strong sense of family solidarity and honor, the author elicited comparisons to Mark Twain and Booth Tarkington. *Aram* evoked the trusting world of childhood while pointing to the pitfalls of innocence. The comic incongruities of "Saroyanesque" ethnic characters like the narrator's uncle, described as "too imaginative and poetic for his own good," enhanced their human qualities. Moved by instinctive feelings and traditions, the author's Old World heroes live off the knowledge and wisdom of their own culture.

Saroyan's rich characterizations also found their way onto the stage. The Group Theater's production of *My Heart's in the Highlands* (1939) was set in the run-down rural home of a Fresno Armenian family facing dispossession. Combining commonplace reality with the poetic language of everyday life, the drama revealed how impoverished people could be generous, spiritually endowed, and emotionally strong. The grandmother's stoicism in the face of eviction, for example, recalled the tragic history of displaced Armenians. Saroyan's theatrics pointed to the enchantment of life, no matter what the circumstances, and the possibility that people could retain human dignity by holding on to their dreams. A second production, the Pulitzer Prize-winning *The Time of Your Life* (1939), took a group of pat characters in a San Francisco bar and exposed the tender feelings behind their tough exteriors. Although life placed humans in molds and assigned roles, it suggested, their individuality kept surfacing. Insisting on the emotional complexity of ordinary people, *The Time of Your Life* placed faith in the transformative power of romantic love and the ultimate emergence of the soul.

Thornton Wilder's *Our Town* (1938) also received a Pulitzer Prize. Born in 1897 in Madison, Wisconsin, Wilder had an affluent upbringing: his father was an editor and diplomat, his mother the daughter of a Hudson River Valley minister. Schooled in Berkeley, California, and Shanghai, he attended Oberlin College and graduated from Yale before receiving an M.A. in French at Princeton. Not long after embarking upon a writing career, Wilder received his first Pulitzer in drama for *The Bridge of San Luis Rey* (1927) before accepting an academic post in literature at the University of Chicago. *Our Town* described commonplace events in the lives of ordinary people in a New Hampshire village in the early twentieth century. Introduced by colloquial conversations between the milkman, local constable, paper boy, and other characters, each act offered a scene in the lives of two families. A Stage Manager served as narrator and interpreter, even answering questions from "plants" in the audience. *Our Town* suggested that the smallest events and rituals of daily existence were of value, and that life was simultaneously imperfect but priceless, trivial but significant, absurd but noble, and mundane but miraculous.

OTHER ROADS

The ties of folk culture had long been a major theme of Native American literature. Yet in the 1930s two non-Indians were instrumental in calling attention to the indigenous heritage. Anthropologist John Collier, the New Deal Commissioner of Indian Affairs, prevailed upon Congress in 1934 to reverse the detribalizing legacy of the Dawes Act by guaranteeing tribal sovereignty and increasing Native American education funding. Meanwhile, Harvard-trained anthropologist Oliver La Farge turned to fiction to celebrate the vitality of Indian customs and culture. In the Pulitzer Prize-winning novel *Laughing Boy* (1929), La Farge told the story of an Americanized Navajo woman who marries a traditional warrior-craftsman and masters ancient handicrafts. The book suggested that the living traditions of "the People" could provide the tools for survival in the modern age. La Farge's short stories in *All the Young Men* (1935) and his novel *The Enemy Gods* (1937) explored how Navajo ways could induce conflict with Anglo civilization. Yet his text for Helen M. Post's photographs in *As Long as the Grass Shall Grow* (1940) pleaded once again for the preservation of Indian culture in the face of white oppression.

The idea that Native American cultural survival depended upon resistance to assimilation was a key theme of 1930s Indian novelist John Joseph Matthews, the Oklahoma Osage author of *Sundown* (1934). D'Arcy McNickle also explored bicultural conflict with an incisive eye. Born on the Flathead Indian Reservation in northwest Montana in 1904, McNickle was the son of a Cree and Salish mother and an Anglo father. After attending an Indian boarding school in Oregon and studying at the University of Montana and at Oxford, he followed a variety of careers as an academic anthropologist, archivist, historian, and administrator for the Bureau of Indian Affairs. It was not until publication of *The Surrounded* (1936) that McNickle converted his passion for Native American life into fiction. The novel centered on a young man of Spanish and Indian ethnicity who returns to the Flathead Reservation for a visit, where his Salish mother has retreated to native ways. Exposed to storytelling and the recital of oral legends at a special festival held in his honor, and drawn to a young Indian woman, he is caught between the two cultures of his upbringing but unable to leave the reservation.

Native American literature contained an implicit critique of modernization and the cult of progress. Nowhere were such sentiments expressed so clearly as in John G. Neihardt's *Black Elk Speaks: Being the Life Story of a Holy Man of the Oglala Sioux* (1932). Selected as Nebraska's poet laureate in the 1920s, Neihardt believed that the insights of art consciousness could be applied to society's problems. *Black Elk* presented the narrated autobiography of a blind fourth-generation Lakota healer, visionary, teacher, and medicine man. The book's narrator had been born in 1863, visualized an uprising of his people at the age of seventeen, joined Buffalo Bill's *Wild West Show*, mourned the Wounded Knee massacre of 1890, and converted to Catholicism fourteen years later. His life was dedicated to reconciling native traditions and spirituality with Christianity and the reality of white dominance.

Much of *Black Elk* explored a Native American world of the spirit that was accessible through dreams or the rhythms and tones of a drumbeat, dance, or chant. The medicine man saw "the whole hoop of the world … the sacred shapes of all things in the spirit." In a natural cosmos in which time was circular instead of linear, all tribes were encompassed by the sacred hoop—"one mighty flowering tree to shelter all the children of one mother and one father." "In the old days when we were a strong and happy people," recalled Black Elk, the nation flourished and the hoop was unbroken. Following the military disasters of the 1890s and the expropriation of Sioux lands, hope seemed lost. Yet the holy man heard a voice that heralded "a good nation walking in a sacred manner in a good land!" Restoration of the people's wholeness, he believed, would accompany comprehension that all living things were tied to each other in community.

Given little progress in Thirties race relations, several black writers attributed particular importance to ordinary people in their work. Heralded as the leading folk poet of Negro life, Sterling A. Brown published *Southern Road* in 1932. The son of a Tennessee minister and former slave, Brown was born in Washington, D.C. in 1901 and educated at Williams College and Harvard. After holding several academic positions, he began teaching literature at historically black Howard University in 1929. *Southern Road* borrowed from African American folk ballads, work songs, spirituals, blues, and jazz to render the inner life of southern people of color in eloquent plain speech. Brown's verse substituted the ironic humor, detachment, and understatement of workers in cabins and cotton fields for maudlin sentimentality. "White man tells me—humh—/Damn yo' soul/," a chain gang piece proclaimed, "Got no need,

Zora Neale Hurston

bebby,/To be tole [told]." "Ma Rainey" addressed the centrality of the blues: "Now you's back/Whah you belong,/Git way inside us,/Keep us strong." In "Memphis Blues" Brown caught the offhand style of working-class life: "Memphis go,/ Memphis come back,/Ain' no skin,/Off de nigger's back."

After years of research on African American folk culture, Zora Neale Hurston published *Mules and Men* in 1935. Hurston argued that southern blacks had developed their own language modifications, religious practices, food preparation techniques, and medical procedures. For example, she insisted that the development of blues, jazz, and authentic Negro dance forms could be traced to the region's "Jook joints" and cabarets. Hurston's first novel, *Their Eyes Were Watching God* (1937), merged her study of the black South with childhood memories. "Honey," an old bluesman declares, "we don't know nothin' but what we see." Much of the book's action takes place at the general store, where the locals trade stories. "Everybody indulged in mule talk," the narrator explains. "He was next to the Mayor in prominence, and made better talking." The novel follows Jamie, a strong female protagonist who elopes with the irresponsible Tea Cake. Defying community censure, she relishes the chance to be a full partner in a relationship built on unqualified respect, companionship, and love.

Richard Wright also began his writing career depicting southern blacks. Wright was born in 1908 into a sharecropping family on a cotton plantation near Natchez, Mississippi. When he was eight years old his father deserted the family. As a child, Wright witnessed the lynching of his step-uncle and the brother of a neighborhood friend. At seventeen he left for Memphis, where he worked as a dishwasher and messenger and began to educate himself. Two years later he moved to Chicago, where he got a job as a post office clerk. Joining the Communist Party and becoming executive secretary of the Chicago branch of the John Reed Club, Wright published poetry and fiction in movement organs like the *New Masses* and signed on with the Federal Writers Project. When he relocated to New York in 1937, the aspiring author became the Harlem editor of the Communist *Daily Worker*.

Wright's first novel was *Uncle Tom's Children* (1938), a compilation of four stories about the endurance of southern blacks that offered the hope that fear could lead to courage and acts of manly rebellion against white violence. After receiving a Guggenheim Fellowship, Wright completed his masterpiece, *Native Son* (1940), the first work by an African American to be selected for the Book-of-the-Month Club. The novel's protagonist was Bigger Thomas, a young black man whose father has been lynched in the South and who lives on relief in a single room on Chicago's South Side with his sister, brother, and mother. "Half the time I feel like I'm on the outside of the world peeping in through a knot-hole in the fence," the character explains. Thomas dreams of a better life despite an inability to keep a job or stay out of trouble. "They just don't let us do *nothing*," he exclaims. "I just can't get used to it." Offered employment as a chauffeur by a white social worker, he winds up driving for the owners of his tenement, who hire "wayward boys" as a charity gesture.

The ensuing tragedy of *Native Son* brilliantly invokes the burdensome weight of race and class. Seeing Thomas as revolutionary fodder, the family's daughter Mary insists on sharing the front seat with the chauffeur and demanding that he sing Negro spirituals while driving her Marxist boyfriend and herself to the South Side. Bigger can't get past the thought "that they kill us for women like her." When the drunken Mary makes an effort to seduce Thomas and he maneuvers the young woman into her room, her blind mother calls out her daughter's name. Panicking out of instinctive fear, Bigger inadvertently kills her by smothering her face with a pillow, and then hacks her body to pieces and burns it in the basement furnace. As a protection against the world he formerly feared, Thomas develops a new aggressiveness and murders the girlfriend who has joined him in a plot to extort money from his employers. Facing execution without remorse, he finally experiences a sense of manhood. Wright wanted the ruthlessness of his story to shock readers and serve as a warning about the explosive potential of the seemingly timid young men who walked the streets of South Side Chicago and New York's Harlem.

DOCUMENTED LIVES, PEOPLE'S THEATER

With the advent of the Works Progress Administration (WPA) in 1935, the Roosevelt administration initiated a massive jobs relief program that extended to the creative arts. By hiring writers, actors, musicians, and visual artists to produce non-commercial work, the federal government sought to honor the vitality of ordinary Americans and democratize formal culture. The centrality of the concept of "the people" was evident in the Federal Writers Project's (FWP) 150-volume "Life of America" series, which included state guidebooks, local histories, studies of ethnic minorities, stories about the disenfranchised, and folklore collections. *These Are Our Lives* (1939), for example, presented sketches designed to demonstrate how the Depression had impacted "real people" in the South. The Project's folklore unit was administered by Benjamin Botkin. A socially conscious Boston Jew who had studied at Harvard and Columbia, Botkin began teaching literature at the University of Oklahoma in 1921, where he became interested in what he defined as "the peculiar disposition and expressions" of the American people and particular localities.

The Federal Theater Project (FTP) presented another opportunity for bringing formal culture to the masses. Under the director of Vasaar College's Hallie Flanagan, the Project mounted plays, ballets, puppet shows, vaudeville presentations, and circuses for twenty-five million Americans at a nominal price or free of charge. The FTP produced two plays on Abraham Lincoln: E.P. Conkle's *Prologue to Glory* (1937) and Popular Front activist Howard Koch's more politicized *The Lonely Man* (1937).

Flanagan also created a Negro Theater Unit headed by stage director and screen writer John Houseman and staffed by writers such as Countee Cullen and Zora Neale Hurston. Houseman hired twenty-year-old actor Orson Welles to direct *Macbeth* (1935), an all-black version of Shakespeare's play in which a former Haitian slave leads an insurrection and becomes a ruthless dictator. Integrating light, movement, décor, and the sound of voodoo drums, the hit drama moved on to a road version seen by a hundred thousand people. Houseman's black troupe also produced Frank Wilson's folk drama, *Walk Together, Chillun* (1936).

With half of the FTP's personnel and budget concentrated in New York City, the theater project's politics were shaped by a stable of Popular Front writers, including Albert Maltz, John Howard Lawson, Clifford Odets, Michael Gold, and Marc Blitzstein. The program's close relationship with the labor movement was demonstrated by the fact that radical plays such as the Yiddish version of *Awake and Sing!* often were block-booked by progressive unions and organizations. One of the unit's first productions was Sinclair Lewis' *It Can't Happen Here* (1936). Lewis' controversial novel about middle-class impotency in confronting a hypothetical fascist uprising had been published a year earlier, but Hollywood had scrapped plans to film it. Seizing upon the surrounding publicity, the FTP opened the drama in eighteen cities nationwide. Another production, George Sklar's *Life and Death of an American* (1937, 1939) began with a police shooting and traced the protagonist's life backwards through a series of flashbacks. Through this device, the martyred main character came to appreciate that capitalism no longer rewarded the deserving and that worker solidarity was the only solution.

Some of the most controversial Project dramatizations involved the Living Newspapers. Addressed to recent news events, these plays used generic male characters like the Farmer or Worker to suggest that upward mobility was an illusion, and that the greatest test of moral and physical courage came with collective action. In *Triple-A Plowed Under* (1936), the central character turned out to be the entire nation and economic system. Invoking a call for heroic manhood, the drama preached that agrarian and industrial workers shared common interests. While the production flattered economically dependent and disenfranchised white farmers as "the people," it did so only to suggest that they, not a hostile federal judiciary, should rule on the constitutionality of federal agricultural policy. Another Living Newspaper, *One-Third of a Nation* (1938), borrowed its title from President Roosevelt's reference to the proportion of Americans suffering from poverty. The script suggested that both workers and the beleaguered white-collar class were powerless to fight the money and power of wealthy bankers and factory owners by themselves, but could unite together in common cause.

Community stage companies sought to address the plight of ordinary people as well. In New York the African American Theater Union produced *Stevedore* (1934), a stark drama about New Orleans dockworkers. The following year, the Negro People's Theater of Harlem mounted a black version of *Waiting for Lefty* (1935). Meanwhile, poet

Langston Hughes turned his writing talents to polemical works like *Mulatto* (1935), a drama of southern interracial sex that remained the longest-running Broadway play by an African American until the 1960s. Other Hughes efforts included *Soul Gone Home* (1937) and *Don't You Want to Be Free?* (1938), a plea for class unity between whites and blacks produced by the poet's own Harlem Suitcase Theater.

THE AMERICAN SCENE

The New Deal ideal of a common citizenship of "the people" found its most significant outlet in publicly sponsored visual art. By making "the creation of beauty" part of the daily lives of all Americans, the government sought to bring economic revitalization to a depressed cultural industry and sustain social morale during hard times. One example of such activity was the Index of American Design—a collection of twenty-two thousand watercolors and drawings of historic handicrafts that the WPA's Federal Art Project (FAP) distributed to popular venues like department stores. The FAP also established six hundred arts and crafts instructional centers nationwide and marketed print reproductions of drawings and paintings at reasonable prices. The heart of New Deal arts activity rested with the commissions, stipends, or wages awarded to individual artists. Through Treasury Department building subsidies, the Public Works of Art program, and the FAP, thousands of federally funded paintings, murals, and sculptures found their way into 1930s housing projects, schools, correctional facilities, post offices, and government offices.

Seeking to document the experiences and culture of ordinary people through representational forms, New Deal art leaned toward aesthetic realism, a style derived from Precisionist painters such as Charles Sheeler. In influential pieces such as *Upper Deck* (1929), Sheeler had sought to reproduce accurate images of the industrial landscape. The detailed work of the Precisionists inspired American Scene artists and Regionalists to celebrate the unique qualities of the natural environment and the plain virtues of rural culture. Regionalist interest in provincial folk types was most explicitly rendered in the work of Grant Wood, an Iowa artist who had studied in Europe before turning to domestic themes. Wood's *American Gothic* (1930), one of the most commonly recognized images of the nation's cultural heritage, offered an iconographic portrait of a stoic father and his spinster daughter standing in front of a nineteenth-century farmhouse with gothic windows. Other pieces, such as *Fall Plowing* (1931), *Dinner for Threshers* (1933), and the lithograph *Seed Time and Harvest* (1937), illustrated Wood's fascination with the self-reliant work ethic of the rural working class.

Midwest artist John Steuart Curry painted dramatic scenes of the prairie landscape in canvases such as *Baptism in Kansas* (1928), *The Stockman* (1929), *Spring Shower* (1931), and *Wisconsin Landscape* (1938–39). Yet the most idealized versions of Regionalist art appeared in the work of Thomas Hart Benton. Born in Missouri in 1889,

Benton studied at the Art Institute of Chicago and Paris before settling in New York. His *America Today* (1930–31), a colorful wall painting completed for a life insurance building, conveyed a rugged naturalism in its depiction of earthy, muscular male figures. Benton's mural for the Whitney Museum library, *The Arts of Life in America* (1932), presented a survey of popular and folk arts from the nation's far-flung regions that incorporated craps shooting, burlesque, and bronco busting. Another panel, entitled *Political Business and Intellectual Ballyhoo*, revealed the artist's contempt for cosmopolitan culture with sly references to "literary playboys" and "Greenwich Village proletarians." Returning to Missouri in 1935 to re-establish ties with the heartland, Benton completed a mural for the state Capitol building that aroused a storm of controversy for exposing the violent and seamy side of the region's history.

Edward Hopper brought the realism of the American Scene to the urban environment. Born in 1882 into a middle-class family in New York's Hudson River Valley, Hopper studied art with Robert Henri, who steered him toward everyday life. Influenced by the Impressionists on several trips to Paris, he returned to New York as a magazine illustrator and commercial artist. Hopper began painting pictures of elevated subway lines, trains, and bridges in the late 1920s, and gradually focused on working people in ordinary urban settings. His canvases seemed to suggest the loneliness of modern public places such as cafes, restaurants, hot-dog stands, offices, hotel rooms, movie theaters, trains, gas stations, or beauty shops. *Early Sunday Morning* (1930) presented a collection of Seventh

Edward Hopper (1882–1967), *Early Sunday Morning* (1930)   Oil on canvas, Whitney Museum of American Art, New York; purchase, with funds from Gertrude Vanderbilt Whitney 31.426. Photograph by Geoffrey Clements.

Avenue storefronts and tenements reminiscent of the stage set for Elmer Rice's *Street Scene. Hotel Room* (1931) depicted a woman seated on a bed in near resignation. *Room in Brooklyn* (1932) pictured a woman holding a piece of paper as she sits alone by a bay window. *New York Movie* (1939) provided a glimpse of a young female usher lost in thought as she stands in the foyer of a near empty theater.

By revealing the private realm of ordinary subjects in the most commonplace settings, Hopper hinted at the complexity of stories to be unearthed in the great American city. Although his people were exclusively white and middle class, they appeared to be transients who were not at home anywhere. Such an impression pervaded Hopper's masterpiece, *Nighthawks* (1942), a canvas modeled on a restaurant in New York's Greenwich Village. Viewed from a perspective outside the café's plate-glass window, the painting featured three subdued patrons seated at the counter in the presence of a uniformed food server. In this late-night setting nobody appears to be talking with anyone else, and there is no suggestion of an ongoing narrative. Characterized by a lack of adornment and cold precision, the picture suggests the calculated efficiency of Hemingway's prose, a writer for whom Hopper had profound admiration.

American Scene painting easily lent itself to social realism and the portrayal of ordinary people. Several New York artists came to incorporate such work in the Depression decade. Born in Russia, Raphael Soyer arrived in New York in 1913, when his father assumed a teaching position at Yeshiva College. Employed on the Lower East Side in the late Twenties, Soyer joined the John Reed Club and began to paint homeless and unemployed people. A typical result of these efforts was *In the City Park* (1934), an oil portrait of four vagrants seated on a bench. *How Long Since You Wrote to Mother?* (1934) took its title from a stenciled message on a mission house wall. *Transients* (1936) depicted several men on rickety wooden chairs waiting for a flophouse bed. Soyer's refusal to treat downtrodden subjects as "types" was clearly illustrated in *Bus Passengers* (1938), an intimate portrait of a working-class woman with an infant on her lap, and *Reading from Left to Right* (1938), a glimpse of three unemployed men whose distinct features mark their individuality. In *Office Girls* (1936) the artist conveyed the self-assured gait of working-class clerical employees on the way to their jobs.

Soyer shared an interest in Manhattan's Union Square neighborhood with his brother Moses, Reginald Marsh, and Isabel Bishop, the group of "Fourteenth Street" artists with whom he came to be identified. A schoolteacher's daughter, Bishop was born in Cincinnati in 1902 and raised in Detroit. At the age of sixteen she came to New York to study applied design but switched to the Art Students League, where her instructors emphasized the importance of the urban scene. Although her compatriot Reginald Marsh gravitated to portraits of rowdy crowds and honky-tonks, Bishop was more interested in street scenes featuring working-class women. Paintings like *Two Girls* (1935) and *Lunch Hour* (1939) showed modestly but fashionably dressed women office workers lounging on public benches, reading, chatting, or briskly proceeding to their destinations. Rather than picturing workers as grotesque victims of a harsh society, Bishop caught the dignity and self-possession of her subjects' individual make-up. In a similar fashion, Pennsylvania native Alice Neel provided intimate portraits of the people of her East Harlem neighborhood with paintings such as *Woman with Blue Hat* (1934).

Ben Shahn was the most well-known social realist of the 1930s. Born in Lithuania in 1898, Shahn arrived in New York at the age of eight, where he lived with his family in a series of cold-water flats. His father, an Orthodox Jewish woodcarver, carpenter, writer, and socialist, introduced him to the mythic past of the Old Testament. Attending night school at the socialist Educational Alliance, Shahn was able to work his way through high school and college as an apprentice lithographer. During the 1920s he studied art and traveled across the world. His first exhibit did not come until 1930, when he mounted a one-man show of sketches and watercolors completed in North Africa. Sharing a studio with photographer Walker Evans, he learned to integrate his work with storytelling and the particular situation of individual lives. The first result of this transformation was a series of watercolors about the Alfred Dreyfus Affair of the 1890s, a notorious scandal that had exposed the entrenched anti-Semitism of the French political elite. The painter's next project consisted of two large panels and twenty-three canvases in commemoration of the trial and execution of Sacco and Vanzetti.

Influenced by the broad canvases of Mexican muralist Diego Rivera, Shahn deployed simplified colors and outlined shapes to present the drama of the famous case through its principal characters. The paintings included portraits of the judge, the defense attorney, six female witnesses, the special review committee headed by Harvard President A. Lawrence Lowell, and those protesting the tragic outcome. The most celebrated image of the series, "The Passion of Sacco and Vanzetti" (1931–32), pictured the two martyrs as ordinary men lying in open coffins presided over by Lowell and the other two other members of the review panel. Becoming increasingly political, Shahn joined the editorial staff of *Art Front*, the publication of the radical Artists Union. He then completed a series of gouache canvases about imprisoned labor activist Tom Mooney in which he contrasted the sincerity of powerless people with the pretensions of politicians by focusing upon the subject's relationship with his mother and wife.

PUBLIC ARTISTS

Shahn's career as a publicly funded artist began in 1933, when he completed eight tempera paintings on Prohibition as a study for a mural for New York City's Central Park Casino. The local Public Works of Art Project never approved the installation, but in 1935 Shahn began a three-year stint as a photographer for the New Deal's Resettlement Administration (RA) and Farm Security Administration (FSA) that resulted in the painting *Scotts Run, West Virginia* (1937), a picture of idle men in an impoverished mining town watching a freight train pass. Between 1937 and 1938 he also completed a massive fresco for Jersey Homesteads, the community center of a garment workers' housing project in a RA model town, about the history of working-class Jewish immigration and the consequent struggles for labor rights and social justice.

Even after leaving the FSA, Shahn used photographs he had taken as models for paintings such as *Sunday Football* (1938), a tempera of sports fans peering through the knothole of a wooden fence; *WPA Sunday* (1939), a portrait of black men sitting on a curb in church clothes; and *Pretty Girl Milking a Cow* (1940), a picture of a farmhand watching the painting's subject as he blows a harmonica. Between 1938 and 1942 he worked on a series of wall paintings reflecting his political sensibilities. *Resources of America* (1939), an ambitious mural executed with his wife, Bernarda, for the Bronx Central Annex Post Office, mixed a survey of the nation's male craft and industrial occupations with a stanza of Whitman poetry. In a similar mode, Shahn's installation for the new Social Security Building in Washington, D.C. (1940–42) depicted the challenges of unemployment, child labor, and old age that awaited government action.

New Deal arts administrators saw the vernacular tradition of the union movement as a source of accessible pubic art for a broad popular audience. Accordingly, they encouraged images that depicted the strength and dignity of working people and that promoted the idea of a nation unified by shared labor. Steering away from controversial topics like poor working conditions or class struggle, art officials preferred to endorse depictions of industrious and independent male craft workers. Significantly, public murals often portrayed vocations like the building trades, mining, and industrial work that had been hit hardest by the Depression, and generally ignored white-collar employment, women's wage labor, or menial service work. The purpose of his Pennsylvania mural *Local Industry* (1936), explained Treasury artist Paul Mays, was to express "the force and vitality of the working people in this valley of factories and furnaces." Howard Cook's *Steel Industry* (1936) portrayed industrial technology as the extension of the power of manly workers. Even the twenty-one frescoes for New York's socialist New Workers School concentrated on positive working-class contributions to American life.

The producer ethic was most evident in federally sponsored art about country life. Radical commitments could produce a small piece such as *Land of Plenty* (1935), a woodcut by former Diego Rivera assistant Lucienne Bloch in which a barbed-wire fence separated a poor migrant family from a cornfield and power lines. Rural post office murals, in contrast, usually celebrated pioneer efforts in building settlements and preparing fields for agriculture, particularly in the Midwest. Representing the land as the basis of American democracy, public art approached the family farm as an icon of continuity and generational harmony in which neighborly male settlers labored together on heavy tasks while the womenfolk gathered the harvest and carried baskets or stalks of corn. Kansas muralist Lumen Winter reflected such a disposition when he advised aspiring artists to "go somewhere where people are working for a living" for inspiration. Public art's desire to convey hope and well-being was epitomized by Arnold Blanch's *One Hundredth Anniversary* (1940), a Wisconsin post office mural showing a staid farming couple framed by the tableau of a neat dairy farm and pasture.

Although white muralists were encouraged to portray Native Americans as romantic primitives who were close to nature and cooperative with settlers, art administrators occasionally awarded commissions to Indian artists. Under Treasury Department auspices, Oklahoma Kiowa Stephen Mopope and four assistants were given free reign in a series of post office installations that used nineteenth-century Plains techniques of hide painting and two-dimensional ledger drawing to trace the history and contemporary life of the people. Similarly, Navajo artist Gerald Nailor recaptured the decorative quality of traditional mural-making in work executed in 1940 for the Washington headquarters of the Department of Interior.

Whatever the limitations of their perspective, New Deal officials viewed awareness of the nation's diverse folk heritage as an important step toward cultural renewal and the revitalization of artisan traditions. One example of such interest was *Negro River Music* (1940), white artist Gustaf Dalstrom's contribution to a multi-panel post office mural depicting the history of St. Joseph, Missouri. Dalstrom's fresco featured eight rural black men seated on a wooden bench and crate playing banjos, harmonica, and clapping hands. When middle-class African Americans in the area objected to the work as a stereotypical portrait of lazy blacks who only wanted to sing, dance, and clown, art administrators ignored their protests and let the piece stand.

Despite continuing criticism of racial stereotypes, several black painters remained fascinated with the seamy urban settings portrayed on canvas during the early years of the Harlem Renaissance. In *Blues* (1929), Archibald Motley, Jr. sought to capture the feel of a nightclub as a couple danced close to the bandstand. His *Black Belt* (1934) pictured a "Bronzeville" street corner of cabarets, drug stores, and hotels on Chicago's South Side. Another Motley painting, *Saturday Night Street Scene* (1936), conveyed the spontaneous bustle of city pavements as a group of people moved to the rhythm of a band of musicians gathered in front of a beauty shop. Edward Burra's *Harlem* (1934) presented an urban landscape in which friendly neighbors relaxed on the front steps of a tenement as the elevated subway loomed in the background.

Although black artists such as Motley and Burra relished the raucous life of the cities, federal sponsorship normally steered away from such images. One of the few African American beneficiaries of the public art program was Aaron Douglas. In *Aspects of Negro Life* (1934), four Federal Art Project wall paintings for the Harlem Public Library, Douglas traced the black struggle for social justice and human rights. It fell upon the artist's young protégé Jacob Lawrence, however, to become the most prominent black recipient of federal art funding. Born in 1917, Lawrence grew up in Harlem, where his single mother alternated between domestic service and relief. Discovering an interest in art at a settlement house day-care program, the young student incorporated the bright colors of his mother's throw rugs into carefree poster paintings. At fifteen Lawrence became involved in the Harlem Art Workshop, where he was influenced by Aaron Douglas, as well as by Langston Hughes and Richard Wright. Dropping out of high school to support his mother, he was accepted into the Civilian Conservation Corps for a six-month stint before winning a two-year scholarship to the American Artists School.

Lawrence began to paint Harlem life as a social realist. Focusing on human figures, street life, and portraits of social inequity, he produced small easel works such as *Street Scene – Restaurant* (1936), a picture of three prostitutes observing the world while relaxing on the front steps of a tenement. Other paintings detailed the interior scenes of dingy apartments or brothels. In 1937 Lawrence pursued a growing interest in black history and culture with a series of forty-one tempera canvases depicting Toussaint L'Ouverture and the struggle for Haitian independence. Hired the next year by the Federal Art Project, the twenty-one-year-old artist produced two paintings every six weeks. Among them was a historical series on Negro abolitionist leaders Frederick Douglass and Harriet Tubman. *The Migration of the Negro* (1940–41), a sixty-panel mural detailing the African American exodus from the South, was completed under the auspices of a Rosenwald Foundation fellowship. In *Tombstones* and *Pool Parlor,* two of thirty works comprising *Harlem Scenes* (1942–43), Lawrence demonstrated his detailed eye for the community's crowded streets and recreational sites.

Although New Deal art administrators normally followed a consensual approach to cultural affairs, they were not always able to avoid controversy. Seeking to honor fire fighters at San Francisco's Coit Tower, the local public art program commissioned the largest federally sponsored mural project in the country. The completed second-floor frescoes included generic scenes of leisure and entertainment or landscape and seascape portraits. Yet the entry-level murals were executed by artists influenced by Diego Rivera in the midst of organized labor's city-wide general strike of 1934. *City Life,* a fresco by Ukranian immigrant Victor Arnautoff, captured the chaos of the streets during the protests. John Langley Howard's *California Industrial Scenes* contrasted the industrial progress of the Shasta Dam with a poor miner's family reduced to living in a tent. Another mural contained a replica of the communist hammer and sickle, leading officials to hold up the Tower's opening for four months until the offending artist agreed to remove the revolutionary symbol.

THE CAMERA EYE

Depression social commentary lent itself more easily to documentary photography than to painting or mural creation. Since the 1920s, camera artists such as Dorothea Lange, Walker Evans, Ansel Adams, and Edward Weston had followed Alfred Stieglitz's lead in seeking out subjects among immigrants, urban scenes, desert landscapes, and struggling farmers. Doris Ulmann also experimented with realist photography. Trained in New

York by camera pioneer Clarence White in the 1910s, Ulmann refused to use a light meter or automatic shutter in portraits of Appalachian Mountain and South Carolina working people. Driven to her extended field trips by a chauffeur and accompanied by her maid, the wealthy socialite nevertheless succeeded in putting subjects at ease by asking what they did in the way of work and whether they enjoyed it. Invited to photograph the Gullah people on a friend's Carolina plantation, Ulmann assembled a collection of portraits entitled *Roll, Jordan, Roll* (1934), which appeared in a limited edition of 350 volumes. Photographs such as *Baptism Scene, South Carolina* (1929–30) revealed a remarkable feel for the religious rituals of southern African Americans.

Margaret Bourke-White was another Clarence White protégé. The daughter of a Bronx engineer who designed printing machinery, she studied biology and zoology at Columbia and several other universities before earning a degree in 1927. Having taken White's photography classes at Columbia, Bourke-White worked as an industrial photographer in the Cleveland steel mills before being hired in 1930 as the first staff photographer for Henry Luce's *Fortune* magazine. Her assignments ranged from the routine of an auto factory spray painter, to workers constructing the Empire State Building, to the daily life of an Illinois farm household, to the impact of the Great Plains draught, to an urban family on relief. As the star photographer of Luce's new *Life* magazine after 1936, she revolutionized modern journalism with the first use of the photo-essay.

Affected by the human misery of the Depression, Bourke-White teamed up with Erskine Caldwell to document the ravages of southern tenant farming and sharecropping. The resulting publication, *You Have Seen Their Faces* (1937), offered a startling juxtaposition of prose and photographic imagery. Caldwell's captions provided the author's conception of the sentiments held by the poor whites and African Americans pictured in the book. Beneath *Maiden Lane, Georgia*, a picture of ramshackle huts, for example, one could find the observation that "a man learns not to expect much after he's farmed cotton most of his life." Seeking to induce public shame by making the reader a first-hand witness to terrible conditions, Caldwell's descriptions of the ragged clothes and haggard faces of the southern poor left nothing to the imagination. Meanwhile, Bourke-White's images portrayed tenants and sharecroppers as people in abject poverty and despair whose only outlet was revivalist religion.

The narrative style of *Their Faces* was influenced by Lewis Hine's photographic survey of construction workers and engine builders in *Men at Work* (1932) and the documentary film work of Pare Lorentz. A West Virginia college graduate, Lorentz had come to New York in the 1920s to write movie critiques for newspapers and magazines. In 1933 he published a photography book of social protest images. Two years later he was hired as motion picture consultant to the Resettlement Administration, the New Deal agency that sought to reorganize small agriculture by transferring poor farmers to more productive zones and improving cultivation techniques. Under the leadership of economist Rexford Tugwell, the bureau sought to instill a populist spirit of solidarity for its goals through publicity. Having failed to convince the Hollywood studios to support a Dust Bowl documentary, Lorentz turned to a group of radical New York filmmakers and undertook the work himself on a $6000 budget.

The result of these efforts was *The Plow That Broke the Plains* (1936), a film shot on location from Montana to Amarillo, Texas. Casting professional actors as the migrants who had left the Dust Bowl years earlier, Lorentz imported stock Hollywood footage for historical background. As the cameras focused on images of parched earth, dust-blowing prairie, sun-bleached cattle bones, rusting plows, and abandoned farm machinery, a lyrical narrator explained that machines had destroyed the vital grasslands, which then had been ravaged by drought and dust storms. Lorentz worked with Virgil Thomson, a Paris-trained modernist composer, on tightly integrating the lush score, including excerpts from cowboy and folk tunes, into the action. When the finished product was rejected by major distributors, the director managed to open the film in an independent theater in New York, where it was cheered by audiences at every performance. Following this success, *Plow* gained nationwide distribution to three thousand educational centers, federal agencies, and small movie houses.

Lorentz's second project was *The River* (1937), a survey of the ecological casualties of deforestation and flooding across the far-flung Mississippi Valley. Reciting a Whitmanesque list of tree names, cities, and rivers as Thomson's score weaved folk ballads and popular songs into the orchestration, the narration pressed viewers to acknowledge the importance of the New Deal's rehabilitation efforts. "You cannot plan for water unless you plan for land," it declared, "But you cannot plan for water and land unless you plan for people." Distributed by Paramount Pictures, *The River* won praise as another Lorentz masterpiece, leading to his appointment in 1937 as director of the U.S. Film Service.

The Resettlement Administration's most important contribution to the documentary form came through the photography project initiated under the leadership of Roy Emerson Stryker. Born into a Populist Kansas family in 1893 and raised in Colorado, Stryker punched cattle on his own homestead for several years while pursuing a career in gold mining. After serving in the World War I infantry, he earned a Columbia economics degree and became Rexford Tugwell's graduate assistant. In the process of collecting photographs for Tugwell's progressive economics textbook and preparing for his classes, Stryker familiarized himself with the photographs of Jacob Riis and Lewis Hine. Recruited by his former mentor to provide visual evidence of the Resettlement Administration's accomplishments to Congress and the pubic, Stryker broadened the mission into a campaign to establish the historical record of the agency's activities.

Hiring a dozen photographers, Stryker set out to portray the suffering of rural Americans in terms understandable to the urban middle class. Under the influence of Columbia rural sociologist Robert Lynd, however, he insisted on the need to balance images of economic distress with evidence of the survival of traditional values and family cohe-

Arthur Rothstein, *Man and Model T Ford that makes 200 miles a day in flight from grasshopper- and drought-ridden area of South Dakota; Highway 10, Missoula, Montana, 1936.*

sion. "We photographed destitute migrants and average American townspeople," he later recalled, "sharecroppers and prosperous farmers, eroded land and fertile land, human misery and human elation." Photographers for the Resettlement Administration and its successor Farm Security Administration amassed an unprecedented documentation of American life though some 270,000 pictures. Stryker's ground rules stipulated that no representation ridicule its object or present a cliché. While subjects encompassed the poor in both industrial cities and the countryside, therefore, they also included mountain fiddlers and harmonica quintets, singing coal miners, barn siding muralists, wrestling matches, barroom poker games, dinner political discussions, county fairs, local movie houses, traveling salesmen, café proprietors, and traveling evangelists.

As artists, propagandists, and documentary reporters, government photographers often experienced inherent contradictions. Ben Shahn discovered to his dismay that the "enchanting" storytelling arts of the South co-existed with "hopeless prejudices, bigotry, and ignorance." The left-wing progressive also found that many poor people maintained "a transcendent indifference to their lot in life"—a realization that led him to rethink his theoretical political notions and begin the transition from social realism to a style focusing upon people's individual qualities. Hired as a twenty-one-year-old Columbia graduate, Arthur Rothstein saw himself more as a documentary historian than an artist. Nevertheless, he was convinced that a successful photograph required a dramatic esthetic. Seeking to represent the drought's eradication of South Dakota's cattle herds, Rothstein moved the location of a cow's skull so that its shadow fell on the parched soil. Although several others of his photos pictured healthy sheep in the vicinity, the local press accused the government of fabricating drought conditions. In Oklahoma, Rothstein staged *Fleeing a Dust Storm* (1936), a picture that became an icon of the Dust Bowl exodus.

IN PRAISE OF THE PEOPLE

"It was our job to document the problems of the Depression," Rothstein later observed, "so that we could justify the New Deal legislation that was designed to alleviate them." Russell Lee, however, sought to emphasize the traditions of rugged individualism and community cooperation upon which reform efforts could be built. An economically independent engineer from Illinois, Lee became the most prolific of Stryker's picture takers. The positive mindset he brought to his work emerged in *Lumberjacks—Saturday Night—Minnesota* (1937), a portrait emphasizing the jaunty and convivial aspects of working-class social life that ignored the excessive drinking and scars of violence visible in several unused pictures. A series of photographs of Pie Town, New Mexico (1940) also demonstrated the power of selectivity by focusing on a community supper that had to be arranged specifically for the shoot by the local Farm Bureau.

The project's most well-known photographer, Dorothea Lange, also placed a distinct imprint on her portraits. Born Dorothea Nutzhorn in Hoboken, New Jersey in 1895, she experienced a bout with polio at age seven that left her with a slight, life-long limp. Five years later her father abandoned the family. Undeterred from her goal of becoming a camera artist, Lange found work as a photographer's assistant in New York studios and took classes from Clarence White at Columbia. After adopting her German mother's maiden name at the age of twenty-three, she moved to San Francisco, where she found a job in a photo supply house before establishing her own studio and specializing in portraits of the social elite. By the early 1930s, however, Lange's populist sensibilities led her into the streets to record images of poor, unemployed, and migrant families. Photographs such as *White Angel Breadline, San Francisco* (1933) co-existed with her pictures of May Day demonstrators and stenographers to demonstrate the dignity and emotional complexity of ordinary people. In 1935 she married Berkeley economist Paul Taylor, with whom she undertook an extended illustrated study of Dust Bowl migrants.

Hired by Roy Stryker, Lange continued to focus on migrant families. In *Toward Los Angeles* (1937) she depicted two ragged hitchhikers striding past a highway billboard that read "Next Time Try the Train—Relax." Another famous image showed a family carrying their clothing in a wagon and baby carriage as they moved on foot down an

Oklahoma highway. Lange's most widely acclaimed photograph was *Migrant Mother* (1936), a picture taken in Nippomo, California, that remains the single most significant icon of the Great Depression. Searching in vain for a pea-pickers camp, Lange came across a woman and several children in front of a lean-to shelter. Ignoring the teenage daughter of the family, she posed the mother with the infant in her lap and two small children burying their heads in her shoulders. To preserve an image of dignity in the face of social neglect, Lange eliminated unseemly distractions such as a pile of dirty clothes, the stained portion of the tent canvas, a battered trunk, and an empty pie plate. A desired sense of intimacy was enhanced by having the mother raise her right hand to her face.

In a session lasting no more than ten minutes, Lange never discovered that the migrant mother's name was Florence Thompson. Nor did she inquire about Thompson's personal history. Instead, the photographer's sole intention was to dramatize the contrast between the woman's inner strength and pride and the impoverished nature of her surroundings. A similar motif characterized *An American Exodus* (1939), the culmination of Lange's collaboration with Taylor, in which the photographs appeared above captions containing gritty quotes from the subjects of the study's profiles. Instead of coming off as hopeless and pitiable sharecroppers, however, the subjects of *An American Exodus* appeared as handsome, tough, competent, shrewd, and humorous people who could even seem belligerent at times.

Lange's pictures were included among the FSA photographs reproduced in Archibald MacLeish's politically infused *The Land of the Free* (1938), Sherwood Anderson's sentimentalized *Home Town* (1940), and Richard Wright's race-conscious *12 Million Black Voices: A Folk History of the Negro in the United States* (1941). Using images assembled by FSA photographer and exhibit manager Edwin Rosskam as the basis of his text, Wright pleaded for the extension of human rights to African Americans. Through the pictures, he wrote, white Americans were able to see black people looking at them "from the dark mirror of our lives!" In the same year in which *12 Million Black Voices* was published, James Agee and Walker Evans released the long-delayed *Let Us Now Praise Famous Men: Three Tenant Families* (1941).

Born in St. Louis and raised in a wealthy Chicago suburb, Evans studied literature at Williams College and the Sorbonne before returning to New York in the late 1920s to take up photography. Rejecting an aesthetic approach to the craft, he preferred to take outdoor pictures in natural light and to concentrate on artifacts of commercial culture and the industrial landscape. Evans' desire to capture the beauty of the commonplace led him to Roy Stryker's photographic unit in 1935, where he set out to document the human impact of soil depletion in West Virginia, Mississippi, and Alabama. The following year he agreed to collaborate with James Agee on a *Fortune* magazine photo-essay on the daily life of a typical white tenant farm family. Agee was from a middle-class family in Knoxville. His father, who died in an auto accident when his son was only six, had come from a Tennessee mountain family with seventeenth-century roots. Agee's mother, a devout Episcopalian and a businessman's daughter, was a drama and music graduate of the state university. After schooling at Phillips Exeter Academy and graduation from Harvard in 1932, Agee accepted his first job offer to become a reporter for *Fortune.*

Despite his affluence, Agee was familiar with manual labor from summer jobs harvesting wheat on the Great Plains. Like Evans, he saw beauty and pathos in ordinary life. After the duo spent two months with three Alabama families, however, *Fortune* rejected the manuscript as excessively long. Refusing to cast his subjects in patronizing terms, Agee had sought to make readers feel what it was like to be poor, and had written about sharecroppers as real people. Under headings like Money, Work, Cotton, Planting, Cultivation, and Picking Season, he catalogued the work habits of his subjects and described their homes and household contents in exhaustive detail. Recounting conversations and chance meetings as they "happened," he insisted that he was recording the tenant life "for its own sake, not for art's sake." Agee considered the personal lives of the tenants more important than the details of their economic oppression or work relationships. He made no attempt to seduce the reader with appeals to sentiment, social consciousness, guilt, or calls for reform, and offered no solutions to tenancy. His only interest was in the human dignity of the people he had chosen to describe.

Like Agee, Evans sought to show people in normal human situations, instead of depicting them as degraded victims of circumstance. Given to removing objects when a scene appeared too cluttered or adding others to achieve balance, Evans was intent on showing the order and beauty that lay beneath the surface of poverty. He often accomplished this by focusing the camera on people's household surroundings and possessions. By conveying the idea that the underprivileged had an aesthetic quality to their lives, he hoped to return dignity to the poor and demonstrate that the meaning of particular images could transcend their immediate circumstances. Evans believed it was important to show that people could be clean and decently presented, even if they had no running water or sanitary facilities, and that tenants took pride in their appearance. In *Laura Minnie Lee Tengle, Hale County Alabama,* he sought to capture the combination of suffering and endurance that he found so compelling in his Alabama subjects.

Once *Fortune* rejected Agee's text, the author expanded its length. Yet book editors preferred stories about helpless and brutalized victims of social conditions. By the time Houghton Mifflin agreed to publish the work, Agee had turned the project into an exercise on writing a book about tenancy. Not content to provide descriptions of what he had seen, the author felt compelled to explain how he had responded. Picturing himself as "a spy, traveling as a journalist" and Evans as "a counterspy, traveling as a photographer," Agree raised moral questions about prying into people's lives. In the end, he concluded that any attempt to promote an accurate record of his observations was doomed. There was no "average white tenant family," Agee declared, only the dignity of their "actuality." Adding the poem whose title gave the largely ignored volume its name, he mourned those who had "no memorial; who perished as though they had never been." "But these were merciful men whose righteousness hath not been forgotten," he protested. "Their bodies are buried in peace; but their name liveth for evermore."

SOURCES AND SUGGESTED READINGS

Working-class social values and consumer habits in the Great Depression constitute the focus of Lizabeth Cohen, *Making a New Deal: Industrial Workers in Chicago, 1919–1939* (1990). Overviews of the era's intellectuals and socially oriented writers and artists include Richard Pells, *Radical Visions and the American Dream: Culture and Social Thought in the Depression Years* (1973), the relevant essays in Lawrence W. Levine, *Unpredictable Past: Explorations in American Cultural History* (1993), and Warren I. Susman, *Culture as History: The Transformation of American Society in the Twentieth Century* (1984).

Michael Deming, *The Cultural Front: The Laboring of American Culture in the Twentieth Century* (1997) offers a definitive survey of dissident Thirties literature and drama. See also Laura Browder, *Rousing the Nation: Radical Culture in Depression America* (1998) and Malcolm Cowley, *The Dream of the Golden Mountains: Remembering the 1930s* (1980). Selections of protest literature appear in Harvey Swados, ed., *The American Writer and the Great Depression* (1966) and Louis Filler, ed., *The Anxious Years: America in the Nineteen Thirties—A Collection of Contemporary Writings* (1963). Radical women writers receive profiles in Laura Hapke, *Daughters of the Great Depression: Women, Work and Fiction in the American 1930s* (1995); Paula Rabinowitz, *Labor and Desire: Women's Revolutionary Fiction in Depression America* (1991); and Elinor Langer, *Josephine Herbst* (1984).

The relevant portions of Howard Pollack's biographical *Aaron Copland: The Life and Work of an Uncommon Man* (1999) set the folk-oriented ballets and suites of America's leading composer of the Thirties in social context. The period's radical folk balladeers elicit study in portions of R. Serge Denisoff, *Great Day Coming: Folk Music and the American Left* (1971) and the more recent Robbie Lieberman, *"My Song is My Weapon": People's Songs, American Communism, and the Politics of Culture, 1930–1950* (1989). See also Joe Klein, *Woody Guthrie, A Life* (1980).

Depression literary regionalism and realism receive treatment in Robert L. Dorman, *Revolt of the Provinces: The Regionalist Movement in America, 1920–1945* (1993). Specific studies include Nona Balakian, *The World of William Saroyan* (1998); Jay Parini, *John Steinbeck: A Biography* (1995); Richard Wilser, *Thomas Wolfe: An Introduction and Interpretation* (1961); and North Callahan, *Carl Sandburg: His Life and Works* (1987). For samples of the documentary tradition among American Indian and African American writers, respectively, see Oliver La Farge, *As Long as the Grass Shall Grow* (1940) and Richard Wright, *A Million Black Voices* (1941).

Descriptions of the Federal Theater Project appear in Barbara Melosh, *Engendering Culture: Manhood and Womanhood in New Deal Public Art and Theater* (1991) and E. Quita Craig, *Black Drama of the Federal Theater Era* (1980). Two socially engaged dramatists of the period warrant profiles in Anthony F.R. Palmieri, *Elmer Rice: A Playwright's Vision of America* (1980) and Rex Burbank, *Thornton Wilder*, 2ⁿᵈ ed. (1978).

For overviews of social realism in Thirties painting, see the relevant portions of Francis Pohl, *Framing America: A Social History of American Art* (2002) and Terry Smith, *Making the Modern: Industry, Art, and Design in America* (1993). Two of the leading realists are the subject of works by Francis Pohl, *Ben Shahn* (1993); Susan Charlowe, *Common Man, Mythic Vision: The Paintings of Ben Shahn* (1998); Robert Hobbs, *Edward Hopper* (1987); and Deborah Lyons, *Edward Hopper and the American Imagination* (1995). See also Samantha Baskind, *Raphael Soyer and the Search for Modern American Art* (2004) and Ellen Harkins Wheat, *Jacob Lawrence, American Painter* (1986). For the public art movement, see Jonathan Harris, *Federal Art and National Culture: The Politics of Identity in New Deal America* (1995). Both Barbara Melosh, *Engendering Culture: Manhood and Womanhood in New Deal Public Art and Theater* (1991) and Marlene Park and Gerald E. Markowitz, *Democratic Vistas: Post Offices and Public Art in the New Deal* (1984) offer provocative analyses of government-sponsored murals and paintings.

Depression documentary photography has attracted considerable attention. Leading studies include William Stott, *Documentary Expression in Thirties America* (1986); Colleen McDannell, *Picturing Faith: Photography and the Great Depression* (2004); and segments of Maren Stange, *Symbols of Ideal Life: Social Documentary Photography in America, 1890–1950* (1989). For the photographic projects of the Farm Security Administration, see James Curtis, *Mind's Eye, Mind's Truth: F.S.A. Photography Reconsidered* (1989) and the samples in Carl Fleischhauer and Beverly W. Brannans, eds., *Documentary America, 1935–1943* (1988). Individual photographers elicit consideration in Vicki Goldberg, *Margaret Bourke-White: A Biography* (1986); Milton Meltzer, *Dorothea Lange: A Photographer's Life* (1978); and Belinda Rathbone, *Walker Evans: A Biography* (1995). For Evans' most noted prose collaborator, see Victor A. Kramer, *James Agee* (1975).

6

Blue Horizons:
Popular Culture as
Great Depression Savior

"A word that's soft and gentle makes it easier to bear." So went the lyric to "Try a Little Tenderness" (1932), a Tin Pan Alley favorite of the early Depression. As much as New Deal reformers, political activists, and creative artists sought to address the suffering induced by the economic collapse, their efforts did not always penetrate beyond their own constituencies. Popular cultural forms were far more likely to impact the consciousness of ordinary Americans. Detective stories provided a venue for progressives and other literary figures to convert the vernacular phrasing of the proletarian novel into more accessible and commercial forms. Cartoon strips and comic books offered coded messages about survival in hard times. African American blues, black swing, and white country music provided fans with tools for successful life strategies or opportunities to forget the daily grind. The same emphases on survival and transcendence marked the contributions of Tin Pan Alley and the Broadway musical theater. Yet the primary role of Depression healer fell to the motion picture industry through emotionally laden films infused with comedy, musical themes, social realism, political drama, and human interest.

PULP FICTION

Left-wing essayists of the 1930s often took a condescending view toward mass culture. Literary critic Edmund Wilson, for example, despised detective stories as rubbish and a waste of time. Yet writers like Dashiell Hammett and Raymond Chandler used the genre for pungent social commentary. Pulp magazines such as *Black Mask* provided the initial venue for detective fiction. Descended from the dime novels, the cheaply produced pulps compensated for poor advertising revenues with huge circulations — an estimated total of ten million between 1918 and 1941. Since contributors were paid by the word, they normally saw themselves as producing a commodity instead of a literary creation. Indeed, few pulp writers could claim a college education. Mainly male subscribers usually came from working-class backgrounds and often were immigrants. Surveys showed that more than half the pulp readers of the 1930s had only a grade-school education, and only a sixth had been to college. Ads for correspondence schools, job training, and self-improvement for speech, manners, and dress emphasized the class orientation of the customer base.

Magazine detective tales conveyed details from everyday life, colloquial speech, and hostility to authority and social decorum. Authors communicated in what Raymond Chandler called "American language." Rebelling against the popularity of British women's mysteries and the nuances of emotion, private life, and domesticity, the male-oriented pulps conferred the dignity of print on the discourse and experiences of ordinary people. Detective fiction invoked cities overrun by criminal gangs, underworld slang, and murder mysteries defying rational deduction or logical calculation. Stories usually took the form of a series of linked episodes instead of a coherent narrative, a fragmented approach that may have appealed to readers used to specialized work tasks. American writers preferred action-packed scenes replete with violence, heavy drinking, and tough talk. The terse language and taciturn dialogue that gave the genre its identity helped to shape realistic characters defined by a code of manliness, autonomy, and honor. Unpretentious and direct, lower-middle-class detective heroes inhabited shabby offices and refused bribes that hindered their freedom of action or compromised their principles.

The terse, skeptical tone of detective fiction often was associated with Dashiell Hammett. A Maryland native, Hammett left home at the age of thirteen to work his way across the country. He spent most of the 1920s as a private detective, an experience that provided intimate knowledge of both criminals and the police. Hammett began his literary career as a comic strip writer and contributor to *Black Mask,* the pulp in which his first book, *Red Harvest* (1929), was originally serialized. Set in the violent labor confrontations and class politics of the Wild West, the novel demonstrated a skill for vernacular prose that stripped literary language of all affectation. Hammett's hard-bitten protagonists were not always virtuous, but their pragmatic worldview offered a perfect foil for exposing the hypocrisies and naiveté of middle-class culture. Most important, his realistic plots and characterizations explained exactly why people murdered.

In *The Maltese Falcon* (1930), Hammett introduced Sam Spade, a tough but romantic "private eye" with a code of loyalty and honor. Seeking justice for the murder of his

Dashiell Hammett

partner, Spade surrenders the woman he loves to police. "I'll have some rotten nights," he tells her, "but that'll pass …I won't play the sap for you." The ironic ending to the plot suggested a world founded upon a void. Hammett's next book, *The Glass Key* (1931), implied that society's pervasive corruption and crime were symptoms of systemic problems beyond the reach of liberal humanism or well-intentioned individuals.

A similar pessimism underlay the work of Raymond Thornton Chandler. Born in Chicago in 1888, Chandler spent his youth in England before returning to the United States. He began writing short stories for *Black Mask* in 1933, when he lost his job as a California oil company executive. *The Big Sleep* (1939) introduced Los Angeles detective hero Philip Marlowe. Searching for a missing person, Marlowe negotiates his way through a nefarious underworld of blackmail, drug addiction, and murder amid southern California's gangsters, corrupt police, and wealthy parasites.

The unsentimental realism and hard-bitten approach of Depression-era detective fiction presented Los Angeles as the nightmare at the end of American history—an urban hell instead of a golden land of opportunity. James M. Cain captured such disillusionment in *The Postman Always Rings Twice* (1934) and *Double Indemnity* (1936). The first novel told the story of a drifter whose affair with a café proprietor's sexy but greedy wife leads to the murder of her older husband and the protagonist's undoing. *Double Indemnity* portrayed a scruffy insurance salesman whose sexual fixation plays into the hands of an alluring wife who wants to kill her wealthy husband for the hefty pay-off on his policy. L.A.'s cozy-looking bungalows, suggested Cain, hid the tragic consequences of unscrupulous Depression marriages of convenience between ambitious young working-class women and older men desperate for love or the pride of possession.

COMIC HEROES, SUPERMEN, AND CARTOON ANTICS

Hard-boiled mysteries made it into the comic strips in 1931 with the inauguration of Chester Gould's realistically drawn *Dick Tracy,* the serialized story of a populist police detective who hounds gangsters when the top brass and politicians are helpless. Although adventure series like *Buck Rogers* (1929+), *Tarzan* (1929+), and *Flash Gordon* (1933+) captivated large numbers of readers, comedies and domestic sagas continued to dominate the comic pages. Readers delighted in following the everyday experiences of semi-respectable but vulnerable blue-collar or middle-class citizens like Caspar Milquetoast or Boob McNutt, who appeared overwhelmed by everything in their mundane environment. Chic Young's *Blondie* (1930+) switched the action to the suburbs, where hen-pecked husband and incompetent office worker Dagwood Bumstead repeatedly served as the unfortunate fall guy. Meanwhile, the successful *Barney Google* strip turned its attention to the hillbilly couple Snuffy and Loweezy Smith. While Snuffy's wife did all the work, her no-account husband slept, played poker, made moonshine, and coined colloquial verbal gems such as "the heebie-jeebies," "fiddlin' around," and "times a-wastin'."

Two of the era's most lasting strips were *Popeye the Sailor,* first appearing in *The Thimble Theater* in 1929, and *L'il Abner,* which debuted in 1934. *Popeye* presented a working-class superman whose strength came from the consumption of spinach. Yet the strip's hero was continually humanized by his hilarious attempts to escape Olive Oyl's marriage plans. *Li'l Abner* was the work of Al Capp. Born Alfred Gerald Caplin in New Haven, Capp studied at several art schools before becoming a comic strip artist in 1932. After drawing working-class characters for Ham Fisher's *Joe Palooka*, he got the idea of creating a series about hillbillies. *Li'l Abner,* the cartoon's title character, was the sweetheart of the buxom and hour-glass figured Daisy Mae and the son of the invincible matriarch, Mammy Yokum, whose husband Pappy was only interested in food. The secret to Capp's success lay in placing his characters in melodramatic situations and allowing them to solve problems in their own way. He also went out of his way to parody business tycoons, politicians, gangsters, self-professed experts, and the upper class. Even Dick Tracy came in for lampooning through the character of detective Fearless Fosdick.

Encouraged in the early 1930s by the massive popularity of the comics, pulp magazine houses began to issue collected reprints of favorite strips. By the end of the decade, several publishers had come upon the idea of incorporating original story lines into their publications. Among the first to do so were *Detective Comics* (1937+) and *Donald Duck* (1938+). The latter employed the "fall guy" motif for its title character—the poor, unlucky nephew of rich Uncle Scrooge forced to rely on ingenuity in overcoming a host of obstacles, only to have his minor triumphs lead to further setbacks.

The greatest success story of the genre was achieved by DC Comics, which began to feature the Superman character in its *Action Comics* series in 1938. *Superman* was the creation of writer Jerry Siegel and illustrator Joe Shuster, two lower-middle-class Jews from immigrant families in Cleveland. Siegel's father had been shot to death in a robbery at his clothing store months after the stockmarket crash. As shy and spectacled teens, the two friends were among many Depression young men who harbored covert fantasies of power, success, and justice.

After conceiving Superman as a hard-boiled detective, Siegel and Shuster transformed the character into an exile of the doomed planet Krypton, a man of steel with x-ray eyes who could fly faster than the speed of light. The alter ego of mild-mannered reporter Clark Kent, the noble and gentle hero defended the weak and oppressed and resolved the problems of the urban jungle. In his initial appearance, Superman liberated a falsely accused prisoner from a lynch mob, helped to free an innocent woman from Death Row, and rescued a wife about to be beaten by her husband. The second issue had him expose a cabal of politicians and munitions makers seeking to embroil the nation in a Latin American war. Other episodes included a confrontation with a mine owner who refused to adopt proper safety measures and a battle with corrupt and incompetent city officials over slum tenements. Although Siegel's story line required a leap of faith, toughened Depression readers could accept the feature's premises because of its sense of humor and intentional excesses. One of the first popular culture products to be directed at the youth market, the bimonthly pulp amassed an average readership of 1.3 million.

Walt Disney's animated films provided the widest exposure of Depression-era graphic arts. Born in Chicago but raised on a Missouri farm, Disney began making crude cartoon features in Kansas City in the early 1920s. Moving to Hollywood, he created an independent production company that benefited from a team of highly talented artists. *Steamboat Willie* (1928) and *Plane Crazy* (1928) pioneered the use of sound in animated shorts and introduced viewers to Mickey Mouse. By combining a sweet disposition with saucy impudence, Mickey embodied the common traits of the ordinary person, as did subsequent characters like Donald Duck, Pluto, and Goofy. As Franklin Roosevelt inaugurated the first one hundred days of the New Deal, Disney scored another hit with *Three Little Pigs* (1933), an animated allegory of resourcefulness in a time of crisis.

RADIO DAYS

In the same year as *Three Little Pigs* premiered in movie theaters, *The Lone Ranger* debuted on radio. Created by writer George W. Trendle, the enormously popular series featured the title character as the single survivor of a criminal gang's massacre of six

Texas rangers, including the hero's own brother. The ranger had been rescued with the help of Tonto, an Indian whose life had once been saved by the same man. The "lone ranger" and Tonto now team up to track down the murderers of the five officers and to battle all law-breakers. Taking a new name and donning a mask in disguise, the avenging officer mounts a white stallion named Silver and shoots silver bullets, although he only aims to wound or disarm, not kill.

Before the decade ended, 86 percent of the nation's homes had a radio receiver. The impact of wireless communication was evident by the fact that 70 percent of Americans reported in the late 1930s that radio provided their prime source of news. Polls indicated that low-income listeners were the medium's most avid fans. Radio exerted a direct impact on people's lives through its presence in their living rooms. By providing intimate contact with popular performers from vaudeville, musical comedy, and film, it helped to alleviate the chaotic insecurity of the economic collapse and introduce an element of regularity into the daily routine. Like the popular culture forms that preceded it, broadcasting played a role in sensitizing Americans to the nation's ethnic diversity and suggesting the prospect of national cohesion.

Among the first popular radio personalities were two white men pretending to be African American. Charles Correll, who was born in Peoria, Illinois, was of Scots-Irish background and had family roots in the Deep South. As a boy, he had served as an usher in a vaudeville theater. He later worked as a bricklayer, stenographer, and director of Iowa amateur minstrel shows. Freeman Gosden was from a middle-class Richmond, Virginia, family, but his father had died when the boy was twelve and his mother and sister were killed in an auto accident before he reached eighteen. After serving in the Navy in World War I, Gosden also directed amateur minstrel extravaganzas. He and Correll met on the blackface circuit in 1920, and both subsequently moved to the Chicago headquarters of their production company. They soon began a radio career as a singing duo and staged a popular musical theater revue called *Red Hot* (1925) infused with blues and jazz styles. As Correll and Gosden began to insert humorous banter and black stage dialect between their on-the-air musical numbers, they were approached about a serial drama and came up with the idea of basing it on two African American characters.

Sam 'n' Henry debuted on a Chicago radio station in 1926. Its ten-minute segments came on the air six nights a week at 7 p.m. The show presented the adventures of two recent migrants from Alabama: the hard-working and sentimental Sam and the lazy, pretentious, and domineering Henry. Exploited by sharp city folk, the two men find work at a construction site and meatpacking plant and share a room in a South Side boarding house. With the use of a rickety, horse-drawn wagon, however, they open a traveling barber service. Two years after the program began, Correll and Gosden moved to a rival radio station and fashioned the characters of Amos and Andy, two Atlanta émigrés who operated a Chicago taxi business with a roofless jalopy. Ten weeks before the 1929 stockmarket crash, the show premiered on the NBC radio network in a fifteen-minute live broadcast. Reset in Harlem, the program would run five or six nights a week for the next fourteen years and reach a peak audience of forty million listeners.

Taking over Henry's shallow vanity, Andy now came off as something of a minstrel caricature. Unscrupulous, superstitious, ignorant, greedy, shiftless, and incessantly talkative, he vainly sought the respect befitting his title as Kingfish of the Mystic Knights of the Sea fraternal order. Amos, in contrast, occasionally sounded like the docile, slow-witted, and gullible buffoons of blackface tradition. Yet *Amos 'n' Andy* also transcended predictable stereotypes. In portraying the Great Migration in intimate detail, the series humanized its characters and touched on universal themes. Like other Americans on the move, Amos and Andy looked to improving their economic condition, worried about the unknown, expressed reluctance about leaving friends and home, and became confused by the adjustments of big-city life. Realistic story lines involved responses to everyday crises of illness, failure, potential destitution, or separation that were understandable to all listeners. Through Amos, audiences could be moved by a black entrepreneur's self-respecting attempts to succeed despite the Depression. The character's commitment to a marriage of mutual respect and devotion further defied racist premises.

Although Andy was often the butt of the show's humor, his ill-conceived get-rich-quick schemes could be taken as a parody of contemporary business practices, lodge association scams, or unreliable political panaceas. In one memorable episode, the Kingfish professed to enlighten Amos about socialists, who put everyone on the "same basin" in the "social-risk" party. If he had no money, explained Andy, and Amos had four dollars and gave him two, his partner could then be a "social-risk." Amos answered that he'd better go back to the Democrats. The open-ended nature of *Amos 'n' Andy* undoubtedly contributed to the show's enormous African American following, whether among middle-class blacks laughing at those beneath them, working-class listeners joining in the fun, or members of both groups given to their own interpretations of episodes. Black leaders disagreed as to whether the series was racially demeaning or spoke to a universal human dignity. Attempting to drive *Amos 'n' Andy* off the air, a petition drive by the African American *Pittsburgh Courier* netted over 740,000 signatures, but such efforts proved fruitless in the face of the program's widespread popularity.

The radio commentary of Will Rogers provided another balm for Depression anxiety. On-stage experience had taught Rogers that humor had to have some truth to be funny, and that ideas were best communicated when they sounded casual and off-handed. "Here a few years ago," he began in one of the twelve radio talks he delivered in 1930, "we were so afraid that the poor people was liable to take a drink that now we've fixed it so that they can't even get something to eat." The Depression, he remarked the following year, had been brought on by "the big boys," not "the working classes." President Herbert Hoover's passivity in confronting the emergency, he said, had resulted in nothing but "the rich always getting richer, and the poor always getting poorer." In 1933 Rogers turned over proceeds from seven radio broadcasts to Red Cross and Salvation Army funds for the unemployed. Yet he refused to support Upton Sinclair's anti-poverty campaign for the California governorship. "I tell you folks," he told a radio audience in 1934, "all politics is applesauce." It was not surprising that Damon Runyon referred to the former rope twirler as "America's most complete human document."

Radio listeners were extremely loyal to star performers. The urban counterpart to Will Rogers was fellow vaudevillian Eddie Cantor. In 1931 Cantor became host of the popular Chase and Sanborn variety show. Casting himself as a "man of the people," the entertainer pretended to be running for president. He also struck an intimacy with audiences by talking about his family and working life. In the "Night Court" segment of the show, Cantor acted as a judge given to absurd pronouncements and sly commentaries. As the Depression deepened, however, the cases increasingly concerned poverty or personal tragedy. One episode involved a forty-six-year-old unemployed breadwinner who had attempted suicide. Cantor responded that men in their forties had become business leaders and great artists, and that no one should give his family another burden by killing himself. Never past the fear that he might be discovered as a fake and asked to return his wealth, Cantor retained a lasting identification with the poor and downtrodden.

The Goldbergs (1929+) tied the theme of survival to working-class Jews on the Lower East Side. The radio series was conceived by Columbia-educated Gertrude Berg, who had mastered the use of dialect humor in vaudeville. Seeking to overcome anti-Semitic stereotypes. Berg came up with the idea of presenting a loving Jewish family whose material ambitions did not threaten its spiritual identity. The series focused on the interactions of family matriarch Molly, the financial plight of her husband Jake, romantic mix-ups among the younger Goldbergs, and ethical issues like offering false impressions to prospective business clients. Sunday evening's *Jack Benny Show* (1932+) offered a more unusual family format. Cast as a successful but penny-pinching entertainer, Benny was willing to do anything for money, including being a dogcatcher, waiting tables, picking fruit, playing violin, or taking in boarders. Rendered powerless by artifacts of the modern world such as department stores or mass transit, he stored his money in a sock rather than trust banks. In the final absurdity, Benny's saucy and independent black valet, Rochester, ran his employer's life and got the best of all interactions between the two.

By 1940 the majority of broadcast programming was devoted to the soap opera. As women became a target of daytime radio advertisers in the early 1930s, serial dramas increasingly addressed the family experiences of everyday people, defined as members of the broad white middle class. "This is *your* story—this is *you*," the announcer for *Rosemary* declared at the start of each show. The episodic plots of series like *Helen Trent* had no beginnings or endings, thereby resembling the interpersonal dealings of normal life. Story lines suggested that it was possible to prevail over adversity, but that suffering was an inherent part of life over which there was no ultimate triumph. In this respect the serials took on qualities of oral folklore or even the blues. Through its dramatic role models, daytime radio offered examples of courage designed to inspire listeners to deal with their own life crises. In the sharing of troubles and partial solutions, the Depression soap opera helped to foster a sense of community amid lingering uncertainties.

COUNTRY MUSIC AND THE BLUES

The psychological burden of hard times often compelled people to turn to popular forms of musical expression for reassurance. In San Antonio, Los Angeles, and other southwestern cities, Mexican Americans flocked to large ballrooms to dance to urbane ethnic orchestras. In contrast, Hispanic agricultural workers in south and central Texas were more likely to attend events where they could dance to *conjunto* (Tex-Mex), a musical style featuring a lead accordion and a twelve-string rhythm guitar, bass, and drums. Working-class bandleaders like the self-taught Mexican native Narcisco Martinez popularized the *conjunto* by setting Spanish-language verses to the tempo of German and Czech polkas, waltzes, and schottisches. In Los Angeles, Stockton, and other California venues, meanwhile, single Filipino men sought relief from long hours of farm labor by attending Saturday night dances that featured traditional music from the homeland.

Country music fulfilled similar needs for the white working class. Through radio, recordings, and the movies, rural harmonies found new adherents beyond their original strongholds. Nevertheless, traditional styling remained an important part of the country mix. Oklahoma's Albert E. Brumley demonstrated the persistence of gospel themes with "I'll Fly Away" (1931), a major hit that hinted at release from present-day troubles. The Carter Family continued to produce inspirational music with classics such as "Keep on the Sunny Side" and "Will the Circle Be Unbroken" (1935). Other popular performers included country fiddler Dr. Humphrey Bate and vocalist Roy Acuff, who began hosting the Grand Ole Opry in 1938. Acuff's mournful mountain style of singing was perfectly suited to the plaintive tales of death and sorrow dominating his repertoire.

Despite the popularity of traditional gospel and mountain forms, western music cast a major influence on Depression-era country styling. During hard times, plain spoken and simply dressed cowboy heroes provided a reassuring symbol of inspiration and endurance. Gene Autry, a former Texas telegraph operator and Oklahoma radio host, won public acclaim for his hit recording of "That Silver-Haired Daddy of Mine" (1931). Billed as "the Singing Cowboy," Autry moved on to Hollywood to make musical westerns such as *Tumbling Tumbleweeds* (1935) and *Boots and Saddle* (1937). These films romanticized western settlers and ranchers as shy and congenial men of the highest morality who corralled evildoers in between musical numbers. Roy Rogers, a native of Duck Run, Ohio, with the given name of Leonard Slye, rose to fame as one of the three harmonizing Sons of the Pioneers before going on to portray clean-cut singing cowboys in movies like *Under Western Stars* (1938).

Western singer Patsy Montana provided the female counterpart to the mythic cowboy. The only girl among eleven children raised on a farm near Hope, Arkansas, Montana arrived in Chicago without means of support in 1930. In the next several years, she drifted from one country music ensemble to another—singing with the Montana Cowgirls in Los Angeles and then joining a country string jazz band that performed on the radio in Shreveport, Louisiana, and Chicago. Montana's big break came with the recording of "I Want to Be a Cowboy's Sweetheart" (1935), a lively polka that appealed to European ethnics as well as fans of western music. The record became the first million-selling disc by a female country music performer and helped to popularize western swing. Additional Montana songs described the thrills of roping cattle and riding the range with a companion cowboy.

Like country music, the blues continued to appeal to a working-class audience. Despite the pressures of the economic collapse, the Great Migration had facilitated the spread of a nation-wide African American popular culture. Through successful black recording artists such as Blind Lemon Jefferson, Peetie Wheatstraw, Kokomo Arnold, and Leroy Carr and Scrapper Blackwell, the blues remained an essential part of the cultural mix. Interaction among regional performing styles was most evident in the work of the relatively unknown Robert Johnson. His mother's eleventh child, Johnson was born out of wedlock in 1911 near Jackson, Mississippi. After turning seven, he moved with his family to the Mississippi Delta region, where he began toying with musical instruments. The first beat-up guitar he owned had two strings missing. Although Johnson married at nineteen, his young wife died in childbirth and he soon took to the road. After seven years playing jukebox joints and house parties as an itinerant musician, he received an invitation to record with a national label in San Antonio.

Johnson spent five days in late 1936 and early 1937 cutting twenty-nine songs. Vocalizing in a high, ghostly voice and improvising complex melodic lines with a rhythmic backing on guitar, he produced a series of original compositions that would take their place among the great blues classics. "Terraplane Blues," his first release, mobilized several sexual metaphors to express a profound sense of longing, as did seductive numbers like "Come On in My Kitchen" and "Kind Hearted Woman Blues." "Love in Vain" intimately conveyed the pain of emotional loss, while "Hell Hound on My Trail" confronted the lurking presence of evil with chilling detail. Meanwhile, up-tempo selections like "Sweet Home Chicago" and "I Believe I'll Dust My Broom" featured the driving boogie beat that would define urban black music long after Johnson's death from poisoning in 1938 at the hand of a club owner jealous over a suspected liaison between the performer and his wife.

SWING TIME

"It don't mean a thing if it ain't got that swing," the lyric to a Duke Ellington tune announced in 1932. The blues-based form of jazz known as swing dominated African American nightlife during the Depression decade. Swing had originated in the 1920s with the hot dance music performed at Harlem's Roseland Ballroom by the Fletcher Henderson Orchestra. Henderson's arrangements featured four brass and three reed instruments whose short, repeated refrains or "riffs" provided the response to improvisations by free-style soloists like Louis Armstrong. The lilting but primitive rhythmic drive of the horns, "walking" bass, guitar, piano, and drums gave swing music its distinctive feel and name. Its foremost interpreter and composer was Edward Kennedy "Duke" Ellington. Born in Washington, D.C. in 1899, Ellington took piano lessons as a teen, worked odd jobs, and played small nightclubs. After forming the Washingtonians in 1918, he brought the group to New York, performed in a number of Harlem and midtown jazz spots, and established the band as the reigning musical force of the Cotton Club between 1927 and 1932.

Through recordings, radio broadcasts, and movie shorts like *Black and Tan* (1929), Ellington's twelve-piece orchestra brought acceptance of swing among whites as well as blacks. The growling horns and elaborate rhythm section of the Ellington sound became the hallmark of hit dance numbers like "The Mooche," (1928), "Mood Indigo" (1930), "Rockin' In Rhythm" (1931), and "Sophisticated Lady" (1933). Another Cotton Club bandleader, Cab Calloway, popularized the "jitterbug," an updated "lindy hop" executed with syncopated swings and turns. At Harlem's Savoy Ballroom, where the Chick Webb Band held uncontested supremacy, local gangs sought prestige in fiercely contested dance competitions. Once Webb hired eighteen-year-old Ella Fitzgerald as the band's lead singer, she became the swing era's top female vocalist. Jazz assumed a more experimental tone in the after-hours jam sessions of Harlem's small clubs, cafes, and Sunday breakfast dances. Meanwhile, pianist Bill "Count" Basie organized a band featuring drummer Jo Jones and tenor sax player Lester Young whose hard-driving blues, fast-moving riffs, and subtle accompaniment became synonymous with swing.

One of Basie's featured vocalists was Billie Holiday. Born Eleanora Fagan in Philadelphia in 1915, the singer grew up in impoverished surroundings in Baltimore, where her mother, a domestic servant, waitress, and factory worker, was abandoned by her musician husband. After a stint in reform school and several jobs scrubbing brothel floors, Holiday accompanied her mother to Harlem in 1929. Influenced at a young age by Bessie Smith's feeling and Louis Armstrong's style, she began singing in speakeasies and nightclubs. Holiday's vocal improvisations emulated the timbre, fluidity, and phrasings of a jazz horn. Recording with Benny Goodman, Teddy Wilson, Lester Young, and others for the black jukebox market, she covered Tin Pan Alley standards like "What a Little Moonlight Can Do" (1935), "I Cried for You" (1936), "Summertime" (1936), "A Fine Romance" (1936), and "He's Funny That Way" (1937) with complete originality.

In 1939 the twenty-three-year-old Holiday began appearing at New York's Café Society, a gathering spot for left-wing artists and intellectuals and one of the first racially integrated nightclubs in the city. Normally derisive of political ideology, the vocalist believed that popular music offered more room for artistic individuality than blues or folk. Indeed, many of her songs dealt with universal laments of desire and betrayals of love. At the same time, Holiday had sufficient experience with racial discrimination to identify herself as a "race woman." Therefore, when Popular Front poet Lewis Allan presented her with a stark anti-lynching poem entitled "Strange Fruit," she agreed after some hesitation to help set the lyric to music. The European-style cabaret number became the performer's signature act and an audience favorite. Holiday also recorded "God Bless the Child" (1941), a song for which she had written the words. "Yes, the strong gets more, while the weak ones fade," the verse stated with working-class realism, "empty pockets don't ever make the grade." "Money had lots o' friends, crowdin' 'round the door," she sang, but when it was gone "and spendin' ends, they don't come no more."

Swing entered the national spotlight when the Benny Goodman Orchestra performed at the Palomar Ballroom in Los Angeles in 1935. A clarinet child prodigy from a working-class Jewish family in Chicago, Goodman barely survived as a free-lance jazz musician before 1934, when he formed a dance band that included drummer Gene Krupa and black pianist Teddy Wilson. Using Fletcher Henderson arrangements, Goodman directed entire musical sections to improvise off the clear melodic beat. As the stars of "Let's Dance," a weekly network radio show, the band went on tour in 1935, only to find audiences unfamiliar with the up-tempo rhythms of their late-night radio broadcasts. In California, however, where a thriving African American swing scene held sway, "Let's Dance" came on the air three hours earlier than back East, and a mix of "bobby-soxers," "jitterbugs," and people of varying social backgrounds were already devoted fans.

Soon billed as the "King of Swing," Goodman presented the first jazz versions of Tin Pan Alley hits for audiences who preferred to move to the music rather than merely listen. In a 1937 concert before twenty thousand people at New York's Paramount Theater, euphoric patrons danced in the aisles. The next year twenty-three thousand fans attended New York's Carnival of Swing, where twenty-five bands performed for six hours. The big band sound received additional exposure when producer John Hammond organized "From Spirituals to Swing" (1938), a Carnegie Hall extravaganza that traced the evolution of black music from its origins to the latest jazz forms. Religious traditionalists alleged that the primitive rhythms, jarring harmonies, and sensual appeal of the fad were leading to a breakdown of moral discipline among the young. By

Billie Holiday

the end of the decade, however, white bandleaders like Jimmy Dorsey, Tommy Dorsey, and Glen Miller had joined Goodman, Ellington, and Basie as the leading representatives of swing, and the music had become the dominant expression of American popular culture.

PENNIES FROM HEAVEN

"Once I built a railroad, made it run, made it race against time," began the words of "Brother, Can You Spare a Dime? (1932), Yip Harburg's penetrating comment on the human impact of the Great Depression. Assuming the persona of a World War I veteran reduced to panhandling, the narrator recalled the experience of "sloggin' thru Hell" as a soldier. "Say, don't you remember," he pleaded, "they called me Al/it was Al all the time." "Say, don't you remember," he repeated, "I'm your pal!" Written for *Americana,* a Broadway satirical revue based on Franklin Roosevelt's rhetorical invocation of the "Forgotten Man," the song described the bitter plight of an ordinary citizen who had dutifully pursued the American Dream and been cast aside to fend for himself.

Although Harburg's stark lyrics provided a graphic example of Depression social consciousness, they did not typify most Tin Pan Alley creations of the period. Seeking to recover from declining record sales and the competition of radio's live orchestra broadcasts, the recording industry increasingly turned to advanced microphone technologies to produce a more intimate sound that personalized the role of vocal soloists. By the end of the decade, budget-conscious radio stations had begun to hire disc jockeys to play recorded music for a broad audience. As a result, popular songs of the Depression often contained an appealing mix of romantic fantasy, escape, and hope while infrequent references to hard times were normally oblique and light-hearted.

"How can you lose what you've never owned?" asked the lyric to "Life Is Just a Bowl of Cherries" (1931), a flippant Broadway revue number that became a popular favorite. Life was "delirious," advised the song, "don't take it serious." A similar sentiment pervaded Yip Harburg and Billy Rose's carefree "It's Only a Paper Moon" (1933). More frequently, popular songs had fun with Depression settings. "Potatoes are cheaper, tomatoes are cheaper," declared the words to "Now's the Time to Fall in Love" (1931), a comical ditty introduced on Eddie Cantor's radio show. Herman Hupfield's "Let's Put Out the Lights" (1932) described the plight of a Depression couple with "no more money in the bank" and nothing to do but go to sleep. "I Found a Million Dollar Baby—In a Five and Ten Cent Store" (1931), a number from a Billy Rose Broadway revue, celebrated the wonders to be found in the most ordinary places. In "Nice Work If You Can Get It" (1937), a selection from the film *Damsels in Distress,* Ira Gershwin cleverly translated one of the most common expressions of the times into a love song about life's simple pleasures.

Popular songwriters preferred to express inspirational themes in metaphoric terms, as in "Beyond the Blue Horizon" (1930), a Leo Robin lyric from the film *Monte Carlo.* In a jaunty number from a 1930 Broadway revue, Dorothy Fields turned slang phrasing toward Depression optimism. "If I never have a cent," the song's narrator boasted, "I'll be rich as Rockefeller,/Gold dust at my feet,/On the sunny side of the street." "Try a Little Tenderness" (1932) commiserated with a common plight of the economic crisis. "You know she's waiting, just anticipating,/Things she may never possess," the lyric advised anxious husbands, "While she's without them, try a little tenderness." "Pennies from Heaven" (1936), a song from a movie of the same name, reminded listeners that "If you want the things you love, you must have showers." Perhaps the most eloquent expression of Depression fortitude came in Yip Harburg's "Over the Rainbow," a piece written for Judy Garland in *The Wizard of Oz* (1939). Envisioning a place "where skies are blue" and "where troubles melt like lemon-drops," Garland sought to be where "the dreams that you dare to dream really do come true."

Tin Pan Alley songwriters like Lorenz Hart could not be confined by the conventions of inspirational verse. Indeed, Hart never abandoned his interest in mocking sentimental verse. In "Ten Cents a Dance" (1930), a number performed by Ruth Etting in Broadway's *Simple Simon,* the lyricist depicted a weary and cynical taxi-dancer with uncompromising honesty. Following an unsuccessful stint in Hollywood, Hart and

Richard Rodgers returned to the musical theater with *Babes in Arms* (1937), a revue about a group of young people who resist participation in a New Deal youth project by putting on their own stage production. *Babes'* cast of unknowns, including four African American tap-dancers, sought to mirror the ethnic and class diversity of the fictional community's young rebels. The show's love song, the lyrical "My Funny Valentine," sustained the cheerful but iconoclastic tone with a less-than-ideal description of a lover with a "figure less than Greek" and a "mouth a little weak."

Songwriters like lyricist Ted Koehler and composer Harold Arlen found an inspiration for emotional realism in African American music. The son of a Jewish cantor, Arlen had been a jazz musician before he and Koehler joined forces at the Cotton Club in the early Thirties. The duo's first hit, "I Gotta Right to Sing the Blues" (1932), was followed by "Stormy Weather" (1933), a number popularized by Ethel Waters. "Don't know why/there's no sun up in the sky," sang Waters, "Stormy weather,/Just can't get my poor self together." An even more ambitious expropriation of black culture appeared in George Gershwin's folk opera *Porgy and Bess* (1935). Eighty years earlier Walt Whitman had predicted that Negro dialect would someday be the basis of a new English language and musical tradition that would produce "a native grand opera." After black performers appeared on Broadway in Marc Connelly's *Green Pastures* (1930), Hall Johnson's *Run, Little Chillun'* (1933), and a revival of *Show Boat* with Paul Robeson, New York's Theater Guild offered to produce a musical version of *Porgy*, a 1925 novel by white South Carolinian DuBose Heyward adopted as a stage drama two years later.

Written in vernacular verse, *Porgy* was set among the Gullah people of the Carolina coast. Excited about composing a folk opera based on the expression "of the people," George Gershwin set out for the Sea Islands in 1934 to absorb the local culture. Gershwin even joined a Gullah "shout" revival on one occasion, to the delight of the participants. Always willing to acknowledge his debt to Negro musical tradition, the composer limited the opera's singing parts to its black characters. He also insisted that only African Americans play these roles, although he had to teach northern black performers to affect a southern dialect. About a third of the work's lyrics, including moving odes like "Summertime," "My Man's Gone Now," and "I Loves You, Porgy," were directly taken from Heyward's poetry, although Ira Gershwin had to be called in to enhance the musicality of particular lines. Ira also wrote complete sets of lyrics for "I Got Plenty of Nuttin'," "It Ain't Necessarily So," and "There's a Boat Dat's Leavin' Soon for New York," three of the light-hearted and irreverent numbers that offset the production's prevailing solemnity.

Porgy played to white stereotypes by contrasting the morally pure and physically maimed character of Porgy with the corrupt, materialistic, and overtly sexualized Sportin' Life. Indeed, the opera's use of rural black dialect proved offensive to northern artists like Duke Ellington, who condemned the work's "lampblack Negroisms." By combining operatic and popular forms, however, George Gershwin's inspired score allowed *Porgy's* protagonists to express the full power of their dignity, passion, and sense of tragedy, potentially fulfilling James W. Johnson's hope that dialect could be used for a complete range of emotion. Unprepared for the opera's fusion of philharmonic traditions and vernacular forms, audiences and critics gave the production mixed reviews, and the extravaganza was a financial flop. Nevertheless, by treating African American culture simultaneously as a subject of high art and a source of lyrical vitality, *Porgy and Bess* would exert an incalculable impact on American popular song, jazz, and concert music.

HARD-TIME COMEDY

By the early 1930s, Hollywood had learned to market westerns, horror films, adventure stories, crime dramas, comedies, musicals, and other features that appealed to particular tastes. Yet since the advent of sound coincided with the impact of the stock market crash, the industry struggled to offset falling box office receipts. Even when attendance recovered, Depression audiences tended to be less affluent than in the past, leading to double-bills and the distribution of free china and gifts as added inducements to patronage. Exhibitors also reported that Thirties audiences had little tolerance for the "Broadway English" of arty stars who came off well in silent features but sounded as if they were snooty or aloof when speaking with upper-class diction.

Preferring folksy personalities, early Depression theatergoers chose Will Rogers as their favorite male movie star. Rogers had begun his sound career with *They Had to See Paris* (1929) and an adaptation of Mark Twain's *A Connecticut Yankee* (1931) in which he lassoed a Knight of the Round Table. In *State Fair* (1933) he once again delighted fans with his customary role as a quiet and ordinary man who stood up to bullies, liars, and hypocrites. One review of the movie commented that Rogers was "what Americans think other Americans are like." The former cowpuncher scored another hit in John Ford's *Judge Priest* (1934), when he portrayed a turn-of-the-century small-town Kentucky jurist who steps down from the bench to defend a local war hero.

As sound movies facilitated rapid-fire dialogue, comedies often took on a frenetic pace. No performers exploited this opportunity with greater success than the Marx Brothers. Raised in the slums of the Lower East Side, the four siblings moved from a musical vaudeville act to comedy, eventually establishing their reputation in the Broadway revue *Coconuts* (1925). The anarchic foursome displayed a manic brand of slapstick humor that poked fun at pretentious respectability, the upper classes, and social convention. Their early Hollywood hits, ultimately recognized as their best efforts, included *Animal Crackers* (1930), *Horse Feathers* (1932), and *Duck Soup* (1933), the latter a film in which Groucho gratuitously ruled the mythical principality of Freedonia. "If you think this country's bad off now," the wisecracking president announced to his subjects, "just wait till I get through with it." In the world of Marx Brothers comedy, there was no meaning to war, nationhood, patriotism, or anything but laughs.

Like Groucho, Harpo, Chico, and Zeppo, W.C. Fields had little respect for social pretensions. Fields' early sound pictures were remakes of old vaudeville routines and musical revue sketches. Set in the Arctic, Mack Sennett's *The Fatal Glass of Beer* (1933) parodied conventional melodrama. By the late Thirties, however, Fields had merged the roles of the knave and the fool. On one hand, he was the bulbous-nosed, raspy-voiced, transparent windbag who made his living as a swindler, confidence man, pool hustler, pitchman, card shark, petty chiseler, or snake-oil salesman. Yet he also played underdogs bullied by nagging wives, criticized by harping mothers-in-law, attacked by dogs, or out-maneuvered by babies. In classic comedies such as *You Can't Cheat an Honest Man* (1939), *My Little Chickadee* (1940), *The Bank Dick* (1940), and *Never Give a Sucker an Even Break* (1941), Fields satirized fraud and humbug while simultaneously using mock-genteel pronouncements, illiterate speech, cliché, and irrelevant patter to parody cultural affectation, formal social ceremony, and hypocrisy.

Mae West provided the perfect counterpart to Fields in *My Little Chickadee*. Born into a working-class family in Brooklyn in 1893, West performed as a child actor and formed her own vaudeville act at the age of nineteen. Addressing audiences with songs and patter infused with sexual innuendo, she assumed a tough and defiantly sensual demeanor that simultaneously made light of men's erotic fixations. "It isn't what you do; it how's you do it," she drawled at the close of every act. Featured in a Broadway show in 1917, West introduced audiences to the shimmy dances of Chicago's black jazz clubs. After several roles in Twenties revues, she opened her own play, *Sex* (1927), in New Haven, but was closed down and served a brief jail sentence for violating local censorship laws. The following year West wrote and starred in *Diamond Lil,* a Broadway production about a sultry underworld saloonkeeper of the 1890s that enjoyed a successful national tour.

"When I'm good I'm very, very good," the buxom vamp with platinum-blonde hair liked to purr with a roll of the eyes, "but when I'm bad I'm better." At she turned forty, West moved to Hollywood, where she synthesized traits and gestures from blues singers Ida Cox and Bessie Smith, silent screen star Clara Bow, and vaudeville queens Eva Tanguay and Sophie Tucker into a movie persona. West's screen roles embodied a mischievous scorn for formal occasions and an insistence on doing what she pleased. "Goodness!" a nightclub hat-checker exclaimed, as she admired Mae's diamonds in *Night After Night* (1932). "Honey," the star responded, "Goodness had nothing to do with it." While *She Done Him Wrong* (1933) offered a film version of *Diamond Lil, I'm No Angel* (1933) told the story of a lady lion tamer who became a Broadway star and exposed everyone surrounding her as hypocrites, prudes, or snobs. By 1935, the statuesque Hollywood comedienne was the highest paid woman in the United States.

Mae West   *(New York Public Library Archives)*

Depression realities provided the backdrop to the material-minded characters portrayed by Mae West. In *Gold Diggers of 1933*, a musical choreographed by Busby Berkeley, the chorus line opened with an ironic version of "We're in the Money." The movie centered on the efforts of the chorus-girl daughters of a mail carrier, saloonkeeper, and laundress to convince an "angel" to stage a new production after their show closes in rehearsal. Hollywood's most celebrated gold-digger was Jean Harlow. The daughter of a Kansas City dentist, Harlow was born Harlean Carpenter in 1911. Married at sixteen to a wealthy broker, she moved to Los Angeles, where she worked as a movie extra and in minor short comedy roles. After divorcing her husband and taking her mother's maiden name, Harlow was discovered by Howard Hughes, who cast her as the love interest in the aviation film *Hell's Angels* (1930). As the platinum-blonde siren in *Dinner at Eight* (1933), the star added a twist to the normal gold-digger role. Playing a hard-boiled and sharp-tongued former hat-checker, Harlow prevails upon her self-made tycoon spouse to release a benevolent shipping company owner from his financial clutches.

CITY BOYS

Cinema audiences also knew Jean Harlow from *The Public Enemy* (1931), one of three enormously popular crime dramas of the early Thirties. Shot in documentary style, gangster films like *Public Enemy* purported to depict the environment in which crime festered without glorifying the gangster. Yet by showing how prejudice discouraged working-class immigrants from achieving a share of the American Dream, and by demonstrating traits of toughness in overcoming Depression adversity, the genre gave voice to normally silenced features of American life. Hollywood gangsters all spoke in street vernacular. Their broken grammar and colorful accents reflected the common experiences of ordinary city people; their rage and bravado provided perspective on a society whose exclusionary tendencies appeared to violate its own democratic principles.

The first gangster talkie was *Little Caesar* (1930), a film drawn from a novel by W.R. Burnett, an author intent on producing a writing style "based on the American people spoke—not literary English." Portraying the world through the gangster's eyes, the movie told the story of Italian American crime operator Rico Bandello. Instead of trying to escape the slums, fight back against social injustice, achieve money or women, or best the law, Rico's sole aim was to "be somebody" and win social recognition. With Edward G. Robinson, a Lower East Side immigrant Jew with experience in the Yiddish stage and Broadway in the lead role, the film traced the criminal's ruthless rise from robbing small-town gas stations to big-city Prohibition kingpin. In the end Rico's vanity and quest for notoriety lead to his demise, and he dies in the gutter amid a hail of gunfire.

Public Enemy starred James Cagney. An Irish American Catholic from the Lower East Side, Cagney sold newspapers and shined shoes on city streets as a teenager. After successfully auditioning for a chorus boy slot in a downtown vaudeville act, he appeared in several Broadway revues. Cagney played small-time gangsters in minor roles in his first two movies, *Sinner's Holiday* (1930) and *Doorway to Hell* (1930). His nervous energy and cocky self-confidence suited *Public Enemy's* lead character, Tommy Powers, a figure based on a real-life Irish competitor of Chicago's Al Capone. The movie showed Powers and his best friend as Chicago slum kids who drift into a life of petty crime and move on to robbery. By the 1920s Tommy sees Prohibition and racketeering as a way to "make it" out of the ghetto. Hard work, he declares, is the same as "learning how to be poor" and making someone else rich. He also rejects love as "sappy" and treats mistress Jean Harlow accordingly. Viciously preying upon shopkeepers and outsmarting other gangs, the ruthless Powers rises to the top of the heap, only to be gunned down by rivals.

One year after triumphing in *Public Enemy*, Cagney appeared in *Taxi!* (1932), a film in which a group of independent drivers resist control by a criminal combine. That same year Paul Muni starred in *Scarface* (1932), a gangster movie directed by Howard Hawks and written by Ben Hecht. Born to Jewish immigrants on the Lower East Side in 1893, Hecht grew up in Racine, Wisconsin, where his parents ran a small woman's fashion business. After completing high school he moved to Chicago, where he worked as a newspaper photographer, crime reporter, and columnist. Publishing in the *Little*

Review, Hecht founded the *Chicago Literary Times* and collected his newspaper columns and sketches in *1001 Afternoons in Chicago* (1922), *Tales of the Chicago Streets* (1924), and *Broken Necks and Other Stories* (1924). Moving to New York, he joined Charles MacArthur in writing *Front Page* (1928), a Broadway play that recalled the cynical, wisecracking, and blasphemous police reporters he had known in his early days. Hecht also helped turn a story he had written about Al Capone into an Academy Award-winning screenplay for *Underworld* (1927), the silent film that inaugurated the gangster genre.

Scarface, another movie based on Capone's rise to power, came out of Hecht's experiences as a Chicago crime reporter and his familiarity with mobster and boxing figures in New York. The writer's hard-boiled prose was perfectly suited to depicting the intense gangland warfare associated with Prohibition. The film's protagonist, Tony Camonte, was played by Paul Muni, a Lower East Side immigrant seasoned in the Yiddish theater. Rising up through Chicago's gang hierarchy, Camonte declares that the town is "up for grabs." His machine gun, he boasts, is a "little typewriter ... I'm gonna write my name all over this town in big letters." The violence and somber shadings of *Scarface* were so pronounced that studio censors delayed its release until a final scene could be added in which civic activists delivered a moral diatribe on the evils of crime.

Through their involvement in bootlegging, the numbers racket, nightclubs, and gambling, Hollywood's gangsters reflected the new world of urban leisure. In *Manhattan Melodrama* (1934) Clark Gable portrayed "Blackie" Gallagher—a freewheeling Lower East Side racketeer who defies state control and socializes at boxing matches, ice-hockey rinks, and racetracks. With the installation in 1934 of the self-policing Production Code Administration (PCA), however, the motion picture industry imposed strict limitations on displays of sex, violence, and "immorality," leading to changes in the gangster genre. Films such as *G-Men* (1935), *Bullets or Ballots* (1936), and *Bordertown* (1936) were compelled to evade PCA regulations by turning criminal characters into lawful figures. *Bordertown* featured Paul Muni as a Los Angeles Chicano tough named Johnny Ramirez who goes to night school and becomes a defense lawyer for working-class Mexican Americans. Stymied by a powerful Anglo elite, he "makes it" by running a border gambling house. Still failing to win the acceptance of the Anglo establishment, however, he returns to the barrio to found a law school to protect the legal rights of his community.

Two African American gangster films followed similar moral conventions. Singer-dancer Ralph Cooper's *Dark Manhattan* (1937), the first black motion picture set in present-day Harlem, used contemporary fashions, urban slang, swing music, and a cast of ordinary people to convey its social realism. Cooper played a slum kid who emerges from "the jungle" to rise through the ranks of the crime syndicate by doing "whatever it takes." In the end, however, his greed and arrogance leads him to break with the other numbers racketeers, and he is brought down. In *Moon Over Harlem*

(1940), a populist gangster movie set in the city streets, a New Negro "race man" seeks to unite Harlem residents against the racketeers who have made their lives miserable.

TROUBLE IN PARADISE

The advent of sound enhanced the social realism of Hollywood productions. In one of the starkest portraits of trench warfare ever brought to the screen, *All Quiet on the Western Front* (1930) exposed viewers to the full brunt of hunger, lice, rats, smoke, endless bombardment, machine gun fire, and the chaos of battle. The film's cast of unknowns portrayed the helplessness of ordinary soldiers caught up in the brutality of World War I and the humanity of men on both sides facing slow death. *I Am a Fugitive from a Chain Gang* (1932) dealt with social injustice at home. The film starred Paul Muni in a story taken from a book about a World War I veteran sentenced to a Georgia chain gang for a $5 hold-up. In the movie an ex-soldier quits his former factory job because he wants to build bridges. On the road a drifter forces him at gunpoint to stage a robbery, and he is caught with the money. Sentenced to ten years of hard labor, he escapes and flees to Chicago to become head of a construction firm. When his girlfriend learns his secret, she blackmails him into marriage and turns him in when he falls in love with a socialite. Returned to prison, he escapes again, but knows he will never be free—"they'll always be after me."

King Vidor's *Our Daily Bread* (1934) was one of the most politically oriented motion pictures of the Thirties. Vidor had directed *The Big Parade* (1925), a realistic silent feature re-issued with a sound score in 1931 that placed a mill owner's son, a heavy-set Irish bartender, and a tobacco-chewing ironworker in the muddy trenches of World War I. Self-financed by the director and distributed by Charles Chaplin's United Artists, *Our Daily Bread* told the story of a group of unemployed city workers who organize an agricultural cooperative. "I don't want any favors," the lead character declares. "All I want is a chance to work." When the county sheriff tries to sell the co-op's land at a bankruptcy auction, the local people control the bidding with the implied use of force. The final sequence of the movie shows the triumphant farmers cutting a two-mile irrigation canal for their commonly owned corn fields.

Director Michael Curtiz worked with Paul Muni in *Black Fury* (1935), another film with a strong social theme. Muni portrayed a Slovak Pennsylvania coal miner who leads a strike to protest unsafe working conditions, fraudulent weighing practices, and lack of pay for separating slate from the coal. When the brutal owners bring in strikebreakers, the entire community riots and the miners' families are evicted from company housing. Nevertheless, the strike is won when Muni enters the mine with explosives and threatens to blow it up. *Riff Raff* (1935), starring Spencer Tracy and Jean Harlow, offered a variation of the labor solidarity theme. The story concerned a California tuna fisherman who rejects radical calls for a wildcat strike but decides to lead a walkout for higher pay when the cannery owner attempts to intrude on his illicit relationship with the woman he loves. Because the rank-and-file don't trust the would-be leader, however, they reject his efforts to take charge of the protest, and he retreats to a hobo camp, only to return to support his wife and rejoin the union.

Charles Chaplin sought to turn his attention to social realism in *Modern Times* (1936), a silent film with a few sound inserts. The movie concerned an ex-convict who gets a job tightening nuts at a factory where the owner is obsessed with assembly line productivity. While telling this story, Chaplin submitted viewers to Depression images of closed-down factories, police brutality against jobless demonstrators, and striking workers. Beyond contrasting the affluent dream houses of the rich with the shack that the hero and his love are forced to live in, the film suggested that working people were drawn to theft in order to survive. Nevertheless, Chaplin's sense of irony has the couple lose their secure jobs once the plant re-opens because the labor union calls a strike.

Although the *Our Gang* series of lovable urchins and Shirley Temple films like *The Little Colonel* (1935) approached childhood from a largely sentimental perspective, two social problem movies of the late Thirties sought to address urban youth crime. Director William Wyler's adoption of the Broadway hit *Dead End* (1937) portrayed tough delinquents as kids with tender hearts whose problems were rooted in the slum environment. After establishing the movie's realism with opening shots of ordinary tenement residents in their daily routines, Weyler showed how the homes of his young principals were full of rodents, crying babies, and bawling parents. Michael Curtiz's *Angels with Dirty Faces* (1938) conveyed the same message. The movie cast James Cagney as an unremorseful gangster who returns to his home turf, where is idolized by the young neighborhood hoodlums. In the end, however, the local priest (Pat O'Brien) asks Cagney to pretend that he is going to the death chamber as a coward, so that the boys will think twice about a life outside the law.

THE PEOPLE, THE FAMILY, THE LAND

The most successful social problem movie of the Depression was John Ford's *The Grapes of Wrath* (1940), a film based on John Steinbeck's 1939 novel of the same name. Steinbeck was born into a middle-class family in Salinas, California, in 1902. After working as a ranch hand and fruit picker, he spent several years at Stanford University, but was an inconsistent student and never graduated. Steinbeck then put in a stint as a lodge caretaker before joining the crew of a freighter leaving for New York, where he arrived in 1925 with ambitions of becoming a writer. After working as a reporter, bricklayer, and assorted jobs, he returned to California, where he holed up in an unused cabin in the hills above Monterrey. Steinbeck's first major work was *Tortilla Flat* (1935), a series of folk tales about the local Mexican *paisanos* that made its way to the screen seven years later. Despite the hard drinking and shiftlessness of several of the book's characters, the author conveyed admiration for their chivalric traditions and sense of community. Yet the novel demonstrated that even a cohesive social ethos could be subject to the temptations of excessive individualism and selfishness.

Steinbeck's next project, *In Dubious Battle* (1936), was a protest novel based on a recent Salinas lettuce pickers' strike. Although the book sympathized with the plight of white "crop tramps" and their abuse by the local power structure of banks, courts, police, and the affluent, it portrayed the manipulations of Communist Party union organizers in painful detail. Amid a cycle of recriminations and mob violence, the protagonist of the story sacrifices his life for the "people," while the strike tacticians predictably use his death for their own political agenda. In *Mice and Men* (1937) Steinbeck drew on his own traveling experiences with hobos and migrant farm workers to provide a completely non-patronizing portrait of two "bindle stiffs," George and the slow-witted Lennie. Taking readers inside the bunkhouse, the novella described two ordinary men whose delusions were mixed with fantasies about owning their own land to share in the American Dream.

Joining a Hollywood committee to help Dust Bowl migrants, Steinbeck toured California labor camps in preparation for a *Life* photo-essay, which he planned to expand into a book-length documentary. When the magazine refused to publish the piece, however, he turned it into a pamphlet entitled *Their Blood Is Strong* (1938) and began to work on the novel that would become *The Grapes of Wrath* (1939). Steinbeck's story dealt with a family of ordinary white Protestants from east central Oklahoma that experiences the Depression as a natural disaster. In a society worshipping profit and efficiency, people like the Joads are tossed aside, and human needs become secondary to economic priorities. Steinbeck's foreclosed small farmers make the epic journey west on Route 66 in the company of former minister Preacher Jim Casy. Once in California, they watch government agents dump kerosene-doused potatoes, damaged oranges, and slaughtered pigs because overproduction has made it unprofitable to market these goods, despite the fact that millions are hungry. "In the souls of the people the grapes of wrath are filling and growing heavy, growing heavy for the vintage," observes Steinbeck.

Having reached their destination, the Joads find the only way to survive is to join the migrant agricultural labor force picking fruit, cotton, and vegetables for abysmal wages in terrible working conditions. The story climaxes when Preacher Casy sacrifices his life in a poorly conceived attempt to lead a farm workers' strike, and labor organizer Tom Joad retaliates by killing the perpetrator. Tom recalls the martyr's homespun philosophy—a practical American working out of faith in deeds. "Two are better than one, because they have a good reward for their labor," readers learn, "for if they fall, the one will lift up his fellow, but woe to him that is alone when he falleth, for he hath not another to help him up." "Man reaches, stumbles forward, painfully, mistakenly sometimes," Tom recalls of Casy's philosophy. "Having stepped forward, he may slip back, but only a half step, never the full step back."

Henry Fonda in *The Grapes of Wrath*   (*Photofest*)

As Tom Joad prepares to go on the lam, he leaves his mother with one of the most stirring radical manifestos in American literature. "I'll be around in the dark," he assures her. "I'll be everywhere. Whenever there's a fight so hungry people can eat, I'll be there. Whenever there's a cop beatin' a guy, I'll be there. I'll be in the way guys yell when they're mad; I'll be in the way kids laugh when they know supper's ready." Yet it is Ma Joad, not Tom or Casy, who provides the moral center to the story. Knowing that her daughter has delivered a stillborn baby as the family finds refuge in a flooded box-car, Ma insists that Rose of Sharon give her milk to a starving stranger. "We ain't gonna die out," she insists when all hope seems lost. "People is going' on—changin' a little, maybe, but going' right on."

The Grapes of Wrath sought to depict the evolving human quest for self-realization as one of individuals as well as groups. For Steinbeck the pride, generosity, and courage of the Joads embodied the fortitude and endurance that were the greatest strengths of the American people. Family cohesion, love of simple pleasures, and the poetry of people's language made life meaningful, he suggested. Yet once people lost their roots in the soil they lost everything else as well.

The very same notions were close to the heart of John Ford. A master of silent westerns of the Twenties, Ford had worked with Will Rogers in *Judge Priest* (1934) and *Steamboat Round the Bend* (1939). In *Young Mr. Lincoln* (1939) the director used Henry Fonda to capture the folksy humor and humility of the Great Emancipator during his days on the Illinois frontier. *Stagecoach* (1939) provided Ford with the opportunity to mold John Wayne into a legendary figure. Based on an Ernest Haycox story, the movie provided the sort of character study in which the director excelled. Its plot centered on The Ringo Kid—a dirt farmer wrongly convicted of murder who escapes prison so that he can revenge the killing of his father and brother. When the Kid's horse dies, he is allowed to join a stage whose other passengers include an alcoholic doctor, a liquor salesman, a southern gambler, and a prostitute just run out of town. As fate would have it, Apaches attack the coach, and the most disreputable members of the party turn out to be the only reliable allies in meeting the crisis. As the local marshal buys the doctor a drink at the close of the film, he allows the Kid and the prostitute to escape to the Mexican border.

Grapes of Wrath reminded Ford of Ireland, where, he said, "they threw people off the land and left them wandering on the roads to starve." Yet his version of Steinbeck's novel focused more on a family than on social problems, on the folk memory of national ideals rather class politics. Ford saw the story of the Joads as a celebration of belonging and a reaffirmation of traditional populist values. Using Henry Fonda once more, he emphasized Steinbeck's commitment to the People, the Family, and the Land. Instead of ending the story in a barren boxcar, Ford had the Joads drive off from a government labor camp. The movie assured its place as an American classic and won an Academy Award for Best Picture when producer Darryl Zanuck prevailed upon the director to close out the final scene with Ma Joad's tribute to the people's ability to survive.

TODAY AND TOMORROW

The Joad family matriarch perfectly embodied the prevailing view that women were responsible for maintaining social morale during the Depression. Yet Hollywood's female leads portrayed a wide variety of responses to the crisis. Barbara Stanwyck seemed particularly suited to conveying the angst of working women. Born in Brooklyn, New York as Ruby Stevens, Stanwyck grew up in foster homes after she was orphaned at age two. At thirteen, she got her first job wrapping bundles in a department store. By the time Stanwyck was fifteen, she was in a nightclub chorus line. A stint with the touring company of the Ziegfeld Follies soon followed. In 1926, at the age of nineteen, she appeared in a Broadway gangland melodrama. After a co-starring role in a play entitled *Burlesque* (1927), the aspiring performer moved to Hollywood, where she began appearing in low-budget silent films.

Stanwyck's first sound movie was Frank Capra's *Ladies of Leisure* (1930). The story centered on a disheveled working-class woman who escapes a wild boat party, only to run into a wealthy socialite who has walked out of a decadent penthouse social gathering. An opportunist and "Follies girl" who lives off men, she charms him while stealing his wallet. In the end their relationship blossoms, but only when she wins the respect of the man she hopes to love. In *Baby Face* (1933), Stanwyck played a far more desperate character—a young woman looking to escape a violent and degrading proletarian environment in Erie, Pennsylvania, where she waits tables at her father's speakeasy and sleeps with local politicians for protection for the business. "Nothing but men, dirty rotten men," she complains. Grasping at her chance, she leaves for New York with an African American woman friend and uses her sexuality to fight her way to the top. After marrying a financier, however, she winds up back in a grimy industrial town when her husband asks her to use the wealth she has accrued to bail out his failing bank, a sacrifice she willingly makes in the interest of love.

Bette Davis played another tough working-class character in *Marked Woman* (1937, the story of a struggling dance-hall hostess. Despite the gangster owner's violence and exploitation, the entertainers would rather work at the seedy establishment than slave away at local factories or wind up in dead-end and abusive marriages. When the protagonist's sister is killed for refusing the advances of one of the club owner's stooges, the women take the management to court and see them sent to prison. Nevertheless, their futures are uncertain as they walk off into the city fog.

Few actresses embodied the harsh struggle for survival better than Joan Crawford. In *Mannequin* (1937), Crawford took on the role of a Lower East Side garment worker. Trapped in a world of factory whistles, crying babies, leaky kitchen faucets, and dirty, foul-smelling tenement hallways, she vows she's "gonna get out." Her first ticket out of the ghetto comes through a marriage to a small-time boxing promoter, but Crawford leaves him because of his gambling. "Live your life for yourself," her mother advises. Entering a liaison with a wealthy business figure, she becomes a successful fashion model.

Gregory La Cava's *Stage Door* (1937) brought the class struggle to a theatrical boarding house. A former Ashcan painting student, boxer, newspaper cartoonist, and cohort of Damon Runyon and Grantland Rice, La Cava had a distinct feel for vernacular culture. *Stage Door* featured Katharine Hepburn. The daughter of a prominent Hartford physician and a suffragist and Bryn Mawr graduate, Hepburn perfectly suited the role of an aristocratic young woman seeking a dramatic career. Through her strained interactions with a fast-talking working-class housemate played by Ginger Rogers, Hepburn's character learns that solidarity with her less fortunate sisters is more important than success. An antidote to Depression class tensions, George S. Kaufman's witty script emphasized that democratic values and attributes such as courtesy, loyalty, tolerance, wit, common sense, energy, innovation, and a sense of adventure were not limited to nor excluded those with background, money, or social pretensions. In the end, both the haughty Hepburn and the feisty Rogers soften their hard exteriors through an awareness of their common plight.

The two most celebrated women's films of the Great Depression involved complex dramas of race and class. Taken from a Fannie Hurst novel, *Imitation of Life* (1934) starred Claudette Colbert as Bea—a struggling widow who supports herself and an infant daughter by selling maple syrup to local businesses. In a gesture mixed with self-interest and charity, she hires Delilah—the black mother of a young daughter—as a live-in housekeeper. Through Delilah's pancake recipe, Bea develops a prosperous line of products. Portrayed by Louise Beavers, the plump, religious, and stoic servant shared some of the racial stereotypes of the southern "mammy," including those depicted in advertisements for "Aunt Jemima" pancake mix. Yet Hurst had given the character life with rural expressions picked up from Zora Neale Hurston. More to the point, Delilah serves as Bea's full business partner—receiving ten times the prevailing wage for domestics and substantial amounts of stock in their mutually run enterprise. Although the movie places Delilah's bedroom downstairs, the racially integrated household boasts a democratic equality and social intimacy rarely witnessed by American film audiences.

The great bond between the two women is the troubled relationship each has with her offspring. Bea's immersion in her entrepreneurial interests alienates her daughter to the point where the young woman eventually seduces her mother's business manager. In turn, Delilah's light-skinned Peola wants to "pass" as white and rejects her mother's insistence that she learn to accept her place as a "colored" person. By positing the tension between an African American culture of deference and the desire to cross the color line, *Imitation of Life* struck a sensitive chord among black viewers. Peola was played by Fredi Washington, a Savannah-born actress who was educated in a Philadelphia convent before moving to Harlem to live with her grandmother and working as a secretary at W.C. Handy's Swan Records. Washington broke into show business as a chorus dancer in the black musical revue *Shuffle Along*, performed in Manhattan nightclubs, and appeared in the film *Black and Tan* (1929) with Duke Ellington. Insisting that Peola wanted "white opportunities" instead of rejecting her racial heritage, she prevailed upon *Imitation of Life* director John Stahl to change her lines to reinforce such an interpretation.

Despite Washington's innovations, Hollywood's version of Hurst's novel occasionally sentimentalized race relations. In contrast to the book, the movie provided no white love interest for Peola, and has her rush to her mother's elaborately staged funeral in a final gesture of tearful reconciliation. Critics wondered if *Imitation of Life* offered a condemnation of racial prejudice or a reinforcement of black stereotypes like the "tragic mulatto." Yet African American audiences appeared to rally to the story's depiction of universal human emotions of love and devotion, as well as its portrait of courageous women struggling for success against enormous odds. In this respect, *Imitation of Life* was a worthy predecessor to the decade's signature motion picture, *Gone With the Wind* (1939), a four-hour Technicolor Civil War extravaganza that garnered eight Academy Awards and was the highest-grossing movie of the year.

Published three years earlier, Margaret Mitchell's 1036-page novel sold a million copies in six months (ultimately approaching thirty million in sales) and won the Pulitzer Prize for fiction. The daughter of a southern suffragist, Mitchell was a former Jazz Age flapper, Atlanta journalist, and society matron who spent ten years working on the book's chapters in reverse order. *Gone with the Wind* told the story of Scarlett O'Hara, an upwardly mobile daughter of Irish immigrants struggling to survive the massive upheavals of the Civil War. Scarlett vacillates between the attractions of the free-wheeling capitalist economy and nostalgia for the family-based traditions she herself has rejected. Amid the chaos of war and poverty, she reduces the plantation ethos of the Old South to a love of home and land, her beloved Tara. As Scarlett refuses to submit to outside forces and vows never to be hungry again, her struggle becomes a model for Depression triumph over adversity. "Burdens are for shoulders strong enough to carry them," she remarks. Dismissing the past, Scarlett declines to dwell upon the prospect of a bleak future. "I'll think of it tomorrow," she concludes. "After all, tomorrow is another day."

Fearing another *Birth of a Nation,* the black press condemned Mitchell's novel for romanticizing slavery with house servants who denounce freedom and identify with the Confederacy. Yet the film's producers went out of their way to remove offensive racial caricatures from the production. Although *Gone With the Wind* idealized the plantation legend that Mitchell had debunked, the studio boasted that the primary African American characters would be presented as "loveable, faithful, high-minded people." The complex make-up of the black principals surfaced in the relationship between Scarlett (Vivien Leigh) and Mammy (Hattie McDaniel). The daughter of a Colorado black minstrel company director, McDaniel brought an emotional depth to the part that enabled her to serve as an all-knowing confidante to Scarlett, chastising her when appropriate and acting as an ethical compass in regard to her mistress's troubled marriage to Clark Gable's Rhett Butler. Like Bea and Delilah in *Imitation of Life,* Scarlett and Mammy recognized each other's moral agency. In *Gone with the Wind*, blackness served as a virtue to be emulated and respected, not denigrated.

COMMON CAUSE

Responding to a feared loss of faith during the Depression, young film directors like George Stevens, Gregory La Cava, Leo McCarey, Frank Capra, and Preston Sturges churned out light-hearted comedies that nevertheless spoke to important social issues. By emphasizing the transcendent qualities of romantic love and male-female collaboration, their humorous explorations of human nature pointed to the positive values of social cooperation and solidarity in the face of crisis. Down-to-earth women stars like Barbara Stanwyck, Claudette Colbert, Myrna Loy, Katharine Hepburn, Ginger Rogers, Jean Arthur, Carole Lombard, and Irene Dunne brought a vibrant sense of character, self-assurance, and wit to many of these movies. Portraying feisty but vulnerable women as news reporters, sales clerks, manicurists, ballroom dance teachers, or even comradely heiresses, they re-emphasized the validity of "feminine" emotions in constructing the common good.

Social class assumed a major role in Depression human relations comedies. The opening credits for Gregory La Cava's *My Man Godfrey* (1936) appeared as warehouse building signs in an etching of Manhattan's East River waterfront. As the camera panned to the chimneys of an adjoining shantytown, the image dissolved into a live scene of vagrants moving around a dump heap and several bonfires. One of the scruffy men, played by William Powell, turns out to be an unemployed Harvard graduate who had come close to suicide after a failed love affair, but been inspired by the optimism and sincere values of the homeless. As Powell and his bedraggled cohorts discuss the prospects of returning prosperity, two limousines filled with Fifth Avenue debutantes interrupt the conversation in search of a "lost man" for a charity scavenger hunt. Tired of rich people humiliating the poor with discourteous treatment, Powell denounces the inability of privileged "nitwits" to acknowledge the extent of Depression suffering. Nevertheless, he winds up as the butler for the family of two of the socialite sisters.

As the servant of the eccentric Bullocks, "Godfrey" quietly teaches his charges the virtues of discipline and humility. Unmoved by daughter Irene's loose talk of socialism and revolution, he insists that only capitalism offers the chance for personal dignity. After rescuing the family patriarch from financial ruin, Godfrey turns a back-to-work scheme for the unemployed into a highly profitable enterprise by opening a posh waterfront nightclub called The Dump. Morrie Ryskind's ironic script resolves when Godfrey agrees to marry the zany but sincere Irene, played by Carole Lombard. As in *Stage Door,* La Cava relished stories that showed the potential for social collaboration once characters discarded elitist snobbery or class-conscious fanaticism.

Similar themes pervaded *The Philadelphia Story* (1940), a film based on a Philip Barry stage play of the same name. After partly underwriting the theatrical production in which she starred, Katharine Hepburn bought the rights to the film and approved the assignment of director George Cukor and co-lead Cary Grant. The story concerned the prospective wedding of Tracy Lord, the daughter of a prominent Main Line family, to an arrogant self-made man. Into the picture comes a tough working-class spy magazine reporter, played by Jimmy Stewart, with nothing but contempt for "the privileged classes enjoying their privileges." Meanwhile, Grant presents a low-key portrait of Tracy's ex-husband Dexter Haven, who presides over the action like a benevolent angel. In a fast-paced drama that never lags, the reporter learns to acknowledge the essential humanity of even the rich, Tracy comes to appreciate the universality of human vulnerability and frailty and the need to be loved instead of worshipped, and Dexter overcomes his upper-class reserve to reassert his desire to remarry the woman he has never stopped loving. Character, not wealth or status, determines "class" in this upbeat Depression morality tale.

The most artistically and commercially successful director of the 1930s was Frank Capra. A turn-of-the-century Sicilian immigrant, Capra arrived in the United States with his family at age six. "I hated being poor," he recalled of his humble beginnings. After working his way through college for a chemical engineering degree, he survived in San Francisco as a cardsharp and salesman. Relocating to Hollywood in the 1920s, he became a scriptwriter and editor for Mack Sennett's silent film comedies. Capra wrote and directed *The Strong Man* (1926), a movie starring Harry Langdon as a self-less character who overcomes the temptations of the city to find the girl of his dreams in a small town. The turning point in the young moviemaker's career came when he signed with Harry Cohn's upstart Columbia Pictures, a small studio that initially produced B-pictures for double-bills in Depression-era neighborhood theaters. Cohn preached that "if your story has novelty, human appeal, humor, and pathos, without being too morbid, your chances are very good."

Abandoning rural protagonists for tough, cynical, and shrewd city dwellers with golden hearts and benign motives, Capra flourished at Columbia. One of his first projects featured Jean Harlow in *Platinum Blond* (1931). Another film, *American Madness* (1931), suggested that ordinary people had the power to fight the Depression by contributing their savings to keep the banks solvent. In *Lady for a Day* (1933), a script based on a Damon Runyon piece, a gang of Broadway pickpockets, hustlers, and rogues mounted an elaborate masquerade to marry off the daughter of an elderly street beggar to a Spanish nobleman. The attempt to present Apple Annie as a wealthy social-ite provided the perfect arena for demonstrating the resourcefulness and humanity of Capra's underclass characters. Yet the director did not score his first major hit until 1934, when Claudette Colbert and Clark Gable starred in the Academy Award-winning box-office smash *It Happened One Night*.

Based on the story of a runaway heiress who finds herself on a long-distance bus ride with a hard-bitten news reporter, *It Happened One Night* incorporated screenwriter Robert Riskin's feel for rapid-fire dialogue, real-life personalities, and tightly constructed plots in a parable of American social democracy. Gable's Peter Warne is a hard-drinking, tough-talking, wily news veteran who tells off his boss, dunks his doughnuts in his coffee, and delights in giving piggyback rides. "I never met a rich man yet who could give piggybacks," he confides. A working-class cynic, he assumes the role of a tender male protector, as Colbert's willful and privileged Ellie Andrews must fend for herself amid unfriendly and vulnerable circumstances. In turn, Andrews learns to rely on resourcefulness and improvisation in response to life's challenges.

Although *It Happened One Night* concentrated on the plight of a wealthy socialite, the film is replete with Depression images. From the shabbiness of a nighttime bus station in the opening scenes, the action shifts to the hardships of the bus ride itself. At a grimy late-night rest stop, the camera pans from a trailer with a neon-lit hot dog sign to Ellie leaning against the bus, slowly dragging upon a cigarette. Once the journey resumes, social class distinctions evaporate when the instant community of passengers joins Warne in a rowdy version of "The Man on the Flying Trapeze." After the bus runs off the road, everyone repairs to an auto court of rundown cabins, scattered refuse, noisy children, and barking dogs. The next morning, Ellie takes her place with the women in bathrobes patiently lining up outside the single shower. The female lead's rejection of a marriage to an upper-class aviator signals her independence from the extravagant, snobbish life of the social elite. Instead, she chooses a union with Warne based on love, honesty, mutual respect, and resistance to adversity. Capra's light-hearted cross-class romance offered a personal approach to dealing with painful Depression divisions.

The director's next hit, *Mr. Deeds Goes to Town* (1936), starred Gary Cooper as a small-town Vermonter who inherits $20 million. Surprised in the mansion he has inherited, Deeds hears the accusation of an impoverished farmer that "you never gave a thought to all of those starving people standing in the breadlines, not knowing where their next meal is coming from, not able to feed their wife and kids." Suitably moved, he decides to give away his wealth by distributing ten-acre plots to the poor. Yet leaders of the cultural elite only ridicule his tuba playing and writing of sentimental greeting-card verse while his benefactor's family accuses him of insanity. "That's fine," answers Deeds. "Just because I want to give this money to people who need it, they think I'm crazy." Aided by Jean Arthur, who plays a salty woman reporter who guides him through the judicial hearing over the disputed will, Deeds offers a near-thirty-minute defense by humbly dramatizing the need for altruism in times of crisis. Once the judge concludes that the philanthropist is "the sanest man that ever walked into this courtroom," jubilant farmers celebrate by carrying the shy Deeds on their shoulders.

THE LAST LAUGH

The affirmative tone of the Riskin-Capra collaboration resurfaced in *Lost Horizon* (1937), the story of a man who finds himself in Tibet's Shangri-La after a hijacking and plane crash. Captivated by a society with no striving after power, success, or material goods, he nevertheless escapes, only to find civilization empty and devoid of peace of mind. The film's last image shows Ronald Colman's protagonist struggling through a snowstorm to find his way back to paradise. Similar idealism marked Riskin's adoption of *You Can't Take It With You* (1938), a feature based on a Pulitzer Prize-winning play by Moss Hart and George S. Kaufman. The story depicted the families of a young couple portrayed by Jimmy Stewart and Jean Arthur. Stewart's senior, a munitions-maker and land developer, wants to tear down the house belonging to Arthur's eccentric father to build a skyscraper. Lionel Barrymore's non-conformist character has not paid income tax for twenty-two years—"I don't believe in it," he proclaims, as he demands that the tax collector show him value for his money. In the end, the couple marries, and the tycoon learns to play the harmonica. "Life is simple and kind of beautiful if you let it come to you," he declares.

Capra's masterpiece, *Mr. Smith Goes to Washington* (1939), offered a parable pitting the virtue and decency of ordinary people against the blighted world of American politics. Sidney Buchman's screenplay stemmed from a short story loosely based on the early career of Montana populist Burton K. Wheeler. Like *Mr. Deeds,* the movie featured an honest and naïve man threatened by powerful and wealthy interests. The plot focused on Jimmy Stewart's Jefferson Smith, a homespun character whose state political ring names him as a patsy to complete the term of a deceased U.S. senator. Arriving in Washington, Smith makes his way to the Lincoln Memorial, where he observes an elderly black man reading the words of the Gettysburg Address to his grandson. Inspired by the example of the Great Emancipator, the young solon effuses that "liberty's too precious a thing to be buried in books."

Smith hopes to build a boys' camp in his home state to contribute to the spread of American civic pride. When he discovers that the political machine has ordered his senior counterpart to introduce a rider to an appropriations bill to fund the construction of a dam on the same property, his world begins to collapse. Things deteriorate further when the ring frames him as the owner of the land, mounts a lethal media propaganda campaign against him, resorts to violence to suppress attempts by the boys' clubs to get out the truth, and uses its corrupt influence to initiate hearings for his expulsion from the Senate. Defeated, demoralized, and completely isolated, Smith makes a last visit, suitcase in hand, to see "Mr. Lincoln." The scene embodies the tendency of Capra heroes to fall into an abyss of humiliation and despair when it appears that powerful forces of self-interest have subverted the common good. Just at that moment, however, Jean Arthur, who plays Saunders, his quick-witted, fast-talking and cynical administrative aide, comes to the rescue. Invoking the example of Lincoln and the Founding Fathers, she convinces him to return to the Capitol to conduct a filibuster while grass-roots support builds for his cause.

As a love-smitten Saunders prompts Smith on Senate protocol from the gallery, he holds the floor for twenty-three continuous hours of improvised reflections and readings from the Declaration of Independence and the Constitution. Deliberately low-key and self-deprecatory, he pleads for the future of democracy, even as the odds against him mount. The only causes worth fighting for are lost causes, he reminds his colleagues. As Smith's body weakens, he falls back on a Christ-like appeal for "plain ordinary kindness … and looking out for the other fella too." Just as the senator collapses from exhaustion, his senior counterpart confesses his role in the nefarious land deal and the campaign against his colleague and the boys' clubs who have packed the galleries burst into applause. Critics have complained that Capra's films never offered specific solutions to the nation's difficulties and over-sentimentalized the issues. Yet *Mr. Smith's* reassertion of core populist values and moral aspirations seemed comforting to Depression audiences, making the film the second highest grossing feature of 1939.

Capra subsequently acknowledged that his pictures sought to "lift the human spirit." His work addressed an American civil religion in which the common people sustained folk heroes against corrupt rackets and politicians, and democracy belonged to everyone. In focusing upon the tension between private interest and the common welfare, however, the director allowed moments of pessimism to creep into his stories. Accented by cinematographer Joseph Walker's dark and shadowy lighting, Capra's movies provided despairing glimpses of American poverty, class struggle, vulgarity, frenzied mobs, the manipulation of public opinion, and social violence. "Whenever things go wrong," agonized Lionel Barrymore's character in *You Can't Take It With You,* "people turn to an ism, Fascism or Communism… . Why don't they ever think of Americanism?"

Such was the theme of *Meet John Doe* (1941), the last Capra feature before U.S. entry into World War II. When an oil and finance magnate with political ambitions takes over a newspaper and fires most of the staff, reporter Barbara Stanwyck authors a letter to the editor in the name of a fictional John Doe, who threatens to protest rampant corruption and social injustice by jumping off the City Hall tower on Christmas Eve. To fill the role of the anonymous figure, Stanwyck produces a fading baseball player portrayed by Gary Cooper, and composes a series of articles under his name preaching the philosophy of good neighborliness. Once John Doe clubs spring up all over the country, however, the unscrupulous tycoon sees Cooper's character as a convenient front man for the fascist movement he and his cronies hope to foist upon the American people. When John Doe tries to expose these efforts, the media mogul uses the police and his private army to keep him from speaking and exposes him as a fake. Demoralized and defeated, the ballplayer prepares to end his life as the letter proposed. Yet Stanwyck convinces him that if Jesus died for the same ideals, they were "worth living for." As ordinary citizens rally around John Doe, they beg him to help revive the movement begun in his name.

With a Dimitri Tiomkin score incorporating Stephen Foster's "Hard Times Come Again No More," *Meet John Doe* conveyed the melancholy despair of a world in which fascism seemed on the move. Capra, in fact, toyed with five different endings, including one in which the seemingly futile hero does commit suicide. Ultimately, however, he chose to sustain a cautious faith in American democracy. "Yes, sir, I'm a sucker for this country," the veteran newspaper editor tells Gary Cooper in a barroom confession. "I'm a sucker for the Star Spangled Banner… . I like what we got here! I like it! A guy can say what he wants—and do what he wants—without having a bayonet shoved through his belly." When anyone tries to change things," he continues, "I get boiling mad... I get mad for a guy named Washington and a guy named Jefferson and Lincoln… lighthouses in a foggy world." As the crowd of supporters impels a cowering John Doe toward action, the editor turns to the fascist publisher in a final gesture of defiance. "There you are, Norton, the people! Try and lick that!" Idealizations of how things *might* be and how people *might* behave, Capra had discovered, offered a fundamental ray of hope in hard times.

The threat of impending fascism and the fragile fate of democracy led Frank Capra close to despair in *Meet John Doe*. It took screenwriter and director Preston Sturges to point the way toward Hollywood's proper role amidst social crisis. Sturges had spent his childhood with his divorced mother in wealthy bohemian circles in Europe and Chicago. Known as a genteel bum after a failed marriage to a socialite, he scored a Broadway hit in 1929 with a comedy about a female waif adopted by the good-hearted denizens of an Italian speakeasy. After a marriage to a second heiress left him penniless, he went to Hollywood in the late Thirties and wrote several successful romantic comedies. *Remember the Night* (1939) told the story of a woman thief befriended by a prosecutor and saved by love. *The Lady Eve* (1941) and *The Palm Beach Story* (1942), two of the first movies Sturges directed, suggested that "class" in America involved good manners, courtesy, and a sense of fun that allowed people to flourish.

It was not until he directed *Sullivan's Travels* (1942), however, that Sturges found a way to produce a socially conscious film without an overt political theme. The movie told the story of John L. Sullivan, a Hollywood comedy director who wants to make a feature called "Brother, Where Art Thou?" as "a commentary on modern conditions" and "the suffering of humanity." To research his material, he disguises himself as a hobo, a device that allows the film to highlight the Depression's impact on ordinary people in documentary style. The plot thickens, however, when a series of mishaps and mistaken identities results in Sullivan's sentence to a chain gang for an attack on a railroad guard. One Saturday night, prison guards herd the director and fellow convicts to a dilapidated country church. As a somber pump organ plays, the hosting black minister asks the poor congregants to welcome their guests in the spirit of love and acceptance. Just as we anticipate an extended sermon on Christian forgiveness and compassion, a wobbly movie projector

Joel McCrae and Veronica Lake in *Sullivan's Travels* (1942)   (*Photofest*)

appears in the center aisle, a sheet is thrown up as an improvised screen, and the bespectacled pastor introduces the night's treat—a one-reel Mickey Mouse cartoon.

As rolls of laughter crescendo wildly across the room, Sullivan initially appears bewildered that people with such heavy burdens could find this sort of escape entertaining. It does not take long, however, for the director to join in the infectious response to the on-screen slapstick, or for viewers to sense that the would-be humanitarian has had a profound change of heart. Once returned to Hollywood, Sullivan vows to make a comedy. "There's a lot to be said for making people laugh," he announces. "Did you know that's all some people have? It isn't much but it's better than nothing in this cockeyed caravan." *Sullivan's Travels* closes with portraits of the poor, sick, and suffering in abandoned laughter. Sturges had stumbled upon the fundamental insight that movies provided an indispensable service by helping to relieve people's pain, even if the fix was only temporary. The Depression taught Hollywood that sustenance of people's morale was one of the most important gifts it had to offer.

SOURCES AND SUGGESTED READINGS

Geoffrey O'Brien, *Hardboiled America: Lurid Paperbacks and the Masters of Noir* (1997); Erin A. Smith, *Hard-Boiled: Working-Class Readers and Pulp Magazines* (2000); and Paula Rabinowitz, *Black and White and Noir: America's Pulp Modernism* (2002): each describes the roots of 1930s detective fiction. See also the relevant portions of Mike Davis, *City of Quartz: Excavating the Future in Los Angeles* (1990). An extensive literature on the role of Depression cartoon strips and comic books includes Gerard Jones, *Men of Tomorrow: Geeks, Gangsters, and the Birth of the Comic Book* (2004) and relevant portions of Gerard Jones and Will Jacobs, *The Comic Book Heroes* (1997). See also Dean Young and Rick Marshall, *Blondie and Dagwood's America* (1981). Other useful sources include the appropriate segments of Reinhold Reitberger and Wolfgang Fuchs, *Comics: Anatomy of a Mass Medium* (1972); Jerry Robinson, *The Comics: An Illustrated History of Comic Strip Art* (1974); and Ian Gordon, *Comic Strips and Consumer Culture, 1890–1945* (1998).

Depression-era radio comes under scrutiny in the relevant segments of Fred J. MacDonald, *Don't Touch That Dial: Radio Programming in American Life from 1920 to 1960* (1979) and Alice G. Marquis, *Hopes and Ashes: The Birth of Modern Times, 1929–1939* (1986). For a superb view of one of the period's most popular radio shows, see Melvin Patrick Ely, *The Adventures of Amos 'n 'Andy: A Social History of an American Phenomenon* (1991). The appropriate portions of Bill C. Malone, *Country Music U.S.A.*, 2nd rev. ed. (2002) describe the growing popularity of the hillbilly genre. For the continuing influence of the blues, see the relevant segments of Elijah Wald, *Escaping the Delta: Robert Johnson and the Invention of the Blues* (2004) and Peter Guralnick, *Feel Like Going Home: Portraits in Blues and Rock 'n' Roll* (1999).

Sources on African American swing jazz include Donald Clark, *Wishing on the Moon: The Life and Times of Billie Holiday* (1994) and John Edward Hasse, *Beyond Category: The Life and Genius of Duke Ellington* (1993). David W. Stowe, *Swing Changes: Big Band Jazz in New Deal America* (1994) explores the social significance of 1930s dance music. Tin Pan Alley's Depression songs receive consideration in Charles Hamm, *Yesterdays: Popular Song in America* (1979) and *Putting Popular Music in Its Place* (1995); as well as in Philip Furia, *The Poets of Tin Pan Alley: A History of America's Greatest Lyricists* (1990). For a portrait of the era's most successful female lyricist, see Deborah Grace Winer, *On the Sunnyside of the Street: The Life and Lyrics of Dorothy Fields* (1997). Depression musical theater comes under scrutiny in segments of Andrea Most, *Making Americans: Jews and the Broadway Musical* (2004).

Overviews of 1930s film appear in Andrew Bergman, *We're in the Money: Depression America and Its Films* (1971) and the relevant chapters of Robert Sklar, *Movie-Made America: A Cultural History of American Movies*, rev. ed. (1994) and Andrew Sarris, *You Ain't Heard Nothin' Yet: The American Talking Film: History & Memory, 1927–1949* (1998). For crime movies and working-class themes, see Robert Sklar, *City Boys: Cagney, Bogart, Garfield* (1992); Jonathan Munby, *Public Enemies, Public Heroes: Screening the Gangster from* Little Caesar *to* Touch of Evil (1999); and the passages on the 1930s in John Bodnar, *Blue-Collar Hollywood: Liberalism, Democracy, and Working People in American Film* (2003). Synopses of significant Thirties films appear in David Zinman, *50 Classic Motion Pictures: The Stuff That Dreams Are Made Of* (1970).

Profiles of two leading Depression comic film performers appear in Marybeth Hamilton, *"When I'm Bad, I'm Better": Mae West, Sex, and American Entertainment* (1996) and Simon Louvish, *Man on the Flying Trapeze: The Life and Times of W.C. Fields* (1997). See also the insightful commentary in Elizabeth Kendall, *The Runaway Bride: Hollywood Romantic Comedy of the 1930s* (1990). Racial themes in *Gone with the Wind* and other Thirties features are the focus of the relevant segments of Donald Bogle, *Toms, Coons, Mulattoes, Mammies, and Bucks: An Interpretive History of Blacks in American* Films, rev. ed. (2002) and Linda Williams, *Playing the Race Card: Melodramas of Black and White from Uncle Tom to O.J. Simpson* (2001).

Two of the most successful comic screenwriters of the period receive their due in Rhoda-Gale Pollack, *George S. Kaufman* (1988) and William MacAdams, *Ben Hecht: The Man Behind the Legend* (1990). The central role of populist themes in Hollywood merits attention in Robert Sklar and Vita Zagarrio, eds., *Frank Capra: Authorship and the Studio System* (1998); Jeffrey Richards, *Visions of Yesterday* (1973); Lee Lourdeaux, *Italian and Irish Filmmakers in America: Ford, Capra, Coppola, and Scorcese* (1990); and Guiliana Muscio, *Hollywood's New Deal* (1997). See also the segments on Thirties motion pictures and popular culture in Lawrence W. Levine, *Unpredictable Past: Explorations in American Cultural History* (1993) and Warren Susman, *Culture as History: The Transformation of American Society in the Twentieth Century* (1984).

7

The Cultural Home Front of the People's War, 1941–1945

Allied resistance to Nazi Germany and Imperial Japan in World War II, declared Vice President Henry A. Wallace, marked the dawn of the "Century of the Common Man." Emphasizing the need for wartime unity and collective sacrifice, American political leaders articulated a faith in the ability of democratic capitalism to serve the welfare and interests of ordinary people. As in the Great Depression, many writers, filmmakers, painters, musicians, and others joined the effort to foster national morale by focusing upon the virtue, resilience, and common interests of everyday citizens, whether in the military or civilian life. The federal government reinforced such tendencies by encouraging awareness of ethnic diversity as a source of national strength. Nevertheless, a number of Popular Front and minority activists turned to vernacular cultural forms to expedite the slow progress of inclusion or to carve out self-defined niches for their constituencies. The resulting output of folk music, hipster jive, and bebop offered a significant alternative to the affirmative tone of home front cultural expression.

WHY WE FIGHT

The rise of overseas military dictatorships and the outbreak of the European war in 1939 led many American writers and artists to conclude that human rights had far brighter prospects at home than elsewhere. Books like John Dos Passos' *The Ground We Stand On* (1941) emphasized a national heritage of democratic pluralism and individualism. Ethnic and religious diversity, wrote Eleanor Roosevelt and Frances Macgregor in a collection of photographs entitled *This Is America* (1942), were "not our weakness, but our strength." The volume reinforced such a message with an array of images including a Vermont farmer, a Pacific beach, a Negro, an Indian, a German American, a synagogue, a European refugee, a New England main street, and a volunteer plane spotter. The egalitarian virtues of American life also were the subject of Stephen Vincent Benét's *Western Star* (1943), a free-verse epic poem that attributed a romantic allure to the settling of the continent by ordinary people.

Norman Rockwell's illustrations offered equally reassuring views of the survival of American cultural values in a perilous world. Born in New York City in 1895, Rockwell received formal training before becoming art director of the Boy Scouts magazine at age nineteen. Starting in 1917, he completed 317 covers for the *Saturday Evening Post*. Influenced by the Farm Security Administration photographs of small-town life in the 1930s, Rockwell sought to convey a sense of well-being in wartime America by picturing a healthy, democratic nation of cohesive communities. *Freedom from Want* (1943), an iconic oil used as the model for an Office of War Information (OWI) poster, depicted a grandmother serving a turkey dinner in a prosperous farmhouse as a fatherly figure prepares to carve up the bird. The artist's interest in common experiences surfaced in his 1943 *Post* cover portrait of "Rosie the Riveter," an idealization of the thousands of female welders who carried on wartime tasks. In the Pacific Northwest, radical shipyard painters Arthur Runquist and Martina Gangle also celebrated the grit of the labor force, but offered a more critical perspective on the human toll of defense work.

Radio offered a lucrative arena for fusing wartime cohesion with democratic vistas. Since the late Thirties, politically oriented scriptwriters like poet Archibald MacLeish consistently had linked antifascism with American social values. Populist sentiments also characterized the broadcast version of Carl Sandburg's *The People Yes,* assembled in 1941 by Stephen Vincent Benét and composer Earl Robinson. Following Pearl Harbor, the networks ran public service war dramas by writers such as Edna St. Vincent Millay, Maxwell Anderson, Dorothy Parker, Pare Lorentz, James Thurber, and Benét. Designed to foster unity by highlighting the selfless contributions of the diverse members of the typical combat platoon, these productions invariably featured a ritualistic listing of names from the nation's multi-ethnic melting pot. Radio series such as *Fighting Men* (1943) and *They Call Me Joe* (1944) made particular use of blacks and other minorities in depicting the battlefield experience.

Motion pictures turned out to be the most important agent of wartime unity and democratic pluralism. Although only fifty of Hollywood's 1100 films between 1938 and 1941 dealt with fascism or the European war, Orson Welles' *March of Time* newsreels and features such as *The Man I Married [I Married a Nazi]* (1940) and *Escape* (1940) personalized Hitler's threat to the lives of ordinary people. "There are those who will say we have nothing to fear—that we are immune—that we are protected by vast oceans from the bacteria of aggressive dictatorships and totalitarian states," warned the government prosecutor in *Confessions of a Nazi Spy* (1939), a movie starring Edward G. Robinson as an FBI agent who uncovers a domestic German espionage ring. "But we … have seen the mirror of history in Europe … America is not simply one of the remaining democracies, America is democracy."

Citizen Kane (1941), Orson Welles' first feature film, suggested how the dictatorial ambitions of irresponsible elites at home mimicked the methods of fascist demagogues overseas. Loosely based on the life of newspaper and media magnate William Randolph Hearst, the movie presented the story of a powerful capitalist who wedded cynical showmanship to right-wing obstructionism and the rhetorical service of European strongmen. A Wisconsin native, Welles had forgone a college education in the early 1930s for world travel. As a director with the WPA's Federal Theater Project, he founded the Mercury Theater and produced modernized versions of Shakespearean drama to illustrate the threat of fascist manipulation of public opinion. His controversial radio production of H.G. Wells' *War of the Worlds* (1938), designed to dramatize mass susceptibility to media propaganda, was so realistic that millions of listeners believed that an invasion from Mars had actually taken place.

Welles insisted that fascist politics amounted to no more than a parade. By portraying one-time reformer Charles Foster Kane as a power-obsessed figure who exploited public opinion for its own sake, the director issued a stark warning about the subversion of American democracy by foreign ideologies. His fusion of Popular Front politics and homegrown populism climaxed in the biting criticism Kane's chief assistant delivers to his boss as the film nears its tragic resolution. "You talk about the people as though they belong to you … as though you could make a present of liberty," scolds the aide. Yet when the "precious underprivileged really do get together," he warns, "that's going to add up to something bigger than your privilege."

Seeking to counter non-interventionist sentiment, director Howard Hawks offered an apt war morality tale in *Sergeant York* (1941). Set during World War I, the film starred Gary Cooper as a shy Tennessee backwoodsman with religious scruples about killing who learns to accept a secular faith in government "of the people, by the people, and for the people." Convinced that ordinary citizens must defend their mutual rights, York fights for his country without sacrificing his individualist values or ties to home and family, ultimately capturing one hundred Germans. After Pearl Harbor, Hollywood viewed expressions of national unity as important goodwill gestures that could discourage the risks of federal regulation. Dependent upon official and military cooperation for the production of newsreels and combat features, studio heads formed a special committee to work with Washington's defense needs. In turn, the government recognized filmdom's relevance to the war effort by classifying it as an "essential industry." By the last year of the conflict, annual box office receipts had nearly doubled, eighty million Americans saw a movie every week, and three hundred thousand soldiers viewed a movie each night.

Intent on motivating troops behind the democratic cause, Army Chief of Staff George C. Marshall commissioned director Frank Capra as a lieutenant colonel and asked him to produce a series of documentaries explaining U.S. war aims. The six-part *Why We Fight* (1942–45) fashioned the conflict as a struggle against oppression in the name of the liberty, equality, and security of the common people. As explained by the narrator of the first installment, the commercially successful *Prelude to War*, Americans were fighting

> freedom's oldest enemy—the passion of the *few* to rule the *many*. This isn't just a war. This is a common man's life and death struggle against those who would put him back in slavery. We lose it, and we lose everything—our homes, the jobs we want to go back to, the books we read, the very food we eat, the hopes we have for our kids, the kids themselves—they won't be ours anymore. That's what's at stake. It's *us* against *them*. The chips are down. Two worlds stand against each other. One must live. One must die—170 years of freedom decrees our answer.

THE PEOPLE'S WAR

Capra's documentaries pointed to the use of populist democracy and consumer abundance as rallying points for the U.S. war effort. The films complemented President Roosevelt's distrust of government propaganda and his suspicion that Americans primarily supported the conflict out of solidarity with the troops. In *Casablanca* (1942), the Academy Award-winning Best Picture by Hungarian-born director Michael Curtiz, Hollywood demonstrated how memorable characterizations, a compelling story, and the invocation of basic human values could engage an audience in international affairs. Featuring Humphrey Bogart as Rick Blaine, the outwardly cynical American operator of a café in Occupied French Morocco, *Casablanca* ultimately won recognition as the greatest American motion picture of World War II.

Bogart proved to be a perfect choice for the part. Born on Manhattan's Upper West Side in 1899 to a physician and an illustrator, he had attended the exclusive Phillips Academy before enlisting in the navy during World War I. Moving on to Broadway, Bogart played genteel upper-class characters in a number of romantic comedies, including one in which he popularized the famous query, "Tennis, anyone?" The actor's arrival in Hollywood in the early 1930s did little to change his persona, although he ultimately won parts as a gangster henchman in *Three on a Match* (1932) and a surly ranch foreman in *A Holy Terror* (1934). It was not until he returned to Broadway to appear as Duke Mantee in Robert E. Sherwood's *Petrified Forest* (1934) that Bogart approached stardom.

Sherwood's play depicted a slow-speaking, menacing gangster on the run to Mexico who holes up in a family-run gas station in the Arizona desert, where intellectual Leslie

Howard philosophizes about him as a primitive American. Once Bogart appeared in the movie version of the drama in 1936, he won a series of working-class roles. In *Black Legion* (1937), a Warner Brothers "social problem" film, he played an ordinary factory worker who runs a drill press, dries the dishes at home, and listens to radio adventure serials with his son. Resentful and envious of the competition of Jews and Catholics at work, however, he joins a violent native fascist movement that leads to his self-destruction. In another part, Bogart portrayed a shadowy gangster henchman to Edward G. Robinson in *Kid Galahad* (1937). He then starred as "Baby Face" Martin in *Dead End* (1937), a screen adoption of Sidney Kingsley's Broadway play about the effects of slum conditions on the young. Here Bogart portrayed a morose and hesitant professional criminal given to sudden bursts of anger and violence.

Inexplicably, the actor's appearances over the next four years were limited to supporting roles in uninspiring "B" pictures. In 1941, however, he starred in *High Sierra* as Roy Earle, a former farm boy paroled after an eight-year sentence for bank robbery. Returning to see his old homestead, he learns that the current owner is about to lose his mortgage. In California, Earle befriends a family driven off its Indiana farm. Despite such benevolence, the gangster leads a robbery of an exclusive California desert resort that goes badly, setting the stage for his shooting by authorities during a futile escape to the mountains. In *The Maltese Falcon* (1941), director John Houston's first movie,

Humphrey Bogart (far right) in *The Maltese Falcon*   (*Photofest*)

Bogart portrayed Sam Spade, Dashiell Hammett's laconic detective anti-hero. Living halfway outside the law and convention, the street-smart Spade saves his energy for moments of concentrated action. In a dark tale of human greed, corruption, and duplicity, Bogart captured the moral ambivalence of a man who turns over his partner's murderer to the police, despite the fact that he is in love with her. He tells the woman that he will wait for her. If on the other hand, "they hang you," he adds, "I'll always remember you."

Bogart's affectation of a tough exterior worked brilliantly in *Casablanca,* where he played a glum, sour, and cold individualist seemingly fixated on his own interests. "I stick my neck out for nobody," Rick explains when asked to hide an associate pursued by the Nazis. Yet the reappearance of Ingrid Bergman's Ilsa, his former love in Paris, reignites both his romantic passion and his political commitment. In Popular Front screenwriter Howard Koch's reworking of the original script, it turns out that Rick had served as an anti-fascist fighter in Spain and earned a price on his head from the Gestapo. Now he must decide whether to transfer two stolen letters of transit in his possession to Ilsa and her husband, a Czech resistance leader the Germans desperately wish to question. The choice becomes even more difficult when Ilsa explains that as the Nazis marched into Paris, she failed to meet him at the train station as planned because she learned that her husband had escaped from a concentration camp and was still alive.

A key to Rick's democratic sensibility lies in his close relationship with his black piano player and bandleader Sam, portrayed without the slightest hint of caricature by Dooley Wilson. As the film concludes, Bogart pretends that he plans to use the transit documents for Ilsa and himself. At the airport, however, he forces her to do the right thing and escape with her patriot husband, so that the work of the resistance can continue. In one of the most eloquent statements of personal sacrifice in cinema history, the hard-bitten Rick explains to the only woman he has ever loved that "it doesn't take much to see that the problems of three little people don't amount to a hill of beans in this crazy world." As Bogart's anti-hero shoots the German commander who threatens to intercept the fleeing couple, he and Claude Rains—the corrupt but endearing police chief—disappear into the fog arm in arm in search of the Free French Forces. An enormous cult favorite well into the twenty-first century, *Casablanca* offered the most credible fusion of populist individualism and international idealism Hollywood ever produced and turned Bogart into one of the world's most revered celebrities.

G.I. JOE

Americans were fascinated with the plight of the two million soldiers and sailors (12 percent of the total force) that experienced direct combat in World War II. Comic book series such as *Private Breger,* the feature that popularized the term "G.I. Joe" (G.I. stood for Government Issue), and *Sad Sack* concentrated on the everyday routine of the front lines. *Green Lantern* and *Captain Marvel,* in turn, offered battlefront adventure. Yet no comic had the impact of the jingoistic and action-packed *Captain America*. A collaboration between two Jews, writer Joe Simon and illustrator Jack Kirby, the series started its run in 1941 with a cover of its belligerent superhero socking Hitler in the face. Subsequent issues caricatured Japanese troops as sinister, ugly, and subhuman creatures given to sadistic cruelty. Appealing to the emotions of young male readers unsettled by the uncertainties of war, *Captain America* reached sales of a million a month.

Bill Mauldin's Pulitzer Prize-winning cartoons in the military press provided a more grounded version of combat life. Through Willie and Joe, two gritty but stoic infantry grunts, Mauldin detailed the drudgery of endless and seemingly pointless long marches through mud and rain and the daily tedium of warfare. Similar realism marked the dispatches of *Time* correspondent John Hersey, who collected his reports from the Pacific and European theaters in *Men on Bataan* (1942) and *Into the Valley* (1943). Turning to fiction, Hersey won a Pulitzer Prize for *A Bell for Adano* (1944), the story of an American unit's humane approach to the restoration of order in an Italian village. Hollywood quickly converted the novel into a critically acclaimed and popular movie.

Syndicated newspaper columnist Ernie Pyle ranked as the favorite war correspondent of American G.I.s. Born in Indiana in 1900, Pyle briefly attended college before becoming a reporter and aviation editor. His Pulitzer Prize-winning dispatches from the front embraced the experiences of ordinary soldiers in every phase of the struggle, "the guys the war can't be won without." In accessible, plain, and understated language, Pyle captured the essence of battlefield humor. Writing about mosquitoes on one occasion, he dryly observed there were "lots of things besides bullets that make war hell." Soldiers looked upon combat as a job they must do and get done quickly, fighting mainly for each other and killing to stay alive, he reported. American troops were not struggling for democracy or international ideals, but simply to return home to blueberry pie, "a blonde," books, music, generosity, good pay, and creature comforts, the journalist insisted. Pyle's columns found their way into book form in *Here Is Your War* (1943) and *Brave Men* (1944) before the popular writer fell to Japanese machine-gun fire on a small island near Okinawa in the final year of the conflict.

Actor Burgess Meredith portrayed Ernie Pyle in *The Story of G.I. Joe* (1945), a movie with a script by budding playwright Arthur Miller. World War II films often emphasized the common man's role in protecting nation, home, and family. In *Joe Smith, American* (1942), Robert Young played an aircraft plant chief kidnapped by Nazi agents seeking the blueprint for a secret bombsight apparatus. In the end, Young escapes and helps to arrest the perpetrators. *The Fighting Seabees* (1944) featured John Wayne as a fiery construction foreman who overcomes the objections of navy bureaucrats and leads an armed crew on a mission to repair a key installation near Japanese lines. Working-class resilience and sentimentality also characterized *The Sullivans* (1944), a movie retracing the lives of five brothers killed in a single Pacific naval battle. Idealizing the atmosphere of a loving and cooperative Irish-Catholic family in

Waterloo, Iowa, the film showed the boys absorbing discipline from their father and love and respect from their mother. When the older Sullivan learns of the death of his sons, no one is surprised that he continues to run the train he operates to ensure the delivery of vital war materiel.

Many combat features modeled their detailed explorations of ordinary Americans on the film and photo documentaries of the late 1930s. Because the war involved an unprecedented use of racial and ethnic minorities in both the military and the civilian labor force, however, the federal government pushed for an approach that pictured blacks, Hispanics, and others as more than unfortunate victims of social conditions. The Office of War Information acknowledged changing realities in 1943 when it directed movie studios to "depict democracy" by showing people of different races, religions, and economic status "mingling on even terms in factory or other war service," as well as "in settings of everyday life." One response was Frank Capra's *The Negro Soldier* (1944), a documentary celebrating African American heroes of the past that provided a tour of contemporary military life from the perspective of the black G.I.

Responding to government prodding, several Hollywood war movies went out of the way to work members of the melting pot into the national crusade. Howard Hawks' patriotic *Air Force* (1943), which began with the singing of the antislavery "Battle Hymn of the Republic" and with excerpts from Lincoln's Gettysburg Address, featured a multi-ethnic bomber crew that listened to Duke Ellington's "It Don't Mean a Thing (If It Ain't Got That Swing)" as it flew to Pearl Harbor following President Roosevelt's declaration of war. *Air Force* starred John Garfield as a Polish American enlisted man who is initially angry at his rejection for a pilot training program but rises to fill the role of an indispensable tail-gunner. Diversity also characterized Robert Taylor's unit in *Bataan* (1943), in which a Pittsburgh Pole, a Mexican American from California, a New York Jew, and an African American all cooperate to delay a Japanese advance across a key bridge. Both the submarine drama *Destination Tokyo* (1943) and *Pride of the Marines* (1945) featured Garfield in stories in which ordinary citizens overcame ethnic, regional, or class differences to band together.

STAR SPANGLED JIVE

The broad publicity given to black boxing champion Joe Louis' visits to military bases pointed to the evolving definition of wartime nationhood. The son of Alabama sharecroppers, Louis migrated with his mother and seven siblings to Detroit at age twelve. Dropping out of school in sixth grade, he roamed the streets and worked at an auto factory before turning to the ring. As the reputation of prizefighting deteriorated in the 1930s, trainers groomed Louis in the opposite image of the legendary Jack Johnson. A God-fearing, clean-living, humble competitor, he achieved acclaim as "a credit to his race." Meanwhile, Louis won twenty-two bouts in a row, leading to national attention in

1935 when he knocked out a self-declared representative of Mussolini's fascist Italy. Louis followed the victory by defeating ex-champ Max Baer in a contest broadcast live over network radio. Louis lost to Germany's Max Schmeling in a 1936 bout the Nazis promoted as a test of Aryan supremacy, but after fighting his way to the heavyweight title, won a rematch two years later. "I'm backing up America against Germany, so you know I am going to town," he declared before flooring his rival in just over two minutes.

A black man's triumph over Schmeling led to wild street celebrations among African Americans, but also turned Joe Louis into a national hero. Known as the "Brown Bomber," the fighter enthusiastically embraced the struggle against Nazi racial ideology with appearances at military installations and financial contributions to armed service relief funds. Louis' celebrity even resulted in a skit appearance in *This Is the Army* (1943), one of several Hollywood films designed to boost home front morale. Directed by *Casablanca's* Michael Curtiz, the movie replicated the score and story line of Irving Berlin's *This Is the Army, Mr. Jones* (1942), a Broadway show replete with Harlem rhythms and high-stepping dancers.

Hollywood's salutes to unity frequently highlighted African American entertainers as representatives of the nation's democratic energies and vitality. *Star Spangled Rhythm* (1942) featured Eddie Bracken and a host of white stars in a loosely constructed plot, but climaxed with Eddie "Rochester" Anderson performing a highly spirited jitterbug, after which he discards his hipster's outfit for an Army uniform. *Stage Door Canteen* (1943), a salute to the armed forces and war service workers that won the approval of civil rights advocates, featured an appearance by vocalist Ethel Waters and footage of an interracial audience of G.I. jitterbugs grooving to the swing rhythms of Count Basie and Benny Goodman.

Two wartime movies featured all-black casts. *Cabin in the Sky* (1943), director Vincente Minnelli's first film, teamed Eddie Anderson with Ethel Waters and vocalist Lena Horne. Born out of wedlock in 1896, Waters ran errands for Philadelphia prostitutes as a child. Married at thirteen and divorced two years later, she first made a living as a hotel domestic. Waters' life changed, however, when she moved to New York in the early 1920s to sing blues under the name "Sweet Mama Stringbean." Known for understated phrasing, she recorded standards such as "St. Louis Blues," "Dinah," and "Am I Blue?" *Cabin in the Sky* featured the singer's heartfelt rendition of "Happiness Is Just a Thing Called Joe," a haunting lament by lyricist Yip Harburg and composer Harold Arlen. Lena Horne was a youthful counterpart to the veteran Waters. Born in Brooklyn in 1917, she joined the Cotton Club chorus line at sixteen before becoming a top big-band singer in the mid-Thirties. After an appearance in the Broadway revue *Blackbirds of 1939*, Horne parlayed her vocal talents and light skin into a film contract.

Minnelli rounded out the star-studded cast of *Cabin the Sky* with Louis Armstrong and Duke Ellington, who appeared as musicians in the film's bawdy nightclub scenes. Restating a conventional theme, the movie addressed the duality of sacred and profane elements in African American culture by depicting a struggle between God and the Devil for a gambler's soul. The popularity of gospel performers like Thomas Dorsey, the pervasiveness of urban Holiness and storefront churches, and the success of evangelical preachers like Father Divine certainly pointed to the central role of spirituality in modern African American life. Yet some critics complained that Minnelli's portrait of the black psyche suffered from the movie industry's over-reliance upon excessive idealization and outworn caricatures in matters of race.

Similar issues related to *Stormy Weather* (1943), a musical built around a sentimentalized biography of legendary tap dancer Bill "Bojangles" Robinson. Born in Richmond, Virginia in 1878, Robinson became an orphan at an early age and fell under his grandmother's care. Learning to dance on the street for pennies, he ran away to Washington, D.C. when he was eight. After observing traveling blackface performers, Robinson created a highly rhythmic, syncopated style of footwork that appeared effortless and carefree. He incorporated these techniques in tap dance and soft-shoe routines in countless minstrel shows, vaudeville appearances, and Broadway revues. Drawn to Hollywood in 1930, Robinson made fourteen movies, four in which he co-starred with Shirley Temple. Enhanced by a Ted Koehler and Harold Arlen score from the Cotton Club revue of 1933, a smoky rendering of the title song by Ethel Waters, and inspiring performances by Robinson, Lena Horne, Fats Waller, the Nicholas Brothers dance team, and hipster song-and-dance man Cab Calloway, *Stormy Weather* nevertheless suffered from an excessively thin plot and facile characterizations.

Despite the awkwardness with which Hollywood approached African American life, performers like the Nicholas Brothers and Cab Calloway succeeded in broadening the appeal of black culture and laying the groundwork for the style eventually known as "G.I. Jive." The Nat Cole Trio played a key role in popularizing the new music. Born in Montgomery, Alabama and raised in Chicago, Cole relocated to Los Angeles, where he organized his own jazz combo in the late Thirties. Mastering a relaxed but upbeat approach, the pianist and vocalist produced a collection of wartime hits that included "Gone with the Draft," "Hit That Jive, Jack," "Straighten Up and Fly Right," and "Sweet Lorraine." Meanwhile, Duke Ellington provided the most important link between swing and mainstream audiences through tunes like "I've Got It Bad" (1941) and "Don't Get Around Much Anymore" (1942), a syncopated lament of home front loneliness recorded by the popular black vocal group the Ink Spots. Ellington's esteemed status prompted the Musician's Union to sponsor his weekly radio program directed at African Americans in which he promoted war bond sales as a way to ensure support for human rights at home.

African American swing and jive dominated wartime popular music to the extent that white musicians, songwriters, and vocalists felt compelled to adopt its styling. In *Stage Door Canteen,* Peggy Lee sounded a good deal like Billie Holiday when she teamed up with the Benny Goodman Orchestra to sing "Why Don't You Do Right?" a number written by Joe McCoy, a member of a Harlem rhythm and blues vocal group. The film also featured Goodman's band performing a Fletcher Henderson arrangement of the "Bugle Call Rag." Perhaps the high point of wartime interracial collaboration came when white lyricist Johnny Mercer wrote "G.I. Jive" (1944), a song set to a boogie-woogie accompaniment and recorded as a mainstream hit by black musician Louis Jordan.

Born in 1909 into a comfortable middle-class family in Savannah, Georgia, Mercer listened to race records as a young man and developed an ear for the nuances of language and rhyme. Learning the importance of musical phrasing in the early 1930s as a vocalist for the Paul Whiteman Orchestra, he moved on to Hollywood, where he polished the lyrics to such standards as "Too Marvelous for Words" (1937) and "Jeepers Creepers" (1938). Wartime collaborations with Harold Arlen like "That Old Black Magic" (1942) and "One for My Baby" (1943) led Mercer to extract literacy from everyday language. "Blues in the Night" (1941), written with Arlen for the film of the same name, most completely reflected Mercer's feel for African American vernacular. "From Natchez to Mobile, from Memphis to St. Joe,/Wherever the four winds blow," the number began, "I been in some big towns, an' heard me some big talk,/But there is one thing I know. A woman's [man is] a two-face, a worrisome thing that leads you to sing the blues in the night."

HOME, SWEET HOME

The most popular interpreters of G.I. Jive may have been the singing Andrews Sisters, three show business veterans from a Greek-Norwegian family in Minneapolis. Through hits like "Don't Sit Under the Apple Tree" (1942) and "Shoo-Shoo Baby" (1943), the harmonizing trio helped to foster morale with upbeat vocals about the fate of romance during wartime. Their syncopated rendition of "Boogie Woogie Bugle Boy," introduced in a movie in 1941, personified the impact of African American phrasing and furthered the image of a democratically inclusive military. "He was a famous trumpet man from out Chicago way" and "the top man of his craft," the song began, until "his number came up" and "he was gone with the draft." "Now the company jumps when he plays reveille," sang the Andrews. "He's the boogie woogie bugle boy of Company B."

Like the Andrews Sisters, Glenn Miller's Army Air Force Band pointed to swing's penetration of military life. Born in Iowa in 1904, Miller paid for his first trombone by milking cows. After attending the University of Colorado, he played music on the West Coast before joining several bands in Chicago and New York as a section man and arranger. In the late Thirties Miller organized an orchestra fronted by lead singer Marion Hutton. His insistence on intricate teamwork and musical precision led to a national radio show and enormous success. Yet Miller disbanded the group, accepted a captain's rank in the Army, and assembled a band of men in uniform. Arranging swinging marches of jazz standards like "Tuxedo Junction" (1940), "Chattanooga Choo-Choo" (1941), and "That Old Black Magic" (1942), he revolutionized the nature of military music. The rhythmic punch of "(I've Got a Gal in) Kalamazoo" provided a particularly brilliant example of Miller's fusion of small-town sentiment and hard-edged jive. When the bandleader's plane disappeared over the English Channel in 1944, he instantly achieved iconic status as an American cultural hero.

The jive rhythms of swing jazz coexisted with romantic ballads depicting wartime separation. Helen Forrest, lead vocalist with the Harry James Band, popularized the Frank Loesser and Julie Styne ballad "I Don't Want to Walk Without You" (1941). The heartfelt "This Love of Mine" (1941) featured lyrics by Hoboken, New Jersey-saloon singer Frank Sinatra. The son of Italian immigrants, Sinatra sent "bobby-soxers" into ecstasy by caressing the microphone and thrusting his hips as he performed, while projecting the innocence of the "boy next door." Backed by the Tommy Dorsey Orchestra, he popularized the dreamy "I'll Be Seeing You" (1943). Crooner Dick Haymes provided another wartime hit with the intimately phrased "You'll Never Know" (1943). Meanwhile, rising stars Dinah Shore and Doris Day recorded "I'll Walk Alone" (1944) and "Sentimental Journey" (1944), jukebox favorites that ranked alongside the Mills Brothers' "Till Then" (1944). As hostilities ended, Kitty Kallen and the Harry James Band collaborated on "It's Been a Long, Long Time" (1945), a Sammy Cahn and Julie Styne tune idealizing the anticipated reunion of sweethearts and spouses.

Hollywood sought to enhance home front morale with portraits of family loyalty, hard work, solidarity, and sacrifice. In *Tender Comrade* (1943), a film written and directed by Popular Front activists Dalton Trumbo and Edward Dmytryk, respectively, Ginger Rogers played one of four women aircraft plant workers who pool their resources to "share and share alike" in a rented house in the absence of their spouses. Learning of her husband's death, Rogers tells her young son that his father "went out and died so you could have a better break when you grow up." Stalwart women also accepted the loss of loved ones in *Since You Went Away* (1944), a movie starring Claudette Colbert and Jennifer Jones. In *Pittsburgh* (1942), John Wayne and Randolph Scott played two feuding Pennsylvania mine operators who unite forces to serve the country after Pearl Harbor. King Vidor's *American Romance* (1944), in turn, described an immigrant ex-steel worker who converts his auto factory into an aircraft plant after losing his eldest son in combat. In William Saroyan's *The Human Comedy* (1943), in contrast, the military conflict is merely the backdrop for a story about the humble residents of a California valley.

Star-studded productions like *Stage Door Canteen* and *Hollywood Canteen* (1944) served the war effort by casting leading show-business personalities as ordinary citizens imbued with homespun values and love of country. The twin virtues of democracy and nationalism received their most explicit treatment in *This Is the Army.* Asked by singer Kate Smith for a patriotic number as the threat of European fascism escalated in

1938, Irving Berlin recycled a piece he had filed away during World War I as "too corny." Five years later, Smith's on-screen performance of "God Bless America" helped to make *This Is the Army* the number one-ranking feature of the war years. While storm clouds gathered overseas, suggested Berlin's lyric, citizens could swear allegiance to "a land that's free." "Stand beside her and guide her," proclaimed the prayer-like rousing chorus, "God Bless America,/My home sweet home."

YOUR LAND, MY LAND

Irving Berlin's tribute to the homeland imagined an immigrant's gratitude for a place of refuge in a dangerous world. Folksinger Woody Guthrie saw America's potential in radically different terms. Arriving in New York City early in 1940, shortly after the outbreak of World War II and the signing of a nonaggression pact between Nazi Germany and the Soviet Union, Guthrie angrily responded to the perceived piety of Berlin's hymn with a parody set to an old Carter Family standard. The song began by listing the country's wondrous geographic treasures. As the narrator proceeds along "the ribbon of highway," however, he sees long relief lines and private property signs instead of a land where the fruits of labor belong to the people. "God Blessed America for me!" the last line concludes in protest.

Guthrie put his lyric away for four years. Meanwhile, he began to make a name for himself in radical circles as a creator and singer of "People's Ballads." Attending a "Grapes of Wrath Evening" to benefit John Steinbeck's committee for migrant workers, he met Huddie Ledbetter and shared the stage with prominent folk artists and personalities. The event marked the first gathering of its kind for a mainstream audience. Guthrie also appeared with Leadbelly, Josh White, Burl Ives, W.C. Handy, and others in *Cavalcade of Song* (1940), a Broadway production that helped to spur the folk revival. A frequent guest on "We the People" and other New York-based network radio shows, he received a request to record a "Grapes of Wrath" song for a commercial label. The singer responded with "Tom Joad," a seventeen-verse ballad about organizing migrant laborers. Guthrie's two-record set, *Dust Bowl Ballads* (1940), soon became a favorite in progressive schools and summer camps.

Building on the success of his record within the radical political movement, Guthrie toured the country in the spring of 1941 with folksinger Pete Seeger. The grandson of a sugar refinery baron with a vast Hudson Valley estate, Seeger had attended private boarding schools, where he learned to play the banjo. After two years at Harvard in the mid–1930s, he followed the path of his father, Charles, a prominent ethnomusicologist, by joining Alan Lomax to record folk music for the Library of Congress. Hearing Guthrie perform in 1940, Seeger decided that he had found "his kind of music." Once on tour, the genteel young man became fascinated with Guthrie's class-based politics, folk music skills, and ability to relate with working people.

Later that spring, Guthrie received a $266 federal contract to travel to Portland, Oregon, to write a series of songs about the construction of the Columbia River's Bonneville Dam. Personally inspecting different portions of the waterway over the course of a month, he produced more than two dozen pieces. In "The Grand Coulee Dam," the songwriter listed the variety of waterfalls and factories along the great river's course in Washington State. His masterpiece, however, was "Roll on, Columbia," an anthem set to a melody closely resembling Leadbelly's "Goodnight, Irene." Striving for poetic detail in the fashion of Walt Whitman, Guthrie listed all the river's tributaries, several, like the Klickitat, with Indian names. The song reiterated the promise that hydroelectric power ensured jobs and prosperity for working people. Northwest dams, proclaimed the chorus, were "turning our darkness to dawn."

Guthrie's western sojourn inspired a period of creativity. "Hard Traveling" presented the details of working life. "Pastures of Plenty," a dirge-like adaptation of the traditional "Pretty Polly," traced the migrant experience. "It's a mighty hard row that my poor hands have hoed," sang Guthrie. "My poor feet have traveled a hot dusty road." The song's terse lines offered a tribute to those who "worked in your orchards of peaches and prunes," who "slept on the ground in the light of the moon." By the summer of 1941, Guthrie was ready to join the Almanac Singers, America's first urban folk-singing ensemble. Comprised of middle-class activists like Seeger, Bess Lomax, and Lee Hays, the group believed that "the people," "the folk," and "the workers" had an indigenous culture and politics normally ignored by the commercial market. To cement their identity as progressive artists in touch with ordinary Americans, members adopted rural and proletarian personas, dressed informally, and sometimes spoke with a southern lilt.

Although the repertoire of the Almanac Singers featured traditional ballads and work songs, the bulk of material tended to be old tunes with updated lyrics, a pattern evident in the class-conscious album *Taking Union* (1941). The group's polemical edge also surfaced in "Reuben James," a song issued several months after Soviet entrance into the war on the Allied side. Having abandoned non-interventionism and returned to the Popular Front alliance between liberals and communists, the Almanacs now asked listeners to remember the names of the ninety-five U.S. seamen lost in a ship sunk by German torpedoes in the North Atlantic. Beyond such populist gestures, the Almanacs fostered cohesiveness in the radical community with spontaneous songfests known as "hootenannies." Seeger and Guthrie had picked up the term at a Seattle singing party and been told it referred to Hootin' Annie, an itinerant prostitute who had been a legendary inspiration to Pacific Northwest lumber workers. Back in New York, the Almanacs used the name for Sunday afternoon rent parties and soon expanded participatory mass singing to concerts, fund-raisers, and a national tour of progressive union halls.

Following Pearl Harbor, the Almanac Singers broadcast "We, the People," a network radio show devoted to the folk tradition, and reached an estimated audience of thirty million in the opening installment of "This Is War," a program billed as an anthology of "music belonging to the United Peoples." Shortly thereafter, however, the group came under fire for ties to the communist movement. Internal problems furthered its difficulties. Ever wary that he had "camped out along the trail of the intellectuals," Guthrie wanted folk songs to include more detail about factory life. He also feared that an excessively internationalized repertoire would alienate American workers. Indeed, the Almanacs suffered from the contradiction of supporting a progressive ideological line in lyrical content while seeking to express the actual concerns of ordinary people and the "inarticulate." Choosing selections on narrowly political grounds, moreover, often led to poor performance standards and dwindling audiences.

Seeking to tell the story of his upbringing and adventures, Guthrie published his autobiography, *Bound for Glory* (1943). The songwriter also recorded a version of "God Blessed America," changing the title, at Seeger's suggestion, to "This Land Is Your Land" (1944). "From California to the New York island," the first verse proclaimed, "This land was made for you and me." Ironically, the radical anthem's celebration of the nation's geographic splendor made it a favorite selection of postwar school assemblies and mainstream political gatherings. Whatever the song's fate, the wartime rebirth of the Popular Front had demonstrated that music could be a tool of political consciousness, and that expressions of people's culture continued to arouse public interest.

SIMPLE GIFTS

Unlike Woody Guthrie and the radical folksingers, former Popular Front activist Aaron Copland sought to convey the essence of American democratic culture in less sectarian terms. After the success of *Billy the Kid,* Copland had become the nation's most recognized composer, producing incidental music for the documentary film *The City* (1939), as well as for Hollywood features *Of Mice and Men* (1939) and *Our Town* (1940). His score for the dramatic narrative *Lincoln Portrait* (1942) expanded his interest in folk material by incorporating ballads like "Springfield Mountain" and Stephen Foster's "Camptown Races." Copland's feel for the vernacular led Agnes de Mille to talk the musician into collaborating on her new ballet, *Rodeo* (1942). The niece of film director Cecil B. De Mille, the choreographer had been an avant-garde performer in the 1920s before turning to a fusion of modern and popular dance forms. In *American Street* (1938), de Mille developed the ability to extract dramatic meaning from commonplace physical gestures. The acceptance of her scenario for *Rodeo* allowed the artist to become the first American choreographer retained by the prestigious Ballet Russe de Monte Carlo.

Visualizing the rodeo as a courtship ceremony and rite of spring, de Mille saw the production as a patriotic celebration of American social harmony. Her sense of realism led to the insistence that the Russian dancers learn to walk and move their bodies like American cowboys, using their backs "the way a pitcher does in baseball … one of the

Agnes de Mille in *Rodeo* (1942)   (*Photofest*)

things the Americans do." Copland incorporated even more folk tunes and railroad songs into *Rodeo* than he had in *Billy the Kid.* The production's original music blended irony and a respect for prairie culture. To accomplish this, Copland had harp fragments resemble a guitar, woodwinds sound like an accordion, and violins emulate country fiddles. The popular ballet received twenty curtain calls and repeated standing ovations at its sold-out New York opening, followed by a successful national tour.

Two years after *Rodeo's* triumph, Copland composed a Pulitzer Prize-winning score for Martha Graham's *Appalachian Spring* (1944). Raised in Pittsburgh and Santa Barbara, California, Graham studied dance in Los Angeles, where she learned to appreciate American folk and vernacular styles. Founding her own dance school in New York in the mid-Twenties, she developed the "Graham technique" in which the stomach and torso were subjected to spasmodic movements, while the dancer assumed a series of innovative kneeling and sitting positions. Graham believed that dance reflected a people's soul and that the nation's rhythmic legacy derived largely from American Indian and African American roots. After choreographing *Primitive Mysteries* (1931), a ballet inspired by Native American ritual, she mounted a series of productions focusing upon the frontier and the national folk heritage. One of these, *American Document* (1937), broke the traditional silence of dance with a spoken narrative taken from the Bible, Walt Whitman, and several key American texts.

Graham found the title for *Appalachian Spring* in "The Dance," a poem in Hart Crane's *The Bridge* (1930). The ballet sought to celebrate the humor, joy, and tenderness of a shared national past and "the American feeling of place." It included dramatizations of a revivalist sermon, a courtship, the wedding of a nineteenth-century Pennsylvania farm couple, and a house-raising. Anxious to establish authenticity, Graham incorporated excerpts from the Virginia Reel and utilized the up-tempo gyrations of a sailors' hornpipe and the jitterbug. Copland responded by sprinkling the score with country fiddle tunes, simple harmonies, folk songs, and the Shaker hymn "Simple Gifts." After converting *Appalachian Spring* into an orchestral suite, the composer completed his *Third Symphony* (1946), a work he described as a representation of the "euphoric spirit of the country" at the close of World War II. The final movement of the piece incorporated *Fanfare for the Common Man* (1942), a hymn-like prayer and patriotic tribute to the struggle against oppression that Copland had written during the uncertain early days of the conflict.

GOLDEN SKIES

Intrigued by *Rodeo's* union of dance and folk art, the new songwriting team of Richard Rodgers and Oscar Hammerstein hired Agnes de Mille to choreograph *Oklahoma!* (1943). Rodgers' last musical had been *Pal Joey* (1940), a collaborative effort with lyricist Lorenz Hart that was halfway between a collection of production numbers and concept-based musical theater. Based on a John O'Hara novel set in Depression Chicago, *Pal Joey* had centered upon the relationship of a ruthless nightclub operator and an adventurous socialite, both of whom used the opposite sex for mere physical pleasure. Although the clever lyrics of self-demeaning songs like "Bewitched" complemented the show's good-natured cynicism, the story lacked romantic resolution. Hart subsequently rejected Rodgers' idea of a musical version of *Green Grows the Lilacs,* a folk-drama of pre-statehood Oklahoma produced by the Theater Guild in 1931. Sensing that wartime tastes involved a shift from urbane sophistication to more positive affirmations, Rodgers sought out *Show Boat* lyricist Hammerstein.

Both men concluded that *Oklahoma!* would be a "folk" musical highlighting homespun American characters, values, and ideals. As a celebration of communal cohesion and the unity resulting from the submerging of differences, the show would communicate the feelings of ordinary people in vernacular language and basic harmonies. Fusing traditional musical comedy with realist drama, Rodgers and Hammerstein envisioned an integration of melody and narrative that went far beyond the pioneering efforts of *Show Boat* and *Pal Joey.* Songs and extended dance routines would introduce and define characters, trace the interaction of psychologically motivated protagonists, and drive the plot toward resolution. The production would be an ensemble performance with no stars or gag lines, one replacing the chorus line with a ballet troupe.

The opening moments of *Oklahoma!* demonstrated the extent to which Rodgers and Hammerstein had revolutionized musical theater. Instead of Broadway's customary production number, the action commenced with a mature woman churning butter amidst a set reminiscent of a Thomas Hart Benton or Grant Wood painting. Meanwhile, an unaccompanied voice in the wings began to sing "Oh, What a Beautiful Morning." "There's a bright golden haze on the meadow," the cowhand began, slowly repeating the initial phrase as he approached the stage. "The corn is as high as an elephant's eye,/An' it looks like it's climbin' clear up to the sky." "All the sounds of the earth are like music," he mused; "the cattle are standin' like statues." The mix of simple metaphor and folk melody defined the brimming optimism of the song's resolution. "I got a beautiful feelin'," sang the cowboy, "everything's goin' my way."

Although *Oklahoma!* referred back to the semi-mythical past of the pioneer era, the musical dealt with well-defined characters in recognizable life situations facing the dilemmas of everyday people. "You cain't deserve the sweet and tender things in life less'n you're tough," observes crusty Aunt Eller. A nominal story of conflict between farmers and cattle ranchers, the show expressed the essence of wartime democratic nationalism. "I don't say I'm no better than anybody else," Eller sings in "The Farmer and the Cowman," "but I'll be damned if I ain't just as good!" The production's title theme song, added as an afterthought, conveyed the nation's faith in itself amid the uncertainties of war. "We know we belong to the land," sang the ensemble, "And the land we belong to is grand!"

Within five years, more than eight million people had seen the Broadway or road version of *Oklahoma!* By then Rodgers and Hammerstein had a new success. Resetting a nineteenth-century Hungarian play to a Maine fishing village of the 1880s, *Carousel* (1945) revolved around an ill-fated romance between a carnival barker and a wistful young mill worker. Although a quarter of the production consisted of dialogue, musical numbers dominated the show. Once again, Rodgers and Hammerstein broke new ground, forgoing the customary overture for an opening pantomime enacted to the cacophony of an out-of-tune merry-go-round. The team's insistence on psychological realism resulted in one of the exalted moments of American musical theater. In the extended soliloquy "My Boy Bill," the prospective father sings about his dreams for a son or daughter only to realize that he has no means to support a child. As the piece reaches its emotional climax, he swears that his kid "won't be dragged up in slums" with "a lot o' bums like me." He will find the money, he vows, if he has to "make it or steal it … take it or *die!*"

Shot in a failed robbery, Billy receives heavenly permission for one day on Earth to pass on the lessons of love and resilience. He chooses to attend his daughter's graduation, where he sings the hymn "You'll Never Walk Alone." "When you walk through a storm," the lyrics instruct, "Keep your chin up high/And don't be afraid of the dark … Walk on, Walk on,/With hope in your heart,/And you'll never walk alone." A perennial favorite at weddings, graduations, and funerals, the inspirational anthem suggested that present sacrifices could produce a better future. It also offered a degree of consolation for those whose loved ones could only return in spirit from military service. Remade as a movie in 1956 and revived on Broadway two years later, *Carousel* became a mainstay of high school dramatic presentations and a fixture of American folklore.

JUKEBOX RHYTHMS

In *Juke Girl* (1942), a film with a more contemporary view of working-class life than the Rodgers and Hammerstein musicals, Ronald Reagan played a former migrant labor organizer who settles down on a farm with Anne Sheridan, a local dancer from a jukebox joint. A product of the fall-off in Depression record sales, jukeboxes were an important fixture of wartime popular culture. With over three-hundred thousand of the devices spread across the country in cafés, soda shops, and bars, working people gained access to recorded dance music and the latest performances of their favorite artists for a fraction of the cost of buying a record. The new genres of country and western music and rhythm and blues became the most important beneficiaries of the jukebox revolution.

By the early 1940s, wartime shellac shortages and declining interest along Tin Pan Alley had contributed to the virtual abandonment of "hillbilly" music to independent record labels and publishers. As the influential Roy Acuff severed ties with New York, Nashville rapidly became the business nexus of country music. In turn, local radio stations in the South, Midwest, and elsewhere appealed to the regional tastes of listeners by playing records produced in Nashville studios. As the wartime expansion of manufacturing and service jobs increased real incomes, moreover, a booming nightlife created new demand for dance tunes, one that received its most extensive exposure in the honky-tonk.

Coined in reference to a ragtime piano style of the 1920s, the term "honky-tonk" came to stand for a disreputable southern roadside tavern for working-class whites on the outskirts of town. Whether supplied by live bands or the jukebox, the dance music of the honky-tonks required heightened volume to drown out the din of carousing laborers, loggers, and farm hands. Live musicians responded with the rhythmic punctuation of a "rinky-dink" piano and electric guitars. Although the new sound embraced European polka music as well as Mexican and Cajun styles, it discarded the flowery sentiments and innocence of traditional ballads. Instead, honky-tonk numbers often described the self-pity or guilt associated with infidelity, alcoholism, divorce, or plain loneliness. Torn between evangelical religiosity and a hell-raising hostility to authority, singers vacillated between idealizations of domestic bliss and a restless urge for freedom.

Ernest Tubb emerged as one of the era's prime country music innovators. Born in central Texas in 1914, Tubb was inspired to play and sing like Jimmie Rodgers. To support his musical hobby, he took odd jobs selling mattresses, digging ditches, and working in a drug store while he entertained in the honky-tonks of the nearby oil fields for $1.25 a night. After help from Rodgers' widow, Tubb won a spot on a Fort Worth radio show. Once recording a few sides, however, his career stalled until he broke into the hit charts with "Walking the Floor Over You" (1941), a plaintive lament that incorporated the electric guitar into recorded popular music and marked one of the first examples of "country and western" styling. The bluesy tone of Tubb's material stemmed in part from western swing, a dance music emerging out of the booming oil towns of East Texas and Oklahoma. Combining string band instrumentation with saxophones, trumpets, and a driving rhythm, country swing fused jazz techniques with traditional breakdowns.

The undisputed champion of the country swing style was Texan Bob Wills. An experienced fiddler in medicine shows and string bands, Wills brought his Texas Playboys to Tulsa in 1934, where he hosted a radio show while the band held forth at a local ballroom. Tommy Duncan, a Jimmie Rodgers disciple whom Wills discovered singing for tips at a Fort Worth root-beer stand, served as the group's lead vocalist. In recorded classics such as "Take Me Back to Tulsa," "Ida Red," and "San Antonio Rose" (1940), Wills punctuated Duncan's vocals with verbal patter designed to sustain the fierce tempo of the band's shuffle boogies and rhythmic jump tunes. Influenced by the Texas Playboys, western swing spread across the taverns, dance halls, and rural nightclubs of the Southwest. When Wills relocated to Bakersfield, California, in 1943, the booming oil and agricultural town became a major center of working-class music.

The wails, moans, shouts, cries, slurred phrases, and bent notes of honky-tonk music and western swing borrowed significantly from traditional African American techniques. Like their white counterparts, however, black musicians responded to wartime conditions by experimenting with new styles. Building on the familiar twelve-bar chord format, big-city performers began to play rhythm and blues, an innovation that relied on the electric guitar for greater volume and intensity. To produce a danceable sound for noisy rent parties, juke joints, and nightclubs, drummers accented the second and fourth "off-beats" of each phrase instead of the first or third. Like country music, rhythm and blues benefited not merely from the effects of wartime prosperity and migration, but from the growth of independent record labels, local radio stations, and nightlife establishments catering to regional musical tastes.

Popular performers of the new musical style included boogie-woogie pianist Albert Ammons, alto sax player and singer Eddie Vinson, keyboardist Jay McShann, and Ella Mae Morse, the vocalist who sang the original version of the popular "Cow Cow Boogie" (1942). The most charismatic of the rhythm and blues artists may have been T-Bone Walker. Born to two musicians near Dallas in 1910, Walker learned blues guitar at an early age before joining medicine shows and performing as a side man for live performances. Moving to Los Angeles in 1936, he played the black club circuit with Les Hite and other local bands. The first blues musician to record with the electric guitar, Walker scored a major hit with "Mean Old World Blues" (1945). Like Walker, Louis Jordan reflected the up-tempo pace of wartime life. An Arkansas native and veteran saxophonist, Jordan formed his own jazz combo in 1938 and drifted toward boo-gie-woogie and jump blues. Recording hot dance numbers like "Caldonia Boogie" (1945) and "Choo Choo Ch'Boogie" (1946), he produced the perfect music for fish fries and house parties, while simultaneously appealing to white audiences.

RACE MATTERS

Although the expanding wartime economy increased opportunities for working peo-ple, non-European ethnic groups continued to bear the burdens of prejudice and dis-crimination. Prevailing opinion often viewed Asian Americans, Hispanics, and African Americans as "nonwhites" with biologically determined characteristics. Even though Congress repealed the Chinese Exclusion Act in 1943 and the Army accepted Filipino Americans for service in the Pacific, Japanese Americans remained in a sepa-rate category. Pronouncements by military and government officials in Washington, D.C. and the Pacific Coast states depicted the nation's 127,000 Japanese Americans as an unassimilated, tightly knit racial group tied to an enemy nation. A presidential order in 1942 interned almost all West Coast Japanese in relocation centers, including the Ni-sei—the 63 percent of the community who were legal citizens by virtue of their birth on U.S. soil.

Many older camp residents had fostered traditional cultural ties to the homeland by patronizing Japanese classical plays, attending sumo wrestling matches, and partici-pating in annual social gatherings and picnics. Once incarcerated, 22 percent of draft-eligible Nisei refused to serve in the armed forces, some professing loyalty to the Emperor. Nevertheless, a significant portion of the Japanese American community sought to embrace the American Way of Life. Thirty-three thousand Nisei men volun-teered for military duty, many experiencing high casualty rates on the European front. Seeking to humanize the residents of the internment camps, California wilderness pho-tographer Ansel Adams published *Born Free and Equal: Photographs of the Loyal Japanese-Americans at Manzanar Relocation Center* (1944). Addressed to "the aver-age American citizen," the book presented a complimentary portrait of ordinary detain-ees as gentle, bright-eyed, intelligent, and non-embittered victims of social injustice.

Anxious to be included in the national mainstream, four hundred thousand Mexican Americans enlisted for military service. Yet the legacy of discrimination and a sense of alienation among young Chicanos in the Southwest helped to generate a rebellious sub-culture. Identifying themselves as Pachucos, groups of working-class Hispanics af-fected the hipster slang and colorful metaphors of an El Paso marijuana gang with the same name. Legend held that male members of the secret society sported tattooed crosses between the thumb and forefinger. More obviously, self-styled Pachucos flaunted conventional standards by styling their slick long hair in ducktails, donning wide-brimmed hats, and wearing zoot suits—a uniform distinguished by long coats pleated at the waist and draped over the knees with baggy trousers tightly pegged at the cuff. Women counterparts, in turn, dressed in oversize coats, draped slacks, huarache sandals ("zombie slippers"), and pompadour hairdos.

Arousing the resentment of wartime authorities as decadent "slackers" and dope fiends, hundreds of Mexican American youth confronted a police roundup in 1942, when an unidentified assailant killed a white man at Los Angeles' Sleepy Lagoon. Twelve defendants faced murder charges and extensive prison sentences before officials ultimately overturned the false convictions. A year later, white sailors responded to a confrontation in the Los Angeles barrio with a series of un-policed attacks on the Mexican American community that lasted for a week before military authorities called a halt to the violence. Despite such repression, zoot suit fashions spread to some Hispanic musicians and performers, and combined with elements of swing and boogie-woogie culture to lay the foundations for the postwar hipster underground.

Seven hundred thousand African Americans served in World War II, but the Army imposed quotas on black recruitment and placed Negro soldiers in racially segregated units with white officers. Because military officials considered nonwhites too docile to fight, they initially confined blacks to labor units. Even as African Americans took their place on the front lines, they received no recognition for combat service. In a period in which the Red Cross separated blood along racial lines, the Army also insisted on the enforcement of local segregation ordinances, prohibiting African Americans in uniform from using public eating facilities where prevailing custom or law forbade the practice. In the civilian sector, "hate strikes" in shipyards and defense plants sometimes protested the hiring of black workers or the integration of public housing.

Racial tensions erupted in rioting in Harlem and Detroit in 1943, killing forty-one people and injuring over a thousand. Meanwhile, trade unionist A. Philip Randolph initiated a Double V campaign for victory over enemies at home as well as on foreign battlefields. "This is every man's war" for "full freedom for all people," declared Paul Robeson. Refusing to sing for segregated audiences, Robeson attacked Hollywood for the persistence of "child-like and innocent" Negro stereotypes in the movies. Meanwhile, civil rights activists integrated war-service canteens in New York and Hollywood, as well as several West Coast jazz clubs. After Billie Holiday declared that she was "a race woman," some fans interpreted her Los Angeles recording of "Travellin' Light" (1942) as a protest against segregated public accommodations.

Richard Wright's text to *12 Million Black Voices: A Folk History of the Negro in the United States* (1941) set the tone for the political assertiveness of the war years. Wright's commentaries on a collection of Farm Security Administration photographs sought to introduce white readers to the realities of African American culture. "Our history is far stranger than you suspect, and we are not what we seem," he warned. "Beneath the garb of the black laborer, the black cook, and the black elevator operator" lay "an uneasily tied knot of pain and hope," suggested the author. Wright intended "to seize upon that which is qualitative and abiding in the Negro experience" by looking at the "triumphs and defeats" of the "humble folk," the "broad masses" who struggled for survival. The accompanying images of his book traced the migration of cotton share-croppers to the northern metropolis and their "slow death on the city pavements." "We watch strange moods fill our children," confessed Wright, "and our hearts swell with pain." The swift speech and impatient eyes of the young, he contended, revealed a bit-terness and frustration "at the sight of the alluring hopes and prizes denied them."

The psychological costs of discrimination dominated the writing of Chester Himes. Dropping out of college in Ohio in the early 1930s, Himes worked as a bellhop and street hustler before drifting into a life of violent crime. While serving nine years time for armed robbery, he published stories about his prison experiences in *Esquire*. Himes went to Hollywood in 1940 to become a screenwriter, but failing to break into the movie business, earned a living as an unskilled laborer in the California shipyards. The "mental corrosion of race prejudice," he later wrote of the white violence he encoun-tered, left him "bitter and saturated with hate." Himes' first novel, *If He Hollers Let Him Go* (1945), described the victimization of a black "leaderman" in the yards. A se-quel, *Lonely Crusade* (1947), conveyed the psychotic dynamics of white racism in the nightmare setting of Los Angeles' racially tense home front economy.

Intent on confronting racial stereotyping in the world of entertainment, Duke Ellington created *Jump for Joy,* a musical revue that played to an integrated Los An-geles audience in 1941. The composer envisioned the extravaganza as a merger of a Cotton Club stage show and the politically minded *Pins and Needles. Jump for Joy* of-fered a history of African American music from spirituals and country blues to boo-gie-woogie and contemporary swing. Purged of racial dialect and blackface, it celebrated liberation from the Jim Crow South and plantation tradition, and included skits marking the deaths of Stephen Foster and Uncle Tom. Two years later, Ellington produced an original score for *Black, Brown, and Beige* (1943) to serve as backdrop to a history of the American Negro. His insistence on portraying the dignified elements of black life came through most clearly in "Come Sunday," a haunting piece that captured the mood of the single day in which ordinary people rested and engaged their spiritual concerns.

BEBOP PROTOTYPES

Ellington's syntheses of African American expression came just as innovative forms were emerging among black musicians. Since the late 1930s, jam sessions at Harlem chili houses and after-hours jazz clubs had nurtured a phenomenon later christened as bebop. Aggressive, provocative, and belligerent in presentation and attitude, the new jazz transcended conventional Western harmonies with complex chords used by pia-nists like Bud Powell and Thelonious Monk. In long improvised solos, horn players

Duke Ellington   (*Photofest*)

such as Lester Young, Charles Parker, and Dizzy Gillespie contributed to the dissonant emphasis by distorting or "flatting" the fifths and ninths of the musical scale and consciously eliminating most of the showy vibrato from their performance. Meanwhile, percussionists like Kenny Clarke imparted a frantic pace to the music by replacing the heavy sound of the bass drum with the more limber top cymbal. Led by Gillespie, bop musicians reinforced the non-Western flavor by experimenting with Afro-Cuban polyrhythm, unpredictable tempos, and offbeat accents.

Bebop practitioners alternated between covering Tin Pan Alley standards and performing their own compositions. Intent on the integrity of the music, players rejected the stereotype of the black entertainer and affected total boredom. Accordingly, they showed no interest in announcing tunes or acknowledging applause, and submitted visiting players to sudden key changes, interrupted choruses, and broken-off solos. Bop's hipster rebellion had roots in the pain of racial discrimination, as well as a reaction to the regimentation of wartime swing bands and military life. It enabled black jazz artists to create a community of avant-garde outsiders and produce a style that few whites could imitate. Like the Pachucos, musicians favored an insider's language of "jive talk." Varying the meaning of words and resorting to internal rhymes, exaggeration, and ungrammatical familiarity, they devised coded terms such as "hip" for street wise, "cool" for composed, "cat" for male, "chick" for female, "crazy" for good, and "dig" for beneath-the-surface understanding. Adopted as the linguistic code of working-class blacks, the jargon of the hipsters ultimately would emerge as America's unofficial slang.

SOURCES AND SUGGESTED READINGS

The application of cultural resources to wartime mobilization figures in Paul D. Casdorph, *Let the Good Times Roll: Life at Home in America during World War II* (1989). Office of War Information photographs appear in the later portions of Carl Fleischhauer and Beverly W. Brannans, eds., *Documentary America, 1935–1943* (1988). See the relevant segments of Jeffrey T. Sammons, *Beyond the Ring: The Role of Boxing in American Society* (1988) for the supportive wartime activities of Joe Louis, while Lewis A. Erenberg contextualizes the champion's status as a national symbol in *The Greatest Fight of Our Generation: Louis vs. Schmeling* (2006).

Hollywood's substantial role in sustaining wartime morale is the subject of Bernard F. Dick, *The Star Spangled Screen: The American World War II Film* (1985) and Jordan Braverman, *To Hasten the Homecoming: How Americans Fought World War II Through the Media* (1996). More critical assessments appear in Clayton R. Koppes and Gregory D. Black, *Hollywood Goes to War: How Politics, Profits and Propaganda Shaped World War II Movies* (1987) and Thomas Doherty, *Projections of War: Hollywood, American Culture, and World War II* (1993). Wartime statements of inclusion receive consideration in the relevant sections of John Bodnar, *Blue-Collar Hollywood: Liberalism, Democracy, and Working People in American Film* (2003). For racial pluralism in home-front movies, see the relevant segments of Thomas Cripps, *Making Movies Black: The Hollywood Message Movie from World War II to the Civil Rights Era* (1993); Bruce M. Tyler, *From Harlem to Hollywood: The Struggle for Racial and Cultural Democracy, 1920–1943* (1992); and Donald Bogle, *Bright Boulevards, Bold Dreams: The Story of Black Hollywood* (2005).

Lewis A. Erenberg points to the democratic influence of wartime popular music in *Swingin' the Dream: Big Band Jazz and the Rebirth of American Culture* (1990). See also Kathleen E.R. Smith, *God Bless America: Tin Pan Alley Goes to War* (2003). For wartime folk balladeers, see R. Serge Denisoff, *Great Day Coming: Folk Music and the American Left* (1971); Robbie Lieberman, *"My Song Is My Weapon": People's Songs, American Communism, and the Politics of Culture, 1930–1950* (1989); and Joe Klein, *Woody Guthrie, A Life* (1980). Useful profiles of the period's musical influences appear in portions of Howard Pollack, *Aaron Copland: The Life and Work of an Uncommon Man* (1999) and Ethan Mordden, *Rodgers and Hammerstein* (1992).

The growing popularity of wartime country music and rhythm and blues is one of the key themes of George Lipsitz, *Rainbow at Midnight: Labor and Culture in the 1940s* (1994). For the Nashville sound, see the relevant chapters of Bill C. Malone, *Country Music U.S.A.*, 2nd rev. ed. (2002) and Dorothy Horstman, *Sing Your Heart Out, Country Boy*, rev. ed. (1996). Descriptions of the period's black popular music appear in Peter Guralnick, *Feel Like Going Home: Portraits in Blues and Rock 'n' Roll* (1999).

For Japanese American internment, see the relevant portions of Ronald Takaki, *Strangers from a Different Shore: A History of Asian Americans* (1989). Useful studies of the Pachuco movement include Marricio Mazón, *The Zoot Suit Riots: The Psychology of Symbolic Annihilation* (1984) and Eduardo Obregón Pagán, *Murder at the Sleepy Lagoon: Zoot Suits, Race, and Riot in Wartime L.A.* (2003). For material on two of the era's key African American cultural figures, see Martin B. Duberman, *Paul Robeson* (1988) and James Sallis, *Chester Himes, A Life* (2001). Portions of Ellen Harkins Wheat's *Jacob Lawrence, American Painter* (1986) describe the mural creations of the foremost African American visual artist of the war years. For the leading black wartime musical figure, see the relevant portions of John Edward Hasse, *Beyond Category: The Life and Genius of Duke Ellington* (1993). Two volumes, Ben Sidran's *Black Talk* (1981) and Ira Gitler's *Swing to Bop: An Oral History of the Transition in Jazz in the 1940s* (1985), depict bebop's revolutionary musical and cultural innovations.

8

Beyond Consensus: Making It Real in Cold War America

"We'll sit and dream—the things that ev'ry dad and mother dream," an aspiring couple sings in "When the Children Are Asleep," a light-hearted musical number in Broadway's *Carousel.* The song's evocation of domestic bliss captured the desires of millions of Americans following the immense dislocations of World War II. Indeed, paintings, westerns, television programs, Broadway musicals, and Hollywood movies all conveyed a widespread quest for stability and traditional anchors in the years between 1945 and 1960. Yet the period's expressive culture reflected a surprising degree of complexity. Ethnic working-class life and middle-class unrest received substantial exposure in the new medium of television, as well as in the psychological and social settings of Hollywood crime sagas, film noir, realist dramas, and even science fiction. In the end, the postwar era experienced a full airing of the controversies and anxieties surrounding the place of ordinary Americans in society's uncertain future.

THE BEST YEARS

Peacetime inaugurated a period of prosperity that afforded middle-class status to millions of people. As Americans spent wartime savings on appliances, automobiles, furniture, and other durable goods, consumer indebtedness returned to 1920s levels. Through low-interest government mortgage loans to veterans, home ownership spread to the point that a majority of Americans soon owned the houses in which they lived.

Federally subsidized highway construction enabled the suburbs to become the focal point of the postwar boom. Political leaders hailed the suburban nuclear family as a key fixture of democratic capitalism and a major reason why the United States had achieved the world's highest living standard.

Idealizations of middle-class life were particularly evident in Norman Rockwell's iconic cover illustrations for the *Saturday Evening Post* and *Look* and his continuing contributions to the *Boy Scout Calendar.* With the exception of Rockwell, the most widely recognized artist of the postwar period was "Grandma" Moses. Born Anna Mary Robertson in 1860, Moses did not turn to easel painting until her husband died when she was sixty-seven. Eleven years later, an art collector discovered her work in a drug store in upstate New York. Bridging folk and popular art techniques, Moses achieved massive popularity by using Currier and Ives prints and magazine clippings as models for portraits of rural and small-town life. Altogether, Grandma Moses completed over 1,500 paintings and reached millions of people with mass-produced greeting card designs.

As peacetime marked the end of widespread separation from loved ones, a variety of popular culture forms explored the importance of family ties to social well-being. Several of the postwar period's most popular fiction and movies equated healthy middle-class family life with the democratic lifestyle. In *Meet Me in St. Louis* (1944), Judy Garland's performance of unpretentious musical numbers like "The Boy Next Door" and "The Trolley Song" complemented a nostalgic view of the early twentieth century as a period in which people valued each other's welfare over wealth or social status. In the popular *Life With Father* (1947), William Powell portrayed a stern but eccentric and loving patriarch of a New York clan of the same era. *A Death in the Family* (1957), James Agee's autobiographical account of the loss of his father in an automobile accident, won the Pulitzer Prize for Fiction and found its way onto stage and screen in the early 1960s as the homespun *All the Way Home.*

Broadway musicals provided some of the most robust celebrations of family virtue and democratic values. Returning to the stage, Irving Berlin produced the score for *Annie Get Your Gun* (1946), a show about sharpshooter Annie Oakley's rise to stardom in the Buffalo Bill *Wild West Show* and her subsequent conversion to domesticity. With numbers like "Doin' What Comes Natur'lly," "The Girl That I Marry," "I Got the Sun in the Morning," and "I Can Do Anything You Can Do," Berlin continued to fuse simple melodies with believable lyrics from everyday language. In "There's No Business Like Show Business," the songwriter produced a perennial standard that spoke to the egalitarian opportunities of an open society. "Yesterday they told you you would not go far," sang lead performer Ethel Merman, "That night you open and there you are/Next day on your dressing room they've hung a star ..."

Annie Get Your Gun received a popular Hollywood treatment in 1950. By then, two more smash-hit musicals were thriving on Broadway. *South Pacific* (1949), the third collaboration between Richard Rodgers and Oscar Hammerstein, took its characters and plot from a Pulitzer Prize winning collection of World War II sketches by fiction writer James Michener. Fashioning the nation's uniformed men and women as representatives of a hardy democracy, the production highlighted Mary Martin's brassy vocals in simply phrased show-stoppers like "Cockeyed Optimist," "Honey Bun," "A Wonderful Guy," and "I'm Gonna Wash That Man Right Outta My Hair." Meanwhile, the egalitarian camaraderie of men at war came forth in hearty chorus numbers like "Bloody Mary" and "There's Nothing Like a Dame." In contrast, Frank Loesser's score in *Guys and Dolls* (1950) gave musical form to the low-life characters of Damon Runyon's Broadway, only to have the story resolve with dual weddings for the show's four principals. Screen versions of *Guys and Dolls* (1955), *Oklahoma!* (1955), *Carousel* (1956), *South Pacific* (1958), and *West Side Story* (1961) brought musical theater to far larger audiences.

As demonstrated by the musicals, popular culture sustained much of its attraction by mining the experiences of everyday life. Director Elia Kazan's first feature film, *A Tree Grows in Brooklyn* (1945), an adaptation of a best-selling wartime novel, offered a telling example. Influenced by the characterizations of Thomas Wolfe and by Henry Roth's *Call It Sleep*, author Betty Smith had set her tale of a World War I-era Irish and German family in the Williamsburg tenements of Brooklyn. The ethnic and working-class slant of Smith's book appealed to Kazan. Of Greek ethnicity, he had migrated with his family from Turkey to the United States as a child. Drawn to radical politics in the Thirties, he joined the Group Theater, but broke with the Communist Party when movement leaders tried him for failing to instigate a strike. After directing a documentary short on miners and a government feature about food rationing, Kazan staged the Broadway production of Thornton Wilder's *The Skin of Our Teeth* (1942) before accepting his initial feature-length assignment in Hollywood.

"There's a tree that grows in Brooklyn, which struggles to reach the sky," states Smith's thirteen-year-old narrator Francie Nolan. Embedded in cement and surviving without sun, water, or earth, it flourishes only in the slums, she explains, because "it likes poor people." The novel affectionately contrasted Katie, Francie's no-nonsense mother, who is obsessed with the survival of her family, with her father, Johnny, an intermittently employed singing waiter, a charming alcoholic, and a perennial dreamer. Although the family suffers scorn and humiliation because of its poverty, the children rise above these affronts and never experience a sense of shame. Nevertheless, Katie informs her husband that Francie will have to quit school and get a job to help the family make ends meet.

Determined to keep his daughter in school, Johnny spends three days walking the streets in search of work, contacts pneumonia, and in a weakened condition from alcohol abuse, dies a few days later. "He had nothing to give but himself," Francie declares in homage to her beloved father, "but of this he gave generously like a king." Working afternoons in a saloon, she manages to graduate high school, receiving a bouquet of flowers that Johnny had ordered for the occasion long before his death. Unlike much of the work of the Thirties, *A Tree Grows in Brooklyn* did not present a sociological treatise on class privilege so much as a tribute to the ethic of self-help and self-improvement. For Smith and Kazan alike, family affection, hard work, saving, education, and neighborly compassion, not collective political solutions, provided dignity to the working class.

TV FAMILIES

Born Yesterday (1950), a Hollywood film based on a stage play by Garson Kanin, presented a more political treatment of working-class aspirations. The movie starred Judy Holliday in an Academy Award-winning performance as Billie Dawn—a New York chorus girl and mistress of a shady scrap iron dealer (Broderick Crawford) who comes to Washington to assist the tycoon's attempts to lobby Congress for special favors. Fearing that the "dumb blonde" needs more of a cultural veneer, Crawford hires a tutor (William Holden) to smooth out her rough edges. In a female version of *Mr. Smith Goes to Washington,* however, Billie takes to heart her teacher's lessons about democracy, and after touring the capital's monuments, asserts her own will over the machinations of her corrupt benefactor. In the end, Billie Dawn's earthy wit and unfailing honesty enable her to take control of the tycoon's legitimate enterprises while winning the heart of her tutor.

Like comedians Milton Berle, Sid Caesar, Danny Kaye, Red Buttons, Jerry Lewis, and Buddy Hackett, playwright Garson Kanin had roots in the working-class Jewish resorts of New York's Catskill Mountains, where the vernacular traditions of Broadway, vaudeville, and radio long had flourished. The hyperactive pace of Catskill comedy proved highly effective in the new medium of television, which rapidly emerged as America's primary entertainment form in the postwar era. By 1954, thirty million households had a TV set; at the end of the decade, 86 percent of all homes boasted access to the medium. Laced with slapstick skits and rapid-fire dialogue, Milton Berle's weekly Texaco Star Theater (1948–56) became television's first commonly watched program. Nevertheless, Broadway humor and New York ethnicity tended to wear thin west of the Hudson River. Accordingly, television's converted radio shows like *The Goldbergs* (1949–57), *The Jack Benny Program* (1950–64), and *George Burns and Gracie Allen* (1950–58) tended to de-emphasize the Jewish character of their leading protagonists.

Seeking as wide an audience as possible, early television programmers favored generic portraits of working-class life. *Mama* (1949–56), a popular weekly prime-time series, described a struggling Norwegian American family in early-twentieth-century San Francisco. The show traced its origins to *Mama's Bank Account* (1943), a short story collection by Kathryn Forbes. Born in 1909 and raised in foster homes, Forbes created a family saga of sacrifice, mutual respect, and solidarity from anecdotes passed on by her grandmother. Her book's title referred to mama's use of an imaginary savings account to provide a carpenter's family with a sense of security during hard times. Facing the need to reconcile individual desires with family needs, the Hansons combined old country values like hard work, courage, and honesty with American traits like economic self-sufficiency and the importance of education for sons and daughters alike. First presented as a Broadway "folk play" in 1944 and in the film *I Remember Mama* (1948), the show's realistic acting, slice-of-life tales, and character-driven plots pointed to the moral strengths of the immigrant family and pragmatic mothers as foundations of democracy.

The situation comedy *I Love Lucy* (1951–61) combined farcical treatments of middle-class family life with subtle parodies of conventional gender roles. As the slightly wacky wife to her real-life husband, Cuban American bandleader Desi Arnaz, Lucille Ball constantly tested the limits of domesticity through her comic antics and expressions of an essential humanity. Several episodes revolved around the character's ill-fated attempts to become a professional entertainer against the wishes of her husband. Others involved cases where Lucy's well-intentioned motives caused confusion. In one memorable sequence, a panic-stricken Lucy sneaks out of the house to sleep in the doghouse so the barking of the abandoned pet she has adopted won't prompt Desi to force her to get rid of the lonely animal.

Just as *I Love Lucy* used humor in dealing with the expectations society placed on women, the black actors of TV's *Amos 'n' Andy* (1951–53) presented African Americans in a slightly more human context than the one to which most viewers were accustomed. *The Life of Riley* (1949–50, 1953–58), a weekly series about an Irish American airplane riveter in southern California, may have done the same for blue-collar workers. In its original run before William Bendix popularized the role, *The Life of Riley* starred Jackie Gleason. A native of Brooklyn, New York, Gleason left school during the Depression when he won a talent contest at age fifteen. Serving a long apprenticeship as a stand-up comic in carnivals and nightclubs, he came to the attention of television producers following a featured role in the Broadway show *Follow the Girls* (1945).

On his own in the fall of 1949, Gleason hosted a variety show, an opportunity he used to introduce television audiences to characters from his nightclub act, such as Joe the Bartender and Charlie the Loudmouth. Beginning in 1952, *The Jackie Gleason Show* included a skit called "The Honeymooners" in which the performer played the boisterous, scheming, and self-defeating Ralph Kramden—a heavy-set bus driver who shares a dingy apartment with his acerbic wife, Alice, and whose best friend and neighbor is a slow-witted but dutifully loyal sewer worker named Norton. Gleason's brilliant characterization allowed viewers to laugh at Ralph's bravado while sympathizing with his human vulnerability. Only moderately successful as its

The Honeymooners   *(Courtesy of CBS Broadcasting,Inc.)*

own series in 1955–56, *The Honeymooners* became far more popular in syndicated reruns a generation later.

RED RIVER VALLEY

Led by *Gunsmoke,* which took to the air in 1955, western adventure series increasingly played a major role on television. The broad acceptance of the postwar western accompanied the widespread popularity of comic book heroes like Gene Autry, Roy Rogers, Hopalong Cassidy, Red Ryder, and Tom Mix. Louis D. L'Amour's best-selling fiction offered another indication of the genre's immense hold. Born in North Dakota, L'Amour left home at age fifteen and traveled around the world as a seaman, logger, elephant handler, cattle skinner, miner, and professional boxer before serving in the World War II military. Best-selling books like *Hondo* (1953) and *Heller with a Gun* (1955) portrayed the stark survival of western protagonists who lived for the moment and faced death or pain with honor and courage, fused body and mind in moments of crisis, and exerted individual will against impersonal forces. L'Amour chose to describe his hard-bitten protagonists as working people—"the men who built a nation."

   The most important venue for the postwar western was the movies. Director John Ford had garnered new respect for the genre with *Stagecoach* (1939). A second important western appeared with William A. Wellman's *The Oxbow Incident* (1943), the story of Henry Fonda and another cowboy who amble into a frontier Nevada town and hear about the murder of a popular local rancher. In the absence of the sheriff, an ex-Confederate officer leads a posse to search for the culprits. Apprehending a young cowboy, a defiant Mexican American who is a wanted criminal (Anthony Quinn), and an old man around a homesteaders' campfire, they convict the three on the spot and give them time to write letters to their loved ones before hanging them. When the sheriff returns to town, he informs the mob that there had been no murder. Fonda then reads the letter the young cowboy wrote to his wife and silently rides out of town to deliver it.

Fonda returned to the western motif with John Ford's *My Darling Clementine* (1946), a film in which he played a comically awkward Marshal Wyatt Earp. Another Ford feature, *Wagon Master* (1950), utilized a score of western hymns and folk songs in a story of two cowhands who join a group of Mormons traveling to the Utah Territory. The director's most memorable western movies, however, involved the intense screen presence of John Wayne. Born Marion Morrison in Iowa in 1907, Wayne moved to southern California with his family when he was only seven. After his parents' divorce, he earned a football scholarship to the University of Southern California, but failed to stick with the team after his first year. Drifting to Hollywood in the late Twenties, he worked as a prop man and an occasional extra, drinking and playing cards in his free time with a group of cronies that included John Ford, Henry Fonda, and Ward Bond.

It was not until 1929 that director Raoul Walsh discovered Morrison's potential as an actor. Assigning him the stage name of John Wayne, Walsh created a starring role for the young performer in *The Big Trail* (1930), in which he played a peaceful scout who heads off an Indian attack. In his first major film appearance, Wayne tells the children of the wagon train that "the Indian was my friend" who "taught me all I know about the woods." Expressing a mystical love of nature, he rhapsodizes about the "trees out there, big tall pines, just a-reachin' and reachin' as if they wanted to climb right through the gates of heaven." After nearly a decade of mediocre western and adventure films, Wayne won recognition for his starring role in *Stagecoach,* followed by popular World War II features like *Flying Tigers* (1942), *The Fighting Seabees* (1944), and *Back to Bataan* (1945). He did not become a superstar, however, until he reached the age of forty and teamed up again with Ford in four mythic postwar western motion pictures.

In *Fort Apache* (1948), Ford cast John Wayne as a seasoned Indian fighter who confronts a pretentious, rigid, and vain Cavalry officer played by Henry Fonda. Once again taking the role of someone who "knew" and respected Indian adversaries, Wayne defends promises made to the Apaches and advises against tactics that will jeopardize the safety of his comrades. When disaster ensues, nevertheless, he covers up the foolish incompetence of the fallen commanding officer in the interests of morale. A second Southwest Texas story, *She Wore a Yellow Ribbon* (1949), cast Wayne as an aging Cavalry veteran about to retire from the service. A father figure to the men who toughens up subordinates for their own good, he walks stiffly from aching joints, wears a Lincoln shawl, hugs grieving widows, and consistently demonstrates reason and humility. The depth of Wayne's characterization becomes apparent in a scene in which the captain shares memories with the old Cheyenne chief, whose warrior son has cast him aside in a reckless march to war.

Rio Grande (1950), the final work of the Cavalry trilogy, recast Wayne in the role of a tough-minded but sentimental and emotionally vulnerable military officer. As a Southwest Texas fort commander, he schools his son in the discipline of regiment life while courting Maureen O'Hara, his estranged wife of fifteen years. Made at the height of the Cold War, the film offered Ford's homage to the sense of duty and camaraderie among men who perform hard and hazardous tasks against difficult odds. In contrast, *The Searchers* (1956), a movie ranked as an American cinema classic, turned the Wayne persona upside-down. The film told the story of a hard-bitten, hateful Confederate veteran and farmer out to recapture his niece, a kidnap victim of raiding Comanches who have murdered her parents and older sister. Yet Wayne is compelled to share the search with the part-Indian orphan who grew up in the besieged family and who insists on finding his adopted sister.

Enduring seven years of hardship, dead-ends, and double-crosses, the two men tough it out despite the horrendous costs. Life is "blood and death and a cold wind blowing and a gun in the hand," explains Wayne. In one of the lasting performances of his long career, the actor transformed himself into a hero who knew the truth of things instinctively. The choppy rhythms, hard-bitten diction, and slow pace of Wayne's slang-infused colloquialisms became a model of mid-century male virility. "That'll be the day," he murmurs, in a line that became a mainstay of American vernacular. Nevertheless, when Wayne discovers that his niece has accepted life among the Comanches, he tries to kill her to save her from the perceived disgrace of "savage" life. Repelled in the attempt by the young orphan, he begins to learn lessons of tolerance and humanity. In another twist of the plot, however, the young woman's adopted brother kills her captor, allowing Wayne to return her "home." Plagued by too many demons, nevertheless, the ex-soldier cannot bring himself to rejoin the human community of peaceful farmers.

In a career that included nearly two hundred feature films, John Wayne remained a box office favorite. His craggy face and huge frame suggested strength, assurance, and self-reliant authority although his physical power seemed balanced by self-restraint and the wisdom of experience. Above all, the quiet, measured, and understated tone of Wayne's speech reinforced an image of sincerity and adherence to traditional virtues like discipline and duty. In *Red River* (1948), the first western directed by Howard Hawks, the actor played a ruthless old cattle driver out to kill the adopted orphan who had laid claim to his Texas ranch. Following a climactic brawl between the two, however, the rancher reconciles with his hated adversary and forgets the past. *Rio Bravo* (1959), another Hawks film, placed Wayne as the sheriff of a Texas border town who arrests a bullying cattle baron for murder. When the outlaw's gang comes to rescue their leader, the law official rejects help out of personal pride, but his sense of responsibility leads to victory when he accepts the aid of a young gunman, an old "sidekick," and a drunken deputy.

FILM NOIR'S FALLEN ANGELS

"Someday fate, or some mysterious force, can put the finger on you or me for no reason at all." So explains the first-person narrator of *Detour* (1945), a movie exemplifying the dark, bleak, pessimistic, and morally ambiguous tone to many postwar pictures. Influenced by a new generation of European directors and increasing interest in psychological realism, several moviemakers gravitated to a style described as "film noir." Rather than celebrating western-style heroes or loving families, these productions focused on alienated, disillusioned, corrupt, or emotionally unstable protagonists from the underside of American life. Their isolated male characters frequently found themselves trapped in webs of paranoia and fear, unable to distinguish the guilty from the innocent, and powerless to confront hostile or incompetent authorities. In the murky world of film noir, even the most physically enticing women were capable of the most treacherous deceit, betrayal, or malevolence. Taking their cue from the dream-like surrealism of *Citizen Kane* and European cinema, directors infused a claustrophobic and constricted tone into their work with tight framing, extreme angles, and shadowy lighting.

Much of the psychological impetus of film noir stemmed from the war-induced fear that modern existence had dehumanized people to the point of no return, and that greed, perversion, and brutality were essential ingredients of the human personality. Movies such as *I'll Be Seeing You* (1944) and *The Best Years of Our Lives* (1946) had introduced viewers to the nightmare qualities of warfare and the difficulties of adjustment for returning veterans. In Edward Dmytryk's *Till the End of Time* (1946), an ex-Marine comes home to find materialistic family members and neighbors abandoning wartime camaraderie in pursuit of their own narrow interests. By examining ordinary life with both social realism and a surrealist lens, film noir directors dissented from Hollywood's often-expressed confidence that domestic stability, social cohesion, and benevolent cooperation defined American society. Instead, a number of the era's most talented filmmakers became fascinated with the dark motives, obsessions, and violent tendencies masked in the superficial activities of the daily routine, particularly those associated with the troubled relationship between men and women.

British director Alfred Hitchcock offered an early preview of film noir in *Suspicion* (1941), a movie in which Joan Fontaine suspects husband Cary Grant of plotting to kill her. Hitchcock's *Shadow of a Doubt* (1943), in turn, used a script by Thornton Wilder to introduce the specter of evil into the everyday life of a typical American small town. When "Uncle Charlie," played by Joseph Cotten, comes west to visit his middle-class sister in California, he is welcomed into the community as an erudite travelogue lecturer. Gradually, however, his adoring niece begins to unravel the fact that he is the

"Merry Widow Killer" on the lam following his latest deed. Beneath the sunny routines of a bucolic existence, we learn, may lurk cynically greedy and power-obsessed monsters with nothing but contempt for their vulnerable targets. Hitchcock's *Strangers on a Train* (1951) offered another view of the troubled male psyche in a film in which a casual conversation between two travelers leads to tragic consequences. "What's a life or two, Guy? Some people are better off dead," volunteers playboy Robert Walker, as he proposes a dual murder plot to address the personal dilemmas of both men.

Pictures like Otto Preminger's *Laura* (1944) and *Fallen Angel* (1945) presented normally appearing men as pathological killers motivated by a possessive obsession with beauty. In *Mildred Pierce* (1945), Joan Crawford portrayed a struggling divorcé betrayed by her second husband. More often, however, film noir focused on men's susceptibility to untrustworthy women who hid their greed behind a tantalizing sensuality. The first of these was Billy Wilder's *Double Indemnity* (1944), a film that Wilder and Raymond Chandler adapted for the screen from James Cain's novel. Through the matter-of-fact narration of an amoral insurance broker, played by Fred MacMurray, viewers learn that he and an older man's seductive wife (Barbara Stanwyck) have convinced the husband to take out a policy awarding double payment in case of death in a railroad mishap. When the company balks at paying the claim following the murder, the agent wants out of the deal, only to have his co-conspirator warn that it is too late to "get off the trolley car." In the end, the two principals shoot each other. Mortally wounded, MacMurray staggers to his office, where he dictates a memo to his boss with a full confession.

Another first-person perspective in *Detour* relayed the story of a young piano player hitchhiking west to join his fiancé. When an older driver picks him up but suddenly dies in the passenger seat after the narrator takes the wheel, the hitchhiker steals the man's wallet, hides the body, and takes the vehicle. He then gives a ride to the seductive Ann Savage, who recognizes the car as belonging to the driver who had earlier made a pass at her when giving her a lift. "That's life! Whichever way you turn, Fate sticks out its foot to trip you," the narrator comments in a parody of free will. Aware of his subterfuge, Savage taunts the protagonist into pretending that he is the heir to the fortune that the original driver was about to inherit. After the two get into a fight, however, the storyteller accidentally kills the woman, forcing him to flee to Reno, where he hitches a ride on the highway, only to find his lift is a police car.

Otto Preminger's *Fallen Angel* cast Dana Andrews as another drifter—a penniless press agent who winds up in a California coastal town of seedy hotels, run-down cafés, and smoky bars. Falling for a sultry waitress (Linda Darnell), he accepts her insistence that she will only have him once she is free of her dead-end job and life, which the film documents in excruciating detail. To provide her with the things she desires, the protagonist marries one of two wealthy sisters in hope of stealing her money, divorcing her, and marrying the waitress. When Darnell is murdered, however, a hard-nosed detective frames Andrews for the crime, until his own investigation reveals that the love-smitten accuser killed the woman because he was driven mad by her casual dalliances with men.

In screenwriter Preston Sturges' adaptation of James Cain's *The Postman Always Rings Twice* (1946), John Garfield plays a hapless drifter who finds a job at a roadside diner outside Los Angeles. Falling in love with the proprietor's young blonde wife (Lana Turner), he joins a plot to kill the older man for the life insurance. After bungling their first attempt, the duo succeeds by staging an auto accident. Acquitted for the crime, they have a real car wreck that takes the woman's life. This time, however, the doorbell "rings twice": the courts convict Garfield of first-degree murder and sentence him to death. Female betrayal also characterized *The Killers* (1946), in which Ava Gardner starred as Kitty, a nightclub singer associated with a petty mobster, and Burt Lancaster plays a Philadelphia street kid and ex-boxer forced into a payroll robbery. When Kitty falsely claims that Lancaster's cohorts are going to steal his share of the proceeds, he grabs the money and flees, and she conspires to have him gunned down so that she can take all the booty. Another film noir, *The Blue Dahlia* (1946), featured a returning soldier who finds his wife in an affair with a club owner and becomes the key suspect in her murder.

James Cain worked on the script for *Out of the Past* (1947), a story of female duplicity starring Robert Mitchum. Born in Hell's Kitchen, Mitchum lost his father when he was two. After surviving as factory worker, boxer, astrological assistant, and wartime sheet-metal worker, he won several bit parts in westerns and war movies, including a supporting role in *The Story of G.I. Joe* (1945). Known for a sardonic delivery, bedroom eyes, and a menacing drawl, Mitchum was perfectly suited for film noir. *Out of the Past* cast him as a former private detective whom a gambler hires to track down his ex-mistress, played by Jane Greer, who has shot and robbed him of $40,000. When Mitchum catches up with the woman in Mexico, he falls in love, and the two run away, only to have her leave, cash in tow, to reunite with her benefactor. When the protagonist returns home to Connecticut to run a gas station, the gambler, played by Kirk Douglas, approaches him to do a job in San Francisco in which Mitchum winds up as the "fall-guy." All three characters ultimately come to their demise, fulfilling the detective's observation that life offers no chance of winning, only "a way to lose more slowly."

Similar treachery marked Rita Hayworth's role in *The Lady from Shanghai* (1948), a production co-starring her husband, Orson Welles, who also wrote, directed, and produced the film. The story concerned a philosophic Irish seaman whom a beautiful, young rich woman talks into serving as the captain of her disabled older husband's yacht on a cruise to San Francisco. Once the sailor has fallen under the charms of the alluring Hayworth, he agrees to help her husband's law partner fake his own death in return for a cash payment so he can support the woman in high style. Yet he discovers that Hayworth and the man are secret lovers and have plotted to kill her husband and set up the sailor for the blame. The frame-up comes very close to succeeding, but Welles escapes legal custody, only to witness a shoot-out between the mismatched spouses in a climactic scene inside San Francisco's Fun House Hall of Mirrors. Leaving Hayworth to die, he ruminates that "the only way to stay out of trouble is to grow old, so I guess I'll concentrate on that. Maybe I'll live so long that I'll forget her—maybe I'll die trying."

FORCE OF EVIL

If sexual women threatened the complete disarray of society, the pervasiveness of male crime pointed to a social order without apparent rules or controls. Film noir lent itself to distinct approaches to lawlessness. Although few moviemakers continued to rely on social class as an explanation for behavior, several used criminality to point to the excessive importance of money and materialism. One of the first to do so was *Deadline at Dawn* (1946), a motion picture scripted by Group Theater dramatist Clifford Odets and directed by Harold Clurman, the ensemble's founder. With the shadowy nightlife of New York City as background, the film presented the tale of a naïve small-town sailor (Bill Williams) who wakes up with over a thousand dollars in his pocket after someone has drugged him in a rigged poker game. In the company of a sympathetic dance hall girl (Susan Hayward) and a friendly cab driver (Paul Lukas), he goes to the apartment of the club owner's sister to return the money, but finds her murdered and himself the key suspect. Yet the cabbie finally confesses that the victim had been carrying on an affair with his son-in-law, and that he killed her to save his daughter from pain.

Like several prewar predecessors, including *Kid Galahad* (1937), *Golden Boy* (1939), and *City of Conquest* (1940), *Body and Soul* (1947) used the vicious competition and corruption of prizefighting as a metaphor of capitalism. Produced by Enterprise Studios, an independent collective of Hollywood progressives, the film combined the talents of writer Abraham Polonsky and actor John Garfield. The son of an immigrant Jewish pharmacist, Polonsky graduated from New York's City College in 1932. Viewing himself as an intellectual aesthete who placed art over politics, he taught English night school classes to finance law studies at Columbia University. A member of the Communist Party after 1936, Polonsky began work at a law firm, where he received an assignment to prepare a radio courtroom scene for *The Goldbergs*. Subsequently hired as a regular writer for the show, he became a full-time radio dramatist. Before initiating his Hollywood career, Polonsky completed several mystery and war novels, helped mount government propaganda broadcasts in occupied Germany, and worked on a postwar network radio series about the psychological adjustment of returning veterans.

Like Polonsky, John Garfield was a product of the Lower East Side and East Bronx. The son of a clothes-presser, he became an apprentice actor in the Group Theater in the early Thirties and played the young working-class idealist in Clifford Odets' *Awake and Sing* (1935). Once Garfield arrived in Hollywood, the studios groomed him as a successor to James Cagney. His first role as a doomed and despairing musician in *Four*

Daughters (1938) won him an Academy Award nomination for best supporting actor. In *They Made Me a Criminal* (1939), a film in which Garfield played a prizefighter framed for murder, he exuded a self-assured working-class masculinity with a touch of vulnerability that won him a reputation as the "people's star." A similar characterization colored his role in *Dust Be My Destiny* (1939), the story of an inmate of a county work farm falsely imprisoned for a homicide. Looking straight into the camera, Garfield delivers a lengthy defense of society's "nobodies."

Body and Soul portrayed the son of a Lower East Side candy store proprietor mowed down by gangsters and a mother forced to live off charity. Growing up in poolrooms and in the "jungle" of Depression streets, he becomes obsessed with making money and does whatever it takes to become a champion boxer, at the cost of alienating his family, loved ones, friends, and community. When the syndicate orders him to throw the next fight, however, Garfield hesitates in realization that his life has "gone down the drain" and that he is nothing more than a walking corpse. The character's moral turning point comes when his African American sparring partner, played by former middleweight Canada Lee, denounces the rampant corruption of the ring. "I don't scare no more," the battered ex-champion announces just before suffering a lethal stroke. Garfield then confronts the mob. "What are you going to do, kill me?" he taunts his backers. "Everybody dies." Intent on winning back self-esteem, the boxer also fights for the neighborhood people who have bet their savings on his behalf. In this allegory of the corruption of human values, Garfield struggles for everyone the system has ground down.

Director Robert Rossen produced a newsreel quality in *Body and Soul* that complemented the staccato rhythms of the film's urban street talk and terse dialogue. A similar tone permeated *Force of Evil* (1948), a movie marking Polonsky's debut as a director. As in *Body and Soul,* the dark, grim, gritty images of shadowy and deserted New York streets perfectly fit the austere narrative. *Force of Evil* starred Garfield as Joe Morse, a syndicate lawyer whose boss is taking over the local numbers racket. The tension in the story comes from the fact that the attorney's brother Leo, a candy store proprietor who has put him through law school to get him off the streets, resists the organization's takeover of his modest operation. Morse pleads with his sibling to cooperate, but to no avail. When the mob kills Leo, Joe guns down the murderers and walks down to the riverside to retrieve his brother's body before giving himself up to the police. "If a man's life could be lived so long and come out this way—like rubbish"—he reasons, "then something was horrible, and had to be ended one way or another."

From the opening shots of Wall Street, *Force of Evil* tied crime to an economic system built upon greed and envy. Nicholas Ray's *They Live By Night* (1949) also offered a nuanced view of criminality. Ray had been part of the left theater movement of the 1930s and worked on wartime folk music radio broadcasts. In his directorial debut, he emulated the comic strips with abrupt cuts and made ample use of street talk and Woody Guthrie songs. Set in the Depression, the film cast Farley Granger as a twenty-three-year-old who has spent seven years in prison for accidentally killing a man. When he escapes a Southwest prison with two hardened criminals, Granger falls in love with the daughter of an outside accomplice (Cathy O'Donnell). Although he wants to go straight, he joins several bank robberies to raise the money to hire a lawyer to clear himself of the original charge. As the couple goes underground, Ray's camera lingers on the back roads, tourist camps, and bleak motels of the surrounding country-side. Betrayed by the wife of one of the gunmen in an effort to gain a pardon for her own husband, Granger comes to a tragic end, reinforcing the belief that poor people are pawns of forces beyond their own control.

Nicholas Ray worked familiar ground in *Knock on Any Door* (1949), a production starring Humphrey Bogart as a successful lawyer who returns to his old neighborhood to defend an Italian American friend accused of killing a police officer. It turns out that the father of Bogart's pal had been sent to prison for defending himself against an at-tacker and had died in incarceration. Raised in poverty, the son had resorted to a life of petty crime until he married a supportive woman and found a job as a warehouse loader. Looking for quick money, however, the young man turned to gambling and crime, and informed his wife that he did not want the child she was carrying, leading to her suicide. When Bogart's client admits to the murder, the lawyer tells the court that the defendant is guilty, but that society also shares the blame "for what they have done to him." Until people wipe out the slums, lectures Bogart, poor neighborhoods will continue to pro-duce criminals. In a similar fashion, Cyril Endfield's *Try and Get Me* (1951) traced the tragedy of an unemployed ordinary family man who reluctantly participates in a series of robberies that lead to a kidnapping and murder and the lynching of the perpetrators.

NAKED CITY

Several of the most intense noir films rejected political statements about social envi-ronment and focused on matters of moral degeneracy or pathological behavior. In *The Big Sleep* (1946), Howard Hawks brought Raymond Chandler's first novel to the screen with an adaptation assisted by William Faulkner. The movie starred Humphrey Bogart as Philip Marlowe, a down-and-out, tough-talking but romantic Los Angeles private eye repeatedly let down by the women of his dreams. When Marlowe takes on an assignment to track down the blackmailers of a dying millionaire's beautiful daugh-ters, played by Lauren Bacall and Martha Vickers, he falls into a convoluted world of moral decadence, corruption, treachery, and casual violence. In this compromised set-ting of betrayal and the suave double-cross, the working-class detective can only rely on his instinct for self-preservation. A different sort of pathology pervaded Edward Dmytryk's *Crossfire* (1947), a film in which Robert Ryan played an ignorant and fear-ful anti-Semitic ex-soldier who beats a Jewish war veteran to death out of pure hatred, and then covers up the murder by killing one of his buddies.

Jules Dassin's *The Naked City* (1948) explored the moral trespasses of both the privileged and the working class. Taken from Arthur "Weegee" Fellig's realist novel about the Lower East Side, the movie's script was written with the help of Hollywood leftist Albert Maltz; its producer was Mark Ellinger, a former New York tabloid crime reporter. *The Naked City* set its mood with documentary shots of the tenements, police stations, docks, bridges, and streets of the teeming metropolis, a technique repeatedly imitated in Hollywood films and in the television series (1958–63) that took its name from the original production. When police discover the body of a young woman in her bathtub, they learn that she had deserted her working-class Polish American family in New Jersey for the wild life of the city. They eventually trace the murder to a brutal Italian American head of a burglary ring who works in conjunction with a corrupt physician, who later commits suicide. In this conservative morality tale, the police become the last defense of traditional values amid the spread of big-city vice and crime.

In *White Heat* (1949), a movie starring James Cagney as Cody Jarrett, a criminal gang leader who rages at society while whimpering at the knee of his beloved "Ma," director Raoul Walsh minimized moral judgments. With documentary detail, Walsh's camera recorded the daily routines of prison life, the minute planning of the robbery of a chemical plant payroll office, and the military precision in executing a job. As the fleeing Jarrett ascends a huge gasoline storage tank, he calls out to his late mother: "Made it, Ma! On top of the world!" Just then, a bullet explodes the tank into an inferno, providing a symbolic finale to the era of the individual gangster. In contrast, *The Asphalt Jungle* (1950) offered a glimpse of organized criminality. Based on a novel by W.R. Burnett, the picture placed Sterling Hayden and Sam Jaffe in a collection of small-time gangsters brought together to pull off an intricately planned jewel robbery with the financial support of a corrupt lawyer. Skillfully drawing out the talents, loyalties, and duplicities of the participants, director John Houston heightened the film's grainy realism by setting much of the action in a night world of dingy rooms and naked light bulbs.

D.O.A. (1950) abandoned psychological insight for a meaningless universe of chance and accident. When an accountant from a small California desert town, played by Edmund O'Brien, takes a San Francisco vacation to break up the tedium of his existence, he drops in at a cellar jazz club where a sinister-looking man switches drinks with him. Advised by a physician the next day that he has radiation poisoning for which there is no antidote, he decides to spend his remaining hours discovering the identity and motivation of his killer. After running frantically through the streets, O'Brien learns that he previously had notarized the bill of sale for a shipment of iridium, which subsequently wound up stolen. He then traces the assailant's trail to the deserted warehouses and downtown streets of nighttime Los Angeles, where he confronts the man and shoots him, before staggering to the police station to report his own murder. "All I did was notarize one little paper, one little paper out of hundreds," he exclaims with his last breath, as he falls to the floor D.O.A.—Dead on Arrival.

Edmond O'Brien in *D.O.A.*   *(Photofest)*

By the early 1950s, crime features had become the dominant focus of film noir. Hard-boiled movies like *Kiss Tomorrow Good-bye* (1950), *Dark City* (1951), and *The Strip* (1951) presented profiles of a psychologically damaged society with intense social realism. William Wyler's *Detective Story* (1951) turned the psychoanalytic tables on the police. Adopted from a Broadway play by Sidney Kingsley, the film starred Kirk Douglas as Jim McLeod, an obsessed, emotionally unstable New York City police detective stalking a physician dealing in black-market babies. Without the means to relate to his wife and unable to benefit from the counseling of a benevolent superior, McLeod appears psychologically indistinguishable from the criminals he seeks to put behind bars. Joseph Losey's *The Prowler* (1951) pursued a similar theme in a portrait of a car patrol officer who complains about the "lousy breaks" life has dealt him. When a beautiful married woman summons him to find a house prowler, he seduces her and conspires to kill her rich husband so that he can use the dead man's life insurance to purchase the Las Vegas motel he has always dreamed of owning.

In Fritz Lang's *The Big Heat* (1953), Glenn Ford played another rogue cop. When he begins to ask questions about the suicide of a seemingly honest colleague, Ford returns home to discover that his wife has been the victim of a bomb blast meant for him. He then defies his superiors by vowing to bring to justice those responsible. Relieved of his duties and acting on his own, he targets the powerful criminal gambling and extortion syndicate that controls the police commissioner and other politicians. In one famous scene, a crude mob boss played by Lee Marvin hurls boiling coffee into the eyes of his girlfriend (Gloria Grahame). Yet Ford learns that the key figure in the rackets is a legitimate business figure and family head whose operations Ford eventually exposes.

UNDERWORLD U.S.A.

Two films based on Mickey Spillane novels, *I, the Jury* (1953) and *Kiss Me Deadly* (1955), took the vigilante detective formula to its logical conclusions. In the seven years after 1948, Spillane produced seven of the best-selling books of all time. His blue-collar private eye, Mike Hammer, brutally punished communist traitors and immoral women. *I, the Jury* told the story of Hammer's hunt for the murderer of his best friend. In the end, he shoots a voluptuous woman whom he suspects of complicity in the killing as she prepares to embrace him. When she asks how he could do such a thing, Hammer tells her "It was easy." Directed by Robert Aldrich, *Kiss Me Deadly* begins when the detective picks up a hitchhiker who has escaped "the laughing house" (mental institution) with a secret. When drug dealers run his car off the road and torture the young woman to death, Hammer follows the victim's trail and brings the perpetrators to his own brand of justice.

Orson Welles memorably portrayed the potential viciousness of law enforcement officials in *Touch of Evil* (1958). The movie featured the actor/director as Hank Quinlan, a corrupt, powerful, and overbearing local police captain in a seedy Texas border town. When Mike Vargas, a Mexican narcotics agent played by Charleton Heston, crosses the border with his new bride (Janet Leigh), he witnesses a car bombing that kills a local millionaire. Once Vargas volunteers to help solve the murder, he enters a power struggle with Quinlan and a local crime family that takes place within a setting of drug smuggling, prostitution, and terrorism. After the police captain implicates a Mexican shoe clerk in the murder by planting evidence, the gang drugs and kidnaps Vargas' wife. Suspecting ties between Quinlan and the syndicate, Vargas uses an informant to induce a taped confession from the corrupt police officer, whose dead body winds up floating in a canal. Claustrophobic, hypnotic, and ominous, the movie remains morally ambiguous to the end, and ranks as the last recognized film noir classic.

No one presented the criminal underside of American life with more relish than Samuel Fuller. Born in Worcester, Massachusetts, in 1911, Fuller moved to New York when his father died when he was eleven. Starting work as a newspaper copyboy, he became the city's youngest crime reporter at age seventeen. During the 1930s, Fuller served as a crime and waterfront reporter in San Diego and traveled across the country covering criminal trials. Arriving in Hollywood in 1935, he produced several screenplays before enlisting in the World War II Army. Back in Hollywood in 1946, Fuller made a series of realistic "B" westerns and war movies designed to serve as the second feature at theater showings. His specialty, however, became the crime film. As an urban reporter, he had discovered a sense of community and mutuality in working-class neighborhoods amid the ethnic rivalries and tensions of big-city life. Fuller's films used such relationships as the context for their stories.

In *Pickup on South Street* (1953), the director featured Richard Widmark as a Skid Row pickpocket who inadvertently acquires a top-secret microfilm on its way to communist spies. Shot in slum apartments, on the subway, under the Brooklyn Bridge, and on the East River waterfront, the film offered an inside look at the world of prostitutes, street peddlers, and petty criminals. Yet Fuller broke film convention and morality by portraying the beauty at the margins of the decaying city. His protagonists, moreover, shared the intuitions and full range of emotions of the people they confronted. In *Crimson Kimono* (1959), Fuller used the shooting of a stripper in Los Angeles' "Little Tokyo" to explore the complex relationship between the Japanese American community and the Anglo detectives sent to break the case.

Underworld U.S.A. (1960) depicted the distinctions between crime and law enforcement in more ambiguous terms. The film concerned the story of Tolly Devlin (Cliff Robertson), a man who seeks to avenge his father's beating death in an alley. While in prison, he learns that three of the gangsters who killed his father have become big shots in a syndicate that markets drugs to teenagers and recruits under-age girls for prostitution. Intent on infiltrating the gang, he goes to work at the club owned by one of the culprits and arranges with a federal agent to doctor the men's files, thereby setting them up for assassination as disloyal subordinates of the lawless kingpin. When the crime boss then orders Devlin to kill the gang moll who has become his girlfriend, he drowns the gangster in his penthouse pool, but takes a bullet from the man's hired thug. Fuller's grim tale ends with Devlin dying in the arms of the woman he loves in the same alley where his father met his demise.

DEMONOLOGY

Beyond the conventions of film noir and crime drama, several works of postwar literature, stage, and film depicted the passions, disappointments, and private pain lurking beneath the surfaces of everyday life. Three white women fiction writers of the South excelled in such efforts. The child of two Jackson, Mississippi schoolteachers, Eudora Welty was born in 1909. After college graduation, Welty endured a brief stint at Columbia University Business School before assuming several jobs in advertising, radio, and journalism. Inspired by her work as a WPA publicity agent, she began publishing stories about local Mississippi folk in 1936. With a sharp eye and ear for detail and a feel for humor and pathos, Welty captured the cadence of southern vernacular among the region's decaying gentry, middle-class denizens, and black and white poor. *Delta Wedding* (1946), her first novel, described the separation and isolation of individuals within an extended family. *The Ponder Heart* (1955) contrasted the simple-minded benevolence of its main character with the greed and selfishness surrounding him.

Flannery O'Connor offered a view of southern character embracing elements of the grotesque. Born in Savannah in 1925, O'Connor lived most of her life on her mother's farm in Milledgeville, Georgia, where she wrote and raised peacocks. Infusing her work with Catholic spirituality and Gothic coloring, she described the familiar people of her small-town community—from county judges and landowners to farm hands, gas-station operatives, and Protestant evangelists. Because O'Connor suffered from a rare form of lupus, which left her in constant pain before she died at thirty-nine, she only managed to produce two novels, *Wise Blood* (1952) and *The Violent Bear It Away* (1960), and the short story collection *A Good Man Is Hard to Find* (1955).

The fiction of Carson McCullers provided another entry into southern folk life. Born Lulu Carson Smith in Columbus, Georgia, in 1917, McCullers was the daughter of a watchmaker and jewelry store owner. Studying to be a concert pianist, she moved to New York at age seventeen, took creative writing classes at Columbia University night school, and began to publish short stories. Despite a life of intense physical ailments and emotional instability, McCullers produced an impressive body of work that blended aspects of poetic and prosaic prose, combining formal and colloquial forms with both allegory and realism. *The Heart Is a Lonely Hunter* (1940), McCullers' first novel, took place in a shabby boarding house. The story centered on an all-night café proprietor, a carnival worker, a black physician, and a young girl with artistic aspirations, each of whom confides their hopes, plans, and grief to a deaf-mute jeweler.

By painting her everyday characters as individuals searching for selfless love and spiritual understanding, McCullers highlighted both isolation and occasional heroism in interpersonal relations. The author's next work, *The Member of the Wedding* (1946), depicted the complexity of human behavior through a series of kitchen dialogues among three characters—Frankie Addams, a twelve-year-old tomboy; her six-year-old cousin John Henry; and her father's black housekeeper, Berenice Sadie Brown—over an August weekend in a southern town during World War II. As the three play cards and talk about the upcoming nuptials of the young girl's older brother, Frankie and Berenice confess their mutual hopes, preoccupations, and fears. Although the servant occasionally lashes out at her charge's untamed aspirations and youthful bravado, neither is willing to accept life as a passive victim.

McCullers' *The Ballad of the Sad Café* (1951), a short story volume blending reality and myth, combined archaic diction with colloquial forms. Set in an eating spot where several mill hands relaxed outside work, the book focused on the difficulty of escaping isolation through love and on the need to laugh at life's strange quirks. Meanwhile, the stage production of *Member of the Wedding* debuted in 1950 with Julie Harris and Ethel Waters in lead roles, followed by a film version two years later. Indeed, psychological themes characterized a number of postwar movies. Billy Wilder's *Lost Weekend* (1945) starred Ray Milland as a writer struggling with a liquor habit. *Come Back Little Sheba* (1952), based on a play about a shabby boarding house by William Inge, featured Burt

Lancaster and Academic Award-winner Shirley Booth as a loveless couple plagued by alcoholism, illusion, and loneliness. In *The Man With the Golden Arm* (1955), Otto Preminger's adaptation of a Nelson Algren novel, Frank Sinatra starred as a Mafia card shark and junkie who returns home to get off heroin. Fred Zinnemann's *A Hatful of Rain* (1957), in turn, traced the impact of drug addiction on a single family.

The disastrous consequences of an ill-conceived marriage provided the subject of *Niagara* (1953), one of the few color movies of the postwar era with a noir plot. *Niagara* starred Marilyn Monroe as Rose, a voluptuous but unprincipled siren who has reached for material security by marrying a sullen, unstable war veteran (Joseph Cotten). Born Norma Jean Mortenson in Los Angeles in 1926, Monroe experienced a troubled childhood in foster homes and orphanages. Married at sixteen, she worked in a World War II defense plant until an Army photographer asked her to pose for a poster for the troops. A modeling vocation and an uneventful movie career followed until she gained minor stardom in *Niagara.* The movie brought a honeymooning couple to a motel near the famous tourist spot, where Rose and her young lover plot her husband's murder over the telephone. Monroe's adulterous search for human affection appears completely uncontainable. Yet her spouse learns of the scheme and throws her paramour to his death over the falls. Then he stalks Rose, finally trapping her in a bell tower, where he strangles her in a darkened corner before eventually meeting his own demise.

The Rose Tattoo (1955), a film adaptation of a Tennessee Williams play, dealt with the need to transcend romantic illusion. The movie featured Anna Magnani as the wife of a Gulf Coast truck driver who supports her family by taking in sewing, but who loses her husband to a life of crime and an affair with a Texas blackjack dealer. When her spouse dies in a shoot-out with police, Magnani's character cherishes his memory until she learns that his former lover now wears the same tattoo as he did. In the depth of despair, nevertheless, she begins to acknowledge the love, affection, and comfort offered by a sincere trucker, portrayed by Burt Lancaster, who supports his grandmother, father, and sister on low wages, but who promises to devout himself to the aggrieved widow.

Adopted from a Clifford Odets play produced in 1941 for the Group Theater, Fritz Lang's *Clash By Night* (1952) introduced the theme of redemption into the gritty atmosphere of Monterrey Bay's working harbor and canneries. Mae Doyle (Barbara Stanwyck) is a former beauty who returns to her birthplace in need of "rest." "Home is where you come when you run out of places," she cracks. "You don't know what jungle I'm from," Mae warns burly Italian fishing boat operator, Paul Douglass, who begins to take an interest in her. An experienced woman of the world, Doyle admits that her "big ideas" produced "small results." Agreeing to marriage, she nevertheless enters a romantic liaison with a like-minded cynic (Robert Ryan), who has sadistic contempt for women but still needs them. "They keep animals separated in cages in the zoo so they don't hurt each other," observes Doyle. Acknowledging that she "mistook boredom for love," she sees a world in which "everybody's lonely, lost." Yet at the film's conclusion, Mae successfully pleads for the chance to return to a loving home and the ties of domesticity.

DAY AFTER DAY

Sidney "Paddy" Chayefsky focused on loneliness in the big city. The son of Jewish immigrants and a political progressive, Chayefsky sought to go beyond conventional romances about the affluent by writing "the most ordinary love story in the world." Through everyday speech and by immersion in "the marvelous world of the ordinary," he hoped to demonstrate that love among real people involved more than physical attraction. Having written the television play *Marty* about a Jewish butcher, Chayefsky saw no problem with movie director Delbert Mann's conversion of the main character to an Italian, since the playwright believed that Italians, Jews, and the Irish shared close kinship ties and emotional volatility. Produced in 1955 on a low budget, the Hollywood version of the drama told the story of a balding, heavy-set, and shy bachelor (Ernest Borgnine), who breaks from his parents and street pals to court a homely woman (Betsy Blair), whom he comes to see as the perfect mate. Understated throughout the movie, Borgnine allows his emotions to explode in the final scene, when he emerges onto the street after Blair has agreed to a second date and triumphantly slams his fist into a "STOP" sign.

Marty's naturalistic style garnered Academy Awards for Best Picture, Best Director, Best Actor, and Best Screenplay. The following year, Borgnine joined with Betty Davis to appear in *A Catered Affair* (1956), a film adaptation of a second Chayefsky television drama. The movie told the story of a Bronx Irish American couple whose daughter is about to be married. The bride's father is a taxi driver trying to save enough money to own his own cab. Her uncle, a house painter who lives with the family in the cramped apartment, simply wants enough cash to buy an electric refrigerator. Davis, in turn, sees an elaborate hotel wedding as a chance to achieve the pride and respectability long denied her. Besides, she wants her daughter to have memories "when the bad years come." Nevertheless, Davis gives in to the objections of the intended couple and the rest of her family. "You gotta start making sacrifices," she agrees. "You can't throw money around." Without frugality, she adds with a nod to the dingy apartment, "this is the way it's always going to be, just like this, day after day."

Although dramatist Eugene O'Neill had ceased writing plays for the live theater during World War II, his work continued to dominate the postwar era. The son of a prominent traveling actor, O'Neill was born in New York City in 1888. After attending Catholic boarding school and a private academy, he spent an unsuccessful year at Princeton University. Taking to the sea as a sailor, he traveled and worked in South Africa, Central America, and Argentina. After a stint as a reporter in New London, Connecticut, and as a drama student at Harvard, O'Neill helped form the experimental

Provincetown Players on Cape Cod, where several of his short pieces presented vernacular treatments of the life of the sea. He spent much of the late 1910s in the bohemian saloons of Greenwich Village in the company of prostitutes and self-avowed anarchists. By 1920, O'Neill was prepared to create the full-length plays that would establish his reputation for penetrating the inner human psyche.

Beyond the Horizon (1920) dealt with the futile dreams of a farm family. *The Emperor Jones* (1920), in contrast, illustrated the impossibility of living without illusions. *Anna Christie* (1921) discussed the concept of redemption through the slang musings of a prostitute. *The Hairy Ape* (1922) delved into the inner feelings of a ship's stoker. *Desire Under the Elms* (1925) stripped New England farm life of surface pieties. *Strange Interlude* (1928) traced a woman's quest for happiness through the stages of her life. *Morning Becomes Electra* (1931) used themes from Greek mythology to depict a New England family's confrontation with death during the Civil War. *Ah, Wilderness!* (1933) emphasized the life-giving values of a conventional American family at the start of the twentieth century.

After 1933, O'Neill entered a period of isolation. Influenced by Russian dramatist Maxim Gorky, his next work, *The Iceman Cometh* (1946, 1956), incorporated memories of Lower Manhattan saloon culture. The play described the persistence of death-defying pipe dreams among even the most lowly, and suggested that all life was an illusion. Three years after O'Neill's death, his masterpiece, *Long Day's Journey Into Night* (1956), appeared on Broadway at the initiative of the playwright's widow, who overruled his instructions against ever producing it. Written in the early 1940s, the autobiographical drama described an early twentieth-century Irish American family with similarities to the playwright's own. The intense interactions centered on a father who was a failed actor, a mother with a morphine habit, an alcoholic older son, and the younger sibling—a philosophical ex-sailor. Made into a film in 1962 with Ralph Richardson and Katharine Hepburn, the powerful drama emphasized the need to transcend cynicism and despair once moral conventions were exposed. O'Neill reminded the world that matters of emotion superseded intellect in the make-up of commonplace but tragic characters.

Lost opportunities also figured strongly in Arthur Miller's Pulitzer Prize-winning drama, *Death of a Salesman* (1949). Born into a middle-class family of New York Jews in 1915, Miller graduated from the University of Michigan and spent much of the 1930s in a variety of journalism and radio jobs, including a stint with the Federal Theater Project. The screenwriter for *The Story of G.I. Joe,* he learned from the example of playwright Tennessee Williams that dramatic storytelling did not have to embrace pedantic language. Miller's first full-scale foray into the theater, *All My Sons* (1947), used contemporary American idiom to describe a search for truth and social responsibility amid the corruptions of the wartime home front. *Death of a Salesman* took on a more ambitious agenda—the human costs of America's obsession with material prosperity and self-sufficiency.

Directed by Elia Kazan, co-founder of the innovative Actor's Studio, the play focused on Willy Loman, an old-style New York salesman used to getting by "on a smile and a shoeshine." Miller's self-deceiving protagonist has internalized the business community's self-help clichés about magnetic personalities reaching the attainment of their goals. Yet he faces a postwar world devoid of the personal relationships and individual enterprise that prevailed at the start of his career. The character's moral limitations, moreover, prevent him from fulfillment as a father or a breadwinner. *Death of a Salesman* focuses on Willie's inability to face the fact that his life-long dreams of success are nothing more than illusions.

Despite Willie's bravado and fakery, Miller's fully rounded characterization induced far more empathy for the role than the author anticipated. Nurturing his dreams even when she knows they are delusions, the protagonist's wife, Linda, underscores the tragic quality of her husband's life shortly before his ultimate demise. "Attention must be paid," she scolds her failed sons. "I don't say he's a great man. Willy Loman never made a lot of money," she exclaims. "His name was never in the paper. He's not the finest character that ever lived. But he's a human being, and a terrible thing is happening to him ... A small man can be just as exhausted as a great man." Adopted for the screen in 1951 with Fredric March in the lead role, *Death of a Salesman* raised the experiences and language of ordinary people to sheer poetry. Originally conceived as a critique of market capitalism, Miller's work took on universal implications as a somber tale of misplaced human aspirations.

CONTENDERS

The psychological costs of surface achievements received extended treatment in George Stevens' *A Place in the Sun* (1951), a film loosely based on Theodore Dreiser's *An American Tragedy*. The plot centered on George Eastman (Montgomery Clift), an innocent slum boy who comes to work in a small-town factory owned by his uncle. After impregnating a fellow worker (Shelley Winters), Eastman falls in love with the wealthy Angela (Elizabeth Taylor). When he fails to save his pregnant girlfriend in a boating accident, he tortures himself with the notion that although he did not murder her, he wanted her to die. Instead of following Dreiser's denunciation of an oppressive class system, *Place in the Sun* presented a confused victim of circumstance—an intense, troubled outsider who pays the ultimate price for a crime of omission.

Picnic (1956), a film version of a Pulitzer Prize-winning play by William Inge, also dealt with the moral issues arising from questions of status. The movie told the story of a drifter (William Holden) who comes to a small Kansas town hoping to find a job at the processing plant owned by the family of his former college roommate. Instead, he seduces his friend's fiancé (Kim Novak) in a sizzling slow dance at the Labor Day celebration, stripping away the community's sentimental façade and pietistic hypocrisy in the process. Bullied into a fight with his old friend, he runs from the police, tells the woman he is a liar and a bum, and hops a freight train going west. In the end, however, Novak tosses away all hopes of future stability and security and decides to meet up with him over at the next town.

Like William Holden and Montgomery Clift, Marlon Brando gravitated to anti-heroic roles. Born in Omaha, Nebraska, Brando attended military school, but grew up on jazz, swing, and blues records and hoped to become a drummer. When his sister went to New York to study drama, he followed. Enrolling at the Actor's Studio, Brando became a disciple of "method" acting, a style that required performers to work toward complete emotional and spiritual identification with the characters they portrayed. The young actor first appeared on Broadway in *I Remember Mama* (1944). Three years later, he achieved stardom under the guiding hand of director Elia Kazan as Stanley Kowalski in *A Streetcar Named Desire* (1947), a searing drama of working-class life by Tennessee Williams. In depicting the play's blue-collar brute, Brando combined the menacing anger, sensuality, and cool detachment of the hipster with an infusion of animalistic energy and raw spontaneity. When Kazan brought the production to the screen in 1951, Brando once again excelled as the brooding and mercurial Kowalski.

On the Waterfront (1954) enabled both actor and director to make their greatest contribution to cinema history. The script for the Academy Award-winning Best Picture was the work of Budd Schulberg. The son of the head of Paramount Studios, Schulberg graduated from Dartmouth College in 1936, but returned to Hollywood to turn the story of a movie tycoon into his first novel, *What Made Sammy Run?* (1941). Drawn to the world of boxing, Schulberg co-managed a fighter. His second novel, *The Harder They Fall* (1947), described the domination of the ring by unsavory business interests. The idea for *On the Waterfront* originated with a Pulitzer Prize-winning newspaper series by reporter Malcolm Johnson that focused on collusion between corrupt labor unions, racketeers, and shipping companies on the New York docks. Johnson detailed a system by which predatory labor bosses extorted kickbacks from the hourly wages of longshoremen and charged exorbitant interest on loans to the same workers. For Schulberg, the waterfront offered a microcosm of the greed and graft of American politics and business in general.

Hanging out in waterfront bars, where he befriended off-duty dockworkers with knowledgeable discussions of boxing, Schulberg composed a latter-day version of a Popular Front pastoral. In fact, the social realism of the script was so overwhelming that the major studios rejected it as pro-communist. Independently produced by Sam Spiegel for Columbia Pictures, *On the Waterfront* told the story of Terry Malloy, an ex-boxer who is part of the retinue of corrupt labor boss Johnny Friendly. Malloy has not been able to face the fact that he compromised himself years ago by throwing a fight for the mob. His odyssey begins when he unwittingly sets up the murder of a fellow worker who was about to "rat" to the police. Confronted by the victim's sister and a

Marlon Brando and Karl Malden in *On the Waterfront* (1954)   *(Photofest)*

fast-talking, crusading Catholic priest who chain-smokes and downs beers, Malloy be-gins to have second thoughts about his loyalties. He wavers further in the hold when he witnesses the killing of a cohort attempting to organize against the labor bosses.

Marlon Brando's Academy Award performance as Malloy brought as much realism to the portrait of working-class life as the screen has ever witnessed. With his battered face, slouching walk, shrugging gestures, half-spoken sentences, gum-chewing arro-gance, and uncertain half-smile, Brando personified the agony of a barely articulate so-cial outcast desperately struggling to regain his dignity and self-esteem. When Father Barry, played by Karl Malden, rushes to the hold following the "accident," Malloy winds up protecting the priest from thrown refuse and a tossed beer can as the cleric de-livers an impromptu version of the Sermon on the Mount:

> But remember, fellows, Christ is always with you—Christ is in the shape-up, He's in the hatch—He's in the union hall—He's kneeling here beside Dugan—and He's saying with all of you—If you do it to the least of mine, you do it to me! What they did to Joey, what they did to Dugan, they're doing to you. And you. And YOU. And only you, with God's help, have the power to knock 'em off for good.

Unsure of how to respond to a subpoena from the crime commission, Malloy agrees to meet with his brother, Charlie (Rod Steiger), Johnny Friendly's chief legal adviser.

In one of the most frequently cited clips of American motion picture history, the former boxer castigates his brother for forcing him to take "the fall" in the bout that would have led to a chance at the championship. "See! You don't understand!" he protests. "I could have had class. I coulda been a contender. I coulda had class and been somebody. Real class. Instead of a bum—which is what I am." When Charlie is murdered because he failed to carry out orders to silence his brother, Malloy vows that "I'll take it out of their skulls!" a phrase Schulberg learned on the waterfront. Convinced by Father Barry that the only way to obtain revenge is to testify before the commission, Malloy returns to the docks to confront Johnny Friendly. Beaten nearly to a pulp, he is cradled Christ-like in the arms of the priest, who tells him that the mob will be defeated if he can lead the workers back to handling cargo. As Leonard Bernstein's score punctuates the drama, Molloy blindly lurches to the gates of the loading dock, and the men follow.

NIGHTMARE IN RED

"Something is happening!" Dr. Miles Bennel screams into the telephone in *Invasion of the Body Snatchers* (1956), an electrifying film that illustrated postwar Hollywood's fixation on external threats to the national well-being. Commencing with widely publicized hearings by the House Committee on Un-American Activities (HUAC) in 1947, the movie industry became a focal point of a crusade to purge communists and their allies from positions of influence in public life. When the Justice Department successfully prosecuted ten writers and directors for contempt of Congress for failing to respond to HUAC questions about their political affiliations, studio leaders initiated a Hollywood Blacklist to prevent anyone with communist ties from working in motion pictures. As the list expanded during the 1950s, over three hundred film professionals, including Hollywood Ten defendants Dalton Trumbo, Edward Dymytryk, and Albert Maltz, came under the ban. Hundreds more progressives in the media, advertising, academia, government service, and labor unions also lost their livelihood.

Although victims of the red scare sought to defend themselves along free speech lines, critics contended that association with the communist movement was not merely a matter of heresy among an intellectual elite, but a commitment to the interests of the totalitarian Soviet Union, a foe in the emerging Cold War. The Korean War (1950–53) against communist aggression in North Korea intensified such charges. Comic books offered one lucrative means for dramatizing the perceived threat of the Red Menace. Although light-hearted series like *Archie*, which limited themselves to the romantic dramas of teenage life, were among the most popular comics, war features embraced the Korean police action with a passion. Portraying the conflict as a meaningless but bloody campaign in hostile terrain, the comics cast enemy officers as brutal, subhuman, godless, and stupid creatures who were capable of any atrocity and vulnerable to murder by their own men. By the mid-Fifties, however, comic book imagery had become so graphic that government pressure forced the industry to engage in self-censorship and the popularity of war serials began to decline.

HUAC's influence and the presence of the Blacklist shaped the political content of Hollywood films. Director Robert Rossen's Academy Award Best Picture, *All the King's Men* (1949), expressed the era's impatience with radical utopianism in an adaptation of Robert Penn Warren's Pulitzer Prize novel of the same name. Based on the life of Louisiana's colorful Huey P. Long, the movie told the story of Willie Stark, a populist demagogue who rides to the governor's chair as a defender of the people but becomes obsessed with his own power. *A Face in the Crowd* (1957) reunited screenwriter Budd Schulberg and director Elia Kazan in a cautionary tale about political chicanery of all stripes. The production starred Andy Griffith as "Lonesome Rhodes," a country music radio and television performer who entertains rural folk with funny songs and witty chatter. Pushed to fame through the power of the broadcast media, Griffith becomes the front man for a presidential candidate with fascist sympathies. In the end, the populist hero is unmasked as a cynically ambitious man who sees the public as gullible idiots and mere toys in his quest for raw power.

The only motion picture to defy the Hollywood purge was *Salt of the Earth* (1953), an independently made collaboration between exiled writer Michael Wilson, producer Paul Jarrico, and director Herbert J. Biberman, each a victim of the Blacklist. The film based its plot on the actual events of a strike of Mexican American zinc miners in New Mexico in the early 1950s. Frustrated by a lack of plumbing and sanitation in employee housing, an endless cycle of debt at the company store, poor safety conditions, and assignment of the most dangerous tasks to Hispanics, laborers initiated a walkout with the support of the Union of Mine, Mill, and Smelt Workers. In response, the mining firm evicted families from company housing and brought in strike breakers. Meanwhile, local police disrupted pickets and arrested protest leaders for resisting arrest. When many of the strikers received jail time for violating federal anti-labor injunctions, the women of the community took over the picket line, ultimately forcing a negotiated settlement.

Intent on making films "based in actuality," the production team allowed miners and their families to play themselves and to participate in the script's editing. The project's only professional performer was a Mexican actress deported by the federal government at the conclusion of filming. Humanizing the story of the strike, the movie focused on the plight of a Mexican American family reluctantly drawn into the struggle. Nevertheless, the political background of the production's creators and the film's graphic illustration of the living conditions of impoverished miners guaranteed a negative response in Cold War Hollywood. Deprived of processing and other services by the major studios, the makers of *Salt of the Earth* faced a near-total boycott by distributors and exhibitors, and only managed to show the completed work in thirteen locations.

As threats of government censorship of film content appeared to escalate between 1947 and 1954, Hollywood sought to placate conservative critics with fifty low-budget explicitly anticommunist movies. These features normally pictured FBI and HUAC investigators as courageous defenders of democracy and average Americans, against the machinations of privileged spies and traitors. *The Iron Curtain* (1948), one of the first of the genre, cast Dana Andrews as a valuable Soviet defector whose life American agents sought to protect. *The Red Menace* (1949) employed a narration by a member of the Los Angeles City Council to tell the story of a well-meaning veteran duped by the communists. Another documentary-style saga, *I Was a Communist for the FBI* (1951), portrayed government efforts to bust a Soviet spy ring. Meanwhile, George Murphy starred in the espionage thriller *Walk East on Beacon* (1952), and John Wayne and James Arness portrayed HUAC investigators of a red ring in Hawaii in *Big Jim McCain* (1952).

THEM!

The most melodramatic anticommunist production of the postwar era may have been Leo McCarey's *My Son John* (1952). Through comedy and human-interest classics such as *Duck Soup* (1933), *Ruggles of Red Gap* (1935), *The Awful Truth* (1937), *Going My Way* (1943), and *The Bells of St. Mary* (1945), McCarey had achieved enormous popularity as a director of light-hearted and sentimental favorites. In contrast, the turgid *My Son John* told the tale of the offspring of a small-town Catholic family, portrayed by Robert Walker, who becomes a brilliant young official in the federal government. When his mother, played by Broadway veteran Helen Hayes, discovers that her son's lofty pronouncements are rooted in his involvement in the communist movement, she convinces him to denounce his subversive ties. Before turning himself over to authorities, however, the idealistic young man succumbs to communist gunfire on the steps of the Lincoln Memorial. A pre-recorded speech blames his betrayal of the people on a misguided association with pseudo-intellectuals.

Hollywood's characterizations of communists were unusually heavy-handed and scarcely believable. Pictured mainly as gangster villains, America's internal enemies invariably appeared as pudgy, haggard, mechanically humorless, cynically cruel and loveless creatures without children who used sex only to entice recruits, hid their thirst for political power behind moral causes like civil rights, murdered each other at random, and were contagiously insane. Science fiction features, in contrast, provided a far more effective arena for filmmakers to work out the "us versus them" psychology of the Cold War. By dramatizing the dangers of invasion by aliens, movies simultaneously articulated the fear of outside takeover and delivered warnings about the prospective destruction of the human spirit and the risks of oppressive conformity in collectively planned utopias.

Cold War anxieties surfaced in *The Thing From Another World* (1951), in which a beast from space tries to take over the planet by assuming the form of a bloodsucking vegetable and spreading its reproductive seeds. To meet the threat, rank-and-file Air Force personnel must overcome the appeasement strategies of an amoral scientist who sports a goatee, dressing gown, and ascot. In the end, the people's heroes improvise an electric explosion to take out the carnivorous carrot. *Them!* (1954) used the insect metaphor as a stand-in for communism. When atomic radiation mutates a colony of ants into oversized monsters and they set up a base in the Los Angeles sewer system from which to attack humans, two children inadvertently wander into harm's way. Ants provided a particularly apt symbol for the dangers of collectivism because of their propensity for social organization. After authorities declare a national emergency to deal with the threat, however, a conflict ensues between the military, which hopes to blast away the giant creatures with gunfire, and scientists, who want to use gas. In this case, the more subtle technique prevails, and a courageous FBI agent rescues the children.

In *Invaders from Mars* (1953), a child warns against Martians who implant crystals in the brains of parents and authorities that program them into becoming traitors and "slaves" to the will of their extraterrestrial masters. Don Siegel's *Invasion of the Body Snatchers* took such fears to unimagined heights with a riveting parable of modern depersonalization. When a local physician returns from a medical convention to a small California valley town, he gradually notices that a number of residents appear emotionless and drained of all their humanity. To his horror, he discovers that alien pods have cloned his sleeping neighbors into physically identical replicas of themselves and that they want him to join them as part of a plan to take over the planet. "People are nothing but problems," explains the town's converted psychiatrist. In the "untroubled world" of the pod people, "there's no pain" and "everyone is the same." As for love, the therapist declaims, "life is simpler without it."

Without free will, individuality, a soul, or family ties, human beings will be free to participate in building a new order based on peace and tranquility. Yet Dr. Bennel is unwilling to make the sacrifice. With all communication with the outside world cut off and his lady friend under the spell of the invaders, the desperate physician escapes to Los Angeles, where he frantically dodges speeding traffic on the crowded freeways while attempting to alert the world to the impending threat. Siegel originally intended to end the movie by having Kevin McCarthy's Bennel stare into the camera and scream *"You're next!"* Overruled by the studio, the director added a scene in which the state patrol discovers a truckload of pods, and psychiatrists at the hospital where Bunnel is pleading his story allow him to grab the telephone and ask for the Federal Bureau of Investigation. However it ended, *Invasion of the Body Snatchers* carried the implicit warning that depersonalization and conformity were not necessarily the exclusive properties of totalitarian communists.

SOURCES AND SELECTED READINGS

The aspirations of the post-World War II middle class constitute the focus of Lizabeth Cohen, *A Consumer's Republic: The Politics of Mass Consumption in Postwar*

America (2003) and Lary May, *The Big Tomorrow: Hollywood and the Politics of the American Way* (2000). For a regional case study, see segments of Becky M. Nicolaides, *My Blue Heaven: Life and Politics in the Working-Class Suburbs of Los Angeles, 1920–1965* (2002). The work of Norman Rockwell and Grandma Moses elicits commentary in Frances K. Pohl, *Framing America: A Social History of American Art* (2002).

Musical comedy's golden age receives consideration in the relevant portions of Gerald Mast, *Can't Help Singin': The American Musical on Stage and Screen* (1987) and Andrea Most, *Making Americans: Jews and the Broadway Musical* (2004). For portraits of the genre's leading creators, see Meryle Secrest, *Somewhere for Me: A Biography of Richard Rodgers* (2001); Hugh Fordin, *Getting to Know Him: A Biography of Oscar Hammerstein II* (1986); and Ethan Mordden, *Rodgers and Hammerstein* (1992).

A provocative introduction to the most significant postwar media appears in Lynn Spiegel, *Make Room for TV: Television and the Family Ideal in Postwar America* (1992). See also Karal Ann Marling, *As Seen on TV: The Visual Culture of Everyday Life in the 1950s* (1994) and Judith E. Smith, *Visions of Belonging: Family Stories, Popular Culture, and Postwar Democracy, 1940–1960* (2004). For the advent and cultural significance of situation comedies, see David Marc, *Comic Visions: Television Comedy and American Culture*, 2d ed. (1997) and portions of George Lipsitz, *Time Passages: Collective Memory and Popular Culture* (1990). Lawrence J. Epstein, *The Haunted Smile: The Story of Jewish Comedians in America* (2001) provides useful insight on the background of many of television's earliest stars.

The years following World War II saw the maturation of the motion picture western, a development described in the relevant segments of Andrew Sarris, *You Ain't Heard Nothin' Yet: The American Talking Film: History & Memory, 1927–1949* (1998). See also Steven Cohan, *Masked Men: Masculinity and the Movies in the Fifties* (1997). For biographical portraits of the western's key figures, see the section on John Ford in Lee Lourdeaux, *Italian and Irish Filmmakers in America: Ford, Capra, Coppola, and Scorsese* (1990); Garry Wills, *John Wayne's America* (1997); and Randy Roberts and James S. Olson, *John Wayne, American* (1995).

Readers can find an excellent introduction to film noir in the brief section on the subject in George Lipsitz, *Rainbow at Midnight: Labor and Culture in the 1940s* (1994). For plot synopses, see Robert Ottoson, *A Reference Guide to the American Film Noir: 1940–1958* (1981). Several studies set the genre within a social and cultural framework. See Jon Truska, *Dark Cinema: American Film Noir in Cultural Perspective* (1984); James Naremore, *More Than Night: Film Noir in Its Contexts* (1998); Nicholas Christopher, *Somewhere in the Night: Film Noir and the American City* (1997); and Foster Hirsch, *Detours and Lost Highways: A Map of Neo-Noir* (1999). See also Frank Krutnik, *In a Lonely Street: Film Noir, Genre, Masculinity* (1991) and Eddie Muller, *Dark City: The Lost World of Film Noir* (1998). The genre's roots in noir fiction receives exposure in David Cochran, *American Noir: Underground Writers and Film-*

makers of the Postwar Era (2000); Paula Rabinowitz, *Black and White and Noir: America's Pulp Modernism* (2002); and portions of Mike Davis, *City of Quartz: Excavating the Future in Los Angeles* (1990).

Postwar interest in crime films comes into focus in the relevant segments of John Bodnar, *Blue-Collar Hollywood: Liberalism, Democracy, and Working People in American Film* (2003) and Jonathan Munby, *Public Enemies, Public Heroes: Screening the Gangster from* Little Caesar *to* Touch of Evil (1999). See the portrait of John Garfield in Robert Sklar, *City Boys: Cagney, Bogart, Garfield* (1992). Paul Buhle and Dave Wagner, *A Very Dangerous Citizen: Abraham Lincoln Polonsky and the Hollywood Left* (2001) present a detailed look at one of the most brilliant film creators of the 1940s. For crime feature director Samuel Fuller, see the profile in George Lipsitz, *Time Passages: Collective Memory and Popular Culture* (1990). Max Allan Collins and James L. Traylor, *One Lonely Knight: Mickey Spillane's Mike Hammer* (1984) sheds light on the leading icon of Fifties pulp fiction.

America's two most esteemed dramatists elicit portraits in Leonard Moss, *Arthur Miller*, rev. ed. (1980) and Frederic I. Carpenter, *Eugene O'Neill*, rev. ed. (1979). See also Margaret B. McDowell, *Carson McCullers* (1980). For a major postwar chronicler of southern life, see Ruth M. Vande Kieft, *Eudora Welty*, rev. ed. (1987). A useful overview of 1950s motion pictures is Douglas Brode, *The Films of the Fifties:* Sunset Boulevard *to* On the Beach (1976). For an inside look at the decade's leading working-class feature, see Joanna E. Rapf, ed., *On the Waterfront* (2003). Leonard Bernstein's musical score for the film is one of many topics covered in Joan Peyser, *Bernstein: A Biography: Revised & Updated* (1998).

Material on postwar comic books appears in William W. Savage, Jr., *Commies, Cowboys, and Jungle Queens: Comic Books and America, 1945–1954* (1998) and the relevant segments of Bradford W. Wright, *Comic Book Nation: The Transformation of Youth Culture in America* (2001). Peter Biskind, *Seeing Is Believing: How Hollywood Taught Us to Stop Worrying and Love the Fifties* (1983) contains a number of insightful and entertaining analyses of anticommunist and science fiction films.

9

Subterranean Nation:
The Challenge of Cultural
Populism: 1945–1960

Beneath the surface tranquility of the years following World War II, American society experienced profound ferment. A subculture of Beat generation literary figures sought to reclaim a national identity by exploring life on the margins. A number of Hispanic, Asian American, and African American authors sought a coherent ethnic identity by revealing the shared cultural traditions of their respective communities. Meanwhile, progressive political activists responded to Cold War repression with an outpouring of folk music sung and fashioned in the name of the people. Finally, country and western, rhythm and blues, rock and roll, and rockabilly musical expressions all figured in the rise of a youth-oriented popular culture with populist overtones and future promises.

BEATIFIC AMERICA

When New York's Museum of Modern Art assembled 503 photographic portraits of individuals from sixty-eight nations, the exhibit proved so popular that its catalogue, *The Family of Man* (1955), sold three million copies. As in the 1930s, the postwar period fostered a profound interest in pictorial representations of ordinary people. In 1948, Gordon Parks became *Life* magazine's first African American photographer, a position he used to document black working life and the throbbing culture of the city streets.

Born in Kansas in 1912, Parks was the youngest of fifteen children. Moving to Minne-apolis at age fifteen, he supported himself as a bellhop, waiter, piano player, and bas-ketball player. After learning to use a camera and compiling a portfolio of images of poor people, Parks won a photography fellowship in 1941. His *American Gothic* (1942) featured a black cleaning woman holding a mop in front of an American flag. During World War II, he shot documentary portraits of black women welders and other wartime workers for the Office of War Information. The subjects of his early work at *Life* included a sixteen-year-old Harlem gang leader and the effects of segregation on an Alabama black family.

The son of Eastern European Jews, Jerome Liebling followed similar interests. En-rolling at Brooklyn College on the G.I. Bill, Liebling studied with photographer Walter Rosenblum, who promoted the fusion of aesthetic considerations with social concerns. When the young artist joined the radical Photo League, he became fixated on realistic treatments of everyday life. Liebling's early work included a series entitled "Ruthie Schwartz Wedding" (1947), street scenes of his native Brooklyn, and a portrait of a young black boy with his coat proudly unfurled. Hired to teach at the University of Minnesota in 1949, Liebling turned his camera to grain handlers, migrant field hands, coal workers, and stockyard laborers. "I want people to feel their own humanity," he commented, "the diversity of what life is all about." As a documentary artist, he looked to separate reality from intellectualism. In Red Lake, Minnesota, Liebling made con-tact with Chippewa Indian elders, whose awareness of the "old ways" fascinated him. The experience led to his participation in the making of a film entitled *The Tree Is Dead* (1953) and his own *Pow-Wow* (1960), a short documentary on Indian burial practices.

Swiss immigrant and photographer Robert Frank provided a darker approach to ev-eryday existence. Settling in the United States in 1947, Frank worked in New York fashion and advertising circles before pursuing independent projects in Europe and South America. Once gaining an international reputation, he succeeded in obtaining a Guggenheim Fellowship to support a cross-country automobile tour in 1955 and 1956. The result was *The Americans* (1959), a collection of unsentimental and revealing im-ages that occasionally recorded the full range of ordinary experience. The photographs captured a rodeo cowboy rolling a cigarette outside Madison Square Garden, a bare-chested and tattooed young man sleeping on the grass in a Cleveland park, a black worker on break outside his Detroit factory, and a Memphis washroom attendant shin-ing a customer's shoes amid a bank of urinals. Other images showed a bored young woman running a Miami Beach elevator, a lonely waitress behind a coffee shop counter in Indianapolis, a group of bench-sitters leaning on their canes in St. Petersburg, and a number of passengers peering out of an open-air trolley in New Orleans.

While recording the mundane life of cafés, bars, political meetings, drive-in movie theaters, and funerals, Frank also focused on extraordinary moments. His camera caught a gathering of young boys enchanted by the jukebox at a New York City candy store, a working-class family from Montana on a Sunday excursion in a battered car, several young couples frolicking in the grass on a day's outing, and a black man and woman gazing into the camera from the seats of a shiny motorcycle. Frank "sucked a poem right out of America onto film," exulted writer Jack Kerouac in the introduction to the volume. For Kerouac, the photographs perfectly captured the humor and sadness of life—"that crazy feeling in America when the sun is hot on the streets and music comes out of the jukebox or from a nearby funeral."

Jack Kerouac was the most obvious representative of a subculture of writers, artists, intellectuals, and philosophic rebels known as the Beat Generation. Nurtured in the shadows of the Cold War's domestic ideal, the Beats sought to fashion an alternative lifestyle that defied prevailing social expectations. Like the bebop musicians they revered, America's most visible nonconformists affected a cool detachment from a materialistic society that appeared to worship authority and to deny fundamental qualities of intuition and emotion. Seeking to tap the raw, primitive energy of the subconscious mind, they turned to writing to express contempt for the rigid social roles and psychic repression they detected in postwar life. "The point of Beat," declared poet Allen Ginsberg, "is that you get beat down to a certain nakedness where you are actually able to see the world in a visionary way …what happens in the dark night of the soul."

Adhering to the protocols of bebop, Beat writers refused to cast their art as entertainment. Instead, they evaded the perceived superficiality of middle-class culture with explorations of urban street life, including the extremes of criminality, drug use, and insanity. Rather than retreating to bohemian enclaves like New York's Greenwich Village, they pursued a fascination with direct experience, whether in late-night forays to places like Times Square, or Harlem, or the tenements of Lower Manhattan, or San Francisco's North Beach. Their poetry and prose consequently relied on emotion, intensity, and unadulterated language, rather than controlled skill or artifice. The act of writing, according to Kerouac and his compatriot Neal Cassady, involved the truthful telling of a tale and a chronicle of thoughts and impressions, a spontaneous record of spoken speech. "There is only one thing a writer can write about," observed Beat novelist and hipster William Burroughs, "what is in front of his senses at the moment of writing."

The first Beat chronicle appeared with *Go* (1952), a loosely integrated novel by John Clellon Holmes. Three years later, Allen Ginsberg, the son of an academic Jewish poet, brought the movement to public light in San Francisco when he read his epic work, *Howl*. "I saw the best minds of my generation destroyed by madness," recited Ginsberg, "—starving, mystical, naked—who dragged themselves through the angry streets at dawn looking for a negro fix." Using free-form verse in the style of Walt Whitman and William Carlos Williams, *Howl* denounced militarism, sterile conformity, materialism, and the apocalyptic forces eating away at the human spirit. Published in paperback as *Howl and Other Poems* (1956) by City Lights bookstore owner and poet Lawrence Ferlinghetti, the volume became the target of a U.S. Customs obscenity prosecution, although a federal judge ultimately ruled that the poem was a legitimate tool of social criticism.

Like Ginsberg's work, much of Beat poetry invoked the commonplace experiences of ordinary people. Ferlinghetti's own *Pictures of the Gone World* (1955), the initial volume of the City Lights Pocket Poet Series, lingered on rooftops "rigged with clotheslines" and other images of the life of North Beach's Italian American neighborhood. "The world is a beautiful place/to be born into/if you don't mind happiness/not always being/very much fun," wrote Ferlinghetti. Kenneth Patchen, the Niles, Ohio native whose work City Lights published as *Poems of Humor and Protest* (1956), described North Beach's vibrant street life in loving detail. Ferlinghetti also published the work of Denise Levertov, an English immigrant whose collection in *Here and Now* (1957) offered a glimpse of Lower Manhattan's sights and smells through the perspective of two gypsy women sitting by the window of their apartment. City Lights solidified its populist credentials by reprinting the work of poet William Carlos Williams.

Allen Ginsberg's former Columbia University cohort, Jack Kerouac, produced the single work most readily identified with the Beat Generation. A working-class French Canadian Catholic from Lowell, Massachusetts, Kerouac had come to Columbia on a football scholarship before turning his attention elsewhere. After several trips across the country between 1949 and 1950, the young writer composed an extended letter about his adventures. Once entered on a 120-foot roll of paper, the sparsely punctuated manuscript became *On the Road* (1957), a novel that Ginsberg helped to bring to the attention of a publisher. Subsequently heralded as "a postmodern western" and "a classic tale of innocence on the lam," the book relied on fictional narrator Sol Paradise to cast Neal Casssady as Dean Moriarty—a quick-talking, wide-eyed, handsome, mercurial womanizer and car thief whose life strategy involved staying on the move.

Although Beat writers often placed themselves on a higher spiritual plane than less developed souls, Kerouac revealed a profound love for America's landscape and promise. "I love to read boxcars and I love to read the names on them like Missouri Pacific, Great Northern, Rock Island Line," confessed Sol Paradise. Denver appeared to him "like the Promised Land, way out there beneath the stars," across the Great Plains. Paradise relished "the hiss of the steam outside, and the creak of the old wood" of his cheap midwestern hotel. He comes across "Mississippi Gene," an itinerant traveler who spends his life "crossing and re-crossing the country every year, south in the winter and north in the summer." Bull, an old-timer, reminisces about the time when things were "wild and brawling and free, with abundance and any kind of freedom for everyone." Yet the narrator still enthuses about raw "Frisco fogs" and "the great buzzing and vibrating hum" of a city offering chili beans, red-hot French-fried potatoes, and steamed clams. Los Angeles appeals to him with its "stucco houses and palms and drive-ins, … red brick, dirty characters drifting by, trolleys grating in the hopeless dawn."

Jack Kerouac   (*Photofest*)

THE FAMILY OF MAN

In a widely quoted section of *On the Road*, narrator Paradise mused that the white world lacked sufficient life, joy, "kicks," darkness, or music, and that he wished he were "a Negro" or a "Denver Mexican." Beat generation adventurers were among the era's few Anglos to acknowledge Mexican American culture in any fashion. Between 1942 and the early 1960s, the federal government recruited more than four million *braceros* to come north to serve mainly as temporary agricultural workers. California social historian Carey McWilliams detailed the abusive conditions prevailing in the migrant labor fields of the early postwar period. Meanwhile, many Mexican immigrants gravitated to industrial and food processing jobs in southwestern cities such as San Antonio, Denver, and Los Angeles. As middle-class residents of these urban centers pressed for full citizenship and educational rights, Spanish-language radio stations bridged the gap between assimilation and cultural autonomy by airing a mix of traditional Mexican rural music and American popular standards.

Divisions in musical taste reflected important class differences. Played in cantinas from rural Texas to Los Angeles, *musico ranchero* or *conjunto* country music relied on accordions and guitars for the thumping polka beat and waltz tempos that working-class immigrants preferred as their favorite dance numbers. Leading interpreters of the popular style included Texas bandleaders Valerio Longovia and Tony de la Rosa. In contrast, middle-class and Anglicized Mexican Americans leaned toward the bilingual and hybrid sounds of *orquesta* music. Developed by Texas saxophonist Beto Villa, these performances fused the ranchero elements of the accordion ensembles with up-tempo fox trots and boleros featuring swing-band horns. As innovators like Isidro López incorporated more elements of country influences into the *orquesta* sound, the style assumed the name "Tex-Mex Ranchero" and became the most commonly recorded postwar Mexican American popular music.

The tension between ethnic identity and the absorption of modern cultural traits constituted a major theme of Hispanic literature. Josephina Niggli's *Mexican Village* (1945) relayed ten stories about an Anglo Mexican young man seeking his roots in his grandmother's village south of the border. Imbued with "nostalgia of the blood," the protagonist reclaims his cultural heritage through local folklore. Yet he maintains his adopted country's irreverence for custom, ritual, and threats to individuality. Mario Suarez's tales of the Tucson barrio, which began appearing in the *Arizona Quarterly* in 1947, were among the first to use the term *Chicano,* originally a disrespectful reference to recent Mexican migrants with a poor, Indian background. In a style reminiscent of John Steinbeck's *Tortilla Flat* and the sketches of Monterrey street life in *Cannery Row* (1945), Suarez offered intimate portraits of eccentric bicultural figures, such as a pachuco rebel, participants in a cockfight betting party, and a philosophic barber.

It fell to Mexican American writer José Antonio Villarreal to produce the first acknowledged Chicano novel. Set in the late 1930s, *Pocho* (1959) focused on a young man's ambivalence over a desire for individuality and the ethical obligations imposed upon him by his family and community. The complexities of assimilation in a hostile environment likewise concerned Filipino author Carlos Bulosan, whose memoir, *America Is in the Heart* (1946), pictured the life of migrant farm laborers and cannery workers in Washington State in the 1920s and '30s. To be a Filipino, wrote Bulosan, was to "feel like a criminal running away from a crime I did not commit." In the short story "The Romance of Magno Rubio," the author recalled the experience of "crawling on our knees like brown beetles" to pick peas.

Chinese American writing contained an equivalent interest in the clash between old and new. In *Fifth Chinese Daughter* (1945), Mills College graduate Jade Snow Wong turned to autobiography to focus on the split between cultures, the impact of racial discrimination, and the place of women in traditional Chinese society. An immigrant to the United States in 1943 who earned a graduate literature degree at Yale, Chin Yang Lee sought to respond to conventional literary and film caricatures of the Chinese in his adopted country. His first novel, *Flower Drum Song* (1957), provided the basis for a Rodgers and Hammerstein Broadway musical in 1959 and a movie two years later. Lee's story concerned a wealthy man in San Francisco's Chinatown who refuses to adjust to American ways and insists upon filial obligations and family devotion from his younger son. Fond of hamburgers and baseball, the young man reads from the Declaration of Independence when his father requires him to recite a chapter from an arithmetic book.

Laced with irony and humor, *Flower Drum Song* demonstrated empathy for both sides of the generational conflict. Lee's second work, *Lover's Point* (1958), embodied a darker mood but sustained a comparable sensitivity to human foibles. Named for a secluded parking lot for romantic couples in Orange Grove, California, the book described a lonely language instructor's love for a prostitute. Without overriding moral judgments, it presented a complex psychological portrait of an immigrant that infused its English dialogue with the peculiar cadences of Chinese language. Completely isolated and desperate for companionship, Lee's protagonist expresses "a strong compassion for the sinners, the criminals, the cynics, the suicides …" Similar realism marked Louis Chu's *Eat a Bowl of Tea* (1961). Employing a coarse, unadorned vernacular language stripped of all clichés, Chu offered an unsentimental view of Chinatown's bachelor waiters, cooks, and laundry workers whose only escape from life's tedium lay in gambling or the patronage of white prostitutes.

The persistence of cultural traditions among ordinary people constituted a major theme of the short stories assembled by Toshio Mori in *Yokohama, California* (1949). Born to Japanese immigrants near Oakland in 1910, Mori followed his parents into the tree nursery business. His sketches of characters he knew in the late 1930s and early '40s contained a "spoken" quality that embraced local gossip, humor, and folk legend as well as the distinctive phrasing that the community's tightly knit families and clans brought to American English. Lawson Fusao Inada's profile, "The Woman Who Makes Swell Doughnuts," in turn, conveyed the resilience of people inundated by the burdens of labor. Inada described the face of his elderly protagonist as one that was "coarse with hard water." Having given birth to six children and worked with "her man" for forty years, he explained, she ran a household that was "completely her little world." Such a person, concluded the writer, contained "the force capable of stirring the earth and the people."

In "Las Vegas Charley" (1961), highly acclaimed short story writer Hisaye Yamamoto described a lowly dishwasher who worked ten hours a night at a Chinese restaurant. The daughter of Japanese immigrants, Yamamoto was born in 1921 in Redondo Beach, California. Her story concerned an alienated character that has lost touch with his community, family, and even his personal identity. In the end, however, the protagonist's son comes "to understand that his father was not an evil man, only one man among so many who lived from day to day as best they could, limited, restricted, by the meager gifts Fate or God had doled out to them."

Several works of Japanese American literature reflected wartime traumas. One of the first was Monica Sone's autobiography, *Nisei Daughter* (1953). Born Kazuko Monica Itoi in 1904 in the Seattle hotel her father managed, Sone offered an intimate glimpse of life at a relocation facility in Minidoka, Idaho. The camps also provided the context for John Okada's *No-No Boy* (1957), the first Japanese American novel in U.S.

history and the only published work by the author. Born in Seattle in 1923, where his family ran a boarding hotel, Okada earned an M.A. in English at Columbia University and served as an Army sergeant while his parents survived an internment camp. *No-No Boy* told the story of Ichiro, a Nisei who refuses service in the armed forces and chooses prison instead. Returning to Seattle after two years, he experiences the postwar fragmentation of Japanese American personal and community identity. Nevertheless, Ichiro begins to take responsibility for his own decisions and the direction of his life. Phrased in vernacular language and borrowing heavily from oral tradition, Okada's sparsely selling novel offered a first step in making Japanese America whole again.

The short stories of Kim Yong Ik, a Korean immigrant who arrived in the United States in 1928 and became an academically trained fiction writer, embodied another perspective on the continuing conflict between cultural tradition and adjustment to modern ways. "The Wedding Shoes" (1958), Ik's first success, recounted the tale of a butcher's son who falls in love with the daughter of a neighboring shoemaker. Although the cobbler consents to the courtship and allows his loved one to work as a domestic servant to pay off his debts, his pride and stubbornness lead to a tragic conclusion. Ik reinforced the pathos of the story with the acknowledgement that the demand for ceremonial, hand-made shoes slackened after the Korean War. Although the author was ambivalent about the contemporary relevance of traditional culture, his writing captured the rhythms of the Korean language, as well as images of the land that immigrants kept in their memory. Another example of bittersweet reminiscence appeared in *You Lovely People* (1955), a collection of short stories by Filipino writer Bienvenido N. Santos.

BRONZEVILLE TO THE MOUNTAIN

"My aim … is to write poems that will somehow successfully 'call' … all black people; black people in taverns, black people in alleys, black people in gutters, schools, offices, factories, prisons, the consulates," Gwendolyn Brooks once explained. "I wish to reach black people in pulpits, black people in mines, on farms, on thrones; not always to 'teach' – I shall wish often to entertain, to illumine." The leading African American poet of the immediate postwar period, Brooks was born in Topeka, Kansas, in 1917 but moved to Chicago with her parents, a schoolteacher and a janitor, five weeks after her birth. Publishing her first verse in a children's magazine at age thirteen, she made regular poetry contributions to the African American *Chicago Defender* while still in high school and received personal encouragement from James Weldon Johnson and Langston Hughes. After graduating from junior college in 1936, Brooks worked for a self-styled spiritual adviser and marketer of charms and potions as a domestic servant and secretary. Two years later, she married an aspiring fellow poet and settled down in a South Side kitchenette apartment above a real estate agency.

Seeking to develop her craft in the early 1940s, Brooks attended writers workshops, mingled with the modernist intellectuals of *Poetry* magazine, won a midwestern regional prize for verse, and received a Guggenheim Fellowship. In 1945, a publisher in search of "Negro poems" released her first collection of work. Endorsed by Richard Wright, *A Street in Bronzeville* (1945) incorporated elegant but spare rhythms to elucidate the lives of South Side beauticians, domestics, preachers, and everyday folk. "I wrote about what I saw and heard in the street," Brooks recalled. One piece, "The Sundays of Satin-Legs Smith," described the ritual of a man who emerges from his cheap hotel quarters once a week for a meal at his favorite café and a movie before returning home, where the only beauty in his life comes from the fine clothes and brightly colored fabrics that adorn his room. Another poem, "We Real Cool," captured the terse phrasing of seven young pool sharks.

Building on Paul Laurence Dunbar's use of black folk traditions and the presence of urban blues and jazz poetry in the work of Langston Hughes, Brooks continued to show interest in the ordinary life of the urban dispossessed. Following *Annie Allen* (1949), the recipient of a Pulitzer Prize for Poetry, she published *Maud Martha* (1953), a lyrical but stark narrative of a dark-skinned young woman's passage into adulthood. Set in the cramped apartments, beauty parlors, nightclubs, and shops of the South Side, the novel avoided either debasing or revering African American life. *The Bean Eaters* (1960), a third collection of poetry, merged blues phrasing and folk ballads with more traditional forms of verse to tell the story of an older married couple's survival of hardship and pain. Intent on unmasking the inner lives of "the un-heroic," Brooks insisted on publishing thin and affordable volumes of work because she believed that poetry should never be the sole province of the privileged and educated few.

Printmaker Elizabeth Catlett shared a similar philosophy. "Art can't be the exclusive domain of the elect," she once declared. "It has to belong to everyone ... Artists should work to the end that ... all people take joy in full participation in the rich material, intellectual, and spiritual resources of this world's lands, peoples, and goods." The granddaughter of slaves, Catlett was born into a middle-class family in Washington, D.C. in 1915. After completing an art degree at Howard University in 1935, she did graduate work under Grant Wood at the University of Iowa with a specialty in sculpture. From there Catlett moved to Chicago's South Side to work at a community art center and align herself with the "Chicago Renaissance" of politically aware African American writers and artists of the early 1940s. A successive stint as the administrator of the George Washington Carver School in New York increased her interest in art for non-elites. Catlett pursued these concerns after 1946, when she won a Rosenwald Fellowship to study printmaking in Mexico, where she became fascinated with muralist traditions combining images of ordinary people with liberationist politics.

Remaining south of the border as a permanent resident, Catlett enrolled at the politically radical People's Graphic Arts Workshop. Her first major work, *The Negro Woman*

(1946–47), consisted of a print series of fifteen linoleum cuts illustrating the living and working conditions of African American women. "I am the Negro woman," read the accompanying text. "My right is a future of equality with other Americans." Undaunted by harassment by the U.S. embassy for alleged communist ties, Catlett proceeded to complete linocuts and other studies of black sharecroppers, field workers, domestic servants, musicians, students, victims of white terrorism, and African American liberationist leaders like Sojourner Truth and Harriet Tubman.

"I ain't nobody but myself," declared the character of Trueblood, a singer of spirituals and blues in Ralph Ellison's *Invisible Man* (1952). Born in Oklahoma City in 1914, Ellison attended Tuskegee Institute before moving to New York in 1936, where he joined the Federal Writers Project and contributed to the radical *New Masses.* After serving in the Merchant Marine during World War II, he received a Rosenwald Fellowship to work on the novel that became *Invisible Man*, a subsequent winner of the National Book Award for Fiction. Ellison's story concerned a young black man's odyssey from the rural South to New York. Embittered by society's insistence on defining him in racial terms, he isolates himself in a basement apartment on the edge of Harlem. In a world in which irrational social institutions masked arbitrary power, suggested the novel, things were not what they seemed. Accordingly, black people needed to rely on their own experiences and shared folklore to define reality, particularly, as Ellison explained in an essay in *Shadow and Act* (1953), on the "near-tragic, near-comic lyricism" of the blues.

Beyond its racial themes, Ellison's surrealist prose addressed the powerlessness of all human beings in achieving personal identity in modern civilization. For this reason, the author refused categorization as a "black" novelist. In contrast, James Baldwin proved far more willing to align himself with African American consciousness. Born in Harlem in 1924, Baldwin became a Pentecostal minister after a religious conversion at age fourteen. Never attending college, he moved to Greenwich Village during World War II, where he worked at a series of odd jobs to support his writing. The recipient of a Rosenwald Fellowship, the aspiring author lived in Paris between 1948 and 1956, where he came to terms with his roots as a Negro after spending an entire night in a hotel room listening to Bessie Smith sing the blues.

Baldwin's first novel, the autobiographical *Go Tell It on the Mountain* (1953), described a young black man's rejection of his preacher father's hatred of white society. Through his religious enthusiasm, however, the protagonist comes to accept a destiny as a leader of his people—"the despised and rejected, the wretched and the spat upon." He rests his faith on the belief that the multitude one day "would compel the earth to heave upward and surrender the waiting dead." Baldwin saw his work as a celebration of the spontaneity and capacity for love and joy among black people, in contrast to white society's fear and hate. In a series of essays in *Notes of a Native Son* (1955) and *Nobody Knows My Name* (1961), he expanded upon these themes by arguing that blackness was part of American identity, and that people of color were both black and American.

Baldwin published his essays as the American struggle for civil rights began to gather momentum. Following massive black participation in the armed forces and home front labor force of World War II, Jackie Robinson's integration of major league baseball served as a major turning point in U.S. race relations. The grandson of a slave and the son of Georgia sharecroppers, Robinson moved with his mother and siblings to Pasadena, California, in 1920 when his father deserted the family. While his mother supported the children as a domestic servant, Robinson ran with local street gangs. Nevertheless, he managed to enroll at Pasadena City College and then won an athletic scholarship to the University of California at Los Angeles (UCLA), where he played football, basketball, track, and baseball on integrated teams. Drafted into the Army, he graduated officer candidate school although the camp baseball club at Ft. Hood, Texas, excluded him on racial grounds. When Robinson refused to move to the back of a city bus, moreover, he faced a court-martial proceeding but ultimately won an acquittal.

Following his release from the Army, Robinson played with the all-Negro Kansas City Monarchs but found the experience degrading. Signed to a contract by Brooklyn Dodgers president Branch Rickey in 1945, he spent a year in the minor leagues, where he endured racial taunts by both players and fans. When baseball commissioner Happy Chandler overruled fifteen of the sixteen major league club owners and allowed Rickey to bring Robinson up to the parent club in 1947, the young player agreed to refrain from responding to verbal insults. In his first year, Robinson won the Rookie of the Year Award and became the National League's Most Valuable Player two years later. Bringing the speed, daring, and fierce competitive spirit of the Negro Leagues to the majors, he capped a spectacular career by stealing home in the 1955 World Series and leading the Dodgers to their first national championship.

HOLLYWOOD ON RACE

"A life is not important except in the impact it has on other lives," Jackie Robinson wrote in his memoirs. Following the erosion of baseball's color line, Americans witnessed the integration of the Army; a Supreme Court decision condemning public school segregation; a grassroots crusade to end segregated bus seating in Montgomery, Alabama; the use of federal troops to permit black students to attend a Little Rock high school; and passage of moderate civil rights legislation in 1957 and 1960. Hollywood responded to these milestones in a gradual and cautious manner. Despite wartime efforts to portray African Americans with dignity and respect, the Disney studio resorted to more traditional racial imagery with *Song of the South* (1946), a semi-animated color musical based on Joel Chandler Harris' Uncle Remus stories. A highlight of the movie was the singing of "Zip-A-Dee-Doo-Dah," a lively ditty taken from the nonsensical chorus of "Zip Coon," a blackface standard of mid-nineteenth-century minstrels. Not surprisingly, black organizations objected to the film's romanticizing of slavery and Reconstruction.

Home of the Brave (1949) marked the first Hollywood feature to address race relations from an African American perspective. Independently produced by Hell's Kitchen native Stanley Kramer and written by Carl Foreman, the film originated with a Broadway play focusing on anti-Semitism. *Home of the Brave* starred James Edwards, a former steelworker, union activist, and combat veteran, in the first title role for a black actor in a Hollywood drama. The screenplay centered on the story of a single Negro in a five-man unit assigned to infiltrate a Japanese-occupied Pacific island. Targeted by racial harassment, the soldier suffers an emotional breakdown. "I learned that if you're colored you stink. You're not like other people," he snaps. "Well, you make us different, you rats." In the end, however, a white comrade reaches out to the black man. "Underneath we're all guys," he concludes.

Shot in documentary style in Portsmouth, New Hampshire, where a light-skinned Negro physician and his family had lived as whites for twenty years, *Lost Boundaries* (1949) centered on the furor that resulted when the Navy rejected the doctor's attempt to enlist and his secret emerged. In the end, a white minister delivers a plea for racial tolerance, and small-town harmony prevails. Yet the film's producers felt compelled to cast white actors as the black principals to encourage empathy for the characters among general audiences. Likewise, Elia Kazan's *Pinky* (1949) starred white performer Jeanne Crain as a light-skinned black nurse who returns to the Deep South to visit her grandmother (Ethel Waters), who has been taking in laundry to help support the young woman up North, where she has been passing for white. Crain winds up caring for an impoverished but crusty white patrician nearing death, an experience that strengthens both her sense of worth and her racial identity. When the nurse inherits the old woman's crumbling mansion, she breaks off her engagement to a northern white man, starts a black health clinic, and vows to remain in the South to work with her own people.

Black empowerment also constituted the focus of *Intruder in the Dust* (1949), the screen adaptation of William Faulkner's introspective novel of the Deep South. Filmed near Faulkner's Oxford, Mississippi, where the locals served as extras, the movie traced the plight of a successful and proud African American farmer, played by Juano Hernandez, accused of killing a white man. Never doubting his self-worth, integrity, or complete equality with anyone else, the protagonist refuses to bend to white pressures as the townspeople prepare for a lynching. His resourcefulness ultimately produces results when he convinces a young boy he once saved from drowning and an elderly, female schoolteacher to help prove his innocence.

Stanley Kramer's *The Defiant Ones* (1956) teamed white actor Tony Curtis with Sidney Poitier, the first black man to share billing with a major film star, in an intense drama of interracial solidarity that drew upon Method acting performances and the cinema techniques of Italian neo-realism. The screenplay focused on two convicts, one black and one white, who escape through the swamps of the Deep South. Chained together, they must overcome mutual bigotry and accept each other as human beings, as hostile lynch mobs, a relentless posse, and vicious bloodhounds pursue them. In a moving final sequence, Poitier fails in an effort to lift the running Curtis onto a passing freight and purposefully falls back to the ground to remain with his mate, certain of capture.

For all of its experimentation, Hollywood preferred to deal indirectly with matters of color. In *Broken Arrow* (1950), cooperative Apache Indians stood in for African Americans as the intended objects of racial tolerance. *Giant* (1956), George Stevens' Academy Award adaptation of an epic Edna Ferber novel about a Texas ranching family, substituted Mexican Americans for blacks in a pluralist plea for racial understanding. Musicals offered another way for movies to speak in the interests of interracial harmony. After lyricist Oscar Hammerstein produced an all-black version of Georges Bizet's opera *Carmen* for the Broadway stage, Otto Preminger's *Carmen Jones* (1954) starred Dorothy Dandridge, Harry Belafonte, and Pearl Bailey in the tragic tale of a black soldier's ill-fated love for a seductive but faithless factory worker.

The screening of *South Pacific* (1958) offered a powerful nostrum for a message equating racial pluralism with American democracy. The musical featured an Army nurse from Arkansas who initially recoils from marriage to a French planter when she discovers that he has two children from a previous liaison with a Polynesian woman. A subplot centered on an Army lieutenant from Philadelphia who backs away from courting the daughter of a Tonkinese woman, only to realize before his death that prejudice can be unlearned. The officer's epiphany leads to a bitter rendering of "Carefully Taught," a tersely phrased Hammerstein lyric set to a child-like Richard Rodgers melody. "You've got to be taught to hate and fear, you've got to be taught from year to year," the song begins. "It's got to be drummed in your dear little ear. You've got to be carefully taught." "You've got to be taught to be afraid," it states, "of people whose eyes are oddly made, and people whose skin is a different shade." "You've got to be taught before it's too late, before you are six, or seven, or eight," it concludes, "to hate all the people your relatives hate, you've got to be carefully taught."

THE PEOPLE'S MUSIC

"Like a tree that's standing in the water, we shall not be moved." So went the words to an old Negro hymn recycled as a protest song in the early 1950s by folksinger Pete Seeger and The Weavers. In the years immediately following World War II, progressive cultural activists sought to use folk music to return America's musical heritage to "the people," to educate the public about important political issues, and to encourage creativity and effective organizing within the movement itself. Through the independent People's Songs, Inc., culturally minded elements of the Left sought to disseminate topical music that supported labor, civil rights, civil liberties, and peace. Between 1946 and 1949, the organization enrolled over two hundred thousand members and produced recordings, published songsheets, conducted classes, and held concerts that offered hope and a vision of an alternative society to socialists and their allies.

People's Songs defined folk music as a non-commercial form that addressed "life as it really is," and that expressed the lives, struggles, and highest aspirations of society's most humble members. Although political communists limited definitions of the people to the revolutionary working class, cultural progressives preferred to follow the example of poet Carl Sandburg by including everyone in the category except powerful capitalists and racists. In contrast to the Communist Party, moreover, which viewed folksingers merely as entertainers for political gatherings, the activists at People's Songs believed that they were building a movement culture whose music could reach participants emotionally as well as intellectually. In a foreword to *The People's Songbook* (1948), scholar and archivist Alan Lomax heralded the advent of "a folk-culture of high moral and political content" associated with "a new kind of human being."

Through institutions such as Tennessee's Highlander Folk School, progressive activists sought to teach labor leaders to use folk music as an organizing tool. Yet in a period in which unions sought stability, respectability, and independence from the left, organized labor failed to embrace either the musical idiom or the political message of folk songs. People's Songs proved more effective in staging hootenannies, particularly during Henry A. Wallace's Progressive Party presidential campaign of 1948. Although communal sing-outs bolstered a sense of community among participants, however, performances mainly inspired those already committed to left-wing causes. As the communist movement became more isolated in the face of Cold War repression, moreover, hootenannies primarily served as a source of ideological solidarity for an increasingly beleaguered minority. Responding to these trends, Woody Guthrie called for an infusion of "Cowboy-Hillbilly-Religious" hoots.

With the collapse of People's Songs, banjo player Pete Seeger organized The Weavers, a folk music ensemble that included guitarist Fred Hellerman and vocalists Lee Hays and Ronnie Gilbert. After performances at New York's Village Vanguard, the group scored a major hit in 1950 when their recording of Huddie Ledbetter's "Good Night Irene" sold two million copies. Harassed for alleged communist ties, The Weavers disbanded, but reunited in 1955 at Carnegie Hall. With album sales surpassing four million, the group helped to popularize the laments of southern farmers and miners, former slaves, and industrial workers, as well as songs from across the globe. Seeger also played a role in the creation of People's Artists (1949–56), an umbrella organization that sponsored concerts, printed a songbook entitled *Lift Every Voice*, and published the periodical protest music broadside *Sing Out!* The first edition of the new publication featured "The Hammer Song" (1950), a collaboration between Seeger and Hays. "If I had a hammer," went the lyric, "I'd hammer in the morning, I'd hammer in the evening … I'd hammer out love between my brothers and sisters—all over this land."

While the urban folk music community tended to romanticize working-class resistance to capitalism, the South produced a number of indigenous songwriters and performers whose social commentary leaned more to fatalism than protest. Merle Travis, a musician from a family of Kentucky coal miners, composed two pieces in 1947 that conveyed the experience of the pits with poetic austerity. "It'll form as a habit and seep in your soul, till the stream of your blood is as black as the coal," began the first. "It's dark as a dungeon and damp as the dew, where danger is double and pleasures are few." "Like a fiend with his dope and a drunkard his wine," sang Travis, "a man will have lust for the lure of the mine." "Sixteen Tons," a song that Tennessee Ernie Ford recorded as a popular single in 1955, comprised the companion piece to "Dark as a Dungeon." "Some people say a man is made out of mud, a poor man's made out of muscle and blood," it began. "You load sixteen tons and what do you get?—another day older and deeper in debt. St. Peter don't you call me 'cause I can't go. I owe my soul to the company store."

Another Kentucky balladeer, Jean Ritchie, came from a family of traditional Cumberland Mountain singers. The youngest of eleven daughters, Ritchie completed a social work degree at the University of Kentucky before moving to New York in 1946 and joining the folk music revival. Her dulcimer accompaniment to classics like "Shady Grove" made her a favorite at the Newport (Rhode Island) Folk Festival, a yearly gathering Pete Seeger helped to establish. Ritchie's passionate commitment to the land of her ancestors ultimately produced her haunting lament "Black Waters" (1977), a bitter commentary on the effects of open-pit mining on the countryside and people.

It fell to Bill Monroe to bring traditional mountain music to a broad popular audience. The son of a female ballad musician, Monroe was born on a western Kentucky farm in 1911. Orphaned at the age of eleven, the young boy went to live with his uncle, a fiddler who performed at local dances with a black blues guitarist named Arnold Schultz. Within a year, Monroe had joined the group as a mandolin player. During the early 1930s, he sang and played with his brothers in an acoustic string band, perfecting the staccato style of performance that would become his trademark. His own group, the Blue Grass Boys, became a permanent fixture of the Grand Ole Opry radio show in 1939 and scored a smash hit with their recording of "Mule Skinner Blues" (1940). Monroe infused Appalachian music with a hard-driving beat, a gospel sound taken from the Holiness revivals of his youth, and a touch of the blues. The straightforward and laconic tenor vocals of original numbers such as "Blue Moon of Kentucky" (1945) and "Footprints in the Snow" (1945) conveyed what the group's songwriter and lead singer described as a "high, lonesome sound."

By 1945, the Blue Grass Boys had added the services of fiddler Charles Wise, bass guitar player Howard Watts (Cedric Rainwater), rhythm guitarist Lester Flatt, and five-string banjo virtuoso Earl Scruggs. A North Carolina farm boy, Scruggs used a three-fingered style for both improvisation and the melodic lead, an innovation that transformed the banjo from an instrument linked with comedy into a legitimate component of a string band ensemble. The Blue Grass Boys developed a reputation for intricate vocal harmonies and fever-pitched, fast-paced mandolin, banjo, and fiddle solos. Performing at country music venues in the Upper South and in southern-styled honky-tonks in Detroit, southern Ohio, Baltimore, and elsewhere, the band came to personify the musical genre that Monroe named "bluegrass." By the late 1950s and early 1960s, the bluegrass style had attracted artists like the Stanley Brothers and fostered widespread imitation among folk music adherents on college campuses.

HONKY-TONK HEROES AND ANGELS

"You sing about the things," country vocalist Webb Pierce once explained, that people "think about most, but don't talk about." By 1949, 650 American radio stations were carrying live and recorded performances by rural artists. Stimulated by independent ownership of broadcasting outlets, the spread of small recording studios, and the expansion of industrial and service jobs beyond the Northeast and Midwest, postwar country music thrived. Working-class culture had particular resonance in the recently urbanized South. The advent of the National Association for Stock Car Auto Racing (NASCAR) in Daytona Beach, Florida, in 1947 embodied the suspicion of authority and gentility prevalent among the region's white laboring classes. Initially drawing its talent from one-time mountain bootleg runners and auto mechanics, NASCAR celebrated the exploits of untamed competitors whose status as uncouth but successful outsiders appealed to fans who saw themselves in similar terms.

Baseball broadcaster Dizzy Dean offered another role model for white southerners. The son of a sawmill worker and log hauler, Dean moved with his family from Arkansas to Oklahoma, where he picked cotton and never got past the seventh grade. As a boy, he fashioned homemade baseballs and bats and participated in the sport in his bare feet. At sixteen, Dean joined the Army, where he earned his nickname as a regimental pitcher. Dean's legendary season with the St. Louis Cardinals came in 1934, when he won thirty games and, with his brother Paul, pitched the "Gas House Gang" to a come-from-behind National League pennant and a World Series victory in seven games. Moving to the broadcast booth in 1941, the self-styled "white-haired boy of the overflowing Mississippi" reinvented baseball lingo. His colorful down-home expressions included "lollapalooza" for a spectacular play, "side-wheeler" for a lefty pitcher, "tools of ignorance" for the catcher's equipment, "whammy" for a jinx, "blooper" for a fluke hit, "duster" for a brush-back pitch, "can of corn" for a lazy outfield fly, "belly-whopper" for a head-first approach to the next base, and, "slud" for the act of sliding.

At the height of Dean's baseball prowess, he organized the Missouri Mudcats, a hill-billy band with Oklahoma-born infielder Pepper Martin on washboard and himself on vocals. The humble origins of the Mudcats were common to country music performers of the postwar period. Rose Maddox, for example, came from a family of Alabama sharecroppers who moved to California when Rose was six. Once out West, the family took refuge with a community of indigents who lived inside drainage culverts before finding work near Modesto as fruit pickers. Rose began singing in the migrant labor camps at the age of eight. When she was ten, the young vocalist and her four brothers won a spot on a local radio show; by 1939, the group had their own syndicated West Coast program. Chaperoned through the central California honky-tonks by their mother, the Maddox Brothers and Rose played a broad repertoire of country music, even incorporating Woody Guthrie's "Philadelphia Lawyer" once they had seen the songwriter perform on the rodeo circuit. As the group moved up to big barns and dancehalls after 1945, Rose began wearing Mexican-styled cowboy costumes, and the band traveled in a fleet of five black Cadillac sedans.

Country music audiences maintained a strong sense of roots through Minnie Pearl. Born Sara Ophelia Colley in 1912 to an affluent family near Grinder's Switch, Tennessee, the young socialite pursued drama studies at a Nashville finishing school before serving as the stage director of a traveling theater company. The character of Minnie Pearl, developed in the late 1930s, harkened back to the "hillbilly girl" persona of vaudeville tradition and Depression radio barn dances. Appearing in a signature straw hat with a $1.98 price tag attached to it, Pearl personified the small-town spinster in search of a man. Yet her country bumpkin repeatedly subjected more sophisticated and cosmopolitan folk to ridicule. In exposing people with "airs," Minnie Pearl personified a long-standing brand of humor that expressed hostility toward the wealthy and power-ful and belief in the intrinsic worth of ordinary people. The first woman to take her place as a regular member of the Grand Ole Opry in 1940, she became a central fixture of the country music establishment.

Nashville's emergence as a major entertainment center helped to foster a shared cul-ture that took on the appearance of a vast extended family. Inspirational songs played a key role in cementing these bonds. "How many times have you heard someone say?" began "A Satisfied Mind" (1955), a gospel-flavored number popularized by both Red Foley and Porter Wagoner, "'if I had his money, I would do things my way.'" Each verse of the song suggested that spiritual peace was a greater treasure than money or fame. Ferlin Husky's best-selling "On the Wings of a Dove" (1959) carried the lesson that God did not forget ordinary people during the hard times "when troubles surround us." Even more frequently, country music emphasized romantic heartbreak and the frailties of human relationships. By one estimate, in fact, tragic love ballads have ac-counted for half to two-thirds of all country songs ever written. Sincere and gritty tributes to personal endurance and survival offered inspiration and hopes of better times for music audiences who often saw themselves as society's underdogs.

Chronicling the joys and pitfalls of romantic love and nightlife culture, the honky-tonk style dominated country music's postwar era. With the advent of the Fender electric bass guitar in 1951 and the ongoing impact of Ernest Tubb's hard Texas sound, industry trade magazines began to place "hillbilly" listings under the "country and western" heading. William Orville "Lefty" Frizzell became one of the music's most popular interpreters. The son of an itinerant East Texas oil driller, Frizzell grew up idolizing Jimmy Rodgers. After an apprenticeship in southwestern honky-tonks and dance halls, he signed a recording contract when he was only twenty-two. By 1951, Frizzell had four of the top ten hits on the country charts and shared lead billing on tour with Hank Williams. His first number, "If You've Got the Money, I've Got the Time" (1950), came directly from his experiences in smoky honky-tonks. The record's second side, "I Love You a Thousand Ways" (1950), allegedly stemmed from a remorseful overnight stay in a county jail. Frizzell's nuanced phrasing and intimate styling produced a string of hits, ranging from "I Want To Be With You Always" (1951) to "Long Black Veil" (1959).

With backing from the danceable beat of the Wandering Boys, the wailing tenor of Louisiana-born Webb Pierce helped to set the tone for Fifties honky-tonk. Popularizing the use of the gut-wrenching pedal steel guitar, Pierce sang about the forbidden subject of adulterous relationships in "Back Street Affair" (1952). "There Stands the Glass" (1953), another hit, dealt with drinking as a healing balm for romantic heartbreak. Pierce's version of the Jimmy Rodgers classic "In the Jailhouse Now" (1955) cemented the performer's status as an icon of the southern working class. Waco, Texas vocalist Hank Thompson and the Brazos Valley Boys also immortalized the hard drinking, cheating male culture of highway watering holes. In William Warren's "The Wild Side of Life" (1952), however, Thompson turned the tables with a bitter lament about one of God's "honky-tonk angels," a woman who forsakes the man who adores her for the glamorous nightlife, where she waits "to be anybody's baby."

To the surprise of the country music establishment, Thompson's rueful lyric elicited a response from a thirty-three-year-old wife and mother of three. Kitty Wells had been born into a Nashville family of musicians as Muriel Deason. Dropping out of school at fifteen, she worked in a factory ironing shirts for nine dollars a week. In 1936, however, she began to sing on local radio and took the name Kitty Wells from an old parlor song featured on the Grand Ole Opry. J.D. Miller's "It Wasn't God Who Made Honky-Tonk Angels" (1952) was the first recording by Wells. "It's a shame that all the blame is on us women," began the final verse. "It's not true that only you men feel the same; from the start most ev'ry heart that's ever broken, was because there always was a man to blame." Despite an Opry ban, Wells scored a major hit and reigned as the first female superstar of country music for the next thirteen years. Dressed in prewar gingham as an unpretentious home-maker, the singer conveyed enormous gospel power with tight-lipped intensity and tear-ful restraint. Her emotional honesty produced eighty-one hits, including classics such as "Release Me" (1954) and "I Can't Stop Loving You" (1958).

LOVESICK BLUES

"Country music relates to people because they think that what happened in the songs might have happened to them or to somebody they know," observed Kitty Wells. Pee Wee King's "Tennessee Waltz" (1948), a number subsequently recorded by pop star Patti Page, illustrated the wisdom of the Wells adage with the plaintive tale of a woman who loses her sweetheart to a friend during the course of one ill-fated dance. "You Don't Know Me" (1955), a collaborative effort between vocalist Eddie Arnold and Nashville songwriter Cindy Walker, provided another glimpse into the private emo-tions that people often recall or recognize from their own life experience. With total economy of phrasing, the painful lyric described the hidden desires of "just a friend" who had never summoned the nerve to reveal himself to the woman he loved.

No single country performer explored the vicissitudes of emotional life more than Hank Williams. Born in 1923 in a small Alabama town, Williams was the son of a World War I soldier who suffered from shell shock. After working at an assortment of jobs in the logging industry, his father entered a veterans hospital for a period of ten years when his son was seven. Brought up by a strong-willed mother who introduced him to the hymns and gospel melodies of the fundamentalist Baptist Church, the young Williams sold peanuts, hawked newspapers, shined shoes, and picked strawberries. At fourteen, he formed a costumed hillbilly band called the Drifting Cowboys. Influenced by a local black street singer and inspired by the styling of Roy Acuff and Ernest Tubb, Williams sang lead vocals as the group performed at medicine shows, school dances, and local clubs. After dropping out of high school and serving a stint in Mobile's war-time shipyards, the aspiring musician resumed playing in the rough southern Alabama honky-tonks he called the "blood buckets." At the age of twenty-four, he traveled to Nashville to become a songwriter and wound up with a recording contract.

The Williams debut single was "Move It On Over" (1947), an up-tempo novelty num-ber based on a blues chord structure. In 1948, the singer joined Shreveport's Louisiana Hayride, a popular country radio show among southwestern oil and gas industry workers. "Lovesick Blues" (1949), his first major hit, fused a strain of self-mockery with a western swing version of a Jimmy Rodgers yodel. As Williams moved on to regular appearances on the Grand Ole Opry, he sold eleven million records in the next four years, including danceable jukebox hits like "Honky Tonkin'," "Mind Your Own Business," "Jambalaya (On the Bayou)," "Settin' the Woods On Fire," and "Hey, Good Lookin'." Beyond cele-brations of drinking and earthy pleasure, however, he bonded with fans with austere de-

Hank Williams   (*Photofest*)

pictions of romantic loneliness, betrayal, and despair. As surveys hinted that less than one-third of working-class couples were happily married in the Fifties, Williams penetrated beneath the era's façade of domestic bliss with an unpolished voice whose twists and turns conveyed the pain that many felt but could not express.

The sincerity of a Hank Williams song, his humble upbringing, and widely publicized marital troubles contributed to the widespread belief that the singer "lived" his music. Williams perpetuated this impression with a series of recitations under the pseudonym "Luke the Drifter." More to the point, he recorded a number of simply stated but soulful laments, including "Your Cheatin' Heart," "Half as Much," "I Can't Help It (If I'm Still in Love With You),"and "Cold, Cold Heart." "The more I learn to care for you," a verse from the last song began, "the more we drift apart." In "I'm So Lonesome I Could Cry" (1949), Williams raised his lyrical artistry to the sublime. Working within a subtly stated blues motif, the country music star fashioned some of the starkest metaphors of emotional abandonment ever to appear in an American song. "Did you ever see a robin weep, when leaves begin to die?" asked the lyric. "That means he's lost the will to live, I'm so lonesome I could cry." The song's chilling final verse continues to arouse awe to this day. "The silence of a falling star, lights up a purple sky," he sang. "And as I wonder where you are, I'm so lonesome I could cry."

Suffering from a painful congenital spinal defect and the personal trauma of a broken marriage, Williams failed to reverse a spiraling descent into alcoholism. He died of a heart attack on New Years Day 1953, eight months before his thirtieth birthday. The popular icon's funeral at the Montgomery Auditorium attracted a crowd of twenty-five thousand people, many forced to stand outside the overflowing facility. Inside, a black gospel quartet performed, while African Americans fans paid their respects in the segregated balcony. The proceedings closed with Roy Acuff leading an array of country celebrities in a rendition of "I Saw the Light," one of the twenty-one gospel songs Hank Williams bequeathed to posterity.

LET THE GOOD TIMES ROLL

By 1949, *Billboard* magazine had placed its "race" record listings under the "rhythm and blues" designation. With expanded African American consumer power in the postwar period, independent record companies like Atlantic, Chess, and Specialty took advantage of cheap magnetic tape technology to market an updated blend of urban music. Their target audience focused on black migrants from the South who helped to shape the urban street culture of communities in the Northeast, Midwest, and Pacific Coast. The spread of non-network radio stations provided record producers with a viable means of merchandising the new sound. By the mid-Fifties, 90 percent of all African Americans had access to a radio. After Memphis' white-owned WDIA switched to black programming in 1948, over sixty stations followed suit, allowing rhythm and blues to become the first major musical style popularized by disc jockeys.

Two styles permeated postwar black popular music. The first took its cues from gospel harmonies popularized during World War II by the Ink Spots and Mills Brothers. The slow romantic ballads of vocal ensembles like the Orioles, Five Keys, Ravens, Five Satins, and Harptones idealized stable love relationships as an essential ingredient of economic success and middle-class stability. Not surprisingly, the optimism and respectable demeanor of these groups contributed to their popularity among white audiences. By the mid–1950s, independent record labels were recruiting black street ensembles from across the nation in emulation of successful "doo-wop" ballads like "Sincerely" (1954), a smash hit by the Moonglows, and "Earth Angel" (1954), a best-seller by the Penguins.

Energized by electric guitars and drums, up-tempo blues shouters presented the second approach of postwar black music. In contrast to the romantic longings of the vocal groups, these performers conveyed a realistic, nearly cynical honesty and a frank desire for immediate emotional release and bodily pleasure. With his best-selling version of Sam Theard's "Let the Good Times Roll" (1946), Louis Jordan recorded the first postwar song to hit the top of both the rhythm and blues and popular music charts. "Don't sit there mumblin' and talkin' trash," he sang, "if you wanna have a ball ya gotta go out and spend some cash." Jordan's own "Saturday Night Fish Fry" (1949), another crossover sensation, presented the ludicrous details of a wild late-night party to a boogie beat. "You never seen such scuffin' and shufflin' till the break of dawn," marveled the singing hipster.

Jordan's immediate successor was Wynonie Harris, a charismatic blues shouter who recorded bandleader Roy Brown's "Good Rockin' Tonight" (1947), a song written as the theme song for Brown's Galveston radio show. Thirty-two years old when he sang "Good Rockin'," Harris was the son of devout Omaha Baptists. After two years of a pre-med course, he had left college and become a dancer in the Kansas City clubs, turned to vocals, and moved to Los Angeles to perform up-tempo blues. Cultivating a reputation as a man who "stirred up" women, Harris toured the South as a superstar. "I heard the news, there's good rockin' tonight," he sang in his signature number. "So meet me in the alley, behind the barn, don't be afraid, I'll do you no harm." "Let's drink some mash and talk some trash," Harris proposed in "Wynonie' Blues." In the outrageous "Loving Machine," which the singer introduced as a "real gone" number, he proclaimed that he "got hip to the trip" and built his own mechanical device for pleasing female visitors.

Harris' raspy voice resembled that of Mississippi Delta electric blues artists Muddy Waters and B.B. King, who infused their work with the masculine sensibility that traditionally defined the genre. Jackie Brenston's boastful "Rocket '88'" (1951) provided another example. In Jesse Stone's bouncy "Money Honey" (1953), Clyde McPhatter and the Drifters offered an equally hard-edged view of romance on the streets. "It's money, honey," shouted McPhatter, "if you wanna get along with me." Ray Charles took on a similar edge in his debut hit "I've Got a Woman" (1955). Born in Albany, Georgia, in 1930, Charles lost his sight from glaucoma at age seven. After studying classical piano at a Florida institute for the blind, he left school at age fifteen and formed his own trio. Charles ingenuously combined elements of gospel, country, and jazz in bluesy keyboard phrasing and a gravelly voice that sometimes gave way to wild, falsetto shrieks. The feel of "I've Got a Woman," ironically, came right out of the church. Yet its sexually charged lyric boasted of a female friend "way over town" who "give me money when I'm in need" but who never goes "running in the streets."

As in much of honky-tonk, up-tempo rhythm and blues steered away from the conventions of sentimental romance. Taking off on the obvious metaphors of "Work With Me, Annie" (1954) by Hank Ballard and the Midnighters, Etta James scored a major hit with the euphemized but nevertheless suggestive "Dance With Me, Henry" (1955). LaVern Baker, the niece of blues great "Memphis Minnie" and an experienced church choir vocalist and nightclub singer, playfully celebrated the lure of physical relations in "Tweedle Dee" (1955) and "Jim Dandy" (1956). Yet it fell to Ruth Brown—"the fabulous Miss Rhythm"—to express the full contradictions of male-female intimacy. Born the oldest of eight children in 1928, Brown sang spirituals in Baptist and Methodist church choirs as a teenager. After winning an amateur night at Harlem's Apollo Theater, she launched a career as a band singer, but switched to rhythm and blues in the late

1940s. Brown recorded eighty hits for Atlantic Records, but her greatest success came with the punchy "(Mama) He Treats Your Daughter Mean" (1953), a syncopated portrait of a woman hopelessly addicted to the love making of an abusive man.

"Big Joe" Turner's original version of Charles Calhoun's "Shake, Rattle, and Roll" (1954), the most influential rhythm and blues hit of the Fifties, expressed the anxieties of working-class romance within the tradition of the male blues shout. Born in Kansas City in 1911, Turner lost his father in a car crash and spent much of his adolescence shining shoes, hawking newspapers, and working as a hotel breakfast cook. He began to sing in local nightclubs with boogie-woogie pianist Pete Johnson in the late Twenties while tending bar and running bootleg whisky. Discovered in 1938 by music producer John Hammond, Turner performed solo blues vocals for big band recordings like "Corrine, Corrina" and "Cherry Red." By the time the singer scored a major hit with "Chains of Love" (1951), he had recorded fifty singles.

"Get outta that bed, wash your face and hands," began the first line of "Shake, Rattle, and Roll," "get in that kitchen, make some noise with the pots and pans." "Well, you wear low dresses, the sun comes shining through," Turner sang in the second verse, "I can't believe my eyes, all that mess belongs to you." "I believe to my soul you're a devil in nylon hose," continued the lyric, "the harder I work, the faster my money goes." After repeating the song's title four times in the chorus, Turner launched into the emotional heart of Calhoun's earthy jump tune. "I'm like a one-eyed cat peepin' in a seafood store," he shouted, "I can look at you and tell you ain't no child no more." Coming around to the punchy chorus for the third time, the song concluded with Turner's lament that "you won't do right to save your doggone soul."

ROCK AND ROLL NATION

Not long after Turner's hit, Bill Haley and the Comets, a Pennsylvania country and western band, recorded a modified version of "Shake, Rattle, and Roll" for white radio play. Haley's version replaced the line about getting out of bed with one about making breakfast for a hungry man. Instead of Calhoun's revealingly low dresses, the new version referred to "those dresses" and "your hair done up so nice," adding the lament that "You look so warm but your heart is cold as ice." Haley completely omitted the verse about "a devil in nylon hose." Instead, he opened the last stanza by repeating, "I believe you're doing me wrong and now I know," followed by "the more I work the faster my money goes."

The Comets captured the spirit of the rhythm and blues sound with an extended instrumental break featuring wild tenor saxophone and lead guitar solos. Meanwhile, another white group, the Crewcuts, cut an old jailhouse song called "Sh-Boom" (1954) initially introduced by the Chords, a six-man, black rhythm and blues vocal group from the West Bronx. These "cover" recordings marked the start of popular music's transition to "rock and roll." A major departure from the bland, soothing, over-orchestrated numbers that characterized most of Tin Pan Alley fare in the postwar period, the revolution in listening taste drew its sustenance from an emerging youth culture, the availability of 45 rpm. records and portable radios, and the ability of a group of enterprising marketers to anticipate the new direction of popular culture.

Long a blues term for sexual intercourse, "rock and roll" became synonymous with rhythm and blues when disc jockey Alan Freed adopted the designation in the early Fifties. A former trombone player, Freed had been raised in Ohio by a Welsh mother and an eastern European Jewish father. After several jobs at small radio stations, he arrived in Cleveland in 1950, where he followed the advice of a local record dealer and began to program rhythm and blues for the city's large African American and southern white population. Interspersing each record with manic howling and banter, the disc jockey called attention to the offbeat accent of the music by pounding a telephone book with a gloved hand. As the musical format of Cleveland's "Moondog Show" attracted imitators across the country, Freed moved his program to the huge New York City market, where his ceaseless efforts to promote rock and roll included the production of live holiday stage shows featuring top rhythm and blues performers.

Songwriter, guitar player, and vocalist Bo Diddley became one of the first stars of rock and roll. Born Ellas Bates in McComb, Mississippi, the young boy moved to Chicago in the early Depression when relatives adopted him, only to drop out of school at fifteen to sing on street corners. Once Bates began to record, he took a new name from the "diddley bow," a southern African American folk instrument. "Bo Diddley" (1955), his first hit, backed its blues phrasing with a hypnotic, primitive, and pulsating "hambone" beat influenced by Latin rhythms and the electrified music of the Pentecostal churches. Follow-up records such as "I'm a Man" (1955) and "Who Do You Love" (1956) accented the same hyper-male posture, particularly when Bo Diddley swiveled his hips in a suggestive fashion when laying down guitar licks in live performances.

As a sexualized black man of the 1950s, Bo Diddley undoubtedly compromised his ability to succeed in the white-oriented popular music market. In contrast, New Orleans piano player and vocalist Antoine "Fats" Domino, the era's most successful African American rock and roll performer, proved far less threatening because of his rotund appearance. A former bedspring factory worker, Domino combined a rocking voice and a dance-oriented boogie-woogie piano style reminiscent of Crescent City legend Professor Longhair (Roeland Byrd). Mastering the integration of blues phrasing with bouncy New Orleans Cajun and Caribbean influences, Domino scored nine rhythm and blues hits between 1950 and 1953. He then rose to the top of the pop charts with foot-stomping numbers like "Ain't That a Shame" (1955), "I'm Walkin'" (1957), and "I Hear You Knockin'" (1957), all recorded before he reached thirty years of age.

Like Fats Domino, Little Richard managed to convey the physicality of rhythm and blues in a non-threatening manner. One of twelve children, Richard Wayne Penniman was born in Macon, Georgia, in 1932. Although his grandfather and two uncles were Seventh Day Adventist preachers, his father made a living as a bartender who sold bootleg whisky. In turmoil over his sexual identity, Penniman ran away from home as a young adolescent and sang gospel music at carnivals and medicine shows, until the white owners of a Macon rhythm and blues club adopted the aspiring singer and piano player and billed him as "Little Richard." In 1951, at age nineteen, the vocalist signed with his first record label, but it was not until a Specialty Records recording session four years later that he stumbled upon his own style with a spontaneous version of "Tutti Frutti" (1956), an obscene homosexual ditty he liked to sing on breaks.

Improvising the opening phrase, "A wop bop alu bop a wop bam boom!" Little Richard belted out the slightly sanitized but playful lyrics of "Tutti Frutti," punctuating the rhythmic effect of the words with falsetto shrieks, impromptu wails, and a manic string of triplet piano chords. "I've got a gal/Named Daisy," he sang, as a hard-driving guitar, saxophone, and drums fueled the pace, "She almost drives me crazy." His next release, "Long Tall Sally" (1956), sustained an even more frenetic tempo with comic images of sexual byplay in the streets and alleys. "Rip It Up" (1956), another hit on both the rhythm and blues and pop charts, opened with the inviting, "It's Saturday night and I just got paid." Other Little Richard classics included "Lucille" (1957), "Keep a Knockin'" (1957), and "Good Golly, Miss Molly" (1958). The rock and roll idol sustained an exotic stage persona by wearing makeup and mascara, sporting a six-inch pompadour hairdo, and standing at the piano as he pounded the keys with wild abandon.

Rock and roll's most representative figure was Charles Edward Anderson "Chuck" Berry. Born into a lower-middle-class black family in St. Louis in 1926, Berry did a stint in reform school before earning a degree in hairdressing and cosmetology. Quitting his job as an autoworker, he supported himself as a beautician while fronting a trio that mixed country music and the blues. In 1955, Berry and piano player Johnnie Johnson traveled to Chicago with a demonstration record of an old country standby, "Ida Red." Rerecorded at Chess Records as "Maybelline" (1955), with partial rights assigned to Alan Freed, the song's big beat, car theme, and playful twists propelled it to Number One on the rhythm and blues, country and western, and pop charts. Berry contributed to his appeal by adopting the "duck walk" dance step that would become his on-stage trademark. Meanwhile, he molded his lyrics into a generic celebration of rock and roll youth culture with anthems like "Roll Over Beethoven" (1956), "Rock and Roll Music" (1957), "School Day" (1957), and "Johnny B. Goode" (1958). "Hail! hail! rock and roll!" Berry sang in "School Day," "deliver me from the days of old."

ROCKABILLY HEAVEN

Chuck Berry's universal appeal pointed to the varied nature of the rock and roll constituency. Inner-city doo-wop groups, from the Cadillacs to the Clovers, contributed a mix of up-tempo hits and slow ballads, including "Speedoo" (1955), "Story Untold" (1955), "Why Do Fools Falls in Love" (1956), "In the Still of the Night" (1956), "A Casual Look" (1956), "Searchin'" (1957), "Book of Love" (1958), "Get a Job" (1958), and "Love Potion No. 9" (1959). Mexican Americans, in turn, rallied to groups like the Emerals, as well as to Ritchie (Valenzeula) Valens, a San Fernando Valley rocker whose recordings of "La Bamba" and "Donna" (1958) created a nationwide following. A third strain of the music came in the fusion of white country and blues known as rockabilly. Played at an accelerated tempo with a slapping bass to accent the offbeat, rockabilly featured intense guitar virtuosity and vocalists who supplemented their performances with echo chamber effects and verbal hiccups and stutters.

Rockabilly tunes accounted for many of the most popular rock and roll hits of the mid to late Fifties. They included Carl Perkins' "Blue Suede Shoes" (1956), Gene Vincent's "Be-Bop-a-Lula" (1956), Jerry Lee Lewis' "Whole Lot of Shakin' Going On" (1957), Dale Hawkins' "Susie-Q" (1957), the Everly Brothers' "Bye, Bye Love" (1957), and Buddy Holly's "That'll Be the Day" (1957) and "Peggy Sue" (1957). The genre's musical birthplace was Memphis, where fledgling record producer Sam Phillips recruited talent from the city's mix of rural white and black migrants. A radio engineer raised near a black church in Florence, Alabama, Phillips opened a recording studio for the "Negro artists" of the Beale Street blues scene in 1950, thereby launching the careers of B.B. King, Howlin' Wolf, Bobby "Blue" Bland, Little Junior Parker, and others. Two years later, Phillips converted his downtown storefront into the independent Sun Records, a shoestring operation that depended upon his driving seventy thousand miles a year to keep in close contact with disc jockeys, distributors, record stores, and jukebox operators.

During the summer of 1953, an eighteen-year-old off-duty machine shop operator walked into Sun with a beat-up, undersized guitar to cut a record as a gift to his mother. Like many of the white teens who frequented downtown Memphis, he had absorbed a taste for the "cat clothes" and bebop speech of Beale Street's hipsters. When Phillips asked what sort of music he played, the visitor answered that he sang "hillbilly" but did not sound like anybody else. His name was Elvis Aaron Presley. Born in 1935 in the rough environs of East Tupelo, Mississippi, Presley had grown up in a succession of cheap rented houses while his father scratched out a living at an assortment of jobs. As a boy, Elvis sang in the First Assembly Church, where the minister helped him learn guitar. Once given his own instrument on his eleventh birthday, he became a regular at the weekly radio amateur shows broadcast from the county courthouse. Shortly after that, the family moved to Tupelo, where the young boy absorbed the gospel harmonies of nearby black street revivals and the country music of the area's first radio station.

Once the Presleys relocated to a Memphis public housing project in 1948, Elvis' musical universe expanded. As he reached high school, he regularly attended monthly gospel shows at the city auditorium, where he particularly enjoyed The Statesmen—a sharply dressed white vocal group whose showmanship and smooth body movements conveyed the urgency of black spirituals. Other influences included the Ink Spots, Fats Domino, and Ivory Joe Hunter. By the time Sun Records put Presley in the studio with two other musicians in mid–1954, he was driving a delivery truck for an electrical supplies contractor. After several attempts to record a ballad, the singer broke into a spontaneous version of "That's All Right," an old blues standard by Arthur "Big Boy" Crudup. Once Memphis disc jockey Dewey Phillips played the tape on his popular radio show, Sun had an instant hit. For the second side of the disc, the trio abandoned the waltz tempo of Bill Monroe's revered "Blue Moon of Kentucky" and performed the song at breakneck speed with an echo effect.

Following the Sun sessions, Presley elicited pandemonium at his first country music show when he shook and wriggled his legs to keep time. The singer's gyrations also produced a torrent of screams among thousands of teenage girls attending his appearance at a Memphis shopping center opening. Presley and his backup musicians now began playing fraternal societies, school and church recreational halls, and Friday night intermissions at a local club. Although Phillips found it hard to get the vocalist's "rough" sound on country radio, "That' All Right" sold well in east Tennessee, and "Blue Moon" rose to Number One on the Memphis country charts. A second record, a cover of the rhythm and blues standard "Good Rockin' Tonight" (1954), led to a one-year contract on the Louisiana Hayride and tours across Mississippi, Arkansas, and Texas. As Presley picked up the skill of winning an audience, he returned to Memphis in early 1955 and bought up all the rhythm and blues records he could find. A third recording date at Sun produced "I Forgot to Remember" (1955), a country song in which the snare drums accented the offbeat, and "Mystery Train" (1955), a cover of a Little Junior Parker blues.

By the fall of 1955, Elvis Presley had signed on with promoter Tom Parker, who arranged for RCA to buy out the Sun contract for $35,000 and $5,000 in back royalties. Although RCA engineers were not sure how to reproduce the "slap-back" echo sound of their Sun predecessors, Presley continued to fuse a unique blend of rhythm and blues, country music, and pop throughout 1956. His records included the anguished "Heartbreak Hotel," a Number One hit in all three genres, as well as covers of "Money Honey" and "I've Got a Woman." After a thunderous rendition of "Shake, Rattle, and Roll" on television's Dorsey Brothers Show, Presley recorded Carl Perkins' "Blue Suede Shoes" on an extended play disc. His next record, "Hound Dog" (1956), covered a Jerry Leiber and Mike Stoller hit by blues shouter Willie Mae "Big Mama" Thornton, with "Don't Be Cruel," a creation of rhythm and blues songwriter Otis Blackwell, on the second side.

Although artists like Louis Jordan, Fats Domino, Little Richard, and Chuck Berry played a major role in introducing black popular music to white audiences in the postwar era, no single figure had as much influence on public taste as Elvis Presley. When he attracted criticism for singing unintelligible lyrics with grunts and groans, Presley protested that "the colored folks been singing it and playing it just like I'm doin' now, man, for more years than I know. They played it like that in the shanties and in their juke joints, and nobody paid it no mind 'til I goosed it up. I got it from them." There were "low-down people and high-up people," he insisted, "but all of them get the kind of feeling this rock 'n' roll music tells about."

THE MAKING OF YOUTH CULTURE

"This is a real decent, fine boy …a very nice person," TV host Ed Sullivan said of Elvis Presley as he put his arms around the teen idol during a live presentation of his popular variety show in 1957. Caught up in the controversy over the singer's on-stage gyrations, Sullivan censored coverage of the star's performances by ordering the cameras to shoot the singer from the waist up. Older middle-class whites tended to associate Presley's pelvic twists and surly demeanor with the distasteful antics of the lower orders. Whether white or black, however, most poor and working-class southerners understood that the entertainer's bodily movements had originated in the performance styles of gospel singers in the sanctified churches. Combining religiosity with sexuality, youthful rebellion with love of family, and a humble background with newly earned wealth, Elvis remained a hero to these fans for the rest of his life.

The furor over "Elvis the Pelvis" ran parallel to an emerging cross-class cultural divide along generational lines. Performed to racially mixed audiences, rock and roll defied mainstream standards of propriety by tempting young people with the promise of sexual and social independence. Blunt sexual imagery in recordings like Shirley and Lee's "Let the Good Times Roll" (1956) and Mickey and Sylvia's "Love is Strange" (1957) contributed to the fear that traditional American values of family cohesion, deference to authority, sobriety, chastity, and personal decorum had run aground. The fact that young performers flaunted their working-class backgrounds and operated outside the entertainment industry's normal channels brought additional resentment. Castigating the lyrics of rock and roll as sly, lewd, and dirty, pop vocalist Frank Sinatra dismissed the music as the work of "cretinous goons."

By the late Fifties, the major record labels had recovered from the intrusion of the independents by recruiting their own teenage pop idols. Occasionally, as in Danny and the Juniors' "At the Hop" (1957) and Eddie Cochran's "Summertime Blues" (1958), the results sustained the passion and intensity of rock and roll's representation of urban street life. In most cases, however, innocuously desexualized performers like Paul Anka, Bobby Vinton, Frankie Avalon, Bobby Rydell, and Fabian came to dominate both the radio and television dance shows like Philadelphia's "American Bandstand." Hollywood also sought to tap into the youth market without appearing socially irresponsible. The trend began with *Blackboard Jungle* (1955), a film about juvenile delinquency that created a national sensation by using Bill Haley's "Rock Around the Clock" for the opening credits. Within the year, a flurry of "teenpics" sought to establish the compatibility of rock and roll with prevailing national values.

Low-budget producer Sam Katzman created the first explicitly teenage film with *Rock Around the Clock* (1956). Despite a contrived plot about an unknown band's rise to stardom, the movie cast rock and roll as a democratic style of music. In the end, performers like Bill Haley and the Comets and the Platters teamed up with Alan Freed to show up the staid Establishment for its immersion in the past and its suspicion of the benevolent intention of teenagers. Anxious to expose black artists like Fats Domino and Chuck Berry, Freed also played himself in *Rock, Rock, Rock* (1956). In still another film, *Don't Knock the Rock* (1956), he appeared alongside Bill Haley and Little Richard to plead that rock and roll was "a harmless outlet for today's kids." Hollywood sought to reach several constituencies at once with *The Girl Can't Help It* (1956), a thinly constructed story about a gangster seeking to impose his voluptuous but tone-deaf girl friend singer (Jayne Mansfield) on gullible teens. Only genuine performances by an all-star cast of rock and roll personalities saved the feature from complete obscurity.

Elvis Presley took to the screen in the same year the rock and roll movies debuted. He sang the title song of *Love Me Tender* (1956) while portraying a member of a family torn apart by the Civil War. *Loving You* (1957) offered Elvis a semi-autobiographical role as a southern gas station attendant who rises to pop music fame. In *Jailhouse Rock* (1957), usually considered the performer's best movie, he played a gritty ex-convict who becomes an egocentric rock star. Another feature, *King Creole* (1958), based on the Harold Robbins novel *A Stone for Danny Fisher*, cast Elvis as a New Orleans busboy who makes his way to troubled stardom as a singer in a mob club.

Several early Elvis films exploited the sullen, brooding, and menacing qualities fashioned in the Memphis years. "You can't be a rebel if you grin," the budding movie star explained. Presley frankly acknowledged that his persona shared commonalities with Marlon Brando and James Dean. In *The Wild One* (1954), Brando played the leader of a motorcycle gang "looking for trouble" with the "squares" of a small California town, whom the group terrorizes. Pressed as to what he would do when they left, he answers that "we're just gonna go … You just go … The idea is to have a ball." When asked what he was rebelling against, Brando simply replied, "What've you got?" Exhibitors marketed *The Wild One* with a poster of the movie's lead character straddled over his cycle in a brooding, alienated and confrontational pose. The rebel "look" also overshadowed the purported message of juvenile delinquency movies from *Blackboard Jungle* to *Crime in the Streets* (1956) to *Hot Rod Girl* (1956) to *High School Hellcats* (1958) to *High School Confidential* (1958). Yet no film of the 1950s left a greater impact on popular youth culture than *Rebel Without a Cause* (1955).

Directed by Nicholas Ray, *Rebel* starred James Dean as a confused and wistful middle-class adolescent who sadly observes the pathetic world of his parents. Dean was a

James Dean in *Rebel Without a Cause* (1955)   (*Photofest*)

perfect match for the role. Born in Marion, Indiana, in 1931, he lost his mother to breast cancer when he was young and grew up with relatives on an Iowa farm. Moving to Los Angeles in 1949, he attended college and received a few bit parts in Hollywood films. Two years later, Dean relocated to New York, where he worked as a busboy, observed classes as the Actor's Studio, did some television drama with writer Rod Serling, and appeared in the Broadway production *The Immoralist* (1954). A screen test with Elia Kazan resulted in a featured role in the movie *East of Eden* (1955), an adaptation of a John Steinbeck novel in which Dean portrayed a brooding son seeking his father's love. In *Rebel*, the budding superstar applied the naturalistic techniques of the Actor's Studio to a character whose tenderness and sensitivity helped to create a new definition of youthful masculinity. Dean immediately drew a cult following of fans that empathized with his anguish and saw their own lives portrayed in the vulnerability he represented.

HIPSTER VISIONS

For all their controversy, rock and roll and rockabilly normally celebrated mainstream desires for physical mobility, everyday pleasures, and stable love relationships. Record and motion picture producers, moreover, usually succeeded in channeling adolescent impulses into containable (and profitable) forms. Nevertheless, attacks on youth culture and the perceived blandness of conventional society helped to foster solidarity and a collective identity among dissenting young people, opening the door to alternative voices. The manic comedy of *Mad* magazine provided an early entry into dissident culture. Formed in New York in 1952, *Mad* specialized in cartoon spoofs of pomposity, fraud, and complacency in movies, advertising, and suburban life. Another source of marginality surfaced in the Beatnik phenomenon of the late Fifties. Extending the lifestyle of the Beat coffee houses into the public arena, young nonconformists began to sport the berets, sandals, and dark clothing of European bohemians. Meanwhile, hipster street talk increasingly characterized the discourse of middle-class insurgence.

Hip morality received its most explicit exposure in Norman Mailer's essay "The White Negro" (1957). Raised in Long Branch, New Jersey, and Brooklyn by a middle-class Jewish family, Mailer entered Harvard at sixteen and graduated with a degree in aeronautical engineering. As a revolutionary socialist, he began composing stories along the lines of James T. Farrell's *Studs Lonigan*. Drafted into the Army, Mailer served in the Pacific theater, where he volunteered for a reconnaissance unit to amass writing material. The result was *The Naked and the Dead* (1948), a novel describing the make-up and background of several soldiers preparing for an attack behind enemy lines. Following the example of John Dos Passos, the author presented contextualized biographies of the book's four lead characters, providing a geographic and ethnic survey of America from the slums of Boston to the comfortable homes of the midwestern middle class. Mailer's story identified with the common soldier, but pointed to the confusion and sense of helplessness generated by the brutality and violence of war.

Following the release of two unsuccessful novels in 1951 and 1955, Mailer co-founded the alternative *Village Voice* newspaper. The writer's columns for the publication strayed from a liberal and socialist political orientation to emphasize the instinctual side of the human condition instead of reason. "The White Negro" pursued these themes by celebrating the perceived virtues of the black street hustler, the juvenile delinquent, and the cultural bohemian. The only sane response to deadening materialism, obsessive security-mindedness, conforming timidity, and sexual repression, argued Mailer, was a life dedicated to immediate pleasure rather than the work ethic and the postponement of gratification. The hipster's taste for jazz, sex, drugs, slang, and pending danger, he insisted, provided the only avenue of psychic liberation for the beleaguered middle class.

With the emergence of hip morality, speculated Mailer, the country might witness "a psychically armed rebellion" against every bastion of institutional power. The resulting animosities and conflicts, he predicted, could inaugurate a "time of violence, new hysteria, confusion, and rebellion." Mailer's prophecy of a democratic culture war received endorsement in Jack Kerouac's second novel, *Dharma Bums* (1958). "I see a vision of a great rucksack revolution," wrote Kerouac, "thousands or even millions of young Americans wandering around with rucksacks … who go about writing poems that happen to appear in their heads for no reason." Both Mailer and Kerouac expressed a faith that America's salvation lay with its nonconforming youth. Drawing its strength from the vitality of non-elites, a vanguard of intrepid souls would go about the work of restructuring the moral basis of American society through a participatory cultural revolution. To a degree, perhaps, that neither writer fully anticipated, the coming decade would usher in a series of social movements that would invoke the name of the people to set in motion the changes outlined by both visionaries.

SOURCES AND SUGGESTED READINGS

Examples of postwar documentary photography appear in *Jerome Liebling: Photographs 1947–1977* (1978); Jerome Liebling, *The People, Yes* (1995); and Robert Frank, *The Americans* (1959). For a concise introduction to the Fifties literary underground, see "The Beat Generation" in David Halberstam, *The Fifties* (1993). A detailed overview appears in *The Beat Generation: A Gale Critical Companion*, Vols. 1–3 (2003). The counterculture qualities of the literary scene concern Michael Davidson, *The San Francisco Renaissance: Poetics and Community at Mid-Century* (1989) and the relevant segments of Daniel Belgrad, *The Culture of Spontaneity: Improvisation and the Arts in Postwar America* (1998). Biographies of the movement's leading figure include Barry Miles, *Jack Kerouac: King of the Beats* (1998) and Dennis McNaly, *Desolate Angel: Jack Kerouac, the Beat Generation, and America* (1979). For 1950s jazz culture, see the relevant portion of Andrew Ross, *No Respect: Intellectuals and Popular Culture* (1989).

Readers can survey Mexican American writers of the Fifties in a number of the listings in Nicolás Kanellos, *Hispanic Literature of the United States: A Comprehensive Reference* (2003). For popular music, see Manuel Peña, *The Mexican American Orquesta: Music, Culture, and the Dialectic of Conflict* (1999). Literary figures of Asian descent garner attention in Esther Mikyung Ghymn, *The Shapes and Styles of Asian American Prose Fiction* (1992) and Shawn Wong, *Asian American Literature: A Brief Introduction and Anthology* (1996). See also the Fifties writers under study in Houston A. Baker, Jr., ed., *Three American Literatures: Essays in Chicano, Native American, and Asian-American Literature for Teachers of American Literature* (1982).

For black fiction and poetry, see Henry Louis Gates and Nellie Y. McKay, eds., *The Norton Anthology of African American Literature* (1997). Two central black literary figures of the postwar era are the subjects of essay collections in Maria K. Mootry and Gary Smith, eds., *A Life Distilled: Gwendolyn Brooks, Her Poetry and Fiction* (1987) and Kimberly W. Bentson, ed., *Speaking for You: The Vision of Ralph Ellison* (1987). See also James Campbell, *Talking at the Gates: A Life of James Baldwin* (1991), a work that can be supplemented by the insightful David Chappell, *A Stone of Hope: Prophetic Religion and the Death of Jim Crow* (2004). The African American connection to 1950s cinema warrants attention in Thomas Cripps, *Making Movies Black: The Holly-*

wood Message Movie from World War II to the Civil Rights Era (1993) and the relevant sections of Donald Bogle, *Toms, Coons, Mulattoes, Mammies, and Bucks: An Interpretive History of Blacks in American Film*, rev. ed. (2002).

Political folk music of the postwar era marks the focus of Robbie Lieberman, *"My Song Is My Weapon": People's Songs, American Communism, and the Politics of Culture, 1930–1950* (1989) and R. Serge Denisoff, *Great Day Coming: Folk Music and the American Left* (1971). For the origins of bluegrass, see the portraits of Bill Monroe and Earl Scruggs in Nicholas Dawidoff, *In the Country of Country: People and Places in American Music* (1997). Nashville's role in southern culture is one of the topics addressed in Pete Daniel, *Lost Revolutions: The South in the 1950s* (2000). Bill C. Malone, *Country Music, U.S.A.*, 2nd rev. ed. (2002) and Dorothy Horstman, *Sing Your Heart Out, Country Boy*, rev. ed. (1996) offer helpful overviews. See also Cheto Flippo, *Your Cheatin' Heart: A Biography of Hank Williams* (1981); Daniel Cooper, *Lefty Frizzell: The Honky Tonk Life of Country Music's Greatest Singer* (1995); and profiles of Rose Maddox and Kitty Wells in Nicholas Dawidoff, *In the Country of Country: People and Places in American Music* (1997).

Among the works tracing the manner in which rhythm and blues shaped 1950s rock 'n' roll and popular music are Nelson George, *The Death of Rhythm and Blues* (1988); Brian Ward, *Just My Soul Responding: Rhythm and Blues, Black Consciousness, and Race Relations* (1998); and James Miller, *Flowers in the Dustbin: The Rise of Rock and Roll, 1947–1977* (1999). For profiles of performers like Ruth Brown and La Vern Baker, see Chip Defaa, *Blue Rhythms: Six Lives in Rhythm and Blues* (1996). The extensive literature on the most influential vernacular music of the Fifties includes Charlie Gillett, *The Sound of the City: The Rise of Rock and Roll* (1983); Philip H. Ennis, *The Seventh Stream: The Emergence of Rocknroll in American Popular Music* (1992); and Nik Cohn, *Awopbopaloobop alopbam boom: The Golden Age of Rock* (1996). See also Davin Seay and Mary Neeley, *The Spiritual Roots of Rock and Roll* (1986). Two studies placing the music in the context of Fifties society are David P. Szatunary, *Rockin' in Time: A Social History of Rock-and-Roll*, 2nd ed. (1991) and Glenn C. Altschuler, *All Shook Up: How Rock 'n' Roll Changed America* (2003).

Profiles of individual rock 'n' roll performers appear in Peter Guralnick, *Feel Like Going Home: Portraits in Blues and Rock 'n' Roll* (1999); Nick Tosches, *Unsung Heroes of Rock 'n' Roll* (1984); and James M. Salem, *The Late Great Johnny Ace and the Transition from Rhythm & Blues to Rock 'n' Roll* (1999). For popular music's greatest star, see Peter Guralnick, *Last Train to Memphis: The Rise of Elvis Presley* (1994); Michael T. Bertrand, *Race, Rock, and Elvis* (2000); and Charles L. Ponce de Leon, *Fortunate Son: The Life of Elvis Presley* (2006).

Lawrence Grossberg's *We Gotta Get Out of This Place: Popular Conservatism and Postmodern Culture* (1992) argues that Fifties youth culture solidified the era's a-political and consumerist mindset. See also the section on rock 'n' roll in George

Lipsitz, *Rainbow at Midnight: Labor and Culture in the 1940s* (1994). Hollywood merchandising of adolescent culture is the subject of Thomas Doherty, *Teenagers and Teenpics: The Juvenilization of American Movies in the 1950s* (1988); R. Serge Denisoff, *Risky Business: Rock in the Film Industry* (1990); and the portions on youth movies in Peter Biskind, *Seeing Is Believing: How Hollywood Taught Us to Stop Worrying and Love the Fifties* (1983). For the leading Fifties prophet of hipster rebellion, see Carl Rollyson, *The Lives of Norman Mailer: A Biography* (1991) and Robert Merrill, *Norman Mailer* (1978).

10

Power to the People: Sixties Liberation and Popular Culture

Few periods of American history began with such optimism over the potential of ordinary citizens as the 1960s. The early portion of the decade witnessed a grassroots civil rights crusade in the South, an urban folk music revival, and the advent of a student movement committed to participatory democracy. In the years that followed, assertions of African American racial consciousness exerted a major influence on both the literary and popular arts. Meanwhile, the white working class responded to the rapid pace of social change through country music. By the late Sixties, disaffection with the war in Vietnam and a hunger for sexual and lifestyle experiment led large numbers of middle-class youth to participate in an emerging counterculture. Invoking the name of the people and laying a claim to core American social values, Woodstock Nation helped to shape a national popular culture, but in doing so, unwittingly laid the foundation for future discord.

GATES OF EDEN

As John F. Kennedy won the White House after eight years of Republican rule in 1960, many Americans welcomed the president's appeal to youthful idealism in the service of national goals. For a generation nurtured on expectations of self-fulfilling, adventurous, and challenging lives, Kennedy's New Frontier suggested not a reinvigorated approach to the Cold War but a dynamic and precedent-setting world fresh with possibility. In the social arena, these aspirations extended to the enrichment of democracy, the elimination of poverty, the expansion of opportunities for self-realization, and the implementation of reason in public policy. By the early Sixties, the civil rights struggle had become the single most significant embodiment of such hopes.

Under the leadership of Reverend Martin Luther King, Jr., a community of activists sought to end racial discrimination and ensure equal rights of citizenship in a broadly based movement that embraced spiritual redemption, personal sacrifice, and moral witness. The goal of restructuring power relationships while transforming human relations became the operating principle of the Student Nonviolent Coordinating Committee (SNCC), an organization of southern black college students devoted to the idea of participatory democracy. Following a series of lunch-counter sit-ins, "freedom rides" to integrate interstate bus travel, and widely publicized street demonstrations in Birmingham, Alabama, King led over 250,000 protesters in the celebrated March on Washington in 1963. One year later, Congress passed a civil rights law desegregating public accommodations. Meanwhile, SNCC and other rights groups recruited northern white college students during the summer of 1964 for a massive voter registration drive in Mississippi. A series of racially motivated murders and terrorist bombings in the Deep South helped to bring about the Voting Rights Act of 1965.

Protest music played an essential role in sustaining the morale of the civil rights cause at marches, mass meetings, sit-ins, prayer vigils, and jailhouse protests. Several hymns originated with Monteagle, Tennessee's Highlander Folk School, which passed on traditional African American and labor songs for use by grassroots organizers. Spirituals such as "This Little Light of Mine," "Amazing Grace," "Ain't Gonna Let Nobody Turn Me 'Round," "Wade in the Water," and "Keep Your Eyes on the Prize" lent themselves to group sings and the building of camaraderie. The movement standard "We Shall Not Be Moved" had been a religious hymn expressing faith in Jesus. Turned into a protest song on behalf of tenant farmers in the 1930s, the piece became a rallying cry thirty years later. "I'll Overcome Some Day," a gospel number once sung by striking North Carolina tobacco workers, had evolved into "I Will Overcome" until Pete Seeger changed the title to "We Shall Overcome." Taught to student leaders of Nashville's sit-in movement in 1960 by Highlander musical director and folk singer Guy Carawan, the hymn became the unofficial anthem of the civil rights crusade.

With a strong base in southern churches and the region's middle-class African American college students, SNCC cultural workers rallied support with religiously based "freedom songs," rather than cater to a black working-class audience of rhythm and blues fans. Gospel-flavored music also projected an image of high-minded respectability that appealed to affluent white financial contributors and the movement's allies on northern campuses. Partly due to Pete Seeger's efforts to awaken college students to the rich heritage of labor songs and non-commercial balladry, the folk music revival intensified during the age of civil rights protest. Along with calypso singer Harry Belafonte and the powerful African American balladeer Odetta, Joan Baez dominated the urban folk music scene of the early Sixties. The daughter of a Virginia Quaker and physicist of Mexican descent, Baez attended Boston University and began her career as a performer in the coffeehouses of nearby Cambridge. Appearing at the Newport Folk Festival in 1959, she stunned audiences with a haunting voice and sparse versions of traditional ballads such as "Wagoner's Lad," "Silver Dagger," and "Wildwood Flower."

The period's most exciting interpreter of American folk music was the offspring of Jewish shopkeepers in northern Minnesota. Born in Duluth in 1941 and raised in the dying Iron Range town of Hibbing, Robert Zimmerman grew up listening to late-night country music radio and the songs of Hank Williams. After mastering rudimentary piano and guitar, he pursued a fascination with Little Richard and James Dean by forming several rock and roll combos in high school. Interested in the roots of the music, Zimmerman gravitated to blues and folk ballads, forms that seemed to offer more creative freedom than commercial music. During a brief stay at the University of Minnesota, he avoided classes and spent much of his time reading Romantic poetry. At this point Zimmerman took on the name Bob Dylan and discovered the Dust Bowl ballads of Woody Guthrie and songs of Cisco Houston. After devouring Guthrie's *Bound for Glory* in a single day, Dylan gradually remade himself into Woody's image, dressing in the way he imagined his idol to have appeared and holding his guitar in the manner pictured in photographs of the veteran troubadour.

As Dylan began his nasal-voiced performances at Minneapolis coffeehouses and Beat gatherings, he invented a well-traveled rambling past for himself and fantasized about being part of the 1930s labor movement, going so far as to compose a "Song to Woody." He followed up this fixation by leaving Minnesota to visit Guthrie in a New Jersey hospital, where the performer was in the later stages of Huntington's chorea, an incurable nerve disorder. Early in 1961, Dylan surfaced in the Greenwich Village folk music club scene, where he joined artists like "Rambling" Jack Elliott and Dave Van Ronk. By now, he had fashioned a comic persona somewhere between Huck Finn and Charlie Chaplin. Steered to Columbia Records producer John Hammond in 1962, Dylan released a debut album whose selections leaned heavily on the traditional repertoire of country blues.

As the civil rights movement captured the young performer's imagination, he befriended Bernice Reagon and other SNCC cultural workers. Once Dylan met Pete Seeger, he submitted several topical songs to *Broadside* magazine, a mimeographed publication founded by former Almanac singer and Dust Bowl migrant "Sis" Cunningham. His second album, *The Freewheelin' Bob Dylan* (1963), reflected these political commitments. "How many roads must a man walk down before you call him a man?" he asked in "Blowin' In the Wind," the collection's signature anthem. Three

Bob Dylan   *(Photofest)*

other pieces, "A Hard Rain's A Gonna Fall," "Masters of War," and "With God on Our Side," offered metaphorical explorations of militarism and moral arrogance. Introduced to the 1963 Newport Folk Festival by Joan Baez, Dylan joined the SNCC Freedom Singers and others for a finale rendition of "We Shall Overcome." He then accompanied Pete Seeger to a SNCC gathering in the cotton fields near Greenwood, Mississippi, where he sang "Only a Pawn in Their Game," a ballad about the racist murder of state NAACP leader Medgar Evers that he had composed for the occasion.

Dylan's third album, *The Times They Are A-Changin'* (1964), included the homage to Evers as well as "The Lonesome Death of Hattie Carroll," a protest against poverty and powerlessness. As groups like Students for a Democratic Society (SDS) and the Student Peace Union (SPU) translated the moral call of the civil rights cause into a broader movement for social justice and peace, the collection's title song cast the human rights struggles of ordinary people in apocalyptic terms. "There's a battle/Outside and it's ragin'," Dylan sang in the album's lead piece, "The order is rapidly fadin'." "For the loser now/Will be later to win," he prophesized. Dylan challenged elders not to "criticize/What you can't understand./Your sons and daughters/Are beyond your command." Yet in *Another Side of Bob Dylan* (1964), the songwriter sought artistic freedom outside the limits of political balladry. One piece, "Chimes of Freedom," universalized the social struggle into a pastiche of images about "ev'ry underdog soldier in the night." Drawn toward allegorical narratives and introspective lyrics about intensely personal relationships, the folk icon began to look for "new directions home."

NOTHING BUT A MAN

Like the early work of Bob Dylan, film treatments of race reflected the biracial optimism of the early Sixties civil rights movement. The screen version of Lorraine Hansberry's *A Raisin in the Sun* (1961), the first Broadway play written by a black woman, became the first movie to introduce mainstream white audiences to the idea that African Americans could be "ordinary" people. Hansberry's middle-class parents had left the South for Chicago during World War I, after which her father became a successful banker and realtor. Drawn to left-wing theater circles in the late Forties, she sought to create an alternative to the suggestion of powerlessness in *Death of a Salesman* and to counter prevailing stereotypes about exotic, trivialized, or criminalized black characters. Setting its action in a crowded three-room apartment on Chicago's South Side, the film dealt with working-class African Americans seeking the American Dream of upward mobility and equal opportunity.

The story of *Raisin in the Sun* centered on the desire of the Younger family matriarch (Claudia McNeil) to use her late husband's life insurance to find a home outside the ghetto and to pay for her daughter's medical school education. When Lena Younger's son Walter Lee (Sidney Poitier) wants to invest in a liquor store as a way of asserting leadership of the family, a series of animated discussions introduces battling social perspectives on matters of morality and black pride. Things become even more complicated when it becomes apparent that Younger's daughter Beneatha (Diana Sands) is a free thinker who rejects her mother's belief in God and accepts the racialist views of her African boyfriend. A popular hit with a biracial audience of both working people and the middle class, *Raisin in the Sun* emphasized collective African American resources of hope, pride, humor, and solidarity, particularly through the dignity, loving endurance, and strength of black women. In the end, the family achieves an element of harmony when Walter Lee loses a portion of the settlement, but Lena succeeds in using the rest for a down payment on a house in a white neighborhood.

Horton Foote's screenplay adaptation of Harper Lee's *To Kill a Mockingbird* (1962) shifted the focus of race relations back to the South. A white Alabama native who had studied law at the state university, Lee won a Pulitzer Prize for the only novel she ever wrote. Incorporating elements of Mark Twain, William Faulkner, and John Steinbeck, her semi-autobiographical masterpiece set a coming-of-age tale of two white children in a grubby southern small town of the early Depression. The film featured Gregory Peck in an Academy Award-winning portrait of Atticus Finch, a soft-spoken lawyer and widowed father trying to raise ten-year-old Jem and six-year-old Scout in a terrifying atmosphere of bigotry and economic deprivation. When Atticus, as the youngsters call him, defies social pressure by agreeing to defend Tom Robinson, a sensitive and articulate black farmer (Brock Peters) wrongly accused of raping a white woman, the entire family becomes involved in the ensuing drama.

As seen through daughter Scout's eyes, wrenching testimony demonstrates that Robinson's only crime was to have felt pity for a lonely poor young white woman who has used her caste privilege to order him to help with some minor house chores. Never abandoning his civilized restraint and self-dignity, Atticus brings out the humanity of both accuser and defendant, while easing his way around threats of a lynching. All comes to naught, however, when an all-white jury disregards the overwhelming burden of the evidence and finds the black man guilty. Once the main floor of the courtroom empties, Atticus quietly gathers his papers and painfully makes his way toward the door. As the camera pans to Scout leaning against the front rail of the segregated balcony, however, viewers witness a rare moment in which a Hollywood film bestows agency upon the powerless. "Stand up," the town's Negro reverend prompts the young girl, as the entire gallery rises in a gesture of respect that is also a silent protest, "your father is passing."

Director Sidney Lumet's *The Pawnbroker* (1965) placed the subject of interracial bonding in the tumultuous setting of East Harlem. The film starred Rod Steiger as Sol Nazerman, a bitter and emotionally spent Holocaust survivor who has witnessed the brutal murder of his family and best friend in a Nazi concentration camp. Looking upon people as "scum," the Jewish shopkeeper maintains an icy exterior while treating anyone who tries to get close to him as cruelly and offensively as possible. The story centers on Nazerman's relationship to his assistant, a black Puerto Rican named Jesus Ortiz (Jaime Sánchez), who seeks to break through the façade and learn the trade from his employer. Although Nazerman characteristically rejects these overtures, Ortiz sacrifices his own life when he steps in to protect his boss during an armed robbery. Through this tragedy, the pawnbroker realizes the shame of his complete isolation from other human beings.

Steiger captured an Academy Award for his lead role as a southern police chief in Norman Jewison's *In the Heat of the Night* (1967), a film that also won Best Picture laurels. Yet much of the movie's edge rested with Sidney Poitier's characterization of Virgil Tibbs. Poitier had earned the first Oscar ever awarded an African American male actor for *Lillies of the Field* (1963), a light-hearted feature about a black Army veteran and drifter who volunteers to build a southwestern desert chapel for five East German nuns. In *Heat of the Night*, sheriff's deputies mistakenly pick up Tibbs, a Philadelphia police detective passing through a Mississippi town, on suspicion of murder. Pressed to find the killer of a wealthy industrialist who had planned to start a racially integrated textile mill, the chief of police reluctantly agrees to bring the outsider into the case. Yet Tibbs must deal with deep-seated local prejudices. When Steiger taunts his new partner by asking how they address him in Philadelphia, the black man answers with calculated rage, "They call me MISTER Tibbs!" In another moment of movie history, Poitier responds to a slap in the face from a white aristocrat by smacking the man back.

Nothing But a Man (1964), a low-budget independent feature shot by white filmmakers Robert Young and Michael Roemer, dealt more directly with African American life in the South. The film starred Ivan Dixon as Duff Anderson, a young Alabama railroad worker struggling to make a life for himself in the early Sixties. Despite a reluctance to assume the responsibilities of a family, Anderson marries a minister's daughter (Abbey Lincoln) over the objections of her father. After getting a sawmill job, however, his attempt to organize the laborers against racist treatment prompts his white employers to fire him as a "troublemaker." Forced to work at a gas station, he faces continual harassment by hostile locals. In rage and frustration, he begins beating his wife. The story takes a crucial turn when Anderson travels to Birmingham to see his father, who is dying after a life of unskilled labor, unemployment, and alcoholism. Awakened to manhood, he reclaims his abandoned illegitimate son and returns to make amends at home. Shot in the dirty streets, gin mills, and decrepit apartments of the urban South, *Nothing But a Man* achieved vast emotional power through understated realism.

RACE POWER AND IDENTITY

Despite the positive messages of early Sixties movies, repeated atrocities by white supremacists and the intransigence of racist practices took an enormous toll. For the black working class and poor of the urban ghettos, the incremental reforms of a nonviolent and integrationist struggle offered little hope amid rampant unemployment, decrepit housing, inadequate social services, police brutality, and other abuses. James Baldwin had warned of the consequences of unabated racial discrimination in *The Fire Next Time* (1963), a series of essays blending the language of the spirituals, gospel, and blues with Old Testament prophecies of retribution. Two of Baldwin's Broadway plays, *Blues for Mr. Charley* (1964) and *The Amen Corner* (1965), conveyed black disillusionment with the American Dream in the strongest terms. As predicted, racial tensions exploded in a series of inner city race riots that erupted in Harlem in 1964 and spread with devastating impact to the Watts section of South Central Los Angeles the next year.

The experience of growing up in the ghetto received graphic treatment in Claude Brown's uncensored memoir, *Manchild in the Promised Land* (1965). The son of a Harlem railroad laborer and a domestic worker, Brown survived a troubled childhood and adolescence before graduating from Howard University and launching a writing career. Yet *Manchild* never achieved nearly the exposure of *The Autobiography of Malcolm X* (1965). Born Malcolm Little in Omaha in 1925, the future activist relocated to Lansing, Michigan, as a boy, where his father, a Baptist minister and follower of black nationalist Marcus Garvey, was murdered. After stints in a foster home and reform school, Malcolm moved in with a half-sister outside Boston, where he shined shoes, worked on railroad dining cars, and fell into petty crime. Moving on to Harlem when he was seventeen, he took the name "Detroit Red" while dealing drugs, pimping, and pulling off armed robberies. Malcolm's propensity to crime eventually resulted in a ten-year sentence for burglary. In prison, he educated himself by copying the entire dictionary by hand and reading voraciously about black history, slavery, and racial oppression.

Malcolm's prison experience also resulted in his conversion to the Nation of Islam—a religious order advocating Muslim teachings, black separatism, and self-help. Moving to Detroit upon his release, he assumed the name Malcolm X and rose to become the group's national spokesperson. As a Black Muslim, Malcolm preached that Negroes needed to develop their own institutions and social values apart from racist America. Rejecting integration, nonviolence, and cooperation with whites, he called for a black political revolution. When Malcolm formed his own Muslim organization in 1964, he continued to castigate whites as devils. A subsequent trip to Mecca, however, led him to acknowledge bonds of brotherhood with white socialists and anti-colonialists. He now advised blacks to join the global struggle for freedom "by any means necessary" and promoted the idea that "black is beautiful." These precepts marked the core of the activist's best-selling autobiography, which black journalist Alex Haley published weeks after Malcolm's assassination in 1965 by three men linked to the Nation of Islam.

Malcolm X's insistence on self-defense, black political autonomy, and assertive racial identity influenced the emergence of Black Power, a concept initially identified with SNCC leader Stokely Carmichael. Taken up in 1966 by Huey Newton and Bobby Seale, two Oakland college students who formed the Black Panther Party, the ideology called for African Americans to resist outside control of their urban communities, to serve the people with grassroots social institutions, and to build up the vitality of a distinct black culture. Eldridge Cleaver provided a fitting expression of such sentiments in the popular *Soul on Ice* (1968). Raised in Arkansas and Los Angeles, Cleaver served a twelve-year prison sentence for rape and selling marijuana. Converting to the Nation of Islam, he joined the Black Panther Party upon his release in 1966 and became the organization's Minister of Information. First published in the radical magazine *Ramparts*, the essays in *Soul on Ice* celebrated the distinctive vitality of black culture, in contrast to the perceived blandness of white middle-class life.

The violence of Panther rhetoric, media posturing by Party leaders, and armed confrontations with police aroused profound controversy and contributed to a wave of reprisal killings initiated by government agents. Yet Black Panther health clinics, breakfast programs, newspapers, and public rallies helped to instill fundamental precepts of racial pride and popularized the doctrine of "power to the people," particularly as rioting spread to racially tense areas of Detroit, Newark, and other cities in the late Sixties. The precepts of Black Nationalism likely received the greatest degree of exposure through the person of Muhammad Ali. Born Cassius Clay in Louisville in 1942, the future champion learned boxing skills at a Police Athletic League gym and went on to win six Kentucky Gold Glove titles. At eighteen, Clay took home a gold medal and the light heavyweight boxing title of the 1960 Olympics.

Turning professional, the fighter defeated veteran Archie Moore in 1962, composing doggerel poetry preceding and following the match. "Some get mad, some lose their money," he proclaimed, "But Cassius is still sweet as honey." Clay even appeared at a Greenwich Village café to recite his verse. When the boxer met Malcolm X at a Detroit mosque in 1963, he joined the Nation of Islam. Changing his name to Cassius X, he predicted that he would knock out heavyweight champion Sonny Liston in his next fight. "I am the greatest! I shook up the world!" he declared after making good on his boast. Rejecting the role of the humble Negro warrior, Clay merged the oral traditions of the black church and pool hall with the playful banter of a Las Vegas wrestler. He could "float like a butterfly and sting like a bee," he declared.

Following the Liston victory, Clay agreed to take the Muslim name of Muhammad Ali. In his next bout with Floyd Patterson, a black integrationist who had married a white woman, Ali let the fight continue for twelve rounds before sealing the victory. Although the light-footed champion studiously avoided alcohol, drugs, cigarettes, and white women, his Black Muslim ties and verbal taunts aroused public furor. As the Vietnam War raged in 1967, the Selective Service reclassified Ali as 1-A and announced its intention to draft him. When the boxer replied that "I ain't got no quarrel with the Viet Cong" and applied for conscientious objector status as a Muslim minister, federal prosecutors successfully pursued a draft evasion conviction. Despite the fact that the five-year prison sentence was under appeal, New York state boxing authorities stripped Ali of his title. When the courts threw out the ban three years later and subsequently reversed his conviction, the fighter initiated a comeback that led to his reclaiming the heavyweight championship on two separate occasions. By the time Ali retired in 1980, he had earned a reputation as the greatest boxer ever to enter the ring.

BLACK FIRE

Muhammad Ali's celebrated feats made him a folk hero to millions of people worldwide. At home, Ali's verbal theatrics and uncompromised principles spoke to an emerging African American cultural pride. The enhanced racial consciousness of the Sixties had particular relevance for the arts. In photography, Gordon Parks filled the pages of *Life* with images of Harlem poverty, the Black Muslims, Malcolm X, Martin Luther King, Jr., and Muhammad Ali. Visual artists such as Romare Bearden, Faith Ringgold, and Elizabeth Catlett turned to innovative forms, including photomontages, quilts, hanging panels, textile sculptures, and print media to depict the full scope of the African American experience. Meanwhile, colorful wall murals depicting black historical and cultural figures began to proliferate in urban communities. As workshops for the creative and performing arts spread, and black publishing houses, theater groups, dance troupes, newspapers, journals, and radio stations multiplied, black culture experienced a revitalization not witnessed since the days of the Harlem Renaissance.

Dramatist, poet, and political activist Leroi Jones played a leading role in voicing the demand for a "new black aesthetic." A Newark-born graduate of Howard University, Jones had been a Beat poet in the 1950s. After publishing *Blues People* (1963), a history of the African American oral tradition, he authored two critically acclaimed plays, *Dutchman* (1964) and *The Slave* (1964), both exploring the legacy of racism. Following Malcolm X's death, Jones urged artists to serve the community with revolutionary work that reflected black consciousness and resonated with the experience of ordinary readers. Taking the African name Imamu Ameer (later Amiri) Baraka in 1967, he called for the replacement of the European literary canon with African-derived models and uniquely black forms of expression. Inspired by a renewed racial identity, some black cultural activists followed Baraka's example by assuming African or Islamic names, wearing African robes and other ceremonial clothing, or sporting natural "Afro" hairdos. In 1966, Black Nationalist Maulana Karenga transformed the traditional African fruit harvest celebration of Kwanzaa into a modern holiday beginning the day after Christmas.

Nationalist intellectuals like Amiri Baraka and Maulana Karanga heralded either African musical forms or modern jazz as the keys to black cultural liberation. During the late 1950s, a group of African American jazz musicians had rebelled against the "cool" sound of white instrumentalists like Dave Brubeck and Gerry Mulligan by incorporating blues and black church elements into the genre known as "hard bop." By the Sixties, avant-garde players like John Coltrane, McCoy Tyner, Sonny Rollins, Miles Davis, Charles Mingus, and Max Roach saw themselves as practitioners of a "New Black Music"—a "people's" art that rejected commercial tastes but derived its stridency from the African American experience.

Although hard bop attracted a coterie of white hipsters, intellectuals, and musicians, it made little headway elsewhere. Baraka's vision of a vital African American culture had far more success in the literary arts. The Black Arts Movement, a result of the Black Writer's Conference of 1967, advanced a collective literary aesthetic of racial pride, solidarity, and self-determination. Its primary Bible was *Black Fire* (1968), an anthology of race-conscious poetry edited by Baraka and poet/critic Larry Neal. Neal had arrived in Harlem in the 1960s after graduate work in politics and folklore. Endowing *Black Fire* with the same importance *The New Negro* had assumed in the Twenties, he described the Black Arts Movement as Black Power's "spiritual sister." Accordingly, much of the volume looked to African communal and spiritual traditions. Neal's own collections, *Black Boogaloo: Notes on Black Liberation* (1969) and *Hoodoo Hollerin': Bebop Chants* (1971), sustained the focus on black cultural forms with repeated nods to jazz and African American folk figures. In a similar fashion, the poems in Baraka's *Black Magic* (1969) captured the cadences of black street idiom and jazz.

Vernacular language dominated both *Cotton Comes to Harlem* (1965) and *Blind Man With a Pistol* (1969), two race-conscious detective novels by Chester Himes. James McPherson's prize-winning *Hue and Cry: Short Stories* (1970), drawn from the author's student experiences as a railroad car waiter, also conveyed the inflections of normal banter. Yet poetry provided the best examples of the Black Arts Movement's interest in African American oral tradition. Experimenting with "rap" or urban street jive, Movement pioneer Gwendolyn Brooks included a long piece about the Chicago street gang, the Blackstone Rangers, in her *In the Mecca* (1968). Nikki Giovanni also chose to write in a highly accessible style. Born in Knoxville, Giovanni graduated from Fisk University before pursuing graduate studies in social work and fine arts. Her first two collections of verse, *Black Feeling, Black Talk* (1967) and *Black Judgment* (1968), fused jazz and blues rhythms with revolutionary militancy and nationalist consciousness. "I wanta say just gotta say something," she rhapsodized, "bout those beautiful beautiful beautiful outasight/black men/with they afros/walking down the street."

Another of Giovanni's poems, "For Saundra," speculated whether the poet "shouldn't write/at all/but clean my gun/and check my kerosene supply." Perhaps these were "not poetic/times at all," the piece suggested. Nevertheless seeking a broader audience, Giovanni recorded the political *Truth Is On Its Way* (1971), a spoken word album backed by African drums and a gospel choir. Still another record anthology, *The Last Poets* (1970), sold over eight-hundred thousand copies with the militant verse of figures like Jabal "Lightin' Rod" Uridin. One of the album's best-known selections, "When the Revolution Comes," merged a political appeal with furious conga rhythms. Gil Scott-Heron's "The Revolution Will Not Be Televised," the lead work of his best-selling album, *A New Black Poet: Small Talk at 125ᵗʰ Street and Lenox* (1970), offered a prime example of poetic street talk. Musical influences also merged with higher spiritual realities in Al Young's *Dancing* (1969) and *The Song Turning Back into Itself* (1971).

SWEET SOUL MUSIC

As the early civil rights movement raised expectations about integration, racial harmony, and black opportunity between 1956 and 1964, African American popular music veered away from the earthy lyrics and style that characterized much of rhythm and blues. In the most racially integrated period of American commercial music history, young audiences of both races bought records by both black and white artists. White songwriters like Mike Stoller, Carole King, Barry Mann, and Phil Spector often provided the material for these recordings. Although lyrics frequently referred to ghetto life, prevailing themes revolved around non-sexual issues like young love, dance crazes, or fashion trends. As in the case of post-World War II doo-wop, black popular music of the early Sixties held out the hope that conventional domesticity might provide the road out of racial oppression and denial.

Sam Cooke ranked as one of the leading stars of the evolving genre. The son of a Baptist minister who relocated from Mississippi to Chicago, Cooke sang in the church choir before joining a traveling gospel ensemble. His initial venture into secular music, "You Send Me" (1957), became an immediate hit. Over the next seven years, Cooke blended his smooth tenor voice into a series of chart-toppers like "Chain Gang" (1960) and "Bring It on Home to Me" (1962). The Drifters provided another example of the broad appeal of black popular music. With Ben E. King replacing Clyde McPhatter as lead vocalist, the group used material from white songwriters in urban-flavored hits like "Save the Last Dance for Me" (1960), "Up on the Roof" (1963), and "Under the Boardwalk" (1964). King also recorded a solo version of Phil Spector's "Spanish Harlem" (1961). An independent producer, Spector had innovated the "wall of sound," a technique for layering and overdubbing musical instrumentation. The results included "Be My Baby" (1963) by the black female group the Ronnettes, and the Righteous Brothers' "You've Lost That Lovin' Feeling" (1964), a hit marketed as "blue-eyed" soul.

Detroit's Motown Records became the most successful marketer of black music to biracial audiences. The label's founder, Berry Gordy, Jr., was born in Detroit in 1929, the son of a recent Georgia emigrant who ran a grocery store named after Booker T. Washington. Dropping out of school in eleventh grade, Gordy sought to make it as a boxer and a jazz record store owner before going to work at a Ford assembly plant. After rhythm and blues vocalist Jackie Wilson recorded two of his songs in the late Fifties, the aspiring entrepreneur gained entry into the music business and produced a number for the Miracles, who became one of the first groups to record for Motown following its inception in 1959. Within a few years, the company had become the largest African American owned enterprise in the United States.

Motown's accomplishment rested upon an urbane synthesis of gospel, rhythm and blues, and popular music forms through dance tunes that conveyed universal messages of love, loneliness, joy, and belonging. Gordy ingeniously sensed that white audiences thirsted for the vitality offered by black music, and that African American styles fit easily into mainstream tastes. He looked for catchy melodies, original phrasing or rhythm, and a simple lyric cast in the present tense. Several Motown groups, including the Miracles, the Temptations, and the Supremes, came out of Detroit high schools. Recordings like the Miracles' "Shop Around" (1961), Martha and the Vandellas' "Heat Wave" (1963) and "Dancing in the Street" (1964), the Temptations' "My Girl" (1965), Gladys Knight and the Pips' "I Heard It Through the Grapevine" (1967), and the Supremes' "Baby Love" (1964) and "You Can't Hurry Love" (1966) depicted everyday situations in terms most people readily understood.

In "Can I Get a Witness?" (1963), Motown artist Marvin Gaye, the son of a Pentecostal minister, harkened back to the gospel influences of black popular music. Gaye also borrowed from Ray Charles, whose call-and-response classic "What'd I Say, Part I" (1959) demonstrated the persistent relevance of church-derived forms. Curtis Mayfield, writer and lead vocalist for the Impressions and a self-acknowledged creator of "songs of faith and inspiration," provided another example of the religious roots of African American popular culture. "People Get Ready" (1965), a Mayfield production that presented an intricately harmonized plea for black national unity and trust in a better day, became a subsequent rallying point for many politically conscious African Americans. "River Deep—Mountain High" (1966), the Ike and Tina Turner number produced by Phil Spector, conveyed a similar gospel feel.

Some of the most significant innovations of Sixties African American popular music originated with New York's Atlantic Records and the Memphis-based Stax studios, the prime innovators of the "soul" sound. Backed by Stax's racially mixed house band, Booker T. and the MGs, whose instrumental "Green Onions" (1962) achieved cult status, Detroit rhythm and blues vocalist Wilson Pickett became one of the prime exponents of the style through records like "In the Midnight Hour" (1965). Like Pickett, Otis Redding excelled at fusing gospel and blues forms into the new style. Rising from poverty in Macon, Georgia, to become a mainstay of the southern black club circuit, Redding first made the charts with his Stax recording of the old Depression standby "Try a Little Tenderness" (1967). When the singer was killed in a plane crash later the same year, his single "(Sittin' On) The Dock of the Bay" (1967) rose to Number One.

"Respect" (1967), another Redding composition, soon became a million-seller for Aretha Franklin. The daughter of a prominent Detroit evangelist, Franklin popularized the spirited use of gospel call-and-response in heartfelt numbers like "A Natural Woman" (1967) and "I Never Loved a Man (the Way I Love You)" (1967). By the late Sixties, pervasive optimism about racial integration had given way to the attractions of Black Power and Black Pride. "Respect" reflected the new mood of militancy with an insistent demand for recognition and acknowledgment. "Find out what it means to me!" snapped Franklin, as her raspy voice spelled out the letters R-E-S-P-E-C-T, a message with dual meaning given, the vocalist's status as a woman and an African American.

Like "Respect," Arthur Conley's "Sweet Soul Music" (1967) took its place as a signature representation of the new musical style. By now, however, James Brown had claimed the title of "Godfather of Soul." Raised in poverty in Augusta, Georgia, Brown shined shoes and danced in the streets as a youngster. After release from jail for a series of juvenile crimes, he decided to become a musician. His first group, the Famous Flames, performed gospel tunes, but Brown launched a rhythm and blues recording career in the mid-Fifties. Fusing blues and gospel into the style that would become "soul," he scored an impressive string of hits that included "Out of Sight" (1964), "Papa's Got a Brand New Bag" (1965), "It's a Man's Man's Man's World" (1966), and "Say It Loud, I'm Black and I'm Proud" (1968). As front man for the James Brown Revue, the singer transformed the repetitive phrasing and coarse voicing of black spiritual and secular harmonies into a frenzied pursuit of ecstasy and a communal celebration of blackness that imparted a cohesive quality to African American culture.

Sly and the Family Stone provided a variant of soul with the upbeat anthem "Dance to the Music" (1968). As a group assigning a variety of roles to its mixed racial and gendered personnel, the Stone stood out as an early symbol of multiculturalism. In the populist plea for mutual tolerance in "Everyday People" (1968), Sly fashioned one of the era's lasting catch phrases when he playfully preached "different strokes for different folks." Yet as the assassination of Martin Luther King in 1968 and the apparent failure of social activists to reverse the poverty and hopelessness of the inner city further punctured the dream of racial integration, performers like Sly increasingly reverted to macho postures and an emphasis on rhythmic complexity. The overlapping voices and intense beat of the Stone's "I Want to Take You Higher" (1969), for example, helped prepare the way for the funk styles of the succeeding decade.

CHICANO ROOTS, INDIAN TRADITIONS

Profoundly influenced by Black Power, politically conscious young Mexican Americans pursued their own goals of cultural autonomy. Identifying themselves as Chicanos, activists sought to recapture the ethnically based folk culture and values rooted in the long history of Mexico's indigenous people. In the realm of social action, Cesar Chavez and Delores Huerta recruited California grape pickers into the United Farm Workers, a union appealing to the Chicano heritage of poor, unassimilated Mexican American field laborers. Other leaders, like New Mexico's Reies Lopez Tijerina, La Raza Unida Party organizer José Angel Guiterrez of Texas, and Denver's Rodolfo "Corky" Gonzales, combined economic grievances with calls for cultural pride and empowerment, as did the militant Brown Berets, a barrio youth group modeled along Panther lines.

Romantic nationalism found an expressive outlet in the Chicano Renaissance or Art Movement, which looked to ordinary people as the transmitters of traditional culture. The contemporary barrio preserved such a heritage, declared dramatist Louis Valdez, through such practices as tortilla consumption, marijuana use, and worship of the Virgin of Guadalupe. Born into a family of California agricultural laborers, Valdez founded a farm workers theater to publicize field conditions when he allied with Cesar Chavez in 1965. The search for Chicano identity led other cultural activists to written literature. José Antonio Villarreal's novel *Pocho* (1959) graphically illustrated the pull between Chicano and Anglo culture in Mexican immigrant life. Through poetry collections such as *You Can Reach Heaven on Foot* (1966) and *Love and Ecuador* (1966), New Mexico's Sabine Ulibarri sought to recapture oral traditions via the prism of childhood memories. The conversational verse of San Antonio's Angela de Hoyos also provided a voice to the powerless through the cross-cultural perspectives of non-elites.

The most influential Chicano work of the 1960s was Corky Gonzales' bilingual epic poem *I am Joaquin* (1967). By tracing an urban worker's search for ethnic solidarity and identity, Gonzales presented a historical overview of exploitation from pre-Columbian times to the most recent Mexican American experiences. Publication of *I Am Joaquin* helped to inspire the formation of Quinto Sol Productions in 1967, a Chicano publishing house that opened its doors to poets such as José Montaya, Rudolfo Anaya, Lorna Dee Cervantes, and Cherrie Moraga. Another milestone occurred with release of "The Spiritual Plan of Aztlan" (1969) by Denver's Chicano Youth Conference. The manifesto urged writers and artists to rededicate themselves to the people by renouncing Anglo values and reorienting their work toward an indigenous Indo-Mexican culture. Nationalist perspectives also prompted southwest self-help groups to install thousands of community murals in the following years.

Like Chicano activists, organizers of native peoples campaigned for a dual agenda of political empowerment and cultural sovereignty. Responding to complaints about police brutality, the American Indian Movement (AIM) formed its first chapter in Minneapolis in 1968. The group soon broadened its goals to include Native American political self-determination and the dissemination of Indian cultural awareness through the education programs of "survival schools" and culture centers. Vine Deloria, Jr., a Lakota Sioux, conveyed these aspirations to a general audience through *Custer Died for Yours Sins* (1969), a best-selling treatise advocating Native American self-determination, pan-Indian nationalism, and the revival of tribal traditions.

N. Scott Momaday

Up through the early 1960s, only nine novels by Indian authors had reached print in over a century. The awarding of a Pulitzer Prize in Fiction to N. Scott Momaday, therefore, marked a major event in Native American cultural history. The son of an Oklahoma Kiowa art instructor/painter and a part-Cherokee teacher/writer, Momaday attended a southwestern military academy, graduated from the University of New Mexico, and completed an English Ph.D. at Harvard. His initial publication in 1967 presented a compilation of Kiowa folk tales. Momaday also published *The Way to Rainy Mountain* (1969), a first-person narrative pointing to the reverence for natural order and beauty in three hundred years of Kiowa history, sacred myths, and tribal customs. *House Made of Dawn* (1968), his prize-winning debut novel, told the story of a young Native man who serves in World War II, only to receive a prison sentence for murder upon his release. Freed from incarceration, he attempts to integrate in white society in Los Angeles, but experiences a form of spiritual suicide. He then returns to his tribal home, where multiple voices from the past and oral flashbacks help him forge a coherent identity.

STAND BY YOUR MAN

"'Hoss," country singer Patsy Cline instructed protégé Dottie West, "if you can't do it with feeling, *don't*." The most soulful female performer in country music history, Cline personified the universality of the search for cultural identity in the 1960s. Born Virginia Patterson Hensley to a sixteen-year-old young white woman in northern Virginia in 1932, she began performing at age eleven, worked at a chicken-processing plant at thirteen, appeared on the radio when she was fourteen, and quit school to sing at clubs and dances by the time she was sixteen. Cline signed a record contract in 1954 following a regular spot on a Washington, D.C. country radio show. After several guest appearances on the Grand Ole Opry, she took first prize on Arthur Godfrey's *Talents Scouts* by singing the bluesy "Walkin' After Midnight." Three years later, her record of "I Fall to Pieces" (1960) rose to the top of the country charts. Other memorable hits included Willie Nelson's "Crazy" (1961) and Don Gibson's "Sweet Dreams (Of You)" (1963).

Having experienced numerous sexual affairs, miscarriages, and nervous breakdowns during and after two tumultuous marriages, Patsy Cline nursed her share of broken dreams. A brassy and plainspoken woman with street smarts and an outrageous sense of humor, she carried a pint of whiskey in her purse and swore profusely. Yet friends and fans also detected the tenderness and sentimentality of someone given to acts of incredible generosity. Cline's genius lay in the ability to convey the full range of these emotions in her singing. Audiences sensed the vocalist's authenticity through the growls, sobs, sighs, rhythmic pauses, bent notes, and volume shifts worked into her throaty but controlled delivery. Supplanting Kitty Wells as the queen of country music, Cline addressed the pains of compliant femininity with complete honesty. Through the guidance of record producer Owen Bradley, who introduced orchestral strings into her songs for a more cosmopolitan sound, Cline was moving toward mainstream popular acceptance when the plane returning her from a benefit performance crashed in the Tennessee hills in 1963, killing everyone on board.

Loretta Lynn was one of the rising stars befriended by Patsy Cline. As described in her song "Coal Miner's Daughter" (1970), the title of a 1976 autobiography and the name of a Hollywood movie made about her life four years later, Lynn was born in a log cabin papered with movie magazines in the Kentucky mountain community of Butcher Holler. Her mother named the baby after film personality Loretta Young. At age thirteen, Loretta married and moved with her husband to Washington State, where she soon had her first child and three others by the time she reached eighteen. Accustomed to cleaning house, picking berries, and taking in laundry, she began singing when given a guitar for her eighteenth birthday. By the late 1950s, Lynn's husband was arranging her singing dates in local clubs and Grange halls. Her first record, "I'm a Honky-Tonk Girl" (1960), appeared on a small label owned by a local lumberman. To promote the single for radio airplay, the couple drove across the country in an old-model Mercury, surviving on bologna sandwiches and sleeping in the car. Befriended in Nashville by Patsy Cline, Lynn signed with Decca and placed herself under the direction of Owen Bradley.

"I think I reach people because I'm with 'em, not apart from 'em," Loretta once observed. Writing her own material, she recorded disarmingly honest songs about the frequent pregnancies, tedium, and drudgery shaping the lives of many working-class women. Yet her music expressed pride in her humble background, earthy humor and warmth, and a sassy self-assertiveness that female fans adored. Early hits included "You Ain't Woman Enough" (1965) and "Don't Come Home a-Drinkin' With Lovin' On Your Mind" (1966). After "Coal Miner's Daughter," Loretta recorded "One's On the Way" (1971), a plaintive contrast between the plight of overworked mothers and the cosmopolitan life of the modern woman. Her most controversial song was "The Pill" (1972), a single banned by many radio stations because it brashly celebrated the fact that wives had a new bargaining chip in the battle to keep men at home. Mixing the controlled vocal style of Kitty Wells with the exuberance associated with Patsy Cline, Loretta Lynn geared her live shows to working-class women, who, she implied, should always stand up for the respect they were due.

Some forty years after its release, surveys continued to indicate that fans ranked "Stand By Your Man" (1968), history's biggest-selling country music single by a female artist, as one of the greatest records of all time. Tammy Wynette, the performer who immortalized the song, was born Virginia Wynette Pugh in a rural shack in eastern Mississippi in 1942. After her father died of a brain tumor when she was nine months old, Virginia stayed with grandparents while her mother worked in a Memphis defense plant. As a child, Tammy worked in the family cotton patch, an experience she retained by keeping a copper dish of cotton on her mantle. Wedded at seventeen a month before high school graduation, she had three children in rapid succession. After the marriage

Tammy Wynette   (*Photofest*)

collapsed, Pugh worked her way through a Birmingham beauty college and began singing in local clubs and on radio. Arriving in Nashville in 1966, she successfully auditioned for a record contract with producer Billy Sherrill, the son of an Alabama preacher and a veteran of an apprenticeship at Sun Records.

Under Sherrill's direction, Wynette's quivering voice explored female pain and vulnerability in hits like "Apartment #9" (1966), "I Don't Wanna Play House" (1967), "Your Good Girl's Gonna Go Bad" (1967), and "D-I-V-O-R-C-E" (1968). Yet no one anticipated the phenomenal success of "Stand By Your Man," a song Wynette co-wrote with Sherrill. "Sometimes it's hard to be a woman," Tammy began in a husky voice. Painfully chronicling the heartaches and disappointments of a working-class marriage, the lyric suggested that each woman needed to forgive and protect her mate because, in the end, "he's just a man." Although "Stand By Your Man" attracted criticism for reinforcing traditional gender roles, Sherrill insisted that the song spoke for women who were secure enough in their identity to identify with expressions of unqualified love. For her part, Wynette saw the lyric addressing the need for support and understanding, not passivity or deference, among emotionally vulnerable people with limited life options. Marrying five times, the singer kept her beauty license current for the rest of her life in case her time in Nashville ever played itself out.

GOOD TIMES AND BAD

In 1967, a bluesy ballad with Mississippi Delta phrasing and acoustic guitar backing catapulted to the top of both the country and pop charts. "Ode to Billie Joe" was the product of singer-songwriter Bobby Gentry. Born Roberta Streeter in Chickasaw County, Gentry moved with her family to the California desert community of Palm Springs in the mid-Fifties. After studying philosophy at UCLA and classical music at a Los Angeles conservatory, she drifted to Las Vegas, where she became a showgirl and nightclub singer. A conversational narrative laced with a Delta drawl, "Ode to Billie Joe" captured the life rhythms and surroundings of a poor white family of cotton farmers. The song used the cyclical techniques of oral tradition to sketch out scattered details of Billie Joe's furtive meeting with the ballad's storyteller and his subsequent suicide off the Tallahatchie Bridge.

Bobby Gentry's song hinted at the hidden passions and demons that men rarely revealed. Yet several male country artists of the Sixties delved into the emotional make-up of their male counterparts. Faron Young's recording of songwriter Willie Nelson's "Hello Walls" (1961) conveyed the stark emptiness of a loveless life. Dave Dudley's "Six Days on the Road" (1963) captured the urgency of a cross-country trucker desperate to get back home. In "Detroit City" (1963), Bobby Bare expressed the lonely desperation of a southern migrant to the industrial heartland. "By day I make the cars," sang Bare, "by night I make the bars." In turn, Porter Wagoner's version of Curley Putnam's "Green, Green Grass of Home" (1965) described the sentimental longings of a condemned prisoner who will never see his loved ones again. In recitations and songs like "Phantom 309" (1967), moreover, country singer Red Sovine immortalized the mystique of the long-distance truck drivers referred to in Dudley's hit.

No single performer identified with the everyday figures of male culture with as much artistry as Johnny Cash. Born into a family of poor cotton farmers in Depression Arkansas, Cash worked briefly in a Michigan auto plant before enlisting in the Air Force. Upon his return to civilian life in 1954, he began playing music and recorded with Sun Records the next year. His early releases included "Cry Cry Cry" (1955) and "Folsom Prison Blues" (1955), but Cash did not score a major hit until "I Walk the Line" (1958), a rockabilly tune with a slapping bass and strongly accented rhythm guitar. Known as the "Man in Black," the singer took on the role of a tragic troubadour mourning for the poor and the dispossessed. His live album, *At Folsom Prison* (1968), featured songs about convicts and other characters trapped by desire or loneliness complete with Cash's impromptu cracks about prison wardens and assorted figures of authority.

Like Johnny Cash, Roger Miller conveyed a profound empathy for the underdog in whimsical creations set to catchy tunes. Born in Texas and raised in Oklahoma, Miller grew up on the music of Bob Wills and learned to play guitar from country performer Sheb Wooley, his cousin's husband. Entertaining fellow soldiers in Korea in the mid-Fifties, he returned to Texas and joined Ray Price as a backup musician. Once in Nashville, Miller played fiddle for Minnie Pearl's road band, began writing songs, and initiated a recording career. Perfecting an original scat delivery of vernacular lyrics, he scored spectacular successes with "Dang Me" (1964) and "King of the Road" (1965), the latter a tongue-in-cheek tale of a resilient hobo who sweeps floors in exchange for "an eight by twelve, four-bit room."

Tom T. Hall's conversational songs offered one of country music's most offbeat views of everyday life. Hall had dropped out of high school in Kentucky to work as a bluegrass musician and disc jockey. Influenced by Ernest Hemingway's economical prose, he began writing lyrics during an Army hitch in Germany in the late Fifties. Once in Nashville, Hall had his first hit with "Harper Valley PTA" (1968), a feisty parody of small-town hypocrisy recorded by Jeannie C. Riley. He subsequently made his own versions of first-person narratives like "A Week in a County Jail," "Shoe Shine Man," and "That's How I Got To Memphis." In "Margie's at the Lincoln Park Inn" (1968), Hall described the torture of a devout family man trying to break off an illicit affair. "Ballad of Forty Dollars" (1968) offered a gravedigger's frank response to a new arrival. "I hope he rests in peace," sings the narrator, "but trouble is the fella owes me forty bucks." Other Hall classics included an ode to café waitresses in "Listen Betty" (1970), a tribute to a childhood mentor in "The Year That Clayton Delaney Died" (1971), and a distillation of barstool philosophy in "Old Dogs, Children, and Watermelon Wine" (1973).

Few songwriters ever have approximated the simple eloquence of Johnny Cash, Roger Miller, or Tom T. Hall. While emulating the direct phrasing of these masters, however, the work of Kris Kristofferson introduced an unprecedented degree of personal intimacy into country music. The son of an Air Force officer, Kristofferson was born in Brownsville, Texas but raised in California. A Rhodes Scholar in English literature, he spent five years as an Army helicopter pilot while preparing for a West Point instructorship. Sidetracked to Nashville, he flew for offshore oilrigs in the Gulf of Mexico while trying to sell his songs. The first break in his career came in 1969, when Roger Miller recorded "Me and Bobby McGee," a saga of life and freely given love on the open road. "Freedom's just another word for nuthin' left to lose," went the chorus, "And nuthin' ain't worth nuthin,' but it's free."

Having idolized Hank Williams as a youngster, Kristofferson leaned toward images of loneliness, alienation, and pain. Yet his lyrics also celebrated the liberating effect of honest relationships. Both features surfaced in Ray Price's recording of "For the Good Times" (1970). An East Texan brought up in Dallas, Price began performing in the early Fifties as a hard-core country artist in the Hank Williams mold. In hits like "Crazy Arms" (1956), he used pedal steel guitar, fiddles, and an electric walking bass to service a shuffle-beat perfect for close couple dancing. Augmented by strings and a backup chorus, "For the Good Times" crossed over toward the top of the pop music charts. "Lay your head upon my pillow," sang Price, "And make believe you love me one more time."

Kristofferson's talent for unadorned imagery underlay the success of Johnny Cash's single "Sunday Morning Coming Down" (1970), a Country Music Association Song of the Year. Without rhyme, artifice, or sentimentality, the song recorded the plaintive impressions of a hard-drinking soul longing for the solace of human community. "'Cause there's something in a Sunday," sang Cash, "That makes a body feel alone." Sammi Smith's recording of "Help Me Make It Through the Night" (1971), the fourth major Kristofferson hit within two years, tied an unvarnished portrayal of loneliness to the frank desire for physical intimacy. Born in southern California in 1943, Smith had started singing in bars when she was twelve. Married at fifteen and the mother of three children before an early divorce, she developed a smoky and sorrowful vocal style that perfectly suited the emotional vulnerability expressed in the songs she favored. "I don't care who's right or wrong," Smith sang in her smash hit, "Let the devil take tomorrow,/Lord, tonight I need a friend."

IN THE SHADOWS

Intimate portraits of ordinary existence also penetrated 1960s popular fiction. In the novella and four short stories published in *Goodbye, Columbus* (1959), Philip Roth proved to be a master of such an approach. Emulating portraits of urban Jewish life in Saul Bellows' *The Adventures of Augie March* (1953) and Bernard Malamud's *The Assistant* (1957), Roth's writing drew upon his own background in 1940s Newark. In creating a mixture of reality and fantasy about everyday life, however, he sought to deal with the moral significance of materialism and obsessions with status. The collection's title piece, converted into a motion picture in 1969, concerned a young librarian who combined acquisitiveness and opportunism with a desire to be a free spirit. Pursuing an affluent young woman out of both lust and desire for social advancement, he must come to terms with the fact that she will never sacrifice her comfortable lifestyle and family for his sake. The protagonist must also address his own embrace of the same middle-class conformity he professes to condemn.

A darker view of social pressure surfaced in Joseph Heller's cult classic, *Catch-22* (1961), a best-selling novel about World War II brought to the screen in 1970. Here the lead character must respond to an irrational bureaucracy bent on death. Oblivious to the fact that enemy pilots are shooting at everyone, Heller's innocent protagonist refuses to participate in additional bombing missions because "they're trying to kill me." When he seeks release from his duties on grounds of emotional instability, he learns of "Catch-22"—a rule that anyone rational enough to want to be grounded could not possibly be insane and therefore was fit to fly. Oregon writer Ken Kesey's *One Flew Over the Cuckoo's Nest* (1962), converted into a movie in 1975, placed the issue of bureaucratic uniformity in a mental hospital referred to as the "Combine"—a symbol of the collective insanity and repression of mainstream society. Kesey's book traced the valiant efforts of an American Indian inmate who falls back upon his cultural resources, defies the control of "Big Nurse," and tries his best to live outside the detested system.

Although Sixties Hollywood often focused on stories about the affluent, several movies turned to society's margins. John Cassavetes' independent film *Shadows* (1960) provided one example. Born into a middle-class New York Greek family, Cassavetes began an acting career after college. Appearing on late-night radio host Jean Shepherd's show in 1957, he boasted that he could make "a movie about people" if listeners sent in a dollar or two. Cassavetes then dipped into his earnings as a TV actor to produce the film of his dreams. Shot in documentary style, *Shadows* described a week in the life of three African American characters—a struggling jazz vocalist, a brooding hipster musician, and their impulsive light-skinned younger sister. Despite the racial context, the drama centered on the way people hid their emotional vulnerabilities behind outer masks. Cassavetes forged new ground by compelling audiences to share the experiences of his characters without dictating how viewers should react. Intensifying the feel of city streets with the driving sounds of jazz bassist Charles Mingus, the film explored the "small feelings" of people like café waitresses, car-park attendants, and taxi drivers.

Robert Rossen's *The Hustler* (1961) brought viewers directly into the grimy world of pool hall culture. Described as a mix between Ernest Hemingway and Clifford Odets, the story revolved around the desire of a young shark, "Fast" Eddie Felson (Paul Newman), to challenge the great Minnesota Fats (Jackie Gleason). Overconfident after winning several matches, he loses all his money to his wily competitor and returns to a life of small-time hustling. When he has both thumbs broken in a barroom fight and reaches rock bottom, Eddie agrees to take to the road with ruthless manager and bankroller Bert Gordon (George C. Scott). Despite the vicious nature of the game in which they find themselves, both Eddie and Minnesota Fats exhibit a grace and nobility that sustains the picture's edge. In the end, the aspiring champion defeats Fats but receives a lifetime ban from pool competition. Having won his adversary's respect, he realizes that the victory, like all such battles, ultimately is hollow.

Newman portrayed another hard-bitten character in *Hud* (1963), a film based on *Horseman, Pass By* (1961), a novel by Larry McMurtry. Reared in a cattle-ranching family near Wichita Falls, Texas, McMurtry combined an academic career in literature with fictional explorations of the mythologies of the cowboy West and the traumas of leaving the land. Both the book and film contrasted the amoral and hedonistic lifestyle of the opportunistic Hud (Newman) with his father, Homer (Melvyn Douglas), an old-school rancher who wants his money "to come from something that keeps a man doing for himself." Hud's lack of principle also emerges in an ill-advised pursuit of the family housekeeper (Patricia Neal). In *Cool Hand Luke* (1967), Newman played still another roustabout, in the case a stubborn working-class rebel who refuses to defer to the sadistic guards running a convict labor camp.

Despite the continuing appeal of middle-class suburban family situation comedies like *Leave It to Beaver* (1957–63) and *The Donna Reed Show* (1958–66), western serials were some of the most watched television programs of the 1960s. As Larry McMurtry acknowledged, the Old West held a penetrating grip on the American psyche because it represented an era associated with individualism, one in which ordinary people appeared to play heroic roles. *Gunsmoke* (1955-75) involved a close-knit community of characters in legendary Dodge City. *Bonanza* (1959-73) revolved around a father and three sons who managed a Nevada ranch. *Rawhide* (1959-66) featured Clint Eastwood as a hotheaded but handsome young cowboy on a cattle drive. The unconventional *Maverick* (1957-62) and *Have Gun, Will Travel* (1957-63), in turn, depicted ruddy individualists with introverted dispositions.

Television treatments of the West led to a new series of movie westerns that revitalized the genre. The key figure in these efforts was actor Clint Eastwood. Born in 1930 in San Francisco, Eastwood had spent much of his youth with his father, pumping gas up and down the West Coast. After graduating high school, he held jobs as a logger, steel-furnace stoker, and gas-station attendant. Following four years in the Army Special Services, he arrived in Hollywood in 1954. *Fistful of Dollars* (1964), the first of director Sergio Leone's Italian-made "spaghetti" westerns, starred Eastwood as the "Man with No Name," an amoral mercenary of few words and no discernible past. Arriving in a town beset by a power struggle between two warring families, he sides first with one and then the other before destroying both and riding off in silence. *For a Few Dollars More* (1965) also cast Eastwood as a bounty hunter who teams up with a rival to bring down a psychopathic bandit. In *The Good, Bad, and the Ugly* (1966), Eastwood played one of three drifters whose quest for a hidden fortune is interrupted by the Civil War. Leone also directed Henry Fonda as a cold-blooded killer in *Once Upon a Time in the West* (1969).

TECHNOCRACY'S CHILDREN

Society's marginalized men received their most sympathetic film treatment in John Schlesinger's *Midnight Cowboy* (1969), an Academy Award Best Picture that provided an intimate view of the subculture of hustlers in New York's Times Square. Joe Buck (Jon Voight), a slow-witted but restless Texas dishwasher formerly abandoned by his mother, arrives in New York under the illusion that he can service rich women as a male prostitute. Finding otherwise, he agrees to allow "Ratso" Rizzo (Dustin Hoffman), the son of an illiterate shoe shiner and a seasoned veteran of the streets, to serve as his manager. To his dismay, Buck learns that the only clients who will pay for his favors are men. Nevertheless, he develops a touching friendship with the poverty-stricken Rizzo, who is suffering from tuberculosis. Buck's moral redemption lies in the compassion and love he demonstrates when he takes his dying compatriot on a final bus ride to Miami, the object of the older man's life-long dream of a warm weather haven.

Offbeat movies like *Midnight Cowboy* attracted audiences open to alternative perspectives. The social ferment associated with the Sixties first took form in the political phenomenon known as the New Left. Inspired by the moral vision and empowering doctrines of the struggle for racial justice, a small group of middle-class college activists formed Students for a Democratic Society (SDS) in 1962. Invoking the civil rights movement's notion of participatory democracy, the organization called for a grassroots transformation of society and the ultimate eradication of racism, poverty, militarism, and imperialism. Once President Lyndon B. Johnson expanded U.S. involvement in Vietnam and draft quotas increased in 1965, the self-styled New Left adopted the war as a metaphor of American society's pathological drive for power. Recruiting hundreds of thousands of college students and peace activists, a broad coalition denounced bombing and ground assaults against Vietnamese civilians, organized resistance to the Selective Service system, and used the cry of "Power to the People" to rally support for a complete reconstruction of the economic and social system.

The New Left distinguished itself from radical predecessors by fusing political goals with a profound interest in social values and lifestyle issues. In doing so, its activities overlapped with an emerging cultural revolution built upon the anti-materialist legacy and spiritual quests of the Beats and bohemians. Identifying with democratic principles of individualism and voluntary cooperation, an articulate minority of Sixties youth sought to link utopian social aspirations with a quest for personal freedom. Like the Beats, the rebels parodied mindless conformity and psychic repression and encouraged people to seek direct experience, oneness with nature, and spiritual enlightenment. In contrast to their predecessors, however, advocates of the alternative culture hoped to democratize the dissident lifestyle far beyond the boundaries of bohemia's literary elites.

Insisting that people should forge their own values, the counterculture sought liberation from the family, religion, and society. Mixing ascetic and democratic arguments in the popular treatise *The Making of a Counter Culture* (1969), historian Theodore Roszak contended that youth's liberated lifestyle would free America of its deadening "technocracy." Charles Reich, a Yale law school professor and author of *The Greening of America* (1970), insisted that the new spiritual awakening would generate a revolution in social values and extricate Americans from passive deference to mechanization and social status. In *The Pursuit of Loneliness: American Culture at the Breaking Point* (1970), sociologist Philip Slater called for an assault on the establishment combining political activity with creativity and consciousness raising. As the counterculture gained headway on college campuses, in sectors of the urban economy, and among a growing number of rural communes, hundreds of underground newspapers and publications like the *Whole Earth Catalogue* served millions of readers with practical hints and inspirational messages devoted to the creation of the alternative society.

Word of the emerging lifestyle spread with media coverage of the "hippies" and "flower children" of San Francisco's Haight-Ashbury. Formed out of the street theatrics of the San Francisco Mime Troupe, the anarchist Diggers sought to demonstrate the alternative community's independence from the capitalist market by giving away free food and clothing. "Our fight," the group declared, "is with those who would kill us through dumb work, insane war, dull money morality." The hippie revolution celebrated the creativity, sexual vitality, and compassion of every person. Long hair, costume jewelry, headbands, capes, and unconventional garb therefore symbolized rejection of manageability or moderation. The euphoria, heightened perceptions, and introspection induced by marijuana provided an additional source of solidarity, while the use of hallucinogenic mushrooms and the chemical compound LSD ("acid") led adherents to believe they were in touch with their inner selves. Advising the young to "tune in, turn on, drop out," ex-Harvard psychologist Timothy Leary promoted LSD as a consciousness-expanding tool that allowed everyone to transcend the ruts of ordinary perception.

Many young people first learned about LSD from journalist Tom Wolfe's *Electric Kool-Aid Acid Test* (1968). The book detailed a cross-country tour by author Ken Kesey preceeding the publication of his *Sometimes a Great Notion* (1964), an epic novel about Oregon's anarchic coastal loggers. Recruiting friends from his California drug commune, Kesey outfitted a vintage 1939 bus with tapes of the Grateful Dead rock band, strobe lights, slides, and tabs of still-legal LSD, and asked legendary Beat personality Neal Cassady to act as driver. As Kesey and his "Merry Pranksters" traversed America, they staged a series of free "happenings" or "acid-tests" to advertise the wonders of hallucinogenic drugs and rock music.

In the same year in which *Acid Test* appeared, Carlos Castaneda published *The Teachings of Don Juan: A Yaqui Way of Knowledge* (1968), a first-person account of an anthropology graduate student's dialogues with an elderly Indian medicine man in Sonora, Mexico. Learning about the traditional uses of peyote, jimson weed, and other hallucinogenic plants in opening the doors of perception, the narrator described the "non-ordinary reality" beyond rational empiricism and the secrets to becoming "a man of knowledge."

PURPLE HAZE

Ken Kesey's Merry Pranksters fully anticipated the key role rock music played in the counterculture. Based on an amplified fusion of rhythm and blues and country and western forms, rock began as a frank celebration of physical sexuality and good times. The genre's earliest devotees included the Beach Boys, a southern California band whose innocent vocal harmonies and musical virtuosity fueled a series of early and mid-Sixties "surfing" hits. When the Beatles inaugurated the British Invasion on American television in 1964, they introduced audiences to a spate of tuneful up-tempo melodies in the Buddy Holly and Chuck Berry tradition. The Rolling Stones then added a heavy rhythm and blues emphasis with sexually infused hits like "(I Can't Get No) Satisfaction" (1965) and "Let's Spend the Night Together" (1967). Meanwhile, British bands like the Who, the Kinks, and the Animals reworked blues styling into contemporary electric guitar rock hits that leaped to the top of the pop charts.

Inspired by the Beatles and blues musicians like B.B. King and John Hammond, Jr., Bob Dylan began to experiment with amplification. With backing from the Paul Butterfield Blues Band, Dylan introduced a rock version of "Maggie's Farm" at the 1965 Newport Folk Festival. The performer's declaration of independence from folk music split the crowd: half rose to its feet to dance to the beat, while the other half booed their former idol's departure from "non-commercial" material. Returning alone to the stage for a second set, Dylan sang an acoustic version of "It's All Over Now, Baby Blue" and quickly departed. His next album, *Bringing It All Back Home* (1965), devoted one side to amplified selections and another to acoustic. Yet by now, Dylan had completely lost interest in "protest" music in favor of oblique reflections on urban street life and intensely metaphorical descriptions of social outcasts.

In the Chuck Berry-styled boogie "Subterranean Homesick Blues," Dylan threw out a rapid-fire pastiche of one-liners whose contents came to constitute a part of American popular culture. "You don't need a weatherman to know which way the wind blows," he sputtered. "Twenty years of schoolin' and they put you on the day shift." "Don't follow leaders, watch the parking meters." The "skippin' reels of rhyme" in "Mr. Tambourine Man," in turn, suggested a growing counterculture influence with masked references to alternate states of consciousness and death. The title of Dylan's next album, the completely amplified *Highway 61 Revisited* (1965), paid homage to the historic northern migration of blues from the Mississippi Delta. Beyond its nod to drug culture and altered perceptions, the collection featured the allegorical "Desolation Row," a nightmarish parade of underground caricatures reminiscent of Beat poetics.

"Like a Rolling Stone," *Highway 61's* Top 40 single, used the language of the streets to describe a generation "with no direction home." Along with the Beatles and Stones, Dylan democratized explorations of surrealist absurdity by fusing sardonic wit with traditional musical forms. With backing from Nashville session musicians, *Blonde on Blonde* (1966), the performer's next album, employed archetypes like the tramp, adventurer, and clown to present dense personal odysseys of life on the edge. The collection's masterpieces included "Visions of Johanna," "Stuck Inside of Mobile with the Memphis Blues Again," and "Sad-Eyed Lady of the Lowlands." Meanwhile, electric Haight-Ashbury bands like the Jefferson Airplane, the Grateful Dead, Moby Grape, and Big Brother and the Holding Company forged an identity between rock and drugs with a blues-based "psychedelic" style. The powerful sound of the San Francisco groups merged feedback, distortion, and multiple recording tracks with frank references to intense personal relationships and LSD.

"Feed your head," the Jefferson Airplane sang in "White Rabbit" (1967), a song based on passages from *Alice in Wonderland.* A product of the free hippie "be-ins" and "happenings" at San Francisco's Golden Gate Park, the psychedelic bands bonded with audiences with explorations of alternative consciousness and social commentary. In "Somebody to Love" (1967), the Airplane counseled the importance of human ties amid society's hypocritical untruths. Big Brother's Janis Joplin tied such feelings of emotional vulnerability to the oral traditions of the blues. Born into a middle-class family in Port Arthur, Texas, Joplin grew up on Odetta and Leadbelly records and began performing folk songs and Jimmie Rodgers tunes in Austin and Houston clubs. Settling in San Francisco in 1966, the singer met a group of musicians at a party and formed Big Brother, a band whose first major label album, *Cheap Thrills* (1968), spawned the hit single "Piece of My Heart." Joplin's untrained voice and sudden rise to fame suggested that anyone could become an artist, but her robust mastery of falsetto, call and response, and bent-note blues forms ranked her as one of the genre's great white interpreters.

As evidenced at the Monterey International Pop Festival of 1967, women fans viewed Joplin, one of rock music's few prominent female artists, as a cultural icon. Nevertheless, Jimi Hendrix stole the show. Of African American and American Indian background and the son of an aircraft assembly line operative, Hendrix grew up in a Seattle housing project. After a stint in the Army ended in the early Sixties, he served as a touring backup guitarist for an array of artists, including Little Richard, Ike Turner, Wilson Pickett, Jackie Wilson, and the Isley Brothers. Relocating to England, the musician put together the Jimi Hendrix Experience as an electric rock band with a unique approach. Deeply immersed in the blues, Hendrix used feedback, high volume, and distortion to impart an otherworldly sensuality to guitar virtuosity.

Jimi Hendrix   (*Photofest*)

Hendrix's first album, *Are You Experienced?* (1967), featured the smash single, the psychedelic "Purple Haze," as well as "Hey Joe," a straight-ahead slow blues sustained by a torturous rhythmic buildup. Following his appearance at Monterey, where he climaxed the set by burning his instrument, the performer achieved legendary status as a counterculture hero. As the precursor of the aggressive guitar emphasis of heavy metal, Hendrix helped to shape a musical revolution in which Carlos Santana emerged as an immediate successor. Leading the band Santana, the Mexican American performer merged a metallic sound with tight Latin and jazz rhythms, thereby introducing the psychedelic sound to working-class Hispanics and blacks. Another Hendrix contemporary, Jim Morrison and The Doors, resorted to electric blues in "Soul Kitchen" (1967) but scored their greatest success with the erotic "Light My Fire" (1967).

BATTLE LINES

Late Sixties hard rock co-existed with the genre's absorption of the mellower sounds of folk and country music. At the start of the decade, the smooth arrangements of commercial groups like the Kingston Trio, the New Christy Minstrels, and the Chad Mitchell Trio introduced folk music to a Top 40 audience. Peter, Paul, and Mary's cover of "Blowin' in the Wind" (1963) consolidated the trend. Two years later, The Byrds scored a major hit on the singles charts with an amplified twelve-string guitar version of "Mr. Tambourine Man" (1965). The group then repeated the feat with "Turn! Turn! Turn!" (1965), a song adapted from the Biblical *Ecclesiastes* and set to music by Pete Seeger. "To everything there is a season and a time to every purpose under heaven," the lyric proclaimed, "A time of war, and a time of peace/I swear it's not too late!"

Once The Byrds established the foundations of folk rock, the vocal harmonizing of (Paul) Simon and (Art) Garfunkel dominated the genre for the remainder of the decade. A rock and roll fan from his teen days in Queens, New York, Simon served as lyricist, composer, musician, and backup singer behind the lead vocals of his childhood friend. Some of the duo's records, like the "59th Street Bridge Song (Feelin' Groovy)" (1966), expressed mere playfulness. Yet Simon's feel for the vernacular framed the group's initial Number One hit, "The Sounds of Silence" (1964, 1966). Starting with the haunting "Hello darkness, my old friend," the song built to a powerful apocalyptic climax. "The words of the prophets are written on the subway walls, and tenement halls," the lyric stated. Simon also demonstrated an uncanny ability to capture conversational intimacy in "America" (1968), a quiet piece about a young couple crossing the country by Greyhound. "'Kathy I'm lost,' I said,/Though I knew she was sleeping," the song's protagonist declared, "'I'm empty and aching and I don't know why.'"

Folk rock's use of personal emotion helped to stimulate broader interest in traditional musical forms. Modeled on a country jug band, John Sebastian and the Lovin' Spoonful combined cheery melodic hooks and bouncy songs of romance in best-selling singles like "Do You Believe in Magic?" (1965), "Summer in the City" (1966), and "Nashville Cats" (1966). Old-time harmonies and rags found additional outlets in groups like the Jim Kweskin Jug Band, the Holy Modal Rounders, and the Nitty Gritty Dirt Band. Toward the end of the decade, even the Grateful Dead began to abandon psychedelic rock for an acoustic repertoire of blues, rags, and dance tunes. Bob Dylan also played a major role in the return to fundamentals. Recording again in Nashville after a two-year recuperation from a motorcycle accident, Dylan produced *John Wesley Harding* (1968), an unplugged collection of mystically oriented narratives, and *Nashville Skyline* (1969), a salute to the artist's early love of country and western. "Love is all there is—it makes the world go 'round," Dylan declared in "I Threw It All Away," an acknowledgment of romantic bliss as the spiritual force providing the meaning of life.

For performers of a more ideological bent, love served as a metaphor of collective solidarity and generational empowerment. "C'mon people now/Smile on your brother," the Youngbloods and Jefferson Airplane sang in separate recordings of "Let's Get Together" (1967), "Everybody get together/Try and love one another right now." Amid spiraling racial violence, student ferment, and anti-Vietnam agitation in the mid-to-late Sixties, several folk rock and urban folk artists turned to populist imagery and phrasing to make political statements. The leaders of the trend included socially conscious folksingers like Pete Seeger, Joan Baez, and Phil Ochs, each of whom played permanent roles at antiwar gatherings and demonstrations. "Call it 'Peace' or call it 'Treason,'/Call it 'Love' or call it 'Reason,'" sang Ochs in one of the movement's most empowering pieces, "I Ain't Marching Anymore" (1965).

As draft resistance intensified in college communities, antiwar lyrics assumed a sharper tone. Merging folk melody, jug-band music, and acid rock with a manic overlay of dark humor, Berkeley's Country Joe and the Fish created the ultimate Vietnam-era standard with their recording of the "I-Feel-Like I'm-Fixin'-To-Die Rag" (1967). Group leader Joe McDonald worked the cadence of a circus pitchman into a mock call to rescue Uncle Sam, stuck "in a terrible jam/Way down yonder in Vietnam." "And it's one, two, three,/What are we fighting for?" shouted Country Joe. "Don't ask me, I don't give a damn,/Next stop is Vietnam." "And it's five, six, seven,/Open up the pearly gates,/Well there ain't no time to wonder why/Whoopee! we're all gonna die."

Using the traditional talking blues form and wit associated with his father, Woody, Arlo Guthrie took on the guise of bemused innocence in another antiwar classic, "Alice's Restaurant" (1967). Guthrie began with a rousing chorus about his favorite place to eat, "just a half a mile down the railroad track." In the mode of a tall tale, the song presented an extensive recounting of a free Thanksgiving dinner that resulted in a police citation when the narrator and his friends dump the remains of the meal at a local landfill closed for the holiday. After describing their ultimate day in court and a fine for illegally disposing of refuse, Arlo brings the story around to a summons to Selective

Service headquarters in Lower Manhattan. "Injected, inspected, detected, infested, neglected, and selected," he receives a classification as unfit for Vietnam military service because of a littering record, and finds that murderers, rapists, and vicious criminals are afraid to sit next to him. The point of the song, instructs Guthrie, is to spread the word about resisting the draft. "You can get anything you want," he reminds listeners in the tongue-in-cheek final chorus, "at Alice's Restaurant."

In contrast to the dry humor of Guthrie's tour de force, Stephen Stills' "For What It's Worth" (1967) pointed to the paranoia and violence associated with liberation politics. The piece arose out of a confrontation between Los Angeles police and street people on the Sunset Strip. Recorded by the folk rock band Buffalo Springfield, the song captured the foreboding sense of doom accompanying an encounter with overwhelming power. "There's something happening here," wrote Stills, "What it is ain't exactly clear./There's a man with a gun over there,/Tellin' me I've got to beware." "I think it's time we stop," he continued—"Hey, what's that sound?/Everybody look what's going down." Although the movement ultimately embraced "For What It's Worth" as its own anthem, the song transcended the era's passions. "There's battle lines being drawn," warned Stills, "Nobody's right if everybody's wrong."

Whether intentional or not, the references to random violence in "For What It's Worth" spoke to the everyday experiences of American troops in Vietnam, where the song was a huge favorite. With the dramatic increase in draft calls after 1965 and the enactment of deferments for college students, 80 percent of the U.S. fighting force was comprised of poor or working-class young men. One of the few folk rock artists to acknowledge this reality was John Fogarty. Forming the Creedence Clearwater Revival at his high school in an industrial suburb of Oakland in the early Sixties, Fogarty fused rhythm and blues and rockabilly into something he called "swamp music." In doing so, the band completely rejected counterculture trappings. Instead, its single records targeted A.M. radio audiences, avoided avant-garde pretension, omitted references to drugs, and raised matters of social class and privilege to a central concern.

By decade's end, Creedence Clearwater was the nation's most popular rock group. In 1969 alone, the band scored major hits with "Proud Mary," "Born on the Bayou," "Bad Moon Rising," "Down on the Corner." and "Green River." Each of these songs featured Fogarty's gravely voice in a celebration of American working-class roots and culture. In "Fortunate Son" (1969), the masterful songwriter, vocalist, and musician took on the class basis of the draft. "Some folks are born,/made to wave the flag,/Ooh, they're red, white, and blue," the song began. "And when the band plays 'Hail to the Chief,'/they point the cannon at you." "It ain't me,/it ain't me," protested the chorus, "I ain't no senator's son." "It ain't me,/it ain't me," it repeated, "I ain't no fortunate one." "Some folks inherit/star spangled eyes," another verse proclaimed, "Ooh, they send you down to war,/And when you ask them,/'How much should we give?'/They only answer 'More! More! More!'"

WOODSTOCK NATION

By the time the Sixties ended, rock music had evolved into a billion-dollar industry and the cult of self-liberation had inundated Madison Avenue, where advertisers learned to equate hip consumerism with authenticity and emotional gratification. Just as some elements of the counterculture expressed hostility to the market, pop art practitioners sought to incorporate the materials of ordinary life into painting and printmaking. Beginning in the early Sixties, painter Roy Lichtenstein infused canvases with a mass-produced appearance by using comic strip figures, newspaper print, and patterns of colored dots. In a similar fashion, pop artist Andy Warhol took inspiration from billboards, product labels, and celebrity personalities. Using commonly available media like vinyl, Plexiglas, and neon, Warhol elevated consumer objects to the level of art. The legendary figure built a cottage industry around widely disseminated silkscreen replicas of soup and soda cans and images of Marilyn Monroe, winning praise as an egalitarian commemorator of everyday life and a rebel against the elitist art establishment.

Comic book art also weathered profound changes in the 1960s. After years of formulaic violence, the comics began to move toward more nuanced portraits in 1962, when Marvel combined ordinary and superhero traits in the same characters. *The Amazing Spider-Man* focused on a spectacled orphan and high school student accustomed to rejection, inadequacy, and loneliness. Subjected to a radioactive spider bite while attending a science fair, he takes on the creature's strength, speed, and agility – including the ability to cling to sheer surfaces. Once a burglar murders Spider-Man's uncle, the secret hero decides to use his enhanced powers to serve humanity. Yet his alter ego remains an awkward teenager who is constantly broke and has trouble getting dates. Even when shedding his glasses and taking on a James Dean look, Spider-Man maintains an irreverent, self-deprecating, and introspective sense of humor.

A comparable transformation lay behind the powers of *The Incredible Hulk*, a gentle and bespectacled atomic physicist accidentally exposed to radioactivity during a nuclear bomb test in the New Mexico desert. The effects of contamination turn the mild-mannered scientist into a green-skinned, muscle-bound monster whenever his temper flares. Yet the Hulk only wants people to leave him alone and only engages in battle when attacked by power-hungry villains. The impact of the counterculture changed comic book format more radically toward the end of the decade, when Robert Crumb initiated *Underground Comix*. Presenting a collection of funky characters like "Fritz the Cat" and "Mr. Natural" in a world surrounded by psychedelic drugs, sexual freedom, and radical politics, the irreverent Crumb played a major role in fostering the hippie mystique through his comic book series and frequent appearances in underground newspapers.

Even the conservative medium of television experimented with alternative tastes. Both Rod Serling's *The Twilight Zone* (1959–1964) and Gene Roddenberry's *Star Trek*

(1966–1969) pioneered the use of veiled but imaginative explorations of expanded consciousness and transcendent values. The culture revolution's most explicit TV treatment, however, took the form of the short-lived *Smothers Brothers Comedy Hour* (1967–1969). Working with a playful script by comic writer Steve Martin, the program's short-haired and non-threatening principals Tommy and Dickie courted a youthful audience with controversial references to the Vietnam War, marijuana, and sex. Guest stars ranged from Pete Seeger and Joan Baez to the Jefferson Airplane and The Doors. Nevertheless, the show's departure from consensual-minded entertainment induced network cancellation in 1969.

While commercial television's search for mass audiences discouraged niche programming, Hollywood found it easier to tap the counterculture market. Mike Nichols' *The Graduate* (1967) scored a spectacular box office success with such an approach. Although Benjamin (Dustin Hoffman), the movie's protagonist, is a materially comfortable creature of the suburban middle class, his growing frustration over pious hypocrisy, mindless acquisitiveness, narrow-minded conformity, and social decorum gradually takes on populist overtones. With a soundtrack highlighting Simon and Garfunkel's "Sounds of Silence" and "Mrs. Robinson," *The Graduate* described a young man who regards adulthood as an empty game with rules that make no sense. The film climaxes with a wedding scene reminiscent of *It Happened One Night.* Just as the minister is finalizing the marriage of Benjamin's heartthrob to a pipe-smoking graduate student, the awakened hero rises to the rescue. Swinging a large cross to clear the path to the church door, Benjamin runs off with the bride and hails a city bus. The action ends with a shot of the two silently settled in the rear seat.

A saga of alienation, violence, and sexual desire, Arthur Penn's *Bonnie and Clyde* (1967) brought millions more young viewers to theaters with a glossy color treatment of 1930s bank robbers Bonnie Parker (Faye Dunaway) and Clyde Barrow (Warren Beatty). Penn engineered sympathy for the film's principals by having the couple serve as Robin Hoods to the common folks and displaced families of Depression hobo camps. Pictured as romantic revolutionaries on the run, Bonnie and Clyde come off as witty leaders of a communal family who refuse to succumb to the petty property concerns of small-minded townsfolk and the ruthless treachery of law enforcement officials. To emphasize the free spirit of the graphically rendered violence, Penn used bluegrass musicians Lester Flatt and Earl Scruggs to perform a frenzied version of "Foggy Mountain Breakdown" for the precedent-setting soundtrack.

Another counterculture favorite, *Easy Rider* (1969), featured a script by Texas fiction writer Terry Southern and actors Peter Fonda and Dennis Hopper. The movie described two cocaine dealers, bikers "Captain America" (Fonda) and Billy (Hopper), who hit the open road after scoring a major sale. The succeeding journey to New Orleans produces a cross-country odyssey that includes a Texas ranch, a hippie commune, and a small town jail, where the duo meets a drunken but charming civil rights lawyer

(Jack Nicholson), whom they subsequently turn on to some weed. After dropping LSD with two prostitutes in a Crescent City cemetery, the duo returns to the road. At this point, the emptiness of their search comes home to Captain America. "We blew it," he confides to Billy. Not long after, the two men meet their tragic end on a rural highway.

Easy Rider's pioneering rock soundtrack included Steppenwolf's "The Pusher" (1968) and "Born to Be Wild" (1968), as well as Dylan's "It's Alright Ma." The combination of music and imagery proved so effective that a film version of the Woodstock rock festival, held during August 1969, easily mobilized Hollywood backing. *Woodstock* (1970), an Academy Award-winning documentary that grossed five million dollars in each of its first five months, memorialized the decade's single most important countercultural event. Originally intended for Woodstock, New York, the festival took place on a dairy farm near the Catskills resort of White Lake. As well over three hundred thousand people congregated to form the third largest city in the state, an incredible array of performers graced the stage. Their ranks included Janis Joplin, Arlo Guthrie, John Sebastian, Joan Baez, the Jefferson Airplane, the Grateful Dead, The Band, The Who, Sly and the Family Stone, Richie Havens, Creedence Clearwater, Carlos Santana, Jimi Hendrix, and the recently formed (David) Crosby, (Stephen) Stills, (Graham) Nash, and (Neil) Young (CSNY).

"By the time we got to Woodstock," CSNY recalled in folksinger Joni Mitchell's subsequent salute to the festival, "We were half a million strong/And everywhere there was a song/And celebration." Surviving the challenges of inadequate sanitation, glaring sun, and pervasive mud, the good-natured crowd reveled in the perceived powers of peace and communal solidarity. During a Sunday rainstorm, the entire gathering joined in a spontaneous version of "Let the Sun Shine In," a song featured in *Hair* (1967), a boisterous Broadway rock musical about a tribe of hippies in Central Park. After three days and nights of star-studded performances, the proceedings closed with free-form versions of the "Star Spangled Banner" and "Purple Haze" by Jimi Hendrix.

Promoted as a communal flowering of antiwar sentiment, love, and sharing, Woodstock embodied a vibrant youth culture's attempt to reshape humanity in the name of an entire generation. As ambitious experiments of immense proportions, the counterculture and allied movements for social change would experience profound difficulty in sustaining the idealism surrounding their initial appearance on the American scene. By the end of the Sixties decade, troubling matters of class privilege and moral accountability were beginning to introduce unanticipated questions about the search for an alternative culture by, for, and of the people.

SOURCES AND SUGGESTED READINGS

David Chappell, *A Stone of Hope: Prophetic Religion and the Death of Jim Crow* (2004) contributes valuable perspectives on the early civil rights revolution. Works on folk music's role in the movement include Robert Cantwell, *When We Were Good: The Folk Revival* (1996) and the later segments of R. Serge Denisoff, *Great Day Coming: Folk Music and the American Life* (1971). See also Mark Marquese, *Chimes of Freedom: The Politics of Bob Dylan's Art* (2003) and David Hajdu, *Positively 4th Street: The Lives and Times of Joan Baez, Bob Dylan, Mimi Baez Fariña, and Richard Fariña* (2001).

Hollywood's growing interest in racial themes emerges in the 1960s segments of Donald Bogle, *Toms, Coons, Mulattoes, Mammies, and Bucks: An Interpretive History of Blacks in American Films,* rev. ed. (2002) and Thomas Cripps, *Making Movies Black: The Hollywood Message Movie from World War II to the Civil Rights Era* (1993). Works covering African American literature in the period include James Campbell, *Talking at the Gates: A Life of James Baldwin* (1991); Maria K. Mootry and Gary Smith, eds., *A Life Distilled: Gwendolyn Brooks, Her Poetry and Fiction* (1987); and Judith P. Josephson, *Nikki Giovanni: Poet of the People* (2003). For detective fiction, see James Sallis, *Chester Himes, A Life* (2001). See also the Sixties entries in Henry Louis Gates and Nellie Y. McKay, eds., *The Norton Anthology of African American Literature* (1997).

Background on Black Nationalism appears in Robin D.G. Kelley, *The Black Radical Imagination* (2002) and William L. Van Deburg, *New Day in Babylon: The Black Power Movement and American Culture, 1965–1975* (1992). Studies of Black Nationalist leaders include Michael Eric Dyson, *Making Malcolm: The Myth and Meaning of Malcolm X* (1995) and Kathleen Rout, *Eldridge Cleaver* (1991). See also the essays in Elliott J. Gorn, ed., *Muhammad Ali: The People's Champ* (1995). Woodard Komozi, *A Nation within a Nation: Amiri Baraka (LeRoi Jones) and Black Power Politics* (1999) profiles a key intellectual pioneer of the Black Arts Movement.

Sixties soul music has inspired a number of studies. Overviews include David Guralnick, *Sweet Soul Music: Rhythm and Blues and the Southern Dream of Freedom* (1986); Brian Ward, *Just My Soul Responding: Rhythm and Blues, Black Consciousness, and Race Relations* (1998); and Craig Werner, *A Change Is Gonna Come: Music, Race, and the Soul of America* (1998). The period's dominant black record label receives extended treatment in Gerald Early, *One Nation under a Groove: Motown and American Culture*, rev. ed. (2004) and Suzanne E. Smith, *Dancing in the Street: Motown and the Cultural Politics of Detroit* (1999). Two of soul's top performers inspire biographies in Peter Guralnick, *Dream Boogie: The Triumph of Sam Cooke* (2005) and Michael Eric Dyson, *Mercy Mercy Me: The Art, Loves, and Demons of Marvin Gaye* (2004).

The social background to Chicano awareness in the 1960s emerges in Rodolfo Acuña, *Occupied America: A History of Chicanos*, rev. ed. (2004) and George Mariscal, *Brown-Eyed Children of the Sun: Lessons from the Chicano Movement, 1965–1975* (2005). For Mexican American writing in the period, see Houston A. Baker, Jr., ed., *Three American Literatures: Essays in Chicano, Native American, and Asia-American Literature for Teachers of American Literature* (1982) and the entries in Nicholás Kanellos, *Hispanic Literature of the United States: A Comprehensive Reference* (2003). See also Harry Justin Elam, *Take It to the Streets: The Social Protest Theater of Luis Valdez and Amiri Baraka* (1997). Native American writers like N. Scott Momaday are among those considered in Louis Owens, *Other Destinies: Understanding the American Indian Novel* (1992). See also the entries in Janet Witalec, ed., *Native North American Literature* (1994) and Kathy J. Whitson, *Native American Literatures: An Encyclopedia of Works, Characters, Authors, and Themes* (1999).

Descriptions of Nashville's leading Sixties artists appear in Bill C. Malone, *Country Music, U.S.A.*, 2nd rev. ed. (2002) and Dorothy Horstman, *Sing Your Heart Out, Country Boy*, rev. ed. (1996). See also Mary A. Burwack and Robert K. Oermann, *Finding Her Voice: The Saga of Women in Country Music* (1993). For profile of Patsy Cline and Johnny Cash, see Nicholas Dawidoff, *In the Country of Country: People and Places in American Music* (1997).

For social realism in the period's novels, see Bernard F. Rodgers, Jr., *Philip Roth* (1978); James A. Atlas, *Bellow: A Biography* (2000); and Evelyn Avery, ed., *The Magic Worlds of Bernard Malamud* (2000). Three of the leading comic novelists of the Sixties receive portraits in Robert Merrill, *Joseph Heller* (1987); Stephen L. Tanner, *Ken Kesey* (1983); and Charles D. Peary, *Larry McMurtry* (1977). An analysis of Hollywood's most naturalistic director appears in Ray Carney, *The Films of John Cassavetes: Pragmatism, Modernism, and the Movies* (1994). For the most acclaimed icon of the revitalized motion picture western, see Paul Smith, *Clint Eastwood: A Cultural Production* (1993).

Chapter summaries of Sixties counterculture appear in Maurice Isserman and Michael Kazin, *America Divided: The Civil War of the 1960s* (2000); Douglas T. Miller, *On Our Own: America in the Sixties* (1996); and David Farber, *The Age of Great Dreams: America in the 1960s* (1994). For the role of rock music, see Philip H. Ennis, *The Seventh Stream: The Emergence of Rocknroll in American Popular Music* (1992); David Pichaske, *A Generation in Motion: Popular Music and Culture in the Sixties* (1989); and Herbert London, *Closing the Circle: A Cultural History of the Rock Revolution* (1985). See also Archie Loss, *Pop Dreams: Music, Movies, and the Media in the 1960s* (1999) and David P. Szatunary, *Rockin' in Time: A Social History of Rock-and-Roll*, 2nd ed. (1991.

The best reference work on specific rock performers is Anthony De Curtis, et al, eds., *The Rolling Stone Illustrated History of Rock and Roll: The Definitive History of the Most Important Artists and Their Music*, 3rd ed. (1992). For Janis Joplin and other female performers, see Lucy O'Brien, *She Bop: The Definitive History of Women in Rock, Pop, and Soul* (1996). See also David Reyes and Tom Waldman, *Land of a Thousand Dances: Chicano Rock 'n' Roll from Southern California* (1998). Studies on the decade's most significant rock group include Devin McKinney, *Magic Circles: The*

Beatles in Dream and History (2003) and Jon Weiner, *Come Together: John Lennon in His Time* (1991).

For explorations of counterculture activities beyond rock, see Jay Stevens, *Storming Heaven: LSD and the American Dream* (1987) and Jonah Raskin, *For the Hell of It: The Life and Times of Abbie Hoffman* (1997). For the evolving nature of comic book art figures, see Michael Mallory, *Marvel: The Characters and Their Universe* (2004). For the counterculture and the nation's prime medium, see Amiko Bodroghkozy, *Groove Tube: Sixties Television and the Youth Rebellion* (2001) and Steven D. Stark, *Glued to the Set: The 60 Television Shows and Events That Made Us Who We Are Today* (1997). Advertising's absorption of dissident appeals comprises the main theme of Tom Frank, *The Conquest of Cool: Business Culture, Counterculture, and the Rise of Hip Consumerism* (1997) and Larry Dobrow, *When Advertising Tried Harder: The Sixties, the Golden Age of Advertising* (1984).

11

Blue-Collar America and the
Turbulent Seventies

The social ferment of the 1960s produced new choices for cultural loyalties and opened the door to an unprecedented outpouring of multicultural expression. In the succeeding decade, a vast array of African American, Hispanic, Asian American, and American Indian writers and artists forged independent paths to cultural creativity, while making substantial inroads on popular culture. At the same time, several counterculture singer-songwriters reached for a populist base through the accessible sounds of country rock. Nevertheless, as advocates of social and cultural reconstruction encountered a series of public reverses, American literature, television, film, and country music often focused on urban underdogs and rural outlaws with conservative or apolitical outlooks. Working-class sensibilities also reappeared in southern rock, while in the North, performers like Bob Seger and Bruce Springsteen used their music to depict the poetry of ordinary life.

SHADES OF MEMORY

As African American writers began to move beyond the ideological umbrella of Black Nationalism, several key works focused on the emotional texture of everyday existence. Some of the most significant came in the novels of Toni Morrison. Born Chloe Anthony Wofford in 1931 to a struggling family of former southerners in Lorrain, Ohio, Morrison graduated from Howard University before completing graduate work

Toni Morrison   (*Photofest*)

in literature at Cornell. After a brief academic career, she became a senior editor at Random House. Her immensely successful first book, *The Bluest Eye* (1970), focused on the lives of three young Lorain black girls in the year 1941. Set on neither a plantation or in a ghetto, the story nevertheless embodied the colloquial language and subtle nuances of African American culture. Morrison's next work, *Sula* (1973), described how a friendship between two women survived the refusal of one to defer to community norms. In the critically acclaimed *Song of Solomon* (1977), the novelist drew upon oral and musical traditions to trace the lost history of a family over a century's time. *Tar Baby* (1981), in turn, borrowed from folktale motifs in detailing the chronicle of an ill-fated romance.

The unassuming but powerful style of Maya Angelou's poetry offered additional lessons on the vicissitudes of everyday life. Born Marguerite Annie Johnson in St. Louis in 1928, the poet spent her childhood in rural Arkansas after her parents divorced. As told in her prize-winning autobiography, *I Know Why the Caged Bird Sings* (1970), Angelou became a rape victim at the age of eight at the hand of her mother's boyfriend, whom her uncle then murdered. Traumatized that words had the power to kill, she remained silent for the next five years. After moving with her mother to San Francisco, attending high school, and bearing a child out of wedlock, Angelou became the city's first black streetcar conductor. A nightclub performer in the 1950s, she joined the civil rights movement early in the following decade before becoming a full-time writer. Angelou's first published collection of verse, *Just Give Me a Cool Drink of Wa-*

ter 'fore I Diiie (1971), presented first-person reflections on love and life. *And Still I Rise* (1978), her second book, captured the stance of an assertive woman. "Does my sassiness upset you?" its title poem asked, "'Cause I walk like I've got oil wells/ Pumping in my living room."

"Phenomenal Woman," another piece in Angelou's collection, explored the secrets of personal magnetism by describing "the fire in my eyes, …the flash of my teeth, …the swing in my waist, …the joy in my feet." A similar emphasis on the vitality of African American women characterized *Family Pictures* (1970) and *Aloneness* (1971), two works by veteran poet Gwendolyn Brooks. During the 1970s, Nikki Giovanni also moved away from political material with a focus on the intimate qualities of family life and personal relationships. In *My House* (1972), *The Women and the Men* (1975), and *Cotton Candy on a Rainy Day* (1978), Giovanni strove for a lyrical and rhythmic emphasis previously untapped in her writing. The poet's well-attended public readings seemed to attest to the fact that African American audiences saw her work as a mirror of their own joys, sorrows, and inner strengths.

In verse she described as "womanist," Alice Walker used southern women of color as her main subjects. The daughter of Georgia sharecroppers, Walker attended Spelman and Sarah Lawrence colleges before turning to writing. An admirer of Zora Neale Hurston, she remained fascinated by the artistry of the cooking, gardening, quilting, and storytelling talents of ordinary female family heads. "They were women then," Walker wrote in the appropriately entitled poem "Women" (1970), "My mama's generation/Husky of voice—Stout of/step." Two collections of verse, *Revolutionary Petunias and Other Poems* (1973) and *Good Night Willie Lee, I'll See You in the Morning* (1979), commemorated the resourcefulness of black women. Walker's interest in the personal travails of everyday people resulted in *The Third Life of Grange Copeland* (1970), a novel about a black man's road to emotional maturity. *In Love and Trouble: Stories of Black Women* (1973) included selections like the sketch of a broken and lonely older African American woman who resorts to "root working" (sorcery) to avenge a white Depression relief worker's refusal to relieve her economic distress.

Vernacular African American perspectives played a central role in the work of Ishmael Reed. Born in Chattanooga in 1938, Reed grew up in Buffalo, where he attended university before dropping out to become a civil rights reporter. Moving to New York, he worked as a market researcher, hospital attendant, and unemployment clerk before joining the staff of the alternative *East Village Other.* One of the architects of the Black Arts philosophy, Reed initially came into print as a novelist. His first book, *The Free-Lance Pallbearers* (1967), described life in America's dying cities. A second, *Yellow Back Radio Broke-Down* (1969), took the form of a western parody. Pursuing an interest in oral tradition, Reed published a celebrated collection of poetry in *Conjure* (1972). The volume's signature piece portrayed the legendary African American hero Railroad Bill, a character described as someone who "Could change himself to a tree/…

he could be/ What he wanted to be." Another novel, *The Last Days of Louisiana Red* (1974), mixed images from Greek mythology and pop culture in portraits of contemporary black life.

The fiction of John Edgar Wideman also leaned on oral culture. Raised in Pittsburgh, where his father was a waiter, garbage man, and paperhanger, Wideman graduated from the University of Pennsylvania and became a Rhodes Scholar. His novel *Hurry Home* (1970) told the story of a black janitor and law school graduate who travels to Europe and Africa to merge the two cultures of his heritage. In *The Lynchers* (1973), Wideman focused on a group of Philadelphia ghetto residents who conspire to kill a white police officer in revenge for the taking of thousands of black lives. Like Wideman, Albert Murray used vernacular discourse in *Train Whistle Guitar* (1974), a series of fictional pieces about the Deep South of the 1920s. Adopted by working-class parents, Murray grew up outside Mobile before studying literature at Tuskegee Institute and graduate school. After forging a career as a blues and jazz essayist, he used *Train Whistle* to give life to the stories people traded in barbershops and front rooms. "It was as if you had been born hearing and knowing about trains and train whistles," he wrote, "and the same was also true of saw mills and saw mill whistles."

RHYTHM 'N' ROOTS

Popular music became one of the prime conduits for enhanced African American consciousness. As the conditions of black urban life continued to deteriorate in the 1970s, even a mainstream artist like Marvin Gaye felt called upon to abandon commercial formulas. *What's Going On* (1971), the self-produced original concept album Gaye recorded for Motown, focused on ghetto poverty and rampant drug addiction in the stark "Inner City Blues." Two years later, Stevie Wonder came out with the dark, brooding, and angry "Living for the City" as part of *Innervisions* (1973), another individually conceived Motown product. The song recounted the story of a Mississippi migrant's arrival in New York in search of work. Duped into running drugs by a "brother," he becomes another victim of the brutality of the streets. Offsetting his agonized vocals with the punctuated rhythms of a gospel-infused electric organ, Wonder offered an uncompromising view of ghetto pain and despair that elevated his artistic stature.

Despite excursions into social commentary, black recording artists more often followed the example of M.C., the lead character of Al Young's novel *Snakes* (1970), who relied on his music, not racial or revolutionary ideology, to express his identity. One way of meeting such a goal came through funk, an earthy black dance music resulting from each instrument pursuing a different clipped rhythm with almost no chord changes, detectable melody, or lyrical complexity. The roots of funk and the term itself went back to Fifties jazz artists like Horace Silver and Art Blakely, who based their work on gospel and blues. Early popular music examples included "Funky Broadway"

(1967) by Dyke and the Blazers, James Brown's "Cold Sweat" (1967), and "Express Yourself" (1970), a number by the Watts 103rd Street Band. The hypnotic beat soon worked its way into Sly and the Family Stone's "Thank You (Falettinme Be Mice Elf Again)" (1970) and the album *There's a Riot Going On* (1971). Meanwhile, George Clinton incorporated Hendrix techniques into the sound he labeled "funkadelic," while Kool and the Gang added horns and congas in singles like "Funky Stuff" (1973) and "Higher Plane" (1974).

Even as the hard-driving rhythms of funk achieved musical prominence, soul continued to play an enormous role in black popular culture, possibly because the lyrical romanticism of its more pop-oriented forms appealed to women and upscale listeners. With eight best-selling singles and six highly successful albums, vocalist Al Green became the leading interpreter of African American ballad music in the 1970s. Born on an Arkansas dirt firm, Green moved to Grand Rapids, Michigan, as a child, where he was the lead singer in his family's gospel group. Thrown out of the house for listening to Jackie Wilson records, he gravitated to Memphis and a lucrative recording career. Utilizing a soft, cool, and creamy voice, Green scored smash hits like "Let's Stay Together" (1971) and "I'm Still in Love with You" (1972). At Motown, Stevie Wonder pursued a similar strategy with "Superstition" (1972) and "You Are the Sunshine of My Life" (1973), while Marvin Gaye created an erotic sensation with "Let's Get It On" (1973). Meanwhile, the Philadelphia music scene generated romantic chart-toppers like the Spinners' "I'll Be Around" (1972) and the Ojays' "Love Train" (1973).

The turn to African American consciousness inspired several black film directors to produce movies for and about inner-city folk. Melvin Van Peebles helped to pioneer the genre with *Sweet Sweetback's Baadasssss Song* (1971). An independently produced feature for which Van Peebles served as writer, director, cinema-photographer, and composer, the film concerned a pimp/outlaw who responds in kind to violence from all quarters and triumphs over a corrupt white establishment. A direct reflection of the era's cultural separatism, *Sweetback* identified blackness with ghetto tenements, coded speech mannerisms, and barbed street wit. Gordon Parks, Sr.'s *Shaft* (1971) also romanticized urban life. Accompanied by a popular theme song and soundtrack by soul vocalist Isaac Hayes, the movie focused on a hyper-masculine and fearless black detective who uses a Harlem militant to infiltrate the mob to find the kidnapped daughter of a leading street kingpin. *Superfly* (1972), a film directed by Gordon Parks, Jr., with a Curtis Mayfield score, portrayed the ghetto pavements as a decaying war zone, while celebrating the feats of a cocaine dealer/pimp who prevails over both the grafting police and the Mafia.

In *Silver Streak* (1976), black comic Richard Pryor offered a new take on the mythic African American trickster. Born in 1940 in Peoria, Illinois, Pryor grew up in the brothel owned by his grandmother where his mother worked as a prostitute. After dropping out of school to join the Army, he began appearing in small clubs and bars as a standup comic. Following in the footsteps of Fifties Beat comedian Lenny Bruce, Pryor graduated to Greenwich Village venues and TV talk shows as an ethnic humorist who mirrored the street talk of black pimps, junkies, and winos. In 1972, Pryor played Billie Holiday's pianist in the film *Lady Sings the Blues* and released his first comedy album, *That Nigger Is Crazy*. His performance in *Silver Streak* followed a prize-winning stint as a writer for a Lily Tomlin television special and collaboration on the screenplay for Mel Brooks' *Blazing Saddles* (1974), a parody of the western film genre and race prejudice.

In *Silver Streak,* Pryor played a completely brazen and self-confident petty thief who tries to save a mild-mannered editor (Gene Wilder) from a nefarious murder plot. Trading one-liners with his white co-star, the black comic steals the movie with impeccable timing mastered in years of stand-up performances. For African American audiences, the film's most delicious moment followed the villain's taunting of Pryor's character as an "ignorant nigger," to which the black man responds by whipping out a gun and replying, "You don't know me well enough to call me no nigger." By the Seventies, jokes about white racial stereotypes had become part of mainstream culture and even entered the world of television. *Sanford and Son* (1972–77) starred veteran black comic Redd Foxx as an elderly, penny-pinching, and stubborn Watts junk dealer whose skill at verbal gamesmanship leads him to believe he is outsmarting his grown son and neighborhood friends. Another TV comedy, Norman Lear's *Good Times* (1974–79), depicted the human foibles of a poor black family in Chicago's Cabrini Green housing project who struggle each day to make ends meet.

Although much of black popular culture focused on the urban ghetto, several important works looked to the South. In *Sounder* (1972), a Martin Ritt film with a screenplay by African American writer Lonne Elder III, the setting was Depression-era Louisiana, where an impoverished black family survives by sharecropping, hunting, and taking in wash. The movie featured Cicely Tyson as a woman whose husband receives a year of hard labor for stealing a ham. Desperate to support three children, Tyson must find a way to keep the land going. Meanwhile, the family's eldest son takes to the road with Sounder, the family dog, in an attempt to reunite with his father. Upon returning home, the young boy must decide between accepting an invitation to enroll at a special school for black students or remain on the land and face continuing poverty. By focusing on the strong bonds of an African American family, this critically acclaimed movie countered notions by sociologists like Daniel Patrick Moynihan that slavery had left an irreversible scar on black social structure.

The experience of enslavement provided the topic for two of the major television events of the 1970s. Expropriating a work of fiction by African American writer Ernest Gaines, *The Autobiography of Miss Jane Pittman* (1974) told the story of a 110-year-old ex-slave. With Cicely Tyson in the starring role as the wise and dignified elderly woman, the drama provided a highly accessible narrative of slavery's legacy of economic hardship and racial discrimination. Three years later, network television presented eight consecutive nights of drama based on Alex Haley's Pulitzer Prize-winning and best-selling nonfiction work *Roots: The Saga of an American Family* (1976). A former journalist for *Playboy* magazine and collaborator on Malcolm X's autobiography, Haley incorporated elements of fact, oral tradition, and imagination into a stirring genealogical account of his family's African background and slavery experiences.

Attracting as many as 130 million Americans at a time, the television series relied upon an all-star cast of African American stage and screen actors. The program began by tracing Haley's story to mid-eighteenth century West Africa and the capture of a young man named Kunta Kinte while he searched for wood to make a drum. Beginning with Kinte, members of the transplanted clan relayed the experiences of characters like Miz Kizzy and "Chicken George" and the family's struggle to survive slavery. *Roots* presented a universal tale of people who had lost their home and suffered unimaginable abuse, but had come through the ordeal through hard work and belief in themselves, thereby sustaining the hope of a better life for their children. Once the story described the family's post-emancipation migration to Tennessee, Haley recounted his return to contemporary Gambia, where he listened to villagers recite the tale of the Kinte forebear who had gone to chop wood and disappeared.

HISPANIC CADENCES

By conveying the African American historical experience from a distinctly black perspective, *Roots* provided a model of collective self-esteem for all ethnic groups. As Chicano Studies Programs began to spread through southwestern universities in the Seventies, a flourishing Mexican American literature explored the life of poor immigrants and other marginal figures. Tomás Rivera's novel *And the Earth Did Not Part* (1971) presented a series of sketches about migrant farm workers in south Texas in the 1950s. Employing the barrio's folkloric style of vernacular Spanish, Rivera's sparse proletarian narration offered multidimensional portraits of characters who demonstrated both vitality and fatalism amid hardship and disappointment. The book's strength lay in the author's skill at balancing elements of vulgarity, treachery, and cruelty with the enduring capacities of ordinary people and their determination to achieve human dignity.

In *Sketches of the Valley and Other Works* (1973) and *Generations and Biographies* (1977), Rolando Hinojosa viewed the common people of south Texas as the guardians of Chicano culture. The characters Hinojosa wrote about, he explained, "go to the toilet, they sneeze and blow their noses, they raise families, know how to die with one eye on guard, and they yield with difficulty like most green wood and thus do not crack easily." Bearing one's burden in daily work, he wrote, "doesn't mean that one is a blind fool unaware of what's really going on." Realistic accounts of poverty also pervaded Ricardo Sánchez's bilingual verse in the autobiographical *I Sing and Shout for My Lib-*

eration (1973), the first Chicano poetry released by a mainstream commercial publisher. Born the youngest of thirteen children in the El Paso barrio in 1941, Sánchez was a high school dropout who enlisted in the Army and spent several years in California and Texas prisons before winning parole in 1969. Another El Paso native, Estela Portillo Trambley, the author of the short story collection *Rain of Scorpions and Other Writing* (1975), focused on the liberation of the human spirit and women's autonomy.

Rudolfo A. Anaya's *Bless Me, Ultima* (1972), a best-selling novel written in English, explicitly tied Chicano identity to Spanish and Indian folkloric traditions. Anaya had been born in a rural New Mexico village, where he learned the old ways of Hispanic farming and ranching, a subject that continued to fascinate him as he entered academic life. His book concerned a young boy in post-World War II New Mexico who vacillates between the wanderlust of his rancher father and the traditional ties to the land embodied in the farming heritage of his mother. Placed with the folk healer Ultima, he learns of the people's experiences, customs, and values, with particular emphasis on the mystical legends and folk wisdom of the past. The protagonist then uses these cultural traditions as the basis for pursuing his own identity.

The central role of ethnicity in Hispanic literature appeared most decidedly in *The Elements of San Joaquin* (1977) and *The Tale of Sunlight* (1978), two poetry collections by Gary Soto. Tracing Chicano life from central Mexico to the inland California valleys, the first volume vacillated between warm reminiscences of a Fresno childhood and portraits of squalor, violence, loneliness, degradation, and hopelessness among poor farm workers. In *Sunlight*, the author continued to produce compassionate but unsentimental depictions of impoverished people, yet held out hope that the powers of the imagination were capable of conquering adversity. To emphasize the Mexican origins of the Chicano cultural heritage, Soto detailed a personal odyssey to his ancestral home near Taxco.

Literary interest in Chicano roots coincided with a popular dance music form known as La Onda Chicana, a hybrid of ranchero, folk, and swing jazz styling. The undisputed champion of the genre was Little Joe Hernández, the bandleader whose record "The Clouds" (1972) took on anthem status. Born into rural Texas poverty, Hernández began picking cotton at age seven and formed a ranchero group when he was fourteen. After initial success in performing Top 40 tunes and ranchero standards, he changed the band's name in 1970 to the Spanish equivalent of Little Joe and the Family and began to affect the long hair, hippie clothing, sandals, turquoise jewelry, and overt militancy associated with the Chicano movement. By assuming a counterculture image, Hernández joined Mexican American rock bands like Cannibal and the Headhunters, the Mysterians, and Thee Midniters in celebrations of indigenous culture. As Little Joe and other artists repackaged ranchero dance numbers as working-class music and reflections of ethnic pride, the band dedicated its 1972 album to "the people."

A proletarian identity likewise underscored "Nuyorican" culture. Influenced by the hard-driving rhythms of salsa, a Cuban-based dance music sweeping the Caribbean community, "outlaw" New York Puerto Rican folk poets like Victor Hernández Cruz, Tato Laviera, Sandra Maria Esteves, and Pedro Pietro conducted readings of unapologetically working-class, unschooled, and unpolished verse. While many Nuroyican poets appeared as alienated revolutionaries, others, like Nicholasa Mohr, preferred to explore the hidden side of urban life. Mohr's *Nilda* (1973), the first work by a Hispanic woman printed by a major publisher in modern times, presented the story of a young Puerto Rican girl's coming of age in World War II Spanish Harlem. Two other collections of her verse, *El Bronx Remembered* (1975) and *In Nueva York* (1977), revealed the ability of residents of the Puerto Rican neighborhoods to survive and produce art, folklore, and strong families.

The most prominent Nuyorican dramatist was Miguel Piñero. Born in Puerto Rico in 1946, Piñero grew up on the Lower East Side. When his father abandoned the family, he and his siblings survived on the street. A gang leader and high school dropout, Piñero wound up doing time in Sing Sing for armed robbery. *Short Eyes* (1975), his award-winning Broadway play adapted for the screen two years later, presented a starkly realistic portrait of the brutal fate awaiting a child molester in a men's prison. A spokesperson for Puerto Rican writers, Piñero co-edited the inaugural anthology of Nuyorican literature in 1975 and went on to produce scripts for television crime shows like *Barreta*, *Kojak*, and *Miami Vice*.

ASIAMERICAN GHOSTS, NATIVE AMERICAN SPIRITS

The publication of *Aiiieeeee! An Anthology of Asian American Writers* (1974) demonstrated how the ethnic revivals of the late Sixties inspired literary artists of Asian background to claim their place within American letters. When Asian American authors gathered in a conference in Oakland in 1975, however, they acknowledged the dual nature of their task. Although seeking to overcome a long-standing history of conservative ethnic prejudice, participants also insisted on responding to progressive stereotypes of Asians as backward and traditional people lacking self-esteem. Frank Chin, a fifth-generation Chinese American, already had countered caricatures of Asian men as docile and emasculated in *The Chickencoop Chinaman* (1972), the first Asian American play ever performed on the New York stage. A second work, *Year of the Dragon* (1974), found its way to public television a year after a theatrical opening.

The most significant Chinese American literary figure of the Seventies was Maxine Hong Kingston, author of the best-selling *The Woman Warrior: Memoirs of a Childhood Among Ghosts* (1976). Born Maxine Ting Ting Hong, Kingston grew up in Stockton, California, where her family ran a laundry. Fascinated by her mother's "talk-stories," she began writing at age nine and wound up with a literature degree at Berkeley. The recipient of a National Book Critics Circle award for nonfiction, *The Woman Warrior* merged elements of biography, fantasy, and storytelling through the accounts of five women, including a fictional first-person narrator. Kingston placed these tales in historical settings dating back to the 1930s. Yet the book's central figure was the ghost of Fa Mu Lan, the mythical Chinese guardian who warns that the female warrior must protect herself from those who would pierce her spirit, and must fight to preserve self-esteem. Through these stories, Kingston reconciled the past and the present, tradition and modern society, and mothers and daughters. A subsequent work, *China Men* (1980), brought similar understanding to the inner world of immigrant Chinese male laborers.

Japanese American writers continued to reflect on the traumas of World War II. Lawson Inada's *Before the War: Poems As They Happened* (1971), the first collection of verse published by a U.S.-born author of Japanese background, described the internment experience from the perspective of a third-generation American whose family had been relocated from Fresno to Arkansas and Colorado. Yoshiko Uchida, a second-generation Japanese American, adopted a child's voice in *Journey to Topaz* (1971) to convey the strengths of kinship in the face of discrimination and adversity. In a memorable passage, Uchida's young protagonist recalled how his mother's sense of pride prompted her to clean house the day before the family left for internment in Utah. Once in camp, a traditional code of honor and mutual concern governed people's lives. In *Journey Home* (1978), Uchida tied the inner fortitude and hope he saw in Japanese culture to the theme of postwar reconciliation. Richard Kim, a Korean immigrant who became an American academic figure, provided another first-person childhood narrative of wartime in *Lost Names* (1970), the tale of a family's ordeal under the Japanese occupation of Korea.

Some of the richest expressions of diversity emerged from Native Americans. Influenced by public displays of Black Power and Chicano consciousness, Indian activists began to organize cultural centers and university studies programs to advance autonomous notions of peoplehood and to revive historic traditions of worship, dance, healing, and poetry. For eighteen months between 1969 and 1970, the American Indian Movement (AIM) occupied San Francisco Bay's former Alcatraz prison to demand that the federal government build an Indian cultural facility on the site. Subsequent AIM activities included a takeover of Washington, D.C.'s Bureau of Indian Affairs and an occupation of tribal headquarters at Wounded Knee, South Dakota. Meanwhile, *Black Elk Speaks*, the reminiscences of an Oglala Sioux holy man first published in the 1930s, emerged in a new paperback edition in 1972.

Poet Leslie Marmon Silko ranked as one of the leading figures of the Native American cultural renaissance. Of mixed white, Hispanic, and Indian background, Silko grew up on a New Mexico Laguna Pueblo reservation, where she absorbed tribal legends and traditions from her extended family. After graduating from the University of Mexico in 1969, she incorporated the stories she had learned into *Laguna Woman* (1974), a collection of poetic meditations on the natural landscape. Her first novel, *Cer-*

emony (1977), combined free verse and narrative prose. The book told the story of a World War II veteran of mixed ethnicity who returns to the Southwest. Alienated from the linear world of rational science and embittered by the European conquest of his native land, he nevertheless struggles to come to terms with his Indian roots. Although the protagonist finds a guide to wholeness in the mystical, mythical, and spiritual stories that unite the past with the present and people with the land, he realizes that traditional ways of seeing require adjustments to new circumstances. In the end, Silko's seeker chooses to purge his psyche of mental disease by visualizing the unity of humankind.

The interaction of Native American and white cultures also fascinated poet James Welch, a member of Montana's Blackfeet/Gross Ventre people and a graduate of reservation schools. After obtaining an English degree from the University of Minnesota, Welch worked as a laborer, forest service employee, firefighter, youth counselor, and visiting professor. His first volume of poetry, *Riding the Earthboy 40* (1971), focused on reservation life. Welch's interest in the novel form resulted in *Winter in the Blood* (1974), the story of an unnamed and dispossessed protagonist who discovers the history of his grandparents and reclaims his ancestral past. Set in the wastelands of northern Montana, the book employs an understated narrative to convey the interplay of comedy and tragedy in a world in which people often are foolish. "I was as distant from myself as a hawk from the moon," the protagonist reveals. The narrator's mother tells her son that his dead father "was a wanderer—just like you, just like all these damned Indians." As in *The Death of Jim Coney* (1979), however, Welch saw the reservation as the only place where a person could retrieve a sense of identity and break free from alienation.

The search for alternative values provided a major theme of the work of Simon Ortiz, one of the most widely read Indian poets of the 1970s. Born in New Mexico's Acoma Pueblo in 1941, Ortiz worked in uranium mines and processing plants and served in Vietnam before entering academic life as a literature and creative writing professor. The collection of verse in *Going for the Rain* (1976) used the persona of Coyote, a traditional southwestern Indian trickster and cultural hero, to express reverence for the natural world and to convey the idea that people must respect their relationship to the land and to each other if they are to survive. Tribal traditions and alternative modes of perception also characterized Ortiz's work in *A Good Journey* (1977), while *From Sand Creek: Rising in This Heart Which Is America* (1981) offered the author's vision of all the nation could have been.

Several Native American poets echoed the spiritual quests of Silko, Welch, and Ortiz. In *indian thoughts: the children of god* (1975), part-Cherokee writer Norman Russell invoked ancestral spirits to celebrate the natural world. J. Ivaloo Volborth, a young urban woman of Apache/Comanche descent, celebrated the magical components of a rediscovered native heritage in *Thunder-Root* (1978). The most explicit reference to Indian ghetto life came through the poetry of Barney Bush, a member of the Shawnee-Cayuga nation, a people whose homeland stretched from southern Illinois across Oklahoma to New Mexico. In the verse of *My House and a Jukebox* (1979), Bush presented a first-person blues set in city bars and streets. Writing of broken lives, he described "the grey mystery" of people glancing at each other "over pool tables/and jukeboxes." Yet even in such bleak surroundings, Bush implied, the most important survival tool of Indian consciousness was tribal humor.

BRIDGING THE WATERS

When folksinger John Denver recorded standards like "Take Me Home, Country Roads" (1971), "Back Home Again" (1974), and "Thank God I'm a Country Boy" (1975), he demonstrated a tendency among counterculture artists to return to traditional sources. The retreat from confrontational stances partly resulted from the traumas of the late Sixties and early Seventies. As the Johnson administration held the line in Vietnam, an offshoot of Students for a Democratic Society (SDS) emerged in the Weather Underground, a group that sought to inspire white working-class youth to revolution through largely symbolic bombings against government, military, and police facilities. Other activists joined Abbie Hoffman and Jerry Rubin's YIPPIES (Youth International Party), in antiwar demonstrations at the 1968 Democratic National Convention in Chicago that attempted to fuse counterculture values with radical politics. Yet the only rock group to show up for the protests was John Sinclair's MC5 (Motor City 5), a working-class Detroit garage band whose debut album, *Kick Out the Jams* (1969), merged Hendrix-style rapid-fire blues with radical punk political anthems but experienced little commercial success.

When the Chicago "Festival of Life" turned into a massive police riot and helped to elect Republican president Richard Nixon, the new administration prosecuted Hoffman, Rubin, Bobby Seale, and five other protest leaders in a five-month conspiracy trial the following year. With testimony from alternative culture celebrities like Allen Ginsberg, Phil Ochs, Arlo Guthrie, Country Joe, Timothy Leary, Norman Mailer, folksinger Judy Collins, and others, the defendants vainly sought to win public sympathy for the antiwar movement and counterculture. Yet violent incidents between street people and local authorities in communities surrounding the University of California at Berkeley and Santa Barbara during 1969 further tested public patience with dissident youth. The following year, a deadly confrontation erupted at Kent State University when Ohio National Guardsmen opened fire in the wake of a small campus protest against the expansion of the Vietnam War into Cambodia, wounding nine and killing four people. In response, student strikes closed down four hundred American colleges and universities.

Lyrics on the Jefferson Airplane's *Volunteers* (1969) album captured the mood of radical college students with calls for political revolution. Following Kent State, Crosby, Stills, Nash, and Young incorporated "Ohio," a tribute to the fallen young protesters, in *Déjà Vu* (1970), the group's second anthology. Yet the traditional portrait on the album's sepia-toned cover and the assortment of countrified tunes and harmonies suggested a turn away from ideological commitments. Such a stance had roots in counter-culture decline. By the late Sixties, the Haight had deteriorated into an unsanitary and dangerous haven for runaways, heroin addicts, narcotic agents, petty thieves, and psychopaths. In 1969, a former "love generation" family headed by ex-convict Charles Manson staged the cold-blooded murder of seven people in the Hollywood Hills, including the pregnant film star Sharon Tate, as part of an LSD-induced fantasy to ignite a race war. Later that year, a free Rolling Stones concert at the Altamont Racetrack near Oakland degenerated into an orgy of violence when the beer-drinking Hells Angels security force viciously attacked members of the crowd of three hundred thousand, killing an African American man.

By the end of 1970, both Janis Joplin and Jimi Hendrix had overdosed on drugs, the Beatles had broken up, Paul Simon had gone solo, and Bob Dylan had released the mellow *New Morning* (1970). In the same year, the Grateful Dead incorporated bluesy numbers like "Uncle John's Band," "Casey Jones," and "Truckin'" into *Workingman's Dead* (1970) and *American Beauty* (1970), the two acoustic albums with which the band would forever be linked. The reversion to traditional melodies and themes owed much to the work of The Band, a collection of musicians who had mastered intricate ensemble techniques while playing with Bob Dylan. After releasing *Music from Big Pink* (1968), named after the house that served as their studio near Woodstock, the group went to Los Angeles to record *The Band* (1969), an album whose cover pictured the performers as somber Old West outlaws.

Mixing country harmonies, nineteenth-century parlor songs, and military ballads with lyrical snippets reminiscent of Walt Whitman and Carl Sandburg, the compositions of guitarist J. Robbie Robertson offered mythological portraits and images of frontier life and rural America. In "The Weight" (1968), a bouncy tune sustained by a descending bass, Robertson blended vague Biblical allusions with archaic references to vagabonds and drifters. "Up on Cripple Creek" (1969) described a roustabout's euphoria over a backcountry woman's generosity—"a drunkard's dream if I ever did see one." The Band's masterpiece was "The Night They Drove Old Dixie Down" (1969), a melodious account of the surrender of the South through the eyes of a Tennessee man whose younger brother has been lost to the war. "Virgil Caine is the name," the narrator begins, "And I served on the Danville train/'Til Stoneman's Cavalry came/And tore up the tracks again." "In the winter of sixty-five, we were hungry, just barely alive/By May the tenth, Richmond had fell; it's a time—I remember, oh, so well."

Seattle songwriter Steve Goodman pursued a similar strand of collective memory in the nostalgic "City of New Orleans" (1970), a song about the flagship train of the old Illinois Central Railroad popularized by Arlo Guthrie. "Good mornin', America, how are you?" Guthrie sang, "Say doncha know me, I'm your native son/I'm the train they call the 'City of New Orleans'/I'll be gone five hundred miles when the day is done." As the narrative lingers on the houses, farms, fields, and graveyards of the legendary run out of Chicago, old men in the club car pass around a bottle in a paper bag while playing penny-ante cards without keeping score. In the near-deserted coach, mothers rock their babies to sleep—"the rhythm of the rails is all they feel." In Goodman's lyric, "the sons of Pullman porters" and "the sons of engineers" ride "their fathers' magic carpet made of steel." Yet once they change cars a last time in Memphis and head down the Mississippi, the mood darkens. As the piece ends, "The conductor sings his song again, 'The passengers will please refrain—this train's got the disappearing railroad blues.'"

The relaxed country blues of singer-songwriter James Taylor provided another excursion into traditional Americana. Laced with pedal steel backing and Taylor's lead guitar, laid-back selections like "Carolina in My Mind" (1970) and "Country Road" (1970) spoke to counterculture interest in rural communes, but also suggested an affinity with the customary life of the countryside. "There is a young cowboy who lives on the range," began the lyric to the title song of *Sweet Baby James* (1970), "he works in the saddle and he sleeps in the canyon … he sits by his fire, thinking of women and glasses of beer." Once the chorus takes up the cowhand's salute to "moonlight ladies," a second verse turns the lyric toward all of life's lonely travelers. "There's a song that they sing when they take to the highway," warbles Taylor, "a song that they sing when they take to the sea, a song that they sing of their home in the sky, maybe you can believe it if it helps you to sleep, the singin' works just fine for me."

THE HEART OF SATURDAY NIGHT

James Taylor's version of "You've Got a Friend" (1971), an inspirational hit by singer-songwriter Carole King, provided the perfect fusion of folk music and gospel, a combination that also marked soulful hymns like Paul Simon's "Bridge Over Troubled Water" (1970) and Jackson Browne's "Rock Me on the Water" (1971). Yet several folk-oriented artists of the early Seventies sought an edgier quality. "God is a concept by which we measure our pain," former Beatle John Lennon sang in a solo album in 1970. Another Lennon cut, "Working-Class Hero," mocked those who lived under the illusion that they were "classless and free." In "The Boxer" (1972), Paul Simon provided a stark metaphor of the urban jungle. "I am just a poor boy/Though my story's seldom told," the song began. "When I left my home/And my family,/I was no more than a boy/In the company of strangers … Seeking out the poorer quarters/Where the ragged people go." After a melodic chorus, "The Boxer" returned to the fallen warrior and the reminders of "ev'ry glove that laid him down." "The fighter still remains," Simon concluded.

The human costs of day-to-day survival played a huge role in the work of folk-oriented singer-songwriters. Harry Chapin's "Taxi" (1972) spotlighted a San Francisco cabbie whose late-night fare turns out to be a former girlfriend now on to better things. Trying to maintain his dignity while realizing his youthful dreams are all but over, he is tempted to rebuff her patronizing offer to "keep the change" when she hands him twenty dollars for a $2.50 ride. "Well, another man might have been angry," he confesses, "And another man might have been hurt,/But another man never would have let her go … I stashed the bill in my shirt."

The songs of Chicago folk music performer John Prine offered painfully realistic explorations of the inner emotions of believable and easily recognizable characters. In "Far From Me," a cut on Prine's self-titled 1971 debut album, the singer portrayed the awkward boyfriend of a small-town waitress who knows she is about to dump him. "Ain't it funny," he sings, "how an old broken bottle looks just like a diamond ring." "Hello in There" described the pathos of an elderly couple who lost a son in the Korea War, have another "somewhere on the road," and two more children living in Omaha. "Me and Loretta, we don't talk much more," explains the narrator, "She sits and stares through the back door screen/And all the news just repeats itself/Like some forgotten dream." In the chilling "Sam Stone," Prine sang about a wounded Vietnam vet addicted to morphine. "There's a hole in Daddy's arm/Where all the money goes," the lyric to the startling chorus rings out, "Jesus Christ died for nothing/I suppose … Sweet songs never last too long/On broken radios."

John Prine's signature work was "Angel from Montgomery" (1971), a remembrance of an eternity of dreams and illusions that "just flow by/Like a broken-down dam." "I am an old woman/Named after my mother," the narrative begins, "My old man is another/Child that's grown old." "When I was a young girl," she recalls, "Well I had me a cowboy/He weren't much to look at/Just a free rambling man." "There's flies in the kitchen/I can hear 'em there buzzin'," sings the storyteller, "And I ain't done nothing/Since I woke up today." "How the hell can a person/Go to work in the morning/And come home in the evening/And have nothing to say." "Just give me one thing/That I can hold on to," pleads the chorus, "To believe in this living is just a hard way to go."

Vocal artist Bonnie Raitt popularized "Angel from Montgomery" in an album recorded in 1974. The daughter of musical comedy star John Raitt, she began as a blues artist who learned bottleneck guitar techniques from musicians like John Hurt, John Lee Hooker, and John Hammond, Jr. After working her way into Boston area folk circles, Raitt released a self-titled debut album in 1971 that paid homage to legendary blues woman Sippie Wallace's "Mighty Tight Woman" and "Women Be Wise." Yet it was not until she recorded Randy Newman's "Guilty" (1973) that the singer reached her full potential. Raised in a family of Hollywood film composers, Newman specialized in orchestrations of simple melodies derived from sources as varied as Stephen Foster ballads and rhythm and blues. His piano-led accompaniments complemented dramatic monologues of everyday American characters and rogues often rendered with a New Orleans drawl and a twist of irony.

The sardonic title song of Newman's *Sail Away* (1972) album offered a sea captain's mock invitation to a group of black Africans to ship out to the New World as slaves. "In America you'll get food to eat," it promised, "won't have to run through the jungle and scuff up your feet./You'll just sing about Jesus and drink wine all day; it's great to be an American." In "Old Man," Newman confronted conventional pieties about the end of life. "Don't cry, old man, don't cry," he sang, "ev'rybody dies." The performer's comic irony reached its full potential in "God's Song." "'I burn down your cities; how blind you must be,'" declares the Deity, "'I take from you your children, and you say "how blessed are we."/You all must be crazy to put your faith in me./That's why I love mankind.'"

Newman filled his next album, *Good Old Boys* (1974), with first-person recitations from a variety of lunatics, boors, alcoholics, and yahoos. Blurring the line between empathy and parody, he gave voice to the inner world of the most disreputable outcasts. In the defiant "Rednecks," an Atlanta native mocks elite condescension toward racist governor Lester Maddox, proudly proclaiming that "We talk real funny down here./We drink too much and we laugh too loud./We're too dumb to make it in no Northern town." "We're rednecks, we're rednecks," the taunting chorus declares, "and we don't know our ass from a hole in the ground." Not content to rest the lyric with such caricature, however, Newman reverses the drift in the final verse. Conceding that southerners are "too ignorant" to realize that the North has given the Negro "his dignity" and set him free, the narrator bursts into a sarcastic litany. "Yes, he's free to be put in a cage in Harlem in New York City," he sings. "And he's free to be put in a cage on the South Side of Chicago … /And he's free to be put in a cage in Hough in Cleveland/ … in East St. Louis/ … in Fillmore in San Francisco/ … in Roxbury in Boston."

"Kingfish" provided another entry into the populist psyche. Assuming the persona of former Louisiana governor Huey Long, Newman declares that he is a "friend of the working man," that the state's "gonna be run by little folks like me and you." In "Louisiana 1927," a poor farmer's account of the great Mississippi Flood, President Coolidge appears and asks if it "isn't … a shame—what the river has done to this poor cracker's land." The characterizations of *Good Old Boys* included a steelmill roller in "Birmingham" and a recession victim in "Mr. President (Have Pity on the Working Man)." Its most powerful pieces, however, described the depths of imperfect love. "I'm drunk right now, baby," a character confesses in the lilting waltz "Marie," "but I've got to be, or I never could tell you what you mean to me." "Sometimes I'm crazy," he sings, "but I guess you know, and I'm weak and I'm lazy and I've hurt you so." Similarly, the singer in "Guilty" wonders why "I never do what I'm supposed to do; how come nothin' that I try to do ever turns out right?" "You know I just can't stand myself," the song concludes, "it takes a whole lot of medicine for me to pretend that I'm somebody else."

Although Los Angeles-based songwriter Joni Mitchell normally produced sensitive lyrics of a confessional bent, "Raised on Robbery," a breezy boogie in her *Court and Spark* album (1974), broke the mold with an impersonation of a prostitute's come-on in a hotel lobby. "Hey honey," Mitchell's lady sings, "you've got lots of cash/Bring us a bottle/And we'll have some laughs." "I'm a pretty good cook," she boasts, "Come up to my kitchen/I'll show you my best recipe/ ... I'm rough but I'm pleasin'/I was raised on robbery." Glitzy Los Angeles offered further explorations of the low life through folk-jazz vocalists Rickie Lee Jones and Tom Waits. In his debut album *Closing Time* (1973), Waits combined a New Orleans drawl with a character resembling Charles Bukowski, a self-styled L.A. Beat street poet with a cult following. Three subsequent records, *The Heart of Saturday Night* (1974), *Nighthawks at the Diner* (1975), and *Small Change* (1976), worked sentimental verse and melodies into crusty odes to late-night diners, lounge drinkers, derelicts, and truckers. Meanwhile, L.A. vocalist Linda Ronstadt immortalized rocker Lowell George's tribute to long-haul drivers in "Willing" (1974).

ONE DAY AT A TIME

When CBS inaugurated television's *Mary Tyler Moore Show* (1970–77), the network broke precedent by constructing an entire series around the daily life of an unattached young woman with a promising professional career. The program's innovative approach rested on the early impact of the feminist movement, a significant development among affluent post-World War II baby boomers. As the number of women in the U.S. work force doubled between 1940 and 1960, demands for a woman's rights agenda entered the political arena. The Civil Rights Act of 1964 formally put an end to gender-related job discrimination. Yet poor enforcement led activist Betty Friedan to organize the National Organization of Women (NOW) two years later. Friedan's *The Feminine Mystique* (1963) argued that middle-class women lacked an autonomous sense of identity, and that domestic obligations placed wives in dependent and infantile relationships. By the late Sixties, radical feminists had emerged from the civil rights movement and New Left to envision a class conflict with a male power structure. Capitalism, they insisted, had an intrinsic interest in commodifying women through advertising and the media.

As the call for women's rights gained ground within the white middle class, activists organized consciousness-raising sessions, created women's health clinics, campaigned for abortion rights, and lobbied for an Equal Rights amendment to the Constitution. In the realm of cultural expression, several feminist artists sought to dramatize women's inclusion in the human community. East Harlem painter Alice Neel, for example, used the nude portrait *Margaret Evans Pregnant* (1978) to celebrate the ever-changing female body. A more ambitious statement appeared in Judy (Cohen) Chicago's massive installation *The Dinner Party* (1974–79). Creating place settings at a triangular table more than forty-six feet long on each side, Chicago used the traditional female crafts of painted porcelain and needlework to commemorate thirty-nine women figures from history and mythology. While the plates contained different versions of the ancient symbol of rebirth—a composite vagina/butterfly—the artist worked with some two hundred colleagues in adorning thousands of adjoining tiles with the names of 999 significant women cultural figures throughout recorded time.

The inclusive dimensions of feminist consciousness converged on Broadway with Ntozake Shange's *for colored girls who have considered suicide/when the rainbow is enuf* (1976–77). Born Paulette Williams in 1948 to an African American professional couple in Trenton, New Jersey, Shange assumed a Zulu name while completing her education and launching a career as a dramatist and academic. Her "choreopoem" originated in a series of witty poetry recitations in cafés and bars. Once on stage, the production added music, dance, and lighting to dramatize the stories of seven black women dressed in the hues of the rainbow and the color brown. Shange's highly praised work emphasized the lack of communication between men and women and the pain of unrequited love. Yet it also held out the possibilities of sisterly solidarity and collective self-esteem. A similar theme of empowerment characterized Bob Fosse's musical *A Chorus Line* (1975), in which an assortment of male and female Italian, Jewish, Irish, Hispanic, Chinese, black, and gay dancers from all regions of the country unveiled their personal identities and secrets while auditioning for a musical comedy.

One of the first Hollywood movies to honor a feminist perspective was Martin Scorsese's *Alice Doesn't Live Here Anymore* (1975). The film starred Ellen Burstyn in an Academy Award-winning role as a thirty-five-year-old New Mexico woman whose truck driver husband dies in an accident, leaving his wife and eleven-year-old son penniless. Hoping to find a job as a singer in California, Alice winds up in a sleazy club in Phoenix. When she gets tired of fighting off predatory men, she takes to the road again with her son, only to have the car break down near Tucson. Finding work as a waitress at Mel's Diner, Alice meets a divorced rancher (Kris Kristofferson), who gradually demonstrates his ability to offer love while respecting her personhood and independence.

Scorsese's film made its way to television through *Alice* (1976–85), the popular weekly situation comedy devoted to the title character's daily grind at the café. The show's focus on the life of a woman who worked outside the home complemented the comic *One Day at a Time* (1975–84), a series whose early episodes revolved around a divorcé's struggles in raising two daughters in a cramped Indianapolis apartment amid the pressure of bills, work-place sexism, and unreliable child support. Still another feature, *Laverne and Shirley* (1976–83), earned a huge working-class following with the unpredictable antics of two "spunky" and "sassy" roommates with little tolerance for elitism or class snobbery. These female characters shared qualities with "Eunice," the beleaguered blue-collar wife who played a featured role in the sketches of *The Carol Burnett Show* (1967–79). Bickering with her loser husband and vicious mother over everything from Jell-o flavors to the décor of recreational vehicles, Eunice still manages to aspire to something better in life. Another resilient character, "Ernestine" the telephone operator, marked comedian Lily Tomlin's frequent appearances on Seventies television.

While dramatizing the life of a single woman with a career in television journalism, the *Mary Tyler Moore Show* attached a human face to feminist aspirations. The opening montage of each installment set the show's tone by picturing Mary's exasperation at the price of packaged meat at a big-city supermarket. Nearly all the action, however, took place in the protagonist's Minneapolis apartment or at the office. At home, Mary's tight relationship with neighbor Rhoda (Valerie Harper) showed that women could bond in friendship as important as any relationship with a man. At work, perky Mary had to contend with gruff Lou Grant (Ed Asner)—the hard-bitten, whiskey-drinking former World War II infantryman and Detroit street reporter who ran the TV newsroom. The show's humor derived from Mary's attempts to smooth out all conflict. These included her desire to remain a "nice" person while pursuing an independent professional life, her attempt to balance workplace demands with loyalty to friends, and her need to remain at the disposal of the people she cared for, while maintaining her personal integrity and a concern for her own needs.

FAMILY FEUDS

In the same year that *Mary Tyler Moore* debuted, Hollywood produced the disturbing *Joe* (1970). The film starred Peter Boyle as a World War II veteran, construction worker, and gun collector who feels threatened when a black family moves into the block where he owns his over-mortgaged home. Watching television every night, he fantasizes revenge against welfare cheats who receive government payments to have babies, and affluent white college kids who take drugs and have free sex. When Joe meets an advertising executive whose daughter has run off with a hippie dope dealer, he agrees to help find the pair. The ensuing search leads to the protagonist's participation in a Greenwich Village drug and sex orgy and to his arrival at a rural counterculture commune. As he sits around an open campfire, the executive shows up and unknowingly shoots his daughter.

Halfway through the 1970–71 television season, CBS sought to take advantage of widespread interest in the culture wars by premiering *All in the Family* (1971–79), a situation comedy inspired by Britain's Cockney series *Till Death Do Us Part* (1966–67). The show was the concept of producer Norman Lear, a third-generation Russian Jew who grew up in the Depression and served in the World War II Air Force before becoming a top television and film comedy writer. *All in the Family* emulated predecessors like *The Life of Riley, The Honeymooners,* and *Sgt. Bilko* by featuring a loud and emotive working-class protagonist whose rigid opinions, prejudices, and innumerable blunders belied a decent heart. Despite the comic overlay, Lear and co-producer Bud Yorkin instructed writers to produce "real" and true-to-life scripts.

Audiences responded in the program's first full season by making *All in the Family* the Number One-rated TV show in the nation—a position it maintained for the next four years.

The opening of the influential series began in the style of the Depression film *Dead End*—panning from a shot of the Manhattan skyline to a close-up of the Bunker residence—a row house on a working-class street in Queens. Inside the door, viewers found a drab interior decorated with cheap pictures and worn but comfortable furniture, including the easy chair belonging to the king of the castle. An aging foreman on a warehouse loading-dock, Archie Bunker (Carroll O'Connnor) had been forced to quit school during the Depression to help support his parents, had fought in World War II, and wound up in a dead-end job where the rewards never seemed to complement hard work. Archie experiences the full brunt of Seventies inflation and wage stagnation: he goes on strike, his employers lay him off, he temporarily loses his house insurance, he becomes a mugging victim, and he winds up driving a cab on weekends for extra pay. Convinced that his best days are behind him, fearful of losing his livelihood, and obsessed with keeping his self-respect, he builds defenses around his life to keep things from getting worse. Why extend himself to others, he insists, when no one does anything for him?

The first working-class television character to be white Anglo-Protestant, Archie Bunker embodied the social conservatism normally linked with Irish American Catholics. *All in the Family* brought these views to the surface by demonstrating Archie's difficulty in coping with a changing world, one that seemed to lavish attention upon and unduly reward racial strangers, sexual "deviants," and cultural rebels. The dramatic device for exploring such tensions lay in Archie's verbal contests with his live-in and financially dependent son-in-law Mike (Rob Reiner), a Polish American graduate student who wholeheartedly embraces the secular and liberal academic values Archie detests. Intent on tearing down everything his father-in-law believes, Mike is the one who chortles most loudly when Archie's bigotry runs up against logic-defying situations such as a successful black realtor, a gay drinking pal, or an unqualified white worker at the warehouse.

Beyond the humor of Archie Bunker's inconsistencies and humiliating predicaments, *All in the Family* offered a depth of characterization that rescued its protagonists from mere caricature. The show's writers carefully made Archie into a full human being, one whose benevolence, however reluctant, always seemed to emerge at the end of each episode. They also imbued the lead character with lovable idiosyncrasies, allowing him to lecture his "Meathead" son-in-law on the right way to put on socks and shoes or having him take joy in a small pleasure like getting his bagged lunch to work without the tuna fish oil leaking onto his Twinkie cupcakes. Beyond Archie's personality, however, the series could not have become a classic of television drama without the presence of Edith Bunker (Jean Stapleton), the family matriarch.

On the surface, Edith appeared to be a passive and dim-witted spouse who habitually deferred to her husband in the interests of family harmony. Yet the script drew out Edith's character to the point where her intuitive insight, her ability to learn from all experience, and her acceptance of all human beings provided the moral center of the drama. For Edith, everyone was a potential friend. Her judgments of people relied more on an estimate of their intentions rather than their actions—an understandable perspective for someone who adored Archie as she did. Through Edith, *All in the Family* went beyond pioneering considerations of racial and ethnic tolerance, to deal with intimate matters like abortion, rape, homosexuality, breast cancer, and death. In demonstrating a fair-minded and grounded view of such issues, she either ignored her husband's posturing and did what she thought right, or held her ground and forced him to concede. Either way, Edith usually prevailed. Jean Stapleton insisted that her character dignified homemakers. Such a sensibility, she believed, was central to the women's movement and helped to explain Edith's enormous popularity among a broad range of television fans.

STAYING ALIVE

The deglamorized view of urban life in *All in the Family* found new life in *Columbo* (1971–77), a police detective series directed by John Cassavetes. The series starred Peter Falk in the title role. A former administrator in the Connecticut state budget bureau, Columbo perennially appeared as an unshaven, glass-eyed buffoon who always wore a wrinkled raincoat, packed a homemade lunch, carried an unlit cigar stub, and drove a beat-up sedan. Given to stumbling patter and distracting references to bromides attributed to "the missus," the detective ingeniously threw patronizing evildoers off guard, particularly when making his frequent off-hand request for "just one more thing." In a similar fashion, *Cannon* (1971–76) featured a heavy-set and taciturn investigator rarely taken seriously by the pretentious wrongdoers he eventually snatched. *Kojak* (1973–78), another popular Seventies police show, starred bald-headed Telly Savalas as a hard-bitten but socially conscious New York homicide lieutenant who brought a gritty realism and big-city smarts to the job.

As television rediscovered the working class, *Happy Days* (1974–84) burst on the scene. A nostalgic view of suburban family life before the Sixties culture wars, the show achieved enormous ratings through Henry Winkler's role as Arthur Fonzarelli ("the Fonz"), a leather-jacketed "greaser" from a blue-collar family who confined his rebellion to an appreciation of cars, girls, and rock and roll. Similar readings of the pre-Kennedy era dominated the Broadway musical *Grease* (1972) and Hollywood's *American Graffiti* (1973), both of which converted "hoods" from marginal backgrounds into amiable allies of the white middle class. Set in Brooklyn high school culture in the late Fifties, the low-budget independent film *The Lords of Flatbush* (1974) avoided such sentimentality. The movie teamed Henry Winkler with the previously unknown Sylvester Stallone in an anecdotal portrait of a benign gang of friends who chase girls, hang out in poolrooms and candy stores, heist an occasional car, and engage in a rumble or two. Stallone induces a degree of sympathy for his character when he takes his pregnant girl friend to a jeweler to pick out a ring, or when, like Terry Malloy, he sees to the rooftop pigeons he raises.

The most compelling motion-picture exploration of Seventies blue-collar life emerged in *Saturday Night Fever* (1977), a film starring John Travolta as Tony Manero, a working-class Italian American living with his family in the Bay Ridge section of Brooklyn. Manero's embittered father, an unemployed construction laborer, constantly demeans his younger son for thinking he will make something of himself in a dead-end job as a paint store clerk. Tony himself has no respect for the sycophant gang of friends who gather around him. Yet the lead character of *Saturday Night Fever* has dreams of grandeur illustrated by the film's extended and uncut opening footage. As Manero struts down the street carrying a can of paint, the soundtrack blares out the disco beat of the BeeGees' infectious "Stayin' Alive," for it is only during weekends on the dance floor of the local disco, Odyssey 2001, that Tony experiences the personal transformation that allows him to express himself and achieve a full measure of self-esteem.

A relatively recent phenomenon when *Saturday Night Fever* debuted, disco had originated as the recorded dance music of New York's gay African American clubs. Influenced by the emerging identity politics surrounding youth culture, ethnic minorities, and feminism, the homosexual community began to assert a public presence following the Stonewall Inn Riot of 1969. As the patrons of a Greenwich Village gay men's bar fought off a police raid and identified themselves as "street people," activists formed the Gay Liberation Front (GLF) and called for "complete sexual liberation for all people." Advocating gay pride and the advancement of a full civil rights agenda, homosexuals and lesbians insisted that sexual orientation was a matter of genetics or chosen lifestyle, not a disease, sin, or act of criminality. As many people "came out of the closet," a thriving culture embraced gay choirs, literary and artistic endeavors, folk music, and social clubs.

In its early manifestation, disco involved a style-based dance performance in a communal setting that empowered gay men by encouraging freedom of bodily movement. Although everyone on the floor was a star, the disc jockey's orchestration of music and lighting made him the club's central figure. Relying on audience approval, DJs spun long-playing records with synthesizers and violins overlaying the regular 4/4 beat of an automatic drum machine. High-energy and erotic divas soon emerged as dance-club favorites. Several tunes, including Donna Summer's "Love to Love You Baby" (1976), Gloria Gaynor's "I Will Survive" (1978), and Gino Soccio's "Dancer" (1979) ultimately worked their way out of the disco clubs to the top rungs of the popular music charts.

As a carefree dance form, disco spread to straight 9-to-5 white wage earners, upwardly mobile professionals, and even seniors. Although the heterosexual and non-black setting of *Saturday Night Fever* ignored the music's roots, the film offered a realistic portrait of the working-class culture surrounding some of its most ardent fans. "They got it all locked up," complains one of Tony's friends about his future prospects, "ain't nobody gonna give you a chance." For Mareno, the opportunity for excellence lies in the club dance contest and a potential new partner, Stephanie (Karen Lynn Gorney), a secretary in a posh Manhattan office. Yet Tony's recruiting effort initially fails. "There's a world of difference between us," sniffs Stephanie. "You're nowhere on your way to no place." Eventually, the duo gets together and wins the contest, although Tony relinquishes the prize to the superior but second-ranked Puerto Rican couple whom the judges pass over in deference to the club's majority clientele.

Mareno's willingness to confront his own limitations provides the edge to *Saturday Night Fever.* Through a series of personal crises, including a pointless rumble with a rival gang, the suicide of a friend, his older brother's sudden resignation from the priesthood, and Stephanie's continual rejection, Tony's defenses break down. Once they do, however, Stephanie opens up, admitting to him in an emotional scene that he has no idea how hard it is to cross the East River and "make it" in the calculating world of upscale Manhattan. Helping her move into her own place, a subdued Mareno offers himself as a supportive friend. "I'm an able person," he declares in an effort to convince Stephanie and himself that he shares the ambition to better himself. In the end, the relationship between the two strikes a note of mutual respect but their future as a couple and as individuals seeking the main chance remains unresolved.

WARRIORS

"Everything they do," declares one of the characters in *Blue Collar* (1978), "is meant to keep us in our places." The film starred Harvey Keitel, Richard Pryor, and Yaphet Kotto as three heavily indebted and disillusioned Detroit autoworkers who rob their own union. Instead of cash, the trio finds incriminating evidence of the local's complicity in mob-related loan-sharking. Francis Ford Coppola's *The Godfather* (1972) and *The Godfather, Part II* (1974) \had already presented an epic history of the Mafia's transition from an immigrant protection society to organized criminality. Set amid the greedy collusion of corrupt unions and big business, *Blue Collar* offered a picture of ordinary working-class life with few illusions. In the end, Pryor's character must decide if testifying against the labor bosses will rectify a wrong or simply perpetuate more corruption.

Unlike *Blue Collar, Norma Rae* (1979) presented an upbeat view of working-class unity, but did so by personalizing the story of its lead character. The film's title role belonged to a poorly educated single mother and widow (Sally Field) working in a southern cotton mill. Norma Rae has lost her husband to fatal injuries sustained in a tavern brawl. She also has seen her father, another mill employee, die when he fails to receive adequate medical attention for a job-related illness. Meanwhile, her mother has gone

Sally Field in *Norma Rae* (1979)   (*Photofest*)

hard of hearing from the din of the looms. When Norma Rae hears a labor organizer talk of the benefits that result from solidarity among people of different races and faiths, she hosts a gathering of interested parties in her home. Here black and white women workers pass on stories of spouses who died of the "brown lung." In the end, Norma Rae defiantly raises a "union" placard at her post, and the women take the first steps toward a strike by stopping their machines, prompting the company to recognize their rights.

Peter Yates' *Breaking Away* (1979) delivered a less politicized but equally powerful perspective on working-class culture. The Academy Award-winning screenplay by Steve Tesich revolved around four aimless high school graduates in the university town of Bloomington, Indiana, with no prospects for college or a job. Known as "cutters," because their fathers once worked at the now-abandoned limestone quarry, the four form a bicycle racing team to test their manhood. The protagonist (Dennis Christopher), whose father now operates a used-car lot, meets girls on campus by impersonating an Italian exchange student. Yet once Dave confesses his real identity to the attractive young woman he has charmed, she angrily discards him and returns to her upper-middle-class boyfriend. Reconciling with his son in a time of need, Dave's father proudly shows him the campus building whose stone he once shaped. When the university allows the cutters to compete in its "Little 500" bike race, the underdog "townies" prevail, to the delight of their families and friends.

No sport symbolized working-class grit more than boxing. In the 1950s, heavyweight champion Rocky Marciano and middleweight Rocky Graziano established the mold for rugged and aggressive white ethnic fighters. Defeating Joe Louis in 1951 and taking the title in a bloody thirteenth-round victory the following year, Marciano became the only undefeated heavyweight (49–0) in boxing history. Graziano's colorful brawling style and elevation from a life of street crime won him almost as much popularity, although his fighting skills never approximated those of his cohort's. Paul Newman's portrait of the boxer's rise to fame in *Somebody Up There Likes Me* (1956) helped to publicize the rags-to-riches story and secure Newman's acting reputation.

One year after his appearance in *The Lords of Flatbush*, Sylvester Stallone marketed a screenplay about a kind-hearted boxer with animalistic drive and ferocity. *Rocky* (1976), an Academy Award-winning Best Picture, featured Stallone as a thirty-year-old club fighter who collects delinquent bills for a loan shark in a decaying South Philadelphia neighborhood. Yet Rocky Balboa gets a chance at redemption when the challenger to black heavyweight champion Apollo Creed drops out due to injury, and Creed looks for publicity by replacing him with a "local underdog fighter." Ridiculed by his opponent as "the Italian Stallion," Rocky initiates a rigorous training regimen to prove that he is not "just another bum from the neighborhood." In a series of images that would become part of cinema lore, Rocky works out by pounding slabs of frozen beef in a meatpacking plant, completes excruciating one-arm pushups, and runs miles of city streets every day at dawn, climaxing in a triumphant jog up the concrete stairs of the Philadelphia Art Museum. Meanwhile, he awkwardly courts a friend's shy sister who works in a pet shop, taking her, on one occasion, on a nearly disastrous ice-skating date.

Rocky brought profound responses from film goers who identified with the positive message that a bum could become a contender through hard work and the will to make good. Bringing to mind the inspirational idealism of Frank Capra's Depression tales, the movie also spoke to a sense of neglect and abandonment among white working-class ethnics. In the end, Balboa defies the odds by going the distance with the flashy champion, narrowly losing the match in a split decision but regaining his self-respect. In doing so, Rocky Balboa represented the quest for recognition among all underdogs and marginalized people. By cheering for Rocky, observed Stallone, audiences were cheering for themselves.

Martin Scorcese's *Raging Bull* (1980) offered a more somber view of the ring. Born in Flushing, Queens, in 1942 to Sicilian immigrants, Scorcese grew up in the tenements of Manhattan's Little Italy. He attended parochial schools, briefly enrolled in seminary, and graduated Catholic high school before earning accreditation from the New York University Film School. Scorcese's first major directing task came with *Mean Streets* (1973), a movie starring Robert De Niro and Harvey Keitel. The film presented a drama of the old neighborhood from the perspective of young hoodlums caught between the patriarchy of community elders and the American success ethic. "You don't make up for your sins in church," Keitel's narrator explains in the opening. "You do it in the streets. You do it at home. The rest is bullshit and you know it." Seeking to assert a degree of ethical responsibility while remaining loyal to his friends, the lead character cannot free himself from an endless cycle of gambling, drinking, poolroom fights, and quests for casual sex. Queried by his girlfriend as to who he really is, he responds that he likes "spaghetti and clam sauce ... chicken with lemon and garlic and John Wayne."

Scorsese's next city drama, *Taxi Driver* (1976), featured De Niro as Travis Bickel, an alienated and insomniac ex-Vietnam marine who drives an all-night cab and spends his off-hours in porno theaters or his shabby room. Having witnessed repeated instances of urban violence and convinced that "too much abuse has gone on for too long," Bickel takes it upon himself to restore moral order as a representative of the people's conscience. After befriending and then offending a frosty blonde woman (Cybill Shepherd) who is the top aide of a presidential candidate, Bickel assumes fatherly protection of a twelve-year-old runaway and prostitute (Jodie Foster). As the pressures in his disturbed mind compel him toward action, he attempts to assassinate the politician and shoots the prostitute's pimp and two cohorts, ending the film in an orgy of personal vengeance with no hint as to his own personal fate or the meaning of his acts.

In *Raging Bull*, De Niro won an Academy Award for portraying the rise and fall of middleweight champion Jake La Motta. Starting the story in a Bronx slum in the early Forties, Scorsese emulated the documentary realism of Abraham Polonsky's *Force of Evil.* In graphic and disturbing footage, the film recorded La Motta's primitive style that allowed opponents to spend themselves with a flurry of blows before the fighter retaliated with ruthless brutality. Pursuing success at all costs, La Motta fails to control the mad and self-destructive qualities of his own make-up, a flaw that makes it impossible to sustain loving relationships with anyone. Following the loss of his title, the boxer cuts himself off from his brother-manager (Joe Pesci) and young second wife (Cathy Moriarty) and winds up in a Florida jail for corrupting a minor. Recognition of his inner demons leads the ex-champion to beating his head against the wall. Once released, an overweight La Motta starts a new life as a standup comic in his own Miami club. His redemption seems assured when in the final scene he peers into the dressing room mirror and mocks himself with a recitation of Marlon Brando's "I coulda been a contender" speech.

THE REDDENING OF AMERICA

Although urban imagery and sensibilities pervaded much of Seventies culture, southerners and westerners sought equal footing. In the realm of literature, Eudora Welty continued to relay the lyricism of the Mississippi hill country's natural talkers and storytellers. *Losing Battles* (1970) celebrated the values of reconciliation, forgiveness, and reunion with tales of Depression folk "making do" amid poverty, natural disasters, and poor soil. "We've all just tried to last as long as we can by sticking together," explains Miss Beulah, one of the novel's prime characters. *One Time, One Place* (1971), a collection of Welty's photographs taken while she traveled across the state for the

WPA, pointed to the author's identification with the courage and spirit of the region's poor whites and blacks during hard times. Welty's next novel was the Pulitzer Prize-winning *The Optimist's Daughter* (1972), the story of a professional woman who returns home as her father, an elderly judge who has married a self-centered young woman, is dying. As the protagonist observes the widow's poor-white relatives at the funeral, she learns that love, honor, and the pursuit of truth transcend class, race, or sex.

Small-town life took on another perspective in *The Last Picture Show* (1971), a novel by Larry McMurtry that Peter Bogdanovich brought to the screen in the sparse style of John Ford and Howard Hawks. Set in a dusty West Texas oil town in the 1950s, the film centered on two high school football stars, Sonny (Timothy Bottoms) and Duane (Jeff Bridges), residents of a cheap rooming house who fear they will never get out of the decaying community. As the two pursue Jacy Farrow (Cybill Shepherd), the spoiled daughter of an oil-rich ex-roughneck, they learn about the lost lives and dreams of the previous generation, as well as its sordid secrets and hypocrisies. The turning point in the story comes with the death of Sam the Lion, the pool hall and movie house operator who serves as the boys' surrogate father, followed by the accidental killing of Sam's half-witted young protégé, the victim of a pickup truck that runs him down while he sweeps the road in a dust storm. With the theater closing and an era ending, Duane goes off to Korea, leaving Sonny alone except for a guilt-ridden, on-and-off-again sexual relationship with the neglected wife of the basketball coach.

During the 1960s, several weekly television series celebrated the values of "plain folk" and rural life. *The Real McCoys* (1957–63) followed the California adventures of a transplanted West Virginia farm clan and the collision of the homespun values of elderly patriarch (Walter Brennan) with the suburban aspirations of its peer-conscious offspring. A similar plot marked the popular *Beverly Hillbillies* (1962–71), a program about an Ozarks family that strikes it rich in oil and moves to a Los Angeles mansion. Meanwhile, *The Andy Griffith Show* (1960–68) chronicled the laid-back routines and dry wit of a stoic, small-town North Carolina sheriff. The Seventies produced *The Waltons* (1972–81), the saga of an extended family of sawmill operators in Virginia's Blue Ridge Mountains that struggle to survive the Depression. Based on the boyhood memories of creator Earl Hamner, Jr., the show offered weekly lessons on the common sense and decency of country people. Another series, *Little House on the Prairie* (1974–83), dealt with a Minnesota couple and three daughters homesteading during the 1870s.

One of television's most popular small-market shows was *Hee Haw* (1969–93), a raucous variety hour hosted by country banjo player Roy Clark and guitarist Buck Owens. Beyond its hillbilly comedy routines and array of scantily clad gingham beauties, the program provided a virtual showcase of the rural musical heritage. Like Hollywood's blue-collar films, country music seemed particularly attuned to working-class dignity and self-worth. Celebrating traditional lifestyles and homegrown virtues, Nashville songwriters employed a simple vocabulary to describe concrete situations, personal experiences, and ordinary life as it was, not as anticipated. On stage, performers endeared themselves to audiences by assuming a modest persona and engaging in informal banter about everyday subjects like hunting, fishing, and home life.

Nashville carved a market niche in the 1970s by professing to speak for the "forgotten Americans" or "silent majority" celebrated in the Nixon White House. In a period of rampant social change, country music offered a refuge of traditional values that promoted respect for authority, religious reverence, binding kinship, the certainty of reward and punishment, and heart-felt patriotism. Within this perspective, love took on a redemptive quality that transcended all suffering. Not surprisingly, many fans contrasted these moral standards with the artificiality and pretension they attributed to the counterculture and the media. At the height of campus disruptions in the early Seventies, for example, Al Capp viciously caricatured long-haired students in the popular *L'il Abner* comic strips. Grassroots apprehension about hippie sanitary habits contributed to the posting of "No shirt, no shoes, no service" signs in nearly all the nation's cafés.

It fell to country artist Merle Haggard to find an appropriate musical expression for the conservative cultural mindset. The child of Oklahoma migrants, Haggard was born in the oil and cotton center of Bakersfield, California. Losing his musician father at age nine, he lived in a converted boxcar with his devoutly religious mother. Under the influence of Bob Wills, Ernest Tubb, and Lefty Frizzell, Haggard began to sing and play guitar. Periodically between 1952 and 1960, however, he served time for a series of burglaries and other crimes until an appearance by Johnny Cash at San Quentin prison inspired him to turn around his life. Freed in 1960, he performed as a backup bass player in the Bakersfield honky-tonks before starting to write his own songs.

Haggard's first Number One single, "I'm a Lonesome Fugitive" (1966), complemented public fascination with outlaws. Another, "Mama Tried" (1968), hooked listeners into a semi-autobiographical tale of wrongdoing with the stark opening line, "I turned twenty-one in prison doing life without parole." Known as "the poet of the common man," Haggard had a special talent for chronicling the lives of everyday people with lyrics that pointed to the private pain others experienced but rarely discussed. "Hungry Eyes" (1968) described a mother's silent bearing of a life without bare necessities. Other songs, like "Workin' Man's Blues"(1969), "White Line Fever" (1968), and "If We Make It Through December" (1973), gave voice to hard-working, beer-drinking, patriotic, and proudly individualistic laborers and truckers with disdain for welfare or any other brand of dependency.

Sometime in 1969, Merle Haggard and his road band were diverting themselves as their bus traveled through Oklahoma, when they passed a mileage sign for the next town. "I bet they don't smoke marijuana in Muskogee," someone said. As the musicians joked around with the idea, they came up with "Okie from Muskogee" (1969), the period's most stirring anthem of small-town identity. Swearing off marijuana, LSD, draft-card burning, free love, long hair, hippie beads, and Roman sandals, the song builds to a rousing chorus of affirmation. "I'm proud to be an Okie from Muskogee," it proclaims, "A place where even squares can have a ball./We still wave Ol' Glory down at the courthouse,/And "white lightin's still the biggest thrill of all."

Early the next year Haggard introduced a song that became a rallying cry for critics of the antiwar movement. "I hear people talkin' bad about the way we have to live here in the country," it began, "Harpin' on the wars we fight and gripin' about the way things oughta be." "I don't mind them switchin' sides and standin' up for things they believe in," sang Haggard, "but when they're runnin' down my country, they're walkin' on the fightin' side of me." "They love our milk and honey, but they preach about some other way of livin'," rang the second verse, "When they're running down my country, hoss, they're walkin' on the fightin' side of me." Invited by President Nixon to the White House, the singer refused, protesting that "The Fightin' Side of Me" (1970) was not a political song. All he was trying to say, he explained, was that people who wanted to change the country should help to make it better instead of putting it down.

DESPERADOS AND STRAIGHT-SHOOTING WOMEN

"Take this job and shove it," rough-hewn country artist Johnny Paycheck sang in the David Allan Coe classic (1977) of the same name. Although the song described a man who had no reason to work because his woman had left him, the attention-grabbing title became a stock catch phrase of the times. Facing economic stagnation, spiraling inflation, energy shortages, expanding welfare costs, and a shift of tax burdens to the non-affluent, many Americans felt victimized by circumstances beyond their control. Such feelings of futility contributed to the popularity of horror films like *The Exorcist* (1973), *Carrie* (1976), *The Omen* (1976), *Alien* (1979), *The Shining* (1980), and *Poltergeist* (1982) that rooted their explanations of incomprehensive events in the supernatural. As disillusionment from Vietnam and the Watergate scandal deepened public alienation, screenwriter Paddy Chayefsky found the perfect outlet for the public mood in *Network* (1976). Learning he is to be fired, television news anchor Peter Finch makes a last stand by instructing viewers to go to the nearest window and protest the abuse of ordinary citizens by yelling "I'm mad as hell and I'm not going to take it anymore!"

Amid the disappointments of the Seventies, country music served as an important conduit of non-elite expression. Responding to widespread interest in truckers and CB (Citizen's Band) radio after a nationwide strike of independent drivers, former rocker C.W. McCall released the smash hit "Convoy" (1976), inspiring a Sam Peckinpah movie of the same name (1977). Another set of country stars continued to mine honky-tonk themes. In the tradition of Merle Haggard, Johnny Paycheck recorded "I'm the Only Hell (My Mama Ever Raised)" (1977). Hank Williams, Jr., in turn, defied cautionary moralists with raucous tunes like "Whiskey Bent and Hell Bound" (1979) and "Family Tradition" (1979). East Texan George Jones, who had first topped the charts with "White Lightning" (1959), chronicled his own struggles with dissipation in heart-felt numbers like "If Drinking Don't Kill Me" (1980).

Between 1969 and 1975, George Jones shared a tumultuous marriage with Tammy Wynette, his partner on popular duets such as "We're Gonna Hold On" (1973) and "Golden Ring" (1976). Ironically, the couple's popularity increased in proportion to its marital difficulties. Wynette continued to portray hurt and lonely women in songs like "Till I Can Make It on My Own" (1975). Yet the "born to cry" sound received its most complete treatment in the music of Dottie West. The oldest of ten children, Dorothy Marie Marsh grew up in a central Tennessee farm family whose Depression diet, she remembered, consisted of "corn bread, butter beans, and fiddles." Abandoned by an abusive and alcoholic musician father, she began singing on the radio at age twelve and waited tables in her mother's restaurant through high school and technical college. After West married and her husband found work with a Cleveland steel company, she won a spot on an Ohio country music TV show. Moving to Nashville in 1961, the singer spent time with songwriters Willie Nelson and Roger Miller before scoring her first hit single, "Here Comes My Baby" (1964), and a career-launching album, *Suffer Time* (1966).

Dottie West's emotional delivery lent itself to solo treatments like "The Cold Hand of Fate" (1970). Nevertheless, her most acclaimed material came in the late Seventies when she completed a series of sexually charged duets with Kenny Rogers. A late-comer to country music, Rogers first came to the attention of Nashville audiences with "Lucille" (1977), the story of a young beauty who has deserted her husband, four hungry children, "and a crop in the field" for the chance encounters of a dark cocktail lounge. His next hit, Don Schlitz's "The Gambler" (1978), offered a universal credo. "You gotta know when to hold 'em, know when to fold 'em," explains the song's mentor, "Know when to walk away, know when to run ... 'Cause every hand's a winner, just like every hand's a loser/And the best that you can hope for is to die in your sleep."

Kenny Rogers' next collaborator was Dolly Parton, the creator of their hit "Islands in the Stream" (1983). The fourth of twelve children, Parton was born in the mountains of Tennessee, where her father was a sharecropper and moonshiner. Learning ballads and old-time songs from her mother, a member of the Church of God, she began appearing on local television at age ten. Following high school graduation, Parton moved to Nashville, where she signed a record contract and joined the Porter Wagoner television show. Many of her hits, like "In the Good Old Days (When Times Were Bad)" (1969), "Tennessee Mountain Home" (1973), and "Appalachian Memories" (1983), expressed pride in humble origins and roots. "Coat of Many Colors" (1971), her favorite memory piece, recalled a homemade rag-patch jacket, blessed with a mother's kiss, worn in pride to school despite ridicule from peers. In songs like "Just Because I'm a Woman" (1968), "My Blue Ridge Mountain Boy" (1969), "A Little at a Time" (1972), "I Will Always Love You" (1974), and "Jolene" (1974), Parton honestly expressed romantic and sexual longings, while describing the burdens and hypocritical standards projected on women.

Sporting blonde wigs, heavy makeup, jewelry, spiked heels, and form-fitting costumes in her late Seventies television program, Dolly Parton embodied the fantasies of Americans like herself who had grown up around a scarcity of material goods. "It costs a lot to look this cheap," she told audiences. "People don't come to the show to see you be you," Parton once observed, "they come to see you be them, and what they want to be." Never abandoning her regional idiom, deprecatory humor, or rustic informality, she alternated between a high-pitched yodel and a wistful, plaintive voice, providing performances with an undeniable authenticity, even when the singer moved into the popular music field toward the close of the decade.

Vocalist Jessi Colter provided a western version of country music soul. Born Miriam Johnson in Phoenix in 1947 to a mining engineer and his Pentecostal evangelist wife, Colter named herself after a Wild West ancestor who robbed trains in the 1870s. After playing piano in her mother's tent revivals, she ran off with rock and roll star Duane Eddy at sixteen. Once divorced from Eddy and a single mother, Colter married musician Waylon Jennings. Her first hit, "I'm Not Lisa" (1975), set the stage for an appearance on *Wanted! The Outlaws* (1976), the pioneering album featuring Jennings, Willie Nelson, and Tompall Glaser, on which she sang "I'm Looking for Blue Eyes" and teamed up with Jennings on "Suspicious Minds."

The Outlaws emerged from the western swing revival centered in Austin, Texas, where performers like Asleep at the Wheel and Jerry Jeff Walker introduced old-style music and themes to a mixed young audience of self-styled rednecks and hippies. Walker achieved national exposure with his best-selling record of "Mr. Bojangles" (1968), a tribute to legendary tap dancer Bill Robinson. Songwriter and performer Guy Clark, whose self-titled album appeared in 1975, figured as another key fixture of the Austin scene. In the powerful "Desperados Waiting for a Train," Clark described a nursing home filled with old oil wildcatters who made up stories over games of dominoes as they waited for their demise. Another song, the rollicking "Let Him Roll," described a dying vagrant's dream of heaven as "just a Dallas whore."

Austin's musical vitality coincided with Willie Nelson's return in 1972. Reared in central Texas during the 1930s, Nelson sang in the Baptist Church before playing in polka bands and honky-tonks. After a successful songwriting career, he rose to prominence with *Shotgun Willie* (1973), an album with original pieces like "Sad Songs and Waltzes" and the collection's title number. Willie's cohort, West Texan Waylon Jennings, had been a musician since he was thirteen, played bass with Buddy Holly, worked as a disc jockey, and recorded folk and pop standards in the Sixties. Jennings' first major hit was "Ladies Love Outlaws" (1972), part of an album whose cover depicted the singer as a black-draped western bad man. His next best-seller, "Are You Sure Hank Done It This Way?" (1975), pointed to the excesses of over-produced country music. In *The Outlaws*, Jennings sang solo on "My Heroes Have Always Been Cowboys" and "Honky Tonk Heroes," while teaming up with Nelson on "Good Hearted Woman" and "Heaven and Hell." A follow-up album, *Waylon and Willie* (1978), brought the two together for the playful "Mamas, Don't Let Your Babies Grow Up To Be Cowboys."

BORN TO RUN

Country music's concrete imagery, compassionate egalitarianism, and anti-utopian humility gradually worked their way into rock music. Reacting against "love generation" affectations and inspired by the hard-rocking electric blues of British imports like Led Zeppelin and Black Sabbath, Seventies bands such as Alice Cooper, Kiss, the Blue Oyster Cult, and Aerosmith turned to a furiously aggressive style dubbed as Heavy Metal. Other artists drew inspiration from distinctly American roots and collective pop culture memory. Don McLean's "American Pie" (1971) mourned the loss of rock and roll innocence by recalling when "the three men I admire most … caught the last train for the coast," a reference to the 1959 Iowa plane crash killing Ritchie Valens, the Big Bopper, and Buddy Holly. Hollywood paid homage to the founding spirits of rock and roll in *The Buddy Holly Story* (1978) and in *American Hot Wax* (1978), a tribute to Alan Freed.

The return to rock and roll basics comprised the outstanding element of Southern Rock, a revitalized fusion of rhythm and blues and country and western centered in Macon, Georgia. The genre's most accomplished practitioners were the Allman Brothers Band, a group mixing soulful vocals with dual lead guitars and a gospel organ. Two years after guitar virtuoso Duane Allman's death in a motorcycle accident, the band produced its signature "Ramblin' Man' (1973), a breezy portrait of a marginal character "tryin' to make a livin' as best he can." Both South Carolina's Marshall Tucker Band and Nashville's Charlie Daniels enhanced the southern mystique of whiskey, guns, and trouble-making with skilled musicianship. In "The Devil Went Down to Georgia" (1980), swing fiddler and lead singer Daniels took on the macho swagger of the region's gruff, tobacco-chewing male icons. Yet it fell to Florida's Lynyrd Skynyrd, a group including vocalist Ronnie Van Zant and three lead guitars, to create the defining anthem of white southern manhood in the mega-hit "Sweet Home Alabama" (1974), a song that conveyed regional resentment of outside meddling and patronizing in undisguised terms.

Bob Seger and the Silver Bullet Band provided a midwestern counterpart to the working-class tones of southern music. Raised in Ann Arbor, Michigan, Seger fused a hearty brand of rock and roll with a glance back to the restlessness and boredom of small-town teenage life. In "Night Moves" (1976), the single that accompanied his best-selling album of the same name, he recalled the feeling of "nothing to lose" while parked in the back seat of an old Chevy "out past the cornfields where the woods got heavy." Another cut, "Mainstreet," pictured young pool hall hustlers peering through a glass window to spy on the exotic dancers in an adjoining club. Seger's version of "Old Time Rock and Roll" (1977) became the second most-played jukebox favorite of all time and highlighted the soundtrack to the popular movie *Risky Business* (1983).

The experiences of the northeastern working class received the most complete treatment in the music of Bruce Springsteen. Of Irish and Italian background, Springsteen was born in 1949 to a bus driver and legal secretary in the factory town of Freehold, New Jersey. At seventeen, he began playing guitar in rock bands like Steel Mill in the greaser and surfer bars of the Jersey shoreline. Five years later, Springsteen signed a solo contract on the hood of a car in the unlit parking lot of a cocktail lounge and enrolled sax player Clarence Clemmons in his backup band. The group's inaugural album, *Greetings from Asbury Park, N.J.* (1973), returned to the musical fundamentals of role models Buddy Holly and early Elvis, revitalizing rock's narrative tradition with stories and characters drawn from local hot-rod culture. The protagonist of "Growin' Up" exults about finding "the key to the universe" in "the engine of an old parked car." In "Spirit in the Night," Wild Billy, Crazy Janey, and Hazy Davey escape the daily grind to a lakeside paradise of drinking and sex "about a mile down on the dark side of Route 88." "It's Hard to Be a Saint in the City," in turn, offers a spirited and comical inventory of life on the streets.

Springsteen's ability to convey the night world's romance and grandeur filled his second album, *The Wild, the Innocent, and the E Street Shuffle* (1973). Some selections, like the intimate "4th of July, Asbury Park (Sandy)" and "The E Street Shuffle," continued to chronicle the seedy dramas of the boardwalk. The record's second side shifted the scene across the Hudson River. "New York Serenade" featured Springsteen's piano in an extended treatment of the city's midnight ambience reminiscent of George Gershwin. In contrast, "Incident on 57th Street" depicted a love affair between Spanish Johnny and his Puerto Rican girlfriend Jane, who regrets that all "those romantic young boys … ever wanna do is fight." The record's legacy, however, rested with the inspirational "Rosalita," a song whose electrifying energy ultimately assured its status as a rock anthem and the climactic number in Bruce Springsteen's live stage shows. As the singer pleads for the hand of a woman whose "papa" disapproves of his life in a rock and roll band, he jubilantly tells her that this is her father's "last chance/To get his daughter in a fine romance" because he is about to sign a career-launching record contract.

Born to Run (1975), Springsteen's first commercially successful album, came out as *Time* and *Newsweek* simultaneously featured the rising star on their covers. Parodying the contents of an old punk tattoo, the title song traced a world of drive-in restaurants, movie theaters, and arcades. Yet the vision was a dark one. "In the day we sweat it out on the streets of a runaway American dream," the lyric went. "At night we ride through mansions of glory in suicide machines." With his town nothing but "a death trap," the singer pleads that "tramps like us, baby, we were born to run." Similar restlessness character-

Bruce Springsteen   (*Photofest*)

ized "Thunder Road." The opening lines of the song record the slamming of a screen door as the radio plays and a woman dances across the porch "like a vision." From there the action shifts to the highway. "Show a little faith! There's magic in the night," the driver exclaims, "You ain't a beauty but hey, you're alright." As the piece builds, Springsteen bursts forth in ecstasy. "Roll down your window and let the wind blow back your hair," he sings, "The night's bustin' open/these two lanes will take us anywhere."

The linchpin of *Born to Run* was "Jungleland," a saga of under-class fugitives that also served as a metaphor for the music industry. Once again, Springsteen found a way to extract poetry from commonplace images, as in the line describing a "[b]arefoot girl sitting on the hood of a Dodge/Drinking warm beer in the soft summer rain." He also continued to demonstrate an uncanny ability to use lyrics to convey the emotional intimacy of ordinary characters. "Beneath the city two hearts beat," a couplet suggested, "Soul engines running through a night so tender." "Lonely-hearted lovers/Struggle in dark corners," read another line, "Desperate as the night moves on." The song's most intense segments, backed by an organ crescendo, portrayed an "opera out on the Turnpike," a midnight gang fight staged "'neath that giant Exxon sign." "From the churches to the jails," sang Springsteen, "Tonight all is silence in the world/As we take our stand/Down in Jungleland."

SOURCES AND SUGGESTED READINGS

Two useful surveys of 1970s cultural history are Bruce J. Schulman, *The Seventies: The Great Shift in American Culture, Society, and Politics* (2001) and Peter N. Carroll, *It Seemed Like Nothing Happened: America in the 1970s*, rev. ed. (2000). Henry Louis Gates and Nellie Y. McKay, *The Norton Anthology of African American Literature* (1997) provides profiles of the period's major black authors. For leading black women writers, see Judith P. Josephson, *Nikki Giovanni: Poet of the People* (2003); Linden Peach, *Toni Morrison* (1995; Mary Jane Lipton, *Maya Angelou: A Critical Companion* (1998); and Donna Haisty Winchell, *Alice Walker* (1992). Two significant black male authors receive portraits in Jay Boyer, *Ishmael Reed* (1993) and James W. Coleman, *Blackness and Modernism: The Literary Career of John Edgar Wideman* (1989).

African American popular music of the Seventies is the subject of Peter Guralnick, *Sweet Soul Music: Rhythm and Blues and the Southern Dream of Freedom* (1986); Craig Werner, *A Change Is Gonna Come: Music, Race, and the Soul of America* (1998); and Brian Ward, *Just My Soul Responding: Rhythm and Blues, Black Consciousness, and Race Relations* (1998). See also Michael Eric Dyson, *Mercy Mercy Me: The Art, Loves, and Demons of Marvin Gaye* (2004). For movies with racial themes, including the use of "black angels," see Krin Gabbard, *Black Magic: White Hollywood and African American Culture* (2004) and Donald Bogle, *Toms, Coons, Mulattoes, Mammies, and Bucks: An Interpretive History of Blacks in American Films*, rev. ed. (2002). *Roots* and other television shows dealing with black characters elicit coverage in Donald Bogle, *Primetime Blues: African American Network Television* (2001) and the relevant passages in Linda Williams, *Playing the Race Card: Melodramas of Black and White from Uncle Tom to O.J. Simpson* (2001).

Profiles of Chicano and Nuroyican writers appear in Nicolás Kanellos, *Hispanic Literature of the United States: A Comprehensive Reference* (2003). For a case study, see Margarite Fernández Olmos, *Rudolfo A. Anaya: A Critical Companion* (1999). Chicano popular music is the subject of Manuel Peña, *The Mexican American Orquesta: Music, Culture, and the Dialectic of Conflict* (1999); David Reyes and Tom Waldman, *Land of a Thousand Dances: Chicano Rock 'n' Roll from Southern California* (1998); and Charles M. Tatum, *Chicano Popular Culture: Que Hable el Pueblo* (2001).

For writers of Asian background, see Lawrence J. Trudeau, ed., *Asian American Literature: Reviews and Criticism of Works by American Writers of Asian Descent* (1999); Emmanuel S. Nelson, ed., *Asian American Novelists: A Bio-Bibliographical Critical Sourcebook* (2000); and Shawn Wong, *Asian American Literature: A Brief Introduction and Anthology* (1996). See also Diane Simmons, *Maxine Hong Kingston* (1999). The most complete reference work on American Indian writers is Kathy J. Whitson, *Native American Literatures: An Encyclopedia of Works, Characters, Authors, and Themes* (1999). See also Jane Witalec, ed., *Native North American Literature* (1994) and Kenneth Lincoln, *Native American Renaissance* (1983). For specific studies, consult Gregory Salyer, *Leslie Marmon Silko* (1997); Ron McFarland, *Understanding James Welch* (2000); Andrew Wiget, *Simon Ortiz* (1986); and Robert M. Nelson, *Place and Vision: The Function of Landscape in Native American Fiction* (1993).

Useful works on Seventies folk music and light rock include Robert Cantwell, *When We Were Good: The Folk Revival* (1996) and Peter Doggett, *Are You Reading for the Country: Elvis, Dylan, Parsons, and the Roots of Country Rock* (2000). See also the works on Bob Dylan cited in Chapter 10. Portraits of the decade's leading singer-songwriter and country rock artists appear in Anthony De Curtis, et al. eds., *The Rolling Stone Illustrated History of Rock and Roll: The Definitive History of the Most Important Artists and Their Music*, 3rd ed. (1992). See also Lucy O'Brien, *She-Bop: The Definitive History of Women in Rock, Pop, and Soul* (1996).

Seventies television sitcoms receive extensive treatment in portions of David Marc, *Comic Visions: Television Comedy and American Culture*, 2nd ed. (1997). For particular series, see Steven D. Stark, *Glued to the Set: The 60 Television Shows and Events That Made Us Who We Are Today* (1997); David Marcus, *Happy Days and Wonder Years: The Fifties and Sixties in Contemporary Cultural Politics* (2004); and Donna McCrohan, *Archie & Edith, Mike & Gloria: The Tumultuous History of* All in the Family (1987).

John Bodnar, *Blue-Collar Hollywood: Liberalism, Democracy, and Working People in American Film* (2003) provides descriptions of movies addressing ordinary life in the 1970s. See also Tom Zaniello, *Working Stiffs, Union Maids, Reds, and Riffraff: An Organized Guide to Films About Labor* (1996). For the work of directors Martin Scorcese and Francis Ford Coppola, see Lee Lourdeaux, *Italian and Irish Filmmakers in America: Ford, Capra, Coppola, and Scorcese* (1990) and Jon Lewis, *Whom God Wishes to Destroy …: Francis Coppola and the New Hollywood* (1996).

Post-Sixties working-class country music receives extensive treatment in Bill C. Malone, *Country Music, U.S.A.*, 2nd rev. ed. (2002) and *Don't Get above Your Raisin': Country Music and the Southern Working Class* (2002). See also Dorothy Horstman, *Sing Your Heart Out, Country Boy*, rev. ed. (1996); Curtis W. Ellison, *Country Music Culture: From Hard Times to Heaven* (1995); and Aaron A. Fox, *Real Country: Music and Language in Working-Class Culture* (2004). The genre's involvement in gender issues receives consideration in Mary A. Burwack and Robert K. Oermann, *Finding Her Voice: The Saga of Women in Country Music* (1993). For profiles of George Jones, Emmylou Harris, and others, see Nicholas Dawidoff, *In the Country of Country: People and Places in American Music* (1997).

The performers of heavy metal and Southern rock warrant extensive consideration in Anthony De Curtis, et al. eds., *The Rolling Stone Illustrated History of Rock and Roll: The Definitive History of the Most Important Artists and Their Music*, 3rd ed. (1992). The most comprehensive treatments of rock music's rising star of the 1970s belong to Jim Cullen, *Born in the U.S.A.: Bruce Springsteen and the American Tradition*

(1997) and Bruce Marsh, *Bruce Springsteen/Two Hearts: The Definitive Biography, 1972–2003* (2004). Other commentaries include Robert Coles, *Bruce Springsteen's America: The People Listening, a Poet Singing* (2003) and Bryan K. Gorman, *A Race of Singers: Whitman's Working-Class Hero from Guthrie to Springsteen* (2004).

12

The Disputed Terrain of People's Culture, 1980–2000

As conflict between social conservatives and cultural progressives escalated in the last two decades of the twentieth century, the United States appeared irredeemably polarized. Yet both sides of the culture divide insisted that their outlook derived from "the people." Male heroes in television and the movies frequently embodied values associated with populist conservatism, while their female counterparts more often represented outlooks promoting liberal inclusion and social justice. In contrast, broadcast and film comedies made light of all perspectives. The desire to reflect the experience of ordinary people continued to characterize much of country music, but found more politicized expression in the evolving work of rock star Bruce Springsteen. Meanwhile, a rich outpouring of multicultural expression pervaded literature and the media, climaxing in popular culture's dominant late-century musical form, hip-hop.

IRON MEN

The fusion of conservative and populist political sentiments received its most significant exposure through the presidencies of Ronald Reagan and George H.W. Bush. Reagan's popularity rested on an informal style that expressed calls for optimism and national strength once associated with the likes of Frank Capra and Franklin D. Roosevelt. Bush modeled himself on Gary Cooper's image as a taciturn westerner whose inarticulate manner suggested sincerity and inner fortitude. During the period in which the two Republican presidents held office between 1981 and 1993, they refashioned corporate capitalism as a populist and democratic enterprise that empowered consumers through the free market. Meanwhile, Republican politicians cooperated with evangelical Christians to advance a nostalgic view of the 1950s as a time of sexual innocence, stable families, and moral certainty, in contrast to the dissipation they linked with Sixties counterculture.

South Vietnam's fall to the Communists in 1975 helped to spark the conservative revival. The Vietnam War had penetrated American popular culture as early as 1966, when Sgt. Barry Sadler's record of "The Ballad of the Green Berets," a commemoration of the Special Forces soldier who "died for those oppressed," sold seven million copies within six months. The song received a film treatment in *The Green Berets* (1968), a movie starring John Wayne as a Marine officer called back to duty in Vietnam. Wayne fights the Viet Cong, protects innocent civilians, befriends an orphaned boy, and converts a liberal American journalist to the pro-war cause. As opposition to the military campaign broadened during the Nixon years, however, the Southeast Asian conflict took on a more problematic image, even in comic books, once a mainstay of patriotic loyalty.

As the comic book production code liberalized in the 1970s, several features mixed their heroics with anti-establishment characters. "No matter what I do," the introspective protagonist of *Amazing Spider-Man* bemoans in one episode, "nothing ever changes!" A new series, *Green Arrow* (1970+), described a bearded figure who shames an older colleague into admitting that his quest for law and order has led him to defend vested interests. Marvel's *Silver Surfer* (1968+) even presented a Christ-like scout from another world who seeks to help humans deal with racism, war, and environmental decay. In *Iron Man,* an ex-Cold Warrior lectures a conservative senator that the American people, not the government, make the country great. Vietnam entered the comics when *Spider-Man* agonized whether he should stay behind "while other guys are doing the fighting" or do his duty "in a war that nobody wants ... against an enemy you don't even hate." In one *Iron Man* segment of 1975, the hero buries the innocent victims of a U.S. air attack, places an epitaph on the mass grave reading "WHY?" and pledges to "avenge those whose lives have been lost through the ignorance of men like the man I once was!"

Three movies of the late Seventies expressed similar misgivings about Vietnam. Michael Camino's Academy Award-winning *The Deer Hunter* (1978) traced the story of three Ukrainian American steel workers from western Pennsylvania who wind up in a Viet Cong prisoner-of-war camp. As the film shifts from scenes of the soldiers' ethnic culture back home to their abusive treatment by the Vietnamese, viewers watch the men collapse into a world of corruption, drugs, and gambling. Returning to America as a lost man, one of the three (Robert De Niro) chooses to let a deer escape the sights of his hunting rifle. In Francis Coppola's allegorical *Apocalypse Now* (1979), Americans enter the heart of darkness in Vietnam and go mad from the experience. *Coming Home* (1978) offered another bleak perspective. When a Marine officer's wife (Jane Fonda) volunteers at a veterans hospital, she befriends and then falls in love with a bitter paraplegic (Jon Voight). After helping the patient deal with his situation, she begins to assert herself by speaking out on the war, only to have her wounded and psychologically damaged husband commit suicide upon his return.

The television series *M*A*S*H* (1972–83) also conveyed an antiwar message. Originating in a Robert Altman film in 1970, *M*A*S*H* chronicled the survival of a Korean War medical team amid the insanity of death and bureaucracy. Altman's characters endured the horrendous conditions of war through black humor, liquor, sex, and perverse camaraderie. In the television series, Alan Alda's "Hawkeye" combined the working-class grit of military situation comedy figures like Sgt. Bilko with the cynicism and independence of a Sixties rebel. Although the program depicted a previous Asian conflict, the similarities to Vietnam were obvious when the Army seemed to have no discernible purpose in a vague and abstract military campaign with no resolution.

Sylvester Stallone's *First Blood* (1982) offered a nationalistic response to the frustrations of Vietnam. The film chronicled the false arrest of ex-Green Beret John Rambo in a small northwestern town and his escape into the hinterlands, where he calls upon his military experience to avoid apprehension. "It wasn't my war," he explains. "You

Sylvester Stallone in *First Blood*   (*Photofest*)

asked me, I didn't ask you. And I did what I had to do to win." The sequel, *Rambo: First Blood Part II* (1985), brings the hero to Cambodia on an undercover mission to rescue U.S. prisoners of war and missing in action, men for whom Washington apparently has given up hope. Only the born-again patriotism and toughness of working-class veterans, suggests the movie, can stand up to the duplicitous liberal elites and government officials who have no stomach for retrieving the gallant men who have served their country and been so abandoned.

Rambo's vigilance had much in common with contemporary portraits of the police. The most celebrated of these involved Clint Eastwood. Starring in Don Siegel's *Dirty Harry* (1971), Eastwood portrayed San Francisco detective Harry Callahan, a vicious figure of unwavering resolve who lived outside the confines of law and order. Assigned to the case of a serial sniper, Callahan opposes delivering a $200,000 ransom for the release of a teenage girl because he fears the perpetrator will only make additional demands. Denouncing hippies and liberals as the cause of social immorality, he is reluctant to accept an untested, college-educated Mexican American as his new partner. In the end, Callahan freelances his own route to capturing the killer, violates the criminal's rights, and takes justice into his own hands once the police are compelled to release the defendant. "Go ahead, make my day!" Eastwood's hero declares, placing a phrase in the American lexicon that President Reagan would quote with relish.

Siegel and Eastwood produced a second hit with *Magnum Force* (1973), a film in which the San Francisco detective traced a series of slayings to his own department, and exposed how the courts ignored victims' rights and treated criminals with excessive permissiveness. In *The Enforcer* (1976), Dirty Harry Callahan returned with a female cohort to combat a terrorist group with ties to police superiors. By the early 1980s, however, Hollywood crime films had begun to take on new twists, including the use of humor. African American comedian Eddie Murphy starred in two movies that embodied the light approach to law enforcement. Born in Brooklyn in 1962 and raised in a middle-class family on Long Island, Murphy performed as a musician and stand-up comic as a teenager. After high school, he worked Manhattan comedy clubs and other East Coast venues before spending four years on television's fabled *Saturday Night Live*.

Influenced by Richard Pryor, Murphy assumed the persona of a self-confident, quick-witted, unflappable, and unconquerable black man capable of mastering any situation. In his first movie, *48 Hours* (1982), the comic played the resourceful Reggie Hammond—a convict on a two-day pass to help hard-bitten white police detective Jack Cates (Nick Nolte) capture a couple of onetime Hammond associates who are deranged cop killers. As the partners trade racial insults, the film sweeps through San Francisco's underworld, climaxing in a scene in a redneck bar when Hammond announces that he is the crowd's "worst f——g nightmare ... a nigger with a badge." After playing a clever hustler who exchanges positions with a preppy stockbroker in *Trading Places* (1983), Murphy starred in *Beverly Hills Cop* (1984), a story about a streetwise Detroit police officer who goes to Los Angeles in jeans, sneakers, and a sweatshirt to hunt down a white friend's killer.

Mel Gibson and Danny Glover presented another interracial crime-busting duo in *Lethal Weapon* (1987). Gibson played a former Special Forces assassin unhinged by his wife's accidental death. Intent on bringing down criminals without any interest in whether he lives or dies, the renegade Los Angeles police officer defies his cautious partner's advice and takes off on his own to destroy a drug smuggling ring run by Vietnam veterans. In *Die Hard* (1988), Bruce Willis portrayed a tough, anti-feminist New York cop who has come to L.A. to meet with his estranged wife, a corporate official in a Japanese-owned financial firm. When a dozen international terrorists take over the company's Century City offices in search of $670 million of negotiable bonds in the complex safe, Willis escapes the premises in a T-shirt, slacks, and bare feet and teams up with a black street officer (Reginald Veljohnson) to pick off the culprits one by one. On the opposite side of the law enforcement divide, Francis Ford Coppola's *The Godfather, Part III* (1990), Martin Scorcese's *Goodfellas* (1990), and Robert De Niro's *A Bronx Tale* (1993) each provided empathetic portraits of male bonding within the Mafia.

BUDDIES

In contrast to action-filled crime films, television police shows tended to concentrate on talk and human relations. The scripts for low-key *Barney Miller* (1975–82), for example, mainly reflected stationhouse banter and humor. Steven Bochco's intensely paced *Hill Street Blues* (1981–87), in turn, combined a nuanced approach to the ethical and social issues surrounding a drug-infested inner-city precinct with emphasis on how ordinary police officers responded to unfolding events. A second Bochco production, *NYPD Blue* (1993+), explored how the personal lives of law enforcement agents influenced the way they performed their jobs. Another popular cop show, the long-running *Law and Order* (1990+), earned a reputation for realism by filming on New York City streets.

Hollywood tales of male camaraderie like *The Blues Brothers* (1980), a movie originating in a series of Dan Aykroyd and John Belushi comedy sketches for TV's *Saturday Night Live*, completely abandoned the confines of crime drama. Barry Levinson's late 1950s period film *Diner* (1982) offered another example. The movie revolved around six ex-high school friends who meet regularly in their old Baltimore neighborhood hangout, where they engage in lively discussions on a range of topics, including sex, marriage, gambling, the pangs of approaching adulthood, and limited vocational prospects. The restricted nature of working-class existence also framed *All the Right Moves* (1983), a formula sports film about a Slavic high school football star (Tom Cruise) who wants out of the dying Pennsylvania mill town where his family has worked for generations. Spurring on the team before the big game with an affluent rival, a tough-talking coach (Craig T. Nelson) tells his players that they have endured ethnic and racial slurs long enough. In the end, the team loses, but the gritty coach gets a job at a California college and arranges a scholarship for the hometown hero.

Alex Cox's bizarre cult favorite *Repo Man* (1984) presented male bonding as black comedy. This surrealistic exploration of neon-lit Los Angeles starred Emilio Estevez as Otto, a suburban punk rock musician who has just lost his job as a supermarket checker. Tricked into repossessing his first car, Otto falls under the tutelage of Bud (Harry Dean Stanton), the seasoned proprietor of the Helping Hands Acceptance Company. As Bud leads his charge around the city's underside in a dented, oversized sedan, he consumes huge quantities of cocaine and alcohol and expounds upon the repo man's philosophy and code. It soon becomes clear that Otto's tutor has no life outside work. "The more you drive, the less intelligent you get," Bud observes. Most people, he explains with contempt, avoid confrontation, but repo men are unique because they spend their lives "getting *into* tense situations."

The Color of Money (1986), Martin Scorcese's sequel to *The Hustler,* starred Paul Newman in an Academy Award-winning performance as an older "Fast" Eddie Felson, who now peddles whiskey and bankrolls pool sharks for a percentage of the take. This time around, Eddie takes a young hotshot (Tom Cruise) on the road to show him the ropes. In innumerable scenes in pool halls, diners, and motels stretching from Chicago to the East Coast, the naïve competitor learns that a hustler sometimes must allow himself to lose to set up a victim. In a repeat of the original film, instructor and student break up over repeated differences, only to meet again in the national tournament in Atlantic City, where Eddie has returned to the game and his former charge proves that he has learned his master's lessons well.

Field of Dreams (1989) focused on the father-son relationship implicit in *The Color of Money*. Based on a novel by W.P. Kinsella, the film featured Kevin Costner as an Iowa farmer who hears voices telling him that if he will "build it, they will come." Ray interprets the message to mean that he should lay out a baseball diamond on his cornfield. When he does, legendary "Shoeless" Joe Jackson, the great Chicago White Sox star banned for collusion with gamblers after the 1919 World Series, appears in the mist and asks if his teammates can use the field as well. Meanwhile, Ray travels to Fenway Park and entices a Sixties radical novelist (James Earl Jones) to return with him to Iowa. "Ray, people will come," the writer enthuses after initial cynicism. "They'll come to Iowa for reasons they can't even fathom … as innocent as children, longing for the past … it's peace they'd like … they'll settle in with the children and cheer their heroes … and they'll watch the game and it'll be as if they dipped themselves in magic waters." When Ray's estranged father shows up with his hero, Joe Jackson, father and son engage in a game of catch, a symbol of baseball's ability to restore the country's cohesion.

While *Field of Dreams* recalled Frank Capra's idealism, several movies turned to political populism. Louis Malle's *Alamo Bay* (1985) presented the conflict between Texas shrimp fishing boat operators and their Vietnamese immigrant competitors as one in which both sides sought the American Dream. The irony of Malle's film lay in the fact that many of the Texans turning to the Ku Klux Klan for support were working-class Vietnam veterans.

Following the Rambo movies, a number of Hollywood features attempted to portray the war more creditably. Oliver Stone's *Platoon* (1986) told the story of a college dropout (Charlie Sheen) who volunteered to go to Vietnam because he objected to the fact that student deferment normally exempted young men of his social class. Offering a view of combat from the perspective of a search-and-destroy team, the film presented graphic images of ground fighting and the killing of innocent villagers suspected of harboring Viet Cong guerrillas. Three subsequent productions, Stanley Kubrick's *Full Metal Jacket* (1987), John Irvin's *Hamburger Hill* (1987), and Brian DePalma's *Casualties of War* (1989, also provided extremely realistic battle scenes.

In *Born on the Fourth of July* (1989), Oliver Stone returned to Vietnam with a film based on an autobiographical play by Ron Kovic. The movie traced the experiences of a young Catholic man from a hard-working middle-class family who volunteers for the Marines out of patriotic duty. Once in Vietnam, he sees the accidental slaughter of civilians and inadvertently kills a member of his own company. Left a paraplegic from his injuries, the protagonist comes to see returning veterans as symbols of a discredited and misplaced love of country. Another Stone production, *Heaven and Earth* (1993), sought to humanize the people caught between the fanatical ideologies of the war's two sides. "Different skin, same suffering," observes an aged Vietnamese man.

Three populist motion pictures addressed the plight of ordinary Americans at home. Set in the early 1920s, John Sayles' *Matewan* (1987) focused on a group of Italian immigrants and black migrants who stage a miner's strike in a West Virginia company town. Marked by realistic dialogue and a soundtrack mixing blues, Italian mandolin tunes, traditional Appalachian chants, and labor songs, the film placed working people at the center of the action, as an old-timer recalls details of the conflict. Michael Moore's salacious *Roger and Me* (1989) brought the labor struggle to present-day Flint, Michigan, the birthplace of General Motors. Describing the impact of GM's layoff of thirty thousand workers, the documentary contrasted the affluent lifestyles of company stockholders with the struggles of local families. One segment profiled an ex-autoworker in charge of housing evictions as a deputy sheriff. Another showed unemployed workers hiring themselves out as living statues for an elite garden party. Still another featured the "Bunny Lady," a woman with a store that advertises "Rabbits—Pets or Meat."

"Just when things were beginning to look bleak," Moore declares in the deadpan style of Mark Twain, "Ronald Reagan arrived in Flint and took twelve workers out for a pizza." Much of the footage of *Roger and Me* parodied the facile public relations and booster efforts of corporate and public officials. Dressed in a baseball cap, down jacket, jeans, and sneakers, Moore documented repeated attempts to speak with GM executive officer Roger Smith with no success. The bankruptcy of political leadership also concerned *Dave* (1993), a movie comedy in which Kevin Kline played a presidential look-alike pressed into temporary service when White House staffers try to cover up their superior's sexual dalliances. When a stroke incapacitates the real president, however, the arrangement becomes permanent. The twist to the story comes when Dave realizes he can effect change and connect with people. Convinced that an ordinary man can run the country better than insiders, he balances the budget over bratwurst dinner with an old accountant pal, while the professional politicians posture and accomplish nothing.

Academy Award winner *Forrest Gump* (1994) presented an unabashed satire of political pretensions on all sides. Starring Best Actor Tom Hanks in the title role, the film chronicled the exploits of a slow-witted but benevolent character who participates in the major events of recent U.S. history. As Forrest sits at a Savannah bus stop, he tells his story to anyone who will listen. It turns out he has taught Elvis how to dance, been a college football star, received military honors in Vietnam, become a ping-pong champion, witnessed the Watergate burglary, and run a successful shrimp business. Adhering to the philosophy that "stupid is as stupid does," he goes through life with no personal ambition, social agenda, or political goals. In the simple world of Forrest Gump, where decency, honesty, and fidelity are the only virtues that count, racists are mean-spirited, militarists are foolhardy, and power brokers merely self-serving. Significantly, Forrest views Sixties radicals and counterculture activists through the same lens. In the end, this immensely popular film placed commonplace innocence and virtue above the posturing of politicized ideologues, no matter what their orientation.

WORKING GIRLS

By the early 1980s, the major television networks began to see prime-time women's programming as a lucrative source of market share. For the first time, an all-women police duo graced the TV screen. In *Cagney and Lacey* (1982–88), two streetwise New York City police officers, one single and the other married, established a strong working relationship based on mutual respect and cooperation. Unlike most cop shows, *Cagney and Lacey* featured protagonists who experienced visible emotional growth and changes as they took on their assignments. Hollywood entered the women's workplace with *9 to 5* (1980), a film featuring Dolly Parton's original composition of the same name. With Jane Fonda, Lily Tomlin, and Parton in lead roles, *9 to 5* described a rebellion of three women office employees against sexual exploitation. After kidnapping their chauvinist boss, the trio takes over the business and institutes equal pay for equal work, flextime, a day-care center, and a positive office environment. The irony in the plot lay in the fact that the company chair sees their innovations as morale-boosting reforms, and the boss, once restored to his former place, takes credit for their implementation.

Two films by Mike Nichols offered contrasting views of women's place in corporate America. In *Silkwood* (1983), Meryl Streep portrayed the real-life character of Karen Silkwood, a hard-drinking and profane union officer and lab employee at an Oklahoma plutonium processing plant. Known for toughness and independence of mind, Silkwood lives in a ramshackle house with her boyfriend (Kurt Russell) and best friend Dolly (Cher), a lesbian. Concerned about plant health and safety violations, she spies for documents that can support her suspicions. After claiming to discover photo negatives showing the doctored quality of control welds, however, Silkwood dies in a car crash on the way to a meeting with the reporter to whom she has promised the evidence.

Working Girl (1988) opened with a shot of Tess (Melanie Griffith), an ambitious secretary in a Wall Street investment firm, commuting on the Staten Island Ferry. The clues to the protagonist's status appear in her teased hairdo, excessive jewelry, and flashy clothes. Combined with her gender, these markers help to keep Tess out of the executive training program to which she aspires. When her female boss (Sigourney Weaver), an acquisitions and mergers executive, breaks a leg in a skiing accident, however, Tess takes over her superior's persona, style, and financial portfolio. Through a combination of charm, wit, and street smarts, including a survey of gossip columns for information on Wall Street players and their families, she manages to pull off a spectacular deal with the help of specialist Harrison Ford, with whom she enters a sizzling romance. In sexualizing the world of finance, *Working Girl* was pure fairy tale. Yet in detailing how Tess' striving threatened her relationship with her co-workers, friends, and fisherman fiancé back on Staten Island, the film emphasized the importance of class in American life.

As the popularity of TV's *Alice* and its spin-offs indicated, the working life of the beleaguered waitress remained a favored subject. Set in the Portuguese American community of a Connecticut seaside town, *Mystic Pizza* (1988) provided Julia Roberts with her first major Hollywood role. The film described the last carefree summer of two sisters, Kat and Daisy, and their friend Jojo, who wait on tables and mop floors for a maternal pizza house operator. Jojo is terrified at the prospects of marriage with a local fisherman, Kat has a Yale astronomy scholarship but no common sense with men, and Roberts' Daisy is unsure of the intentions of a young suitor from an uppity family that looks down upon her. The heart of the movie lies in the casual but devoted camaraderie among the three employees and the protective love of the childless proprietor, who produces an envelope to fund Daisy's college education when no other options appear.

In Allison Anders' *Gas Food Lodging* (1992), a divorced and hard-working roadside café waitress valiantly tries to raise two adolescent daughters in a mobile home in dusty Laramie, New Mexico. Restless and bored, the three welcome the arrival of several male strangers, a situation that precipitates initial conflict, the healing of old wounds, and a reassertion of their mutual strengths. Overworked food servers fared better in Andrew Bergman's *It Could Happen to You* (1994) and James L. Brooks' *As Good As It Gets*

(1997). In the first, beat cop Nicholas Cage offers half a lottery ticket to a hard-luck New York waitress (Bridget Fonda), who thinks nothing of the gesture until he wins the jackpot and insists on fulfilling the promise, much to the chagrin of his ambitious wife (Rosie Perez). *As Good As It Gets* told the story of a single mom (Best Actress Helen Hunt) who regularly serves a superstitious, obsessive-compulsive romance novel author (Best Actor Jack Nicholson) at a local café. As a painfully awkward relationship develops between the two, the waitress and the writer's gay neighbor (Greg Kinnear) team up to humanize Nicholson, allowing him to overcome his mental prisons.

PLACES OF THE HEART

As the media turned to ordinary women as viable subject matter, characterizations of female protagonists took on renewed complexity. The TV movie *Lois Gibbs and the Love Canal* (1982) broke new ground with the story of a passive and insecure Niagara Falls homemaker who becomes a self-confident crusader against toxic waste when her son becomes mysteriously ill. Defying her husband, an employee of the offending plant, as well as the local power structure, Gibbs organizes neighboring women to force the federal government to order a site evacuation and cleanup. A more personal kind of activism characterized *The Burning Bed* (1984), a television feature in which Farah Fawcett portrayed a woman brutalized by a jobless husband resentful of her attempts at self-improvement. Taking her three children from the home, she sets fire to the abuser's bed, killing him in the process. In the end, a jury acquits her of all charges on grounds of temporary insanity. *Silent Witness* (1985), another made-for-television film, told the story of a supermarket checkout clerk who witnesses a gang rape in a local bar and defies her family and community by testifying against her husband's brother and two other men.

Interest in fully developed women movie characters resulted in Mary Tyler Moore's role as an affluent suburban mother in denial over her son's mental illness in Robert Redford's Academy Award Best Picture, *Ordinary People* (1980). Another Academy winner, *Terms of Endearment* (1983), an adaptation of a Larry McMurtry novel by James L. Brooks, concentrated upon the intimate relationship between a mother (Best Actress Shirley MacLaine) and her cancer-ridden daughter (Debra Winger), and her simultaneous camaraderie with a former astronaut (Best Supporting Actor Jack Nicholson). In *Places of the Heart* (1984), in turn, Academy Award Best Actress Sally Field played a young Texas widow of the 1930s who bridges both gender and racial barriers. Determined to save her family farm from foreclosure after a drunken black teenager shoots her police officer husband to death, she takes in a blind boarder for ready cash and hires an African American drifter (Danny Glover) to help plant and bring in the cotton crop. When the Ku Klux Klan drives away the black laborer after the successful harvest, Field tries to envision a society without violence and prejudice.

One of the most offbeat male-female relationships occurred in Jim Jarmusch's *Stranger Than Paradise* (1984), a film about a sixteen-year-old Hungarian girl who visits a cousin and his aimless pal in New York. Unperturbed by the fact that her hosts survive by cheating at cards, playing the horses, and betting at the dog track, she pesters them with questions about American customs, insisting, for example, that they explain why packaged frozen meals are called "TV dinners." The visitor soon ingratiates herself by shoplifting food and cigarettes. When she leaves for Cleveland to stay with an elderly aunt, the two men realize how dependent upon her company they have become. Showing up in Ohio, they bring her on a trip to a seedy Atlantic resort in central Florida. "You're someplace new," someone observes in the deadpan style that permeates the film, "and everything looks just the same." As Jarmusch highlights the sublime elements of America's tackiest surroundings with a cast of unknown character actors, he tells a touching love story of people with no pretensions for being other than they are.

Like *Stranger Than Paradise,* Norman Jewison's *Moonstruck* (1987) stripped the emotional life of its principals of all excess. The movie starred Cher in an Academy Award winning performance as Loretta Castorini, a thirty-eight-year-old Italian American widow who works as a bookkeeper at a Brooklyn funeral parlor. Cher had recently triumphed in Peter Bogdanovich's *Mask* (1985), the true story of a drug-taking single biker mom who nurtures her son, Rocky (Eric Stolz), with confidence and unqualified love, despite the fact that a rare and incurable disease has disfigured the boy's face. In *Moonstruck,* Loretta agrees to marry a kind but older man, who first must return to Sicily to tend to his dying mother. In a gesture of reconciliation, the fiancé instructs the bride-to-be to involve his estranged brother Ronny (Nicholas Cage), an embittered bakery worker, in plans for the wedding. In the romance and intense family interactions that follow, viewers learn that the only way to avoid life's pain is to avoid life itself. Although death may be inevitable, these true-to-life characters suggest, people must sustain a concern for the living and the possibilities of love.

Several women's films placed their protagonists on voyages of emotional discovery. Geraldine Page won an Academy Award for her lead role in *The Trip to Bountiful* (1985), screenwriter Horton Foote's adaptation of a play he had written for television in 1953. Page played an elderly woman with a weak heart and a love of hymns sharing a cramped Houston apartment in 1947 with her son and his shrewish wife. Determined to return one last time to the small southeast Texas Gulf town where she grew up, she puts on an old hat and her best dress, absconds with her pension check, and makes her way to the bus station. Once arriving at her destination, she proves surprisingly able to adjust her long-held fantasies to the realities before her.

A far different journey awaited "Baby" (Jennifer Grey), the highly indulged sixteen-year-old daughter of a middle-class Jewish family in the low-budget *Dirty Dancing* (1987). When Baby falls into an affair with the working-class dance instructor (Patrick Swayze) at the Catskills resort where her family summers, she not only experiences her first contact with soul music and sexual arousal, but also assumes an independent identity as a caring and socially aware adult. Joan Micklin Silver's *Crossing Delancey* (1988) coupled Amy Irving, a single Jewish careerist in her early thirties, with another working-class man. Isabelle works at a fashionable bookstore, where she is in awe of the New York literary elite, and rents a tiny uptown apartment, where, according to her Lower East Side grandmother (Reizl Bozyk), she "lives alone ... like a dog." Through the grandmother's intervention, a matchmaker sets Isabelle up with a hard-working, patient, and generous Jewish pickle merchant (Peter Riegert). Initially mortified, the young woman comes to appreciate her suitor's genuine qualities, in preference to the pretensions and hypocrisies of her urbane associates.

The vitality of working-class values also underlay Garry Marshall's romantic fable *Pretty Woman* (1990). The movie starred Julia Roberts as a Sunset Strip hooker retained as an escort by a handsome financier (Richard Gere), who is negotiating a delicate takeover of an old shipbuilding firm. Much of the movie deals with Gere's success in turning a coarse and gawky street hustler into an elegant glamour queen. Yet in the end, the prostitute becomes the moral center of the movie, when her total honesty and directness inspires the buyout wizard to change his mind and propose a partnership with the targeted company to continue producing boats. Just when it looks as if the couple will go their separate ways, Gere rushes to her building and ascends the fire escape to her apartment window. What happened in the fairy tale when the white knight climbed up the tower to rescue the maiden? he asks. "She rescued him right back," she answers.

Just as *Pretty Woman* turned the tables on moral agency, *Thelma and Louise* (1991), a women's road-buddy movie featuring Geena Davis and Susan Sarandon, offered a succinct treatment of gender role reversal. A saucy waitress in an Arkansas coffee shop, Louise talks her timid housewife friend, Thelma, into taking off on a weekend fishing trip that the two undertake in Louise's turquoise Thunderbird convertible. When a cocky regular in a roadside honky-tonk attempts to take liberties with Thelma in the parking lot and taunts Louise into doing something about it, she shoots the offender to death with Thelma's borrowed pistol, leading to a desperate escape across the Southwest. Despite the danger, the ensuing crime spree and adventure prompts the two principals into experiencing life for the first time. When Thelma muses that she has always been "a little crazy," Louise agrees, but adds, "This is just the first time you've ever had to really express yourself." Framed by stark desert scenery and a hearty country music score, *Thelma and Louise* provided a fresh rendering to the tale of the western desperado.

SO-CALLED LIFE

Vernacular storytelling reached its highest form in the radio broadcasts and fiction of Garrison Keillor. During the Fifties, late-night New York radio personality Jean Shepherd had mined the riches of oral tradition with a series of reminiscences about his Indiana boyhood and readings from the work of Booth Tarkington. Shepherd's published tales included *In God We Trust: All Others Pay Cash* (1966) and *Wanda Hickey's Night of Golden Memories and Other Disasters* (1971). In an audiocassette entitled *Jean Shepherd: Shepherd's Pie* (1991), the humorist described how ordinary midwesterners felt doomed to mediocrity and obscurity. Garrison Keillor embodied a similar mentality. Raised outside Minneapolis during the 1940s, Keillor was the son of a railway mail clerk and part-time carpenter. Although the working-class family followed a pietistic brand of Protestantism, the youngster had the freedom to listen to the radio and enjoy the stories of his great uncle, aunt, and grandfather. At age thirteen, he began writing and adopted the name "Garrison" because it sounded distinguished.

A reluctant student at the University of Minnesota in the early Sixties, Keillor worked as a parking lot attendant and served on the student radio station. When he became editor of the campus literary review, he published several pieces satirizing lower-middle-class fundamentalism and small-town ignorance. After obtaining a Master's Degree in English, Keillor placed two humorous pieces in the *New Yorker*. He also began hosting a morning public radio show that featured a wide variety of recorded music. At first, he made fun of the pretentiousness of public radio in brief comedy skits. Gradually, however, Keillor began to develop a broadcasting persona that sounded "like somebody sitting across the breakfast table from you reading an item." Adopting down-home inflections and the informal grammar of the small-town Midwest, he renamed the program *A Prairie Home Companion*. After writing a *New Yorker* piece on the Grand Ole Opry in 1974, Keillor refashioned his program as a friendly gathering reminiscent of old-time radio and moved the broadcast to Saturday evenings.

In the barn dance tradition, *Prairie Home Companion* featured a mix of comedy routines and live acoustic country and folk music. As the show went live on national public radio in 1980, however, Keillor focused on the mythic upstate village of Lake Wobegon—"the little town that time forgot." In the satiric tradition of Mark Twain, the friendly host broadcasted fictional commercials for local sponsors like Bertha's Kitty Boutique, The Fearmonger's Shoppe, Powdermilk Biscuits, and Ralph's Pretty Good Grocery. Gradually, however, Keillor moved from the distance of an announcer's persona to offer weekly updates on the fictional characters and exploits of his adopted hometown. As a loving son in exile and sincere insider, he offered intimate descriptions of home life, heartbreak, and hard times that enabled him to make unpretentious observations about the human condition and the quirks of everyday life.

Artless and informal in presentation, each of the show's monologues began with the greeting, "Well, it has been a quiet week in Lake Wobegon." Listeners learned about the quarrel over Florida vacation plans between Lutheran Pastor David Ingquist and his wife, Judy, the toughness of Norwegian bachelor farmers, the hot tuna "blue plate special" at the Chatterbox Café, and the latest developments at the Our Lady of Perpetual Responsibility Catholic Church. Additional segments concerned holiday celebrations,

Garrison Keillor   (*Courtesy A Prairie Home Companion*)

ice fishing, the fate of the local softball nine, the difficulties of local politicians, tavern gossip, lost loves and opportunities, and eternal family squabbles. Beneath these tales, narratives consistently pointed to lessons of humility and compassion. "Life is basically happy, but you can find tragedy if you go looking for it," Keillor quoted locals Clarence and Arlene Bunsen as saying on one occasion. No matter what direction the presentations assumed, however, each installment ended identically. "Well, that's all the news from Lake Wobegon," concluded Keillor, "where all the women are strong, all the men are good looking, and all the children are above average."

By 1984, 218 public radio stations carried the award-winning *Prairie Home Companion*. Keillor's stories also found their way into print in *Lake Wobegon Days* (1985) and in *Leaving Home* (1987), an edited collection of thirty-six monologues that sold four million copies. After a two-year hiatus, Keillor returned to the air in 1989 with the New York-based American Radio Company of the Air. Four years later, however, the show resumed broadcasts from St. Paul's refurbished World Theater under its original name. With parodies of film noir detectives, politically correct cowboys, snooty French chefs, anxiety-ridden baby boomers, postmodernist theorists, and English graduate students, the program's humor increasingly targeted the urbane audience making up its core following. Such popularity, in fact, led Robert Altman to feature Keillor in a screen version of *A Prairie Home Companion* (2006) written by the radio personality himself.

Several widely viewed television shows concentrated on the lives of everyday Americans. In *Taxi* (1978–83), Danny DeVito played Louie, the wisecracking dispatcher at the Sunshine Cab Company, where drivers like Alex Reiger (Judd Hirsch) hated their jobs because they aspired to better things. Set in a Boston bar owned by a former Red Sox pitcher (Ted Danson), *Cheers* (1981-93) reveled in the hilarious interactions between bartenders, waitresses, and "regulars," including a know-it-all mail carrier, a psychiatrist in a dysfunctional marriage to a therapist, and a disgruntled, overweight, and cranky accountant. As the Fox network reached out to African Americans with *A Different World* (1987-93), *The Fresh Prince of Bel-Air* (1990-96), and *In Living Color* (1990-94), the irreverent *Married ... With Children* (1987-97) focused on a trashy white family. Parodying upbeat family sitcoms (situation comedies), the show depicted the life of Al Bundy, a second-rate shoe clerk at a dying strip mall whose self-centered and sarcastic wife despised housework and her husband, whose precocious teen daughter was an incorrigible slut, and whose teenage son floundered in a sexualized dream world.

One year after the debut of *Married ... With Children, Roseanne* (1988–97) hit prime time. The show evolved from a stand-up comedy routine by executive producer and star, Roseanne Barr, in which a "domestic goddess" offered practical advice on child rearing. Barr intended *Roseanne* as a response to *The Cosby Show* (1984–92), a top-rated program revolving around the supportive parenting of two prosperous African American professionals. In contrast, the Conners were a disorganized mother-centered, working-class family that faced constant debt and threats of unemployment. Dan (John Goodman), Roseanne's husband, starts out as a construction subcontractor who often takes jobs as a sheet-rock installer and later graduates to running a motorcycle shop and owning his own diner. Roseanne works at a plastics factory before moving on to becoming a small café proprietor. As Barr described it, the show's protagonist loves her family, "but they can drive her nuts." A sarcastic and even scornful parent, Roseanne nevertheless provides affection and support when needed. With it all, the family honestly confronts thorny issues like masturbation, cosmetic breast surgery, and gay and lesbian relationships.

Matt Groening's irreverent *The Simpsons* (1990+), an animated comedy first introduced on the *Tracey Ullman Show,* pushed the boundaries of family parody with a take-off on mindless suburban consumerism and social conformity. Nominal family head Homer, a slothful, dull, and vain nuclear plant inspector, quickly popularized the dim-witted catch phrase "d'oh." In contrast, blue-haired wife and mother Marge managed to think the best of people while cleaning up her husband's calamities. Meanwhile, the social responsibility of jazz saxophonist and intellectual daughter, Lisa, diverged from her mischievous but lovable brother, Bart, the star of the show known for excusing misdeeds with a glib "Don't have a cow, man." Mike Judge's animated *The Beavis and Butt-Head Show* (1993–97) parodied the male adolescent audience of its Music Television (MTV) network with a portrait of two dumb high school losers fascinated with violence, sex, and bathroom humor. Through the program, the phrase "it sucks" became a mainstay of everyday language. Another animated feature, *South Park* (1997+) mocked small-town life in Colorado with a portrait of four third-graders and the mantra "nothing is sacred."

Cable television's interest in realism produced the short-lived MTV series *My So-Called Life* (1994–95). Starring Claire Danes, the show offered a non-sentimental portrait of suburban adolescence from the perspective of an awkward fifteen-year-old, Angela Chase. "School is a battlefield for your heart," Angela observes. The program's story line concerned Angela's fixation on Jordan Catalono (Jared Leto), a languid and inarticulate classmate who sings in a rock band and spells danger in the eyes of the young woman's parents. A similar impatience with romantic contrivance characterized the enormously popular *Seinfeld* (1989–98). Building a reputation as a comedian focused on common absurdities and ironies, Jerry Seinfeld worked with fellow comic Larry David to develop a series based on a TV comedy writer's everyday routine. By extracting humor from trivia, casual incidents, the situations of city existence, and the quirky singles life of "30-somethings," the team created one of the most beloved shows of all time. *Friends* (1994–2004), a series about six "20-somethings" who gather at a New York coffee house called Central Perk, offered a comparable account of the lives and loves of Generation X.

TENDER MERCIES

While much of Nineties television comedy concentrated on the urban middle class, country and western took its place as the nation's foremost popular music style. Hollywood had first documented the genre's rise in Robert Altman's *Nashville* (1975), succeeded by *Urban Cowboy* (1981), a film starring John Travolta and Debra Winger as dance-hall regulars at Gilley's Club, a Houston-area hot spot frequented by oil workers. Another movie, *Tender Mercies* (1983), featured Robert Duvall as a divorced, alcoholic, ex-honky-tonk singer who winds up a handyman and devoted husband to a religious widow running a remote Texas motel. Duvall's repentant character bore similarities to country performer George Jones, whose real-life bouts with liquor were legendary. Known for conveying the searing pain of broken love through low moans and high wails delivered through clenched teeth, Jones won a Grammy Award with "He Stopped Loving Her Today" (1980), a Bobby Braddock and Curly Putnam composition subsequently voted the greatest country song of all time. "This time he's over her for good," the sparse lyric concludes of a man in love with the woman who left him until the day he died.

Although country recordings frequently made it to the popular music charts, Nashville continued to rely on gospel roots, particularly as Protestant evangelicals began to reassert a public presence in the Seventies. Accepted as a regular member of the Grand Ole Opry in 1973, comic Jerry Clower reflected such sensibilities. Raised during the

Depression in rural Mississippi by a single mother after his alcoholic father deserted the family, Clower joined the Baptist Church at thirteen, where he met his wife-to-be. A successful fertilizer salesman after World War II, he became a popular banquet speaker across the South and began to record his stories in 1971. Clower's humor chided excesses of religious piety, but spoke to the ingenuity, pride, and gumption of rural and working-class people. Emphasizing the knowledge that came from personal experience instead of formal learning, he extracted folk wisdom from personal mistakes and embarrassments.

By the 1980s, numerous country artists had returned to simple lyrics and old-fashioned styling to express small-town values, continuity with the past, and fellowship with family and loved ones. Kentucky's Ricky Skaggs, a skilled bluegrass mandolin player who performed with the Stanley Brothers as a teenager, merged electric instrumentation with traditional motifs in the best-selling album *Don't Cheat in Our Home Town* (1983). Meanwhile, North Carolina vocalist and guitarist Randy Travis scored a Number One hit with "On the Other Hand" (1986), a song about a man who barely manages to resist the temptations of an extramarital affair when he remembers the vows represented by his marriage ring. In the wedding favorite "Forever and Ever, Amen" (1987), Travis sang about love as constant as old men talking about the weather and old women gossiping about old men. George Strait's "Love Without End, Amen" (1990), in turn, described the life-long commitment of a loving parent.

Lyle Lovett's album *Joshua Judges Ruth* (1992) provided an example of modern country music's sustained interest in traditional themes. In a down-home fusion of Biblical imagery and snippets of everyday life, Lovett's "Since the Last Time" offered a catchy portrait of a man who attended church every Sunday after being "drunk the night before." Such a juxtaposition of religiosity and hard living made sense in the largely Protestant culture of the South, where the promise of salvation normally required acknowledgment of sin. Southern Ohio's Dwight Yoakam, the grandson of a Kentucky coal miner, offered further evidence of the crossover between a traditionalist approach and the attractions of the nightlife with hits like "Honky Tonk Man" (1986) and "Guitars, Cadillacs" (1986), songs that recalled the hard-driving beat of guitarist Buck Owens.

Houston-raised Clint Black, the first of the "new country" performers to sport a perennial cowboy hat, helped to foster the honky-tonk revival with *Killin' Time* (1989), a collection that sold over three million copies. Georgia's Travis Tritt combined hardcore country and rock in barroom favorites like "The Whiskey Ain't Workin'" (1991), a song recorded as a duet with veteran artist Marty Stuart, and "Lord Have Mercy on the Working Man" (2003). Another blue-collar hero, Oklahoman Joe Diffie, released *Honky Tonk Attitude* (1993), while vocalists Brad Paisley and Tim McGraw further mined working-class themes. Meanwhile, the Austin scene continued to produce hard-driving Texas swing and drinking tunes through the performances of country and western stars like Butch Hancock, Dale Watson, Jimmie Dale Gilmore, and Steve Earle.

No matter what genre they assumed, working-class subjects found an inevitable place within modern country music. Even the pop-oriented vocal group Alabama paid tribute to working people who were "worth more than they're paid" in "Forty Hour Week" (1984). Another mainstream artist, Garth Brooks, experimented with vernacular currents in the rowdy "Friends in Low Places" (1990). Nashville's most successful rendering of populist themes, however, came in the blend of musical styles produced by Alan Jackson. The son of a Georgia auto mechanic, Jackson spent over four years as a Nashville mailroom clerk and side-man before recording his first solo album in 1989. Proud of his southern lilt and twang, the singer combined a passion for traditional country material with everyday subjects. *Don't Rock the Jukebox* (1991), Jackson's self-consciously titled second album, included "Working Class Hero," a tribute to his father, and "Midnight in Montgomery," a salute to Hank Williams. A follow-up collection featured "Chattahoochee" (1992), an up-tempo reminiscence of a love-hungry teenager hanging out by the river on Friday nights.

Female singers added another element to country music's portrait of ordinary life. The Birmingham-born daughter of an Army officer, Emmylou Harris mixed contemporary and traditional material and styling. Although Harris' counterculture demeanor appealed to young cosmopolitans, her haunting vocals reflected a working-class sensibility that acknowledged differences between men and women in temperament and attitudes. The mother-daughter team of Naomi and Wynonna Judd, billed as The Judds, also spoke to people with a rural background. Taking off from their Appalachian roots, the duo produced a steady stream of hits that included "Mama, He's Crazy" (1984), "Love Is Alive" (1984), and "John Deere Tractor" (1984).

Lacy J. Dalton, a native of the Pennsylvania Appalachians, cultivated an even more explicit working-class image. Although Dalton's mother earned a living as a beautician and a waitress and her father as a mechanic and hunting guide, both parents were country musicians. Dropping out of college in Utah in the late Sixties to become a hippie folksinger, the aspiring artist wound up as a widowed mother living on food stamps in California's Santa Cruz Mountains at the age of twenty-seven. Once Dalton sent a tape to a Nashville contact, however, she signed a contract and produced her first hit, "Crazy Blue Eyes" (1979). Her next hits, "Hard Times" (1980) and "Hillbilly Girl with the Blues" (1980), coincided with a small film role in *Take This Job and Shove It*. Dalton's *Highway Diner* (1986), an album devoted to the reverses of blue-collar life and farm foreclosures, produced the hit single "Working Class Man." *Survivor* (1989), in turn, focused upon single mothers as symbols of human perseverance. "I come from a working-class background," commented Dalton; "it wasn't long ago that I was waiting on tables for a living."

Country music's female fans helped to elevate Reba McEntire to superstar status. Born on a working Oklahoma ranch in 1955, McEntire sang as a child with her sister and brother. Discovered in 1974 by Red Steagall while performing the national anthem at a rodeo, she won recognition as a "new traditionalist" with *My Kind of Country* (1984), an album featuring hits like "How Blue" and "Somebody Should Leave." In 1991, McEntire recorded "The Greatest Man I Never Knew," a tribute to her father. Most of her songs and videos, however, like "For My Broken Heart" (1993), depicted the pride, hard work, and determination of ordinary women seeking to control their destiny. In doing so, McEntire's lyrics went beyond customary themes of heartbreak and domestic turmoil, to touch on issues like wife beating, prostitution, or the struggles of women emerging from divorce or broken relationships.

Traditional music received further exposure when Dolly Parton returned to her blue-grass roots with two acoustic albums, *The Grass is Blue* (1999) and *The Little Sparrow* (2003). Both Patty Loveless, the daughter of a Kentucky coal miner, and musician-vocalist Alison Krauss further expanded the market for acoustic music with best-selling work. Meanwhile, a new breed of female artists like Faith Hill, Shania Twain, Deana Carter, and Sara Evans sang openly of the desire of ordinary women for sexual pleasure and personal fulfillment, even if it meant defiance of parents or spouses. Raised on a Missouri tobacco farm, Evans invoked the essential definition of country music, *Three Chords and the Truth* (1995), as the title of her debut album. Liberationist strategies also marked the music of Lee Ann Womack, whose lyric for "You Can Fly" (2000) implored her young daughter to take chances in life and pursue her dreams. Martina McBride's controversial "Independence Day" (1993), in turn, pictured a battered wife taking justice into her own hands. Another McBride hit, "When God-Fearin' Women Get the Blues" (2000), amounted to a whimsical model of patriarchal subversion.

AT THE EDGE OF TOWN

Rebelling in the late Seventies against the perceived pretensions, artiness, and senti-mentalized corruption of the rock establishment, bands like Britain's Sex Pistols and New York's Ramones inaugurated the aggressively minimalist and raging sounds of anarchist punk. Elements of the underground's anger and urgency soon found their way to more mainstream channels. Pop musician Billy Joel, a street gang member and wel-terweight boxing champion during his days as a Long Island teenager, scored a major hit with "Allentown," a cut from *Nylon Curtain* (1982), an album focusing on Vietnam veterans, ailing steelmills, and rampant unemployment. The same recession year wit-nessed the release of Indiana musician John Cougar Mellencamp's *American Fool* (1982), a collection of homegrown rock selections featuring the best-selling single "Jack and Diane," a saga of "2 American kids growin' up in the heartland."

"Oh yeah," sang Mellencamp, "life goes on/Long after the thrill of livin' is gone." Despite these examples, no rock performer seemed to capture the bittersweet qualities of working-class existence with the consistency of Bruce Springsteen. In the concept album *Darkness on the Edge of Town* (1978), Springsteen sought to give voice to people shut out of the American Dream who struggled for survival and self-fulfillment against overwhelming odds. "Some guys," he sang in "Factory," they just give up living/And start dying little by little, piece by piece." In "Adam Raised a Cain," Springsteen's protagonist noted the poignancy of ordinary people "born into this life payin' for the sins of somebody else's past." Yet the collection also contained stories of people who broke through social barriers, of those "wanting things that can only be found/In the darkness on the edge of town."

Springsteen's Number One album, *The River* (1980), continued to depict everyday realities of work, struggle, and potential escape. "Drive All Night," with its touching imagery of a narrator's obsessive commitment to his loved one, illustrated a young couple's search for warmth in a cold, unforgiving world. The stark "Point Blank" raised the specter of incipient violence in ordinary existence. In the countrified "Wreck on the Highway," Springsteen brought to mind Frank Capra's *It's a Wonderful Life* with a tableau in which the protagonist sees himself as the victim of a car crash he encounters while driving home. The album's title piece presented the tale of a young working-class protagonist who marries his seventeen-year-old girlfriend after getting her pregnant. Resigned to a construction job to support his family, the narrator loses his meager livelihood during a recession. "Now I just act like I don't remember," he sings of lost hopes, "Mary acts like she don't care." "Is a dream a lie if it don't come true," the young man asks, "Or is it something worse."

Influenced by Flannery O'Connor's stories of isolation and the music of Jimmie Rodgers, Hank Williams, and Woody Guthrie, Springsteen produced the acoustic *Nebraska* (1982). The album's cover featured a two-lane blacktop photographed through a car windshield in the style of a Robert Frank image. *Nebraska* emphasized the impact of place on the development of characters and the tough moral choices confronting people in an imperfect world. "Used Cars" offered a young boy's cynical reflections on a dead-end life. In "Highway Patrolman," a police officer allows his brother's car to escape a crime scene. The album's title song presented a first-hand account of 1950s mass murderer Charlie Starkweather. In "Johnny 99," a song initiated with a Jimmie Rodgers wail, Springsteen told the story of a man laid off by a New Jersey plant closing. Unable to find work, the protagonist gets drunk and shoots a night clerk in an attempted robbery. Without pretending innocence, he tells the judge that he had "debts no honest man could pay" and was about to lose his house. "It was more'n all this that put that gun in my hand," he explains.

Springsteen's most popular recording was *Born in the U.S.A.* (1984), the Number One album that remained in the Top Ten for two years and generated seven best-selling singles. By now, the performer had completely merged his individual persona with that of the white working class. Fusing Fifties rock and roll and rockabilly with Sixties folk rock, Springsteen updated the traditional "greaser" image with an explicitly populist political stance. "I'm on Fire," a song reproduced in a popular music video, described a garage mechanic's longing for a married woman far above his station. In "My Hometown," a father taught his son the rituals of a dying textile mill town victimized by outsourcing. The album's theme of pride in the face of adversity and failure received its most explicit treatment in the collection's title piece. "Born in a dead man's town," the song began, "the first kick I took was when I hit the ground." After a scrape with the law, the narrator does time in Vietnam and returns with "nowhere to run" and "nowhere to go." Yet the lyric ends with the half-ironic, half-defiant "I'm a cool rockin' daddy in the U.S.A."

Despite the troubled content of Springsteen's subject matter, the upbeat cadence of "Born in the U.S.A." prompted reports that the performer had rejected a $12 million offer by the Chrysler Corporation to record the song for a TV commercial. The singer also declined to let the Republican Party use the piece as the theme song for its 1984 convention. By the Eighties, Springsteen saw himself as "a rich man in a poor man's shirt." Having read a biography of Woody Guthrie, he began to incorporate "This Land Is Your Land" in each concert, and recorded Guthrie standards like "I Ain't Got No Home" and "Vigilante Man" for a tribute organized by the Smithsonian Institution. Springsteen's influences also included Dale Maharidge's *Journey to Nowhere* (1985), a book about boxcar hoboes in decaying Youngstown, Ohio, with photographs by Michael Williamson.

Springsteen's identification with Woody Guthrie and marginalized Americans led to *The Ghosts of Tom Joad* (1995), a solo collection backed mainly by acoustic guitar that received a Grammy as the Best Contemporary Folk Album. Writing for the first time about experiences he had not personally shared, the vocalist sang about Hispanics in the Southwest and highways going nowhere. Nevertheless, he continued to focus on a consistent theme—the dreams of ordinary people and their attempts to fulfill them. Springsteen's introduction to the album suggested that his lyrics were about "how people just keep going, keep going." "What are we/without hope in our hearts?" he asked in "Across the Border." Dreams with no chance of coming true, suggested Springsteen, were a form of death because people needed the promise of better times to stay alive.

JARS OF DREAMS

Seventeen years after publication of the first collection of Asian American works, *The Big Aiiieeee! An Anthology of Chinese American and Japanese American Literature* (1991) pointed to the continuing prominence of writers of Asian heritage. Poet Cathy Song provided an example of the new generation's vitality. Born in Hawaii in 1955 to parents of Korean and Chinese ancestry, Song earned a Master's Degree in Creative Writing at Boston University before returning to Honolulu. Her first book, *Picture Bride* (1983), contained thirty-one poems detailing her Korean grandmother's life story. Selections like "The Youngest Daughter" and "The White Porch" focused on ties between young women and mothers, communities, traditions, and the land. Writing in an unpretentious style that relied on natural forms of expression, Song evoked families sitting around the kitchen amid the clatter of dishes, an approach she maintained in two subsequent anthologies, *Frameless Windows, Squares of Light* (1988) and *School Figures* (1994).

Garrett Kaoru Hongo was another Hawaii poet with a vernacular touch. At six, Hongo moved with his Japanese American family to a working-class neighborhood in Los Angeles. In *Yellow Light* (1982), he offered a series of first-person pieces reflecting both cultural pride and bitterness about ethnic prejudice. "Who Among You Know the Essence of Garlic?" lovingly described traditional cuisine ingredients like mushrooms, carrots, chicken grease, ripe pears, steaming noodles, shrimps, guavas, and red onions. "Off from Swing Shift," in contrast, began by detailing the gambling habits of the poet's father before addressing the treatment of native Japanese during World War II. Another collection, *The River of Heaven* (1988), suggested that music and stories could mitigate suffering. Meanwhile, poet and anthologist Janice Mirikitani based three volumes of her work on the gender and racial stereotypes associated with her family's wartime incarceration. The internment experience received a Hollywood treatment in director and writer Alan Parker's *Come See the Paradise* (1990), a film starring Dennis Quaid as a union organizer whose Japanese American wife and daughter spend the war in a camp.

As the influx from a multitude of Asian nations increased once Congress began to liberalize immigration laws in 1965, a diversity of Asian voices entered the American literary scene. With publication of *The City in Which I Loved You* (1990), Li-Young Lee, an Indonesian immigrant born to Chinese parents in 1957, ranked as one of the more evocative of these figures. In "The Clearing," a poem about working at a grocery in a multi-ethnic community, the author described the joy of encountering a man "with my own face" who gossiped like his grandmother. Another portrait of the urban cauldron emerged in the verse of Woon Ping Chin, a Malaysian immigrant born in 1945. *The Naturalization of Camellia Song* (1993) explored how ethnic newcomers struggled to maintain cultural integrity amid the pervasiveness of American popular culture. Chin's work repeatedly included casual references to the city landscape. One poem, "Seven Vietnamese Boys," described a street crossing as the place where a 7–11 parking lot met the Sunoco gas station. "Have you noticed," asked Chin, how the sun setting over a big-city avenue left "a hue as fiery as dragons?"

Asian American writers used personal and family reminiscences as the foundation for several novels describing ethnic communal life. In *A Jar of Dreams* (1981), Japanese American novelist Yoshiko Uchida presented a picture of post-World War II America through the idiomatic narrative of a twelve-year-old girl. Although the storyteller describes herself as a "big nothing," she traces her strength of character to her father's confrontations with racist bigots and a visiting aunt's advice never to "be ashamed of who you are." Another work, *Picture Bride* (1987), described a young girl from a small Japanese village who comes to California in 1917 to marry an older Japanese shopkeeper. Falling in love with a younger man, she remains loyal to her husband, only to suffer later in life when her daughter defies custom by marrying an Italian American.

A twelve-year-old narrator also provided the viewpoint in *The Floating World* (1989), a novel by Japanese American writer Cynthia Kadohata that centered on a family traveling across mid-Fifties America in a battered sedan. Kadohata recalled an adolescent girl's experiences in a small Arkansas town, her work in a chicken factory, and life in an apartment building in ethnic Los Angeles. Maui-born Sylvia Watanabe, in contrast, wrote about the attempt of Japanese American protagonists to define themselves against the currents of tradition in Hawaii. "A Spell of Kona Weather," a colloquial mood piece in a series of stories in *Talking to the Dead* (1992), provided a first-person narrative of the intimate relationship of two sisters and their grandmother. First-person accounts of the Hawaiian experience and the encounter with American ways also figured in the stories of Nora Okja Keller, the Korean American author of *Comfort Woman* (1997). Similar portraits of immigrant problems with assimilation permeated the understated prose of India's Bharati Mukherjee, the author of *Jasmine* (1989), *The Middleman and Other Stories* (1989), and *Leave It to Me* (1997).

The world of novelist Fae Myenne Ng revolved around old-time immigrants and their offspring in San Francisco's Chinatown, where the author had assisted her mother in sweatshop labor as a child. Ng's signature work, *Bone* (1993), referred to the tradition by which the Chinese send the bones of their deceased relatives back home for proper burial. Narrated by one of three daughters, the novel described the humiliation and discrimination experienced by second-generation Americans, long years of unrewarding labor in sweatshops, kitchens, and laundry rooms, and excruciating hours in lines for Social Security and unemployment checks. As the protagonist's family copes with the suicide of one of their daughters, secrets from the past gradually unravel. The pressures of cultural assimilation place further demands on the courage and perseverance of the novel's characters. Writing with great discipline about the triumphs and reversals of ordinary people, Ng somehow succeeds in combining an insider's knowledge of the community she describes with an outsider's dispassion and lack of sentimentality.

Amy Tan emerged as the most commercially successful Asian American storyteller. Born in Oakland, California, in 1952 to Chinese immigrants and raised in Fresno, Oakland, and Berkeley, Tan received a university education at San Jose State and Berkeley. Through most of the 1980s, she worked as a reporter, editor, and free-lance journalist. Her first novel, *The Joy Luck Club* (1989), a national best-seller, explored the generational and cultural differences between Chinese-born mothers and their American daughters. The book centered on a fictional mahjong club organized by four immigrant women in the 1940s. Each narrates how they struggled against family domination and the constricted role of Chinese women in their early lives. Their professional daughters then proceed with their own accounts of the struggle for equality in contemporary life.

The sixteen stories in *The Joy Luck Club* focused on "the art of invisible strength" passed down to the next generation, mothers' perseverance and ingenuity, and their fierce love for their children. Yet these maternal figures also imposed impossible demands, intruded into the lives of their offspring, and insisted on maintaining Old World ways. Tan's second work, *The Kitchen God's Wife* (1991), continued to address the delicate relationship between immigrant mothers and their daughters. The book offered an older woman's description of survival in China before and during World War II. Its novelty rested with the use of Chinese American vernacular as a legitimate dialect, not simply an example of "broken" English. Tan said that she wrote with her mother as the intended reader and used the imagery, speech rhythms, and intent of her parent's thoughts. The popularity of the two novels prompted Hollywood's Oliver Stone to produce a film version of *Joy Luck Club* (1993) under the direction of Hong Kong-born Wayne Wang, an independent filmmaker who had created sensitive portraits of San Francisco's Chinatown in *Chan Is Missing* (1981) and *Dim Sum: A Little Bit of Heart* (1985).

OLD SHIRTS, NEW SKINS

As the American Indian population approached two million by the end of the century, interest in tribal traditions intensified. Leslie Marmon Silko's *Storyteller* (1981) fed curiosity about the old ways in an unusual collection of poems, short stories, anecdotes, folk tales, historical and autobiographical notes, and photographs. "My family are the Marmons at Old Laguna on the Laguna Pueblo Reservation where I grew up," Silko began. "We are mixed blood ... but the way we live is like Marmons and if you are from Laguna Pueblo you will understand what I mean." The title selection of the book offered an intimate glimpse of a jailed Inuit Eskimo woman. "It will take a long time," wrote Silko, "but the story must be told." *Almanac of the Dead* (1991), a novel, offered an apocalyptic vision in which Native Americans reclaimed ancestral lands after whites succumbed to moral decadence and environmental degradation.

Like Silko, N. Scott Momaday continued to write about the psychological dimensions of Indian identity. Momaday's second autobiography, *The Names: A Memoir* (1976), had explored the relationship between naming and self-identity. His second novel, *The Ancient Child* (1989), juxtaposed a story about an Oklahoma Kiowa painter whose world revolves around New York and Paris art galleries, and a young tribal medicine woman who turns into a boy and a bear. Tribal lore also marked the fiction of Louise Erdich. Born in Little Falls, Minnesota, in 1954, Erdich grew up near the Chippewa reservation in North Dakota, where her German-born father and Chippewa mother taught at the local government Indian school. Although Erdich graduated from Dartmouth in 1976 and earned a Johns Hopkins M.A. three years later, her varied work experience included stints as a North Dakota beetfield hand, a waitress, a psychiatric aide, a prison poetry teacher, a lifeguard, and a construction flagger.

Erdich's novels evoked the American landscape and a sense of place through multiple narratives. Depicting tough and funny characters, she developed a reputation for writing the way people thought and talked. *Love Medicine* (1984), her first novel, consisted of fourteen interconnected stories and a fifty-year narrative about members of the Chippewa community. *The Beet Queen* (1986), the first work of a trilogy, presented a series of personal stories about a small North Dakota town between 1932 and 1972. *Tracks* (1988), the second novel in the set, traced the story of two members of a family back to 1912–1924, and offered Erdich the chance to delve into the importance of "mothering" in the life of the community. *The Bingo Palace* (1994), the final work in the trilogy, used a familiar gathering place as an entry point into the lives of its protagonists.

By the 1990s, Sherman Alexie had become one of the most widely read Native American writers. Born in 1966 on the Spokane Indian Reservation in Washington State and a university graduate, Alexie inaugurated his publishing career with *The Business of Fancydancing* (1992), a collection of stories and poems about reservation life. The book did not retreat from the racism, poverty, alcoholism, and sense of loss that pervaded rural Indian existence. Yet Alexie's ironically comic style emphasized

Louise Erdich

the people's survival and hope amid the resilience of shared cultural values and family cohesion. In the poem "Love Song," the author described old blankets that "smell like grandmother." "Gravity," in turn, pictured a reunion of father and son consummated on a basketball court. Other vernacular poetry works included *I Would Steal Horses* (1992), *First Indian on the Moon* (1993), *Old Shirts and New Skins* (1993), *Water Flowing Home* (1995), *The Summer of Black Widows* (1996), and *The Man Who Loves Salmon* (1998).

Although mystery writer Tony Hillerman was not an American Indian, he set more than thirteen short story collections and novels within the culture and topography of Navajo country. Born and educated as a journalist in Oklahoma, Hillerman spent several years as a reporter for southwestern newspapers and served as a university professor before turning to full-time writing. Collections like *The Jim Chee Mysteries* (1993) featured culturally ambivalent Navajo detective heroes who struggle to reconcile an ethnic heritage of spiritual traditions, legends, and rituals with the mindset and requirements of the Anglo world surrounding their government responsibilities.

Like their American Indian counterparts, several Hispanic poets and novelists examined the relationship between ethnic and mainstream culture. Raised during the Fifties in a poor Mexican American family in San Francisco's Mission district, lyrical poet Lorna Dee Cervantes addressed cultural conflict, the difficulties of assimilation, and the experience of immigrant women. A collection entitled *Plumed* (1981) emphasized the consequences of alienation from one's roots, while *From the Cables of Genocide: Poems of Love and Hunger* (1992) offered a female perspective on life, death, social conflict, and poverty. Luis Rodriguez, another Mexican American poet, conveyed his experiences as a young Los Angeles thief, street gang member, and industrial worker into a volume of verse appropriately named *Always Running* (1993).

Oral culture dominated the work of bilingual Nuyorican poet Victor Hernández Cruz, an immigrant raised in New York's Spanish Harlem. Another Puerto Rican poet, Judith Ortiz Cofer, depicted the immigration experience in *Reaching for the Mainland* (1987) and *Terms of Survival* (1987). Cofer's memoir *Silent Dancing: A Remembrance of a Puerto Rican Childhood* (1990) drew upon her upbringing in Paterson, New Jersey. Oscar Hijuelos' autobiographical *The Mambo Kings Play Songs of Love* (1989), the first Hispanic fiction to win the Pulitzer Prize, traced a similar theme. Born in New York in 1951 into a Cuban American working-class family, Hijuelos completed graduate work in English before publishing his first novel, *Our House in the Last World* (1983), the story of a family of Cuban émigrés. *The Mambo Kings* used documentary style to portray two brother musicians from Cuba who come to New York in the 1950s to play in the city's fashionable dance clubs. The novelist's other books included *The Fourteen Sisters of Emilio Montez O'Brien* (1993) and *The Empress of the Splendid Season* (1999), the story of a cleaning woman from Cuba who remembers the beauty and prosperity of her youth.

MY NAME IS MY OWN

African American writers provided additional insights into the impact of modern life on traditionally oriented people. John Edgar Wideman continued to investigate historical settings in his Homewood trilogy of stream-of-consciousness novels. Published in paperback in 1981, *Damballah, Hiding Place* and *Sent for You Yesterday* each jumped back and forth between the 1920s and the Seventies through a series of letters the protagonist sends to a brother serving a life sentence for murder. Wideman's next work, an autobiography entitled *Brothers and Keepers* (1984), pointed to the chasm between the black middle class and under class. Another novel, *Philadelphia Fire* (1990), the recipient of a PEN/Faulkner Award for Fiction, revolved around the real-life bombing by city police of a black sect's headquarters, an event that led to eleven deaths and destruction of much of the neighborhood.

Publication of Al Young's *Seduction by Light* (1988), a novel in which the author assumed the folksy and philosophic voice of Mamie Franklin, a middle-aged African American woman, pointed to increasing literary interest in the experience of black female figures. Rita Dove, the first poet laureate of color in the United States, explored the inner life of African American women within a highly detailed historical and human context. Born in Akron, Ohio, in 1952, Dove was the daughter of a self-educated Goodyear chemist. A graduate of Miami University of Ohio and the Iowa Writers Workshop, she embarked upon a teaching career at Arizona State and the University of Virginia. Despite her academic ties, however, Dove avoided the political considerations and racial or gender issues associated with the Black Arts Movement, gravitating to a more inclusive style of work that concentrated on portraits of individual characters.

Dove's first book of poems, *The Yellow House on the Corner* (1980), merged Biblical imagery with narratives of everyday experience in an autobiographical account of a transition from girlhood to womanhood. In *Museum* (1983), the poet placed a collection of family snapshots amid personal recollections set within the framework of historical developments. The Pulitzer Prize-winning *Thomas and Beulah* (1986) offered a family history from the perspective of the author's maternal grandparents. "They'd left the Tennessee ridge/with nothing to boast of," Dove explained in "The Event," "but good looks and a mandolin." "She wanted a little room for thinking," the poet wrote of her grandmother in "Daystar." "So she lugged a chair behind the garage/to sit out the children's naps." Dove's subsequent collections included *Grace Notes* (1989), a volume describing everyday routines; *Mother Love* (1995), an exploration of family life; and *On the Bus with Rosa Parks* (1999), a series of reflections ranging from the civil rights struggles of the Fifties to a variety of human experiences.

Like Rita Dove's work, the poetry of Sherley Anne Williams placed the lives of its subjects in historical context. Born in 1944, Williams worked alongside her parents in the fruit and cotton fields of Bakersfield, California. Losing her father to tuberculosis when she was eight and experiencing the death of her mother eight years later, she fell into the care of an older sister. After earning a History degree at Fresno State, Williams began writing short stories, completed graduate work, served as a community educator in Washington, D.C., and taught in Brown University's Black Studies Department. *The Peacock Poems* (1975), her first volume of verse, described a Bakersfield childhood. A second book, *Some One Sweet Angel Chile* (1982), offered a series of women's perspectives from different historical eras, including those of blues artist Bessie Smith and her own youthful recollections. In "I Want Aretha to Set This to Music," the poet acknowledged the pain and hurt of womanhood. "But I'll make book," she added, "Bessie did/more than just endure."

While embracing vernacular phrasing, June Jordan placed her poetry in a feminist context. Born in Harlem during the Depression, Jordan was the daughter of a postal clerk and a nurse, both Jamaican immigrants. Losing her mother to suicide at an early age, Jordan quickly took to writing. Her teaching career ranged from writing workshops for children to academic appointments at elite universities. At Berkeley, Jordan ran the Poetry for People program and championed the use of Black English in the classroom. Although she persistently resisted any attempt to categorize her own work, she saw herself in the tradition of Walt Whitman. At the same time, Jordan expressed particular admiration for Zora Neale Hurston and the neglected black women writers of the Harlem Renaissance. Her feisty individualism surfaced in "Poem about My Rights" (1980), a free verse complaint about being "the wrong/sex the wrong age the wrong skin." "I am not wrong. Wrong is not my name," insisted Jordan. "My name is my own my own my own."

The last years of the century witnessed assertions of black female agency in books such as Gloria Naylor's *The Women of Brewster Place* (1982), an award-winning first novel adopted as a TV miniseries later in the decade. Born in New York in 1950, Naylor spent time as a Jehovah's Witness missionary and telephone operator after graduating college. Influenced by Zora Neale Hurston and Toni Morrison, she peopled her first work with a group of black female ghetto residents who share their dreams, desires, and the pain of their oppression by telling stories. In the same year that *The Women of Brewster Place* appeared, Alice Walker published the Pulitzer Prize-winning *The Color Purple* (1982). The novel revolved around the life of a poor southern African American woman, born in 1900, who is raped in her teens by her stepfather and who sells the two children she bears as a result. Forced to marry "Mister," the local landowner, she experiences further abuse. Nevertheless, a friendship with her husband's mistress—a Bayou honky-tonk singer—and a reunion with her sister bring her back to life and lead her to cherish the color purple as a symbol of the unity and enjoyment that is God.

Toni Morrison's *Beloved* (1987) earned another Pulitzer Prize. Set in post-Civil War Ohio, the novel told the story of a former slave and her adolescent daughter haunted by the ghost of a child whose runaway mother had killed her rather than see her return to bondage. Deeply immersed in oral folk tradition, the book explored the painful legacy of slavery. In *Jazz* (1992), Morrison employed multiple perspectives to examine a Harlem love triangle of the 1920s, while she constructed the secret life of a Fifties black seaside resort in *Love* (2003). Terry McMillan's chronicles of black women attained even greater commercial success. Born in Port Huron, Michigan, to working-class parents, McMillan studied journalism at Berkeley and graduated from the Columbia University film school. Her best-selling *Waiting to Exhale* (1992) described the lives and romantic aspirations of four black working-class women through a series of vignettes that merged the sexuality and emotional vulnerability of the central characters. In *How Stella Got Her Groove Back* (1996), McMillan offered another perspective on the resilience of African American women.

SOUL FOOD

Both theatrical producers and Hollywood filmmakers derived inspiration from the post-Sixties explosion of ethnic consciousness. Moving beyond the political drama of the farm worker's movement, Luis Valdez staged the stylized musical *Zoot Suit* in 1978. Mixing commentary by cool hipster El Pachuco with music and dance, *Zoot Suit* revolved around the notorious Sleepy Lagoon Case of 1942 that falsely convicted four young Los Angeles Chicano men of murder. Writer-director Valdez brought the musical play to the screen in 1981 with Edward James Olmos in the lead role. Born in East Los Angeles in 1947, Olmos had thrived in experimental theater roles in the Seventies incorporating street language in rugged characterizations. Following *Zoot Suit,* he starred in *The Ballad of Gregory Cortez* (1982). Based on a true incident immortalized in oral tradition, the independent film traced the misunderstanding that led a young Mexican American to kill a Texas sheriff in 1901 and temporarily elude a posse of six hundred men. Another historical drama, Isaac Artenstein's *Break of Dawn* (1988), told the true-to-life story of Pedro J. Gonzales, a pro-labor Spanish-language radio host framed for rape in the 1930s by racist prosecutors.

Several motion pictures explored Hispanic culture's relationship to mainstream society. *La Bamba* (1987), a Luis Valdez biography of Fifties rock and roll star Ritchie Valens, released in separate English and Spanish versions, pictured the performer's childhood and adolescence in Chicano Los Angeles, his work in the fields, his devotion to his mother and family, and his discovery of his ethnic roots. At the same time, the film dealt with Valens' dilemma over whether to enhance his career by assimilating into Anglo culture. *Born in East L.A.* (1987), a parody of American nativism, featured Richard Marin of the comedy team Cheech and Chong as director and lead character. Accidentally rounded up and deported to Mexico by U.S. immigration agents, Cheech returns by crossing the border with a group of Asians he has trained to act like East L.A.

Chicanos. In *Stand and Deliver* (1988), Edward James Olmos portrayed an inner-city Latino math teacher who inspires his students to excellence, despite the poverty and culture of failure that surrounds them. The challenges of sustaining a separate Cuban American identity, in turn, characterized the filming of *The Mambo Kings* (1992).

Ethnic distinctiveness and personal dignity played key roles in Native American cinema. Gregory Nava's *El Norte* (1983) presented the tale of two Guatemalan refugees—an Indian coffee worker and his sister—who arrive in Los Angeles with the help of a "coyote" who escorts them through a rat-infested sewer. While the young man seeks day jobs at the local pickup spot for illegal immigrants, his sister scrubs clothes by her employer's swimming pool because she cannot figure out the hi-tech washing machine. Jonathan Wacks' low-key *Powwow Highway* (1988) centered on Buddy Red Bow, a Northern Cheyenne Montana political activist fighting mining company encroachments on his reservation. When Buddy learns that authorities in Santa Fe have framed his sister on drug charges, he sets off to rescue her in an oversized old sedan with his friend Philbert Bono, an overweight advocate of traditional Indian warrior spirituality. The journey of self-discovery leads to the sacred Black Hills and to dilapidated Indian prairie communities. Native American themes also surfaced in Sherman Alexie's screenplays for *Smoke Signals* (1998) and *The Business of Fancydancing* (2002).

The dramatic productions of August Wilson provided some of the clearest portraits of African American vernacular experience. Born in 1945 to a German American father and a black mother, Wilson grew up on "the Hill"—a poor, racially mixed Pittsburgh neighborhood. Raised by a black stepfather, he quit his first year at a white suburban high school after a teacher accused him of plagiarism and educated himself at the public library. Wilson absorbed African American oral traditions by listening to the conversation of old men at a local cigar store. Influenced by the Black Power movement, he published poetry and short stories in small journals and organized a black community theater. After moving to Minnesota's Twin Cities in 1978, Wilson initiated his playwriting career by producing scripts for a small ensemble.

Ma Rainey's Black Bottom (1984), Wilson's first Broadway effort, offered a view of the intense racial and artistic tensions plaguing the famed 1920s blues vocalist and her band. After the play garnered the New York Drama Critics Award, Wilson completed a Pulitzer Prize-winning script for *Fences* (1987), a production starring James Earl Jones as a bitter black baseball player from the segregation era who opposes his son's acceptance of a college athletic scholarship. The playwright's interest in the African American cultural legacy resulted in *Joe Turner's Come and Gone* (1988), a drama set in a Pittsburgh boarding house in 1911 whose characters verged on losing their ethnic identity and southern roots. In *The Piano Lesson* (1990), a second Pulitzer Prize winner, Wilson dealt with the impact of history by focusing on a brother and sister who argue whether or not to sell the piano once traded for their slave grandparents. Set in a black Pittsburgh luncheonette in 1969, *Two Trains Running* (1992) recaptured the passions of the Vietnam War and the era's racial conflicts, while *Seven Guitars* (1995) returned to 1948 and the death of legendary Pittsburgh blues guitarist Floyd "Schoolboy" Barton.

Several motion pictures placed African American protagonists in historical settings. Steven Spielberg's *The Color Purple* (1985) starred Whoopi Goldberg, Oprah Winfrey, and Danny Glover in Alice Walker's feminist saga of plantation life in the first half of the twentieth century. The chronology of *Driving Miss Daisy* (1989) took up where Walker's story ended. Based on a Pulitzer Prize-winning off-Broadway play by Alfred Uhry, the film co-starred Academy Award Best Actress Jessica Tandy as a wealthy elderly Jewish woman who reluctantly agrees to hire a black chauffeur (Morgan Freeman). Although Daisy resents the intrusion of her new employee, she gradually comes to admire Hoke's sense of pride, cunning intelligence, and quiet wisdom. As she teaches him to read, he offers lessons in humility and realism. When the older woman expresses shock that her Reform synagogue has been bombed, Hoke responds that such distinctions have no meaning to bigots—"jes' like light or dark we all the same nigger." The relationship between the two ultimately transcends that of employer and servant. In her last days in a nursing home, Daisy confides to Hoke that he is her best friend.

Never servile or self-demeaning, Miss Daisy's chauffeur nevertheless must defer to the racial protocol of the segregated post-World War II South. Similar sensitivity marked Denzel Washington's Easy Rawlins, the Los Angeles area detective who appears as the central character of Carl Franklin's *Devil in a Blue Dress* (1995). Franklin based the film on a novel by Walter Mosley. Raised in South Central Los Angeles of the Fifties by a Jewish mother and African American school custodian, Mosley became interested in film noir. He fashioned Rawlins as a black aircraft mechanic who buys a little house on the G.I. Bill in 1948. Losing his job, the former veteran accepts an assignment from a white man to track down the socialite girlfriend of a local politician. Cruising the Central Avenue world of black clubs, nightspots, and shops, he finds himself in a shadowy milieu of paranoia, corruption, and deceit. Yet even when confronting the absurdities of a dangerous and violent white world, the detective still maintains his poise, dignity, and individuality. After discovering that the subject of his search (Jennifer Beals) prefers the company of dark men, he learns that she is a black woman passing for white.

A more contemporary perspective characterized *Soul Food* (1997), a film written and directed by George Tillman, Jr. The twenty-eight-year-old African American son of a Milwaukee autoworker and a nurse, Tillman fashioned a story about a strong black grandmother (Irma P. Hall) who holds her extended family together over Sunday dinners. When the matriarch falls ill, her grandson (Brandon Hammond) tries his best to fill her shoes. Aided by a rhythm and blues soundtrack by vocalist Kenneth (Babyface) Edmonds, the surprising hit grossed $43 million upon its initial release. Two other popular movies, *Waiting to Exhale* (1995) and *How Stella Got Her Groove Back* (1998), starred African American performers Whitney Houston, Angela Bassett, and Whoopi Goldberg in screen adaptations of Terry McMillan's best-selling novels.

HIP HOP NATION

In his directorial debut in *She's Gotta Have It* (1986), African American movie maker Spike Lee took on the role of a comic rapper. By the mid–1980s, rap music and hip-hop styles had become the dominant forms of African American and Hispanic vernacular expression and key fixtures of global popular culture. Rap emerged in a period of populist ferment in the music industry. Influenced by rebel British groups like the Sex Pistols and The Clash, white American garage bands like Fugazi and Sonic Youth took up hard-core punk, attracting followers identified by tattoos, body piercing, and frenetic slam dancing. While groups like Guns 'n' Roses and Whitesnake adhered to heavy metal, bands like REM, the Red Hot Chili Peppers, Pearl Jam, and Kurt Cobain's Nirvana merged catchy melodies with sardonic and melancholy lyrics reflecting punk alienation. Marketed as grunge, the form spread from independent record labels, college radio stations, and underground clubs to widespread exposure on MTV. Meanwhile, the alternative music scene thrived in movable warehouse dance "raves" fueled by "house" funk rhythms and the mood-enhancing drug "Ecstasy."

While young white musicians rebelled against the dominance of the rock establishment, Hispanic and African American artists sought avenues of expression with ethnic roots. Beginning in the late Sixties, public murals celebrating Chicano consciousness took their place alongside the homemade religious shrines normally associated with traditional Mexican American culture. Increasingly, young Mexican Americans sought to assert an autonomous presence on public life. Low-rider cars offered one way of establishing a unique identity. Customized with multicolor paint jobs, crushed velvet interiors, and chain steering wheels, the vehicles featured hydraulic lifts and suspension systems that enabled drivers to raise, lower, or bounce the chassis while "cruising." Other young barrio residents, particularly adherents of *cholo* gang culture, turned to graffiti as a way of reclaiming public space or conveying coded information about their affiliations and identities.

Assisted by Spanish-language radio, Chicano youth culture found its most intense expression through popular music. As ballroom *orquesta* styling fell out of favor with a generation committed to cross-class unity, and record producers targeted an international Latin market, Mexican American performers reached out to an ethnically diverse young audience. Although working-class immigrants remained loyal to *conjunto* accordion ensembles through the 1990s, Los Angeles witnessed the spread of *banda*, a traditional Mexican brass music updated with synthesizers. Mexican-born Carlos Santana, the son of a mariachi violinist and leader of the Sixties rock group Santana, appealed even more explicitly to Chicano youth. By the time Santana won a Grammy in

2000 for his mixture of rock and ethnic styles, he had sold forty million records. Los Lobos, another popular group that originally performed acoustic Mexican folk songs, branched out into a mix of punk, mystical folk rock, and late Sixties blues in the ground-breaking album *How Will the Wolf Survive?* (1984). Pop vocalist Selena also illustrated the enormous commercial potential of Mexican American music for young audiences.

While Chicano artists catered to the tastes of young Texas and California Hispanics, Caribbean and Latino influences reverberated along the East Coast. Paul Simon's *The Capeman* (1998), a Broadway musical that traced the aftermath of a youth gang murder in 1950s New York, emphasized the importance of Puerto Rican and rock and roll musical traditions to the city's street culture. During the 1990s, New York and Miami dance halls featured *salsa* performers like vocalist Celia Cruz and bandleader Tito Puente, as well as Dominican *merengue* bands like Juan Luis Guerra's 4.40. Gloria Estefan's Miami Sound Machine, whose records mixed upbeat Cuban rhythms with a sophisticated big-band approach, won widespread popularity during the decade, as did Latino dance fads like Brazil's hip-gyrating *lambada* and the infectious *macarena.*

The mellow styles of reggae provided another component to pop music culture. First popularized in the United States by Jimmy Cliff in the film *The Harder They Come* (1973), reggae was a Jamaican form characterized by a loping beat, a rhythm and blues feel, and primitive recording techniques. The music achieved massive exposure through the recordings of Bob Marley and the Wailers, a group whose songs protested Kingston ghetto conditions while celebrating the lifestyle of the Rastafarian religious sect. Although Seventies reggae primarily attracted counterculture whites in the United States, the genre influenced the development of *reggaeton,* a Puerto Rican and Jamaican dance-hall music that fused hip Spanish and English lyrics with a *salsa* and *merengue* beat.

The spread and influence of Hispanic music and lifestyles rested upon the fact that by the 1990s, nearly one-fifth of Americans under thirty-four were U.S.-born Latinos. On the West Coast, *cholo* gang culture introduced such innovations as baggy khaki pants and jeans, oversized shirts, baseball caps, bandanas, and low-riders. In turn, Hispanic performers of East Coast *hurban* music combined the Caribbean accents of *reggaeton* and the hyper-masculine posture of Jamaican dance-hall culture with the wordplay of African American and West Indian dance-club disc jockeys and emcees. The resulting hybrids—rap music and hip-hop culture—constituted the twentieth century's final and perhaps most controversial expressions of populist sensibility.

Originating in New York's South Bronx in the mid-Seventies, rap involved the delivery of rhymed phrases and chants in nonstandard street speech, accompanied by highly rhythmic electronically based music. The genre's sophisticated verbal artistry reenacted the playing of the "dozens," an African-Caribbean rhetorical tradition in which participants mastered self-discipline and emotional control by "toasting" each other with improvisational insults, boasts, and retorts. In the United States, a rich black oral culture of ring games, skip rope rhymes, street poetry, comedy, prison songs, blues, and soul music created the cultural foundation for rap by celebrating "bad-man" heroes and legendary ethnic personalities. Synchronizing their text with the insistent beat, rappers used indirect metaphors, allusions, and imagery to comment on urban life in intensely personal, conversational, and confrontational tones.

Forged in the economic and social dislocation of the South Bronx, but influenced by West Indian dance-hall techniques and African American funk, rap developed through the collaboration of club emcees and disc jockeys like Afrika Bambaataa, Kool "DJ" Herc, and Grandmaster Flash. These pioneers purposely scratched vinyl records, reversed the direction of turntables, sampled fragments or "break beats" from other works, interjected spoken vocals, used mechanical percussion backing, experimented with bass frequencies, and introduced spontaneous sound effects, all at attention-getting high volume. Expropriating Lovebug Starski's incantation "hip, hop, you don't stop—that makes your body rock," Bambaataa envisioned a nonviolent urban youth culture of African and Muslim heritage fashioned from the surrounding desolation. Hip-hop came to represent the mix of vernacular expression and gesture, urban warrior apparel, street names, graffiti art, and break dancing surrounding rap music, a culture that received national exposure in Charlie Ahearn's documentary film *Wild Style* (1982).

The first rap record was the Sugar Hill Gang's "Rapper's Delight" (1979). Within a year, solo artist Kurtis Blow had produced two million-selling twelve-inch single rap records. As the performance style spread from the Bronx to Manhattan disco clubs in the early Eighties, disc jockeys assumed the rhyming functions once employed by emcees. Using neighborhood friends as a supporting crew, Grandmaster Flash became the first deejay to record as an individual artist. "The Message" (1982), as stark a vision of inner-city existence ever heard on vinyl to that point, graphically depicted the full scope of the ghetto environment. "I'm close to the edge," Flash warned in a matter-of-fact tone. Yet the performer communicated pride in the sheer ability to survive. "It's like a jungle sometimes, it makes me wonder/How I keep from going under," he repeated.

Rap's generational rebellion against respectability and stark references to urban poverty, family tensions, male-female conflicts, social injustice, and violence provided an authenticity that few popular culture forms ever achieve. As New York-area black and college radio stations popularized the style, independent record labels provided freedom for street artists to add synthesizers, drum machines, and computerized arcade sounds to their rhythmic poetry. Some of the first popular performers of the 1980s included Run-DMC, a group from Hollis, Queens, who combined heavy metal and rap; L.L. Cool J.; the Fat Boys; and Public Enemy, whose album *Fight the Power* (1989) took on issues of black pride and police brutality. Meanwhile, female rappers like

Queen Latifah and Salt 'N' Pepa explored gender-related tensions over trust, control, and personal autonomy.

INSIDE THE HOOD

In contrast to their East Coast counterparts, black artists from South Central Los Angeles and Oakland produced the laid-back, bass-oriented sound of gangsta rap. The relaxed feel of the music belied uncensored accounts of drug dealers, gang wars, and police confrontations, often delivered over the wail of sirens and the crack of gunfire. By the early 1990s, one third of young African American men were involved in the criminal justice system, black male unemployment surpassed 40 percent in many communities, and crack cocaine had become the central commodity in the inner-city underground economy. "We're telling the real story of what it's like living in places like Compton," explained Ice Cube (O'Shea Jackson), a former art school student and member of the group N.W.A. (Niggaz With Attitude). "Six in the Morning" (1985), the first commercial West Coast gangsta rap recording, originated with South Central's Ice-T, a performer influenced by the tight rhymes of Iceberg Slim, a former L.A. pimp who turned to street poetry in the 1960s. Other practitioners of the genre included N.W.A. founder Dr. Dre, Tone Loc, Snoop Doggy Dog, Tupac Shakur, and Biggie Smalls.

By romanticizing urban crime while calling attention to black-on-black violence, gangsta rap lent itself to dramatization in the movies. By the 1990s, African Americans comprised one fourth of the film-going public. As early as 1973, Hollywood had glamorized the story of an Oakland pimp in the popular "blaxploitation" feature *The Mack*. With a soundtrack provided by Ice-T, Dennis Hopper's *Colors* (1988) marked the first of a series of "hood" films incorporating the music and styles of gangsta rap. Hopper's movie pictured the attempts of two white L.A. police officers (Sean Penn and Robert Duvall) to discourage the nihilistic cycle of violence between the rival Crips and Bloods. *Boyz N the Hood* (1991), a film by twenty-three-year-old black writer and director John Singleton, starred Ice Cube in a profile of the coming of age of three young men amid South Central's dysfunctional poverty, drugs, and violence. Although Singleton presented ghetto street life and problems like police harassment with brooding melancholy, he used "b-boy" dialect, hip-hop clothing styles, and shared attitudes to suggest the intimate camaraderie shared by his principals.

Another hood film, Mario Van Peebles' *New Jack City* (1991), opened with aerial shots of New York City accompanied by a rap by Queen Latifah. Deeply immersed in the aesthetics of black urban street culture, the movie starred Ice-T as a police officer on the trail of a ruthless crack dealer (Wesley Snipes). In nineteen-year-old Matty Rich's *Straight Out of Brooklyn* (1991), a black teenager robs a local drug dealer to get his family out of the Red Hook projects. *Juice* (1992), a film with a soundtrack by Queen Latifah and several rap artists, featured Tupac Shakur as one of four teenage friends who suffer tragic consequences when a store robbery goes out of control. Albert and Allen Hughes' docudrama about Watts, *Menace II Society* (1993), in turn, began with the murder of two Korean convenience store proprietors who treat the protagonist and his cohort as criminals. Characterizing the ghetto as a prison with police-enforced borders, the film suggested that violence was the only means of self-assertion for people without agency or hope. America's nightmare lies in young black men who "don't give a f—," states a character. "The hunt is on and you are the prey."

Spike Lee sprinkled a good deal of moral ambivalence in his tales of ghetto life. In *She's Gotta Have It* (1986), Lee's rapper provided comic relief as one of three male suitors of a young black graphics artist unable to choose a single mate. Set over a twenty-four-hour period in Brooklyn's Bedford-Stuyvesant on a hot summer's day, *Do the Right Thing* (1989) focused on an insider's view of everyday street culture. Lee portrayed the amiable and quiet-spoken Mookie, a pizza delivery boy outfitted in sneakers and a T-shirt. Despite his best intentions, Mookie finds himself caught up by the simmering racial tensions between Sal (Danny Aiello), his Italian American boss, and neighborhood residents. When an argument over the playing of a boom box by rapper Radio Raheem produces a confrontation that results in a police shooting, an angry crowd sets the pizzeria on fire. In an apparent effort to deflect the community's anger away from Sal, Mookie throws a trashcan through the store window. The movie then closes with contrasting quotes from Malcolm X and Martin Luther King on the use of violence.

Lee pursued themes of African American identity with the affirmative *Malcolm X* (1992). In *Get on the Bus* (1996), he presented a series of fictionalized vignettes about the participants in Black Nationalist Louis Farrakhan's Million Man March. Meanwhile, the director sought to bring a humanizing perspective to potentially polarizing issues. *Mo' Better Blues* (1990), a story about a self-centered jazz musician, resolved with a demonstration of the importance of fathers to black family life. *Jungle Fever* (1991) offered a non-judgmental portrait of interracial romance. *Clockers* (1995) tackled the issue of personal responsibility amid the constant shadow of crime in public housing. In *He Got Game* (1998), one of Lee's most eloquent statements of universality, the filmmaker accompanied footage of an inner-city night basketball game with a soundtrack laced with selections from Aaron Copland's cowboy ballets.

Lee's attempts at transcendence helped to set the stage for "post-hood" movies like John Singleton's *Poetic Justice* (1993), a film starring Janet Jackson as a South Central beautician and aspiring poet who returns to the world through the loving attention of mail carrier Tupac Shakur after her boyfriend dies in a shooting. After appearing as Jackson's aunt in *Poetic Justice*, Maya Angelou played a nurturing grandmother in another "post-hood" feature, *Down in the Delta* (1998), a movie originally created for television. Opening in the war zone of burned-out buildings, empty lots, litter, and graffiti surrounding a South Side Chicago housing project, the film follows the visit of a single, unemployed, and desperate mother and her two children to relatives in Missis-

Spike Lee　(*Photofest*)

sippi. As everyone pitches in to help at the family chicken restaurant and Angelou dishes out her brand of folk wisdom, the Chicago refugees seem to take on new life, in effect reversing the disruptions to the extended family generated by the African American migration out of the South. Significantly, between 1990 and 1995 alone, nearly 370,000 black Americans returned to states below the Mason-Dixon Line.

SOURCES AND SUGGESTED READINGS

The cultural conflicts of the 1980s and after receive coverage in James Davison Hunter, *Culture Wars: The Struggle to Define America* (1991) and the final chapter of David A. Horowitz, *America's Political Class Under Fire: The Twentieth Century's Great Culture War* (2003). Comic book innovations attract attention in Michael Mallory, *Marvel: The Characters and Their Universe* (2004). Works about gritty male film protagonists include Tom Zaniello, *Working Stiffs, Union Maids, Reds, and Riffraff: An Organized Guide to Films About Labor* (1996) and David E. James and Rick Berg, eds., *The Hidden Foundation: Cinema and the Question of Class* (1996). See also previously cited material on Clint Eastwood, Martin Scorsese, and Francis Ford Coppola. For television, see Daniel Marcus, *Happy Days and Wonder Years: The Fifties and Sixties in Contemporary Cultural Politics* (2004); David Marc, *Comic Visions: Television Comedy and American Culture*, 2nd ed. (1997); and Kristal Brent Zook, *Color by Fox: The Fox Network and the Revolution in Black Television* (1999).

TV portraits of working-class women figure strongly in Elayne Rapping, *The Movie of the Week: Private Stories/Public Events* (1992) and the books on television cited in Chapter 11. For *Moonstruck* and other women-oriented films, see Kristine Brunouska Karnick and Henry Jenkins, eds., *Classical Hollywood Comedy* (1995). Background on *Prairie Home Companion* appears in Peter A. Scholl, *Garrison Keillor* (1993) and Judith Yaross Lee, *Garrison Keillor: A Voice of America* (1991).

The country music studies cited in Chapter 11 take the story up to the 1990s and beyond. See also Barbara Ching, *"Wrong's What I Do Best": Hard Country Music and Contemporary Culture* (2001) and Bruce Feiler, *Dreaming Out Loud: Garth Brooks, Wynonna Judd, Wade Hayes, and the Changing Face of Nashville* (1998). For Bruce Springsteen's music in the Eighties, see Jim Cullen, *Born in the U.S.A.: Bruce Springsteen and the American Tradition* (1997) and the relevant chapter in Bryan K. Garman, *A Race of Singers: Whitman's Working-Class Hero from Guthrie to Springsteen* (2000). Anthony De Curtis, et al. eds., *The Rolling Stone Illustrated History of Rock and Roll: The Definitive History of the Most Important Artists and Their Music*, 3rd ed. (1992) provides a complete discography and commentary on Springsteen's later work. See also Larry Starr and Christopher Waterman, *American Popular Music: From Minstrelsy to MTV* (2003).

Lisa Lowe describes Asian American life in the 1980s and '90s in *Immigrant Acts: On Asian American Cultural Politics* (1996). The standard reference works on Asian American literature are Emmanuel S. Nelson, ed., *Asian American Novelists: A Bio-Bibliographical Critical Sourcebook* (2000) and Lawrence J. Trudeau, ed., *Asian American Literature: Reviews and Criticism of Works by American Writers of Asian Descent* (1999). See also Shawn Wong, *Asian American Literature: A Brief Introduction and Anthology* (1996). See also Bella Adams, *Amy Tan* (2005). Recent American Indian writers receive profiles in Kathy J. Whitson, *Native American Literatures: An Encyclopedia of Works, Characters, Authors, and Themes* (1999) and Jane Witalec, ed., *Native North American Literature* (1994). Case studies include previously cited work on Scott Momaday and Leslie Marmon Silko, as well as the essay on Louise Erdich in Hans Bak, *Neo-Realism in Contemporary American Fiction* (1992) and Daniel Grassian, *Understanding Sherman Alexie* (2005).

A useful source on Hispanic migration patterns is Alejandro Portes and Robert L. Bach, *Latin Journey: Cuban and Mexican Immigrants in the United States* (1985). For creative writers, see Nicolás Kanellos, *Hispanic Literature of the United States: A Comprehensive Reference* (2003). Specific studies include Margarite Fernández Olmos, *Rudolfo A. Anaya: A Critical Companion* (1999); Miguel Algarin and Bob Holman, eds., *Aloud: Voices from the Nuyorican Poets Café* (1994); and the profiles of Lorna Dee Cervantes and other Mexican American artists in Rafael Pérez-Torres, *Movements in Chicano Poetry* (1995).

For black writing, consult Henry Louis Gates and Nellie Y. McKay, *The Norton Anthology of African American Literature* (1997). Full-length treatments include the works cited in Chapter 11 on Toni Morrison, Alice Walker, and John Edgar Wideman, as well as Malin Pereira's *Rita Dove's Cosmopolitanism* (2003). For studies of two popular black women writers of the 1990s, see Paulette Richards, *Terry McMillan: A Critical Companion* (1999) and Charles E. Wilson, *Gloria Naylor: A Critical Companion* (2000). The period's leading African American dramatist is the subject of Peter Wolfe's *August Wilson* (1999).

Recent African American influences in the movies, including the films of Spike Lee, come under scrutiny in Krin Gabbard, *Black Magic: White Hollywood and African American Culture* (2004) and Donald Bogle, *Toms, Coons, Mulattoes, Mammies, and Bucks: An Interpretive History of Blacks in American Films*, rev. ed. (2002). Other useful studies include Paula J. Massood, *Black City Cinema: African American Urban Experiences in Film* (2003). See Terry McMillan et al., *Five For Five: The Films of Spike Lee* (1990) for a collection of essays on the early work of the foremost African American movie director of the 1980s and '90s.

The most comprehensive introduction to rap music and hip-hop culture is Jeff Chang, *Can't Stop Won't Stop: A History of the Hip-Hop Generation* (2005). Useful analyses include Nelson George, *Hip Hop America* (1998); Tricia Rose, *Black Noise: Rap Music and Black Culture in Contemporary America* (1994); Cheryl L. Keyes, *Rap Music and Street Consciousness* (2002); and Imani Perry, *Prophets of the Hood: Politics and Poetics in Hop Hop* (2004). See also the segment on rap in George Lipsitz, *Dangerous Crossroads: Popular Music, Postmodernism, and the Poetics of Place* (1994). Hip-hop's fusion of art and greed is the subject of Eithne Quinn, *Nuthin' But a "G" Thang: The Culture and Commerce of Gangsta Rap* (2004). A white working-class rapper receives his due in Anthony Bozza, *Whatever You Say I Am: The Life and Times of Eminem* (2003). For hip-hop influences, see Shilpa Davé, et al., eds., *East Main Street: Asian American Popular Culture* (2005).

Epilogue

In the Name of the People

By 2001, annual sales of recorded rap music surpassed three billion dollars. The genre's commercial vitality frequently depended upon financial partnerships between corporate media subsidiaries and independent black labels. Bad Boy Entertainment, a New York studio operated by former Crips gang leader Sean "Puffy" Combs, shared ownership with Arista Records. In Los Angeles, former Blood affiliate Suge Knight forged a similar arrangement between Death Row Records and Universal/MCA. Hip-hop cultural styles received additional exposure when MTV began airing rap videos in 1989. Often shot on buses and subways and in the abandoned buildings, playgrounds, schoolyards, rooftops, and well-known street locations of the inner city, video gave performers and their local "posses" the chance to "represent" their communities as sites of pride and shared identity, not simply centers of poverty and social pathology.

Gangsta rap borrowed from the historical legacy of black folk heroes and "tricksters" like Stagolee and Railroad Bill, who fought back against oppression and confronted social convention. Exploiting the contradiction between lived experience and mainstream ideals of equal opportunity, rappers sometimes presented themselves as stray dogs growling in the face of authority. To some extent, the "bad man" posture, symbolized by the use of the term "nigga," served as a protective shell against harsh inner-city realities. Yet it also served as an attention-getting device for artists combining critical social commentary with a quest for personal authenticity and a drive for profit. Some successful rappers imitated the style of Prohibition-era gangsters or ghetto pimps by dressing "up" with gold jewelry and sagging gear, or by sporting cornrow hairstyles, dread locks, shaved heads, or tattoos. Hip-hop culture also fostered the use of "jeep beats," luxury vehicles with amplified stereo systems that broadcasted ghetto sounds to other neighborhoods in a virtual reclamation of public space.

Despite rap's roots in black culture and experience, white artists like the Beastie Boys, Vanilla Ice (Robert Van Winkle), and Eminem (Marshall Mathers) also utilized the form. By the 1990s, white consumers accounted for more than half of hip-hop sales, a trend contributing to the rise of suburban-style black rappers like DJ Jazzy Jeff and Fresh Prince. Middle-class male teenagers gravitated to gangsta rap's forbidden narratives of easy money, gunplay, partying, and compliant women. Given such popularity, artists were under constant pressure to maintain street credibility and refute charges of "selling out." Violent posturing and a projection of an outlaw image, however, combined with a marketable rivalry between East and West Coast studios to produce unanticipated results. A year after the murder of a bodyguard for Bad Boy Entertainment's Biggie Smalls in 1995, Small's posse and rivals from California's Death Row Records drew weapons during a backstage scuffle at an awards show. Within months, someone shot Death Row's Tupac Shakur, followed by the drive-by killing of Smalls in 1997. Five years later, Run-DMC's "Jam Master Jay" Mizell fell to gunfire in a New York recording studio.

Commentators like African American cultural critic Stanley Crouch and TV personality Bill Cosby have condemned the violent images of gangsta rap and attacked it for demeaning women by linking sexual conquest to material affluence. They argue that a profit-oriented corporate media manipulates hip-hop imagery to conform to prevailing racial notions among whites, thereby producing an updated version of the nation's first popular culture form, the minstrels. Nevertheless, as words like "dis" (put down), "wack" (kill), "chill" (remain cool), and "def" (excellent) entered social discourse, and black cultural expression helped to define popular entertainment, the life of the inner city continued to exert a major hold on the American imagination. Academy Award Best Picture *Crash* (2005) used racially tense Los Angeles as the backdrop for a plot that followed several characters through a series of accidents, shootings, and carjackings over a thirty-six-hour period. *Hustle and Flow* (2005), in turn, featured the Academy Award-winning rap song "It's Hard Out There for a Pimp" to tell the story of a Memphis vice operator and drug dealer named DJay who aspires to becoming a rapper.

As the success of Kanye West, a middle-class African American rap artist with a broadly accessible style indicates, vernacular cultural expressions are easily subject to modification for a mass audience. At the same time, popular music depends upon a projection of authenticity and the ability to speak to ordinary people. Common entertainment forms often face an inherent tension between formula production requirements and the freshness of creative integrity and innovation that allows a product to distinguish itself from competitors. In country music, where television videos emphasized visual appeal and the drive toward mass acceptance tended to smooth out rough edges, such contradictions were particularly evident.

Several Nashville artists have resisted homogenization by reviving traditional themes. In the best-selling *Wide Open Spaces* (1998), the Dixie Chicks paid tribute to Texas honky-tonk with shuffle tunes like "Am I the Only One" and "Tonight the Heartache's On Me." Kenny Chesney's "Back Where I Come From" (1997) and "She Thinks My Tractor's Sexy" (1999) celebrated rural self-identity and pride. Trace Adkins returned to country's confessional roots with the disarming "I'm Tryin'" (2001), while his raucous "Hot Mama" (2003) trumpeted the fires of marital passion. Down-home themes also colored the vocals of (Kit) Brooks and (Ronnie) Dunn in best-selling albums like *Hard Workin' Man* (1993), *Red Dirt Road* (2003), and *Hillbilly Deluxe* (2005). Another duo, (Eddie) Montgomery and (Troy) Gentry, dedicated the popular *My Town* (2002) to veterans, blue-collar workers, and farmers. After recounting the narrator's flight from home after a fight with his father, the album's title song and hit single pictured the protagonist returning to raise a family with his high school sweetheart. The lyric then offered snapshots of the local scene and kinfolk on the way to church.

The terrorist attacks of September 11, 2001 helped to spark a resurgence of moral fervor and militant patriotism. Yet the Grammy Award country song of the year turned out to be Alan Jackson's "Where Were You When the World Stopped Turning?" (2001), a subdued meditation on the event's effect on ordinary people. Several months later, Toby Keith weighed in with a more bellicose tone. A former oil rigger who ultimately sold more than twenty-five million records, Keith had cultivated an Everyman image with macho hits like "You Ain't Much Fun (Since I Stopped Drinkin')" (1994) and "How Do You Like Me Now?" (1999). His "Courtesy of the Red, White, and Blue (The Angry American)" (2002) responded to 9/11 with a salute to soldiers in Afghanistan and a warning to those who "messed with the U.S. of A." Keith subsequently criticized the Dixie Chicks for telling an English concert audience that they were ashamed of President George W. Bush for invading Iraq. A more benign form of populism appeared in country star Gretchen Wilson's "Redneck Woman" (2004) and in "Politically Uncorrect" (2005), a duet with Merle Haggard honoring the Bible, the flag, and "the working man."

Whatever political form populist country music assumed, the genre embodied an historic association with the underdog. Such a sensibility underlay Ethan and Joel Coen's *O Brother, Where Art Thou?* (2000), a film whose title derived from the idealistic movie the fictional director in *Sullivan's Travels* proposed to make. The sons of Minneapolis college professors, the Coens were intellectual filmmakers whose first smash hit had been *Fargo* (1996), the story of a pregnant North Dakota police chief who foils a bizarre kidnapping plot. *O Brother* described the madcap adventures of three quirky prisoners who escape a Mississippi chain gang during the Great Depression and disguise themselves as old-time music performers. Released as a best-selling album, the soundtrack highlighted traditional balladeers and performers like Alison Krauss, Emmylou Harris, Ralph Stanley, and The Whites in a roots-oriented mix of populist country, bluegrass, folk, gospel, and blues known as Americana.

Everyday images continued to permeate television. As competition between network and cable TV intensified, and liberal culture elites came under increasing fire, programmers aspired to new levels of realism. Crime remained a compelling subject. Set in Baltimore, Barry Levinson's *Homicide: Life on the Streets* (1993–99) presented an unsentimental view of police work in which some cases remained unsolved. The Home Box Office (HBO) series *The Sopranos* (1999+) took viewers inside the house and favorite strip club of a suburban New Jersey mobster who experiences a mid-life crisis, sees a psychiatrist, and has problems raising two teenagers. James Gandolfini, the son of a New Jersey cement mason and school lunch server who drove a delivery truck and tended bar before playing "tough guys," portrayed Tony Soprano with convincing authenticity. Another realistic portrait came in Kiefer Sutherland's performance in *24* (2001+) as ruthless federal agent and L.A. Counter Terrorist Unit member Jack Bauer, in a show covering a single day in the character's life each season. Bauer's hard-bitten cop despised superiors who wanted results, but never cared to get their "hands dirty."

Public fascination with lawlessness and the attraction of low production costs encouraged the making of documentary-style TV features like *America's Most Wanted* (1988+), *Unsolved Mysteries* (1987+), and *COPS* (1989+)—an actual video record of police car officers on their daily rounds. Another show, *Rescue 911* (1989–96), recorded the responses of emergency crews. The popularity of shows depicting everyday situations generated a phenomenon known as "reality TV." One of the most popular examples, *The People's Court* (1981+), featured retired judges as arbiters of minor disputes between litigants, who agreed to abide by the magistrate's decision and submit their case to a non-binding vote by the studio audience. In *Who Wants to Marry a Millionaire?* (1999+), female contestants marketed themselves as suitable for wealthy partners. A similar desire to observe ordinary people under competitive stress contributed to the appeal of *Survivor* (2000+), a show that placed participants together in remote locations and required them to vote on sending someone home each week. The power to pick winners on *American Idol: The Search for a Superstar* (2002+), meanwhile, fell to the viewing audience.

Much of turn-of-the-century entertainment pointed to the postmodern breakdown between elite and popular culture. By affording ordinary consumers the ability to create private media files of images, texts, and graphics, communication innovations such as personal Websites, Internet downloading, iPod music storage, cell phones messaging, and compact disc technology helped democratize access to information and the products of expressive culture. Interactive computer video games provided still another avenue of participatory involvement. Whether the communications revolution represents the flowering of a "people's culture" or points to a mere fixation on gadgetry and self-indulgence, remains to be seen. Whatever the case, it is difficult to envision the scope of modern American cultural history without reference to its long-standing preoccupation with, and reflection of, the diverse experiences of ordinary people. Although descriptions of the lives and aspirations of non-elites often surface through the perspective of self-selected representatives, one cannot imagine a thriving culture completely cut off from their contributions and worldviews.

Index